ADVANCED COBOL
FOR STRUCTURED AND
OBJECT-ORIENTED PROGRAMMING

THIRD EDITION

ADVANCED COBOL FOR STRUCTURED AND OBJECT-ORIENTED PROGRAMMING

THIRD EDITION

Gary DeWard Brown

WILEY COMPUTER PUBLISHING

John Wiley & Sons, Inc.
New York • Chichester • Weinheim • Brisbane • Singapore • Toronto

Publisher: Robert Ipsen
Editor: Marjorie Spencer
Assistant Editor: Margaret Hendrey
Managing Editor: Angela Murphy
Text Design & Composition: North Market Street Graphics

Designations used by companies to distinguish their products are often claimed as trademarks. In all instances where John Wiley & Sons, Inc., is aware of a claim, the product names appear in initial capital or ALL CAPITAL LETTERS. Readers, however, should contact the appropriate companies for more complete information regarding trademarks and registration.

This book is printed on acid-free paper. ∞

This publication is designed to provide accurate and authoritative information in regard to the subject matter covered. It is sold with the understanding that the publisher is not engaged in professional services. If professional advice or other expert assistance is required, the services of a competent professional person should be sought.

Library of Congress Cataloging-in-Publication Data:

Brown, Gary DeWard.
    Advanced COBOL for structured and object-oriented programming /
Gary DeWard Brown.
       p.   cm.
    "Wiley computer publishing."
    Includes index.
    ISBN 0-471-31481-1 (paper : alk. paper)
    1. COBOL (Computer program language) 2. Structured programming.
3. Object-oriented programming (Computer science) I. Title.
QA76.73.C25B763   1999
005.13'3—dc21
                                          98-38910

10 9 8 7 6 5 4 3 2 1

CONTENTS

PREFACE

It's your first day on the job as a COBOL programmer. You've located the coffee machine, someone delivered your terminal, a stranger passes you a sealed letter containing your user ID with a password, and you've been escorted to a peripheral cubicle. Somehow during the interview process, they came to believe that you know everything about COBOL. This book can help.

According to the Gartner Group, there are 300 billion lines of computer code. Eighty percent, 240 billion lines, are COBOL. Estimates are that there are 3 million COBOL programmers looking after this code and adding to it. However, a glance at the curriculum of colleges shows that entry-level programmers are being trained in C/C++, Java, Visual Basic, and HTML. Few are being trained in COBOL, and more COBOL programmers are retiring than are being trained. This presents real opportunities for you.

This book is for those who know the basics of programming and want to learn COBOL quickly without wasting time rehashing basic programming techniques. Having advanced beyond the introductory programming manual, they need a book that touches only lightly on the basics of computing, but goes into detail on both programming techniques and the COBOL statements. The book assumes you are familiar with computers, computer applications, and a programming language, not necessarily COBOL. The book describes the COBOL statements in enough detail to enable someone familiar with programming to learn COBOL. Because you likely have some programming background, the book makes it clear where you can skip what you already know. The book is intended to make you a master of COBOL programming skills.

Among the subjects covered in this book are:

- Structured programming in COBOL
- Both the ANSI '85 statements and older statements found in legacy systems
- The new ANSI features for the standard to be implemented sometime in the twenty-first century
- The object-oriented features of COBOL
- The features of IBM, Micro Focus, and Fujitsu COBOL

- Full-screen I/O
- Dates and the year-2000 problem
- Client/server applications, Internet technologies, and application programming interfaces
- The COBOL report writer
- How to read COBOL programs

The solutions to the problems in this book, along with additional problems, are contained in a Web site so that you can download them. A selected reading list is also provided. You can locate the Web site at www.wiley.com/compbooks. Just go to it and select this book's title.

ACKNOWLEDGMENTS

My special thanks go to Sue McGinty for not only contributing material to the book, but also for her time and patience spent in reviewing and making suggestions. I wish to thank Liz Ryan and Johnson Waite for their help and for contributing material to the book. Marjorie Spencer, Margaret Hendrey, and Angela Murphy of John Wiley & Sons are a part of the professional staff whose insights, reviews, and suggestions were invaluable and who also made the book's production a pleasure.

PART I

BASIC COBOL

CHAPTER 1

INTRODUCTION

1.1 WHICH COBOL?

This book describes ANSI COBOL, IBM COBOL, which includes COBOL for OS/390 and VM (formerly VS COBOL II), the COBOL Set for AIX, and VisualAge COBOL for OS/2 and for Windows. Most COBOL programs were developed on the IBM mainframe (predominantly on the MVS operating system, now referred to as OS/390), and so this is assumed as the starting point. This book also includes features of Micro Focus and Fujitsu COBOL. To shorten the descriptions in the book, the following shorthand notations are used:

- *ANSI COBOL* refers to the current 1985 ANSI standard with the proposed changes to the standard due sometime after the year 2000. There are certain to be changes to the standard as it is described in this book before it is published.
- *IBM COBOL* includes COBOL for OS/390 and VM, the COBOL Set for AIX (IBM's UNIX), and VisualAge COBOL for OS/2 and for Windows.
- *Mainframe COBOL* includes COBOL for OS/390 and VM.
- *Workstation COBOL* includes the COBOL Set for AIX and VisualAge COBOL for OS/2 and Windows.
- *PC COBOL* includes Micro Focus, Fujitsu COBOL, and the other PC COBOL compilers, excluding VisualAge COBOL.
- *Nonmainframe COBOL* includes the COBOL Set for AIX, VisualAge COBOL for OS/2, and Windows, and PC COBOL.

For information on the various COBOL compilers, you can visit the following Web sites. However, because Web sites change more frequently than bank names, you can always revert to an Internet subject search.

IBM: www.software.IBM.com, www.mvshelp.com, www2.s390.ibm.com

Micro Focus: www.microfocus.com

Acucobol: www.acucobol.com

Deskware: www.deskware.com

Fujitsu: www.adtools.com

Hitachi: www.hitachi.com

Other useful Web sites are:

American National Standards Institute: www.ansi.org

Technical Committee X3J4 for COBOL Standardization: www.ncits.org

The COBOL Foundation: www.cobol.org

Copy of the new ANSI Standard: osiris.dkuug.dk/jtc1/sc22/wg4/open/n0123

The COBOL Center: www.infogoal.com

1.2 LEGACY SYSTEMS

You will most likely begin your programming career maintaining existing COBOL programs. The term for old programs has been upgraded to *legacy applications,* and early in your career you will likely spend more time maintaining these than in writing new programs. There are many obsolescent features in COBOL that, while still supported, you need no longer use. Unfortunately, you will need to learn about them because they will show up in the old programs you maintain and modify. The book makes it clear which features you shouldn't use, but which may appear in old programs.

Most of the legacy programs will have been written for the IBM mainframe, the dominant hardware when most COBOL programs were written, and many will continue to be run there. Consequently, this book stresses the mainframe environment. Some programs will migrate to the PC, and the book covers this environment too. Even if a program continues to run on the mainframe, you may modify the program on the PC, with its friendlier and less expensive environment, before uploading to the mainframe for production.

1.3 THE DISTRIBUTED ENVIRONMENT

A growing number of programs will be made interactive and will run in a distributed (client/server, Internet, or intranet) environment. As part of their year-2000 projects, many companies plan to migrate their legacy applications to a distributed environment to save costs and make the programs more responsive to their users.

1.4 ANSI STANDARD COBOL

COBOL was developed in the late 1950s and became an ANSI standard in 1968. There was a minor revision in 1974 (COBOL-74), but the major revision was in 1985 (COBOL-85). The 1985 revision gave COBOL statement terminators that made it a viable structured programming language. This book assumes that you are using the 1985 ANSI standard with the object-oriented features. If your installation is still using a pre-1985 COBOL version, the best advice this book can give you is to change jobs. However, because many of the old, obsolescent pre-1985 COBOL features will appear in legacy applications that you are likely to maintain, this book covers these too, with a warning to not write them in new programs.

There is an ongoing effort to update the ANSI standard again to incorporate object-oriented features. However, the earliest the final version will be released is sometime in the twenty-first century. Compiler manufacturers cannot wait this long and have already implemented the object-oriented features, and these too are described in this book. Other features of the new standard are identified and placed where appropriate throughout this book, and Appendix A describes other changes beyond the scope of this book.

While there are many advantages to having an ANSI standard for COBOL, it has an important drawback. Changes to COBOL are extremely slow. Structured programming features came a decade after they were accepted as standard programming practice. Object-oriented features are on the same schedule. One would be foolish to predict when the ANSI COBOL standard will address the Internet.

1.5 A GLIMPSE AT COBOL

How does one approach a language such as COBOL? Scott Adams, in a Dilbert cartoon, depicts the COBOL programmer as a dinosaur. Clearly, COBOL is not a glamorous language. To see why, here is a quick look at one of the simplest COBOL programs you can write.

```
IDENTIFICATION DIVISION.
PROGRAM-ID. Hello.
PROCEDURE DIVISION.
    DISPLAY "hello world."
    GOBACK.
```

Not so bad. However, this simple program gives a rather distorted view of COBOL. For a more realistic preview, here is another program that opens a file, reads a record from it, and performs a calculation. Don't read the program. It does nothing of interest. Just look at it to get an impression of what a COBOL program looks like.

```
IDENTIFICATION DIVISION.
PROGRAM-ID.  EINSTEIN.
ENVIRONMENT DIVISION.
INPUT-OUTPUT SECTION.
FILE-CONTROL.
    SELECT IN-FILE ASSIGN TO INFILE.
DATA DIVISION.
FILE SECTION.
FD  IN-FILE BLOCK CONTAINS 0 RECORDS.
01  IN-REC.
    02  M                           PIC S9(10).
    02  C                           PIC S9(10).
WORKING-STORAGE SECTION.
01  E                               PIC S9(10) PACKED-DECIMAL.
PROCEDURE DIVISION.
BEGIN-PROGRAM.
    OPEN INPUT IN-FILE
    READ IN-FILE
    COMPUTE E = M * (C ** 2)
    CLOSE IN-FILE
    GOBACK.
END PROGRAM EINSTEIN.
```

As you can see, COBOL is ponderous, rigid, and verbose. Most non-COBOL programmers would describe it as stodgy. If you were selecting a language for the joy of programming, it would not be COBOL. COBOL is a mature, stable language that lacks the excitement of new languages such as C/C++, Java, and Visual Basic. It can't compete on excitement, but it can compete in corporate usage and job opportunity.

1.6 WHAT COBOL DOES WELL

COBOL is a serious language for serious applications. Venerable if unexciting, it dates back to a time when the saxophone was the lead instrument in rock and roll bands. It became the most widely used programming language, and, despite its faults, continues to survive for good reasons. It is efficient in dealing with files because of its ability to read and write records without data conversion. It has decimal arithmetic for working with monetary amounts. It is good at formatting reports. It is relatively easy to learn and read for program maintenance and is largely self-documenting, which is of critical importance because at many installations, program documentation is either lost or out of date. It is an industry and ANSI standard. COBOL (COmmon Business Oriented Language) is a language designed for business applications.

What then is a business application? It is any application that facilitates the operation of a business. This includes such traditional applications as accounting, payroll, human resources, inventory, accounts receivable and payable, and fixed assets. It may also include forecasting, planning, sales, and marketing. Business applications are characterized by the following:

- They are transaction driven.
- They are usually classified by function with account numbers, vendor numbers, employee IDs, and so on.
- They involve amounts in discrete units, whether monetary ($1.55), time (2.25 hours), weights and measures (10 units), or percentages (6.65 percent sales tax). Business applications involve the type of calculations that you can perform on a desk calculator, where precision is required to some number of decimal places—rarely more than four. This differs from scientific applications where precision is required to some number of significant digits, often with very large and very small amounts occurring in the same calculation, such as the time it takes light to pass through a thin film.
- Business applications tend to be large, complex, and long lived, which means that they must be constantly changed (maintained), and latent bugs have full opportunity to spring to life.
- Business applications, often critical to the life of an organization, are taken very seriously.

None of these may be your reason for learning COBOL. More likely, you will learn COBOL because there is a demand for COBOL programmers and it opens the way to a well-paying career.

1.7   THE COBOL ENVIRONMENT

The COBOL programming environment is that of production computing for commercial applications. Production programs have a relatively long life, are perhaps more input/output-oriented than computation-oriented, and are more logical than algorithmic. There is often a separation of effort in design, programming, running, maintenance, and even documentation, with different people working on different parts. This makes communication vital. It is this environment for which the programming criteria are derived, and the goal is to improve program maintenance, correctness, reliability, and efficiency.

COBOL was designed as a batch programming language. With a *batch* system, you prepare a complete job and submit it to the computer. The computer's operating system schedules the job and executes it at its convenience, which may be hours later. You have no control over the job once you submit it. Often you submit a job and then hours later, when you get your output, you find that a minor error caused the entire job not to run. Over time, COBOL compilers have provided for interactive compilation in which you submit the program from your computer terminal and stay at the terminal while the job runs, interacting with the job to quickly correct any errors. In addition, the nonmainframe COBOL compilers provide interactivity within the language itself, enabling you to display output on the terminal and accept input from it while the program is running. Nonetheless, most legacy systems with which you will work will be batch systems.

Batch execution is generally looked down upon, but it is great for long-running jobs, especially those run on a routine basis as *production* jobs, and it has several advantages over interactive jobs.

- You don't need to wait at your terminal for your job to complete. You can go away and come back later.
- You can run the job off shift, when computer rates are usually lower.
- You can set up a complex job once and then keep resubmitting it rather than having to retype all the run commands each time.
- The job may run more efficiently because it doesn't require the computer resources of an online job.
- The computer can schedule the jobs at its convenience to make the most effective use of its hardware to maximize throughput.
- Your program will produce an audit trail so you can reconstruct what happened during the run.

1.8   USE OF THIS BOOK

The language features are described with examples—not long examples illustrating applications, but short examples illustrating language features. Applications are important, but as examples they are too long and involved to hold your interest. A few complete programs are included to show how all the COBOL statements look when they are put together in a complete program.

The book is divided into three parts. Part I describes the basic COBOL statements, with emphasis on those used for structured programming. Part II describes advanced COBOL features. Then Part III goes beyond COBOL to describe dates and the year-2000 problem, distributed computing, application programming interfaces, cross-system development, and how to read COBOL programs. Object-oriented COBOL is also covered in this part. To use the book as a textbook, read the chapters in sequence and work the exercises. If you are an experienced programmer, you may wish to choose selected chapters.

The notation in this book requires little explanation. The book shows the statements the way you write them. If there are several forms or options, you are shown each form to let you see how it is coded, without the distraction of braces, brackets, lines, and other items that are not coded. An underline indicates that one of several items may be coded, with the items listed above the dashed lines. Comments that describe the statements are set off in brackets. Language statements are in uppercase letters; lowercase italic type denotes generic terms, such as *name* or *value*.

```
        INPUT
        OUTPUT
OPEN _____ file-name
```

[Explanations are in this typeface. You could code this statement in two ways. You choose the *file-name*.]

```
OPEN OUTPUT OUT-FILE       Or       OPEN INPUT IN-FILE
```

Many COBOL statements have several forms, with optional words that have no effect other than to make the statement read better as an English sentence. Because you must read COBOL programs, the verbose form of the statements is also given, with the optional words shaded.

```
                    ASCENDING
                    DESCENDING
    SORT file-name ON _____ KEY identifier
         WITH DUPLICATES IN ORDER
```

This means you might read programs in which the statement is coded in any of the following ways:

```
SORT file-name ON ASCENDING KEY identifier
     WITH DUPLICATES IN ORDER
SORT file-name ASCENDING identifier DUPLICATES
SORT file-name ON ASCENDING KEY identifier DUPLICATES IN
SORT file-name ASCENDING identifier WITH DUPLICATES ORDER
```

There are also alternative forms of coding the same thing. IN and OF are interchangeable, and IS is coded with a singular form (SPACE IS) and ARE with the plural (SPACES ARE). SPACE and SPACES are also equivalent.

There is so much to COBOL that it daunting, but you will likely never use many of the features. To help you decide what is important, the book divides the items into *Essential, Sometimes Used,* and *Rarely Used.* In addition, there is a category for *Archaic.* These are features that you could forget entirely about except that they may appear in legacy programs. You can read these items as needed.

The vocabulary used to describe COBOL differs from that used with other languages, such as C/C++, Java, FORTRAN, and Pascal. This book generally tries to avoid any specialized vocabulary, but a major difference in COBOL is the vocabulary. Because the COBOL vocabulary is an important part of the COBOL culture, this book describes it where it is needed.

CHAPTER 2

COBOL OVERVIEW

This chapter gives an overview of the COBOL language. If you are already familiar with COBOL, conserve your energy and skip this chapter.

For an overview of what computer programming is all about, let's take a quick tour of a typical (but simplified) application. Computers operate on data and can do incredibly complex things with it, but for business applications, the data itself is simple. There are only two kinds of data: numeric (hours, monetary amounts, and so on) and nonnumeric (names, addresses, employee IDs, and so on).

2.1   NUMERIC OPERATIONS AND THE COMPUTE STATEMENT

The operations you perform on numeric data are the usual ones: addition (+), subtraction (–), division (/), multiplication (∗), and the exponential (∗∗). The following is a typical arithmetic operation in COBOL:

```
COMPUTE A = (((5 + 2) * 4) / 7) ** 2
```

A COBOL statement begins with a verb, such as COMPUTE. There is no statement delimiter. COBOL recognizes the end of a statement by the verb that begins the next statement. This means that COBOL has a long list of reserved words that you cannot use as names. Appendix B contains the complete list.

The computer evaluates the preceding COMPUTE statement as

```
A = (((5 + 2) * 4) / 7) ** 2 =
    ((7 * 4) / 7) ** 2 =
    (28 / 7) ** 2 =
    4 ** 2 = 16                    [The result, 16, is then stored in A.]
```

You use parenthesis to specify the order in which to perform the arithmetic operations, the same as in all programming languages. This covers most of what you need to know about calculations in business applications.

2.2 COBOL DATA

Data items are more complicated. The *A* in the preceding example is a *variable,* although COBOL terms it an *identifier* or *data item.* It is a named storage area in the computer containing the data values. You must explicitly describe all COBOL data items. The numbers in the example statement are *numeric literals.*

Data is often collected by someone entering it from a terminal, such as is shown in the following screen:

```
Employee Name: Smith, Joseph L.
Birth Date (YY/MM/DD): 64/11/21
Hire Date (YY/MM/DD): 95/09/24
```

The computer data is then stored as a record in a file. A *record* is a group of related data. Think of it as a line of data. The following shows how a typical record (line) of data, such as that just entered on the preceding screen, might be stored in a file:

```
Smith, Joseph L.            641121 950924
```

When column headings are placed above the data, you can easily understand what it means:

```
                           Birth  Hire
Employee Name              Date   Date
Smith, Joseph L.           641121 950924
```

There is an employee named Joseph L. Smith who was born on November 21, 1964, and was hired on September 24, 1995. You can also see that you have the makings of a year-2000 problem because the year is stored as two digits. You'll soon see what problems this causes.

Column headings work for humans, but the computer has no use for them, and there is no need to store them in a file. They are useful only when the output is displayed on a screen or printed in a report. Rather than use column headings, the computer wants you to name the variable that is to contain the data, describe its format, and tell it what columns the data occupies in the record. In COBOL, you do this by describing the data with a structure. Data has both relationships and structure. The name field is related to the birth and hire date fields. They are all attributes of the same item—an employee. The name might be a single field, or it could be a substructure: first name, middle initial, last name. A date field is a substructure composed of the year, month, and day. Here is how you might describe the preceding record in COBOL:

```
01  In-Emp.
    02  Emp-Name                PIC X(30).
    02  Birth-Date.
        03  Yr                  PIC 99.
```

```
         03  Mo                  PIC 99.
         03  Dy                  PIC 99.
     02                          PIC X.
     02  Hire-Date.
         03  Yr                  PIC 99.
         03  Mo                  PIC 99.
         03  Dy                  PIC 99.
```

Now examine this data structure in detail to see how COBOL wants its data described. You code a *record description* to describe the data.

01 In-Emp.

[You name the record ***In-Emp.*** If you wanted to do something with the entire record, such as write it out, you would refer to it by this name. The 01 is the level of the structure. Level 01 is the highest.]

02 Emp-Name   PIC X(30).

[You named the employee name field ***Emp-Name.*** The PIC X(30) tells COBOL that the field contains 30 characters. PIC is short for PICTURE. The X signifies characters. The level 02 tells COBOL that this field belongs to the previous 01 level item.]

02 Birth-Date.

[This names the birth date field. The level 02 tells COBOL that this field also belongs to the previous 01 level item.]

   03 Yr   PIC 99.

[This names the year field of ***Birth-Date.*** The PIC 99 tells COBOL that the field contains two numeric digits; each 9 signifies a numeric digit. Because this is a level 03 item, it belongs to the previous level 02 item in the hierarchy.]

   03 Mo   PIC 9(2).

[This names the month field. It is also two numeric digits. PIC 9(2) is identical to PIC 99, PIC 9(3) to PIC 999, and so on.]

   03 Dy   PIC 99.   [This names the day field.]

02   PIC X.

[This item has no name. It is merely a blank column in the data. In a real application, you would likely eliminate this space because the computer doesn't need it. However, for the purpose of illustration, 641121 950924 is easier to see as two dates than 641121950924.]

02 Hire-Date.

[This names the hire date field. Because this is a level 02 item, it is at the same level in the hierarchy as the ***Birth-Date*** field.]

   03 Yr   PIC 99.

[This names the year field of ***Hire-Date.*** The PIC 99 tells COBOL that the field contains two numeric digits. Because it is a level 03 item, it belongs to the previous level 02 item in the hierarchy]

   03 Mo   PIC 99.   [This names the month field.]
   03 Dy   PIC 99.   [This names the day field.]

The data structure is a hierarchy, as shown in Figure 2.1. Now let's see how COBOL knows which columns within the record the data occupies. Here is the record description again.

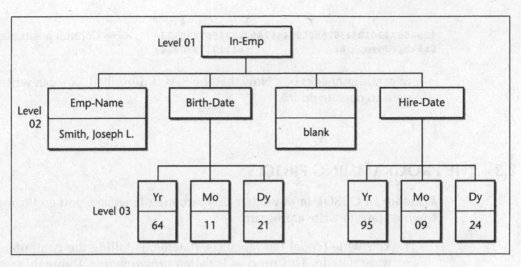

FIGURE 2.1   Data as a structure.

```
01  In-Emp.
        [No data described here. It occupies no column positions.]
    02  Emp-Name              PIC X(30).
        [This item occupies 30 characters. Therefore, it must be in columns 1 through 30.]
    02  Birth-Date.
        03  Yr                PIC 99.
            [This item occupies two digits. Therefore, it must be in the next two
            columns, 31 through 32.]
        03  Mo                PIC 99.
            [This item occupies two digits. Therefore, it must be in the next two
            columns, 33 through 34.]
        03  Dy                PIC 99.
            [This item occupies two digits. Therefore, it must be in the next two
            columns, 35 through 36.]
    02                        PIC X.
            [This item occupies one space. Therefore, it must be in the next col-
            umn, 37.]

    02  Hire-Date.
        03  Yr                PIC 99.
            [This item occupies two digits. Therefore, it must be in the next two
            columns; 38 through 39.]
        03  Mo                PIC 99.
            [This item occupies two digits. Therefore, it must be in the next two
            columns; 40 through 41.]
        03  Dy                PIC 99.
            [This item occupies two digits. Therefore, it must be in the next two
            columns; 42 through 43.]
```

To verify this, you can lay a scale above the record to show the column positions.

```
         1         2         3         4
12345678901234567890123456789012345678901234567890123        <=== Column positions
Smith, Joseph L.                    641121 950924
```

Everything checks out. Now that the data is described, you can write a COBOL program to operate on it.

2.3   THE PROGRAMMING PROCESS

Whether in COBOL or any other programming language, you go through the following steps to write a program:

1. You write (*code*) the language statements telling the computer what you want it to do. This process is called *programming*. Doing this makes you a *programmer*.

2. You *compile* the program, which takes the language statements you wrote and translates them into lower-level commands (machine language commands) that the computer hardware understands. This is an iterative process because the compiler often finds statement errors that you must correct before you can continue.

3. You *link-edit* the program, which brings into your program all the system functions that it will need. A typical system function might obtain the current date, which you might need in the program.

4. Finally, you *execute* (*run*) the program. This, too, is often an iterative process because when you write programs, you make mistakes. A computer error is called a *bug*, and the process of getting the errors out of your program is called *debugging*. You may also decide that the results are not quite what you wanted. Computer output acts as a catalyst, and when you look at it, you see changes you should make.

What has just been described is the *batch* method of programming. You code all your statements and then send them to the computer as a batch to have the computer compile them for you. Other languages, such as BASIC, are *interpretive*. With these, as soon as you write a statement, the computer interprets (compiles) the statement and executes it. This gives you immediate response, but often the response is so stimulating that you don't have time for the reflective thought necessary to write a good program. Because COBOL is a batch programming language, the interpretive method of programming is ignored.

To illustrate how COBOL operates on the data, assume a simple application is needed that reads in the file of data, one record at a time, performs some operation on the data within each record, and writes the record back out as a new file. Almost every COBOL program ever written is a variation on this basic theme. For the operation on the data, assume that you need to calculate the person's age when hired, add this new field to the record, and write it back out into a new file. The program will take an input record such as this:

```
Smith, Joseph L.              641121 950924
```

You'll use the hire and birth dates to calculate the person's age when hired, 30 here. After this, you'll append this field to the old record to form a new record that you'll write into a new file. In computer terminology, the file that you read is called the *input file* and the file that you write is called the *output file*. The record description for the input file has already been given, but you must now write a record description for the output file. It will be identical to that for the input file, except that you must give the record description a different name and add a field to contain the person's age when hired. Name this field *Hire-Age*. Here is the output record description:

```
01    Out-Emp.                   <=== New Name
      [You need to distinguish the output record from the input record named In-Emp.
      Do this by giving it a different name, Out-Emp.]
      02    Emp-Name             PIC X(30).
      02    Birth-Date.
            03    Yr             PIC 99.
            03    Mo             PIC 99.
            03    Dy             PIC 99.
      02                         PIC X.
      02    Hire-Date.
            03    Yr             PIC 99.
            03    Mo             PIC 99.
            03    Dy             PIC 99.
      02    Hire-Age             PIC 999.       <== Added
```

Aside from the record name and the new *Hire-Age* field, the output record is identical to the input record. This field will occupy columns 44 through 46 of the record. Now that the record descriptions are complete, you have to tell COBOL which file's records they describe. To do this, you write a file definition (FD) that names the file and associates the record description with the file.

```
FD In-File BLOCK CONTAINS 0 RECORDS.
      [The FD (File Definition) names the file (In-File seems appropriate) for use within
      the program. The BLOCK CONTAINS is a Mainframe COBOL thing that tells the
      operating system to choose an optimum block size for the file. The description of
      the record immediately follows so that COBOL knows that In-Emp describes the
      record for In-File.]
01    In-Emp.
      02    Emp-Name             PIC X(30).
      02    Birth-Date.
            03    Yr             PIC 99.
            03    Mo             PIC 99.
            03    Dy             PIC 99.
      02                         PIC X.
      02    Hire-Date.
```

```
              03  Yr                      PIC 99.
              03  Mo                      PIC 99.
              03  Dy                      PIC 99.
FD Out-File BLOCK CONTAINS 0 RECORDS.
```

[You write another FD to describe the output file and name it *Out-File*. Notice that the record contains 46 characters because you added the *Hire-Age* field.]

```
01 Out-Emp.
    02  Emp-Name                      PIC X(30).
    02  Birth-Date.
        03  Yr                        PIC 99.
        03  Mo                        PIC 99.
        03  Dy                        PIC 99.
    02                                PIC X.
    02  Hire-Date.
        03  Yr                        PIC 99.
        03  Mo                        PIC 99.
        03  Dy                        PIC 99.
    02  Hire-Age                      PIC 999.
```

2.4 COBOL FILE OPERATIONS: OPEN AND READ

Finally, you can write the COBOL statements to read the input file, compute the employee's age, and write the output file. First, you must open the input file, *In-File,* for input so that the system will locate the actual file on disk and ready it for reading. The COBOL OPEN statement does this.

```
    OPEN INPUT In-File
```

This OPEN statement asks the system to locate the file and prepare it for INPUT processing. You also need to open the output file, *Out-File,* for output. You've probably anticipated how this statement is written:

```
    OPEN OUTPUT Out-File
```

Then you execute a COBOL READ statement to read the next record from the input file.

```
    READ In-File
```

This READ statement reads the next record in the *In-File* file into its record description, *In-Emp.* If the record contained this:

```
Smith, Joseph L.              641121 950924
```

the record description would contain the following:

```
01  In-Emp.
    02  Emp-Name                  PIC X(30).
        [Contains "Smith, Joseph L.      ".]
```

```
02  Birth-Date.
    03  Yr              PIC 99.     [Contains 64.]
    03  Mo              PIC 99.     [Contains 11.]
    03  Dy              PIC 99.     [Contains 21.]
02                      PIC X.      [Contains blank.]
02  Hire-Date.
    03  Yr              PIC 99.     [Contains 95.]
    03  Mo              PIC 99.     [Contains 09.]
    03  Dy              PIC 99.     [Contains 24.]
```

2.5 REFERENCING COBOL DATA ITEMS

You can now process the data in the record. In this application, processing means computing the person's age when hired and storing it in *Hire-Age* in the output record named *Out-Emp*. The *Hire-Age* is the year hired minus the year of birth. You need to write a COMPUTE statement along the lines of:

```
COMPUTE Hire-Age = Yr hired - Yr born
```

How do you tell COBOL which *Yr* you want? You do this by *qualifying* the name. You write the COMPUTE statement as:

```
COMPUTE Hire-Age = Yr IN Hire-Date - Yr IN Birth-Date
```

You must qualify the *Yr* because there is more than one data item named *Yr* in the input record. The IN *Hire-Date* and IN *Birth-Date* qualify the year by telling COBOL which *Yr* you mean.

You need to qualify data items only if they have nonunique names. Because there is only one *Hire-Date* in the data descriptions, you don't need to code *Hire-Date* IN *Out-Emp,* although you could.

Unfortunately, there is also a *Yr* IN *Hire-Date* and *Yr* IN *Birth-Date* in the output record, *Out-Emp.* This means that the COMPUTE statement has not qualified the data items sufficiently and is in error. You must qualify the *Yr* IN *Hire-Date* and *Yr* IN *Birth-Date* to tell COBOL which record you mean. For this, you must write the COMPUTE statement as:

```
COMPUTE Hire-Age = Yr IN Hire-Date IN In-Emp -
                   Yr IN Birth-Date IN In-Emp
```

COBOL terms an item of data (*Yr*) a *data item.* When it is fully qualified (*Yr* IN *Hire-Date* IN *In-Emp*), COBOL terms it an *identifier.*

Although the COMPUTE statement does nothing more than compute the equivalent of $A = B - C,$ the long data names and qualifications make it appear much more complex than it really is. COBOL permits long, descriptive data names, with the downside being that they can make the simplest statement appear complicated. Some people prefer short, less descriptive data names to make the statements appear less complex. Others prefer long, descriptive data names, regardless of how complicated things appear.

Because you need to qualify date items only if the names are not unique, you could eliminate the need for qualifying the names by giving the data items different names in the *Hire-Date* and *Birth-Date* in both the *In-Emp* and *Out-Emp* records. However, the price of this is that you end up with a lot of names for essentially the same data items, and this is generally a bad practice. Nonetheless, this will be done in the example so that the statements don't appear so long-winded. Here are the revised record descriptions with unique names:

```
01  In-Emp.
    02  In-Name                    PIC X(30).
    02  In-Birth-Date.
        03  In-Birth-Yr            PIC 99.
        03  In-Birth-Mo            PIC 99.
        03  In-Birth-Dy            PIC 99.
    02                             PIC X.
    02  In-Hire-Date.
        03  In-Hire-Yr             PIC 99.
        03  In-Hire-Mo             PIC 99.
        03  In-Hire-Dy             PIC 99.
01  Out-Emp.
    02  Out-Name                   PIC X(30).
    02  Out-Birth-Date.
        03  Out-Birth-Yr           PIC 99.
        03  Out-Birth-Mo           PIC 99.
        03  Out-Birth-Dy           PIC 99.
    02                             PIC X.
    02  Out-Hire-Date.
        03  Out-Hire-Yr            PIC 99.
        03  Out-Hire-Mo            PIC 99.
        03  Out-Hire-Dy            PIC 99.
    02  Out-Hire-Age               PIC 999.
```

Now you can write the COMPUTE statement as:

```
COMPUTE Out-Hire-Age = In-Birth-Yr - In-Birth-Yr
```

2.6 THE IF/THEN/ELSE STATEMENT

There is a problem with the way the age is calculated. It has only a 50 percent chance of being correct, which leaves something to be desired. In the record for Joseph L. Smith, the hire date is 95, the birth year is 64, and 95 − 64 is 31. However, the hire date was September 24 and the birth date was November 21, so the person was only 30 when hired. If the month and day hired are equal to or greater than the month and day born, the algorithm will work—which will occur roughly half the time. Not a very good algorithm. You must check whether the month and day hired are less than the month and day born, and if so, you must subtract 1 from the age. For this, you need the most powerful of all computer statements, the IF statement. In the IF statement, you make some comparison, and if it is true, *then* you do one thing; *else* if it is false, you do something else. The IF statement has the following general form:

```
IF comparison
    THEN statements to execute if comparison is true
    ELSE statements to execute is comparison not true
END-IF
```

Because the IF is a compound statement that itself can contain other statements, COBOL needs some way of telling where the statements following the ELSE end. The END-IF does this.

The ELSE and its statements are optional. You could code just the THEN with its statements. The **comparison** for this application needs to test two items to see if one is greater than or equal to the other. Here is the COMPUTE statement again, followed by an IF statement to make the correction for the birth date not occurring before the hire date:

```
COMPUTE Hire-Age = In-Hire-Yr - In-Birth-Yr
IF In-Hire-Mo < In-Birth-Mo
    THEN COMPUTE Hire-Age = Hire-Age - 1
                    [If the month hired is less than (<) than the month born, subtract 1.]
    END-IF
```

Let's see if this is correct. When you write a program, it is a good idea to *desk check* the statements to see if they do what you want. In desk checking, you plug in numbers and do the calculation that the computer would do to see if things turn out correctly. Here is how you might desk check the following statements:

```
COMPUTE Hire-Age = In-Hire-Yr - In-Birth-Yr
                31 = 95        - 64
```
[You perform the calculation of 95 - 64 to see that the result is 31.]
```
IF In-Hire-Mo < In-Birth-Mo
    9           < 11
```
[9 is less than 11, so you execute the THEN statements.]
```
    THEN COMPUTE Hire-Age = Hire-Age - 1
                    30 = 31        - 1
```
[You calculate 31 - 1 = 30, which is the correct age.]
```
    END-IF
```

If all you were dealing with were the year and month, you would be done. However, you must consider the case where the birth and hire month are the same, but the birth day is greater than the hire day. For this, you must also subtract 1 from the age. You can write another IF statement to check for this.

```
IF In-Hire-Mo = In-Birth-Mo
```
[Now if the month born is equal to (=) the month hired, you must check the day.]

```
          THEN IF In-Hire-Dy < In-Birth-Dy
      [This IF lies within the previous IF, which is perfectly legal. It is a nested IF.]
              THEN COMPUTE Hire-Age = Hire-Age - 1      [Subtract 1 again.]
          END-IF      [Marks the end of nested IF.]
  END-IF    [Marks end of original IF. Because you had two IFs, you need two END-
            IFs.]
```

IF statements and logical expressions are the most difficult part of any programming language. Most of the subtle errors that creep into programs are due to them. Even the most experienced programmers make mistakes in such logical statements.

There are other ways you could have written the above statements. One is to avoid the use of the nested IF. The following statement replaces the preceding nested IF.

```
IF In-Hire-Mo = In-Birth-Mo
AND
In-Hire-Dy < In-Birth-Dy
                [Instead of a nested IF, you use the logical AND. For the following
                THEN statement to be executed, the comparisons joined by the
                AND must both be true.]
    THEN COMPUTE Hire-Age = Hire-Age - 1      [Subtract 1 again.]
END-IF
```

This works equally well, and you have correctly computed the age. To do a thorough desk check of the statements, you might want to test the calculations when the birth month is one less, one greater, and equal to the hire month. Then when the months are equal, recheck the calculation when the birth day is one less, one greater, and equal to the hire day.

Now check the year. What will happen with the first person hired in the year 2000? You might have a record like this:

```
Jones, Robert B.                    590814 000716
```

The employee, Robert B. Jones, was born on August 14, 1959, and was hired on July 16, 2000. Let's follow the statements through that compute his age:

```
COMPUTE Hire-Age = In-Hire-Yr - In-Birth-Yr
         -59 = 00       - 59
```

The person's age is computed as −59 years old, which is in error. Had the year been carried as four digits, you would compute **Hire-Age** = 2000 − 1959 = 41, which is correct. This is a typical problem caused by the year 2000 when the year is carried as two digits. There are several ways to correct this, but they can be left for Chapter 26. Ignore the problem for now. So far, you have the following statements:

```
OPEN INPUT In-File, OUTPUT Out-File
READ In-File
COMPUTE Hire-Age = In-Hire-Yr - In-Birth-Yr
IF In-Hire-Mo < In-Birth-Mo
    THEN COMPUTE Hire-Age = Hire-Age - 1
END-IF
IF In-Hire-Mo = In-Birth-Mo
    AND
    In-Hire-Dy < In-Birth-Dy
    THEN COMPUTE Hire-Age = Hire-Age - 1
END-IF
```

More desk checking. Is there any chance you will subtract 1 from *Hire-Age* twice? After all, COMPUTE *Hire-Age = Hire-Age* − 1 appears twice. No, it won't happen because the COMPUTE is executed first if *In-Hire-Mo* is less than *In-Birth-Mo* and is executed the second time if *In-Hire-Mo* equals *In-Birth-Mo,* and the two comparisons are mutually exclusive.

2.7 THE MOVE STATEMENT

Now that you have computed the *Hire-Age,* it is sitting there all alone in the *Out-Emp* record. Before you write the *Out-Emp* record to the output file, you need to move all the other fields from the input record, *In-Emp,* to it. The following COBOL MOVE statement does this.

```
MOVE In-Emp TO Out-Emp
```

Everything in *In-Emp* gets moved to *Out-Emp,* a character at a time. Here is the program with the MOVE statement added:

```
OPEN INPUT In-File, OUTPUT Out-File
READ In-File
COMPUTE Hire-Age = In-Hire-Yr - In-Birth-Yr
IF In-Hire-Mo < In-Birth-Mo
    THEN COMPUTE Hire-Age = Hire-Age - 1
END-IF
IF In-Hire-Mo = In-Birth-Mo
    AND
    In-Hire-Dy < In-Birth-Dy
    THEN COMPUTE Hire-Age = Hire-Age - 1
END-IF
MOVE In-Emp TO Out-Emp  <=== Added
```

Unfortunately, a bug has just been introduced into the program. When COBOL does a MOVE in which the fields are of equal length, it moves all the characters from the sending field to the receiving field. It is more complicated when the fields have different lengths. When the sending field is longer than the receiving field, COBOL chops off (truncates) characters on the right of the data to match the length of the receiving field. No problem here because the sending field, *In-Emp*, is 43 characters, which is not longer than the length of the receiving field, *Out-Emp*, 46 characters.

What about the remaining possibility, in which the sending field is shorter than the receiving field? For this, COBOL pads the data on the right with blanks to match the length of the receiving field. *In-Emp* is shorter than *Out-Emp* by three characters, so COBOL moves the 43 characters from *In-Emp* to *Out-Emp* and fills in the remaining three characters of *Out-Emp* with blanks. This wipes out the *Hire-Age* just stored.

Problems such as this are typical of computer applications. You compute the age, but when you check the record after you write it, the age isn't there—just three blanks. You'll have to solve this bug.

A simple solution would be to move the data from *In-Emp* to *Out-Emp* before you compute the *Hire-Age:*

```
OPEN INPUT In-File, OUTPUT Out-File
READ In-File
MOVE In-Emp TO Out-Emp          ◄
COMPUTE Hire-Age = In-Hire-Yr - In-Birth-Yr
IF In-Hire-Mo < In-Birth-Mo
    THEN COMPUTE Hire-Age = Hire-Age - 1
END-IF
IF In-Hire-Mo = In-Birth-Mo
    AND
    In-Hire-Dy < In-Birth-Dy
    THEN COMPUTE Hire-Age = Hire-Age - 1
END-IF
MOVE In-Emp TO Out-Emp          Move this statement
```

This illustrates that it is not enough to just write correct statements, you must also write them in the proper order. There are other solutions to the problem that might be even better, but let's move on.

2.8   MORE FILE OPERATIONS: THE WRITE AND CLOSE STATEMENTS

The next step is to write the new output record into the output file. The COBOL WRITE statement does this.

```
WRITE Out-Emp
```

When you are done processing the files, you should close them with a CLOSE statement. Closing files makes them ready for processing by another application.

```
CLOSE In-File, Out-File
```

2.9   THE STOP RUN AND GOBACK STATEMENTS

The last thing is to tell the operating system that you have reached the end of the program. Either the STOP RUN or GOBACK statement does this.

```
STOP RUN                    or      GOBACK
```

GOBACK is a more general statement that is supported by the current COBOL compilers and the new ANSI standard, so it is preferable.

2.10   PROGRAMMING LOOPS

Wonderful. You have opened the input file, read a record from it, computed the age at which the employee was hired, moved the data from the input record to the output record, written the output record to the output file, and closed both the input and output files. Here are the statements so far:

```
OPEN INPUT In-File, OUTPUT Out-File
READ In-File
MOVE In-Emp TO Out-Emp
COMPUTE Hire-Age = In-Hire-Yr - In-Birth-Yr
IF In-Hire-Mo < In-Birth-Mo
   THEN COMPUTE Hire-Age = Hire-Age - 1
END-IF
IF In-Hire-Mo = In-Birth-Mo
   AND
   In-Hire-Dy < In-Birth-Dy
   THEN COMPUTE Hire-Age = Hire-Age - 1
END-IF
WRITE Out-Emp
CLOSE In-File, Out-File
GOBACK.
```

There is a big problem. If you were only going to process one record, you would have been better off doing it by hand. There is unlikely to be only one record in the input file. There could be thousands. The computer only comes into its own when endless repetition like this must be done, which is great because we humans hate it.

Because there could be any number of records in the input file, you must modify the program to process however many records there are. For this, you will need to program what is called a *loop*. In a loop, you tell the computer to repeat a group of statements. In this application, you must repeat the statements that read the input record, move the input record to the output record, compute the age, and write the output record. Pictorially, here is what is needed:

```
            OPEN INPUT In-File, OUTPUT Out-File
    Start loop. ◄─────────────────────────────────────────┐
        READ In-File                                       │
        MOVE In-Emp TO Out-Emp                             │
        COMPUTE Hire-Age = In-Hire-Yr - In-Birth-Yr        │
        IF In-Hire-Mo < In-Birth-Mo                        │
            THEN COMPUTE Hire-Age = Hire-Age - 1           │
        END-IF                                             │
        IF In-Hire-Mo = In-Birth-Mo                        │
            AND                                            │
            In-Hire-Dy < In-Birth-Dy                       │
            THEN COMPUTE Hire-Age = Hire-Age - 1           │
        END-IF                                             │
        WRITE Out-Emp                                      │
        Any more records?            Yes ──────────────────┘
                    │
                    ▼
                   No
                    │
                    ▼
        CLOSE In-File, Out-File
        GOBACK.
```

To code this loop, you need two things. First, you need a way to tell COBOL to repeat a group of statements. Second, you need a way to tell when the input file has no more records to read so that you can end the loop. For the latter, the READ statement has a feature to let you tell if there are more records in the file. You can write it as:

```
READ In-File
    AT END statements to execute when no more records to read
    NOT AT END statements to execute when a record was read
END-READ
```

Because the READ statement written this way is a compound statement that can contain other statements, you must tell COBOL where it ends. You do this with the END-READ. For this application, you want the READ statement to operate as:

```
READ In-File
    AT END statements to quit the loop
    NOT AT END statements to process record and write it out
END-READ
```

All you have to do is replace the original READ with this and find some way of coding a loop.

2.11 THE PERFORM STATEMENT

The simplest way of coding a loop in COBOL is the PERFORM statement. You can write the PERFORM for a loop as

```
PERFORM WITH TEST AFTER UNTIL comparison
    statements to execute within the loop
END-PERFORM
```

Because the PERFORM is a compound statement that encloses a group of statements, COBOL needs you to tell it where the statements end by coding the END-PERFORM. The WITH TEST AFTER tells COBOL to make the test to see if the *comparison* is true *after* it has executed the statements following the PERFORM—that is, when the END-PERFORM is reached. Here is how it operates:

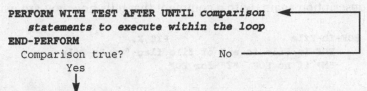

```
PERFORM WITH TEST AFTER UNTIL comparison
    statements to execute within the loop
END-PERFORM
Comparison true?                    No
        Yes
```

The *comparison* is written like the comparison in an IF statement. COBOL continues to execute the statements between the PERFORM and END-PERFORM until the *comparison* is true. Here are the statements with the PERFORM/END-PERFORM and the modified READ:

```
OPEN INPUT In-File, OUTPUT Out-File
    [The first two statements aren't changed.]
PERFORM WITH TEST AFTER UNTIL comparison          <=== Added
    [You perform the loop until the comparison is true. The comparison is the diffi-
    cult part, and you can tackle it later.]
    READ In-File
        AT END statement to make the comparison be true
        NOT AT END
            statement to make the comparison be false
            MOVE In-Emp TO Out-Emp
            COMPUTE Hire-Age = In-Hire-Yr - In-Birth-Yr
            IF In-Hire-Mo < In-Birth-Mo
                THEN COMPUTE Hire-Age = Hire-Age - 1
            END-IF
            IF In-Hire-Mo = In-Birth-Mo AND
                In-Hire-Dy < In-Birth-Dy
                THEN COMPUTE Hire-Age = Hire-Age - 1
            END-IF
            WRITE Out-Emp
    END-READ
END-PERFORM                         [Added to mark the end of the loop.]
CLOSE In-File, Out-File             [These two statements don't change.]
GOBACK.
```

All you need worry about now is the *comparison*. For this, another variable is needed that is set to one value to continue the loop and another value to end the loop. Here is the description of the variable:

```
01  EOF-In-File                     PIC X.
```

EOF-In-File is a single character. Level 01 doesn't need to describe a structure. It can also describe an item of data, termed an *elementary item.* You'll set *EOF-In-File* to "N" to indicate that the last record hasn't been read. The "*N*" is an alphanumeric literal, also called a nonnumeric literal. An *nonnumeric literal* consists of characters enclosed in quotation marks. When the last record is read (termed an *end of file* or EOF condition) you'll set *EOF-In-File* to "Y". It would be nice to tell someone reading the program that you are using *End-In-File* this way. A *comment* does this. A comment is text that you write to explain what is going on within the program, but which has no effect on the program's execution. Here is the *EOF-In-File* description again, with a comment that tells how you are using it:

```
01   EOF-In-File                    PIC X.
*        EOF-In-File is end of file flag for In-File.
*        "N" if no EOF. "Y" for EOF.
```

Now you can code the PERFORM loop as:

```
PERFORM WITH TEST AFTER UNTIL EOF-In-File = "Y"
    READ In-File
        AT END MOVE "Y" TO EOF-In-File
        NOT AT END MOVE "N" TO EOF-In-File
            □  □  □
        END-READ
    END-PERFORM
```

This does exactly what is wanted. The program is now complete, except for some required *housekeeping* statements that COBOL requires you to write.

2.12   A COMPLETE COBOL PROGRAM

Here is the program with all these overhead statements added:

```
IDENTIFICATION DIVISION.
PROGRAM-ID.  Empage.
ENVIRONMENT DIVISION.
INPUT-OUTPUT SECTION.
FILE-CONTROL.
    SELECT In-File ASSIGN TO OLDFILE.
    SELECT Out-File ASSIGN TO NEWFILE.
DATA DIVISION.
FILE SECTION.
FD In-File BLOCK CONTAINS 0 RECORDS.
01   In-Emp.
    02   In-Name                    PIC X(30).
    02   In-Birth-Date.
        03   In-Birth-Yr            PIC 99.
        03   In-Birth-Mo            PIC 99.
        03   In-Birth-Dy            PIC 99.
```

```
      02                            PIC X.
      02  In-Hire-Date.
          03  In-Hire-Yr          PIC 99.
          03  In-Hire-Mo          PIC 99.
          03  In-Hire-Dy          PIC 99.
  FD Out-File BLOCK CONTAINS 0 RECORDS.
  01  Out-Emp.
      02  Out-Name                PIC X(30).
      02  Out-Birth-Date.
          03  Out-Birth-Yr        PIC 99.
          03  Out-Birth-Mo        PIC 99.
          03  Out-Birth-Dy        PIC 99.
      02                          PIC X.
      02 Out-Hire-Date.
          03  Out-Hire-Yr         PIC 99.
          03  Out-Hire-Mo         PIC 99.
          03  Out-Hire-Dy         PIC 99.
      02  Hire-Age                PIC 999.
  WORKING-STORAGE SECTION.
  01  EOF-In-File                 PIC X.
  *       EOF-In-File is end of file flag for In-File.
  *       "N" if no EOF.  "Y" for EOF.
  PROCEDURE DIVISION.
  A00-Begin.
      OPEN INPUT In-File, OUTPUT Out-File
      PERFORM WITH TEST AFTER UNTIL EOF-In-File = "Y"
          READ In-File
            AT END MOVE "Y" TO EOF-In-File
            NOT AT END
              MOVE "N" TO EOF-In-File
              MOVE In-Emp TO Out-Emp
              COMPUTE Hire-Age = In-Hire-Yr - In-Birth-Yr
              IF In-Hire-Mo < In-Birth-Mo
                 THEN COMPUTE Hire-Age = Hire-Age - 1
              END-IF
              IF In-Hire-Mo = In-Birth-Mo AND
                 In-Hire-Dy < In-Birth-Dy
                 THEN COMPUTE Hire-Age = Hire-Age - 1
              END-IF
              WRITE Out-Emp
          END-READ
      END-PERFORM
      CLOSE In-File, Out-File
      GOBACK.
  END PROGRAM Empage.
```

That's it. You have seen most of the COBOL you will need to use. There are hundred of details remaining—most important, how you format numbers for reports—but the essentials are out of the way. If nothing in this chapter makes sense, you should read it again. If you get the general drift, continue on, even if several things may be hazy. Everything will be covered in more detail in the following chapters.

CHAPTER 3

GENERAL LANGUAGE RULES

This chapter contains the essential rules for coding in COBOL. Many were described in the previous chapter and new ones will be pointed out when they are encountered. They are all placed together here for quick reference. You may quickly glance through this chapter and refer back to it when needed.

3.1 COBOL DATA TYPES

Essential

A full description of the COBOL data types is given in Chapters 9 through 11. The following is only a summary to familiarize you with the major types.

- USAGE DISPLAY is character data. (Only character data can be displayed on a terminal or printed.) If you omit the USAGE clause, USAGE DISPLAY is assumed. DISPLAY, along with the BINARY, PACKED-DECIMAL, and so on can be coded alone, without the USAGE. The shaded items here show the words you can omit.

```
01  Name                          PIC X(5) USAGE IS DISPLAY.
```
Same as
```
01  Name                          PIC X(5) USAGE DISPLAY.
```
Same as
```
01  Name                          PIC X(5) DISPLAY.
```
Same as
```
01  Name                          PIC X(5).
```
- BINARY or COMP is a binary number.
```
01  Name                          PIC S9(8) BINARY.
```
- COMP-1 is a single-precision floating-point number.
```
01  Name                          COMP-1.
```

28

- COMP-2 is a double-precision floating-point number.

```
01   Name                              COMP-2.
```

- PACKED-DECIMAL or COMP-3 is a packed-decimal number.

```
01   Name                              PIC S9(9)V99 PACKED-DECIMAL.
```

3.2 STATEMENT FORMAT

The COBOL statement format was designed for punched cards (found today in museums) and must be coded in certain columns.

Essential

- Column 7 indicates the continuation of literals (-), a comment (*), a debugging statement (D), or a page eject (/).
- Columns 8 through 11 are termed the *A area*. Column 8 is termed the *A margin*. The following items must begin somewhere in these columns:

    Identification Division, Environment Division, Data Division, and Procedure Division headers

    Procedure names (the equivalent of statement labels) for sections and paragraphs

    Data description level numbers 01 and 77

    DECLARATIVES and END DECLARATIVES

    END PROGRAM, END CLASS, and END METHOD headers

- Columns 12 through 72 are termed the *B area*. Statements begin in this area. Column 12 is termed the *B margin*.

PROPOSED NEW ANSI STANDARD: Check Compiler to See if Implemented

There was never any need for the A and B margin distinction, and the new ANSI standard eliminates the B margin, keeping only the A margin. Anything that had to start in the B margin in the past can start in the A margin under the new standard.

Archaic

- Columns 1 through 6 contain an optional sequence number. The sequence numbers are an obsolete feature that have no effect on the program. In the old days, they served to help put a card deck back together if it was dropped, but this problem disappeared long ago.
- Columns 73 through 80 are available for program identification. This is also an obsolete feature that you can ignore.

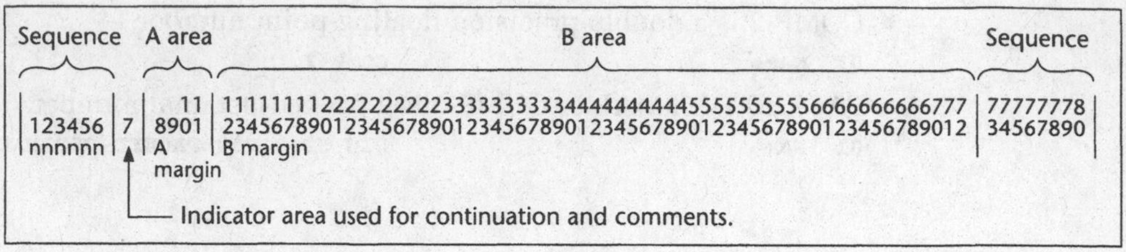

FIGURE 3.1 COBOL coding form.

```
Label-A.                            [Begins in the A margin.]
    MOVE C TO D                     [Begins in the B margin.]
```
Figure 3.1 shows the COBOL coding form.

TIP *Don't code the sequence numbers unless your installation uses them for change control, which is unlikely. They serve no purpose today.*

3.2.1 Continuation

Essential

If a statement exceeds one line, continue the statement on the next line in column 12 or beyond. The last character of the line being continued is assumed to be followed by a space. For readability, break the statement where it is obvious that it is continued, and indent the continuation.

```
COMPUTE A = (Var + 27.6 -
Val) / (Homes -
Rent)
```

Archaic

You can also break a line in any column. Code a hyphen (-) in column 7 of the next line, and continue in column 12. The continuation follows the last nonblank character of the first line. For example, you could also continue the preceding statement by coding:

```
11111111112222222222333333333344444444445555555555666666666777
789012345678901234567890123456789012345678901234567890123456789012
    COMPUTE A = (Var + 27
-    .6 - Val) / (Homes - Rent)
```

To continue an alphanumeric literal, code the literal through column 72, code a hyphen in column 7 of the next line, code a quotation in column 12 or beyond, and continue the literal.

```
11111111112222222222333333333334444444444555555555566666666666777
78901234567890123456789012345678901234567890123456789012345678901
    MOVE "THIS IS THE WINTER OF OUR DISCONTENT. SUMMERS ARE WORS
-   "E." TO A
```

The previous statement is better written as follows:

```
MOVE
"THIS IS THE WINTER OF OUR DISCONTENT. SUMMERS ARE WORSE."
    TO A
```

TIP *Don't continue alphanumeric literals because it increases the chance for error.*

3.2.2 Blanks and Separators

Essential

Blanks in COBOL separate items. Place at least one blank wherever you might expect a blank in an English sentence. You can code multiple blanks wherever a single blank may appear.

```
COMPUTE   A = 1.3    + 13   or   COMPUTE A = 1.3 + 13
```

You can also code a separator comma (comma followed by one or more spaces) wherever a blank can be placed. The comma and semicolon are also interchangeable as separators. Thus, you can separate a series of items with blanks, commas and blanks, or semicolons and blanks.

```
ADD A B C TO D     Same as     ADD A, B, C TO D
                   Same as     ADD A; B; C TO D
```

TIP *Separate a series of items with commas, as is done in most other programming languages.*

Likewise, you can separate statements with commas and blanks or semicolons and blanks.

```
MOVE A TO B, MOVE C TO D     Same as     MOVE A TO B; MOVE C TO D
```

TIP *Don't use commas and semicolons to separate statements because they can only cause problems. Write each statement on a separate line.*

TABLE 3.1 Separator Items in COBOL Statements

Separator	Rules
b	You can code several blanks wherever one blank can appear.
,b	Follow a comma with one or more blanks.
.b	Follow a period with one or more blanks.
;b	Follow a semicolon with one or more blanks.
(	Left parentheses need not be preceded or followed by a blank.
)	Right parentheses need not be preceded or followed by a blank.
:	Colon need not be followed by a blank.
b"	
b'	Precede an opening quotation mark or apostrophe with one or more blanks.
"b	
'b	Follow a closing quotation mark or apostrophe with one or more blanks.
b==	Opening pseudo text delimiter must be preceded by a blank.
==b	Closing pseudo text delimiter must be followed by a blank.

```
MOVE A TO B
MOVE C TO D
```

The characters shown in Table 3.1 are also used as separator items, depending on the context. Several items in the table have yet to be described, but they are included here for completeness. Note that a lowercase *b* indicates a blank.

3.2.3 Free-Form Input

PROPOSED NEW ANSI STANDARD: Check Compiler to See if Implemented

The proposed ANSI standard has free-form statements, allowing you to write COBOL directives, procedure names, and statements anywhere from column 1 to the end of the line. A line is limited to 255 characters. You can switch back and forth between free and fixed form at any time. You request free-form statements by coding the following in column 8:

```
>>SOURCE FORMAT IS FREE
```

Once this is set, you can write statements without regard to column boundaries. Sadly, you must still end a paragraph with a period. You can code a comment wherever you can code a separator (space) by preceding it with the characters *>.

```
*> This is a comment.
MOVE A TO B *> This is a comment too.
```

You denote debugging lines by starting the line with >>D. Debugging lines are lines that contain statements used only to debug the program as described in Chapter 19. You tell COBOL whether you want such lines compiled (for program debugging) or ignored (when the program is ready for production).

```
>>D MOVE A TO B
```

Note that free form will accept all fixed-form statements except the comment and debugging line, so at a minimum, free form lets you code fixed form and not worry about extending beyond column 71. Note that fixed form will not accept free-form statements. You can switch back to fixed form by coding:

```
>>SOURCE FORMAT IS FIXED
```

If you elect to use the free-form format, don't mix it with fixed form because it is unaesthetic and difficult to read. Convert the fixed form to free form by doing the following:

1. Change all * and *D* in column 7 to *>* and >*D* to make the comments and debugging statements free form, and shift them into column 8.
2. Do a column delete of columns 1 through 7 for all the statements to align them on the left margin.
3. Then enter new statements in column 1 as free form.

In the Fujitsu COBOL compiler, you can request free-form input with the SRF compiler option.

3.3   COBOL STATEMENTS

The basic instruction in COBOL is a *statement.* You group COBOL statements into *sentences* and *procedures.*

3.3.1   Statements

Essential

A COBOL statement begins with an English verb, such as COMPUTE, ADD, and MOVE. The rest of the statement may consist of item names, separators (usually the blank), key words, and sometimes optional words. There is no statement terminator in COBOL. COBOL knows where a statement begins only by recognizing the verb that begins the statement. For this reason, all COBOL words are reserved and cannot be used for data names.

You must code COBOL statements in columns 12 through 72. A line may contain a whole statement, part of a statement, or several statements:

```
MOVE X TO Y  MOVE V TO W MOVE M TO N
```

or

```
MOVE X TO
Y  MOVE V TO W MOVE M
TO N
```

TIP *Code a single statement per line to make the statements easier to read.*

```
MOVE X TO Y
MOVE V TO W
MOVE M TO N
```

Sometimes a single statement is made clearer if you continue parts of it on different lines. The COBOL column restrictions often force you to continue statements.

```
PERFORM A10-Do-Loop WITH TEST AFTER
    VARYING Size FROM 1 BY 2 UNTIL SIZE > 100
```

In the days of punched cards, when cards had to be physically pulled, repunched, and replaced, it was easier to change programs when parts of a statement spread across lines.

```
OPEN INPUT In-File,
           Trans-File
```

With a text editor, this is no longer true.

```
OPEN INPUT In-File, Trans-File
```

COBOL also classifies statements into conditional statements and imperative statements. A *conditional statement* is one such as IF/THEN/ELSE that tests a condition and does different things based on the result of the comparison. An *imperative statement* is a statement that specifies an unconditional action to take and executes it as a unit. All conditional statements with an explicit scope terminator are imperative statements. A sequence of imperative statements is itself an imperative statement.

3.3.2 Sentences

Archaic

Long ago, the period was the only means of grouping statements in COBOL. One or more statements terminated by a period are termed a *sentence* in COBOL. The following is a sentence containing three statements:

```
MOVE X TO Y
MOVE V TO W
MOVE M TO N.
```

The choice of a period to delimit a sentence was an unfortunate attempt to emulate English. It is the least visible of any character and is easy to overlook. The period as a delimiter is ambiguous because numeric literals also contain periods as decimal points, so that you must be careful to write 2 or 2.0 rather than 2., which would delimit a sentence. The period as a delimiter also doesn't work well for nesting statements, which is a serious drawback when trying to do structured programming. COBOL now provides explicit scope terminators to mark the end of conditional statements, and you no longer need the period except to end a paragraph.

As an example of the dangers of the period, look at the following statements:

```
IF A = B
    THEN DISPLAY "THIS DISPLAYS WHEN THE VALUE OF A EQUALS B".
DISPLAY "THIS ALWAYS DISPLAYS".
```

The first DISPLAY executes if *A* equals *B* and then control drops through and the second DISPLAY always executes. The programmer made a global change to change *A* to *Ax*.

```
IF Ax = B
    THEN DISPLAY "THIS DISPLAYS WHEN THE VALUE OF Ax EQUALS B".
DISPLAY "THIS ALWAYS DISPLAYS".
```

Suddenly the second DISPLAY began executing as part of the THEN phrase, as if the statements had been written as follows. Can you see why?

```
IF Ax = B
    THEN DISPLAY "THIS DISPLAYS WHEN THE VALUE OF Ax EQUALS B"
        DISPLAY "THIS ALWAYS DISPLAYS".
```

The period of the THEN phrase was pushed into column 73. COBOL ignores anything in column 73, and so it produced no error message. It wasn't obvious from looking at the listing that the period was in column 73. This type of error can drive you crazy. Such an error might lay latent for months until a particular transaction causes the statements to execute, with the resulting error. Maintenance problems like this are one reason why correcting the year-2000 problems is so fraught with dangers.

TIP *Code the period only after the last statement in a paragraph. Place the period on a separate line to make modifications easier. Treat periods in COBOL like little land mines.*

3.3.3 Procedures

A *procedure* consists of a collection of statements executed as a group. Procedures consist of *paragraphs* (one or more sentences) and *sections* (one or more paragraphs).

Paragraphs

Essential

You group together sentences into paragraphs that begin with a *paragraph name,* the COBOL equivalent of a statement label. All the sentences that follow belong to that paragraph up to the next paragraph name. The paragraph name begins anywhere in columns 8 through 11 and must itself end with a period.

```
paragraph-label.
     statements in the paragraph [None of these ever need periods.]
     .
          [Placing the period on a line by itself fulfills the requirement that the paragraph
          end with a period and keeps it from causing problems.]
next-paragraph-label.     [This marks the end of a new paragraph.]
```

By definition, a paragraph contains sentences, and a sentence is defined as one or more statements terminated by a period. Therefore, by definition, the paragraph must end with a period. The compiler doesn't need it. It is just one of those rigid things in COBOL.

Sections

Rarely Used

A section is composed of one or more paragraphs. A section begins with a section name, followed by a paragraph name. It contains all paragraphs up to the next section name. Sections can be used to define the range of the PERFORM statement, similarly to paragraphs, but there is no need. Sections are redundant to paragraphs, except to segment programs. The following example illustrates a section. The section name begins anywhere in columns 8 through 11.

```
A10-part-2 SECTION.
A20-part-2.
   MOVE A TO B
   .                        [Section]
A30-part-2.
   MOVE C TO D
   .

A40-Part-2 SECTION.
       [The next section name delimits the previous section.]
```

COBOL requires paragraph names within a section to be unique, but you can use the same paragraph name in different sections. You must then qualify the paragraph name: *paragraph-name* IN *section-name.* Within the section containing a duplicate paragraph name, you need not qualify the paragraph name.

TIP   *Never use duplicate paragraph names because doing so is confusing.*

Archaic

Sections can *segment* programs to divide a large program into smaller segments and reduce the memory requirement. Today's computers all have very large central storage, so there is no need for this. You might, however, see segments in old programs. Sections are assigned literal priority numbers from 0 to 99. The most frequently used sections should have the lower numbers. Sections having the same priority, termed a *program segment,* are grouped into a single overlay segment by the compiler. Thus, sections that frequently communicate with each other should have the same priority. Sections with priority numbers 0 to 50, and sections not assigned a priority, constitute a fixed portion and reside permanently in memory during execution. Sections 51 to 99 constitute the *independent segments* and are loaded into memory when required. You code sections as follows for segmentation:

```
segment-name SECTION priority.
A10-Task-A SECTION 55.
```

The system would not bring the code in the *A10-task-a* section into memory until required by it or by one of the paragraphs it contains. When the section is brought into memory, it may overlay some other idle section. This reduces the total memory requirement of the program at some cost in extra I/O and slower execution.

3.3.4   Clauses and Phrases

A COBOL *clause,* often optional, consists of the words in a definition that specify attributes. The VALUE in the definition of *The-Age* here is a clause:

```
01 The-Age                    PIC S999 VALUE 21.
```

A *phrase* is a subpart of a COBOL statement and may or may not be optional. For example, THEN is a phrase in the IF statement:

```
IF A = B
    THEN MOVE X TO Y
END-IF
```

3.4 CHARACTERS AND WORDS

Essential

In COBOL, the characters *A* through *Z*, *a* through *z*, and *blank* are alphabetic; *0* through *9* are numeric; and + − * / = $, ; . "()><: are special. The quotation (") delimits character strings. IBM and PC COBOL let you code an apostrophe (') the same as a quotation ("), as does the new ANSI Standard. The upper- and lowercase characters are equivalent, except when they appear in a character string:

```
MOVE "THE END" TO A     Same as          move "THE END" to a
MOVE "The end" TO A     Not the same as  MOVE "THE END" TO A
```

A COBOL word consists of 1 to 30 characters. The characters may be *0* through *9*, *A* through *Z*, *a* through *z*, or the hyphen (-). The hyphen must not be the first or last character, but all other characters may appear in any position. (*-X* and *X-* are invalid, but *X-X* is valid.) COBOL names that identify procedures and data must be COBOL words that conform to the rules.

PROPOSED NEW ANSI STANDARD: Check Compiler to See if Implemented

The new ANSI standard adds the underscore (_) to the COBOL character set, with the same uses and limitation in words as the dash. The new standard also extends the word to 31 characters and adds the colon (:) and ampersand (&) as special characters.

3.5 NAMES

Essential

You must name paragraphs and sections, which are termed *procedure names.* Section names must be unique, and paragraph names must be unique within a section. Begin the procedure names anywhere in columns 8 through 11, and end them with a period:

```
A10-Initialize.
```

Statements may appear on the same line as the procedure name, provided that they begin in column 12 or beyond and are separated from the name and its period.

TIP *Place the procedure name on a line by itself to make it stand out.*

```
Correct, but not as clear:        Better coded as
A20-End.  MOVE 16 TO RETURN-CODE.  A20-End.
                                      MOVE 16 TO RETURN-CODE
```

TIP *Make each procedure contain a functionally related unit of code. The procedure name marks the start of such a functional unit, and the name can indicate what the procedure does. Make the procedure easier to locate in the program by preceding the procedure name with characters or numbers that indicate its position relative to other procedure names.*

```
B10-Initialize.
    PERFORM A20-Zero        [A20 should precede B10 in the program.]
B20-Read-Master.            [B20 should follow B10.]
    PERFORM Z10-Terminate   [Z10 would be much further down in the program.]
```

Data names are also 1 to 30 characters (*A* through *Z*, *a* through *z*, *0* through *9*, -), and the hyphen must not be the first or last character. Data names must be unique within a program or subprogram.

```
09  Total-Amount            PIC X.
01  Eof-Input               PIC X.
```

TIP *Select data names that describe their contents.*

For example, *Counter* only tells you that something is counted. *Page-Count* tells you what is counted, *Report-Page-Count* tells for which report the pages are counted, and *Rpt6-Page-No* conveys the same information by using shorter words and abbreviations.

PROPOSED NEW ANSI STANDARD: Check Compiler to See if Implemented

The new ANSI standard allows names to be as long as 60 characters, and the underscore (_) can be used like the dash.

3.6 COMMENTS

Essential

Write comments one per line by coding an asterisk (*) in column 7 and the comments in the remaining columns of the line.

```
* ASTERISK IN COLUMN 7.
* COMMENTS IN REMAINING COLUMNS OF LINE.
```

TIP *Indent the comment or set it off if it might hide or obscure the statements.*
Write the comments in lowercase to make them distinct from the COBOL
statements (or uppercase if you write the COBOL statements in lowercase).

```
 A10-Initialize.
 ****************************************************
 * Enclosing the comment in asterisks sets it off. *
 ****************************************************
      OPEN INPUT In-File
 * This comment is indented to set it off.
      DISPLAY "FILE OPENED."
 **** Exit
```

You can place comments anywhere within a program.

3.7 SPECIAL WORDS

COBOL has a wide variety of special words.

3.7.1 Abbreviations and Synonyms

Essential

Several long COBOL reserved words can be abbreviated, such as PIC for PICTURE
and THRU for THROUGH. This book uses only one form, generally an abbreviation rather than the long form. When an abbreviation is used, the unnecessary
characters are shaded. Thus, if you see PICTURE, you know you can code PIC or
PICTURE. You can write most words that can be singular or plural either way:
ZERO, ZEROS, or ZEROES, SPACE or SPACES, and so on. Likewise, you can
interchange IS/ARE and OF/IN: *Day* OF *Month* or *Day* IN *Month*.

TIP *In qualifying data names, OF and IN are interchangeable. But in the PIC*
clause, you can only use IN. Forget OF and use IN. IS and ARE are also
interchangeable. Use IS for singular items (ZERO) and ARE for plural (ZEROES).

3.7.2 Reserved Words

Essential

All COBOL defined words are reserved and cannot be used as procedure names or
data names. Appendix B lists COBOL reserved words. New reserved words are
constantly added as COBOL is expanded, and a program that compiles properly
today may not compile properly tomorrow. This is an inherent and frustrating part
of the COBOL language.

There are over 700 COBOL reserved words in the compilers described in this
book, including such common words as TIME, DATE, and ADDRESS, and no one

remembers them all. The following guidelines help in selecting names that are not reserved words.

- None begins with *0* through *9* or *Y.*
- None begins with *Z* except for ZERO, ZEROS, and ZEROES.
- None is a single character.
- None has the dash as the second character (x-) except for words beginning with *I-O* and *B-.*
- None has the dash as the third character (xx-) except for words beginning with *DB-* and *FH-.*
- None has two dashes except for those beginning with *FH—.*

Thus, *9Total-Amount, Ztotal-Amount, A-Total-Amount,* and *Total—Amount* would be relatively safe in never being reserved words, but this technique results in ugly names.

TIP *Select meaningful names and then let the compiler tell you which ones are invalid, or check the name in Appendix B.*

3.7.3 Optional Words

Sometimes Used

COBOL has optional words whose sole purpose is to improve readability. IS is such a word and is always optional.

```
IF A = B THEN ...    Same as    IF A IS = B THEN ...
                     Same as    IF A IS EQUAL TO B THEN ...
```

Optional words make statements more like English language sentences, which may or may not be good. However, they also make programming harder. You must remember the valid optional words, as not just any word will do, and remember where the optional words may be placed.

TIP *Minimize your use of optional words. Then someone reading your program won't have to worry about what they mean.*

3.7.4 Figurative Constants

Essential

COBOL has several figurative constants that assume the value of an alphanumeric or numeric literal when used. Their advantage is that they assume the appropriate attributes for the data type depending on the context in which they are used. For example, ZEROS assumes the value of a numeric zero or zero characters, depending on the context. When used as an alphanumeric literal, ZEROS represents the character literal "000 . . . 0" whose length is that required by the operation. COBOL provides the following figurative constants:

- ZEROS, ZERO, or ZEROES assumes the value of an arithmetic zero or one or more zero characters.

- SPACES or SPACE represents one or more blank characters.

- HIGH-VALUES or HIGH-VALUE represents one or more characters having the highest value in the collating sequence. You can only use HIGH-VALUES as alphanumeric data, not as numeric data.

- LOW-VALUES or LOW-VALUE represents one or more characters having the lowest value in the collating sequence. You can only use LOW-VALUES as alphanumeric data, not as numeric data.

- QUOTES or QUOTE represents one or more of the quotation character ("). The APOST compiler option in IBM and PC COBOL causes QUOTES to represent an apostrophe (') rather than a quotation. Note that although QUOTES represents a quotation character, you cannot code it in a character string. That is, "THE QUOTE." appears as shown, not as "THE".".

- NULLS or NULL represents a null value in storing addresses (not in the ANSI standard).

- ALL *"characters"* repeats the *characters* as often as required by the context in which it appears. You can also precede any of the foregoing with ALL. That is, ALL ZEROS is identical to ZEROS.

```
ALL "AB"      Same as       "ABABAB...AB"
```

ALL is an obsolete item in the ANSI standard when associated with a numeric item with a length greater than one. The reason is that characters may have to be truncated when moved to a numeric item, and the results are often unexpected. For example, suppose you have a numeric item described as

```
01  A                       PIC 99V99.
```

You might then use ALL to move a literal to it, with surprising results. The involved explanation for the results is the reason this use of ALL was made an obsolete item.

```
MOVE ALL "1" TO A           [A contains 11.00.]
MOVE ALL "12" TO A          [A contains 12.00.]
MOVE ALL "123" TO A         [A contains 31.00.]
MOVE ALL "1234" TO A        [A contains 34.00.]
MOVE ALL "12345" TO A       [A contains 45.00.]
```

3.7.5 Special Registers

Sometimes Used

COBOL has several built-in registers, which either are used by statements or provide an interface to the operating system. You don't describe the special registers; you just use them.

- COLUMN-COUNTER is used by the report writer to count the position of characters in a line and is described in Chapter 18. Its built-in description is PIC S9(9) BINARY SYNC.

- DEBUG-ITEM is used for debugging. It is described in Chapter 19 and its built-in description is:

```
01  DEBUG-ITEM.
    02  DEBUG-LINE              PIC X(6).
    02  FILLER                  PIC X VALUE SPACE.
    02  DEBUG-NAME              PIC X(30).
    02  FILLER                  PIC X VALUE SPACE.
    02  DEBUG-SUB-1             PIC S9(4)
                                SIGN LEADING SEPARATE.
    02  FILLER PIC              X VALUE SPACE.
    02  DEBUG-SUB-2             PIC S9(4)
                                SIGN LEADING SEPARATE.
    02  FILLER                  PIC X VALUE SPACE.
    02  DEBUG-SUB-3             PIC S9(4)
                                SIGN LEADING SEPARATE.
    02  FILLER                  PIC X VALUE SPACE.
    02  DEBUG-CONTENTS          PIC X(n).
```

- LINAGE-COUNTER is used in the LINAGE clause of the File Description entry. It is described in Chapter 12 and has the same definition as the LINAGE clause.

- LINE-COUNTER is used by the report writer to count the vertical lines on a page and is described in Chapter 18.

- PAGE-COUNTER is used by the report writer to count the page number and is described in Chapter 18. Its built-in description is PIC S9(9) BINARY SYNC.

The following special registers are not a part of the ANSI standard but are provided in IBM COBOL.

- ADDRESS OF *record* obtains storage address of an item for POINTER data. It is described in Chapter 25 and implicitly defined for each record in the Linkage Section. ADDRESS OF is in Micro Focus COBOL. Fujitsu COBOL provides the ADDR function.

- LENGTH OF *item* obtains the length of a numeric data item. It is described in Chapter 10 and its built-in description is PIC 9(9) BINARY. Don't use this. Use the LENGTH-OF intrinsic function described in Chapter 21.

- RETURN-CODE returns a completion code to the operating system when the run terminates. It is also in PC COBOL. RETURN-CODE is described in Chapter 19 and its built-in description is:

```
01  RETURN-CODE                 PIC S9(4) BINARY VALUE ZERO.
```

To set a return code, just move a value to the RETURN-CODE:

```
    MOVE 16 TO RETURN-CODE
```

- SHIFT-IN and SHIFT-OUT specify unprintable Double-Byte Character Set (DBCS) characters. Their built-in descriptions are:

```
01  SHIFT-IN                        PIC X(1) VALUE X"OF".
01  SHIFT-OUT                       PIC X(1) VALUE X"OE".
```

- SORT-CONTROL contains the ddname of a data set containing the sort control statement. It is described in Chapter 23 and its built-in description is:

```
01  SORT-CONTROL                    PIC X(8) VALUE "IGZSRTCD".
```

- SORT-RETURN sets the return code for a sort. It is described in Chapter 23 and its built-in description is:

```
01  SORT-RETURN                     PIC S9(4) BINARY VALUE ZERO.
```

- SORT-CORE-SIZE sets the number of bytes of memory for the sort. It is described in Chapter 23 and its built-in description is:

```
01  SORT-CORE-SIZE                  PIC S9(8) BINARY VALUE ZERO.
```

- SORT-FILE-SIZE estimates the number of records to be sorted. It is described in Chapter 23 and its built-in description is:

```
01  SORT-FILE-SIZE                  PIC S9(8) BINARY VALUE ZERO.
```

- SORT-MESSAGE specifies the ddname of a data set that the sort program is to use in place of the SYSOUT data set. It is described in Chapter 23 and its built-in description is:

```
01  SORT-MESSAGE                    PIC X(8) VALUE "SYSOUT".
```

- SORT-MODE-SIZE estimates the most frequent record length of variable-length records for sorting. It is described in Chapter 23 and its built-in description is:

```
01  SORT-MODE-SIZE                  PIC S9(5) BINARY VALUE ZERO.
```

- TALLY is an identifier used to store numeric values. Don't use it. Simply define your own identifier. Its built-in description is:

```
01  TALLY                           PIC 9(5) BINARY VALUE ZERO.
```

- WHEN-COMPILED contains the compilation date. Its built-in description is:

```
01  WHEN-COMPILED                   PIC X(16).
```

The date is stored in the form "*mm/dd/yyhh.mm.ss*". Use the WHEN-COMPILED intrinsic function described in Chapter 21.

3.8 PROGRAM ORGANIZATION

Essential

COBOL programs are divided into four divisions, each beginning with a header: Identification Division, Environment Division, Data Division, and Procedure Division. The Identification Division contains comments identifying the program, author, and date written. The Environment Division describes the computer, the I/O devices, and the access methods to be used. The Data Division describes all the data, and you must explicitly describe all data items. The Procedure Division contains the procedures, which in turn contain the executable program statements.

COBOL also provides subprograms (called *subroutines* in other languages), which are invoked by the CALL statement. You share data between the calling program and the subprogram by including the data as parameters (called *arguments* in other languages) in the CALL statement. These are described in Chapter 20.

3.9   SUGGESTIONS FOR WRITING PROGRAMS

TIP   *Keep the following in mind.*

- Keep the documentation inside the program by coding comments. If the documentation is within the program, it is much more likely to be updated when the program is changed, and it won't be lost.

- Begin the program with comments that summarize the program's purpose. Describe the program in enough detail to give the reader the proper background for reading the program. Generally a few paragraphs will do. Add comments if the program is changed during production so that the reader has a record of the major changes made, the date, and who made them.

- Organize the program into paragraphs, and invoke them with PERFORM statements as described in the next chapter. This gives the equivalent of a table of contents to the program, as shown in the following example. Notice how the following few statements give the reader a good idea of what the program is to do and the order in which it is done.

```
PROCEDURE DIVISION.
A00-Begin.
    PERFORM B10-Initialize
    PERFORM C10-Read-In-Tables
    MOVE LOW-VALUES TO Record-Key
    PERFORM D10-Read-Master-File WITH TEST AFTER
            UNTIL Record-Key = HIGH-VALUES
    PERFORM E10-Wrapup
    GOBACK.
```

- Make each main paragraph be a functionally related unit of code, such as initialization or record selection. Make the beginning and ending of each such unit stand out. How you do it is a matter of taste. The following example illustrates one method.

```
D10-Read-Master-File.
*****************************************************************
* PROCEDURE TO READ AND SELECT RECORDS.   *
* Records with Record-Type = "F" selected and displayed. *
* IN:  In-File open.        *
*      SS-name contains person's name.    *
* OUT: Record-Key contains HIGH-VALUES.   *
*      All records in In-File read. Records with *
*      Record-Type = "F" displayed.       *
*****************************************************************
```

```
                    MOVE LOW-VALUES TO Record-Key
                PERFORM WITH TEST BEFORE UNTIL Record-Key = HIGH-VALUES
                    MOVE LOW-VALUES TO Record-Type
                    PERFORM WITH TEST BEFORE UNTIL (Record-Key = HIGH-VALUES)
                                              OR (Record-Type = "F")
                        READ In-File INTO In-Record
                            AT END MOVE HIGH-VALUES TO Record-Key
                            NOT AT END DISPLAY "Record-Key = ", Record-Key
                        END-READ
                    END-PERFORM
                END-PERFORM
                    .
        **** Exit
```

- Organize the program to help the reader. Use blank lines or lines of asterisks to set off paragraphs. Save the reader from having to page back and forth in the program to follow the logical flow by placing the paragraphs of the program in the sequence in which they execute.

3.10 PROTOTYPE COBOL PROGRAM

The statements in a COBOL program must be in the following order:

```
IDENTIFICATION DIVISION.
PROGRAM-ID. program-name.
ENVIRONMENT DIVISION.
CONFIGURATION SECTION.
INPUT-OUTPUT SECTION.
FILE-CONTROL.
    SELECT In-File ASSIGN TO ddname.    [Associates the file with an I/O device.]
    SELECT Out-File ASSIGN TO ddname.
DATA DIVISION.
FILE SECTION.                           [Describe all the files here.]
FD  In-File                            [Code an FD to describe each file.]
    BLOCK CONTAINS 0 RECORDS.
    [This is a required item for Mainframe COBOL that will be described later.]
01  In-Record.
    [This is the record-area. The records placed here describe the preceding FD's
    records.]
    05  K                      PIC X(15).
    [Alphanumeric elementary item.]
    05  L.                     [L is a group item.]
      10  M                    PIC S9.
    [External decimal number elementary item.]
      10  N                    PIC X(4).
    [Alphanumeric elementary item.]
FD  Out-File BLOCK CONTAINS 0 RECORDS.
01  Out-Record               PIC X(20).
WORKING-STORAGE SECTION.     [Describe the data items here.]
01  In-EOF                   PIC X.
*       Flag for end of file. "Y", EOF. "N", no EOF.
```

```
        [Code an * in column 7 for a comment.]
 01  Record-Count                     PIC S9(8).
*        Record-Count counts the records read and written.
 PROCEDURE DIVISION.
        [Program statements of the main body follow this.]
 A00-Begin.
        [The Procedure Division is composed of paragraphs or sections.]
     OPEN INPUT In-File, OUTPUT Out-File
     MOVE "N" TO In-EOF
     MOVE ZEROS to Record-Count
     PERFORM A10-Copy-File WITH TEST AFTER UNTIL In-EOF = "Y"
     CLOSE In-File, Out-File
     DISPLAY "Records copied: ", Record-Count
     GOBACK.
**** End of program execution.
 A10-Copy-File.
     READ In-File
        AT END MOVE "Y" TO In-EOF
                DISPLAY "END OF FILE"
        NOT AT END
                MOVE In-Record TO Out-Record
                WRITE Out-Record
                ADD 1 TO Record-Count
     END-READ
        .
**** Exit
 END PROGRAM program-name.
```

The many required statements give even simple COBOL programs a formidable look, but writing them soon becomes automatic. They do help in reading programs, because you know where to look to find things. A quick look at the Input-Output Section tells which files are used, and the Data Division describes all the data used in the program.

EXERCISES

1. What problems can the reserved words of COBOL cause?
2. Tell which of the following COBOL names are incorrect, and why.

```
FORMULA            Z
2HOT               NOT-HER
PROGRAM-ID         7UP
OH*                UP-OR-DOWN
W-                 EITHER/OR
UP                 TO H24
NOW-OR-LATER       -TO-HERE
TEXT               MEET-ME@4
F-117              AVERAGE-AMOUNT-OF-DOLLARS-REMAINING
HUT_16             HASN'T
```

3. Explain the syntax errors in the following statements.

```
A1.   COMPUTE A = B*C.
      MOVE ZERO TO A.
      IF (B=C) THEN GO TO A1.
      MOVE 1 TO X(1,2).
****  BEGIN COMPUTATIONS
START-IT.
      MOVE X
      TO Y, MOVE V
      TO W
      ADD A, B C TO D.
      ADD E, F, G TO H.
NEW-PART
      ADD I,J TO K.
      ADD X(1) TO Y.
      COMPUTE A = B+C.
      MOVE STRING TO X.
```

CHAPTER 4

CRITERIA

The criteria developed here are used throughout the book, and lead to several rules and guidelines for style. If you are not interested in the why of the programming rules and guidelines used in this book, you can skip this chapter.

4.1 RATIONALE FOR THE CRITERIA

A *rule* is something that there is every reason to observe, with no valid exceptions. Indenting nested IF statements is a rule. A *guideline* has valid reasons for being followed, but in exceptional instances should not be followed. Eliminating the GO TO statement is a guideline.

Some rules and guidelines must be ambiguous. Everyone agrees that IF statements should not be nested to *too* deep a level, but you can argue *how* deep. Either there is no precise definition, or it would take so many words to state the rule as to make it useless. In these instances, use the *reasonable-person rule*. In common law, this rule states that if a reasonable person would find something wrong, it is wrong.

Frequently we find ourselves objecting to something with feelings like those expressed in the childhood ditty:

> *I do not like thee, Doctor Fell;*
> *The reason why, I cannot tell;*
> *But this I know and know full well,*
> *I do not like thee, Doctor Fell.*

Rules give you words to express why you feel as you do about something. Rules are often said to detract from creativity, but creativity is hard to suppress. The poet Homer followed precise rules of meter and rhyme, but that didn't suppress his creativity in writing the *Iliad* and the *Odyssey*. Good rules are not a panacea, but they help.

At first glance, this chapter may appear to be reinventing the wheel. In fact, it does even less—it simply suggests that you use the wheel. None of the criteria developed in this chapter are new. A selected reading list is given on the Web site but many of the criteria have been around since saber-toothed tigers stopped being a menace.

4.2 THE ENVIRONMENT

The COBOL programming environment is that of production computing for commercial applications that have a relatively long life, are more input/output-oriented than computation-oriented, and are more logical than algorithmic. There is often a separation of effort in design, programming, running, maintenance, and even documentation, with different people working on different parts. This makes communication vital. It is this environment for which the criteria are derived, and the goal is to improve program maintenance, correctness, reliability, and efficiency.

Too often, programming techniques are concerned only with the efficiency and implementation of individual language statements. But the life of such knowledge is short, and what was avoided with old compilers may be encouraged with new ones. With computers continuing to double in price-performance every 18 months, much of the concern over which language features are efficient is irrelevant.

COBOL was designed at a time when people were relatively cheap and computers were expensive. In 1965, 1 million computer instructions were roughly equivalent in cost to 15 minutes of a programmer's time. Today the opposite is true. People are expensive and computers are cheap. A million instructions today buys less than a fraction of a millisecond of a programmer's time.

4.3 THE RULES AND GUIDELINES

People often fail to appreciate just how hard programming is. Is the following COBOL statement correct?

```
COMPUTE X = Y / Z
```

Y or Z might not have been assigned values; Z might contain zero; the identifiers might be of improper data types; they might be undefined; or the names might be reserved words. Precision might be lost; an underflow or overflow might occur; the statement might be in the wrong columns; or blanks might not have been properly inserted. The statement might be at the wrong place in the program, or you might have actually wanted $Y * Z$ or Y/W. These are only the obvious errors from a single statement containing no logic. Programs consist of hundreds of statements with logic and interaction, and systems contain thousands. Each statement is like a moving part in a machine, and if a part fails, the entire system may fail. In addition, the job-control language and the interaction with the operating system can be more complex than the programming language. Programming is a difficult undertaking in which nothing is trivial. This leads to the first and most important rule.

TIP   *Simplify.*

Simplifying programs makes them easier to design, maintain, understand, document, and run. Begin simplifying in the design, because simplicity lost here cannot be regained. Simplicity may not always be possible, but you can always eliminate needless complexity.

People tend to regard complexity highly, because human nature holds in awe that which it doesn't comprehend. But accomplishment comes from making things simple rather than complex. Even in science, the great ideas are simple. Sir Isaac Newton expressed three classic laws of physics with a fraction of the complexity found in the 1040 income tax forms. Were he alive today, surely he, too, would have an accountant prepare his income tax returns and his children program his VCR.

The techniques of good expository writing in English also apply to programming. Many of the following rules are borrowed from Strunk and White's *The Elements of Style* (Macmillan, 1959) and George Orwell's essay on "Politics and the English Language" (*A Collection of Essays,* Doubleday, 1954). The essence of good expository writing is to decide what you want to say, and then to say it as simply, concisely, and clearly as possible. This is also the essence of good programming.

Many simple programming techniques appear to be difficult because they are unfamiliar. A binary search is difficult in COBOL only if you are unfamiliar with the SEARCH statement. A goal of this book is to make all COBOL statements familiar by describing them and giving examples of their use.

TIP   *Eliminate the unnecessary.*

That which you eliminate doesn't need to be designed, programmed, documented, and maintained, and costs nothing to run. Never use a long word where a short one will do, such as PICTURE for PIC. Omit unused paragraph names, because they can distract and confuse. A single discounted cash flow subprogram written to be used by many will save effort and likely be both more reliable and more efficient than separate subprograms written for several individual applications.

Eliminating the unnecessary also simplifies. Notice the apparent difference in complexity in the following two descriptions that produce identical results.

```
01  X PICTURE S999999V99 USAGE IS COMPUTATIONAL VALUE IS ZERO.
01  X PIC S9(6)V99 COMP VALUE ZERO.
```

Neither statement is comprehensible to someone unfamiliar with COBOL, but the first appears more complex. PIC for PICTURE and COMP for COMPUTATIONAL become as familiar to COBOL programmers as are Dr. for doctor, Ms. for Miss/Mrs., and COBOL for common business-oriented language.

Eliminate the optional words in COBOL. For example, you'll quickly become familiar with the READ statement written in the following form.

```
READ In-File INTO In-Record
```

Then one day you might see it written like this:

```
READ In-File NEXT RECORD INTO In-Record
```

Is it the same statement? If you aren't familiar with what NEXT RECORD means, you must look it up because it might entirely change the way the statement executes. This wastes your time because it is an optional word that has no effect on execution, being provided only as a perverse form of program documentation.

Eliminate useless repetition. Useless repetition occurs in many ways. For example, data entered into a system may be used in several programs. By validating the data only once as it enters the system rather than at each place it is used in a program, you save effort, save the computer's resources, and make the system easier to change. Useless repetition often creeps in under the guise of flexibility. Many people feel that it is good to provide a variety of ways in which to do something. They are like the old farmer who is asked for directions back to the main road. He doesn't realize that by describing several alternatives, he is making you more lost.

COBOL often gives the appearance of having been designed by that same old farmer. The following statements all add 1 to an identifier:

```
COMPUTE Variable = Variable + 1
ADD 1 TO Variable
ADD 1 TO Variable GIVING Variable
SUBTRACT -1 FROM Variable
SUBTRACT -1 FROM Variable GIVING Variable
SET INDEX-Variable UP BY 1
```

Each statement has its own options and operates on limited data types. What is essentially simple becomes complex with the many ways in which it can be done. You are forced to make an unnecessary choice and then worry whether it was the correct one.

TIP   *Clarify. Write to be read by others.*

Programs are read more frequently than they are written. Even a program's author writes a program only once and then reads it many times during debugging. It follows that it is more important that programs be easily read than that they be easily written. Programs are also likely to be read by someone other than the program's author. Often, programs are considered to be readable if someone who understands what the program is to do can understand how the code accomplishes it. This is the absolute minimum in readability. The goal should be to go beyond this to write programs so that someone can understand what the program is to do from reading the language statements.

Programmers often sacrifice clarity to optimize at the detail level, where the results are rarely measurable. Efficiency should come from the design and not from modification during debugging or production. Programs cost little to change during design but are expensive to change once they have been coded, and it is risky to modify a correct program. Any significant inefficiency is usually localized to a few areas. Avoid cleverness when it is at the expense of clarity.

One way to achieve clarity is to avoid ambiguity. For example, the COBOL statement MULTIPLY *A* BY *B* is ambiguous, because it is not apparent where the result is stored. Surprisingly, it is stored in *B*. The statement COMPUTER $B = B *A$ avoids the ambiguity. Few people remember the hierarchy of logical and arithmetic operations. In what order will the following operations be performed?

```
IF A = B OR C = D AND E = F …
```

Use parentheses to show the hierarchy and remove the ambiguity.

```
IF (A = B) OR ((C = D) AND (E = F)) …
```

Clarify the sequence of execution; things that hide it are bad. This rule is the basis for structured programming. To understand the sequence of instructions at any point in a program, you must know where control came from and where it is going. A good way to clarify the flow of control is to have a single entry and exit in each functional unit of code. This eliminates the threading in and out of statements with a GO TO. For example, if control can reach a paragraph by sequential execution, falling through from the previous paragraph, and by a PERFORM or GO TO, it is difficult to tell where you came from. The following code is typical.

```
A.   IF NOT a-condition THEN GO TO B.
        a-statements.
B.   IF NOT b-condition THEN GO TO C.
        b-statements.
     GO TO D.
C.   c-statements.
D.   d-statements.
```

The code is intertwined and hard to follow. How do you get to *D?* Under what conditions do you execute *C?* Is the preceding a complete unit, or might *C* be the target of a PERFORM or GO TO from somewhere else? Now examine the way the preceding coding reads when you eliminate the unnecessary GO TOs.

```
A.
    IF a-condition
        THEN a-statements
    END-IF
    IF b-condition
        THEN b-statements
        ELSE c-statements
    END-IF
    d-statements
```

Now it is clear that paragraph A is a unit and that the *d-statements* are always executed. The *c-statements* cannot be the target of a PERFORM or GO TO, and you get to the *c-statements* when *b-condition* is false.

Weinberg, in his book *The Psychology of Computer Programming* (Van Nostrand Reinhold, 1971), points out that a linear sequence is easier to follow than a nonlinear one. A program containing many GO TOs is hard to follow, because you must keep track of all the possible paths and page back and forth in the source code. The GO TO is not all bad. It does make it clear where control is going. It is bad only in that it clouds where control came from and distracts the reader by breaking the linearity of the program.

Eliminating unnecessary GO TO is good, but it does not ensure that the flow of control is clear. The following example also hides the sequence of execution.

```
IF Cost IS EQUAL TO ZERO MOVE ZERO TO Page-A, MOVE 1 TO
New-Line, ELSE PERFORM Max-Size, IF Cost IS GREATER THAN
ZERO PERFORM Zero-Cost, ELSE PERFORM Big-Cost.
```

It reads well as an English sentence, but it is difficult to read as a sequence of discrete steps. It is better written as follows:

```
IF Cost = 0
    THEN MOVE 0 TO Page-A
         MOVE 1 TO New-Line
    ELSE PERFORM Max-Size
         IF Cost > 0
             THEN PERFORM Zero-Cost
             ELSE PERFORM Big-Cost
         END-IF
END-IF
```

Now the logical sequence is clear. Computer programs are not read for their contribution to the literature of the English language but to understand the logic and computations within the program. The previous example shows how programs can be made clear by proper indentation. Programs are also more readable if a single statement is contained on a line. If a line must be continued, break the statement at a point where it is obvious that it is continued, and indent the continuation. Thus, you express the logic and continuation of statements by indentation.

Nested IFs are often avoided, but they are good if written so that the intent is clear. The following statement is a nested IF, and it is clear.

```
IF A = B
    THEN MOVE C TO D
         MOVE X TO Y
         IF E = F
             THEN PERFORM M
                  IF G = H
                      THEN PERFORM Z
                      ELSE PERFORM X
                  END-IF
         END-IF
END-IF
```

THEN clauses nested to several levels are usually clear, but ELSE clauses can cause problems, as shown in the following example:

```
IF A = B
    THEN MOVE 1 TO X
         IF C = D
             THEN PERFORM U
                  IF E = F
                      THEN PERFORM V
                           PERFORM W
                      ELSE PERFORM M
                  END-IF
             ELSE PERFORM N
                  MOVE X TO Y
         END-IF
    ELSE PERFORM P
END-IF
```

Each ELSE clause has a corresponding THEN clause, and these clauses are hard to pair up if the ELSE does not immediately follow the THEN. A little astigmatism on the part of the reader, and they would be lost. Nested IFs are good if not nested too deeply and if the corresponding ELSE clause is kept close to its THEN clause.

TIP *Keep the major logic and organization as visible and at as high a level as possible.*

This makes programs easier to follow and change. A good way to do this is to use the PERFORM statement:

```
MOVE "N" TO EOF-Master
PERFORM Read-Master UNTIL EOF-Master = "Y"
```

These statements tell you where you are reading the master file, that it is read within a loop, and that the loop terminates when *EOF-Master* is set to "Y", probably by detecting the end of the file. It clearly indicates the start of the read loop (the beginning of paragraph *Read-Master*), and the end of the loop (the end of paragraph *Read-Master*).

Make the program *modular* by organizing it into distinct functional parts. Invoke the modules with PERFORM statements. This aids in quickly finding your way into a program by giving the equivalent of a table of contents for program execution. It also divides the program into smaller parts that can be readily digested, and it eases maintenance, because you can identify the beginning and end of a functionally related part of the program. In addition, it reduces the interaction, or at least keeps the interacting components together.

You constantly break up long items into shorter parts without giving it much thought. The number 12135550911 becomes relatively easy to remember and comprehend as 1 (213) 555-0911. Dividing a complex program into digestible components makes it much more manageable.

TIP *Convey as much useful information in the coding as possible.*

COBOL is largely self-documenting and is made more so by selecting meaningful names. For example, the paragraph name *Read-Loop* conveys more information than *A1*. *A10-Read-Loop* conveys even more information, because it indicates its location relative to other names if the names are placed in sequential order within the program. By conveying useful information, you lead the reader through the code. Consider the following two examples that show alternative ways to code a loop.

```
MOVE 1 TO K.
A20-Max.
    several-statements
    COMPUTE K = K + 1
    IF K NOT > 20 GO TO A20-Max
```

Not until after plowing through many statements to discover a GO TO back to the start do you discover that it is a loop. The following is a better way to code the loop.

```
PERFORM A20-Max
    VARYING K FROM 1 BY 1
    UNTIL K > 20
□   □   □
```

```
A20-Max.
    several-statements.
```

Now it is clear that a loop controlled by *K* is repeated 20 times. However, the loop is still bad, because the statements comprising the loop do not immediately follow the statement controlling them. In this case, it would be better to use an in-line PERFORM so that the statements can be placed within the loop:

```
PERFORM VARYING K FROM 1 BY 1
        UNTIL K > 20
    several-statements
END-PERFORM
```

TIP   *Keep the reader in context.*

Things are easier to understand when they are in context. The context consists of the surrounding items that, by their presence, tell you something about the item. In the following example, a single word of context is enough to give the word *beagle* three different meanings and, in one case, is enough to indicate a spelling error.

Beagle—dog (a breed of dogs)

Beagle—Darwin (the ship upon which Darwin sailed)

Beagle—hawk (a misspelling of *eagle*)

The first step in making a program understandable is to put the reader in context. A short narrative at the start of the program should tell what the program does, what goes into it, and what comes out of it. Place related items together so that each item contributes to the understanding of the others. Isolating related items also makes them easier to change.

TIP   *Write programs to be changed.*

Change is constant for most programs. In theory, programs are written from a complete set of specifications, and when the programs perform according to the specifications, the job is complete. In practice, it rarely works like this. Specifications are written when the least amount is known about the program, and no specifications can be complete enough to account for all contingencies. Programs evolve during the implementation. The budget might be cut, requiring a less elaborate program. In a personnel program, new legislation could require the addition of new information and the exclusion of old information. A new personnel director might want a different set of reports. This evolution does not end when the program is placed in production but continues over its entire life. Information produced by programs acts as a catalyst, generating a desire for more or different information. After people have worked with the program for a while, they may begin to understand what they really want. Programming is an iterative process.

Maintenance often costs more than development, because a surprising number of items can change. The number of departments and locations within a company can certainly change, but you might forget that the number of states can also change (Puerto Rico). And, of course, the calendar changes each year. About the only things unlikely to change are the number of months in a year (unless the Aztecs stage a comeback) and physical measurements (until the Unites States switches to the metric system).

Facilitating change is very important in the design of data. As a simple example, you should never store a person's age in a data record. This would require updating the record on the person's birthday and, if nothing else, might present some difficult job-scheduling problems. It would be better to store the person's date of birth and then write a subprogram to compute the person's age given the person's birth date and the current date as parameters.

You can make programs easier to change by making data and data descriptions drive programs wherever possible. If a table may change, read it in from a file on disk rather than building it into the program. Then you can make the change in the external data without disturbing the program. Make all items that are likely to change be parameters.

TIP   *Trust the code and not the external documentation.*

Regardless of what a comment says, a program will do as it is directed by the statements. The statements themselves should serve as the documentation where possible, eliminating a separate documentation effort and the possibility that it will be incorrect or outdated. Experienced maintenance programmers know that program flowcharts, while a fine tool for design, are difficult to draw and are rarely kept up to date. Documentation that isn't trusted isn't used.

Make the source statements serve as the documentation. Use comments when the language statements do not make clear what will be done, but never when the statements themselves are clear. Don't let the comments obscure the code. In the following, the comment just restates what the statement does. It doesn't tell you what you really need to know—why the year is being divided by 4.

```
*   Divide Last-Yr by 4.
    DIVIDE Last-Yr BY 4 GIVING A-Num REMAINDER Leap-Flag
```

Better is

```
*  Determine if Last-Yr is a LEAP YEAR. If so, Leap-Flag
*  contains ZERO.
      DIVIDE Last-Yr BY 4 GIVING A-Num REMAINDER Leap-Flag
```

TIP *Don't mislead, surprise, or confuse.*

Human beings have difficulty in noticing the unexpected. You have seen examples such as the following:

PARIS IN THE

THE SPRING

Because you do not expect to find the extra THE, you do not see it. Computers lack this tolerance for ambiguity, and this causes us problems in communicating with them. An example of surprising and confusing the reader is to use an item named *Days* to contain units of months. Exceptions can make programs complex and difficult to follow, and they can contribute heavily to maintenance problems. Eliminate exceptions where possible. Failing this, comment them as exceptions, giving the reason and explaining how they are handled.

Much of the surprise and confusion in programming comes from inconsistency. For example, in COBOL, you must READ a *file-name,* but WRITE a *record-name.* This is inconsistent, and as a result it is easy to confuse the two. Rules, standards, and a confidence in your tools, techniques, and abilities all lead to consistency.

Avoid complex logical expressions, especially those combining NOT with OR or those with double negatives. In the following example, it is not immediately apparent that GOBACK is always executed.

```
    IF (Salary NOT = 0) OR
       (Salary NOT = 1)
       THEN GOBACK
    END-IF
```

Do not force small incompatibilities for small improvements. It sometimes seems as if a cavalier attitude, rather than necessity, is the mother of incompatibility. Often it is better to live with bad features than to undergo the slow torture of minor, incompatible improvements.

TIP *Check for errors where they can occur, on the assumption that things will go wrong.*

One of the frustrating aspects of computer programming is that a program may run correctly hundreds of times and then erupt with an error. This inevitably happens, and you should design and program for it. You do this by checking for errors, recovering if possible, and printing error messages. For example, when you read a table, check for the table exceeding the internal table size. If you divide by a variable, check for zero divide. Validate all raw input data. Don't assume that things have gone correctly. For example, you might think that there is no need to check the sequence of a master file because it is kept in sort order. You forget that the sort key may be updated, an unsorted file may be inadvertently read, or any of a hundred other things may go wrong.

Once you detect an error, print a clear, concise message describing the error. Make error messages relevant and direct them to the person who will read them. The message "TABLE OVERFLOW--ABEND" is ambiguous if the program has more than one table. ABEND means *evening* in German, but little else to nonprogrammers. The error message should describe what went wrong, the transaction or data involved, the action taken within the program, and any action that must be taken outside the program.

TIP *Break any of these rules rather than do anything outright barbarous.*

This is just to say that rules must not stop you from thinking.

4.4 SUMMARY

Before applying the criteria to the COBOL language features and to structured programming, reread them carefully.

- Simplify.
- Eliminate the unnecessary.
- Clarify. Write to be read by others.
- Keep the major logic and organization as visible and at as high a level as possible.
- Convey as much useful information in the coding as possible.
- Keep the reader in context.
- Write programs to be changed.
- Trust the code and not the external documentation.
- Don't mislead, surprise, or confuse.
- Check for errors where they can occur on the assumption that things will go wrong.
- Break any of these rules rather than do anything outright barbarous.

EXERCISES

1. Critique one of the following computer languages using the criteria developed in this chapter.

   ALGOL   COBOL
   APL   FORTRAN
   Assembler language   Pascal
   BASIC   PL/I
   C/C++   RPG

2. Write a paper suggesting additions, deletions, or a complete new set of criteria if you disagree with those in this chapter.

3. Write a paper critiquing the computer operating system or job-control language with which you are familiar, using the criteria developed in this chapter.

CHAPTER 5

DETAILS OF THE BASIC COBOL STATEMENTS

Several basic COBOL statements are described in detail here for reference. Their basic operation was covered in Chapter 2, and this chapter goes into all the nuances. Some of the redundant, obsolescent statements not previously covered are also described here. You can skip through this chapter quickly and refer back to it as needed.

5.1   THE MOVE STATEMENT

Essential

The MOVE statement moves the contents of an item to an identifier. If necessary, COBOL converts the *item* to the data type of the *identifier*.

```
MOVE item TO identifier
```

An *item* may be either a literal or an identifier of an appropriate data type. The following MOVE statements are then valid.

```
MOVE 2 TO X          [Numeric literal moved to an identifier.]
MOVE "A" TO Y        [Nonnumeric literal moved to an identifier.]
MOVE W TO Z          [Identifier moved to another identifier.]
```

But the following statement is invalid.

```
MOVE W TO 2          [Wrong! Can't move an identifier to a literal.]
```

You can assign a single item to several identifiers.

```
MOVE 0 TO Rec-In,          Same as      MOVE 0 TO Rec-In
          Rec-Selected,                 MOVE 0 TO Rec-Selected
          Rec-Ignored                  MOVE 0 TO Rec-Ignored
```

The sending item is converted to the data type of the receiving identifier as appropriate. The MOVE statement can either move single items (an *elementary move*) to an identifier or move one group of items (a *group move*) to another group. The following is an example of a group move:

```
01  A.
    05  B                         PIC X.
    05  C                         PIC X(100).
01  D.
    05  E                         PIC S9(4).
    05  F                         PIC X(50).
    05  G                         PIC S9(4).
    □   □   □
    MOVE D TO A
```

The 52 bytes from *D* are moved to *A*, and the remaining 49 bytes of *A* are padded on the right with blanks. In a group move such as this, COBOL moves the bytes from the sending field to the receiving field without conversion. If the receiving field is shorter than the sending field, COBOL truncates the bytes. If the receiving field is longer, COBOL pads the field with blanks on the right. (If you add the JUST LEFT clause on the description of the receiving field, which left-justifies the data as described in Chapter 10, COBOL pads on the left.)

The results are undefined when the sending and receiving items overlap.

```
01  A.
    05  B                         PIC X.
    05  C                         PIC X VALUE "X".
    05  D                         PIC X(99).
    □   □   □
    MOVE C TO A
```

The results are undefined because C is contained in *A*.

5.2 THE MOVE CORRESPONDING STATEMENT

Sometimes Used

You can move corresponding elements of records by appending CORRESPONDING to the MOVE.

```
01  A.
    05  X                         PIC X.
    05  Y                         PIC X.
    05  V                         PIC X.
01  B.
    05  V                         PIC X.
    05  W                         PIC X.
    05  X                         PIC X.
    □   □   □
```

```
        MOVE CORR A TO B          Same as     MOVE X IN A TO X IN B
                                               MOVE V IN A TO V IN B
```

Notice that the data items on the right in the preceding example are *qualified*. When two records have elements with the same names, you must qualify the element names with the record name so that COBOL can know which element is meant. In the example, you must write element *X* as *X* IN *A* or *X* IN *B* to distinguish the element. You can also code CORR with the ADD and SUBTRACT statements, as described following.

All elementary items that have the same name and qualification, up to but not including the group names, participate in the operation. The elementary items need not be in the same order or be of the same data types. COBOL will convert items of different data types.

```
01   Dates.
     05   Start-Date.
          10   Month            PIC XX.
          10   Days             PIC S999 PACKED-DECIMAL.
          10   Year             PIC S99.
          10   Century          PIC S9(4).
     05   Days-In-Year          PIC S999.
     05   End-Date.
          10   Year             PIC S99.
          10   Month            PIC S99.
          10   Days             PIC S99.
     05   Yrnday.
          10   Days-In-Year     PIC S999.
     □   □   □
     MOVE CORR Start-Date TO End-Date
```

Same as

```
     MOVE Month IN Start-Date TO Month IN End-Date
     MOVE Days IN Start-Date TO Days IN End-Date
     MOVE Year IN Start-Date TO Year IN End-Date
```

Elementary item names must have the same qualification to participate in the operation. *Century* does not participate because it is not an elementary item in *End-Date,* and *Days-In-Year* does not participate because its fully qualified names do not match. If the group names contain tables (arrays, which are described by the OCCURS *n* TIMES clause), the tables are ignored. Any FILLER or unnamed item is likewise ignored.

```
01   Some-Item.
     05   B                     OCCURS 20 TIMES.
          10   C                PIC X.
          10   D                PIC X.
     05   FILLER                PIC X.
     05   E                     PIC X.
```

If *Some-Item* were named in a CORR operation, table *B* and the FILLER would not participate. The group names may be tables or belong to tables, in which case they must be subscripted or indexed. The following statement would be valid for the previous record.

```
MOVE CORR B(1) TO X
```

The CORR phrase can make programs easier to change, especially when corresponding elements are likely to be added or deleted from records. You can make a single change to the data descriptions rather than to the statements scattered throughout the program.

However, CORR has disadvantages. It may not be obvious, when a data description is changed, that the execution of Procedure Division statements that have a CORR phrase may change, too. This can create severe maintenance problems. In practice, CORR always seems to be less useful than it would appear to be because different names always seem to have already been chosen for the file descriptions your program is using. And finally, the coding effort you save by using CORR is often more than offset by having to qualify all the items (*Month* IN *Start-Date*) because they do not have unique names.

TIP *Don't use CORR. The risk of changing program execution when data names are changed outweighs the savings in effort.*

5.3 ARITHMETIC STATEMENTS: COMPUTE

Essential

The COMPUTE statement evaluates an arithmetic expression on the right of the equal sign and assigns it to the identifier on the left. Conversion will occur if necessary to evaluate the expression or assign its value to the identifier. An *arithmetic expression* is either a single item or several items operated on by the arithmetic operations (+, −, *, /, and **). A, $A + D$, and $A + B * 2$ are arithmetic expressions. An arithmetic expression can contain both numeric literals (constants) and identifiers (variables).

```
COMPUTE identifier = arithmetic-expression
COMPUTE A = B * 2
COMPUTE A = B + C / D
```

You can also code multiple receiving fields.

```
COMPUTE A, B = C + D     Same as     COMPUTE A = C + D
                                     COMPUTE B = C + D
                         Or          COMPUTE A = C + D
                                     MOVE A TO B
```

Parentheses specify the order in which the operations are to be performed. Those within inner parentheses are performed first.

```
COMPUTE X = (A + (B - C) * D / E) ** 2
```

The spaces in the COMPUTE statement are important, and the rules for placement are as follows:

- One or more spaces before and after the equal sign: $A = B$ but not $A=B$
- One or more spaces before and after the arithmetic operators +, −, *, /, and **: $A + B$ but not $A+B$

Note that the simplest form of the COMPUTE statement is identical to the MOVE statement, but can be used only for numeric data items.

```
COMPUTE A = B           Same as        MOVE B TO A
```

5.4   ADD, SUBTRACT, MULTIPLY, AND DIVIDE STATEMENTS

Rarely Used

COBOL also has ADD, SUBTRACT, MULTIPLY, and DIVIDE statements, which perform the arithmetic operations implied by their names. They are redundant to COMPUTE, and while they may be more readable to someone who hasn't taken high-school algebra, don't use them. They are to programming what "See Dick and Jane run" are to literature. They make COBOL programmers look bad. COBOL was intended to let the person off the street write computer programs. This didn't happen with COBOL, but it did with spreadsheet tools, and it ensued that the person off the street had no trouble writing in the algebraic form. There are two exceptions to this suggested prohibition.

1. The ADD statement is a convenient shorthand for adding an item to an identifier.

```
ADD item TO identifier    Same as        COMPUTE identifier =
                                                  identifier + item
ADD 1 TO A                                COMPUTE A = A + 1
ADD B TO C                                COMPUTE C = C + B
```

2. You need ADD and SUBTRACT to perform corresponding operations on records with the CORR phrase, because COMPUTE cannot have the CORR phrase.

TIP   *Aside from the simple ADD and SUBTRACT and the CORR phrase, forget about ADD, SUBTRACT, MULTIPLY, and DIVIDE.*

The equivalent COMPUTE statement indicates the operation performed.

```
ADD A TO B                Same as         COMPUTE B = B + A
ADD A, B GIVING C                          COMPUTE C = A + B
ADD A, B, C TO D                           COMPUTE D = D + A + B + C
ADD A, B, C TO D, E                        COMPUTE D = D + A + B + C
                                           COMPUTE E = E + A + B + C
ADD A, B, C GIVING D                       COMPUTE D = A + B + C
ADD A, B, C GIVING D, E                    COMPUTE D = A + B + C
                                           COMPUTE E = A + B + C


SUBTRACT A FROM B         Same as          COMPUTE B = B - A
SUBTRACT A, B, C FROM D                     COMPUTE D = D - A - B - C
SUBTRACT A, B, C FROM D, E                  COMPUTE D = D - A - B - C
                                           COMPUTE E = E - A - B - C
SUBTRACT A FROM B GIVING C                  COMPUTE C = B - A
SUBTRACT A, B, C FROM D                     COMPUTE E = D - A - B - C
  GIVING E
SUBTRACT A, B, C FROM D                     COMPUTE E = D - A - B - C
  GIVING E, F                              COMPUTE F = D - A - B - C


DIVIDE A INTO B           Same as          COMPUTE B = B / A
DIVIDE A INTO B, C                          COMPUTE B = B / A
                                           COMPUTE C = C / A
DIVIDE A INTO B GIVING C                    COMPUTE C = B / A
DIVIDE A INTO B                            COMPUTE C = B / A
  GIVING C, D                              COMPUTE D = B / A
DIVIDE A BY B GIVING C                      COMPUTE C = A / B
DIVIDE A BY B GIVING C, D                   COMPUTE C = A / B
                                           COMPUTE D = A / B


MULTIPLY A BY B           Same as          COMPUTE B = A * B
MULTIPLY A BY B, C                          COMPUTE B = A * B
                                           COMPUTE C = A * C
MULTIPLY A BY B GIVING C                    COMPUTE C = A * B
MULTIPLY A BY B                            COMPUTE C = A * B
  GIVING C, D                              COMPUTE D = A * B
```

The CORR phrase option in the ADD and SUBTRACT statements causes the operation to be performed on corresponding elements of records. Note that CORR can't be used with GIVING.

```
01 A.
   05 X                    PIC 9.
   05 Y                    PIC 9.
   05 V                    PIC 9.
01 B.
   05 V                    PIC 9.
   05 W                    PIC 9.
   05 X                    PIC 9.
   □  □  □
   ADD CORR A TO B         Same as    ADD X IN A TO X IN B
                                      ADD V IN A TO V IN B
   SUBTRACT CORR B FROM A  Same as    SUBTRACT X IN B FROM X IN A
                                      SUBTRACT V IN B FROM V IN A
```

COMPUTE is simpler to write and makes the computation easier to understand than the other statements. COMPUTE also keeps track of any intermediate results and gives more accuracy by extending the precision to 30 digits if necessary. However, the intermediate results are more difficult to keep track of in long COMPUTE statements, especially those with division. It may be better to break up the COMPUTE and define a data item of the desired precision to control the intermediate results, as follows:

```
COMPUTE A = B * (C / D) * E
```

Perhaps this is better written as:

```
01  Temp  PIC S9(5)V9(6) PACKED-DECIMAL.
    □ □ □
    COMPUTE Temp = C / D
    COMPUTE A = B * Temp * E
```

5.5   ARITHMETIC STATEMENT PHRASES

You can add phrases to arithmetic statements to do such things as round the results and detect errors.

5.5.1   Order of Phrases

Essential

For reference, the various phrases described following must be coded in the following order:

```
ADD/SUBTRACT/MULTIPLY/DIVIDE        COMPUTE ROUNDED =
GIVING                              ON SIZE ERROR
ROUNDED                             NOT ON SIZE ERROR
REMAINDER (DIVIDE only)             END-COMPUTE
ON SIZE ERROR
NOT ON SIZE ERROR
END-verb
```

For example:

```
DIVIDE A INTO B                     COMPUTE B ROUNDED = B / A
    GIVING C ROUNDED                    ON SIZE ERROR
    REMAINDER D                             MOVE ZERO TO B
    ON SIZE ERROR                       NOT ON SIZE ERROR
        MOVE ZERO TO B                      MOVE ZERO TO A
    NOT ON SIZE ERROR               END-COMPUTE
        MOVE ZERO TO A
END-DIVIDE
```

5.5.2 The ROUNDED Phrase

Sometimes Used

The final results in arithmetic statements are normally truncated if their precision is greater than that of the identifiers to which they are assigned. Thus, if a resulting identifier has a precision of PIC S999, a result of 22.9 is truncated to 22, and a result of −6.1 is truncated to −6. The ROUNDED phrase rounds the final results rather than truncating them and can be used in the COMPUTE, ADD, SUBTRACT, MULTIPLY, and DIVIDE statements. A 22.9 is rounded to 23, and a −6.1 is rounded to −6. COBOL rounds a value whose rightmost digit is 5 up in absolute magnitude, so that 1.5 is rounded to 2 and −1.5 is rounded to −2. ROUNDED has no effect on COMP-1 and COMP-2 floating-point numbers and is ignored. You code the ROUNDED phrase as follows:

```
COMPUTE A ROUNDED = B + C
ADD A TO B ROUNDED
ADD A TO B GIVING C ROUNDED
SUBTRACT C FROM D ROUNDED
MULTIPLY F BY G ROUNDED
DIVIDE H BY I GIVING J ROUNDED
```

If there are multiple receiving fields, you can code ROUNDED for each:

```
COMPUTE A ROUNDED, B ROUNDED = X / Y
```

Rounding gives more accurate results than does truncation. This is especially important when repetitive operations are performed on numbers. Suppose that in a report, dollars and cents are to be summed, but the numbers are to be printed in units of whole dollars. A common error is to sum the rounded or truncated numbers, as shown in the following columns that might represent the report.

Full Accuracy	Rounded	Truncated
10.00	10	10
10.50	11	10
10.60	11	10
10.10	10	10
10.60	11	10
51.80	53	50

Summing the rounded or truncated numbers gives a wrong total that appears to be correct in that the individual numbers do sum to the total, even though this total is wrong. The correct total is 51.80, which is 52 if rounded or 51 if truncated. When many numbers are summed, the result can be off considerably. Always compute the sum with the full precision and then round or truncate this sum, as shown in the following columns:

Full Accuracy	Rounded	Truncated
10.00	10	10
10.50	11	10
10.60	11	10
10.10	10	10
10.60	11	10
51.80	52	51

This gives the correct totals. Unfortunately, the totals appear to be wrong, because the individual numbers do not equal the total when summed. Reports lose their credibility when someone cannot add a column and obtain the same total that was printed by the computer. The choice between correct totals that appear to be wrong and incorrect totals that appear to be correct is not a happy one. You should choose the correct totals even at the cost of appearing to be wrong.

TIP *Avoid problems with incorrect totals in reports by printing dollars and cents, even though the cents might not be of interest. Don't truncate or round unless you must.*

5.5.3 The ON SIZE ERROR Phrase

Sometimes Used

A *size error* occurs when the magnitude of a result exceeds the size of the identifier into which it is to be stored. You can append the ON SIZE ERROR phrase to an arithmetic statement to execute imperative statements if a size error occurs. Division by zero always causes a size error, as does an improper exponent (0 ** 0). You can code ON SIZE ERROR for the COMPUTE, ADD, SUBTRACT, MULTIPLY, or DIVIDE statements.

```
COMPUTE/ADD/SUBTRACT/MULTIPLY/DIVIDE
   ON SIZE ERROR imperative-statements
   NOT ON SIZE ERROR imperative-statements
END-COMPUTE
```

You can code either the ON SIZE ERROR, the NOT ON SIZE ERROR, or both.

```
COMPUTE A = B / C
   ON SIZE ERROR MOVE C TO D
                 MOVE E TO F
END-COMPUTE
ADD A TO B
   ON SIZE ERROR MOVE C TO D
END-ADD
ADD A TO B
```

```
    NOT ON SIZE ERROR PERFORM A10-Error-Message
END-ADD
```

An *imperative statement* is one that specifies no conditional actions. It may also consist of a sequence of imperative statements. Any conditional statement that is delimited by its explicit scope terminator is an imperative statement. Thus, the following is permitted:

```
COMPUTE A = B / C
   ON SIZE ERROR
      IF C = 0
         THEN DISPLAY "ZERO DENOMINATOR"
         ELSE DISPLAY "INVALID VALUES FOR B OR C."
      END-IF
END-COMPUTE
```

If there is no SIZE ERROR phrase and a size error occurs, IBM COBOL truncates the results. (The ANSI standard leaves the result undefined.) When ON SIZE ERROR occurs, the result of the operation is not stored in the resultant identifier. When the ROUNDED phrase is specified, the rounding occurs before the check is made for a size error.

```
COMPUTE A ROUNDED = B + C * D
   ON SIZE ERROR MOVE ZERO TO A
END-COMPUTE
```

If SIZE ERROR is coded for ADD or SUBTRACT CORR, a size error on any of the data items causes the appropriate SIZE ERROR statements to be executed. However, COBOL executes them only once, after all the corresponding operations are done.

5.5.4 The REMAINDER Phrase

Sometimes Used

The DIVIDE GIVING statement with the REMAINDER phrase computes a remainder. (You can't use REMAINDER with COMP-1 or COMP-2 floating-point data.) In the following example, if *A* contains 6 and *B* contains 17, *D* would contain the remainder 5. REMAINDER must follow any ROUNDED.

```
DIVIDE A INTO B GIVING C REMAINDER D
DIVIDE A INTO B GIVING C ROUNDED REMAINDER D
```

The following is illegal:

```
DIVIDE A INTO B GIVING C REMAINDER D ROUNDED        Error!
```

You don't need to use the DIVIDE statement to get the remainder. The REM intrinsic function described in Chapter 21 calculates the remainder directly:

```
COMPUTE D = FUNCTION REM(B, A)
```

5.6 ARITHMETIC OPERATIONS

Essential

The arithmetic operations are + for add, – for subtract, * for multiply, / for divide, and ** for exponential. You usually code them in COMPUTE and IF statements. Precede and follow them by one or more spaces. COBOL converts the items within the expression to a common numerical base if necessary.

```
COMPUTE X = A + B - C / D ** 2
IF (A + B) = (C - 1)
    THEN PERFORM B10-Zero-Table
END-IF
```

You can precede an arithmetic expression with a plus or minus sign as a prefix, termed a *unary operator.* (A unary sign indicates the sign of the item, not a subtraction or addition. Note that it must also be preceded and followed by a space.) COBOL interprets the following statement as *X* plus a minus *Y.*

```
COMPUTE W = X + - Y
```

5.7 CONDITIONAL OPERATIONS

The following conditions, including the relational condition, the sign condition, the class condition, and the condition-name condition, can appear only in the IF, PERFORM, EVALUATE, and SEARCH statements. (SEARCH is described in Chapter 13.)

5.7.1 Relational Conditions

Essential

<	Less than. You can also write this as IS LESS THAN.
<=	Less than or equal to. You can also write this as NOT > or IS LESS THAN OR EQUAL or IS NOT GREATER THAN.
>	Greater than. You can also write this as IS GREATER THAN.
>=	Greater than or equal to. You can also write this as NOT < or IS GREATER THAN OR EQUAL TO or IS NOT LESS THAN.
=	Equal. You can also write this as IS EQUAL TO.
NOT =	Not equal. You can also write this as IS NOT EQUAL TO.

Some might argue that the long forms are easier to understand, but the >= form is clearer to most people who program. Things like IS EQUAL TO take away from your status as a professional programmer.

TIP *Forget the English terms and use the <, >, and = characters.*

Precede and follow relational conditions with one or more spaces. You can compare identifiers, literals, and arithmetic expressions.

```
IF A = B
    THEN ADD 1 TO C
END-IF
IF (X * Y + Z) = 2
    THEN ADD 1 TO D
END-IF
```

5.7.2 The Sign Condition

Archaic

The *sign condition* tests for positive, negative, or zero values.

TIP *Because it is completely redundant to the relational conditions, don't use it.*

```
IF X IS POSITIVE          Same as        IF X > ZERO
IF X IS NOT POSITIVE                      IF X <= ZERO
IF X IS NEGATIVE                          IF X < ZERO
IF X IS NOT NEGATIVE                      IF X >= ZERO
IF X IS ZERO                              IF X = ZERO
IF X IS NOT ZERO                          IF X NOT = ZERO
```

5.7.3 Class Conditions

A *class condition* tests whether an identifier contains only numeric or alphabetic data.

The NUMERIC Condition

Essential

The NUMERIC condition is true if the identifier contains only the digits 0 to 9, with or without a + or – sign. You can test only identifiers declared as alphanumeric (DISPLAY) or PACKED-DECIMAL numeric for NUMERIC, not alphabetic characters declared as PIC A. (PIC 999 or PIC XXX, but not PIC AAA.) There is no class test for floating-point COMP-1 and COMP-2).

```
IF identifier IS NUMERIC …
IF identifier IS NOT NUMERIC …
```

```
IF X IS NOT NUMERIC
    THEN MOVE B TO C
END-IF
```

For DISPLAY external decimal numbers, the data is considered to be numeric if it is unsigned or has an operational sign carried with the rightmost digit. However, COBOL does not consider them to be numeric if the characters plus (+) or minus (−) are present unless you code the SIGN clause, described in Chapter 9.

The ALPHABETIC Condition

Rarely Used

The ALPHABETIC test is true if the identifier contains only the characters *A* through *Z*, *a* through *z*, and *blank*. ALPHABETIC-UPPER tests for *A* through *Z* and *blank*. ALPHABETIC-LOWER tests for *a* through *z* and *blank*. ALPHABETIC can test only alphanumeric or alphabetic identifiers (DISPLAY) described as PIC A or X (that is, PIC AAA or PIC XXX, but not PIC 999). ALPHABETIC is less useful than it might appear to be because most nonnumeric data, such as names (O'Reilly) contain nonalphabetic characters.

```
IF identifier IS ALPHABETIC …
IF identifier IS NOT ALPHABETIC …
IF identifier IS ALPHABETIC-UPPER …
IF identifier IS NOT ALPHABETIC-LOWER …
IF X IS ALPHABETIC
    THEN MOVE B TO C
END-IF
```

TIP *Forget about alphabetic data.*

5.7.4 Condition-Name Conditions

Sometimes Used

Condition names allow you to specify some of the logic in the data descriptions, and which may or may not make programs easier to read. *Condition-names* are level 88 data items defined for an elementary item and assigned a value. Testing the condition name is the same as testing the data item for the value. The following example illustrates a condition name.

```
01  Thing                        PIC X.
    88  Thing-Is-Big             VALUE "Y".
    □   □   □
    MOVE "N" TO Thing      Same as    MOVE "N" TO Thing
    IF Thing-Is-Big                   IF Thing = "Y"
        THEN MOVE C TO D                  THEN MOVE C TO D
    END-IF                            END-IF
```

You might argue that the example on the left is clearer. But you could also argue that it can't be understood without paging back to the data description to see what the level 88 data item contains. In addition, it is not at all apparent that the MOVE "N" TO *Thing* on the left has any effect on the IF *Thing-Is-Big* statement that follows, whereas this is abundantly clear with the example on the right where you can see exactly what operation is performed.

Rather than set a value that makes the level 88 condition name true, you can set it to true using the COBOL SET statement. COBOL then moves a value to the condition name to make it true.

```
SET Thing-Is-Big TO TRUE    Same as:    MOVE "Y" TO Thing-Is-Big
IF Thing-Is-Big
```

This makes it clear to someone reading the program that the SET statement changes the value for the item being tested. If a field can contain several values, you can set a different level 88 condition name for each value, using a descriptive name. This lets you program using symbolic names for the values.

```
01  Marital-Status              PIC X.
    88 Married                  VALUE "1".
    88 Single                   VALUE "2".
    88 Divorced                 VALUE "3".
    □  □  □
    SET Divorced = TRUE  Same as  MOVE "3" TO Marital-Status
    □  □  □
    IF Married …            Same as   IF Marital-Status = "1" …
    IF Single …                       IF Marital-Status = "2" …
    IF Divorced …                     IF Marital-Status = "3" …
```

PROPOSED NEW ANSI STANDARD: Check Compiler to See if Implemented

The new ANSI Standard lets you set a condition name to FALSE.

```
SET Few TO FALSE
```

You can assign each condition name to a value, a range of values (*n* THRU *m*), several single values, or some combination of these. Within a record, level 88 denotes a condition name and cannot be used for anything else.

```
01  Some-Item                   PIC S9(6) PACKED-DECIMAL.
    88  Few                     VALUE 1.
    88  Lots                    VALUE 1 THRU 10.
    88  Many                    VALUE 1, 3.
    88  Myriad                  VALUE 1, 3, 9 THRU 16, 17,
                                      25 THRU 50.

    □  □  □
    IF Few                 Same as    IF Some-Item = 1
       THEN MOVE C TO D                  THEN MOVE C TO D
    END-IF                            END-IF
```

```
        IF NOT Lots                     IF (Some-Item < 1) OR
           THEN MOVE C TO D                 (Some-Item > 10)
        END-IF                              THEN MOVE C TO D
                                        END-IF


        SET Few TO TRUE         [Some-Item is set to 1.]
        SET Lots TO TRUE        [Some-Item is set to 1. If there are sev-
                                 eral values, the first value is set.]
```

You can also list several condition names in one SET. The effect is as if several SET statements had been written:

```
        SET Many, Myriad TO TRUE    Same as    SET Many TO TRUE
                                               SET Myriad TO TRUE
```

You can also define condition names for group items in a record, but the value must be an alphanumeric literal or a figurative constant. Assigning condition names for group items does not preclude defining condition names for elementary items. However, the elementary items must all be DISPLAY.

```
01  Date-Rec.
    88  New-Year                VALUE "940101".
    05  Year                    PIC XX.
        88  This-Year           VALUE "94".
    05  Month                   PIC XX.
    05  Days                    PIC XX.
```

You can assign condition names to table elements, and you must subscript the condition name when used.

```
    05  Array-A                 PIC X OCCURS 10 TIMES.
    88  Yes                     VALUE "Y".
    □  □  □
    IF Yes(3) THEN …    Same as    IF Array-A(3) = "Y" THEN …
```

Condition names make COBOL programs easier to read as English sentences, but harder to read to understand what is happening in the program. They are convenient for testing several values. They may also make it easier to change the program, because the change can be made in a single place in the Data Division rather than in several places throughout the program.

5.7.5 Logical Operations

Essential

The *logical operations,* also termed *Boolean operations,* can connect the relational, sign, class, and condition-name conditions. They consist of the AND, OR, and NOT.

1. **Logical AND.**   If *X* and *Y* are both true, then *X* AND *Y* has the value true. If either *X* or *Y* or both are false, then *X* AND *Y* has the value false.

```
IF (X = 1) AND (Y = 0)
   THEN PERFORM X10-Done
        [The THEN clause executes only if X equals 1 and Y equals 0.]
END-IF
```

2. **Logical OR.**   If either *X* or *Y* or both are true, then *X* OR *Y* has the value true. If both *X* and *Y* are false, then *X* OR *Y* has the value false.

```
IF (X = 1) OR (Y = 0)
   THEN PERFORM X10-Done
[The THEN clause executes if X equals 1 or if Y equals 0.]
END-IF
```

3. **Logical NOT.**   If *X* is true, then NOT *X* has the value false. If *X* is false, then NOT *X* has the value true.

```
IF NOT ((X = 1) AND (Y = 2))
   THEN PERFORM X10-Done
                [The THEN clause executes if X is not equal to 1 or if Y is not
                equal to 2.]
END-IF
```

4. **Implied relations.**   If the same item is compared to several other items connected by AND, OR, or NOT, you don't need to write the full relational condition for each item; it is implied.

```
A < B OR > C          Same as    (A < B) OR (A > C)
A NOT = B OR > C                  (A NOT = B) OR (A > C)
A = B OR > C AND < D              (A = B) OR
                                  ((A > C) AND (A < D))
```

You can also imply the relational condition itself.

```
A = B OR C            Same as    (A = B) OR (A = C)
A = B AND C AND D                (A = B) AND (A = C) AND
                                 (A = D)
```

In these simple forms, the implied relations improve readability, but they quickly become confusing when used to excess. The following is unclear, because it is not apparent that the last relational operator (>) applies to *D*.

```
A = B AND > C OR D       Same as     (((A = B) AND (A > C)) OR
                                     (A > D))
```

The NOT is especially troublesome. COBOL treats it as part of the relational condition if it precedes the <, =, or >. To be safe, avoid implied conditions containing the NOT.

Complex logical conditions are often a source of error. For example, are the following two logical expressions equivalent?

```
NOT (A = B OR A = C)                (A NOT = B) OR (A NOT = C)
```

TABLE 5.1 Decision Table

A = B	True	False	True	False
A = C	True	True	False	False
NOT (A = B OR A = C)	False	False	False	True
(A NOT = B) OR (A NOT = C)	False	True	True	True

It is not obvious that they are different. The first expression is true only if *A* is not equal to either *B* or *C*. The second expression is true either if *A* is not equal to *B* or if *A* is not equal to *C*. Avoid complex logical expressions, double negatives, and NOT in combination with OR. For example, NOT (*A* NOT = *B*) is better written as *A = B*. Use a decision table to decipher particularly complex conditional statements. The decision table presented in Table 5.1 shows that the previous two expressions are not equivalent.

If you must write a decision table to decipher a logical expression, the expression is not very readable. Try not to write logical expressions that require a decision table to be understood. Recast the logical expression or rewrite it with nested IFs to make it clearer.

```
Unclear                         Better as
IF NOT (A = B OR C)                 IF A = B OR C
    THEN do something                  THEN CONTINUE
END-IF                                 ELSE do something
                                    END-IF
                                Or
                                    IF A NOT = B AND A NOT = C
                                       THEN do something
                                    END-IF
                                Or
                                    IF A NOT = B
                                       THEN IF A NOT = C
                                               THEN do something
                                            END-IF
                                    END-IF
```

5.7.6 Conditional Expression

Essential

A *conditional expression* consists of a relational, sign, class, or condition-name condition, or several relational, sign, class, or condition-name conditions, connected by the AND, OR, or NOT logical operations. For example, *A = B* AND *C = 6*.

5.7.7 Hierarchy of Operations

Essential

The following hierarchy list specifies the order, from highest to lowest, in which operations are performed.

```
Highest:   Unary operator (sign as prefix)         + B or - C
           Exponential                             A ** B
           Multiply, Divide                        A * B / C
           ADD, Subtract                           A + B - C
           Relational, sign, class, condition-name A > B
           conditions
           Logical NOT                             NOT (A > B)
           Logical AND                             A AND B
Lowest:    Logical OR                              A OR B
```

COBOL evaluates operations having equal hierarchy from left to right.

```
A * B * C              Same as    (A * B) * C
A + B - C ** D         Same as    (A + B) - (C ** D)
```

Parentheses override the hierarchy. They specify the hierarchy of operations explicitly, so that you do not have to remember the foregoing rules.

```
Unclear                      Better as
   IF A + B * D = 2 OR A > 6    IF ((A + (B * D)) = 2) OR
      THEN ADD 1 TO X              (A > 6)
   END-IF                          THEN ADD 1 TO X
                                END-IF
```

TIP   *Because there is no question of the hierarchy of operations when you use parentheses, use them to lessen the chance for error.*

EXERCISES

1. What will the identifiers A, B, C, and D contain after each of the following statements has been executed? Assume that each identifier has a precision of S9(4).

```
MOVE 1 TO A, B
COMPUTE B = A + 1
ADD B TO A
MULTIPLY B BY A
DIVIDE A BY 5 GIVING C REMAINDER D
```

2. Place parentheses around the following expressions to indicate the hierarchy of operations. Also insert blanks where necessary.

```
1/2*A*T**2
A**B-2/Y-D
A+2*C**2/B+6*4
A+B=ZERO OR NOT A NOT=1 AND B > A*10-6
```

3. The following statements each contain an actual or an almost certain potential error. Find each error.

```
MULTIPLY A BY 2
ADD "125" TO B
```

```
DIVIDE Budget-Remaining BY Periods-Remaining
MOVE ZERO TO A, B. C
COMPUTE A = B * C ROUNDED
IF A = 2 = C
    THEN ADD 1 TO A
END-IF
```

4. The following table contains paragraph names and associated values of the identifier Switch-A. Perform the proper paragraph name as given by the value of Switch-A, first using IF statements and then an EVALUATE statement.

Value of Switch-A	Paragraph Name
1	Start-it
2	Finish-it
3	Continue-It
4	Proceed-To

5. Use IF statements to set the identifier *Ans* to the appropriate value based on the conditions given. Then do the same using an EVALUATE statement.

Value of Ans	Condition
0	If X equals zero
−1	If X is negative and Y is not greater than zero
−2	If both X and Y + Z are greater than 22
100	If X equals 1 and Y equals 1, or if half of Y + Z equals 1
200	All other conditions

6. Rewrite the following IF statement using condition names.
```
01  X                         PIC S9(5).
    □  □  □
    IF (X = 1) OR
       ((X NOT < 20) AND (X NOT > 30)) OR
       (X = 50 OR 60 OR 61)
       THEN ...
    END-IF
```

7. Write decision tables to show whether the following IF statements are true or false for all possible conditions.
```
    IF (X = 1 AND NOT Y = 1) OR
       NOT (X = 0 OR Y = 1)
       THEN ...
    END-IF
    IF (X NOT = 1 OR Y NOT = 1) OR
       NOT (X = Y)
       THEN ...
    END-IF
```

8. What values will *X* assume within the following loops?

```
PERFORM Loop1 VARYING X FROM -10 BY 3 UNTIL X > 6

PERFORM Loop2 VARYING X FROM 1 BY 1 UNTIL X > 1

MOVE 4 TO Y
PERFORM WITH TEST BEFORE VARYING X FROM 1 BY 1
        UNTIL (X > 10) OR (Y NOT > 0)
   PERFORM VARYING X FROM -3 BY -2 UNTIL X < -7
     imperative-statements
   END-PERFORM
END-PERFORM
```

9. Assume that *Dy, Mo,* and *Yr* contain the day, month, and year of a start date, and that *Dur* contains a duration in days. Assuming 30 days per month, use IF and COMPUTE statements to COMPUTE the end date from the start date and the duration, and store the results back in *Dy, Mo,* and *Yr*.

10. Assume that the day, month, and year of a start date are contained in *S-Dy, S-Mo,* and *S-Yr,* and the end date in *E-Dy, E-Mo,* and *E-Yr.* Write the statements necessary to store the exact duration in days in *Dur,* assuming 30 days per month.

11. An equation is given as $Y = (X - 1)/(X * 2 + 1)$. Write the statements necessary to evaluate the equation for values of *X* ranging from -6 to 10 by steps of 0.5.

12. Rewrite the following statements without using the GO TO statement but using instead the IF, EVALUATE, or PERFORM statements.

```
       MOVE 1 TO X.
Loop1.  MOVE ZERO TO A(X).
       ADD 1 TO X.
       IF X < 10 THEN GO TO Loop1.
       IF B > 6 THEN GO TO Next1.
       IF B < ZERO THEN GO TO Next1.
       IF C = ZERO THEN GO TO Next1.
       IF B > 3 THEN GO TO Next2.
       MOVE ZERO TO D.
       ADD 1 TO B.
       GO TO Next3.
Next1. MOVE ZERO TO E.
       IF X + Y > 0 THEN GO TO Next3.
       ADD 1 TO G.
       GO TO Next3.
Next2. ADD 1 TO G.
       GO TO Next4.
Next3. ADD 1 TO F.
Next4.
```

13. The following IF statement has been coded.

```
IF XX NOT = ZERO AND ZZ = 1 AND XX NOT = 1 OR XX NOT = 2
   THEN PERFORM Fini
END-IF
```

Tell whether the *Fini* paragraph will be executed, based on the following combinations of values of *XX* and *ZZ.*

```
XX          ZZ
0           0
0           1
0           2
0           3
1           0
1           1
1           2
1           3
```

14. What combinations of values will *X*, *Y*, and *Z* have in the loop?

```
PERFORM Loop1 WITH TEST BEFORE
        VARYING X FROM 1 BY 2 UNTIL X > 4
        AFTER Y FROM 0 BY -1 UNTIL Y < -1
        AFTER Z FROM 2 BY 3 UNTIL Z > 7
```

CHAPTER 6

MORE COBOL STATEMENTS

This chapter previews the ACCEPT, DISPLAY, PERFORM, and EVALUATE statements, along with tables. If you are familiar with these, you can skip this chapter.

6.1 PREVIEW OF DISPLAY AND ACCEPT STATEMENTS

Essential

COBOL is essentially a batch programming language with limited features for online, interactive programming consisting of the ACCEPT and DISPLAY statements. Here is an example of how they might be used on the PC. The program in Chapter 2 read in transactions containing both a birth date and a hire date that were two digits in length. You can easily expand the years to four digits by adding the century to the definition.

```
01  Out-Emp.
    02  Out-Name            PIC X(30).
    02  Out-Birth-Date.
        03  Out-Birth-Century   PIC 99.     <== Added
        03  Out-Birth-Yr        PIC 99.
        03  Out-Birth-Mo        PIC 99.
        03  Out-Birth-Dy        PIC 99.
    02                      PIC X.
    02  Out-Hire-Date.
        03  Out-Hire-Century    PIC 99.     <== Added
        03  Out-Hire-Yr         PIC 99.
        03  Out-Hire-Mo         PIC 99.
        03  Out-Hire-Dy         PIC 99.
    02  Hire-Age            PIC 999.
```

Now you have to somehow obtain the two digits for the century. There are various ways to do this, but for now, the brute-force method will be used to illustrate how the DISPLAY and ACCEPT statements can ask someone at the computer terminal to type in the century (19 or 20). This is for illustration only, and better ways are described in Chapter 26. To ask for the century, you would display the following on the terminal:

```
DISPLAY "Enter data for employee ", Out-Name
```
[This displays "Enter data for employee " followed by the employee's name on the next line of the terminal.]
```
DISPLAY "Birth date is: ", Out-Birth-Mo, "/",
        Out-Birth-Dy, "/", Out-Birth-Yr
```
[This displays a new line containing "Birth date is: "mm/dd/yy" on the terminal.]
```
DISPLAY "Enter the century (19 or 20) of the birth date: "
```
[This displays on the next line and tells the person at the terminal what you want entered.]
```
ACCEPT Out-Birth-Century FROM CONSOLE
```
[This positions the cursor to the end of the previous line and waits for the person to type in the century and press ENTER.]

Then you would do the same thing for the *Hire-date.* Of course, humans being what they are, you have to expect that the person at the terminal will type in something wrong. Because you know that the only valid input is 19 or 20, you can check that this is what was entered. Here is a loop to keep asking for the century until the person types in 19 or 20.

```
DISPLAY "Enter data for employee ", Out-Name
DISPLAY "Birth date is: ", Out-Birth-Mo, "/",
        Out-Birth-Dy, "/", Out-Birth-Yr
PERFORM WITH TEST AFTER UNTIL Out-Birth-Century = 19 OR 20
   DISPLAY "Enter the century (19 or 20) of the birth date: "
   ACCEPT Out-Birth-Century FROM CONSOLE
END-PERFORM
```

This is better, but it doesn't tell the person what was done wrong. It just asks for new input. It is a good practice to tell people what they have done wrong before you ask them to redo it. You can add an IF statement to do this.

```
PERFORM WITH TEST AFTER UNTIL Out-Birth-Century = 19 OR 20
   DISPLAY "Enter the century (19 or 20) of the birth date: "
   ACCEPT Out-Birth-Century FROM CONSOLE
   IF Out-Birth-Century NOT = 19 AND
      Out-Birth-Century NOT = 20
      THEN DISPLAY
          "Look stupid! Enter a 19 or 20 for the Century."
   END-IF
END-PERFORM
```

While there is much to recommend honest and succinct error messages, in practice, you would likely phrase it more politely than this.

The ACCEPT and DISPLAY statements provide an easy way of entering data and displaying it. On the mainframe, they can also accept data from the input stream and display it in the printed output. This is handy for testing and debugging programs.

6.2 THE PERFORM WITH TEST BEFORE STATEMENT

Essential

In the previous section, the loop was executed by a PERFORM WITH TEST AFTER statement, and an IF statement was used to display an error message. Suppose that besides displaying an error message when the person enters the century incorrectly, you want to give the person a different prompt, perhaps one that goes into more detail. You can do this with another form of the PERFORM, one with the WITH TEST BEFORE phrase.

```
PERFORM WITH TEST BEFORE UNTIL condition
    imperative-statements
END-PERFORM
```

When the statements immediately follow the PERFORM, as they do here, it is called an *in-line* PERFORM. Previously, an error message was displayed with the following IF statement:

```
IF Out-Birth-Century NOT = 19 AND
    Out-Birth-Century NOT = 20
    THEN DISPLAY
        "Look stupid! Enter a 19 or 20 for the Century."
END-IF
```

Replace this with the following PERFORM WITH TEST BEFORE statement:

```
PERFORM WITH TEST BEFORE UNTIL Out-Birth-Century = 19 OR 20
    DISPLAY "Look stupid! Enter a 19 or 20 for the Century."
    DISPLAY
    "Try again to enter the century of the birth date",
    "(19 for the 1900's, 20 for the 2000's): "
    ACCEPT Out-Birth-Century FROM CONSOLE
END-PERFORM
```

The WITH TEST BEFORE statement tests before any of the statements within the PERFORM are executed. Hence, if the century equals 19 or 20, execution continues following the END-PERFORM and the error message isn't displayed.

6.3 THE OUT-OF-LINE PERFORM STATEMENT

Essential

There is another form of the PERFORM, the *out-of-line* PERFORM. Rather than following the PERFORM with the statements it is to execute, you instead place the statements in a procedure (paragraph or section) and PERFORM the procedure. For this, you write the PERFORM as:

```
PERFORM procedure-name …
```

Then you place the statements in a procedure somewhere else in the program.

```
procedure-name.
    statements to be executed by the PERFORM
```

Here are the statements to request the century by modifying the preceding PERFORM WITH TEST BEFORE and placing the statements in a procedure.

```
PERFORM WITH TEST AFTER UNTIL Out-Birth-Century = 19 OR 20
    DISPLAY "Enter the century (19 or 20) of the birth date: "
    ACCEPT Out-Birth-Century FROM CONSOLE
    PERFORM A10-Get-Century WITH TEST BEFORE
            UNTIL Out-Birth-Century = 19 OR 20
END-PERFORM
```

```
A10-Get-Century.
    DISPLAY "Look stupid! Enter a 19 or 20 for the Century."
    DISPLAY
        "Try again to enter the century of the birth date",
        "(19 for the 1900's, 20 for the 2000's): "
    ACCEPT Out-Birth-Century FROM CONSOLE
```

```
***** EXIT
```
[This comment isn't needed, but it makes it clear that here is where you exit the performed statements. Execution then continues with the statement following the PERFORM that invoked this procedure.]

The out-of-line PERFORM has several important uses. First, if there are many statements, it lets you set them aside so that they don't clutter up the main flow of the program. Second, COBOL allows you to code statements only in columns 12 through 72, and as you indent them, it is easy to force them beyond column 72. To solve this problem, you can place the statements in a procedure and PERFORM them. Finally, you can perform the statements in a procedure from any point in the program. For example, you might write a general error procedure and PERFORM it from many places in the program.

6.4 THE EVALUATE STATEMENT

Essential

Suppose that each time a person makes a mistake entering the century, you want to give them a different error message to encourage them. For this, you might define a new data item to count the errors and examine it to determine which error message to display. Define an item named *Entry-Errors* as follows:

```
01   Entry-Errors                    PIC S999 VALUE 0.
```
[The VALUE 0 assigns an initial value of zero to the item.]

Then you can change the error procedure to display a different error message each time.

```
A10-Get-Century.
    ADD 1 TO Entry-Errors
```
[The ADD statement is a shorthand way of writing COMPUTE *Entry-Errors* = *Entry-Errors* + 1.]

```
    IF Entry-Errors = 1
      THEN DISPLAY
            "Look stupid! Enter a 19 or 20 for the Century."
      ELSE IF Entry-Errors = 2
      THEN DISPLAY
        "Is it that difficult? This isn't rocket science here."
      ELSE IF Entry-Errors = 3
      THEN DISPLAY
            "You're trying my patience. Get it right this time."
      ELSE DISPLAY "I give up."
           DISPLAY
           "I hope you have a hangover and not the alternative,"
           DISPLAY "which is that you are terminally stupid."
           GOBACK
           END-IF
           END-IF
    END-IF
    DISPLAY
        "Please try again to enter the century of the birth date",
        "(19 for the 1900's, 20 for the 2000's): "
    ACCEPT Out-Birth-Century FROM CONSOLE
    .
***** EXIT
```

Nesting IF statements like this is tedious, and there is a better way. The EVALUATE statement evaluates an item and takes action based on its value. You can replace the preceding IF statements with an EVALUATE statement coded as follows:

```
A10-Get-Century.
    ADD 1 TO Entry-Errors
    EVALUATE Entry-Errors
```
[This tells COBOL to look at the *Entry-Errors* item.]
```
      WHEN 1
```
[If the value is 1, execute all the following statements up to the next WHEN.]
```
        DISPLAY
          "Look stupid! Enter a 19 or 20 for the Century."
```
[You can execute several imperative statements here if you wish.]

```
WHEN 2
  DISPLAY
  "Is it that difficult? This isn't rocket science here."
WHEN 3
  DISPLAY
    "You're trying my patience. Get it right this time."
WHEN OTHER
```
            [OTHER is a catch-all. If none of the previous WHEN phrases were
            true, the following statements are executed.]
```
  DISPLAY "I give up."
  DISPLAY
    "I hope you have a hangover and not the alternative,"
  DISPLAY "which is that you are terminally stupid."
  GOBACK
END-EVALUATE
```
      [As with all compound statements, you must code the scope terminator.]
```
DISPLAY "Try again to enter the century of the birth date",
        "(19 for the 1900's, 20 for the 2000's): "
ACCEPT Out-Birth-Century FROM CONSOLE
```
```
***** EXIT
```

6.5 DEFINING TABLES

Essential

Let's add another item of complexity to the program. Suppose that you want to count the number of employees you hired in each month of the year, perhaps to see if hiring over the years is seasonal. One way to do this would be to define 12 data items, such as *January, February, . . . , December* to contain the counts. Then you could use an IF statement to look at the month and if 1, add 1 to *January*, if 2, add 1 to *February*, and so on. Or you could use an EVALUATE statement and WHEN 1, add 1 to *January*, WHEN 2, add 1 to *February*, and so on. However, it is better to use a table (called an *array* in all other programming languages).

The table consists of a single data name that has, for this application, 12 elements, 1 for each month. You can subscript the data name with the month to refer to the item for a particular month. Here's how.

First, you need to define the table with an element for each month. You'll set the elements of the table to zero and then add one to the appropriate element as you read in each employee. To define a table, you add the OCCURS clause to the data definition. The OCCURS cannot be written at level 01 or 77, so it is made a level 05 item here. (Level 77 is a special level that can define only an elementary data item. It does nothing that cannot be done with level 01.) The OCCURS 12 TIMES in the following tells COBOL that the table has 12 elements.

```
01  Month-Table.
    05  Month-Count                     PIC S9(7) OCCURS 12 TIMES.
```

Now if you refer to *Month-Count*(1), you are referencing the first element of the table, January in this application. *Month-Count*(12) references the element for December. The (1) and (12) are termed *subscripts*. When you define a table, the elements have no predictable values. They could contain whatever happened to be in the computer's central storage, left over from other programs. The first step must be to zero the table out so that you can use it for a count. One way to do this would be the brute-force method:

```
MOVE ZERO TO Month-Count(1)
MOVE ZERO TO Month-Count(2)
    .        .       .
MOVE ZERO TO Month-Count(12)
```

Obviously, there is a better way.

6.6 THE PERFORM TIMES STATEMENT

Essential

You will use the PERFORM TIMES statement. It is coded as:

```
PERFORM integer-item TIMES
    statements to execute integer-item times
END-PERFORM
```

The *integer-item* can be a literal or identifier. You can code the following:

```
PERFORM 12 TIMES
    MOVE ZERO TO Month-Count(1)
END-PERFORM
```

This doesn't do much good. You set the count for January to zero 12 times. You need to subscript *Month-Count* with an item that will have values from 1 to 12. Define an item named *Month-Subscript* to use as the subscript.

```
01  Month-Subscript              PIC S9(5).
```

Now code the loop to set all 12 elements of *Month-Count* to 0.

```
COMPUTE Month-Subscript = 1
```
[You must set *Month-Subscript* to an initial value of 1 for the first time into the loop.]
```
PERFORM 12 TIMES
    COMPUTE Month-Count(Month-Subscript) = 0
```
      [When *Month-Subscript* equals 1, you set element 1 of *Month-Count* to 0, when it equals 2, you set element 2 to 0, and so on.]
```
    ADD 1 TO Month-Subscript
```

[You bump the subscript up by 1 each time through the loop.]
```
END-PERFORM
```
[At the end of the loop, all 12 elements will be set to 0.]

The PERFORM TIMES can name an identifier, and the value of the identifier when the PERFORM is executed determines the number of times the loop is performed.

```
PERFORM Some-Value TIMES
```

Changing the value of the identifier within the loop has no effect on the number of times the loop is executed. If the identifier contains zero or a negative number when PERFORM is executed, the loop is not performed, and execution follows the END-PERFORM.

6.7 THE PERFORM VARYING STATEMENT

Essential

There is a simpler way of coding the preceding using another variation of the PERFORM statement, the PERFORM VARYING statement, written as

```
PERFORM WITH TEST BEFORE or AFTER
        VARYING subscript FROM start-value BY increment-value
        UNTIL subscript comparison end-value
```

COBOL begins the loop by setting the *subscript* to the *start-value*. Each time it reaches the end of the loop (at the END-PERFORM), it adds the *increment-value* to the *subscript*. The loop is terminated when the *comparison* is true. Here is how you would code the loop to zero out *Month-Count*:

```
PERFORM WITH TEST AFTER VARYING Month-Subscript FROM 1 BY 1
        UNTIL Month-Subscript > 12
    COMPUTE Month-Count(Month-Subscript) = 0
END-PERFORM
```

COBOL will set *Month-Subscript* to 1 the first time through the loop. When the END-PERFORM is reached, it will add 1 to *Month-Subscript,* and check to see if *Month-Subscript* is greater than 12. If so, it will terminate the loop. The result is that the loop will be executed for *Month-Subscript* containing values of 1, 2, . . . , 12.

Now that you have zeroed out the *Month-Count* elements, you need to add code to the program to count the month in which an employee was born. If you recall, when you read in a record, the birth month is stored in *In-Birth-Month*. Here are the statements to read a record from the file and count birth month for the employee.

```
READ In-file
   AT END MOVE "Y" TO EOF-In-File
    NOT AT END
            MOVE "N" TO EOF-In-File
            MOVE In-Emp TO Out-Emp
            ADD 1 TO Month-Count(In-Birth-Month)     <== Added
```

In-Birth-Month contains the birth month, and you can use it to subscript the table.

EXERCISES

1. Write a loop to display the following characters on the screen.

```
    X
   XXX
  XXXXX
 XXXXXXX
```

2. Write a small program to request a person's telephone number. Use parentheses and dashes to show the person how they are to enter the number: (___) ___-___.

3. Same as problem 2, but make the input field free form. Assume an area code of 800 if the person doesn't enter it. Accept telephone numbers in any of the following forms: 1-800-555-1111, (800) 555-1111, 555-1111, 800/555-1111, and 1-800/555-1111.

4. Are these two groups of statements equivalent?

```
MOVE "N" TO Flag                 MOVE "N" TO Flag
PERFORM WITH TEST BEFORE         PERFORM WITH TEST AFTER
        UNTIL Flag = "Y"                 UNTIL Flag = "Y"
    READ File-I INTO A               READ File-I INTO A
        AT END MOVE "Y" TO Flag          AT END MOVE "Y" TO FLAG
        NOT AT END                       NOT AT END
        ADD 1 TO Count                   ADD 1 TO Count
    END-READ                         END-READ
END-PERFORM                      END-PERFORM
```

5. What will *Count* contain after each of the following loops are executed?

```
MOVE ZERO TO Count               MOVE ZERO TO Count
PERFORM Count TIMES              PERFORM WITH TEST AFTER
    ADD 1 TO Count                       UNTIL Count >= 9
END-PERFORM                          ADD 1 TO Count
                                     END-PERFORM

MOVE ZERO TO Count               MOVE 10 TO Count
PERFORM WITH TEST BEFORE         PERFORM Count TIMES
        UNTIL Count => 9             COMPUTE Count = Count - 1
    ADD 1 TO Count                   END-PERFORM
END-PERFORM

PERFORM WITH TEST AFTER
    VARYING COUNT FROM 1 BY 1 UNTIL COUNT = 10
```

```
        ADD 1 TO Count
    END-PERFORM
```

6. Change the following nested IF statement to an EVALUATE.

```
IF A = 0
    THEN MOVE 1 TO C
ELSE IF A = 1
    THEN MOVE 5 TO C
ELSE IF A = 2
    THEN MOVE 3 TO C
ELSE MOVE 10 TO C
END-IF  END-IF  END-IF
```

CHAPTER 7

DETAILS OF MORE BASIC COBOL STATEMENTS

This chapter describes the ACCEPT, DISPLAY, IF, GO TO, and PERFORM statements in detail.

7.1 THE ACCEPT AND DISPLAY STATEMENTS

In addition to the forms described here, PC COBOL has an extensive facility to accept full-screen input as described in Chapter 24.

7.1.1 The ACCEPT Statement

> **Essential**

For PC and Workstation COBOL, the following form of the ACCEPT statement accepts input from the PC keyboard.

```
ACCEPT identifier
```

The *identifier* is a group item, an elementary alphabetic, alphanumeric, alphanumeric edited, numeric edited, or external decimal numbers. ACCEPT stores the input in *identifier,* truncating or padding the input on the right with blanks, if necessary, to match the length of *identifier.*

In Mainframe COBOL, this form displays an AWAITING REPLY message on the operator's console and suspends program execution until the operator responds. Don't use this form on the mainframe. Mainframe operators are very busy and dislike responding to messages. Most installations carefully control who can request input from the operators and under what circumstances.

To accept input from your terminal's keyboard on the mainframe, you must first define a symbolic name for the terminal in the SPECIAL-NAMES paragraph. SPECIAL-NAMES is fully described in Chapter 24.

```
ENVIRONMENT DIVISION.          [SPECIAL-NAMES is in this division.]
CONFIGURATION SECTION.
```

```
SPECIAL-NAMES.
    SYSTERM IS symbolic-name.
```

Then you use this *symbolic-name* in a FROM phrase of ACCEPT.

```
ACCEPT identifier FROM symbolic-name.
```

Finally, when you execute the program in TSO, you must allocate SYSTERM as follows:

```
ALLOC F(SYSTERM) DA(*)
```

Here is an example:

```
SPECIAL-NAMES.
    SYSTERM IS Terminal.
    □  □  □
    ACCEPT Person-Name FROM Terminal
```

The *symbolic-name* can be coded for the other COBOL compilers, too. It lets you specify other sources for the input. The possibilities are:

CONSOLE. This is the operator's keyboard.

SYSTERM. This is a mainframe TSO terminal keyboard.

SYSIN or **SYSIPT.** On the mainframe, SYSIN and SYSIPT are the system logical input device, the input stream. Input consists of 80-character lines. You must also include a JCL SYSIN or SYSIPT DD statement. JCL (Job Control Language) is an OS/390 mainframe language that you use to run your programs. You can also code SYSIN or SYSIPT for PC or Workstation COBOL, and use the run features of the compiler to direct the input requests to a file.

device. On the mainframe, you can code any ddname and include a DD statement for it to read input from a file. On PC and Workstation COBOL, you use the run features of the compiler to direct the input requests to a file.

TIP   *For CONSOLE input, first use a DISPLAY statement to tell the person at the terminal what is expected before executing the ACCEPT.*

The following example displays a message on the PC terminal and suspends program execution until they respond by typing a message in on the PC keyboard. COBOL then stores this message in *Answer*.

```
01 Answer                        PIC X(114).
    □  □  □
```

```
DISPLAY "WHAT IS YOUR NAME?"
ACCEPT Answer
```

For batch processing on the mainframe, you would ACCEPT input from the input stream. Assume the standard input file SYSIN contains the following line:

```
//GO.SYSIN DD *
244CONTINUE
/*
```

You could then define a symbolic name as SYSIN and write an ACCEPT statement to read the line.

```
SPECIAL-NAMES.
    SYSIN IS File-Input.
□ □ □
 01  Run-Control.
     05  Run-No   PIC 999.
     05  Run-Type PIC X(5).
     □ □ □
    ACCEPT Run-Control FROM File-Input
```

The line is read, and Run-No contains 244. Run-Type contains "CONTI".

Another form of the ACCEPT statement retrieves the date and time. You code it as follows:

```
ACCEPT identifier FROM request
```

The *request* is one of the following:

- *TIME* returns a PIC 9(8) external decimal number in the form *hhmmsstt: hh*, hour (00 to 23); *mm*, minute; *ss*, second; *tt*, hundredths of a second.

- *DATE* returns a PIC S9(6) external decimal number date in the form *yymmdd: yy*, year; *mm*, month; *dd*, day. Note the potential year-2000 problem.

- *DAY* returns a PIC S9(5) external decimal number date (year and day of the year) in the form *yyddd: yy*, year; *ddd*, day of the year (001 to 366). Note the potential year-2000 problem.

- *DAY-OF-WEEK* returns a PIC 9(1) external decimal number representing the day of the week with a value of 1 (Monday) through 7 (Sunday).

```
 01  Week-Day     PIC 9.
     □ □ □
    ACCEPT Week-Day FROM DAY-OF-WEEK
```

IBM has provided an optional subprogram named IGZEDT4 as a patch for Mainframe COBOL to obtain the date with a four-digit year. IGZEDT4 returns the date as eight characters in the form *yyyymmdd*.

```
01  The-Date.
    05  Yr     PIC 9999.
    05  Dy     PIC 99.
    05  Mo     PIC 99.
    □   □   □
    CALL "IGZEDT4" USING The-Date
```

PROPOSED NEW ANSI STANDARD: Check Compiler to See if Implemented

The proposed ANSI standard adds two input date formats:

- *DATE YYYYMMDD* returns a PIC S9(8) external decimal number date in the form *yyyymmdd: yyyy*, year; *mm*, month; *dd*, day.
- *DAY YYYYDDD* returns a PIC S9(7) external decimal number date (year and day of the year) in the form *yyyyddd: yyyy*, year; *ddd*, day of the year (001 to 366).

In addition, you can code the ON EXCEPTION/NOT ON EXCEPTION phrases for the ACCEPT. The PC COBOL compilers provide this now.

7.1.2 The DISPLAY Statement

Essential

For Workstation and PC COBOL, the DISPLAY statement displays the contents of the *items* on the terminal.

```
DISPLAY item, item, …, item
```

The *item* can be any data item, including a literal, except an index. A figurative constant such as SPACES displays as a single character. Numeric literals must be unsigned (1 but not −1). Group items display as alphanumeric. COBOL converts numeric items to external decimal for display. Each DISPLAY statement starts on a new line, and the display continues onto the next line if the line overflows (more than 120 characters for printed output, more than 100 characters for a terminal). If the line is shorter than the line of the device, the line is padded on the right with blanks.

On the mainframe, this form of DISPLAY displays on the operator's terminal. Because the operator doesn't want to receive your output, don't use this form for the mainframe. To display on your TSO terminal, you must define a symbolic name, similar to that for the ACCEPT.

```
SPECIAL-NAMES.
    SYSTERM IS symbolic-name.
```

Then you add the UPON phrase to the DISPLAY statement. You also need to allocate the TSO terminal to SYSTERM, if you have not already done so for the ACCEPT.

```
DISPLAY item, item, …, item UPON symbolic-name
```

The *symbolic-name* specifies where to display. The following are permitted:

CONSOLE. This requests the operator's terminal.

SYSTERM. This is a mainframe TSO terminal.

SYSOUT, SYSLIST, or **SYSIPT.** On the mainframe, SYSOUT, SYSLIST, and SYSLST are the system logical output device, the printer. You must also include a JCL SYSOUT, SYSLIST, or SYSIPT DD statement. You can code these same names for PC or Workstation COBOL, and use the run features of the compiler to direct the output requests to a file or the printer.

device. On the mainframe, you can code any ddname and include a DD statement for it to write output into a file. On PC and Workstation COBOL, you use the run features of the compiler to direct the output requests to a file or the printer.

For batch processing on the mainframe, you usually define a symbolic name for SYSOUT so that the display is printed with your output.

Each DISPLAY statement displays at the current line position and positions to the start of the next line at the end. (The printer spaces before printing.) If you want to leave the display at the end of the displayed line, add the WITH NO ADVANCING clause.

```
DISPLAY "THIS IS A LINE." UPON SYSOUT WITH NO ADVANCING
DISPLAY "THIS IS A CONTINUATION." UPON SYSOUT
```

The display will be "THIS IS A LINE.THIS IS A CONTINUATION.", and the display will then be positioned to the start of the next line.

Identifiers display according to their descriptions in the PIC clause. An item of PIC X(10) would display 10 characters, and PIC S9(5)V99 would display 7 characters (regardless of whether described as DISPLAY, BINARY, or PACKED-DECIMAL) with leading zeros and no decimal point.

The display of the sign depends on the compiler. In Mainframe COBOL, a minus value is indicated in the rightmost digit. (See the discussion of the SIGN clause for external decimal numbers in Chapter 9.) Workstation and PC COBOL and the new ANSI standard display a minus value with a minus sign. If *Value-A* is declared S9(5)V99 and contains 23 and *Value-B* is declared S9(3)V9(4) and contains −23.2345, they display as follows in Mainframe COBOL:

```
DISPLAY Value-A          [Displays as "0002300".]
DISPLAY Value-B          [Displays as "023234N".]
```

The other COBOL compilers display the sign display to the left or right of the item. If *Value-A* and *Value-B* were BINARY, they would display as follows:

```
DISPLAY Value-A          [Displays as "+0002300".]
DISPLAY Value-B          [Displays as "−0232345".]
```

Blanks are not inserted between displayed items, as shown in the following example. It displays as "0002300023234N" in Mainframe COBOL and as "+0002300−0232345" in PC COBOL.

```
DISPLAY Value-A, Value-B
```

TIP *To make numbers readable, separate numeric values with literal blanks. Because only the values of items are displayed, include some text to describe what they signify.*

The following displays as "Value-A = +0002300 Value-B = −0232345" in PC COBOL.

```
DISPLAY "Value-A = ", Value-A, " Value-B = ", Value-B
```

7.2   THE IF STATEMENT

7.2.1   The IF/THEN/ELSE Construct

Essential

The *If/Then/Else* construct executes one or the other of two sets of statements based on the results of a conditional test.

```
IF conditional-expression
    THEN imperative-statements to execute if true
    ELSE imperative-statements to execute if false
END-IF
```

The THEN keyword is optional, and some people prefer to write the IF this way:

```
IF condition
imperative-statements
ELSE
imperative-statements
END-IF
```

It is a matter of personal choice—or company standards.

7.2.2 The CONTINUE Statement

Essential

Either the THEN or ELSE may be null. In COBOL, the THEN must always be present, but you may omit the ELSE. Because CONTINUE is a null statement, you can code it to fulfill the requirement that there be a THEN phrase.

```
IF A = B
    THEN CONTINUE                   [You must code something here.]
    ELSE COMPUTE B = C + D * E
    ADD 1 TO X
END-IF
IF A = B
    THEN ADD X TO Y
        MOVE 2 TO Z
END-IF
```

7.2.3 Conditional Expressions in the IF Statement

Essential

The IF statement tests a condition, or several conditions, connected by AND, OR, or NOT. Try to prevent such logical expressions from becoming too complex. As in English, avoid double negatives. NOT in combination with OR is usually written incorrectly. Be careful not to confuse AND and OR.

TIP   *Structure the logical expression to show the relationship.*

```
IF ((The-Age > 35) OR
    ((The-Weight > 110) AND (The-Height > 5)) OR
    (The-Eyes = "BLUE"))
        AND
    (The-Name = "SMITH")
    THEN PERFORM A30-Select-Person
END-IF
```

Logical expressions are the most difficult part of a computer program to read. They can become so complex that you must write a decision table to understand them. Sometimes it is more straightforward to use the EVALUATE statement than to use the IF. Try to break up long logical expressions into shorter ones that can be more easily understood. Use parentheses, indentation, implied logical operations, and nested IF statements to accomplish this. The following example illustrates an IF statement that is hard to read and recasts it to be more readable.

```
IF The-Sex = "M" AND ((The-Age > 20 AND The-Age < 30) AND
(The-Weight > 90 AND The-Weight < 150) AND (The-Height > 5
AND The-Height < 6)) OR The-Wealth > 1000000 THEN PERFORM
B10-Select-Person END-IF
```

It is much clearer as

```
IF The-Sex = "M"
    THEN IF ((The-Age > 20 AND < 30) AND
            (The-Weight > 90 AND < 150) AND
            (The-Height > 5 AND < 6))
                OR
            (The-Wealth > 1000000)
            THEN PERFORM B10-Select-Person
        END-IF
END-IF
```

7.2.4   Nested IF Statements

Essential

Sometimes a logical expression is clearer if it is written as a nested IF. Each nested IF acts as if it were an AND applied to the previous IF.

```
IF (X = 1) AND (Y = 1)
    THEN PERFORM B10-last
END-IF
```

This is the same as

```
IF X = 1
    THEN IF Y = 1
            THEN PERFORM B10-last
        END-IF
END-IF
```

You can nest IF statements to any level, but an IF statement nested to great depth is hard to follow, and indenting to show the logical flow can soon force the coding beyond column 72. Keep each ELSE close to its related THEN. (Do this by placing some of the inner code in a separate paragraph and executing it with a PERFORM.) Note also that a separate END-IF is required for each IF.

```
IF A = B
    THEN IF X = Y
            THEN MOVE 0 TO A
            ELSE MOVE 1 TO A
        END-IF
    ELSE IF X > Y
            THEN MOVE 2 TO A
            ELSE MOVE 3 TO A
```

```
                    END-IF
           END-IF
```

Alternatively, you can make inner groups be separate paragraphs with the IF statement performing them. You can also nest THEN clauses to several levels with the meaning remaining clear, as shown in the following example.

```
IF A = B
   THEN ADD 1 TO C
        IF C = D
           THEN PERFORM A01-Start
                IF E = F
                   THEN IF G = H
                           THEN MOVE X TO Y
                                IF I = J
                                   THEN PERFORM A20-Next
                                END-IF
                        END-IF
                END-IF
        END-IF
END-IF
```

A common error is to forget to include an END-IF statement delimiter. The result will be no compilation error, but the meaning of the statements will change. For example:

```
IF A = B
   THEN MOVE 0 TO A
   ELSE MOVE 2 TO A
[Missing END-IF here.]
MOVE A TO B
```

The statements are interpreted as

```
IF A = B
   THEN MOVE 0 TO A
   ELSE MOVE 2 TO A
        MOVE A TO B
```

You will often control the logic within a program by using flags. Define such flags as PIC X, and use values for the flags that describe their meaning, such as "Y" for yes and "N" for no. The following example executes one statement the first time it is encountered and another statement from then on.

```
01  First-Time                  PIC X VALUE "Y".
    □   □   □
    IF First-Time = "Y"
       THEN PERFORM A10-Initialize
            MOVE "N" TO First-Time
       ELSE PERFORM A10-Normal
    END-IF
```

7.2.5 Old Forms of the IF Statement

`Archaic`

You can also write the IF statement without the END-IF if you terminate it with a period. However, things get very messy when you try to nest IF statements in this form.

```
IF conditional-expression
    THEN imperative-statements
    ELSE imperative-statements.
```

A common COBOL error was to misplace a period in a conditional statement. The following example illustrates the dangers. The statements on the right are indented to show how the statements on the left are executed. (The indentation, of course, has no effect on the way in which the statements execute.)

```
As coded:                        As executed:
    IF A = B                         IF A = B
        THEN MOVE 100 TO A.              THEN MOVE 100 TO A.
            ADD 2 TO B.              ADD 2 TO B.
```

7.2.6 The NEXT SENTENCE Statement

`Archaic`

COBOL also has a NEXT SENTENCE statement, which was often used in old COBOL programs. You can only place a NEXT SENTENCE in an IF statement that has no END-IF. It acts as a branch to the start of the next sentence—the next statement following a period. Here is an example:

```
IF A = C
    THEN IF B = D
            THEN COMPUTE A = A / B
            ELSE NEXT SENTENCE ─────────────┐
    ELSE IF A = D                           │
            THEN COMPUTE A = A * B           │
            ELSE NEXT SENTENCE. ───────────┐ │
ADD 1 TO A ◄───────────────────────────────┘─┘
```
        [This is the first statement following the period.]

Because it is easy to overlook a period, NEXT SENTENCE led to many errors. With the CONTINUE statement, there is now no reason to use NEXT SENTENCE.

7.3 THE GO TO STATEMENT

`Sometimes Used`

The GO TO statement transfers control to the first executable statement in the named procedure.

```
GO TO label
```

For example:

```
A01-Start.  ◄─────────────┐
    GO TO X10-End-It-All. ─┐ │
X10-End-It-All.  ◄─────────┘ │
    GO TO A01-Start. ────────┘
```

Structured programming has given the GO TO bad press, most of it deserved. However, the GO TO is not all bad, and one need not be fanatical about it.

TIP   *You can use the GO TO, but don't transfer backward or intertwine the code with GO TOs, because this makes the logical flow hard to follow.*

Intertwining occurs when the path of one GO TO crosses the path of another, as shown in the following two examples.

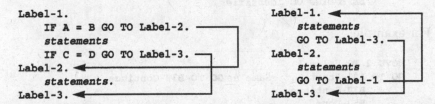

```
Label-1.                          Label-1.  ◄────────────┐
    IF A = B GO TO Label-2. ──┐       statements         │
    statements               │        GO TO Label-3. ──┐ │
    IF C = D GO TO Label-3. ─┐│    Label-2.            │ │
Label-2.  ◄──────────────────┘│        statements      │ │
    statements.              │         GO TO Label-1 ──┘ │
Label-3.  ◄──────────────────┘    Label-3.  ◄───────────┘
```

GO TOs should not exit from a paragraph to several different points outside the paragraph, because this also obscures the logical flow by forcing the reader to follow the various paths. The following example illustrates this:

```
Label-1.
    statements
    IF A = B GO TO Label-3. ──────── Exit here ─────────┐
    statements                                          │
    IF B = C GO TO Label-2. ─────── Exit here ─┐        │
    Statements.                                │        │
**** Exit                                       │        │
 Label-2.  ◄───────────────────────────────────┘        │
    statements.                                          │
 Label-3.  ◄────────────────────────────────────────────┘
    statements.
```

Although the GO TO should be avoided, there are times when it adds clarity to a program. Suppose you encounter a situation where you want to terminate the program. The following is typical.

```
IF some error occurs
    THEN PERFORM Z90-PRINT-ERROR
```

```
END-IF
more-statements
```

Does control return from Z90-PRINT-ERROR and execution continue? Only by looking at the Z90-PRINT-ERROR procedure can you tell. If you coded the following, it is clear that control does not return from the Z90-PRINT-ERROR procedure.

```
IF some error occurs
    THEN GO TO Z90-PRINT-ERROR
END-IF
more-statements
```

The GO TO DEPENDING ON statement transfers to one of several procedures, depending on the contents of a numeric elementary data item:

```
GO TO procedure, procedure, ..., procedure
    DEPENDING ON identifier
```

For example:

```
MOVE 2 TO Value-A
GO TO A01-Start,        Same as GO TO B30-Continue
    B30-Continue,
    B50-Done
    DEPENDING ON Value-A
```

If *Value-A* contains a value other than 1, 2, or 3, the GO TO DEPENDING ON is ignored, and execution continues with the next executable statement.

The GO TO DEPENDING ON statement provides a little of the *Case* construct of structured programming. However, the EVALUATE statement described later in this chapter is far superior.

TIP   *There is no reason to use GO TO DEPENDING ON.*

7.4 THE PERFORM STATEMENT

7.4.1 Execution of Procedures

Essential

The PERFORM statement is a brilliant concept that selectively executes groups of statements. It permits a program to be organized into functional units that are invoked with the PERFORM statement. It is especially useful for invoking functional units from several points within a program to save having to code the same function in several places. Code the *out-of-line* PERFORM as follows:

```
PERFORM procedure
```

The out-of-line PERFORM may invoke either a paragraph or section. A paragraph consists of a paragraph name and all following statements up to the next paragraph name. A section is a collection of paragraphs that begins with a SECTION name and includes all paragraphs up to the next section.

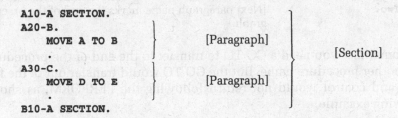

```
A10-A SECTION.
A20-B.
    MOVE A TO B                    [Paragraph]
    .
A30-C.                                               [Section]
    MOVE D TO E                    [Paragraph]
    .

B10-A SECTION.
```

The out-of-line PERFORM transfers control to the first executable statement in the procedure. Control returns to the next executable statement following the PERFORM after the last statement in the procedure executes. The last statement in a procedure is the one preceding the next procedure name. This is a rather passive way of indicating the end of a procedure, especially if the next procedure is on the following page. Use a comment to highlight the end of a procedure invoked by a PERFORM. This tells the reader that control is expected to return to the invoking PERFORM rather than continuing on to the next procedure, as would occur if the procedure were the target of a GO TO.

```
    PERFORM B10-One
    MOVE A TO B
    □  □  □
B10-One.
    MOVE 1 TO A
    COMPUTE B = C + D
    .
**** Exit
B20-Two.
```

The previous statements execute in the following sequence.

```
    PERFORM B10-One
    MOVE 1 TO A
    COMPUTE B = C + D
    MOVE A TO B
```

The out-of-line PERFORM operates as a GO TO, transferring control to the first executable statement in the procedure. At the end of the procedure, COBOL executes another GO TO to transfer back to the next executable statement following the PERFORM. PERFORM operates as follows:

```
    PERFORM B10-One                    [Operates as GO TO B10-One.]
    MOVE A TO B
    □  □  □
B10-One.
    MOVE 1 TO A
    COMPUTE B = C + D
    .      [End of paragraph operates as a GO TO to the statement following the PER-
           FORM.]
**** Exit                                        [The comment has no effect.]
  B20-Two.                [Next paragraph name marks the end of the preceding para-
                          graph.]
```

Sometimes you need a GO TO to transfer to the end of the procedure, requiring another procedure name. But the GO TO would transfer out of the first procedure, and control would not return following the PERFORM, as shown in the following example.

```
    PERFORM B10-One
    □  □  □
B10-One.
    READ In-File INTO In-Record
      AT END GO TO B20-Two
    END-READ
    MOVE In-Record TO Out-Record
    .
**** Exit
B20-Two.
```

If the GO TO is executed, control will not return following the PERFORM, but will continue sequentially in paragraph *B20-Two.* You can solve this problem with the PERFORM THRU, which names a first and last procedure to specify a range of procedures to execute.

```
    PERFORM first-procedure THRU last-procedure
```

Execution begins with the first executable statement in *first-procedure,* and control returns following the PERFORM when the last statement in *last-procedure* executes. The *first-procedure* must precede *last-procedure* in the program. You can now code the following.

```
    PERFORM B10-One THRU B10-One-Exit
    □  □  □
B10-One.
    READ In-File INTO In-Record
      AT END GO TO B10-One-Exit
    END-READ
    MOVE In-Record TO Out-Record
```

```
B10-One-Exit. EXIT.
**** End of B10-One.
```

TIP *Never use the PERFORM THRU form unless the code must contain para-graph labels that are the target of GO TOs.*

EXIT is a special null statement used to terminate a range of procedures. EXIT is not required, just a good practice, and any sequential range of procedures can be executed. The following example executes the *C10-First* paragraph and then the *C20-Second* paragraph.

```
PERFORM C10-First THRU C20-Second
    □  □  □
C10-First.
    MOVE 1 TO A
    COMPUTE B = C + D
    .
**** Exit
 C20-Second.
    MOVE B TO C
    COMPUTE D = A - B
    .
**** Exit
```

Note that the PERFORM *C10-First* THRU *C20-Second* is equivalent to

```
PERFORM C10-First
PERFORM C20-Second
```

This is better, because the goal is to isolate functionally related code, and invoking different ranges of procedures makes it unclear where the functionally related code begins and ends. Are *C10-First* and *C20-Second* separate units, or are they part of a single unit? You cannot tell.

The procedure specified in the THRU clause may optionally contain only an EXIT statement. There is less chance for confusion if the THRU clause names an EXIT statement, which must be the only statement in its procedure; that is, you must precede and follow it with procedure names. If an EXIT statement is executed without being named in a PERFORM, execution continues with the procedure following the EXIT.

TIP *Always use EXIT to terminate procedures invoked by the PERFORM THRU so that it is apparent that the several procedures constitute a unit. Also include the word EXIT in the procedure name to show that it is an EXIT.*

```
        PERFORM C10-First THRU C20-First-Exit
        □  □  □
C10-First.
    READ In-File INTO In-Record
      AT END GO TO C20-First-Exit
    END-READ
    MOVE In-Record TO Out-Record
    MOVE SPACES TO In-Record

C20-First-Exit.  EXIT.
```

Any procedures invoked by a PERFORM execute in sequence if they are encountered during normal execution, but avoid this because it makes the program hard to follow. The following example illustrates this.

```
        PERFORM B10-One THRU B30-Three-Exit.
            [Control returns to the next statement.]
B10-One.   MOVE 1 TO A.              [This is the next statement.]
B20-Two.   MOVE 1 TO B.
B30-Three-Exit.  EXIT.
B40-Four.  MOVE 1 TO C.
```

These statements execute in the following sequence.

```
        PERFORM B10-One THRU B30-Three-Exit.
B10-One.   MOVE 1 TO A.
B20-Two.   MOVE 1 TO B.
B30-Three-Exit.  EXIT.
B10-One.   MOVE 1 TO A.
B20-Two.   MOVE 1 TO B.
B30-Three-Exit.  EXIT.
B40-Four.  MOVE 1 TO C.
```

TIP *Never let control drop through into a paragraph. PERFORM the paragraph.*

To reiterate, if you invoke a procedure with a PERFORM, don't also execute it by letting control fall through from the preceding procedure. Although the GO TO can transfer out of the range of statements being invoked by the PERFORM, this is confusing and you should avoid it. Use the GO TO to transfer out of a procedure only when the flow of control must be broken. For example, use it when you terminate a loop early or when the run terminates because of an error.

7.4.2   The In-Line PERFORM

Essential

The *in-line* PERFORM consists of a PERFORM statement followed by any imperative statements and terminated by an END-PERFORM. (Remember that an imperative statement can be a conditional statement, as long as it is terminated with its END scope terminator.)

```
PERFORM
    imperative-statements
END-PERFORM
```

The in-line PERFORM becomes more interesting when it is used for loops.

7.4.3 Execution of Loops

Essential

The PERFORM also implements loops. The simplest loop is to PERFORM a procedure some number of times:

```
PERFORM integer TIMES
    imperative-statements
END-PERFORM

PERFORM procedure integer TIMES
PERFORM first-procedure THRU last-procedure integer TIMES
```

The loop executes *integer* times. The *integer* may be a numeric integer literal or identifier. If *integer* is zero or negative, the *procedure* is not performed. Once PERFORM is executed, changes in the value of an identifier *integer* have no effect on the number of times the loop executes.

```
01  A                          PIC S9(4) BINARY.
    ☐  ☐  ☐
    MOVE 6 TO A
    PERFORM A TIMES
        ADD 1 TO A
    END-PERFORM
```
[The ADD statement executes six times, even though the value of A is changed within the loop.]
```
    PERFORM A60-Zero-Table Table-Size TIMES
```
[*A60-Zero-Table* executes ten times, even if a new value is assigned to *Table-Size* in the *A60-Zero-Table* paragraph.]

The PERFORM UNTIL executes a procedure until a specified condition is met. The WITH TEST BEFORE or AFTER phrase tells whether to test the condition before or after executing the loop.

```
                    AFTER
                    BEFORE
PERFORM WITH TEST _____ UNTIL condition
    imperative-statements
END-PERFORM
PERFORM procedure WITH TEST BEFORE UNTIL condition
```

The WITH TEST BEFORE is a *Do While* in structured programming terminology.

```
PERFORM first-procedure THRU last-procedure WITH TEST AFTER
        UNTIL condition
```

The WITH TEST AFTER is a *Do Until* in structured programming terminology. If the condition is true when PERFORM is executed, the procedure is not performed.

```
PERFORM A10-TEST WITH TEST AFTER UNTIL End-Flag = "Y"
```

If you omit the WITH TEST phrase, WITH TEST BEFORE is assumed:

```
PERFORM WITH TEST BEFORE UNTIL condition
```

This is the same as

```
PERFORM UNTIL condition
```

In the following example, PERFORM UNTIL is used to read in a file until a desired record is selected or until an end of file is encountered. Note that the WITH TEST AFTER ensures that the loop is performed at least once. (Assume that *In-Record-Key* and *In-Record-Type* are Working-Storage data items within *In-Record*.)

```
PERFORM WITH TEST AFTER
        UNTIL (In-Record-Key = HIGH-VALUES) OR
              (In-Record-Type = "A"
   READ In-File INTO In-Record
     AT END MOVE HIGH-VALUES TO In-Record-Key
   END-READ
END-PERFORM
   .
**** Exit
```

The PERFORM VARYING can loop while incrementing a control identifier. You often use this type of loop to manipulate tables.

```
PERFORM WITH TEST BEFORE or AFTER
        VARYING subscript FROM start BY increment
        UNTIL condition
PERFORM procedure WITH TEST BEFORE or AFTER
        VARYING subscript FROM start BY increment
        UNTIL condition
PERFORM first-procedure THRU last-procedure
        WITH TEST BEFORE or AFTER
        VARYING subscript FROM start BY increment
        UNTIL condition
```

The *subscript* is a numeric identifier or index that is incremented each time through the loop. (Subscripts and indexes are described in detail in Chapter 13.)

The *subscript* is set to the value of *start* at the beginning of the loop. COBOL evaluates the UNTIL condition at the place specified and, if the condition is true, terminates the loop. If the condition is not true, the *increment* is added to *subscript* and the loop continues another iteration. At the end of the loop, *subscript* contains the value that it had when the UNTIL condition became true. (If the condition is true at the start of the loop, *subscript* contains the value of *start*.)

You would usually code the *condition* for a loop as shown here:

```
PERFORM WITH TEST BEFORE or AFTER
        VARYING subscript FROM start BY increment
        UNTIL subscript > end
```

The *start*, *increment*, and *end* may be numeric identifiers, literals, or indexes.

- *start* is the first value that *subscript* is to assume within the loop.
- *increment* is a value added to *subscript* at the end of each pass through the loop.
- *end* is the last value that *subscript* is to assume within the loop.

In the following example, the loop executes ten times, with **Ix** assuming values from 1 to 10. **Ix** contains 11 at the end of the loop.

```
PERFORM WITH TEST BEFORE VARYING Ix FROM 1 BY 1
        UNTIL Ix > 10
    MOVE ZEROS TO Table-1(Ix)
END-PERFORM
```

Valid values for an index are from 1 to the size of the table—that is, it cannot exceed the bounds of the table. However, the loop can increment or decrement the index to be one more or less than this because this is necessary to terminate the loop. For example, consider the following loop to zero out a table of 30 elements:

```
01  A-Table.
    05  Tab-Vals           PIC S9(4) OCCURS 30 TIMES
                           INDEXED BY Tab-X.
    □  □  □
    PERFORM VARYING Tab-X FROM 1 BY 1 UNTIL Tab-X > 30
        MOVE ZEROS TO Tab-Vals(Tab-X)
    END-PERFORM
```

To terminate the loop, *Tab-X* is allowed to contain 31. You could test *Tab-X* outside the loop to see whether it contained 31.

The *increment* may be positive or negative. If negative, *subscript* is decremented, and you should code the UNTIL phrase as UNTIL *subscript* < *end*. The following statement executes the loop 100 times, with *Ix* assuming values from 100 to 1 within the loop. At the end of the loop, *Ix* contains 0. A value of 0 for an index is undefined in the ANSI standard. Therefore, *Ix* may contain garbage. Don't depend on its value if the final value may be zero—use an identifier rather than an index as subscript.

```
PERFORM WITH TEST BEFORE VARYING Ix FROM 100 BY -1
        UNTIL Ix < 1
```

The UNTIL phrase may be any conditional expression. For a WITH TEST BEFORE, the loop is not executed if the UNTIL condition is true. The following loop is not executed, because *Start-It* is greater than 10.

```
MOVE 11 TO Start-It
PERFORM WITH TEST BEFORE VARYING Ix FROM Start-It BY 1
        UNTIL Ix > 10
```

But the loop executes once if a WITH TEST AFTER is used:

```
MOVE 11 TO Start-It
PERFORM WITH TEST AFTER VARYING Ix FROM Start-It BY 1
        UNTIL Ix > 10
```

At the end of the loop, execution continues with the next executable following the PERFORM (for an out-of-line PERFORM) or the END-PERFORM (for an in-line PERFORM). The *subscript* contains the next value greater than *end* (or less than *end* if *increment* is negative). In the following example, the loop executes with *Ix* containing values of 1 to 10. At the termination of the loop, *Ix* will contain 11.

```
PERFORM WITH TEST BEFORE VARYING Ix FROM 1 BY 1 UNTIL Ix > 10
```

If *increment, end,* and *subscript* are identifiers and you change their values within the loop, it will affect the number of times the loop is performed. Changing the value of *start* within the loop has no effect on the loop.

The ANSI standard requires that an in-line or out-of-line PERFORM execute at least one statement, but IBM and PC COBOL don't have this requirement. For some things, such as searching an alphanumeric item to find the first nonblank character, all you want to do is perform the loop without executing a statement. Examples of this are given in Chapter 22.

TIP   *The choice of whether to use an in-line or out-of-line loop depends on the following:*

Use an out-of-line loop when the statements within the loop can be invoked from more than one place in the program.

Use an out-of-line loop when the loop contains a large number of statements. (What constitutes a large number is a matter of choice.)

For most other situations, use an in-line loop. It is easier to read because the statements are placed directly in the line of flow in the source.

You can nest the out-of-line PERFORM to seven levels by coding one VARYING and several AFTER phrases for nested loops. The last AFTER varies most rapidly. Because tables can have seven dimensions, there can be as many as six AFTER clauses. The AFTER/FROM/BY phrase cannot be coded in an in-line PERFORM. It is permitted only in an out-of-line PERFORM.

```
PERFORM paragraph-name WITH TEST BEFORE or AFTER
        VARYING subscript-1 FROM start-1 BY increment-1
        UNTIL condition-1
        AFTER subscript-2 FROM start-2 BY increment-2
        UNTIL condition-2
        AFTER subscript-3 FROM start-3 BY increment-3
        UNTIL condition-3
        . . . . .
        AFTER subscript-7 FROM start-7 BY increment-7
        UNTIL condition-7
```

The *start* values are set for each *subscript,* and then each UNTIL condition is tested to see whether the loop should be performed. The loop is performed with the *subscript* in the last AFTER varying the most rapidly, as shown in the following example.

```
PERFORM A10-Zero-Table WITH TEST BEFORE
        VARYING Ix FROM I BY 1 UNTIL Ix > 5      [This varies last.]
        AFTER Iy FROM 1 BY 1 UNTIL Iy > 4        [This varies next.]
        AFTER Iz FROM 1 BY 1 UNTIL Iz > 8        [This varies first.]
   □ □ □
A10-Zero-Table.
    MOVE ZERO TO Table-A(Ix, Iy, Iz)
    .
**** EXIT
```

The loop is performed 160 times, with the subscripts varying as shown.

```
Ix = 1, Iy = 1, Iz = 1 to 8
Ix = 1, Iy = 2, Iz = 1 to 8
  .      .        .
  .      .        .
Ix = 1, Iy = 4, Iz = 1 to 8
Ix = 2, Iy = 1, Iz = 1 to 8
  .      .        .
  .      .        .
Ix = 5, Iy = 4, Iz = 1 to 8
```

At the end of a PERFORM with AFTER phrases, the VARYING *subscript* will contain the value that caused the UNTIL condition to be true. All the AFTER *subscripts* will contain their appropriate *start* values.

The AFTER/FROM/BY/UNTIL phrase cannot appear in an in-line PERFORM. The following is in error.

```
PERFORM WITH TEST BEFORE VARYING Ix FROM I BY 1 UNTIL Ix > 5
                [VARYING is permitted.]
       AFTER Iy FROM 1 BY 1 UNTIL Iy > 4
                [Error. AFTER not permitted.]
       AFTER Iz FROM 1 BY I UNTIL Iz > 8
                [Error. AFTER not permitted.]
  MOVE ZERO TO Table-A(Ix, Iy, Iz)
END-PERFORM
```

PROPOSED NEW ANSI STANDARD: Check Compiler to See if Implemented

The new ANSI standard allows you to code the AFTER phrase in an in-line PER-FORM.

To perform in-line operations on multidimensional tables, you can nest the PERFORM statements within the loop. Such loops can be nested to any level. This also makes clear the order in which the indexes are to be varied. The embedded PERFORM must perform statements totally included in or totally excluded from the range of statements in the original PERFORM. The following example will do what the preceding one was intended to do:

```
PERFORM WITH TEST BEFORE VARYING Ix FROM 1 BY 1 UNTIL Ix > 5
   PERFORM WITH TEST BEFORE VARYING Iy FROM 1 BY 1
          UNTIL Iy > 4
   PERFORM WITH TEST BEFORE VARYING Iz FROM 1 BY 1
          UNTIL Iz > 8
     MOVE ZERO TO Table-A(Ix, Iy, Iz)
   END-PERFORM
  END-PERFORM
END-PERFORM
```

7.4.4   Breaking Out of Loops and Paragraphs

Essential

There is one major problem associated with the flow of control not covered by the structured programming constructs—how to quit in the middle of a block of code. This can occur inside a nested IF or other conditional statement, inside a paragraph, or inside a loop. A typical example is to read a file and terminate at the end of the file. The following functional need occurs in almost every program:

```
imperative-statements
READ In-File INTO In-Rec
  AT END want to quit paragraph
END-READ
many statements to process record
   .
**** Exit
```

This leads to a more general need to be able to exit from a paragraph or loop anywhere within it, such as the following:

```
paragraph-name.
    statements
    IF condition
        THEN want to exit paragraph
    END-IF
    remainder-of-statements
    .
**** Exit
```

Conditional statements such as the IF can do this by executing the remaining statements in the procedure as a statement group. However, this is often awkward and results in nesting statements to several levels:

```
paragraph-name.
    statements
    IF NOT condition
        THEN remainder-of-statements
    END-IF
    .
**** Exit
```

Often the simplest and most straightforward way of breaking out of conditional statements or a paragraph is to use a GO TO:

```
paragraph-name.
    statements
    IF condition
        THEN GO TO label
    END-IF
    remainder-of-statements
    .
label. EXIT.
```

Just remember to perform such a paragraph with a PERFORM THRU:

```
    PERFORM paragraph-name THRU label
```

The same thing often occurs within loops where you want to jump to the end of the loop and continue or break out of the loop.

```
    PERFORM UNTIL condition
      statements
      IF first-condition
          THEN want to branch to end of loop and continue
      END-IF
      more-statements
      IF second-condition
```

```
            THEN want to break out of loop
      END-IF
      remainder-of-statements
   END-PERFORM
```

Again, you might be able to use IF statements to do this, but it gets very awkward:

```
   PERFORM UNTIL condition
      statements
      IF first-condition
         THEN CONTINUE
         ELSE more-statements
               IF second-condition
                  THEN set condition to end loop
                  ELSE remainder-of-statements
               END-IF
      END-IF
   END-PERFORM
```

You can use a GO TO to break out of a loop. However, you can't use a GO TO to continue an in-line loop, because you can't place a label between PERFORM and END-PERFORM. Sometimes the best way is to separate some of the code into paragraphs and PERFORM it. The following illustrates a GO TO to break out of a loop and a PERFORM to continue it.

```
   PERFORM UNTIL condition
      statements
      IF first-condition
         THEN CONTINUE
         ELSE PERFORM A10-More-Statements
               IF second-condition
                  THEN GO TO A10-Break-Loop
                  ELSE PERFORM A10-Rest-Of-Statements
               END-IF
      END-IF
   END-PERFORM
      .
A10-Break-Loop.
A10-More-Statements.
   more-statements
      .
**** Exit
A10-Rest-Of-Statements.
   remainder-of-statements
      .
**** Exit
```

Using a GO TO and placing code in a paragraph to solve logic problems is not desirable. But do it if the alternatives are less desirable.

The GO TO is also useful for branching to an error exit when a catastrophic error is encountered that breaks the main line of the program. You can use nested

IFs, with the THEN clause as the error routine and the ELSE clause as the remainder of the program. However, this is needlessly complex and holds the least interesting code, the error termination, in front of the reader, forcing him or her to look elsewhere for the remainder of the program. It is better to terminate a program with a GO TO.

```
IF error-condition
    THEN GO TO Z10-Error-Routine
END-IF
```

PROPOSED NEW ANSI STANDARD: Check Compiler to See if Implemented

The new ANSI standard solves the problem of breaking out of a loop or branching to the end of a loop to continue it by providing new forms of the EXIT statement. EXIT can break out of paragraphs, sections, or an in-line PERFORM at any point.

```
PERFORM UNTIL condition
    statements
    IF condition
        THEN EXIT PERFORM          [Breaks out of PERFORM.]
    END-IF
    more-statements
END-PERFORM
```

To branch to the END-PERFORM to continue the loop, you add the CYCLE phrase.

```
EXIT PERFORM CYCLE
```

You can also exit anywhere within a paragraph or section by executing the EXIT PARAGRAPH or EXIT SECTION statements.

```
some-paragraph.
    some-statements
    IF condition
        THEN EXIT PARAGRAPH        [Terminates paragraph.]
    END-IF
    more-statements
    .
**** Exit
```

7.5 THE EVALUATE STATEMENT

Essential

The EVALUATE tests for several conditions and executes different statements for each condition. The simplest form of EVALUATE is

```
EVALUATE expression
   WHEN value imperative-statements
   WHEN value imperative-statements
         .     .     .
   WHEN value imperative-statements
END-EVALUATE
```

Here is an example:

```
EVALUATE A / B
   WHEN 1 PERFORM A10-First          [Executed if A / B equals 1.]
   WHEN ZERO PERFORM A10-Zero        [Executed if A / B equals 0.]
   WHEN -1 PERFORM A10-Negative      [Executed if A / B equals −1.]
END-EVALUATE
```

EVALUATE is extremely handy for organizing the overall logic of a program and performing the appropriate actions.

The expression following the EVALUATE is called the *selection subject.* It can be a literal, an identifier, or an expression. The values following the WHEN phrase are called the *selection objects.* They can be literals, identifiers, or arithmetic expressions, as long as they have a data type that can be compared with the result of the selection subject following the EVALUATE.

```
EVALUATE A * B * C          [The selection subject is a numeric expression.]
   [Therefore, Average-cost must be a numeric identifier.]
   WHEN Average-Cost imperative-statements
   WHEN D / E imperative-statements
   [D / E is valid, because it is an arithmetic expression, whose data type can be
   compared with A * B * C.]
         .     .     .
END-EVALUATE
```

Rather than a single value, the selection objects following the WHEN can be a range of values specified by coding THRU.

```
WHEN 12 THRU 21
WHEN Size-Small THRU Size-Big
WHEN A * B THRU (A * 2) * B
```

COBOL examines each WHEN phrase in turn, and if the value of the subject expression equals a single value or falls within a range of values, it executes the statements following the WHEN phrase. Control then resumes with the next statement following the END-EVALUATE rather than dropping through to the next WHEN. Only one WHEN phrase is executed. The following example illustrates this:

```
EVALUATE Person-Age
   WHEN 15 CONTINUE
   WHEN 13 THRU 19 ADD 8 TO Feeding-Cost
```

```
    WHEN 20 THROUGH 29 SUBTRACT 2 FROM Feeding-Cost
END-EVALUATE
```

If *Person-Age* contains 15, execution immediately resumes following the END-EVALUATE. You can use the CONTINUE null statement to perform no action for WHEN phrases. Even though 15 would be true for the second WHEN, it is never reached, because the previous WHEN executes.

If you want to select any of several discrete values, you can code several WHEN phrases in succession. Stacking the WHEN phrases in front of the imperative statements causes COBOL to treat them as if they were all connected by logical ORs. The following example adds 10 to *Feeding-Cost* if *Person-Age* contains 11, 13, or 19. A value of 20 is added if *Person-Age* contains 12, 14 through 18, or 20.

```
EVALUATE Person-Age
    WHEN 11
    WHEN 13
    WHEN 19
        ADD 10 TO Feeding-Cost
    WHEN 12
    WHEN 14 THRU 18
    WHEN 20 ADD 20 TO Feeding-Cost
END-EVALUATE
```

If no WHEN is selected, execution continues following the END-EVALUATE. You can place a WHEN OTHER phrase last as a catchall to execute statements if none of the previous WHEN phrases executes. Here is the simplest example:

```
EVALUATE A / B                Executes as      IF A / B = ZERO
    WHEN ZERO ADD 1 TO C                           THEN ADD 1 TO C
    WHEN OTHER ADD 2 TO C                          ELSE ADD 2 TO C
END-EVALUATE                                   END-IF
```

You can also precede a selection object in a WHEN phrase with the NOT. The following would catch all values except 15 through 21.

```
WHEN NOT 15 THRU 21
```

There can be several selection subjects, separated from each other by the keyword ALSO. There must be a corresponding number of selection objects on each WHEN, also separated by ALSO. The selection subjects are evaluated and compared with the selection objects one by one. The following example illustrates this. If *Person-Age* equals 21, *Person-Income* equals 100,000, and *Person-State* equals "CA", COBOL executes the WHEN phrase. If any of the comparisons is not true, COBOL goes on to the next WHEN.

```
EVALUATE Person-Age ALSO Person-Income ALSO Person-State
    WHEN 21 ALSO 100000 ALSO "CA"
```

Note that any NOT applies to only a single value or range. For example, WHEN NOT 21 ALSO 100000 is not the same as WHEN NOT 21 ALSO NOT 100000.

Code the keyword ANY in place of any selection object following the WHEN if you want to ignore a particular comparison. The following selects if *Person-Age* equals 21 and *Person-Income* equals 100,000. Any value of *Person-State* is accepted.

```
WHEN 21 ALSO 100000 ALSO ANY
```

So far, the EVALUATE statement has been used to compare expressions as selection subjects with identifiers or literals as expression objects. You can reverse this to use logical expressions following the WHEN as selection objects. You then place TRUE or FALSE as the selection subjects following the EVALUATE to tell what value of the logical expressions you want to select. The advantage is that the WHEN can test different identifiers. The following example illustrates this:

```
EVALUATE TRUE                Same as    EVALUATE FALSE
   WHEN Person-Age = 21                    WHEN Person-Age NOT = 21
      PERFORM A10-First                       PERFORM A10-First
   WHEN Person-Income > 100000             WHEN Person-Income <= 100000
      PERFORM A20-Second                      PERFORM A20-Second
END-EVALUATE                            END-EVALUATE
```

Any logical expression that you can code in an IF statement can be coded with this form of the EVALUATE. The expressions do not need to compare the same identifiers. You can also compare multiple expressions using the ALSO keyword. Each WHEN phrase must contain the same number of logical expressions as there are selection subjects following the EVALUATE:

```
EVALUATE TRUE ALSO FALSE
   WHEN Zip-Code IS NUMERIC ALSO Person-State = "CA"
                    [This WHEN phrase executes if Zip-Code is numeric and the
                    Person-State does not contain "CA".]
      PERFORM A10-First
   WHEN ANY ALSO Person-State = "NY"
                    [This WHEN phrase executes if Person-State contains "NY". Notice
                    that ANY can also be used in place of an expression.]
      PERFORM A20-Second
```

You can also place the logical expressions as the selection subjects following the EVALUATE and code TRUE or FALSE as the selection objects following the WHEN. This is a simple way of writing a decision table.

```
EVALUATE Person-State = "CA" ALSO Person-Age > 21
   WHEN TRUE ALSO TRUE imperative-statements
                    [Person-State = "CA" and Person-Age greater than 21.]
   WHEN TRUE ALSO FALSE imperative-statements
                    [Person-State = "CA" and Person-Age less than or equal to 21.]
```

```
        WHEN FALSE ALSO TRUE imperative-statements
                [Person-State NOT = "CA" and Person-Age greater than 21.]
        WHEN FALSE ALSO FALSE imperative-statements
                [Person-State NOT = "CA" and Person-Age less than or equal to
                21.]
    END-EVALUATE
```

Note that in this example, all cases are accounted for and there would be no need for a WHEN OTHER. You could code one, but it would never execute.

And finally, you can mix and match:

```
EVALUATE FALSE ALSO A * B
    WHEN D > E ALSO 12 THRU 24
                [This WHEN phrase executes when D > E and A * B has a value of
                12 through 24.]
```

7.6 SCOPE TERMINATORS

Essential

Each of the following conditional statements has an associated *explicit scope terminator*. Several of these statements are described later.

ADD	END-ADD	READ	END-READ
CALL	END-CALL	RETURN	END-RETURN
COMPUTE	END-COMPUTE	REWRITE	END-REWRITE
DELETE	END-DELETE	SEARCH	END-SEARCH
DIVIDE	END-DIVIDE	START	END-START
EVALUATE	END-EVALUATE	STRING	END-STRING
IF	END-IF	SUBTRACT	END-SUBTRACT
MULTIPLY	END-MULTIPLY	UNSTRING	END-UNSTRING
PERFORM	END-PERFORM	WRITE	END-WRITE

COBOL can also assume necessary scope terminators for you. These are termed *implicit scope terminators*. Implicit scope terminators are assumed as follows.

A *period* terminates any unterminated statements. For example:

```
PERFORM 10 TIMES        Same as    PERFORM 10 TIMES
    IF F = G                           IF F = G
        THEN MOVE H TO I.                  THEN MOVE H TO I
                                       END-IF        ←Assumed
                                       END-PERFORM   ←Assumed
```

Note that the following would result in an error:

```
PERFORM 10 TIMES        Same as     PERFORM 10 TIMES
   IF F = G                            IF F = G
      THEN MOVE H TO I                    THEN MOVE H TO I
   END-IF                              END-IF
END-PERFORM                           END-PERFORM
                                      END-IF      ←Doesn't close anything
                                      END-PERFORM ←Doesn't close anything
```

Periods can often result in an undetected error. For example, suppose you coded the following:

```
IF F = G                Executed as    IF F = G
   THEN MOVE H TO I                        THEN MOVE H TO I
       MOVE J TO K.                            MOVE J TO K
       MOVE L TO M                      END-IF
                                        MOVE L TO M
```

The unintended period terminates the IF statement with no error message. This type of error is extremely easy to make and difficult to detect.

TIP *Never use periods in language statements except at the end of a paragraph.*

Because each paragraph must end with a period, COBOL assumes implicit scope terminators as needed at the end of a paragraph. COBOL also assumes implicit scope terminators when statements are nested and an explicit scope terminator for the outside statement is encountered. For example:

```
PERFORM 10 TIMES                Same as    PERFORM 10 TIMES
   IF F = G                                   IF F = G
      THEN MOVE H TO I                           THEN MOVE H TO I
END-PERFORM                                   END-IF      ←Assumed
                                           END-PERFORM
```

This can also easily lead to errors, such as the following:

```
PERFORM 10 TIMES     Executed as    PERFORM 10 TIMES
   IF F = G                            IF F = G
      THEN MOVE H TO I                    THEN MOVE H TO I
MOVE J TO K                                 MOVE J TO K
END-PERFORM                            END-IF      ←Assumed
                                       END-PERFORM
```

A new phrase will also cause an implicit scope terminator to be assumed when nesting, as shown in the following example:

```
READ In-File INTO In-Rec    Same as    READ In-File INTO In-Rec
   AT END                                 AT END
```

```
        IF A = B                          IF A = B
            THEN MOVE C TO D                  THEN MOVE C TO D
                 MOVE E TO F                       MOVE E TO F
    NOT AT END MOVE G TO H                  END-IF    ←Assumed
    END-READ                           NOT AT END MOVE G TO H
                                       END-READ
```

The one exception to this is in nested IF statements. ELSE phrases are applied as appropriate to matching THEN phrases, as shown in the following example:

```
IF A = B                Same as    IF A = B
    THEN MOVE C TO D                   THEN MOVE C TO D
        IF E = F                          IF E = F
            THEN MOVE G TO H                  THEN MOVE G TO H
            ELSE MOVE I TO J                  ELSE MOVE I TO J
        ELSE MOVE K TO L                  END-IF    ←Assumed
    END-IF                             ELSE MOVE K TO L
                                       END-IF
```

Implicit scope terminators save coding but are a major source of error, which is not a wise trade-off.

TIP   *Don't rely on implicit scope terminators. Code them explicitly.*

EXERCISES

1. What will the identifiers *A*, *B*, *C*, and *D* contain after each of the following statements has been executed? Assume that each identifier has a precision of S9(4).

```
MOVE 1 TO A, B
COMPUTE B = A + 1
ADD B TO A
MULTIPLY B BY A
DIVIDE A BY 5 GIVING C REMAINDER D
```

2. Place parentheses around the following expressions to indicate the hierarchy of operations. Also, insert blanks where necessary.

```
1/2*A*T**2
A**B-2/Y-D
A+2*C**2/B+6*4
A+B=ZERO OR NOT A NOT=1 AND B > A*10-6
```

3. The following statements each contain an actual or an almost certain potential error. Find each error.

```
MULTIPLY A BY 2
ADD "125" TO B
DIVIDE Budget-Remaining BY Periods-Remaining
```

```
MOVE ZERO TO A, B. C
COMPUTE A = B * C ROUNDED
IF A = 2 = C
   THEN ADD 1 TO A
END-IF
```

4. The following table contains paragraph names and associated values of the identifier *Switch-A.* Perform the proper paragraph name as given by the value of *Switch-A,* first using IF statements and then an EVALUATE statement.

Value of Switch-A	Paragraph Name
1	Start-It
2	Finish-It
3	Continue-It
4	Proceed-To

5. Use IF statements to set the identifier *Ans* to the appropriate value based on the conditions given. Then do the same using an EVALUATE statement.

Value of *ANS*	Condition
0	If X equals zero
−1	If X is negative and Y is not greater than zero
−2	If both X and $Y + Z$ are greater than 22
100	If X equals 1 and Y equals 1, or if half of $Y + Z$ equals 1
200	All other conditions

6. Rewrite the following IF statement using condition names.
```
01  X                        PIC  S9(5).
    □  □  □
    IF (X = 1) OR
       ((X NOT < 20) AND (X NOT > 30)) OR
       (X = 50 OR 60 OR 61)
       THEN …
    END-IF
```

7. Write decision tables to show whether the following IF statements are true or false for all possible conditions.
```
    IF (X = 1 AND NOT Y = 1) OR
       NOT (X = 0 OR Y = 1)
       THEN …
    END-IF
    IF (X NOT = 1 OR Y NOT = 1) OR
       NOT (X = Y)
       THEN …
    END-IF
```

8. What values will X assume within the following loops?

```
PERFORM Loop1 VARYING X FROM -10 BY 3 UNTIL X > 6

PERFORM Loop2 VARYING X FROM 1 BY 1 UNTIL X > 1

MOVE 4 TO Y
PERFORM WITH TEST BEFORE VARYING X FROM 1 BY 1
        UNTIL (X > 10) OR (Y NOT > 0)
    PERFORM VARYING X FROM -3 BY -2 UNTIL X < -7
      imperative-statements
    END-PERFORM
END-PERFORM
```

9. Assume that Dy, Mo, and Yr contain the day, month, and year of a start date, and that Dur contains a duration in days. Assuming 30 days per month, use IF and COMPUTE statements to COMPUTE the end date from the start date and the duration, and store the results back in Dy, Mo, and Yr.

10. Assume that the day, month, and year of a start date are contained in S-Dy, S-Mo, and S-Yr, and the end date in E-Dy, E-Mo, and E-Yr. Write the statements necessary to store the exact duration in days in Dur, assuming 30 days per month.

11. An equation is given as $Y = (X - 1)/(X2 + 1)$. Write the statements necessary to evaluate the equation for values of X ranging from –6 to 10 by steps of 0.5.

12. Rewrite the following statements without using the GO TO statement, but using instead the IF, EVALUATE, or PERFORM statements.

```
    MOVE 1 TO X.
Loop1.  MOVE ZERO TO A(X).
    ADD 1 TO X.
    IF X < 10 THEN GO TO Loop1.
    IF B > 6 THEN GO TO Next1.
    IF B < ZERO THEN GO TO Next1.
    IF C = ZERO THEN GO TO Next1.
    IF B > 3 THEN GO TO Next2.
    MOVE ZERO TO D.
    ADD 1 TO B.
    GO TO Next3.
Next1.  MOVE ZERO TO E.
    IF X + Y > 0 THEN GO TO Next3.
    ADD 1 TO G.
    GO TO Next3.
Next2.  ADD 1 TO G.
    GO TO Next4.
Next3.  ADD 1 TO F.
Next4.
```

13. The following IF statement has been coded.

```
IF XX NOT = ZERO AND ZZ = 1 AND XX NOT = 1 OR XX NOT = 2
    THEN PERFORM Fini
END-IF
```

Tell whether the *Fini* paragraph will be executed, based on the following combinations of values of XX and ZZ.

XX	ZZ
0	0
0	1
0	2
0	3
1	0
1	1
1	2
1	3

14. What combinations of values will *X*, *Y*, and *Z* have in the loop?

```
PERFORM Loop1 WITH TEST BEFORE
        VARYING X FROM 1 BY 2 UNTIL X > 4
        AFTER Y FROM 0 BY -1 UNTIL Y < -1
        AFTER Z FROM 2 BY 3 UNTIL Z > 7
```

CHAPTER 8

STRUCTURED PROGRAMMING IN COBOL

This book takes a wide view of structured programming as a way of organizing thoughts and programs to achieve correct and easily modifiable programs. This is done by applying the criteria in Chapter 4 along with the structured programming constructs to show the purpose of a program by its form. *Structured Programming,* in its most limited definition, consists of a few constructs that specify the flow of control of the program. If you are familiar with structured program and the COBOL statements that support it, you may wish to skip this chapter.

Essential

The major advantages of structured programming are that it gives form, order, uniformity, and discipline to programs and simplifies their logical flow. Another side benefit of structured programming is that it has changed the emphasis from *clever* programming to *clear* programming, where it properly belongs.

Structured programming consists of three primitive forms or constructs that have been mathematically proved to be the minimum required to code all program logic. Because these three constructs can be proved mathematically to be the minimum required, they enable a program to be mathematically proved to be logically correct. However, proving programs to be mathematically correct is impractical and has no relevance to most programming. Also, it does not follow that because these three constructs are the minimum required to write a program, they are the only ones needed. In practice, they are not always the most direct means of programming. Use them only so long as they clarify the sequence of execution.

8.1 SEQUENTIAL EXECUTION OF STATEMENTS

Essential

Sequential execution is the most elementary of the three constructs, and is shown in Figure 8.1.

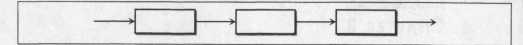

FIGURE 8.1   Sequential execution.

```
ADD X TO Y
PERFORM C10-Totals
COMPUTE B = C + D * E
```

8.2   THE IF/THEN/ELSE CONSTRUCT

Essential

The IF/THEN/ELSE construct executes one or the other of two blocks of code based on the results of a conditional test. Figure 8.2 shows this.

```
IF A = B
    THEN ADD X TO Y
        MOVE 2 TO Z
    ELSE COMPUTE B = C + D * E
        ADD 1 TO X
END-IF
```

8.3   THE DO WHILE CONSTRUCT

Essential

The *Do While* construct repeats an operation while a condition is true. Figure 8.3 shows this. The PERFORM WITH TEST BEFORE does this in COBOL. Note that if the condition is true when the PERFORM is encountered, the PERFORM statements are skipped.

```
PERFORM WITH TEST BEFORE UNTIL EOF-In = "Y"
    imperative-statements
END-PERFORM
```

Any form of the PERFORM is valid.

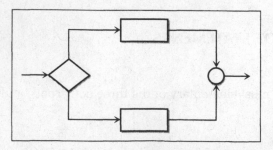

FIGURE 8.2   IF/THEN/ELSE construct.

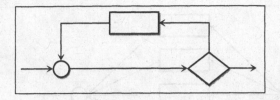

FIGURE 8.3 *Do While* construct.

```
PERFORM WITH TEST BEFORE VARYING I FROM 1 BY 1
        UNTIL Ix > 10
```

Although these three constructs are the minimum required to perform all logical operations, two additional structured programming constructs are provided for convenience.

8.4 THE DO UNTIL CONSTRUCT

Essential

The *Do Until* is identical to the *Do While,* except that the operation is always performed at least once. Figure 8.4 shows this. The PERFORM WITH TEST AFTER is the COBOL form of the *Do Until.*

```
PERFORM WITH TEST AFTER UNTIL EOF-Flag = "Y"
    imperative-statements
END-PERFORM
```

Note that COBOL assumes the WITH TEST AFTER if no WITH TEST phrase is coded. The foregoing PERFORM is the same as

```
PERFORM UNTIL EOF-Flag = "Y"
```

8.5 THE CASE CONSTRUCT

Essential

The *Case* construct executes one of several groups of statements, depending on a value. Figure 8.5 shows this. The EVALUATE statement is the COBOL form of the *Case.* If you want to test a single identifier for several possible values, you usually code the EVALUATE as shown here.

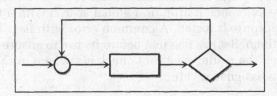

FIGURE 8.4 *Do Until* construct.

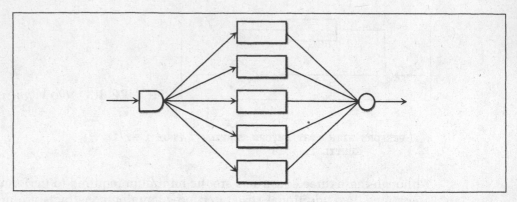

FIGURE 8.5 *Case* construct.

```
EVALUATE The-X
    WHEN "A" PERFORM C20-Max
    WHEN "B" PERFORM C20-Min
    WHEN "C" PERFORM C20-Avg
    WHEN OTHER PERFORM C20-Error
END-EVALUATE
```

If, instead, you want to test for one of several conditions, you usually code the EVALUATE as follows:

```
EVALUATE TRUE
    WHEN The-X <= "A" PERFORM C20-Max
    WHEN The-X >= "Z" PERFORM C20-Min
    WHEN Something-Else = "C" PERFORM C20-Avg
    WHEN OTHER PERFORM C20-Error
END-EVALUATE
```

8.6 WRITING STRUCTURED PROGRAMS

Essential

Flags often control the logic in structured programming, although they can be confusing and lead to errors. But generally they contribute less confusion and errors than would the GO TOs that they replace. Use consistent values for each flag such as "Y" and "N" for yes and no or "T" and "F" for true and false. Define each flag as PIC X to permit such symbolic values to be assigned to it.

Don't reuse a flag for different purposes to conserve storage, because the confusion and error potential outweigh the minimal storage savings. When a flag has a single purpose, the cross-reference listing or a global search with a text editor will show wherever that purpose is tested. A common error with flags is to forget to assign initial values to them. Set the flag just before its use to ensure that it has a proper initial value. Then the reader need not check elsewhere in the program to find the last place it was assigned a value.

The next example illustrates the advantages of structured programming in a rather long example. Assume that an input file *In-File* with a Working-Storage record *In-Rec* is to be copied to *Out-File* with a Working-Storage record *Out-Rec*. A transaction file *Trans-File* with a Working-Storage record *Trans-Rec* identical in format to *In-Rec* is to be read. If a transaction record matches an input record, the input record is displayed and deleted, not written out. If an input record is not matched by a transaction record, the input record is to be displayed and written out. Any transaction records not matching an input record are also to be displayed.

This sounds simple, but the logic is involved. The limiting cases must also be considered, where there may be no input or transaction records. For simplicity, assume that the input and transaction files are in proper sort order. Only the Procedure Division statements are shown. The example omits such niceties as printing the number of records read and written.

Flags are needed to indicate an end of file for the input and transaction files. Rather than defining a separate flag, the record item itself is used and set to HIGH-VALUES when an end of file is encountered. (This requires that the record be defined in the Working-Storage Section; it cannot be defined in the File Section.) Besides eliminating a separate flag, this simplifies the logic. The comparison of the input record against the transaction record works properly when either record has been set to HIGH-VALUES for an end of file. The technique of setting a record to HIGH-VALUES to indicate an end of file often simplifies the logic of matching files. It was commonly used in legacy systems, and works wonderfully as long as no record can contain LOW-VALUES or HIGH-VALUES as legitimate data. The nonstructured programming example is shown first, using GO TOs.

```
PROCEDURE DIVISION.
A00-Begin.
    DISPLAY "BEGINNING TEST PROGRAM"
    OPEN INPUT In-File Trans-File, OUTPUT Out-File
    MOVE LOW-VALUES TO Trans-Rec
    .
A10-Read-Next.
    READ In-File INTO In-Rec
      AT END DISPLAY "EOF IN"
            GO TO A70-Purge-Trans
    END-READ
    IF Trans-Rec = LOW-VALUES
        THEN GO TO A40-Read-Trans
    END-IF
    .
A20-Check-For-Delete.
    IF Trans-Rec < In-Rec
        THEN DISPLAY "TRANSACTION IGNORED: ", Trans-Rec
            GO TO A40-Read-Trans
    END-IF
    IF Trans-Rec = In-Rec
        THEN DISPLAY "DELETING: ", In-Rec
            MOVE LOW-VALUES TO Trans-Rec
            GO TO A10-Read-Next
```

```
        END-IF
      .
A30-Write-Out.
    WRITE Out-Rec FROM In-Rec
    DISPLAY "WRITING: ", In-Rec
    GO TO A10-Read-Next
  .
A40-Read-Trans.
    READ Trans-File INTO Trans-Rec
      AT END MOVE HIGH-VALUES TO Trans-Rec
            DISPLAY "EOF TRANS"
            GO TO A30-Write-Out
    END-READ
    GO TO A20-Check-For-Delete
  .
A70-Purge-Trans.
    IF Trans-Rec = HIGH-VALUES
       THEN GO TO Z90-Stop-Run
    END-IF
  .
A80-Skip-Trans.
    READ Trans-File INTO In-Rec
      AT END GO TO Z90-Stop-Run
    END-READ
    DISPLAY "TRANSACTION IGNORED: ", Trans-Rec
    GO TO A80-Skip-Trans
  .
Z90-Stop-Run.
    DISPLAY "END OF PROGRAM"
    CLOSE In-File, Trans-File, Out-File
    GOBACK.
END PROGRAM TESTPGM.
```

Now to write the program using structured programming. The first step in writing a structured program is to step back and think about what the program is to do, without getting immersed in the details of programming. Before starting the code, the program needs to be specified in more detail.

Many programmers use pseudocode to express the design. Use English, the structured programming constructs, an idealized COBOL, or whatever helps you to express what the program is to do. The pseudocode is often better for designing a program than is a flowchart. The basic approach will be to read an *In-File* record and then read all *Trans-File* records until one is obtained that is equal to or greater than the *In-File* record. Ignore any *Trans-File* records less than the *In-File* record. If a *Trans-File* record matches the *In-File* record, display the *In-File* record as deleted. Otherwise, write it out.

Begin the main program logic by reading each *In-File* record until there are no more. That is, until the EOF (end of file) is reached. This is expressed in pseudocode as

```
Do Until EOF In-File
   Read an In-File record
```

A *Do Until* is used rather than a *Do While* because you must go through the loop to read a record before you can tell if you have reached EOF.

Now examine the next step in detail. After each *In-File* record is read, you want to read *Trans-File* records while they are less than the *In-File* record. You need a *Do While* because you don't want to read any *In-Trans* records if you already have one that is greater than or equal to the *In-File* record. However, you have to prime the pump by making sure you read a *Trans-File* record the first time.

There are two common ways of doing this. One way is to prime the pump by reading the first Trans-File record before entering the loop as shown by the following pseudocode:

```
Read Trans-File record
Do until EOF In-File
   Read an In-File record
   Compare the In-File and Trans-File records
   Read In-File and Trans-File records as necessary
```

The other way is to set a flag indicating that *Trans-File* has not been read and test this flag within the loop.

```
Set No-Record flag for Trans-File
Do until EOF In-File
   Read an In-File record
   If No-Record flag for Trans-File set
      or Trans-File record < In-File record
      Then Read Trans-File
   End-If
```

The If can be replaced by a Do while to continue reading Trans-File records until we get one equal to or greater than the current In-File record.

```
Do while Trans-File record < In-File record
   Read Trans-File record
End Do while
```

Both methods are used and both have their advocates. In the nonstructured program example we are converting, a single flag is used to indicate that a record hasn't been read (the record is set to LOW-VALUES) and that the end of file has been encountered (the record is set to HIGH-VALUES). This simplifies the logic because you can now read Trans-File records until you get one that is greater than or equal to the In-File record. We'll use this second method to write develop the complete pseudocode. LOW-VALUES are moved to the Trans-File record it indicate that it has not been read. This also makes it less than the current In-File record.

```
Move LOW-VALUES to Trans-File record
Do until EOF In-File
   Read an In-File record
   Do while not EOF Trans-File and
```

```
        Trans-File record < In-File record
    Read Trans-File record
```

Now you have either an EOF or a record for the *Trans-File*. If there is a record and it is less than the *In-File* record, you display that you are ignoring it and continue the *Do While* loop. If there is a *Trans-File* EOF or the *Trans-File* record is equal to or greater than the *In-File* record, you do nothing and let the *Do While* loop terminate.

```
Move LOW-VALUES to Trans-File record
Do until EOF In-File
    Read an In-File record
    Do while not EOF Trans-File and
            Trans-File record < In-File record
    Read Trans-File record
        Not at end
            If Trans-File record < In-File record
                Then Display unmatched Trans-File record
            End If
    End Read
End Do While
```

Don't worry about the exceptional cases of an EOF condition yet, and assume that when you drop through the *Do While*, you have both an *In-File* and a *Trans-File* record. The possibilities are now the following:

The *Trans-File* equals the *In-File* record. You display that you are deleting the *In-File* record and continue the *Do Until* loop.

The *Trans-File* record is greater than the *In-File* record. You write the *In-File* record and continue the *Do Until* loop.

The *Trans-File* record is less than the *In-File* record. This can't happen, because the *Do While* continues until this condition is no longer true. Thus, there are only two conditions to test.

You can now add an *If* statement to handle the two possible situations.

```
Move LOW-VALUES to Trans-File record.
Do until EOF In-File
    Read an In-File record
    Do while not EOF Trans-File and
            Trans-File record < In-File record
    Read Trans-File record
        Not at end
            If Trans-File record < In-File record
                Then Display unmatched Trans-File record
            End If
    End Read
End Do While
If Trans-File record = In-File record
```

```
        Then Display deleting In-File record
        Else Display writing In-File record
            Write In-File record into Out-File
    End If
End Do Until
```

Now think about the exceptional cases, such as end of file. Consider the EOF for *In-File* first. When you reach EOF for *In-File* and end the *Do Until* loop, could there still be records left in *Trans-File?* There could, so you need to force all the *Trans-File* records to be read when *In-File* reaches EOF. The simplest way to do this is to move HIGH-VALUES to the *In-File* record when it reaches EOF. This makes the *Trans-File* record always less than the *In-File* record so that the *Do While* continues until *Trans-File* also reaches EOF.

If you initialize the *In-File* record to LOW-VALUES, you can test it for HIGH-VALUES to determine if there is an end of file. The use of LOW-VALUES for the initial condition and HIGH-VALUES for the final condition is a common practice in reading sequential files. The LOW-VALUES and HIGH-VALUES don't disturb any test for the records being in sequence. This method does depend on LOW-VALUES and HIGH-VALUES not being legitimate values within the actual records.

You also need to consider what the conditions are when you drop through the *Do While.* The conditions are as follows:

EOF *In-File*, EOF *Trans-File*. The *In-File* record will contain HIGH-VALUES. You don't want to do anything, and the *Do Until* loop will terminate.

EOF *In-File*, *Trans-File* record read. This can't occur, because an *In-File* EOF forces the *Do While* to continue until *Trans-File* also reaches EOF.

EOF *Trans-File*, *In-File* record read. You need to write out the *In-File* record.

***Trans-File* record read, *In-File* record read.** If the records are equal, you display that you are deleting the *In-File* record; otherwise, you write the *In-File* record.

You can now modify the *If* statement following the end of the *Do While* to handle the possible conditions.

```
Move LOW-VALUES to Trans-File record, In-File record
Do until In-File record = HIGH-VALUES
    Read an In-File record
        At end Move HIGH-VALUES to In-File record
    End Read
    Do while Not EOF Trans-File and
            Trans-File record < In-File record
        Read Trans-File record
            Not at end
                If Trans-File record < In-File record
                    Then Display unmatched Trans-File record
                End If
        End Read
```

```
        End Do While
     If In-File record = HIGH-VALUES
        Then Continue
        Else If Trans-File record = In-File record
                Then Display deleting In-File record
                Else Display writing In-File record
                     Write In-File record into Out-File
              End If
     End If
End Do Until
```

Now consider what happens when you reach EOF for *Trans-File.* You could still have records in *In-File,* but these will be read and written properly. You can simplify the code by also moving HIGH-VALUES to *Trans-File* when it reaches EOF and testing for this as the EOF condition:

```
Do while Trans-File record Not = HIGH-VALUES and
        Trans-File record < In-File record
```

You don't need the *Trans-File record Not = HIGH-VALUES.* When *Trans-File* equals HIGH-VALUES, the *Trans-File record < In-File record* terminates the loop. You can simplify it to

```
Do while Trans-File record < In-File record
```

The pseudocode now becomes

```
Move LOW-VALUES to Trans-File record, In-File record
Do until In-File record = HIGH-VALUES
    Read an In-File record
        At end Move HIGH-VALUES to In-File record
    End Read
    Do while Trans-File record < In-File record
        Read Trans-File record
            At end Move HIGH-VALUES to Trans-File record
            Not at end
                    If Trans-File record < In-File record
                        Then Display unmatched Trans-File record
                    End If
    End Read
    End Do While
    If In-File record = HIGH-VALUES
        Then Continue
        Else If Trans-File record = In-File record
                Then Display deleting In-File record
                Else Display writing In-File record
                     Write In-File record into Out-File
              End If
    End If
End Do Until
```

The nested *If* statement executed when you drop through the *Do While* is needlessly complex. Because you are testing for several conditions, it really should be a *Case* construct. You can replace the nested *If* with the COBOL EVALUATE statement:

```
Evaluate true
  When In-File record = HIGH-VALUES Continue
  When Trans-File record = In-File record
      Display deleting In-File record
  When other
      Display writing In-File record
      Write In-File record into Out-File
End Evaluate
```

Our pseudocode now becomes

```
Move LOW-VALUES to Trans-File record, In-File record
Do until In-File record = HIGH-VALUES
    Read an In-File record
        At end Move HIGH-VALUES to In-File record
    End Read
    Do while Trans-File record < In-File record
        Read Trans-File record
            At end Move HIGH-VALUES to Trans-File record
            Not at end
                If Trans-File record < In-File record
                    Then Display unmatched Trans-File record
                End If
        End Read
    End Do While
    Evaluate true
      When In-File record = HIGH-VALUES Continue
      When Trans-File record = In-File record
          Display deleting In-File record
      When Other
          Display writing In-File record
          Write In-File record into Out-File
    End Evaluate
End Do Until
```

What happens if there are no *In-File* records? You set the *In-File* record to HIGH-VALUES, which forces the *Do While* to continue until *Trans-File* also reaches EOF and you store HIGH-VALUES in its record.

What happens if there are no *Trans-File* records? You set the *Trans-File* record to HIGH-VALUES, which prevents it from executing again. In the EVALUATE statement, the HIGH-VALUES in the *Trans-File* record will always be greater than the *In-File* record, which forces the *In-File* record to be written. Thus, you continue reading all the *In-File* records and writing them out.

What happens when you reach EOF on both the *In-File* and the *Trans-File*? The *Do Until* immediately terminates.

What happens if the *In-File* or the *Trans-File* records are not in the same ascending sort order? The program will not work properly, and so you might think about checking the sort order of these two files. If you wanted to do this, you would add it to our pseudocode as follows.

```
Read an In-File record
    At end Move HIGH-VALUES to In-File record
    Not at end
        If In-File record < last In-File record
            Then Display error message
                Terminate program
            Else Move In-File record to last In-File record
        End If
End Read
```

You would need to initialize the last *In-File* record by moving LOW-VALUES to it at the start of the program. You would also want the same sequence checking for *Trans-File.*

What happens if there are duplicate records in either file? Duplicate *In-File* records are deleted or written properly. Duplicate *Trans-File* records will be displayed, which is probably what you would want. The specifications did not tell us what to do in the event of duplicates, and you might want to resolve this before writing the program—perhaps printing an error message. However, for now the program is probably handling duplicates properly. If you wanted to check for duplicate records, you could change the pseudocode as follows.

```
Read an In-File record
    At end Move HIGH-VALUES to In-File record
    Not at end
        If In-File record < last In-File record
            Then Display error message
                Terminate program
            Else if In-File record = last In-File record
                    Then Display error message
                    ELSE Move In-File record to last In-File record
            End If
        End If
End Read
```

Now you can begin thinking about the code. The *Do Until* in COBOL is a PERFORM WITH TEST AFTER. The *Do While* is a PERFORM WITH TEST BEFORE, but instead of coding *Do While Trans-File record < In-File record,* you must PERFORM UNTIL *Trans-File record >= In-File record:*

```
Do while Trans-File record < In-File record
```

becomes

```
    PERFORM WITH TEST BEFORE UNTIL Trans-File record >= In-File record
```

Assume the record areas for *In-File* and *In-Trans* are *In-Rec* and *Trans-Rec*. You can now make the minor changes in the pseudocode to turn it into true COBOL code. You need to open and close the files and perhaps use DISPLAY to note the progress of the program. To simplify the program structure you can PERFORM the update as a paragraph. The COBOL program is then as follows:

```
PROCEDURE DIVISION.
A00-Begin.
    DISPLAY "BEGINNING TEST PROGRAM"
    OPEN INPUT In-File, Trans-File, OUTPUT Out-File
    MOVE LOW-VALUES TO In-Rec, Trans-Rec
    PERFORM A10-READ-In-File WITH TEST AFTER
            UNTIL In-Rec = HIGH-VALUES
    DISPLAY "END OF PROGRAM"
    CLOSE In-File, Trans-File, Out-File
    GOBACK
    .
**** Exit
A10-Read-In-File.
    READ In-File INTO In-Rec
      AT END MOVE HIGH-VALUES TO In-Rec
    END-READ
    PERFORM WITH TEST BEFORE UNTIL Trans-Rec >= In-Rec
       READ Trans-File INTO Trans-Rec
            AT END MOVE HIGH-VALUES TO Trans-Rec
          NOT AT END
                IF Trans-Rec < In-Rec
                   THEN DISPLAY "TRANSACTION IGNORED:", Trans-Rec
                END-IF
       END-READ
    END-PERFORM
    EVALUATE TRUE
      WHEN In-Rec = HIGH-VALUES CONTINUE
      WHEN Trans-Rec = In-Rec DISPLAY "DELETING:", In-Rec
      WHEN OTHER
            DISPLAY "WRITING: ", In-Rec
            WRITE Out-Rec FROM In-Rec
    END-EVALUATE
    .
**** Exit
END PROGRAM TESTPGM.
```

The nonstructured program contains 32 COBOL verbs and eight paragraph names. The structured program contains only 21 COBOL verbs and two paragraph names. The goal was not to write the program with the fewest statements, but simple, clear programs will generally lead to this. But which is the most efficient? Any differences are so minor that it is not a consideration.

If nothing else, there are two things that you should get out of structured programming. First, you should step back and think about what you want to program without getting immersed in the detail. Second, you should write the program in the simplest, clearest possible way.

EXERCISES

1. Develop a set of rules for using GO TO statements.

2. What changes do you believe should be made to COBOL to enhance its use for structured programming?

3. Write a paper on what, if anything, you believe makes structured programming a better way to program.

4. Write a paper discussing and evaluating one of the following:
   - Structured walk-through
   - Chief programming teams
   - Modular programming
   - HIPO (hierarchical input/process/output) charts, a method of charting programs as a replacement for flowcharts
   - Object-oriented programming
   - Object-oriented design
   - CASE (computer-aided software engineering) tools

5. The following is an excerpt from a typical nonstructured program. Rewrite it as a structured program.

```
Start-It. READ In-File INTO Rec-In AT END GO TO Done.
    IF Rec-Type = " " GO TO Done.
    IF Rec-Type = "A" GO TO Go-On.
    IF Rec-Type = "B" GO TO Start-It.
    IF Rec-Type = "C" GO TO Go-On.
    GO TO Start-It.
Go-On. MOVE 1 TO Ix.
    IF Rec-Name(Ix) = SPACES GO TO Start-It.
Store-Name. MOVE Rec-Name(Ix) TO Save-Name(Ix).
    MOVE 1 TO Iy.
Store-Pop. IF Rec-Pop(Ix, Iy) = SPACES GO TO More-Names.
    MOVE Rec-Pop(Ix, Iy) TO Save-Pop(Ix, Iy).
    ADD 1 TO Iy.
    IF Iy < 11 GO TO Store-Pop.
More-Names. ADD 1 TO Ix.
    IF Ix < 21 GO TO Store-Name.
    MOVE Rec-No TO Save-No.
    GO TO Start-It.
Done.
```

6. Assume that you are attending a symposium on programming techniques. One speaker claims to have a new composite technique that improves programmer productivity, as measured by code produced per day, by an order of magnitude. His method is to use structured, top-down design while regressing stepwise using interactive meditation. This is augmented with the power of positive thinking, organized into online, modular programming teams with frequent work breaks while everyone faces east, links arms with others, and slowly repeats a mystic Hindu chant.

- Assuming that you have some doubts about the productivity claims, what questions would you ask to dispute or verify the claims?
- Assume that the claim of a tenfold improvement in the ability of programmers to write programs is true. What are the possible outcomes of each programmer being able to write ten times the amount of code that he or she can produce today?

7. The last two examples in this chapter are a nonstructured and structured program to update a file. Make the following changes to both programs and discuss the difficulty of making the changes.

- Check the *In-File* and *Trans-File* for ascending sort order.
- Check the *In-File* and *Trans-File* for duplicate records.
- Count the *In-File* and *Trans-File* records read and the number of records written.
- If three consecutive *Trans-File* records do not match an *In-File* record, print an error message and continue.
- If there are no *In-File* records, or if there are no *Trans-File* records, print an error message and continue.

CHAPTER 9

NUMERIC DATA

This chapter describes the packed-decimal, binary, external decimal, and floating-point numeric data used in COBOL. If you are already familiar with these data types, you might skip this chapter.

9.1 OVERVIEW OF NUMERIC DATA

Essential

The ANSI standard does not specify the internal form of numeric data and the precision of intermediate results. This chapter describes the numeric data types for the IBM mainframe that have become standard for COBOL on most other computers. See Chapter 28 for a description of how data is represented internally in the computer.

The numeric data types consist of BINARY (or COMP, COMP-4, or COMP-5), COMP-1 (single-precision floating-point), COMP-2 (double-precision floating-point), PACKED-DECIMAL, and DISPLAY (called *external decimal numbers* and containing numbers as character data). For numeric data, the PIC character string can contain only 9, P, S, and V. PACKED-DECIMAL is usually the most convenient form for monetary data. COMP-1 and COMP-2 floating-point types are supported in most COBOL compilers, although you will seldom use them in COBOL, and the following discussion does not apply to them.

You write numeric literals as decimal numbers with an optional decimal point. The numbers may be signed plus (+) or minus (−) or unsigned (assumed positive).

```
23   175.925   -.00973   +16
MOVE 23 TO A
COMPUTE B = C / 176.925
```

Numeric literals cannot end with the decimal point because COBOL would confuse it with the period that ends a sentence.

```
2 or 2.0, but not 2.
```

You describe elementary numeric data items with a level number, a name, a PIC clause, and the data type (BINARY, PACKED-DECIMAL, or DISPLAY).

```
nn   data-name     PIC string data-type.
```

Verbose form:

```
nn   data-name     PICTURE IS string USAGE data-type.
```

The period at the end of each data description is required.

```
01  State-Population              PIC S999V99 PACKED-DECIMAL.
```

The *nn* level may be 01 through 46 to represent the hierarchy. Level 01, the highest hierarchical level, specifies either an elementary data item or a group item. Higher-level numbers represent lower hierarchical levels. An *elementary item* describes a data element. A *group item* is followed by items with levels 02 through 46 and doesn't describe a data element, but instead has lower-level items (higher-level numbers) following it that describe the elementary items. Levels 02 through 46, in turn, specify either elementary items, or, if followed by higher-level numbers, group items. Levels 02 through 46 must all belong to an 01-level item.

You must code the 01 in the A area (columns 8 through 11). You can code the other levels (02 through 49, 66, 77, and 88) in either the A or B area (columns 8 through 72). Always indent the levels to show the hierarchy.

There are also three special levels: 66, 77, and 88. Level 66 renames data items (described in Chapter 11), level 77 defines an elementary data item, and level 88 defines a condition-name entry (described in Chapter 5). Chapter 11 describes the levels in more detail.

The PIC clause specifies the precision, the number of digits to the left and right of the decimal point, in the form PIC S99 . . . 9V99 . . . 9. The S indicates a signed number, each *9* represents a decimal digit, and the *V* specifies the assumed decimal point. Therefore, S9V999 can contain numbers such as −0.007, 9.265, and 3.000. If you omit the V, the decimal point is assumed on the right, so that S99 and S99V are equivalent. The V does not count in determining the length of a data item. The S also does not count in determining the length unless the SIGN IS LEADING clause, discussed later, is coded. If the S is omitted, the number is unsigned and treated as positive.

TIP *Except for a number that is always positive, such as a length, code the S to make the number signed.*

Unsigned numbers can give surprising results. The following statements make it appear as if −1 + 1 equals 2:

```
01  X                       PIC 999 PACKED-DECIMAL.
    □  □  □
    MOVE ZERO TO X          [X contains 0.]
    SUBTRACT 1 FROM X       [X contains 1, because the minus sign is lost.]
    ADD 1 TO X              [X contains 2.]
```

If there are many 9s, they become tedious to write.

TIP *Code a single 9 and follow it with the number of 9s enclosed in parentheses so you can tell at a glance the number of digits to the left and right of the decimal point.*

```
S9(5)        Same as        S99999
SV9(4)       Same as        SV9999
S(6)V9(8)    Same as        S999999V99999999
```

The maximum number of digits that can be contained in a numeric data item is 18.

PROPOSED NEW ANSI STANDARD: Check Compiler to See if Implemented

The new ANSI standard increases this to 31.

The assumed decimal point can lie outside the number. This allows you to represent very large or small numbers with only a few digits of storage. Code a P to the left or right of the 9s to specify the position of the decimal point when it lies outside the number. Omit the V. P(2)9 represents numbers such as .001 and 9(P2) represents numbers such as 100. For example, SP(5)9(4) permits you to represent the number .000001234 with four digits. The following specifies a data item that contains only three digits, such as 213, but is treated as if it had the value .0000213.

```
01  A     PIC SP(4)999 PACKED-DECIMAL.
```

Place the Ps on the right to specify that the decimal point is to the right of the number. The following specifies a data item that contains only three digits, such as 213, but is treated as if it had the value 21,300,000.

```
01  A     PIC S999P(5) PACKED-DECIMAL.
```

The total number of digits, including those specified by the Ps, cannot exceed 18. The Ps conserve file and central storage, but often the savings are not worth the extra effort and potential confusion. The P itself doesn't count in determining the storage length of the data item.

The VALUE clause assigns initial values to data items. A data item has no predictable value unless you assign it an initial value or until you store a value into it in the Procedure Division. The following initializes *X* with a value of zero.

```
01  X          PIC S9(5) PACKED-DECIMAL
               VALUE 0.
       or VALUE IS 0   or   VALUES ARE 0.
```

Plan the number of digits to carry in data items. Larger numbers require more file and central storage, and you should not be wasteful. But smaller numbers may not allow room for growth, and one way to minimize change is to provide for growth. For example, a company with $500,000 in sales might require a data item of S9(6)V99 today, but what happens if sales grow to over $1,000,000? Inflation alone could cause this. If there is no physical limit on the size of a number, define the item to contain the largest number expected plus at least one or two digits for safety.

Keep the numeric precision consistent, even if some numbers are defined to be larger than necessary. Besides arithmetic operations being more efficient if all the numbers have the same precision, generalized subprograms are also easier to write when all the potential applications have the same precision. For example, if the total revenue of a company is $100,000, but the largest revenue of a division is only $10,000, describe all revenue data items as S9(8)V99 for consistency and safety.

Data items containing dollar amounts should provide two digits to the right of the decimal point (V99) to carry the cents, even if only whole dollar amounts are wanted. Carry the cents to prevent rounding errors and to guard against a future requirement of carrying cents.

9.2 PACKED-DECIMAL NUMBERS

Essential

You can code PACKED-DECIMAL as COMPUTATIONAL-3. COMP-3 was the only way of coding it in old IBM compilers, but PACKED-DECIMAL is now the ANSI standard and you should use it rather than COMP-3.

```
01  A     PIC S9(5)V99 PACKED-DECIMAL.
```

The computer stores packed-decimal numbers with each group of four binary digits (half a byte) representing a single-decimal digit. For example, 0000 represents 0, 0001 represents 1, 0100 represents 4, and 0001 0100 represents 14. The sign also occupies one-half byte. Therefore, S99V9 occupies one and one-half bytes for the digits and one-half byte for the sign, for a total of two bytes. To determine the number of storage bytes for a number, count the number of digits, add 1 for the sign, round up to the next even number if necessary, and divide by 2. Both S9(6)V9(2) and S9(6)V9(3) occupy five bytes.

Specify an odd number of digits so that the number with its sign will occupy an integral number of bytes. S9(4) wastes one-half byte; S9(5) occupies the same three bytes and is more efficient.

TIP *Use packed-decimal for all monetary and most other numeric data except internal counters and subscripts.*

Packed-decimal numbers may contain up to 18 digits. They are efficient in both storage and computations, and they allow a wide range of numbers with integral precision. Packed-decimal numbers, although somewhat less efficient for integer computations than binary numbers, are more flexible. They are also more efficient for input/output, because they do not require alignment and the messy slack bytes described in Chapter 11.

Assign initial values with the VALUE clause. The following initializes *X* with a value of 23.

```
01  X      PIC S9(5) PACKED-DECIMAL
           VALUE 23.
```

Packed-decimal numbers carry the sign in the rightmost four bits. A plus sign is a hexadecimal C, a minus a D, and an unsigned number is represented by an F. The ANSI standard provides for four separate codes for a plus sign and three for a minus. Obviously, this takes considerably more time for the computer to determine whether a number is positive or negative than if a single code specified the plus and minus sign. In IBM COBOL, you can specify the NUMPROC(PFD) compiler option, described in Chapter 33, if your program keeps the plus and minus signs with a single code each. Unless you are reading data generated by an old compiler, use NUMPROC(PFD) to save execution time.

9.3 BINARY NUMBERS

Essential

BINARY (or COMPUTATIONAL) numbers are stored internally in a computer word, half-word, or double word as a group of binary digits (bits) representing the number to the base 2. For example, 101 represents 5 and 1110 represents 14. Binary numbers are the most efficient for arithmetic computations because computers are binary machines. However, they are poor as data in files because their alignment can cause problems as described in Chapter 11.

TIP *Use BINARY only for internal counters and subscripts.*

```
01  A      PIC S9(4) BINARY.
```

The number of bytes needed to contain the value depends on the number of digits, as follows:

- 1 to 4   Half-word or two bytes.
- 5 to 9   Full word or four bytes.
- 10 to 18   Two full words or eight bytes.

The VALUE clause assigns initial values to data items. The following initializes *X* with a value of 100.

```
01  X      PIC S9(4) BINARY VALUE 100.
```

IBM COBOL lets you write BINARY as COMPUTATIONAL-4, but don't. In Workstation COBOL, you can code COMPUTATIONAL-5 for native binary in which the maximum value that can be stored on the number depends on the number of bytes allocated rather than the PIC clause. For example, if you code PIC S999 COMP-5 and a half-word is allocated, you could store the maximum value of 32,767, the largest signed number that a half-word can contain, rather than 999.

PROPOSED NEW ANSI STANDARD: Check Compiler to See if Implemented

The new ANSI standard provides four new ways to define binary data: BINARY-CHAR (one byte long), BINARY-SHORT (two bytes), BINARY-LONG (four bytes), and BINARY-DOUBLE (eight bytes). BINARY-CHAR is especially useful because it allows you to perform arithmetic operations on byte data ("B" − "A" equals 1) as done in C/C++. The numbers can be signed or unsigned, and the maximum values the data can contain are shown in Table 9.1.

TABLE 9.1   Maximum Values for Binary Data

Usage	Max Value, Signed	Max Value, Unsigned
BINARY-CHAR	−128 to +127	255
BINARY-SHORT	−32,768 to +32,767	65,535
BINARY-LONG	−2,147,483,648 to +2,147,483,647	4,294,967,295
BINARY-DOUBLE	-2^{63} to $+2^{63}-1$	$2^{64}-1$

9.4   EXTERNAL DECIMAL NUMBERS

External decimal numbers are also termed DISPLAY numbers, *zoned-decimal* numbers, and *numeric field data.* You use these for source input and printed output. They consist of character data that contains only numeric digits, one digit per byte in storage. You can treat the data as alphanumeric and print it without conversion. When arithmetic operations are performed on external decimal numbers,

COBOL must convert the external decimal number to packed-decimal for the computations. When packed-decimal numbers are displayed or printed, they must be converted to external decimal numbers. Hence, external decimal numbers are inefficient for computations but efficient for display or printing.

9.4.1 Describing External Decimal Numbers

Essential

External decimal number items contain 1 to 18 numeric digits and are described as follows.

```
01  A      PIC S999V99.
```

Their data type is DISPLAY. (DISPLAY is assumed if no type is coded.) The following three forms are identical; all contain five characters.

```
01  B      PIC S9(5).
01  B      PIC S9(5) DISPLAY.
01  B      PIC S99999 USAGE DISPLAY.
```

The VALUE clause assigns initial values to data items. The following initializes *X* with the digits *00006*.

```
01  X      PIC S9(5) VALUE 6.
```

External decimal numbers must always have leading zeros, not leading blanks. You can also treat external decimal numbers as alphanumeric data. The statements that operate on alphanumeric data, such as INSPECT, STRING, and UNSTRING, may also operate on it.

If the number is signed (denoted by a leading S), the operational sign is carried in the left half of the rightmost byte. The S does not count as a character position; both S999V9 and 999V9 occupy four character positions.

The same NUMPROC(PFD) compiler option discussed for PACKED-DECIMAL numbers also applies to external decimal numbers and saves execution time for most applications.

9.4.2 The SIGN IS SEPARATE Clause

Sometimes Used

Before COBOL '85, COBOL expected the minus sign to be overpunched over the rightmost column when external decimal numbers were read. This dated back to when the standard data entry device was a keypunch, and you could punch two characters in the same column. Today, a terminal is the standard input device and has no facility for overpunching. You can, however, type the character that corresponds to the digit with the plus or minus sign overpunched. The sign is stored in the left half-byte of the rightmost digit as a hexadecimal "F", written X"F", if unsigned; an X"C" if positive-signed; and an X"D" if negative-signed. Thus, an unsigned number will have X"F0" to X"F9" as the rightmost digit, which are the EBCDIC characters 0 to 9. A signed number will have X"C0" to X"C9" if positive and X"D0" to X"D9" if negative. X"C1" to X"C9" are the EBCDIC characters A to I, and X"D1" to X"D9" are the EBCDIC characters J to R. (As for the zeros, X"C0" is an EBCDIC left brace {, and X"D0" is a right brace }.) So, if you wanted to enter a −21, you could type 2J. This is a bad way to enter numbers. It is much better to enter the number as people expect to see it (−21).

The SIGN clause is one way around this problem. Another solution is to *de-edit* the number, as described later in this section. The default if you don't code the SIGN clause is for the sign to be carried in the high-order four bits of the trailing numeric digit. The S for the sign then doesn't occupy a character position. You can code this explicitly as:

```
01  X              PIC S9(3) SIGN IS TRAILING.
```
[*X* occupies three character positions.]
```
□  □  □
MOVE -14 TO X      [X contains "−014".]
MOVE 14 TO X       [X contains "+014".]
```

You can also specify that the sign is carried over the high-order four bits of the leading numeric digit.

```
01  X              PIC S9(4) SIGN IS LEADING.
```

The main use for the SIGN clause is to let you code a sign in a fixed position in the field for a DISPLAY data item. For this, you code the SIGN clause as:

```
SIGN IS LEADING SEPARATE CHARACTER
```
Or
```
SIGN IS TRAILING SEPARATE CHARACTER
```

The S for the sign in the PIC string now occupies a character position. You can code this only for an elementary DISPLAY item that has a signed numeric field with an S for sign, or a group item that contains one or more such fields. SIGN for a group item applies to the elementary items unless they contain their own SIGN clause. In the next example, *Y* occupies four character positions. The number can participate in arithmetic operations, even though it contains a nonnumeric character (+ or −).

```
01  Y              PIC S999
                   SIGN IS TRAILING SEPARATE.
□  □  □
MOVE 23 TO Y       [Y contains "023+".]
MOVE -23 TO Y      [Y contains "023−".]
```

If data is moved to an item having the SIGN clause and conversion is necessary, COBOL inserts the sign in the proper position. If data is moved to an item having the SIGN clause without conversion, no sign is set and the job terminates if you perform arithmetic operations on the number. This can occur in a group move or when you read data into an item.

9.4.3   De-editing Edited External Decimal Numbers

Sometimes Used

As described in Chapter 12, you can edit external decimal numbers to insert various nonnumeric characters for display. For example, you can edit the external decimal number "00234480P" to become "−23,448.07". The blank, comma, and period are nonnumeric characters that make the number easy to read for humans. Unfortunately, the computer doesn't accept these nonnumeric characters when it performs computations. To get rid of them, use the NUMVAL or NUMVAL-C intrinsic functions described in Chapter 21 to convert the numeric DISPLAY data. This allows you to use the value in an arithmetic expression.

```
01   Num-Item       PIC S9(9)V99 PACKED-DECIMAL.
     □  □  □
     COMPUTE Num-Item = FUNCTION NUMVAL-C("$1,023.4") * 6.25
```

9.5   COMP-1 AND COMP-2 FLOATING-POINT NUMBERS

Rarely Used

COMPUTATIONAL-1 and COMPUTATIONAL-2 floating-point numbers, normally used in scientific computations, are rare in COBOL. Numbers in scientific computations are often derived from physical measurements that have limited precision. This contrasts with the integral units common in commercial computations, such as dollars and cents. For example, a bicycle might cost exactly $122.98, but the weight might be 21, 21.3, 21.332, or 21.33186 pounds, depending on the accuracy of the scale.

The computer stores floating-point numbers in a computer word in two parts, one representing the significant digits of the number, and the other representing the exponent that determines the magnitude of the number. This corresponds to scientific notation, where, for example, $0.25E - 5$ represents 0.0000025 and −0.25E5 represents −25,000. This notation allows a wide range of numbers to be used in arithmetic computations without losing significant digits of precision.

To add or subtract numbers expressed in this notation, the system must normalize them to the same power of 10. For example, 6E4 + 8E2 would be normalized to .06E2 + 8E2 to equal 8.06E2. To multiply numbers, the exponents are added, so that 6E4 * 8E2 equals 48E6. To divide two numbers, the exponent of the denominator is subtracted from that of the numerator so that 6E4 / 8E2 equals 0.75E2. Thus, to calculate the time in seconds that it takes light, traveling at 11,800,000,000 inches per second, to pass through a film 0.0001 inch thick, the computation is done as 1.0E − 4 / 1.18E10 to equal 0.847E − 14. Computers have special floating-point hardware to do such computations efficiently, and you do not need to worry about normalizing the numbers.

Floating-point numbers are not precise; their precision is limited to some number of significant digits. For example, a computation such as 0.1 + 0.1 may yield a result of 0.19999 when expressed in floating-point, rather than exactly 0.2. This is acceptable in scientific computations, in which answers are given plus or minus some tolerance, but it can be inappropriate for business applications, in which numbers must balance to the penny.

TIP *Because 0.1 + 0.1 may result in 0.19999 rather than 0.2, never compare floating-point numbers solely for equality. Nor should you use them for counters.*

You write a floating-point literal as a decimal number, followed by an E, followed by an exponent. You can sign both the number and the exponent. The number can be a maximum of 16 digits.

```
2E0    -9E0    15.3E5    2.2E-1
```

COMP-1 single-precision numbers occupy a full word of four bytes with the maximum magnitude ranging from 10^{-78} to 10^{+75} for Mainframe COBOL and 1.175E−38 to 3.403E38 for Workstation COBOL. The number has at least 6 decimal digits of precision. COMP-2 double-precision numbers occupy a double word of eight bytes. The maximum magnitude ranges from 10^{-78} to 10^{+75} for Mainframe COBOL and from 2.225E308 to 1.798E308 for Workstation COBOL. The number has at least 16 decimal digits of precision. Specify floating-point data items as COMP-1 (single-precision) or COMP-2 (double-precision). Don't code a PIC clause.

```
01  A    COMP-1.
01  B    COMP-2.
```

You can assign initial values to date items:

```
01  X    COMP-2 VALUE 1.26E+3.
```

The value can only be a floating-point literal or ZERO. You can use floating-point data wherever numeric data is allowed, with the few exceptions noted where appropriate in this book.

> **PROPOSED NEW ANSI STANDARD: Check Compiler to See if Implemented**
>
> The new ANSI standard incorporates floating-point numbers as FLOAT-SHORT (same as COMP-1), FLOAT-LONG (same as COMP-2), and FLOAT-EXTENDED (new and implementation-dependent). Compiler vendors will continue to support COMP-1 and COMP-2 for compatibility.

9.6 DATA CONVERSION AND PRECISION

Essential

Conversion occurs automatically when arithmetic operations are performed on numeric data of different types. This can occur both in arithmetic statements, such as COMPUTE and ADD, and in relational expressions, such as those in the IF statement. The arithmetic statements also result in conversion if the resultant identifier differs from the data type of the data being stored. COBOL converts the data to a common numeric type to perform the operations, according to the following hierarchy.

```
Highest:    COMP-2
            COMP-1
            PACKED-DECIMAL
            DISPLAY      [Converted to packed-decimal for computations.]
Lowest:     BINARY
```

In the statement COMPUTE $A = B + C + D$, if A and B are BINARY, C is PACKED-DECIMAL, and D is COMP-1, COBOL converts B and C to COMP-1 for the arithmetic operation. COBOL then converts this intermediate result to BINARY and stores it in A.

You can convert numeric data to alphanumeric data by moving it to an alphanumeric data item. If the data item is an external decimal number, COBOL aligns the number on the decimal point and sets the sign. If the numeric data is copied to a PIC X alphanumeric data item, the numeric data is converted to character, left-justified, with the decimal point and any sign removed.

```
01  Y                   PIC X(3).
    □  □  □
    MOVE 22 TO Y        [Y contains "22".]
    MOVE -2.1 TO Y      [Y contains "21".]
    MOVE 2345 TO Y      [Y contains "234".]
```

Convert alphanumeric data to numeric by moving it to a numeric data item. (You can't convert data defined as alphabetic PIC A to numeric.) You can convert data contained in a PIC X item to numeric only if it contains the characters 0 to 9. (The SIGN clause further allows the item to contain a + or – in a leading or trailing position.) You can convert only integers to alphanumeric (PIC S99V but not S99V9).

```
01  Y                      PIC S999V.
    □  □  □
    MOVE "023" TO Y        [Y contains a numeric 23.]
```

For alphanumeric data containing such edit characters as the currency sign, commas, and a decimal point, use the NUMVAL or NUMVAL-C intrinsic function described in Chapter 21.

Alphanumeric data cannot appear in arithmetic expressions. Conversion also takes computer time, and excessive conversions can make a program run slower.

Arithmetic precision can be lost during conversion in the low-order digits. In an assignment statement, precision can be lost in both the high- and low-order digits if the data item to which the data is being assigned cannot contain the number being assigned. You can detect the loss of high-order digits by the ON SIZE ERROR phrase, but you can't detect the loss in low-order digits. The following example illustrates how high- and low-order digits are lost.

```
01  X                      PIC S99V99 PACKED-DECIMAL.
    □  □  □
    MOVE 123.456 TO X      [X contains a numeric 23.45.]
```

In the absence of a ROUNDED phrase in arithmetic operations, low-order digits of precision are lost by truncation, not rounding. For example, if the number 1.999 is stored in a data item of precision S9V99, COBOL truncates the number to 1.99. The ROUNDED phrase in the arithmetic statements rounds a number rather than truncating it. Values whose rightmost digit is less than 5 are rounded down in absolute magnitude, and values whose rightmost digit is 5 or greater are rounded up in absolute magnitude. Thus, 1.995 is rounded to 2.00.

When there is more than one arithmetic operation performed in a single statement, COBOL must carry intermediate results. For example, in COMPUTE $X = (A *B) / C$, the $A * B$ is first evaluated and held as an intermediate result. This intermediate result is then divided by C, and the intermediate result from this is stored in X.

Loss of precision and overflow in intermediate results are a common source of error. A grade-school student would give the correct result of the expression 6 * (2 / 4) as 3, but IBM COBOL evaluates it as 0. Assuming the result is stored in an integer item, the 2 / 4 yields an intermediate result of precision PIC S9, the 0.5 is truncated to zero to store the intermediate result, and 0 times 6 yields 0. The ANSI standard leaves the result undefined. PC COBOL evaluates it as 3. The precision of IBM COBOL intermediate results shown for the arithmetic operations in the following examples are given by iVd. The i signifies the number of decimal digits to the left of the decimal point and d the number of digits to the right.

Add, subtract:

$i_1Vd_1 \pm i_2Vd_2$ yields $(max(i_1, i_2) + 1)Vmax(d_1, d_2)$

99V9 + 9V999 yields precision of 9(3)V9(3)

99.9 + 9.999 equals 109.899

Multiply:

$i_1Vd_1 * i_2Vd_2$ yields $(i_1 + i_2)V(d_1 + d_2)$

99V9 * 9V999 yields precision of 9(3)V9(4)

99.9 * 9.999 equals 998.9001

Divide:

i_1Vd_1/i_2Vd_2 yields $(i_1 + d_2)Vmax(d')$

where $max(d')$ is maximum of d_1, d_2 or maximum of any d in the arithmetic expression except that in a divisor or exponent.

99V9 / 9V999, final result of 99V9 yields precision of 9(5)V9(3)

99.9 / 0.001 equals 99900.000

99V9 / 9V999, final result of 99V9(4) yields precision of 9(5)V9(4)

00.1 / 3.000 equals 00000.0333

Exponential:

$x ** n$ with x having precision i_1Vd_1 and n having i_2Vd_2.

- If n is noninteger (d_2 not zero), both the number and the exponent are converted to floating-point for the calculation.
- If x is an identifier with precision i_1Vd_1:

   $i_1Vd_1 ** i_2V$ yields $i_1 * |n|Vd_1 * |n|$.

   25 ** 2 equals 625 as precision 9(4).

   25.1 ** 2 equals 630.01 as precision 9(4)V99.
- If x is a literal of precision i_1Vd_1:

   $i_1Vd_1 ** i_2V$ yields $iVd_1 * |n|$, where i is set to the number of integer digits that result.

   25.3 ** 2 equals 640.09 as precision 9(3)V99.

Except for floating-point numbers, IBM COBOL carries as many as 30 digits of precision in intermediate results. High-order precision is lost only if the intermediate results require more than 30 digits, and the compiler will issue a warning if it is possible for this to occur. Binary numbers are converted to packed-decimal if the intermediate results would require more than 18 digits.

Addition and subtraction generally cause no problems. Multiplication can cause a problem if the result can exceed 30 total digits of precision—unlikely in commercial applications. Division causes the most problems. The result can exceed 30 total digits of precision when a very large number is divided by a very small number. A more likely error is loss in precision caused by a division resulting in a fraction. You have seen how 6 * (2 / 4) yields zero in IBM COBOL. You could obtain the correct result by any or the following.

Coding 6 * (2 / 4.0) to force the intermediate result to be carried to one decimal place.

Defining the final result to have a decimal precision of V9 to force the intermediate result to be carried to one decimal place.

Coding (6 * 2) / 4 to perform the division last. This method is preferable unless the result of the multiplication could exceed 30 total digits of precision. This works equally well for (6 * 1) / 3, whereas the two previous methods would give a result of 1.8.

Define a data item to contain the intermediate result and perform the operation in parts.

```
01  Temp                         PIC S9(4)V9(5) PACKED-DECIMAL.
    □  □  □
    COMPUTE Temp = 6 * 2
    COMPUTE Final-Result = Temp / 4
```

TIP *Be careful with division and, whenever possible, perform the division last in a series of computations.*

An expression such as $X * (Y / Z)$ may lose precision, and you should change it to $(X * Y) / Z$. Except for logical expressions, numeric computations are perhaps the most common source of error. Errors in loss of precision are especially hard to find, because a program runs as expected, but the numbers computed may be off slightly.

TIP *Always hand-calculate critical computations to check the precision.*

PROPOSED NEW ANSI STANDARD: Check Compiler to See if Implemented

The new ANSI standard provides for *standard arithmetic* that yields the same results regardless of the platform. Standard arithmetic is the result that would occur if the numbers involved were converted to floating-point with 32 significant digits of precision, including any intermediate results. Any comparison is done as if the numbers were rounded to 31 significant digits. Because such arithmetic can't be done with the computer's native hardware, standard arithmetic will result in a performance penalty. Standard arithmetic is requested by a new ARITHMETIC clause in a new OPTIONS paragraph in the Identification Division.

```
IDENTIFICATION DIVISION.
PROGRAM-ID.  program-name.
OPTIONS.
    ARITHMETIC IS STANDARD.
```
[You can also code ARITHMETIC IS NATIVE, the default and the way it has been in the past.]

9.7 NUMERIC DATA IN APPLICATIONS

Essential

TIP *Use the precision given here for the following common numeric data types.*

Percentages. Divide percentages by 100 for storage so that you can use them directly in applications. Store percentages as PIC S9V999 PACKED-DECIMAL data items. (That is, carry 50 percent as 0.500.) Three decimal places permit percentages accurate to 1/8 percent.

Dollar amount. Always carry dollar amounts in dollars and cents as PIC S9(n)V99 PACKED-DECIMAL, even if only whole dollars are to appear in reports. Make dollar amounts signed so that you can carry debits and credits.

Hours. If hours are used in calculations, keep them as PIC S9(n)V99 PACKED-DECIMAL data items rather than separately as hours and minutes. The two decimal digits are accurate to the minute, which is sufficient for most business applications. The following statement converts hours and minutes to a decimal number:

```
COMPUTE time = hours + minutes / 60
```

Salary. Although salary is often given in an amount per year, month, week, or day, you must often convert it to an hourly rate for internal use. Carry dollars to four decimal places. (Union contracts sometimes quote hourly rates as low as 1/8 cent.)

EXERCISES

1. Select the data types that would be best for the following uses, and describe why they would be best.
   - A count of the input records read from a file.
   - The population of states contained within a record.
   - Computing rocket trajectories.
   - Computing the interest on a house loan.
   - Reading numbers in from an input line.

2. The equation for a future amount invested at i percent per year for n years is

$$Future\ amount = Investment \left(1 + \frac{i}{100}\right)^n$$

Write the statements necessary to compute the future amount of ten-year investments ranging from $100 to $102 by increments of 5 cents at an interest rate of 7¼ percent.

3. Assume the following items are declared.

```
01  A     PIC S9(6)V999.
01  B     PIC S999V99 PACKED-DECIMAL.
01  C     PIC S9(4) BINARY.
01  D     COMP-1.
01  E     COMP-2.
```

Describe the conversion that will be done in each of the following statements:

```
COMPUTE E = A * D
COMPUTE A = D * B * C
ADD 1 TO C
MOVE B TO A
```

4. Assume that the following data items are described.

```
01  A     PIC S9(4) BINARY.
01  B     PIC S9(6)V9(3)
          PACKED-DECIMAL.
01  C     PIC S999 PACKED-DECIMAL.
```

Show the results of the following statements.

```
COMPUTE A = 3.5
COMPUTE A ROUNDED = 3.5
COMPUTE B = 1254.6 * 3.3235 / 6.43229 + 12.1136
MOVE 12.211 TO B
COMPUTE B = B / 4.395 * 6.4 + 7.1135
COMPUTE A = (12 + .1) / 7
COMPUTE A = (12 / 7) + .1
```

5. The IRS has called you in to do some programming. It feels that it has not been getting a fair shake from the taxpayers. It has decided to pay off the national debt by billing each taxpayer his or her share. You are told that the national debt is $10,627,260,497,937.12. The IRS insists that the national debt be paid off to the penny. The share for each person is to be paid in the proportion of his personal income tax to the total income tax. Under these circumstances, is it possible to pay off the national debt to the penny? Assume that there are 157,916,412 taxpayers. Under the worst possible circumstances, assuming that you round, how much over or under might you collect? If you truncate, how much over or under might you collect?

CHAPTER 10

CHARACTER DATA

10.1 DEFINING CHARACTER DATA

Essential

Character data consists of a string of characters. The names of people, their street addresses, and the words on this page all constitute character data. Character data is not a COBOL term, but is a standard term for describing data in character form. Character data is also termed *character string* and *text data* in other languages. In COBOL, data described as DISPLAY constitutes character data, which can be alphanumeric and alphabetic.

COBOL defines three *classes* of data: alphabetic, alphanumeric, and numeric. Numeric was described in the last chapter. Alphanumeric and alphabetic are described here. Both are DISPLAY data, which is COBOL's term for character data. Throughout this book, the term DISPLAY indicates that the data items may be any of these three types of character data. However, the examples don't code DISPLAY, because it defaults if omitted.

Alphabetic data is described as PIC A. This data can contain only the characters A to Z, a to z, and blank. You rarely need it, both because alphanumeric data serve better and because data containing only alphabetic characters are rare. Even people's names, such as O'Reilly, require alphanumeric data items.

TIP   *Don't use alphabetic data.*

Alphanumeric data can consist of any of the characters in the COBOL character set, including alphabetic and numeric characters. *External decimal numbers,* described in Chapter 11, consist of the digits 0 to 9. *External floating-point* numbers consist of a number with an E for the exponent. Because external numbers contain only numeric digits, they can both participate in arithmetic operations and be displayed.

COBOL further subdivides the alphanumeric class of data into three *categories:* numeric-edited, alphanumeric-edited, and alphanumeric. You can also operate on group items as if it were character data, and the group item is treated as if it contained all alphanumeric data. Table 10.1 summarizes the classes and categories of COBOL character data.

Numeric-edited data, such as "$33,425.37 CR" for a credit, and *alphanumeric-edited* data, such as "11/18/2003" for a date, contain special edit characters coded in the PIC clause. You can display this data but not perform arithmetic operations on it. You can, however, move numeric items to it if the PIC clause contains 9s. Numeric- and alphanumeric-edited data are generally used for display and printing as discussed in Chapter 12. If the alphanumeric data contains no special edit characters, it is termed simply alphanumeric data.

You write alphanumeric literals by enclosing the characters in quotation marks ("). IBM and PC COBOL provide the APOST compiler option, described in Chapter 33, to let you use an apostrophe (') instead. Workstation, PC COBOL, and the new ANSI Standard also allow either the quotation (") or apostrophe (') to be used, as long as the same character is used at the beginning and end of a string.

```
"AT" "FIVE" "ME TO"
```

Specify a double quotation character (") by coding two consecutive quotation marks.

```
"""WHERE IS IT?"""    Becomes    "WHERE IS IT?"
```

The number of X's in the PIC clause specifies the length of alphanumeric data items: PIC XX . . . X or X(*integer*). The *integer* is the number of characters that the data item is to contain.

```
01  data-name                    PIC X(integer).
```

Or

```
01  data-name                    PIC XXX...X.
```

TABLE 10.1 COBOL Data

Level of Item	Class	Category
Elementary	Numeric	
	Alphabetic	
	External decimal and floating-point	
	Alphanumeric	Numeric-edited
		Alphanumeric-edited
		Alphanumeric
Group	Alphanumeric	All data types

In the following example, *B* contains 12 characters, *C* contains 3 characters, and *D* contains 4 characters.

```
01 B PIC X(12) DISPLAY.              Or:    01 B     PIC X(12).
01 C PICTURE XXX USAGE DISPLAY.      Or:    01 C     PIC X(3).
01 D PICTURE XXXX USAGE IS DISPLAY.  Or:    01 D     PIC X(4).
```

You describe alphabetic data items the same as alphanumeric items, except that you code an A rather than an X.

```
01 W     PIC AAAA.                   Or:  01 W     PIC A(4).
```

The PIC clause may contain A or 9 in combination with X, but COBOL treats the item as if it were all Xs.

```
01 Y     PIC XXAA9.               Same as   01 Y     PIC XXXXX.
```

Give alphanumeric data items initial values by appending the VALUE clause to the description. The following example initializes B with the characters "ABCD":

```
01 A                              PIC X(4) VALUE "ABCD".
```

If too few characters are specified, COBOL pads the string out on the right with blanks. If too many characters are specified, the description is in error.

```
01 B                              PIC X(4) VALUE "1".
```
[*B* contains "1bbb".]
```
01 C                              PIC X(4) VALUE "VWXYZ".
```
[*C* is in error.]

PROPOSED NEW ANSI STANDARD: Check Compiler to See if Implemented

The new ANSI standard lets you omit the PIC clause when you code a VALUE with an alphanumeric literal (but not a figurative constant.)

```
01  Some-Item                     PIC X(7) VALUE "THE END".
```

Or

```
01  Some-Item                     VALUE "THE END".
```

10.1.1 The JUSTIFIED Clause

Sometimes Used

If you want data stored right justified in a DISPLAY elementary data item, you can code the JUSTIFIED RIGHT clause. You cannot code it for numeric, numeric-edited, alphanumeric-edited, or index items.

```
01  A       PIC X(6) JUSTIFIED RIGHT.

    MOVE "AB" TO A                          [A contains "bbbbAB".]
```

If a sending item is longer than the JUST RIGHT receiving item, COBOL truncates the leftmost characters; if shorter, it pads the data on the left with blanks.

```
    MOVE "ABCDEFGH" TO A                    [A contains "CDEFGH".]
```

JUST RIGHT has no effect on any initial value set by VALUE:

```
01  A                          PIC X(6) JUST RIGHT VALUE "AB".
```
[A contains "ABbbbb", not "bbbbAB".]

10.1.2 Hexadecimal Literals

Rarely Used

You can write hexadecimal (hex) literals as X"*hex-digits*. There must be two hex digits per byte, and you can specify a maximum of 320 digits.

```
    X"C1C2C3" is the same as "ABC" in Mainframe COBOL.
    X"414243" is the same as  "ABC" in Workstation and PC COBOL.
01  A-Value                    PIC X(4) VALUE X"C1C2C3".
```

Upper- and lowercase characters are treated the same. X"C1" is the same as X"c1".

10.2   THE SPECIAL-NAMES PARAGRAPH

The SPECIAL-NAMES paragraph in the Configuration Section lets you specify your own character set and define figurative constants.

10.2.1 Specifying Your Own Character Set: The ALPHABET Clause

Rarely Used

By default, the character set will be EBCDIC for the IBM mainframe and ASCII for all else. Code the ALPHABET clause in the SPECIAL-NAMES paragraph of the Environment Division to specify another character set.

```
ENVIRONMENT DIVISION.
CONFIGURATION SECTION.
SPECIAL-NAMES.
    ALPHABET alphabet-name IS character-set.
```

The *alphabet-name* is a name you choose to call the character set. The *character-set* can be one of the following:

- STANDARD-1 for ASCII-encoded files
- STANDARD-2 for ISO 7-bit-encoded files
- EBCDIC for EBCDIC—the default for Mainframe COBOL
- ASCII for the PC—the default.
- NATIVE for the computer's native mode; this is the default if you omit CODE-SET (see Chapter 17)

If none of these satisfies you, you can devise your own character set and specify it by coding the *character-set* as

```
ALPHABET alphabet-name IS literal
                       literal THRU literal
            .      .       .
                       literal THRU literal.
```

The *literal* is the character wanted. You can code a single-character literal ("Z") or an unsigned decimal representation of the character you want with a value from 1 to 255. For example, an EBCDIC "Z" is a hex "E9", which is decimal 234. If the entire character set consisted of S through Z, you could code

```
ALPHABET alphabet-name IS 227 THRU 234.
```

Or

```
ALPHABET alphabet-name IS "S" THRU "Z".
```

The collating sequence of the character set depends on the order in which you specify the codes. For example, if you code

```
ALPHABET alphabet-name IS "A", "Z" THRU "S".
```

The collating sequence from low to high is A, Z, Y, X, W, V, U, T, and S. Thus, you can make the collating sequence be whatever you want it. The first character specified is associated with the figurative constant LOW-VALUES and the last character with HIGH-VALUES. If two or more characters are to have the same position in the collating sequence, code them as

```
literal ALSO literal ALSO literal … ALSO literal
```

The following example establishes an alphabet named VOWELS:

```
SPECIAL-NAMES.
    ALPHABET Vowels IS "A", "E", "I", "O", "U".
```

You can code several alphabets. Note that SPECIAL-NAMES is a paragraph, and you code the period at the end of the paragraph.

```
SPECIAL-NAMES.
    ALPHABET Vowels IS "A", "E", "I", "O", "U"
    ALPHABET Consonants IS "B" THRU "D", "F" THRU "H",
            "J" THRU "N", "P" THRU "T", "V" THRU "Z".
```

10.2.2 Defining Figurative Constants: The SYMBOLIC CHARACTERS Clause

Rarely Used

The normal figurative constants that can be used with character data are ZEROS, SPACES, HIGH-VALUES, LOW-VALUES, QUOTES, and ALL. You can also define your own figurative constants with the SYMBOLIC CHARACTERS clause. You code it in the Environment Division in the SPECIAL-NAMES paragraph as follows:

```
ENVIRONMENT DIVISION.
CONFIGURATION SECTION.
SPECIAL-NAMES.
    ALPHABET alphabet-name IS …  [Any ALPHABET must come first.]
    SYMBOLIC CHARACTERS name-1, name-2, …, name-n
            IS/ARE integer-1, integer-2, …, integer-n.
[End SPECIAL-NAMES paragraph with a period.]
```

Each *name* is a unique user-defined word that must contain at least one alphabetic character: 9999A but not 9999. There must be an *integer* corresponding to each *name*. The *integer* is the ordinal position (1 to *n*) of the character in the character set. For example, an EBCDIC dash or minus sign is a hex X"60", which is 96 in decimal. But because the first EBCDIC character is X"00", the ordinal position of the minus is 97. Here is how it could be defined:

```
SYMBOLIC CHARACTERS A-Dash IS 97.
```

Now you could treat *A-Dash* as a figurative constant:

```
MOVE ALL A-Dash TO A-Line          [A-Line would be filled with dashes.]
```

If you use the ALPHABET clause to specify your own alphabet, you can assign a symbolic name to one of these characters. Code the *integer* as the ordinal position (1 – *n*) of the character in the alphabet, and follow *integer* with IN *alphabet-name* to name the alphabet.

```
SPECIAL-NAMES.
    ALPHABET alphabet-name IS literal, literal, …
    SYMBOLIC CHARACTERS name-1, name-2, …, name-n
            IS/ARE integer-1, integer-2, …, integer-n
            IN alphabet-name.
```

Here's an example that creates an alphabet named *Digits* for the numeric digits and assigns the symbolic name *Unity* to the second digit (1) and the symbolic name *Trinity* to the fourth digit (3).

```
SPECIAL-NAMES.
    ALPHABET Digits IS "0" THRU "9"
    SYMBOLIC CHARACTERS Unity IS 2 IN Digits
    SYMBOLIC CHARACTERS Trinity IS 4 IN Digits.
```

10.3   OPERATING ON CHARACTER DATA

COBOL lets you move all or specific characters from one data item to another. You can also compare character data, determine the length of a data item, and place character data from different data items end to end (termed *concatenation*).

10.3.1   Moving Character Data

Essential

The MOVE statement can move alphanumeric identifiers and literals to other alphanumeric identifiers. The following example stores "12345" in *K*.

```
01  K                                    PIC X(5).
01  L                                    PIC X(5) VALUE "12345".
    □    □    □
    MOVE L TO K     Or:     MOVE "12345" TO K
```

In the MOVE statement, COBOL pads identifiers on the right (left if they are declared JUST RIGHT) with blanks if they are assigned a smaller item; it truncates longer items on the right (left if they are declared JUST RIGHT):

```
01  B                                    PIC X(4).
    □    □    □
    MOVE "AB" TO B                       [B contains "ABbb".]
    MOVE "ABCDEF" TO B                   [B contains "ABCD".]
```

To repeat a literal to fill an item, precede the literal with ALL.

```
01  Z                                    PIC X(6) VALUE ALL "1".
    [Z contains "111111".]
    □    □    □
    MOVE ALL "A" TO Z                    [Z contains "AAAAAA".]
```

10.3.2   Reference Modification

Essential

COBOL allows you to refer to substrings of character data by giving the starting character position and the length. The general form for this *reference modification* is *identifier(starting-character:length)*

Both the *starting-character* and *length* are arithmetic expressions. The *starting-character* is the starting character position (the first character is 1), and must result in a value from 1 to the length of the identifier. The *length* must result in a positive, nonzero value. For example:

```
01  A                              PIC X(6) VALUE "ABCDEF".
01  B                              PIC X(6).
    □   □   □
    MOVE A(3:2) TO B    Acts as    MOVE "CD" TO B
```

The *length* is optional. If omitted, COBOL assumes a length from the *starting-character* to the rightmost character. Note that you must always code the colon, even if the length is omitted.

```
MOVE A(2:) TO B     Acts as     MOVE "BCDEF" TO B
                    Same as     MOVE A(2:5) TO B
```

Except when restricted in specific statements, you can use reference modification wherever you can use an alphanumeric identifier. For example:

```
MOVE SPACES TO B
MOVE "XY" TO B(3:2)                  [B now contains "bbXYbb".]
MOVE A(3:2) TO B(1:2)                [B now contains "CDXYbb".]
```

Either the *starting-character* or *length* can be arithmetic expressions. In the following example, the identifier *Bar-String* is filled with 1 to 10 X characters, depending on the value contained in the identifier *Score*.

```
01  Score                          PIC S999 BINARY.
01  X-String                       PIC X(10) VALUE "XXXXXXXXXX".
01  Bar-String                     PIC X(10).
    □   □   □
    IF Score >=1 AND <= 10
       THEN MOVE X-String(1:Score) TO Bar-String
    END-IF
```

You could create bar charts using a technique such as this.

Reference modification is extremely powerful and lets you manipulate individual or groups of characters. Chapter 22 contains additional COBOL statements that operate on characters to do more exotic things, such as searching for specific characters within a string, counting the number of occurrences of specific characters, extracting characters from a string, replacing found characters in a string with other characters, and concatenating one string to the end of the other.

10.3.3   LENGTH OF Special Register (Not in ANSI Standard)

Archaic

The LENGTH OF special register obtains the number of bytes occupied by an identifier—that is, the identifier's length. There is now a LENGTH intrinsic function that is part of the ANSI standard that should be used instead, making

LENGTH OF unnecessary. LENGTH OF is implicitly defined as BINARY PIC 9(9). You write it as

```
LENGTH OF identifier
```

For example

```
01  A                               PIC X(10).
01  B                               PIC S9(4) BINARY.
    □   □   □
    MOVE LENGTH OF A TO B           [Moves 10 to B.]
    MOVE LENGTH OF A(3:) TO B       [Moves 8 to B.]
    MOVE LENGTH OF B TO B           [Moves 2 to B.]
```

For variable-length tables (described in Chapter 13), LENGTH OF gives the current length of the table. However, you cannot use it as a subscript. Suppose you have the following:

```
01  Array-A.
    05  A                           PIC X(4) OCCURS 100 TIMES
                                    DEPENDING ON Len-A.
01  Len-A                           PIC S9(4) BINARY.
    □   □   □
    MOVE LENGTH OF Array-A TO An-Item
```
   [Contents of *An-Item* are undefined, because no value has been stored in *Len-A* to specify the length of the table.]
```
    MOVE 10 TO Len-A
    MOVE LENGTH OF Array-A TO An-Item
```
   [*An-Item* contains 40, because *Array-A* has 10 elements of 4 bytes each.]
```
    MOVE 100 TO Len-A
    MOVE LENGTH OF Array-A TO An-Item
```
   [*An-Item* contains 400, because *Array-A* has 100 elements of 4 bytes each.]

10.3.4 Comparing Character Data

Essential

Relational conditions, such as those in the IF statement, can compare two character strings. COBOL compares the two strings character by character from left to right, according to the collating sequence of the character set. Chapter 23 shows the collating sequence of the EBCDIC and ASCII character sets.

In the relational condition, if the strings are of unequal length, COBOL pads the shorter with blanks on the right to equal the length of the longer string for the comparison. The following example compares the characters "ABCD" with "23bb".

```
01  X                               PIC X(4) VALUE "ABCD".
    □   □   □
    IF X = "23" ...
```

You can test alphanumeric and alphabetic PIC A items to determine if they contain only the alphabetic characters A to Z, a to z, or blank.

```
IF identifier ALPHABETIC THEN …
IF identifier NOT ALPHABETIC THEN …
IF identifier ALPHABETIC-UPPER THEN …
IF identifier NOT ALPHABETIC-LOWER THEN …
```

You can also test alphanumeric and external decimal number items to determine if they contain only the numeric characters 0 to 9.

```
IF identifier NUMERIC THEN …
IF identifier NOT NUMERIC THEN …
```

Table 10.2 summarizes the tests that may be made on alphanumeric, alphabetic, and external decimal numbers.

You can also define your own classes of data in the SPECIAL-NAMES paragraph of the Environment Division. For example, suppose you want to define a class named *Odd-Num* for odd numeric characters. You write the SPECIAL-NAMES paragraph with a CLASS clause as

```
ENVIRONMENT DIVISION.
CONFIGURATION SECTION.
SPECIAL-NAMES.
    ALPHABET …
    SYMBOLIC CHARACTERS …
    CLASS Odd-Num IS "1", "3", "5", "7", "9".
    □  □  □
01  The-Data     PIC X(6).
    □  □  □
    IF The-Data(6:1) IS Odd-Num THEN …
    IF The-Data(6:1) IS NOT Odd-Num THEN …
```

The general form of the CLASS clause is

TABLE 10.2 Alphabetic and Numeric Tests

Type of Item	Permissible Tests
PIC A	ALPHABETIC
	ALPHABETIC-UPPER
	ALPHABETIC-LOWER
PIC X	ALPHABETIC
	NUMERIC
PIC 9	NUMERIC

```
SPECIAL-NAMES.
    CLASS class-name IS literal, literal,
        literal THRU/THROUGH literal, literal, …
```

The *literal* is usually a single-character literal, such as "1" or "%", or multiple characters, such as "13579", that are treated as if the characters had been written separately. The aforementioned CLASS clause could also have been written as

```
CLASS Odd-Num IS "13579"
```

The *literal* cannot be a symbolic character, such as SPACE. It can be an integer that represents the ordinal position of the EBCDIC or ASCII character code, which is one more than the character code. For example, the EBCDIC numeric code for a "%" is 108 and its ordinal position is 109.

```
CLASS class-name IS 109, …
```

In EBCDIC, this is the same as

```
CLASS class-name IS "%", …
```

However, in ASCII, a 108 is a "l", so that the foregoing in ASCII is the same as

```
CLASS class-name IS "1", …
```

You cannot use the *class-name* test for external decimal numbers (PIC 9).

10.3.5   Concatenation Operation

> **PROPOSED NEW ANSI STANDARD: Check Compiler to See if Implemented**
>
> The new ANSI standard lets you concatenate character strings with the & concatenation operator. You can code a concatenation expression anywhere you can code an alphanumeric literal.
>
> ```
> MOVE "ABC" & "DEF" TO A          [Same as MOVE "ABCDEF" TO A]
> ```

10.4   CHARACTER DATA IN APPLICATIONS

Essential

The main problem with text fields is determining their maximum length.

TIP   *Consult the following to determine the maximum length of character data items.*

Dates. Keep dates as a PIC 9(8) item in the form *yyyymmdd.* This is the ISO international standard (ISO, 1988).

Names. Nothing is more insulting than to receive computer-generated output in which your name is truncated. Allow plenty of room in storing names.

- *Last name:* 30 characters. According to the *Guinness Book of World Records,* Featherstonehaugh is the longest English name. However, hyphenated last names after marriage are becoming more common today, so 30 characters should allow for this and foreign names.

- *First name:* 15 characters. Christopher is the longest of the common given names. The 15 characters provide a margin for this.

- *Middle name:* 20 characters. The middle name is often a family name. If you store only the middle initial, you need only a single character.

Address. The following items are usually required for addresses in the United States and most foreign addresses. Allow plenty of room, because it can be extremely offensive to truncate a company, city, or nation name.

- *Company name:* 65 characters. *The Atchison Topeka and Santa Fe Railroad Company* is the longest of the Fortune 500 names. The names of law firms go on forever.

- *Division name:* 65 characters. Same as the company name.

- *Street address:* 40 characters. The longest street name I have encountered is my own: Mandeville Canyon Road. Leave some room for street number and room, suite, or apartment number.

- *City:* 25 characters. Southampton Long Island is the longest name in the United States. Fortunately, El Pueblo de Nuestra Señora la Reina de los Angeles de Porciuncula can be abbreviated L.A. (Wales has longer names, so allow 25 characters to avoid offending the Welsh.)

- *State:* 21 characters. Fifteen characters is sufficient for United States (the Carolinas), but allow 21 to include Canada (Northwest Territories) if the name is spelled out. Allow 2 characters if you need only the post office code for U.S. states.

- *Zip code:* 14 characters. Nine characters are enough for the U.S. ZIP+4 code, but allow 14 for foreign countries.

- *Country:* 30 characters. St. Vincent and the Grenadines is the longest name not usually abbreviated. A full 37 characters are required for the Democratic People's Republic of Yemen (and Korea). (However, People's Republics are an endangered species.) The Russian Soviet Federated Socialist Republic is 43 characters but it went the way of Leningrad and Stalingrad. The longest name of a member of the U.N. requires 38 characters: Byelorussian Soviet Socialist Republic. (Socialist Republics also are on the endangered list.)

This covers the basics of character data. Chapter 22 describes other COBOL statements that operate on data and advanced character manipulation.

10.5 NATIONAL CHARACTERS

PROPOSED NEW ANSI STANDARD: Check Compiler to See if Implemented

The new ANSI standard supports national characters, in addition to the ASCII or EBCDIC character sets of USAGE DISPLAY. National characters might be the French, German, Russian, or Greek alphabets, and are established by the compiler. You specify national characters by coding NATIONAL in place of DISPLAY.

```
01  Some-Data                  NATIONAL PIC X(20).
```

You denote a national literal with an N.

```
    MOVE N"XYZ" TO Some-Data
```

National hexadecimal literals are denoted with an NX.

```
    MOVE NX"234571" TO Some-Data
```

Other than this, you code national characters the same as you would alphanumeric characters.

10.6 BOOLEAN DATA

PROPOSED NEW ANSI STANDARD: Check Compiler to See if Implemented

Boolean data (also called bit string data) consists of a string of bits having a value of 0 or 1. Boolean literals are denoted by a B:

```
B"0101…01"
```

The Boolean operators are B-AND (logical and), B-OR (logical OR), B-XOR (logical exclusive OR), and B-NOT (logical NOT). They operate as follows:

- B-AND Set results bit to 1 if both corresponding bits are 1.
  `"1100" B-AND "0101"` results in `"0100"`.
- B-OR Set results bit to 1 if either corresponding bit is 1.
  `"1100" B-OR "0101"` results in `"1101"`
- B-XOR Set results bit to 1 only if one of the corresponding bits is 1.
  `"1100" B-XOR "0101"` results in `"1001"`
- B-NOT Reverse the value of the bits.
  `B-NOT "1100"` results in `"0011"`

You define Boolean data as follows, where each 1 represents a bit.

```
nn  data-name                  USAGE BIT 111…1.
01  Flag-A                     BIT 1(8) VALUE "00001111".
```

Flag-A consists of a full byte of eight bits. Boolean data can appear in both the MOVE and COMPUTE statement:

```
MOVE B"00000001" TO Flag-A
COMPUTE Flag-A = Flag-A B-AND "00000111"
```

Boolean items can be concatenated with the & concatenation operator.

```
MOVE "111" & "00000" TO Flag-A      [Same as MOVE "11100000" TO Flag-A.]
```

You can also use reference modification with Boolean data.

```
MOVE "111" TO Flag-A(6:3)
```
            ["111" is moved to the sixth, seventh, and eighth bits of *Flag-A*.]

Boolean values can be compared equal or not equal. If the items being compared are of unequal length, the shorter is padded on the right with 0's for the comparison.

```
IF Flag-A = "1" …
```
                        [Executes as if written *Flag-A* = "10000000"]

A Boolean item is aligned on a byte boundary when it follows a non-Boolean item. If it follows a Boolean item, the bits follow contiguously.

```
01  A-Table.
    05  An-Element                  PIC 1 OCCURS 5 TIMES.
```

The first bit in the array is aligned on a byte boundary, and is followed consecutively by the remaining four bits to occupy less than a byte. To align each of the elements on a byte boundary, add the ALIGNED clause.

```
05  An-Element              .        PIC 1 OCCURS 5 TIMES ALIGNED.
```

Now each bit starts on a byte boundary, and the array occupies five bytes. Boolean data is often used for flags. A bit value of "1" is true and "0" is false. The following executes the THEN phrase if *An-Element(3)* is a 1. You can only test Boolean items for true or false if they have a length of 1.

```
IF An-Element(3)
    THEN …
    ELSE …
END-IF
```

EXERCISES

1. Show what these identifiers will contain when initialized as follows.

```
01  A                       PIC X(6) VALUE ZEROS.
01  B                       PIC X(10) VALUE "MARYQUOTES".
01  C                       PIC X(3) VALUE "ABC".
```

```
01  D                          PIC X(6) VALUE ALL "12".
01  E                          PIC X(8) JUST RIGHT
                               VALUE "123".
01  F                          PIC X(6) VALUE "ABC".
01  G                          PIC X(8) VALUE ALL ZEROS.
```

2. Define an identifier named *Text-A* containing 20 characters and an identifier named *State* containing 4 characters. Write the statements necessary to move the data in *State* to *Text-A,* right-justifying it with leading blanks.

3. Define an alphabet named *Hawaiian-Alphabet.* It is to contain only the vowels A, E, I, O, U, and the consonants H, K, L, M, N, P, and W. Also define a class name of *Hawaiian* for the same characters. Test the variable named *City-Name* to see if it contains only *Hawaiian* characters.

4. Use IF statements to examine a variable named *The-Num* defined as PIC S9(5), and set it to blanks if it contains zero. This is to do functionally the same as if you had defined *The-Num* with BLANK WHEN ZERO.

5. Define symbolic parameters named *Dollar* for "$" and *Pound-Sterling* for "£". Assume that you are doing this only for the PC. The ASCII code for the £ is 156.

6. Assume that you must display numbers of precision S9(5), and you want negative numbers to be enclosed in parentheses. Positive numbers are to appear without parentheses. Define an identifier containing seven characters. Store the number in character positions 2 through 6. Place the parentheses in character positions 1 and 7 if the number is negative. Thus, 23 would appear as "bbbb23b" and −23 as "(bbb23)". Repeat this, but let the left parenthesis float so that −23 prints as "bbb(23)".

CHAPTER 11

DATA DESCRIPTIONS AND RECORDS

This chapter explains how to code data descriptions and records. Skip this chapter only if you already have them down pat.

11.1 ORDER OF CODING DATA DESCRIPTION CLAUSES

Essential

For reference, you code the level first in a data description, then the data name or FILLER. If REDEFINES is coded, it must come next.

```
level   data-name/FILLER REDEFINES
```

The remaining clauses can be coded in any order, with the exception of the clauses relating to the OCCURS, which must be coded in the following order:

```
OCCURS, DEPENDING ON, ASCENDING/DESCENDING KEY, INDEXED BY
```

11.2 WRITING DATA DESCRIPTIONS

Essential

You can allocate storage for elementary items, records, and tables. You must explicitly describe all data items. COBOL does not automatically set storage to zero or blanks, and you must initialize each data item or assign a value to it before using it in computations. You write data descriptions as follows. Note that you must always terminate the description with a period.

```
nn  data-name  PIC character-string USAGE clause.
```

The level-number (*nn*) is one or two numeric digits specifying the level. The levels can be 01 through 49 (or 1 through 49), 66, 77, and 88.

The *data-name* is a name containing 1 through 30 characters: 0 through 9, A through Z, a through z, or the hyphen. The hyphen cannot be the first or last character. Begin the *data-name* somewhere in columns 12 through 72. Level numbers 01 and 77 names must be unique. Omit the name, or code FILLER as the data name, to indicate an unnamed item.

The *character-string* represents characters specifying the length or precision of the data item. For example, X(10) specifies 10 characters, and S999V99 specifies a signed number with three digits to the left and two to the right of the assumed decimal point. The maximum length of the character string is 30 characters.

The *USAGE* clause specifies the representation of the data. You can code BINARY, COMP-1 (single-precision floating-point), COMP-2 (double-precision floating-point), PACKED-DECIMAL, or DISPLAY (external decimal numbers, alphanumeric, or alphabetic). Don't code PIC for COMP-1 and COMP-2.

You can code only a single data description entry on a line, but you may continue it onto other lines. Level numbers are used as follows:

- 01 is used for record names and must begin somewhere in columns 8 through 11. They are aligned on a double-word boundary in IBM COBOL.
- 02 through 49 are used for levels within a record. Begin them in columns 8 through 72.
- 66 is used for renaming groups of items within a record. Begin it in columns 8 through 72.
- 77 is used for noncontiguous elementary data items—those not a part of a record. IBM COBOL aligns it on a full-word boundary. Begin it in columns 8 through 11.
- 88 is used for condition names that assign a logical value to the contents of a data item. Begin it in columns 8 through 72. Condition names were described in Chapter 5.

The data descriptions may appear in any of the three sections within the Data Division. The File Section describes I/O records; the Working-Storage Section describes elementary items, records, and tables; and the Linkage Section describes subprogram parameters. Records are described in the File Section as follows:

```
DATA DIVISION.
FILE SECTION.
FD record-descriptions.
01  record-name.
```

Follow each File Description (FD) entry with a data description describing the record. This area for describing records is termed the *record area*. COBOL doesn't allocate storage for the record descriptions, and aside from level 88 condition names, you cannot assign initial values. The *record-name* describes the format of the record within the input or output buffer. A *buffer* is an area of storage automatically allocated by the operating system to hold records for I/O operations.

Records are described in the Working-Storage Section as follows:

```
WORKING-STORAGE SECTION.
77   data-name               PIC ….
01   data-name.
```

COBOL allocates storage to all level 77 items, and you can assign them initial values. They can appear before or after any level 01 descriptions. Level 77 items are a redundant COBOL feature. It makes no difference whether you code a level 01 or 77 item:

```
77   An-Item                 PIC X(4) VALUE "ABCD".
```

Identical to

```
01   An-Item                 PIC X(4) VALUE "ABCD".
```

Records are described in the Linkage Section as follows:

```
LINKAGE SECTION.
77   data-name               PIC ….
01   data-name.
```

You describe all subprogram parameters within a subprogram in the Linkage Section. COBOL doesn't allocate them storage, and aside from level 88 condition names, you cannot assign them initial values. They are associated with the data passed in the parameters of the calling program.

11.3 DESCRIBING RECORDS

Essential

A *record* is a hierarchical collection of related data items, which may be of different data types. You describe I/O records as records. For example, a record describing a person might include the person's name and date of birth. Some items might be group items, as for example the date of birth that consists of a month, a day, and a year. The following example shows how such a record is described. The two records following are identical. Notice how aligning the PIC clauses makes the hierarchical relationship easier to understand.

```
01   Person.
02   The-Name                PIC X(25).
```

```
                    02  Birth-Date.
                    03  Month          PIC X(9).
                03  Days               PIC S99 PACKED-DECIMAL.
                        03  Year       PIC S9(4).
```

Same as

```
    01  Person.
        02  The-Name       PIC X(25).
        02  Birth-Date.
            03  Month       PIC X(9).
            03  Days        PIC S99 PACKED-DECIMAL.
            03  Year        PIC S9(4).
```

11.3.1 Level Numbers

Essential

The record name (*Person* in the previous example) must be level number 01, and all succeeding items within the record must have level numbers greater than 01. The level numbers need not be consecutive, as they serve only to indicate the relative hierarchy of the record. For example, the following record is identical to the previous two.

```
    01  Person.
        05  The-Name       PIC X(25).
        05  Birth-Date.
            10  Month       PIC X(9).
            10  Days        PIC S99 PACKED-DECIMAL.
            10  Year        PIC S9(4).
```

TIP *Increment the levels by a number such as 5 to leave room for subdividing items if later required.*

Items within a record that are not further subdivided are elementary items. They must contain the PIC clause (except for COMP-1 and COMP-2). In the previous record, *The-Name, Month, Days,* and *Year* are elementary items. The group items subdivided into elementary items are referred to by their names. For example, the entire record is referred to by its name, *Person,* in the previous example.

11.3.2 Data Names

Essential

The data name can be 1 through 30 characters including A through Z, a through z, 0 through 9, and the dash (-).

> **PROPOSED NEW ANSI STANDARD: Check Compiler to See if Implemented**
>
> The new ANSI standard allows names to be as long as 60 characters, and the underscore (__) can be used like the dash.

TIP *Use consistent data names.*

If you use the same data name in the Linkage Section of a subprogram as you use in the program calling it, you can easily locate all references to the data item with a global search.

TIP *Prefix the level-01 group name to the elementary data items within it.*

Although this means you can't use CORR (which usually can't be used anyway), it eliminates the need to qualify elementary data names. It also makes it much easier to locate data items with the search facility of a text editor.

11.3.3 FILLER

Essential

The special data name FILLER describes data items in a record that need no name, such as text within a print line. This saves having to make up a name that will never be used. FILLER must be an elementary item and contain the PIC clause. You often use it to pad out records to increase their size. You may assign FILLER an initial value.

```
01  HEADER.
    05  FILLER              PIC X(6) VALUE "DATE: ".
    05  A-Date.
        10  Month           PIC 99.
        10  FILLER          PIC X VALUE "/".
        10  Days            PIC 99.
        10  FILLER          PIC X VALUE "/".
        10  Year            PIC 9(4).
```

You can also omit FILLER, so that the foregoing is identical to:

```
01  HEADER.
    05                      PIC X(6) VALUE "DATE: ".
```

```
05   A-Date.
     10   Month            PIC 99.
     10                    PIC X VALUE "/".
     10   Days             PIC 99.
     10                    PIC X VALUE "/".
     10   Year             PIC 9(4).
```

11.3.4   The PIC Clause

Essential

The PIC clause specifies the number of digits, sign, and decimal point for numeric data items. The maximum length of a numeric or numeric-edited item is 18 digits. For alphanumeric items, it specifies whether the data is alphabetic, numeric, or alphanumeric, the length of the item, any editing to be done, and any characters to be inserted. The string following PIC describing the data can be 30 characters long. The PIC clause is fully described in Chapters 9, 10, and 12 in the context of its use.

PROPOSED NEW ANSI STANDARD: Check Compiler to See if Implemented

The new ANSI standard increases this to 60 characters.

11.3.5   The USAGE Clause

Essential

You code the USAGE clause to specify the data type of an item as BINARY, COMP-1, COMP-2, or PACKED-DECIMAL.

```
01   Test-Data                USAGE IS PACKED-DECIMAL
                              PIC S9(5)V99.
```

You can code USAGE at the group level to apply to all data items within the group. However, it is then easy to mistake the elementary items for external decimal numbers when they are specified to be another data type at the group level.

TIP   *Code the USAGE clause for each elementary data item rather than at a higher level.*

The example on the right makes it clearer that *Y* and *Z* are BINARY.

```
05   X BINARY.        Same as    05  X.
     10   Y   PIC S9(5).              10  Y   PIC S9(5) BINARY.
     10   Z   PIC S9(5).              10  Z   PIC S9(5) BINARY.
```

1.3.6 The VALUE Clause

Essential

You code the VALUE clause as:

```
VALUE IS value or VALUES ARE value
```

You can also code the VALUE clause at the group level if all the group items are alphanumeric data items (DISPLAY). The VALUE at the group level must be a figurative constant or a nonnumeric literal. COBOL initializes the group area without regard to the elementary item data types, as if they were all PIC X. The items within the group cannot contain the VALUE, JUST, or SYNC clauses.

```
01  X VALUE SPACES.     Same as  01  X.
    05  Y    PIC X(3).           05  Y    PIC X(3) VALUE SPACES.
    05  Z    PIC X(2).           05  Z    PIC X(2) VALUE SPACES.
```

1.4   RECORD ALIGNMENT AND THE SYNC CLAUSE

Sometimes Used

COBOL does not automatically align BINARY, COMP-1, and COMP-2. If the numbers are not properly aligned, IBM COBOL moves the numbers to a work area to perform arithmetic operations, which may be inefficient. The SYNC clause is an option coded for elementary items to align data on the proper word boundary. You code it as:

```
SYNC    or    SYNCHRONIZED LEFT    or    SYNCHRONIZED RIGHT
```

IBM COBOL and Micro Focus COBOL, but not the ANSI standard or Fujitsu COBOL, permit SYNC to be coded for a group level. This acts the same as if all elementary items within it had SYNC coded.

Numbers are unaligned if SYNC is omitted. If SYNC is used for a table, each table element is aligned. SYNC aligns only BINARY, COMP-1, and COMP-2 data items. IBM COBOL aligns data types as follows.

BINARY S9 to S9(4)	Half-word
BINARY S9(5) to S9(18)	Full-word
COMP-1	Full-word
COMP-2	Double-word or eight bytes
All else	Byte boundary, no need for SYNC

IBM COBOL aligns the level number 01 for each record on a double-word boundary. It also aligns the first item in the Data Division on a double-word boundary.

It aligns level number 77 items on a full-word boundary. SYNC is in the ANSI standard, but the standard leaves the actual synchronization computer-dependent.

When data items within a record are aligned, some wasted space, termed *slack bytes,* may result. For example, suppose an IBM COBOL data item aligned on a double word is followed by an item aligned on a full word, and then followed by an item aligned on a double word. The result is a full word of 4 slack bytes. You must count these slack bytes in determining the size of a record. The record in the following example is 32 bytes in length.

```
01  A.
    05  B                          COMP-2 SYNC.
        [Aligned on a double word.]
    05  C                          PIC X(2).
        [Two slack bytes inserted here.]
    05  D                          PIC S9(5) BINARY SYNC.
        [Aligned on a full word.]
    05  E                          COMP-1 SYNC.
        [Aligned on a full word.]
[Four slack bytes inserted here.]
    05  F                          COMP-2 SYNC.
        [Aligned on a double word.]
```

TIP   *Slack bytes are confusing. Avoid them by placing all the double-word alignment items first in the record, followed by all the full-word alignment items, followed by all the half-word alignment items, followed by all the remaining items.*

Another alternative is to not code SYNC and live with whatever efficiency penalty results for computations. A final alternative is to not use BINARY, COMP-1, or COMP-2 items in records.

11.5   DOCUMENTING RECORDS

Essential

TIP   *Treat the documentation of records, especially those describing I/O records, as the most important of all program documentation.*

You can read a program and understand the computations done on the data from the statements, but unless you understand the data, the program will have little meaning. There are many ways to document records, and many installations have detailed standards. The following are suggestions.

TIP *Keep as much documentation in the source by using comments so that the documentation gets changed when the program is changed and so that the documentation does not get lost.*

Document the records with comments, placing them on the right side of the page so that they do not distract from the data descriptions. The data descriptions describe the form of the data, and the comments describe its meaning. Include the following in the comments:

- A short description of each data item.
- The meaning of values within the item. This applies mainly to flags and codes.

```
05  FLSA  PIC X.
*       Exemption code.
*       E - Exempt.
*       N - Nonexempt.
05  The-Status   PIC X.
*       Marital status.
*       M - Married.
*       S - Single.
```

You should include three other items for I/O records.

- A short description of the file.
- The record length in bytes. The reader will want to know this, and here is the best place to document it.
- The relative byte location of each data item. You need this to specify the sort fields for external sorts and to locate data items in a file dump. You must do this anyway to compute the record length, and it is little extra effort to document it at the same time. Place the relative byte locations in a comment following the item. If you must insert a field, all the following relative byte locations must be recomputed. Some compilers compute the relative byte locations and print them on the source listing, obviating the need for the relative byte locations.

Give the level 01 items a short name and append this name to all items within the record. This way, it is apparent which record they belong to when they are used in the program.

```
******** PAY is the master payroll file.
******** Record length is 400 bytes.
 01  Pay.
   05  Pay-Name                    PIC X(25).
```

```
*           Name of person.              Bytes 1-25.
 05   Pay-Code                           PIC X.
*           Type of pay.                 Byte 26.
*           H - Hourly.
*           S - Salaried.
 05   Pay-Salary                         PIC S999V99.
*           Hourly rate.                 Bytes 27-31.
```

Documentation of this type is easy to maintain, because it is right there to change when the record description is changed. Keep all the I/O records in a COPY library, as described in Chapter 19, so that all programs using the file will automatically include the file documentation. All the file documentation then exists in one place and is fully descriptive.

11.6 GROUP ITEM OPERATIONS

Essential

You can operate on elementary items within a record the same as any data item, although the data names may have to be qualified to make them unique. Group items named in expressions are treated as elementary alphanumeric data items. Group item names can appear only in nonarithmetic expressions, such as the IF, MOVE, and INSPECT statements. (They may also appear in arithmetic operations that contain the CORR phrase, but this is a different type of operation.) The following example illustrates the treatment of group items in expressions.

```
01  Y.
    05  B         PIC S9(7) PACKED-DECIMAL.
    05  C.
        10  D     PIC X(10).
        10  E     PIC S99.
    □   □   □
```

MOVE SPACES TO Y
[Blanks are moved to the entire record without conversion, just as if Y had been declared as an elementary data item with PIC X(16). Note that this moves blanks into B and E, which are described as numeric items. An error will occur if they are used in an arithmetic expression, because they contain invalid data.]

MOVE ZEROS TO Y
[This moves 16 zero characters to Y. It also moves character data into the PACKED-DECIMAL identifier B, and a data exception will occur if B is used in an arithmetic expression. However, E now contains valid data.]

The IF statement can test group or elementary items. It treats a group item as an elementary alphanumeric data item.

IF Y = SPACES THEN …   [Y is considered to be PIC X(16).]

1.7   INITIALIZING RECORDS

COBOL provides two ways of initializing data items: by using the VALUE clause or the INITIALIZE statement.

1.7.1   Initializing Data Items

Essential

When a record is created as an output record, you must first initialize it, generally by moving spaces to the alphanumeric fields and zeros to the numeric fields. Consider the following record to be initialized:

```
01  A.
    05  B                   PIC X(10).
    05  C                   PIC S9(5) PACKED-DECIMAL.
    05  D                   PIC X(3).
    05  E                   PIC S9(5) PACKED-DECIMAL.
```

You can initialize the record by coding VALUE clauses to assign initial values to the elementary items.

```
01  A.
    05  B                   PIC X(10) VALUE SPACES.
    05  C                   PIC S9(5) PACKED-DECIMAL
                            VALUE ZERO.
    05  D                   PIC X(3) VALUE SPACES.
    05  E                   PIC S9(5) PACKED-DECIMAL
                            VALUE ZERO.
```

You can also initialize a record by moving values to the elementary items:

```
MOVE SPACES TO B, D
MOVE ZEROS TO C, E
```

The easiest way to initialize a record is to move SPACES to the record as a group item and then move ZEROS to the numeric items.

```
MOVE SPACES TO A
MOVE ZEROS TO C, E
```

1.7.2   The INITIALIZE Statement

Essential

The INITIALIZE statement saves you having to write several MOVE statements to initialize data. You write it as

```
INITIALIZE data-name, data-name, …, data-name
```

The *data-name* cannot contain a RENAMES clause or be an index. However, it can be a data item that is itself indexed. INITIALIZE moves SPACES to all alphabetic, alphanumeric, and alphanumeric-edited items; it moves ZEROS to all numeric and numeric-edited items. For example, the record A at the beginning of this section can be initialized as follows:

```
INITIALIZE A     Same as     MOVE SPACES TO B, D
                             MOVE ZEROS TO C, E
```

You can also add the REPLACING clause to the INITIALIZE statement to restrict the initialization to specific types of data and assign values other than SPACES and ZEROS:

```
INITIALIZE data-name REPLACING format DATA BY value
```

The *value* can be an identifier or literal. The *format* can be any of the following: NUMERIC, ALPHABETIC, ALPHANUMERIC, NUMERIC-EDITED, or ALPHANUMERIC-EDITED. The *value* and *format* must be of a compatible data type with the *data-name*. For example:

```
INITIALIZE A REPLACING NUMERIC BY 10
```

Same as

```
MOVE 10 TO C, E
```

You can also write several phrases following REPLACING, but you must use a different category each time. Note also that you code REPLACING only once.

```
INITIALIZE A REPLACING NUMERIC BY 2
                       ALPHANUMERIC BY ALL "X"
```

Same as

```
MOVE 2 TO C, E
MOVE ALL "X" TO B, D
```

When you use the REPLACING for a group item, only elementary items within the group that match the type are initialized. If you use REPLACING for an elementary item and it doesn't match the type, nothing is initialized. The following statement is ignored.

```
INITIALIZE C REPLACING ALPHANUMERIC BY ALL "X"
```

When you initialize a group item, any FILLER or unnamed data items subordinate to it are not initialized. Chapter 13 describes how to assign initial values to tables.

PROPOSED NEW ANSI STANDARD: Check Compiler to See if Implemented

The new ANSI standard lets you initialize FILLER and unnamed data items by adding the FILLER phrase.

```
INITIALIZE data-name WITH FILLER …
```

You can initialize the data-name structure to the initial values coded for it by the VALUE clauses. To do this, you code the DEFAULT phrase.

```
INITIALIZE data-name TO DEFAULT
```

You can initialize all items of one or more *categories* (ALPHABETIC, ALPHANUMERIC, ALPHANUMERIC-EDITED, BOOLEAN, NATIONAL, NATIONAL-EDITED, NUMERIC, NUMERIC-EDITED, or ALL to include them all) to a value by coding the following. If the items in data-name or items subordinate to it contain VALUE clauses, the items are initialized to these values. Those without VALUE clauses are initialized to ZERO or SPACES.

```
INITIALIZE data-name category TO VALUE
```

11.8   REDEFINITION OF STORAGE

11.8.1   The REDEFINES Clause

Essential

The REDEFINES clause assigns different data names and descriptions to the same storage by redefining one data item to occupy the same storage as another. The general form of writing the REDEFINES clause is

```
nn   new-item REDEFINES redefined-item    PIC …
```

As an example, suppose that you wanted to solve a year-2000 problem by storing the year in the form 1999 rather than as two digits in the form 99, and you want to do this without expanding the record in the file. You have the following record description.

```
01  Some-Date.
    05  Year                  PIC 99.
```

The *Year* occupies two bytes. You can redefine it as BINARY and store a number as large as 32,767 in it. The following code shows how:

```
01  Some-Date.
    05  Year                  PIC 99.
    05  Year-Binary REDEFINES Year PIC 9(4) BINARY.
```

Now you can treat the same two bytes of storage as alphanumeric by referring to it as *Year* and as binary by referring to it as *Year-Binary.* Because you can't move *Year* to *Year-Binary,* another item is needed to hold the year while COBOL moves it back and forth.

```
01  A-Year                       PIC 99.
    □   □   □
    MOVE Year TO A-Year
    MOVE A-Year TO Year-Binary  [This converts the two-digit year to binary.]
```

Assuming you know that the earliest date in the file was 1960, the following converts any dates from 60 to 99 to be 1960 to 1999. Dates from 00 to 59 are converted to 2000 to 2059.

```
IF Year-Binary > 60
    THEN ADD 1900 TO Year-Binary
    ELSE ADD 2000 TO Year-Binary
END-IF
```

The level number of the redefining item, the item to the left of the REDE-FINES, must be the same as the level of the redefined item, and they cannot be level 66 or 88. The redefining item can be a data name or FILLER. The redefining item can also be a structure.

```
01  Out-Rec.
    05  Ax                       PIC S9(5) PACKED-DECIMAL.
    05  New-Ax REDEFINES Ax  PIC A(3).
    [It is given a name here.]
    05  FILLER                   REDEFINES Ax.
    [It can also be FILLER.]
    10  First-1              PIC X(2).
    10  Next-1               PIC X.
    05                           REDEFINES Ax.
    [Or you do not need to give it a name.]
    10  First-2              PIC X.
    10  Next-2               PIC X(2).
```

Don't qualify the redefined item following the REDEFINES, even if the name is not unique. COBOL doesn't need the qualification, because it knows which item you mean from where you place the redefining item containing the REDE-FINES.

The redefining item must follow the redefined item, with no intervening nonredefined items. Note that the same area can be redefined more than once.

```
Incorrect:                      Correct:
01  A   PIC X(10).              01  A   PIC X(10).
01  B   PIC X(10).              01  B   REDEFINES A PIC X(10).
01  C   REDEFINES A PIC X(10).  01  C   REDEFINES A PIC X(10).
```

The ANSI standard doesn't let a redefined item contain a REDEFINES. IBM and PC COBOL do. For them, you could code the following for C in the previous correct example.

```
01  C  REDEFINES B       PIC X(10).
```

For a level 01 item, the length of the redefined item can be shorter or longer than the redefining item. (However, the redefining item must not be longer than the redefined item if the redefined item is declared EXTERNAL, as described in Chapter 19.)

```
01  A.                   PIC X(10).
01  B  REDEFINES A       PIC X(2).
    [It can be shorter.]
01  C  REDEFINES A       PIC X(20).
    [It can also be longer.]
```

However, if the level is not 01 or the redefined item is declared EXTERNAL, the redefining item must be equal to or shorter than the redefined item.

```
01  A.
    05  B                PIC X(10).
    05  C REDEFINES B     PIC X(10).      [It can be the same.]
    05  D REDEFINES B     PIC X(2).       [It can be shorter.]
    05  E REDEFINES B     PIC X(20).      [Wrong; can't be longer.]
```

The REDEFINES clause must immediately follow the data name.

```
Incorrect:                    Correct:
01 B PIC X(5) REDEFINES A.    01  B  REDEFINES A PIC X(5).
```

The redefined item can contain a VALUE clause, but the redefining item cannot—unless it is a level 88 item. The redefining item may contain the SYNC clause, as long as the synchronization does not cause the redefining item to extend beyond the redefined item.

Incorrect:
```
01  A                    PIC S9(5) BINARY.
01  B  REDEFINES A       PIC S9(5) BINARY VALUE 10.
```

Correct:
```
01  A                    PIC S9(5) BINARY VALUE 10.
01  B  REDEFINES A       PIC S9(5) BINARY.
```

Although level 88 items cannot be redefined, both the redefining item and the redefined item may have level 88 condition names.

```
01  A                    PIC S9(5) BINARY SYNC
                         VALUE 10.
```

```
      88  BIG-A                         VALUE 200.
      01  B   REDEFINES A               PIC S9(5) BINARY.
          88  BIG-B                     VALUE 100.
```

Redefinition can conserve central storage by allowing the same storage to be reused for different purposes, but you must use it for only one purpose at a time. Avoid such redefinition because it leads to confusion and errors. Central storage is not that scarce a resource.

TIP *Use redefinition only when you need to overlay data of one type with another or when a file can contain more than one record type.*

When a file can contain more than one record type, make each record have a flag that specifies the record type. Then interrogate the flag to determine which redefinition item describes the record. (REDEFINES cannot be used for 01 level items in the record area of the File Section as described in Chapter 15. There, you implicitly redefine level 01 records by placing one after the other.) The following example illustrates a record with a field that may contain two data types.

```
01  Rec.
    05  Rec-Type                    PIC X.
    05  Rec-C                       PIC X(4).
    05  Rec-Num REDEFINES Rec-C     PIC S9(7) PACKED-DECIMAL.
```

This record might contain alphanumeric data, referred to by *Rec-C,* or a packed-decimal number, referred to by *Rec-Num,* depending on the value contained in *Rec-Type.* Redefinition also allows data of one type to be stored in a data item of another type without conversion.

```
      MOVE "ABCD" TO Rec-C      [Rec-Num also contains "ABCD".]
```

You can also redefine tables to occupy the same storage.

```
01  Table-A.
    05  Level-1                  OCCURS 100 TIMES.
        10  X                    PIC S9(5) PACKED-DECIMAL
                                 OCCURS 50 TIMES.
01  Table-B REDEFINES Table-A.
    05  Level-1                  OCCURS 100 TIMES.
        10  Y                    PIC X(3) OCCURS 50 TIMES.
```

The redefined item cannot itself contain an OCCURS clause. However, the redefined item may be subordinate to an item containing an OCCURS clause, but not an OCCURS DEPENDING ON clause. This means that table elements can be redefined.

```
01  Table-A.
    05  Level-1                 OCCURS 100 TIMES.
        10  X                   OCCURS 50 TIMES.
            15  Y               PIC S9(5) PACKED-DECIMAL.
            15  Z  REDEFINES Y  PIC X(2).
```

An OCCURS DEPENDING ON clause cannot be coded for a redefining item, for a redefined item, or for any item subordinate to them.

11.8.2 The RENAMES Clause

Rarely Used

The REDEFINES clause just described redefines one record over the same storage area as another. In contrast, the level 66 RENAMES clause allows a single data name to rename a series of data items within a record. There are two forms. In the first form, *data-name-1* simply renames *data-name-2*. This is not particularly useful.

```
66  data-name-1  RENAMES data-name-2.
```

In the second form, *data-name-1* renames all items from *data-name-2* through *data-name-3*.

```
66  data-name-1  RENAMES data-name-2 THRU data-name-3.
```

The following example illustrates the RENAMES clause.

```
01  A.
    05  B.
        10  C           PIC X(3).
        10  D           PIC X(4).
    05  E               PIC X(5).
    05  F.
        10  G           PIC X(6).
        10  H           PIC X(7).
66  W   RENAMES C.          [W is another name for C.]
66  X   RENAMES B.
        [X is a group item containing 7 characters and is just another name for B.]
66  Y   RENAMES B THRU G.
        [Y is a group item containing 18 characters. It consists of the storage of the C, D,
        E, and G data items.]
```

You cannot use *data-name-1* as a qualifier (*C* IN *X* is invalid). You can only qualify it with the record name within which it renames items (*W* IN *B* is valid). If an elementary item is renamed, the level 66 item assumes the attributes of the item renamed. When group items are renamed, the level 66 item is also a group item.

The level number 66 RENAMES clause must immediately follow the last item in the record description, and you can code several RENAMES clauses for a single record. You cannot rename level numbers 01, 66, 77, and 88 items, but you can rename both elementary items and group items within a record. If the RENAMES *data-name-1* THRU *data-name-2* form is used, *data-name-2* must follow *data-name-1* in the record, and it may be subordinate to it. You cannot rename items that contain an OCCURS clause or are subordinate to an item containing an OCCURS clause. This means that an element of a table cannot be the subject of the RENAMES.

EXERCISES

1. Assume that a record is to contain an employee's name, social security number, age, date of birth, annual salary, and number of dependents. Define and document the record to contain this information. Define the name so that you can retrieve the initials and the last name.

2. Assume that you are being passed a transaction generated by the computer. Each 80-character line contains 10 fields of 8 characters each. The first character of each field describes the data contained in the remaining 7 characters of the field. The fields are as follows:

First Character	Remainder of Field
1	7 characters
2	3 characters, left-justified
3	4 characters, right-justified
4	7-digit number
5	2 numbers, one with 3 digits and one with 4 digits
6	5-digit number, left-justified, with 2 positions to right of assumed decimal point

Define a record to contain this record and allow you to manipulate it. Edit the numeric data to ensure its validity for COBOL.

3. Assume that an old program is run on a new computer, and it terminates with an error. Fortunately, it tells you the statement number at which it terminated. It terminated in the second of the following two statements:

```
MOVE SPACE TO First-Byte
MOVE Left-Part TO Right-Part
```

Next, you look in the Data Division and find the following record:

```
01  Bit-Table.
    05  What-It-Contains    PIC X(200).
    05  Redefine-It   REDEFINES What-It-Contains.
        10  First-Byte      PIC X.
```

```
        10  Right-Part              PIC X(199).
01      Left-Part REDEFINES Bit-Table PIC X(199).
```

What was the programmer attempting to do? Why might it be failing on the new computer? Is this a good programming practice?

4. Two records are defined as follows:

```
01  One.
    02  A.
        03  B                   PIC X(3).
        03  C                   PIC S999 PACKED-DECIMAL.
        03  D.
            04  E               PIC S9(6) PACKED-DECIMAL.
            04  F               PIC X(2).
    02  G                       PIC X(6).
    02  H                       PIC X(6).
01  Two.
    02  J.
        03  D                   PIC X(3).
        03  C                   PIC S9(3) PACKED-DECIMAL.
        03  Q.
            04  E               PIC S9(6) PACKED-DECIMAL.
            04  F               PIC X(2).
    02  R                       PIC X(6).
    02  S                       PIC X(6).
```

Note the elements that participate in the following statements.

```
    MOVE Two TO One
    MOVE CORR Two TO One
    MOVE CORR J TO A IN One
    MOVE S TO G
```

5. Use the INITIALIZE statement to initialize the records in Problem 4 with values as follows:

One. Initialize nonnumeric identifiers to blank and numeric identifiers to 0.

Two. Initialize nonnumeric identifiers to all "−" and numeric identifiers to 1.

CHAPTER 12

PRINTED OUTPUT

Printing reports is one of the most important and difficult parts of programming in COBOL. Don't skip this chapter.

12.1 OVERVIEW

Essential

Printed output, the most common form of output, is often surprisingly complicated. It is read by humans rather than by a computer, and it is two-dimensional, consisting of characters within a line (a line corresponds to a record) and lines on a page. It also requires an aesthetic sense that is not always inherent in the cool logic generally required of programmers. But the most difficult part of printing output is the reaction of the end user to the printed page. Somehow, printed output evokes a response from the reader much like that of newlyweds to a roomful of new furniture. They have definite ideas where each piece should go, but after they see it there, they are apt to change their minds. The same occurs when the reader first sees a report. This is especially true of management reports, which are less standardized and are used for making decisions. It is not necessarily capriciousness on the reader's part to want to make changes to the report. Only by seeing actual numbers and working with them can the reader know what further information is needed. It is hard for a programmer to second-guess the reader. Although readers should be pressed to think about their needs, the needs may not be apparent until the information is used.

The PC has increased the level of expectation for reports. The color graphics display and laser printer, with their pie charts and three-dimensional bar charts, make the typical COBOL report containing rows and columns of numbers look unappealing. Rather than trying to fight this battle using Mainframe COBOL, you would be better off to download the data and use PC software to display the reports.

The first thing to come to terms with in designing reports is that they are likely to change.

TIP *Make the reports easy to change. Consider using one of the various report and graphical packages available on the mainframe and PC as an alternative to generating reports with COBOL or use the COBOL report writer described in Chapter 18.*

12.2   PRINTERS

Essential

Most mainframe printers today are laser printers, which print a page of output at a time. The paper is normally 11 inches wide by 8½ inches, with 66 lines per page and 132 characters per line. However, they can also print 110 and 204 characters per line. Printers can also print 88 lines per page. The paper can be oriented 8½ inches wide by 11 inches for letter format. Other paper sizes are also available, but these are the most common.

There is a wide range of laser and inkjet printers on PCs. They may or may not have the same capability as the mainframe printers. Their usual paper orientation is 8½ inches wide by 11 inches, and some have the ability to print on paper that is 11 inches wide by 8½ inches. Some can also print 14-inch-wide-by-11-inch paper.

You make multiple copies by printing the report several times. In OS/390, you can print a file several times with the COPIES subparameter in the DD statement, as follows:

```
//GO.ddname DD SYSOUT=A,COPIES=copies
```

Special forms can also be made in many sizes and are most widely used to print checks. The special forms can have anything preprinted on them and often come in colors.

TIP *Avoid using special forms if you can. They are expensive and a royal pain to everyone. A report change can mean designing a new form, with the associated design and delivery time.*

12.3   PRINT FILES

Print files require formatting data to fit it on the printed page and are rather involved.

12.3.1   Specifying the Printer

Essential

You must write the SELECT statement for print files, just as for any other file. In Mainframe COBOL, you specify a *ddname* and then code a JCL DD statement as follows. JCL (Job Control Language) is a language used on the OS/390 mainframe to run jobs.

```
SELECT file-name ASSIGN TO ddname.
   □  □  □
//ddname DD SYSOUT=A
```

The SYSOUT=A specifies the standard printer at most installations, but other output classes may be required or available.

In PC COBOL, you specify the printer by coding "LPT*n*:" as the *ddname* for Micro Focus COBOL and PRINTER or LPT*n* or COM*n* for Fujitsu COBOL. The ORGANIZATION IS LINE SEQUENTIAL, described in Chapter 15, is optional, but you should code it for Micro Focus COBOL.

```
SELECT file-name ASSIGN TO "LPT1:"   [Micro Focus]
   ORGANIZATION IS LINE SEQUENTIAL.
SELECT file-name ASSIGN TO PRINTER   [Fujitsu]
```

12.3.2 The FD Entry

Essential

You describe print files the same as normal files, with the record length set to the number of print positions. IBM mainframe printers are controlled by the first character position in each line. Mainframe COBOL automatically accounts for this unless you code the NOADV compile option, described in Chapter 33. NOADV requires you to set aside the first character of each line for the carriage control character controlling the printer. You never need to store anything in this position—the compiler does it for you. If you accept the default ADV compiler option, COBOL automatically adds an extra byte to the record described in the FD for any file that has the LINAGE clause or for which there are WRITE ADVANCING statements. If you are writing an application to be compatible with PC COBOL, code the ADV option for Mainframe COBOL. Here is a typical FD entry.

```
FD  file-name BLOCK CONTAINS 0 RECORDS.
01  print-line                    PIC X(132).
```

You define the print lines as records and move values to the data items within the record. In Mainframe COBOL, the WRITE statement automatically moves a carriage control character to the first character position of the record for the file. You must open print files the same as any other file.

12.3.3 Statements for Printing

For reference, here are the usual statements needed for printing.

```
IDENTIFICATION DIVISION.
PROGRAM-ID.  program-name.
```

```
      INPUT-OUTPUT SECTION.
      FILE-CONTROL.
           SELECT file-name ASSIGN TO ddname.
      DATA DIVISION.
      FILE SECTION.
      FD   file-name
           BLOCK CONTAINS 0 RECORDS.        [Mainframe COBOL only]
      01   print-line   PIC X(132).
      WORKING-STORAGE SECTION.
      01   data-line …
           ☐   ☐   ☐
      PROCEDURE DIVISION.
      A100-Begin.
           OPEN OUTPUT file-name
           WRITE print-line FROM data-line
             AFTER ADVANCING n
           CLOSE file-name
           GOBACK.
      END PROGRAM program-name.
```

12.3.4 The WRITE ADVANCING Statement

Essential

You append the ADVANCING phrase to the WRITE statement to print lines, and
IBM COBOL then inserts the proper carriage control character in the first character position of the printed line. (ADVANCING is not supported in OS/390 VSAM
files. In OS/2, they are not supported for Btrieve files, and BEFORE is not supported for line-sequential files).

```
                              AFTER
                              BEFORE
      WRITE record FROM identifier _____ ADVANCING integer LINES
      WRITE Out-Rec FROM Current-Rec AFTER ADVANCING 1
```

The AFTER prints the line after advancing the *integer* lines, and the BEFORE
prints the line before advancing the *integer* lines. The *integer* is an integer
numeric literal or elementary data item. A value of 0 is valid and the line is left
where it is.

To start a new page before or after printing, you can code

```
                              AFTER
                              BEFORE
      WRITE record FROM identifier _____ ADVANCING PAGE
```

If you omit the ADVANCING phrase, lines are written as if you had coded
AFTER ADVANCING 1 for single spacing. In Micro Focus COBOL and the ANSI
Standard, you can't code WRITE ADVANCING for files with the LINAGE clause.

You can omit the FROM phrase to write directly from the record area as
explained in Chapter 15.

```
      WRITE Print-Line AFTER ADVANCING PAGE
```

12.3.5 Mnemonic Names

Rarely Used

ADVANCING may also specify a mnemonic name that is defined in the SPECIAL-NAMES section and is associated with a carriage control character. The mnemonic names for IBM COBOL are shown here:

```
ENVIRONMENT DIVISION.
CONFIGURATION SECTION.
SPECIAL-NAMES.
    CSP IS name-0        [Suppress spacing.]
    C01 IS name-1        [Eject to a new page.]
    Cnn IS name-nn       [Skip to channel nn, where nn is 02 through 12. The action is
                         installation-defined. In AIX, OS/2, and Windows, it advances
                         one line.]
    AFP-5A IS name.      [Advanced function printing.]
```

The following example uses mnemonic names for suppressing spacing and ejecting to a new page:

```
SPECIAL-NAMES.
    CSP IS Over-Print
    C01 IS New-Page.
    □   □   □
    WRITE Rpt-Record FROM Rpt-Line
          AFTER ADVANCING New-Page
    WRITE Rpt-Record FROM Rpt-Line
          AFTER ADVANCING Over-Print
    WRITE Rpt-Record FROM Rpt-Line
          AFTER ADVANCING 1 LINE
```
[The use of mnemonic names does not preclude the use of *integer* LINES.]

12.3.6 The AT EOP Phrase

Rarely Used

You can add AT EOP (END-OF-PAGE) and NOT AT EOP phrases to specify imperative statements to execute if an end of page occurs. You must then code the LINAGE clause in the FD for the file. In IBM COBOL, but not in PC COBOL or the ANSI standard, you can code EOP with ADVANCING LINES and ADVANCING PAGE. Add the END-WRITE scope terminator if you use EOP.

```
WRITE record FROM identifier
    AFTER
    BEFORE
    _____ ADVANCING integer LINES
    AT EOP imperative-statements
    NOT AT EOP imperative-statements
END-WRITE
```

```
WRITE Rpt-Record FROM Rpt-Line
   AFTER ADVANCING 1 LINE
   AT EOP PERFORM C20-New-Page
END-WRITE
```

EOP is not supported in Workstation COBOL for line-sequential and Btrieve files. In OS/390, it is not supported for VSAM files.

12.3.7   The LINAGE Clause

Sometimes Used

Normally, you don't want to print a full page; you want a margin at the top and bottom. You specify the number of lines per page and top and bottom margins by adding the LINAGE clause to the FD for the print file. LINAGE is also required if you code an EOP phrase in the WRITE statement.

```
FD  Rpt-O BLOCK CONTAINS 0 RECORDS
    LINAGE IS page-lines LINES
            WITH FOOTING AT footing-line       [Optional]
            LINES AT TOP top-margin            [Optional]
            LINES AT BOTTOM bottom-margin.     [Optional]
```

All identifiers or literals must be unsigned integer. The four parts of the LINAGE phrase are all optional and have the following effect:

IS *page-lines* LINES. This specifies the number of lines that can be printed on the page (called the page body) and must be greater than zero. It excludes the margins.

WITH FOOTING AT *footing-line*. This specifies the first line number of the footing area within the body of the page. The *footing-line* must be greater than zero and less than the last line of the page body (*page-lines*). If you omit WITH FOOTING, *page-lines* is assumed.

LINES AT TOP *top-margin*. This specifies the number of lines of top margin to leave and may be zero. Zero is assumed if TOP is omitted.

LINES AT BOTTOM *bottom-margin*. This specifies the number of lines of bottom margin and may be zero. Zero is assumed if BOTTOM is omitted.

Either unsigned literal integers or data items can be used to specify the values. Figure 12.1 shows how the values relate to the page. Note the following equation:

Logical page size = top-margin + page-lines + bottom-margin

In Micro Focus COBOL and the ANSI standard, you can't code WRITE ADVANCING for files with the LINAGE clause. The LINAGE clause causes IBM COBOL to append a carriage control character automatically to each line written

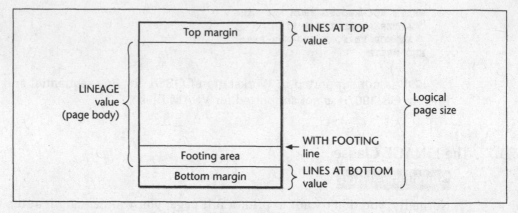

FIGURE 12.1 Phrases of the LINEAGE clause.

for the file. Because of this, IBM COBOL allows you to code WRITE ADVANCING for files with the LINAGE clause. However, if you make the file EXTERNAL and use it in several subprograms, you must code LINAGE with the same values in all the subprograms describing the file. Then you can also intermix WRITE and WRITE ADVANCING statements. If you don't code the LINAGE clause for an EXTERNAL file, then if any subprogram uses a WRITE ADVANCING, all the subprograms for the file must use WRITE ADVANCING.

Here is an example of printing a file with the LINAGE clause:

```
FD  Rpt-O BLOCK CONTAINS 0 RECORDS
    LINAGE IS 55 LINES
    LINES AT TOP 5
    LINES AT BOTTOM 6.
01  Rpt-Record                      PIC X(132).
    □  □  □
WORKING-STORAGE SECTION.
01  Rpt-Line.
    05  FILLER                      PIC X(6) VALUE "NAME: ".
    05  Rpt-Name                    PIC X(5).
    05  FILLER                      PIC X(3) VALUE SPACES.
    05  Rpt-Age                     PIC 999.
    □  □  □
    OPEN OUTPUT Rpt-O
    MOVE "SMITH" TO Rpt-Name
    MOVE 21 TO Rpt-Age
    WRITE Rpt-Record FROM Rpt-Line
      AT EOP MOVE "Y" TO New-Page-Flag
      NOT AT EOP MOVE "N" TO New-Page-Flag
    END-WRITE
```

The following line prints with single spacing:

```
NAME: SMITH    021
```

12.3.8 The LINAGE-COUNTER Special Register

> **Rarely Used**

When you code the LINAGE clause in an FD, COBOL automatically creates a LINAGE-COUNTER special register for the file to contain the current line position in the page body. That is, line 1 is the first line below any top margin. COBOL initializes it to a value of one when you open the file and for each new page. If there is more than one FD with a LINAGE clause, you must qualify the LINAGE-COUNTER to specify which file it belongs to by writing LINAGE-COUNTER IN *file-name.* You can retrieve the value of the LINAGE-COUNTER, but you can't change it. LINAGE-COUNTER has the same PIC and USAGE as the LINAGE identifier (or binary if it is a literal).

```
MOVE LINAGE-COUNTER IN file-name TO identifier
IF LINAGE-COUNTER IN file-name > 30 THEN ...
```

12.4 PRINTING NUMERIC DATA

> **Essential**

You must often edit numeric data for printing to suppress leading zeros and insert commas and decimal points. You edit numbers by defining an item in the print line that contains special editing characters in the PIC clause, and then move the number to the item to convert and edit it. The PIC clause cannot contain more than 30 edit characters. (The new ANSI standard expands this to 60 characters.)

The 9, S, V, and P edit characters are the only ones permitted for external decimal numbers, and they do not preclude arithmetic operations from being performed on the item. These edit characters were described in Chapter 9, and they are included here again for review. Note that you can write the edit characters in upper- or lowercase: S9V9 or s9v9.

12.4.1 Edit Characters for External Decimal Numbers

> **Essential**

9 (Decimal Digit)

The *9* edit character in a PIC clause represents a decimal digit (0 to 9) within the number and occupies a character position. The 9 does not imply a signed number; the S, +, −, DB, or CR edit characters do this.

```
01  X    PIC 9(4).                    [X occupies 4 character positions.]
    □   □   □
    MOVE 2 TO X                        [X contains "0002".]
    MOVE -2 TO X                       [X contains "0002".]
```

S (Sign)

The *S* edit character specifies that the number is signed, but it does not cause the sign to be printed nor to occupy a character position. The sign is carried in the left half of the rightmost byte. The S must be the leftmost edit character if included.

```
01  X    PIC S999.                    [X occupies 3 character positions.]
    □  □  □
    MOVE 2 TO X           [X contains "002" as a positive number.]
    MOVE -2 TO X          [X contains "002" as a negative number.]
```

V (Decimal Alignment)

A single *V* edit character coded in a PIC clause indicates the position of the internal decimal point. If V is not coded, the decimal point is assumed to be to the right of the number. V is not stored as a character and does not occupy a character position.

```
01  X    PIC S999V99.                 [X occupies 5 character positions.]
    □  □  □
    MOVE 2.3 TO X        [X contains "00230" as a positive number.]
    MOVE -2.3 TO X       [X contains "00230" as a negative number.]
```

High- or low-order digits are truncated if the value is too large to be contained in the identifier:

```
    MOVE 1234.123 TO X              [X contains "23412" as a positive number.]
```

P (Scaling Factor)

The *P* edit character specifies a decimal point outside the range of the number. You code the Ps to the left or right of the 9s. The number of Ps indicates the number of places to the left or right of the number the decimal point lies. (The number is limited to 18 total digits, including the positions specified by the P.)

```
01  X    PIC SP(3)999.                [X occupies 3 character positions.]
    □  □  □
    MOVE .000476 TO X
    [X contains "476", but is treated as .000476 in arithmetic computations.]
```

```
01  Y    PIC S999P(3).                [Y occupies 3 character positions.]
    □  □  □
    MOVE 476000 TO Y
    [Y contains "476", but is treated as 476,000 in arithmetic computations.]
```

The V edit character may be coded, but it is not needed, because the P specifies the assumed decimal point. The *X* and *Y* could also be coded as follows:

```
01  X                       PIC SVP(3)999.
01  Y                       PIC S999P(3)V.
```

The next group of edit characters inserts such nonnumeric characters as the comma, decimal point, and blanks for printing numbers. If the data item also contains numeric edit characters, the item is termed a *numeric-edited* data item; otherwise, it is termed an *alphanumeric-edited* data item. (Both types are also referred to as *external* data, because the data is formatted for external display or printing.) You cannot perform arithmetic operations on numeric-edited or alphanumeric-edited data items.

12.4.2 Edit Characters for Numeric-Edited Data

`Essential`

The following edit characters are mainly used for numeric-edited data. Alphabetic data items may contain the B edit character. Alphanumeric-edited data items may contain the 0, B, and / edit characters. Numeric-edited data may have a VALUE clause to assign a value to the item, and the VALUE must be an alphanumeric literal or figurative constant, but not a number. In the following example, the decimal point makes this numeric-edited data so the VALUE clause must be an alphanumeric literal.

```
01  An-Item                        PIC 999.99 VALUE "123".
```

In this example, the PIC describes an external decimal number, and so the VALUE clause must be a numeric literal.

```
01  Another-Item                   PIC 999V99 VALUE 123.
```

You can only assign alphanumeric literal initial values to numeric- or alphanumeric-edited data items. The value is not edited.

```
01  X    PIC ZZ9 VALUE "006".                [X contains "006".]
```

Numeric-edited items may contain any of the following edit characters, subject to their rules of construction, in addition to the edit characters already discussed.

Z (Leading Zero Suppression)
The Z edit character, like the 9 edit character, represents a decimal digit (0 to 9) within the number. However, the Z causes leading zeros to be replaced with blanks. Each Z occupies a character position and cannot appear to the right of a 9 edit character.

```
01  X    PIC ZZ9V99.                          [X occupies 5 character positions.]
    □  □  □
    MOVE 2.31 TO X                            [X contains "bb231".]
    MOVE 26.3 TO X                            [X contains "b2630".]
    MOVE .94 TO X                             [X contains "bb094".]
```

If the item contains all Zs and no 9 edit characters, COBOL sets the entire item to blanks if you store a value of zero in it. This includes any decimal points, commas, or other editing inserted by other edit characters. Coding all Zs is equivalent to coding the BLANK WHEN ZERO clause, described later in this chapter.

```
01  Y     PIC ZZZVZZ.
    □  □  □
    MOVE ZERO TO Y                          [Y contains "bbbbb".]
```

* (Leading Asterisks)

The * edit character is identical to the Z edit character, except that it replaces leading zeros with asterisks rather than blanks and is used for check protection. It cannot appear in the same PIC clause as the Z, nor can it appear to the right of a 9 edit character.

```
01  X     PIC **9V99.                       [X occupies 5 character positions.]
    □  □  □
    MOVE 26.31 TO X                         [X contains "*2631".]
```

If the item contains all *s and no 9 edit characters, COBOL sets the entire item to asterisks, except for any decimal point, if you store a zero value in the item. You cannot code BLANK WHEN ZERO with the * edit character.

```
01  Y                                PIC **.**.
    □  □  □
    MOVE ZERO TO Y                          [Y contains "**.**".]
```

The next group of edit characters—the +, −, DB, and CR—are for signed numbers. Only one can appear in a PIC clause. The S edit character must not be coded in combination with any of these. If the +, −, DB, or CR are not coded, minus numbers print with the minus sign indicated in the rightmost digit, as described earlier in Chapter 7 for the DISPLAY statement. Because no one would like to see −23 print as "2L", use the following edit characters when printing numbers.

− (Minus Sign)

The − edit character indicates a signed number. If the number is negative, a minus sign is inserted where the − appears in the PIC clause; a blank is inserted if the number is positive. The − must be either the first or last character in the PIC string. Code a string of −s on the left to represent numeric digits and suppress leading zeros in the same manner as the Z edit character. The minus is inserted to the left of the first nonzero digit if the number is negative; a blank is inserted if the number is positive. Each minus sign counts as a character position.

```
01  X    PIC ---9.                          [X occupies 4 character positions.]
    □  □  □
    MOVE -2 TO X                            [X contains "bb−2".]
    MOVE 2 TO X                             [X contains "bbb2".]
    MOVE 1234 TO X
```

[*X* contains "b234"; remember that a blank is inserted, not a digit. Also notice that the leading digit is truncated.]

```
01  Y    PIC 999-.                        [Y occupies 4 character positions.]
    □  □  □
    MOVE -2 TO Y                          [Y contains "002–".]
    MOVE 2 TO Y                           [Y contains "002b".]
01  Z                                 PIC -999.
    □  □  □
    MOVE 2 TO Z                           [Z contains "b002".]
    MOVE -2 TO Z                          [Z contains "–002".]
```

+ *(Plus Sign)*

The + edit character is identical to the – except it also inserts a + if the value is positive. The + must be the first or last character in the PIC string. Code a string of +s on the left to represent numeric digits and suppress leading zeros in the same manner as the Z edit character. The sign is inserted to the left of the first nonzero digit. Each plus sign counts as a character position.

```
01  X    PIC +999.                        [X occupies 4 character positions.]
    □  □  □
    MOVE 2 TO X                           [X contains "+002".]
    MOVE -2 TO X                          [X contains "–002".]
```

CR *(Credit Symbol)*

You can code a single *CR* edit character in the rightmost position of the PIC clause. If the number is negative, CR is inserted; otherwise, two blanks are inserted. CR counts as two character positions.

```
01  X    PIC 999CR.                       [X occupies 5 character positions.]
    □  □  □
    MOVE -27 TO X                         [X contains "027CR".]
    MOVE 27 TO X                          [X contains "027bb".]
```

DB *(Debit Symbol)*

The *DB* edit character is identical to the CR edit character, except that the DB is inserted if the number is negative.

```
01  X    PIC 99DB.                        [X occupies 5 character positions.]
    □  □  □
    MOVE -1 TO X                          [X contains "01DB".]
    MOVE 1 TO X                           [X contains "01bb".]
```

. *(Decimal Point)*

The *decimal point* edit character is inserted where it appears in the PIC clause, and it occupies a character position. You can code only one decimal point. It specifies the decimal alignment, so the V edit character must not be used. The decimal point cannot be the rightmost character in a PIC clause.

```
01  X    PIC ZZ9.99.                           [X occupies 6 character positions.]
    □  □  □
    MOVE 22.31 TO X                            [X contains "b22.31".]
```

, (Comma)

The *comma* edit character is inserted where it appears in the PIC clause, and it counts as a character position. If leading zeros are suppressed, the comma is replaced by a blank if all of the characters to the left of the comma are zero. The comma cannot be the rightmost character in the PIC clause.

```
01  X    PIC 9,999.                            [X occupies 5 character positions.]
    □  □  □
    MOVE 4 TO X                                [X contains "0,004".]
    MOVE 4000 TO X                             [X contains "4,000".]

01  Y    PIC Z,ZZ9.                            [Y occupies 5 character positions.]
    □  □  □
    MOVE 4 TO Y                                [Y contains "bbbb4".]
    MOVE 4000 TO Y                             [Y contains "4,000".]

01  W    PIC *,**9.                            [Y occupies 5 character positions.]
    □  □  □
    MOVE 4 TO W                                [W contains "****4".]

01  Z    PIC --,--9.                           [Z occupies 6 character positions.]
    □  □  □
    MOVE -4 TO Z                               [Z contains "bbbb-4".]
    MOVE -4000 TO Z                            [Z contains "-4,000".]
```

$ (Dollar Sign)

A single $ edit character is inserted where it appears in the PIC clause and counts as a character position. A string of $s represents numeric digits, suppressing leading zeros in the same manner as the Z edit character, and a single $ is inserted to the left of the first nonzero digit. The $ must be to the left of all 9 or V edit characters.

```
01  X    PIC $999.                             [X occupies 4 character positions.]
    □  □  □
    MOVE 4 TO X                                [X contains "$004".]

01  Y    PIC $$$9.                             [Y occupies 4 character positions.]
    □  □  □
    MOVE 4 TO Y                                [Y contains "bb$4".]
```

The edit characters +, –, *, Z, and $, when used as floating edit characters, cannot appear in the same PIC clause. That is, they are mutually exclusive (unless there is a single instance of the characters $–+).

B (Blank)

The *B* edit character causes a blank to be inserted wherever it appears in a PIC clause, and it counts as a character position.

```
01  X    PIC B9B9B.                          [X occupies 5 character positions.]
    □  □  □
    MOVE 21 TO X                             [X contains "b2b1b".]
    MOVE 123 TO X                            [X contains "b2b3b".]
```

0 (Zero)

The *0* edit character causes a zero to be inserted wherever it appears in a PIC clause, and it counts as a character position.

```
01  X    PIC 0990.                           [X occupies 4 character positions.]
    □  □  □
    MOVE 21 TO X                             [X contains "0210".]
    MOVE 123 TO X                            [X contains "0230".]
```

E (Floating-Point)

You can display floating-point numbers by coding a single *E* to separate the number from its exponent. The E occupies a character position. You can use either a + or − sign for both the number and its exponent. A + causes either a plus or minus sign to be inserted, and a − causes only minus signs to be inserted. You can't code a BLANK WITH ZERO, JUST, or VALUE clause when you code the E for floating-point. The exponent must be 99. A V or . can be coded to specify the internal or actual decimal point.

```
01  X    PIC +999V99E+99.                    [X occupies 10 character positions.]
01  Y    PIC -9.9999E-99.                    [Y occupies 11 character positions.]
    □  □  □
    MOVE 2.33E6 TO X                         [X contains "+23300E+04".]
    MOVE -2.33E6 TO Y                        [Y contains "−2.330E 06".]
```

X (Alphanumeric Character)

The *X* edit characters represent any alphanumeric character and occupy character positions.

```
01  Y    PIC X999X.                          [Y occupies 5 character positions.]
    □  □  □
    MOVE "(234)" TO Y                        [Y contains "(234)".]
```

A (Alphabetic Character)

The *A* edit characters represent any alphabetic characters or blanks and occupy character positions.

```
01  Y    PIC A999A.                          [Y occupies 5 character positions.]
    □  □  □
    MOVE "Z234Z" TO Y                        [Y contains "Z234Z".]
```

/ (Stroke Edit Character)

The / edit character causes a stroke (slash) character to be inserted wherever it appears in a PIC clause, and it occupies a character position.

```
01  X    PIC 99/99/9999.                    [X occupies 10 character positions.]
    □ □ □
    MOVE "12252003" TO X                    [X contains "12/25/2003".]
```

BLANK WHEN ZERO

The *BLANK WHEN ZEROS* or *ZEROES* clause is not an edit character. You add it to the data description entry to set the entire data item to blanks if a value of zero is stored in it. The * edit character cannot be coded in the PIC character string if BLANK WHEN ZERO is coded.

```
01  X    PIC ZZ9.9 BLANK WHEN ZEROS.        [X contains 5 character positions.]
    □ □ □
    MOVE 1 TO X                             [X contains "bb1.0".]
    MOVE 0 TO X                             [X contains "bbbbb".]
```

Using the SPECIAL-NAMES Section to Redefine Edit Characters

For reference, you must code the phrases in the *SPECIAL-NAMES* paragraph in the following order:

```
SPECIAL-NAMES.
    ALPHABET alphabet-name IS name
    SYMBOLIC CHARACTERS symbolic-character IS integer
    CLASS class-name literal THRU literal
    CURRENCY SIGN IS literal
    DECIMAL-POINT IS COMMA.
```

The SPECIAL-NAMES section may specify a symbol other than the $ to be the currency symbol. It may also specify that the roles of the comma and period are to be reversed as edit characters (9,999,99 becomes 9.999,99) to print numbers in the European manner.

```
SPECIAL-NAMES.
    CURRENCY SIGN IS "character"
    DECIMAL-POINT IS COMMA.
```

You can code CURRENCY SIGN, DECIMAL-POINT, or both. The *character* may be any character except 0 through 9, A through D, P, R, S, V, X, Z, lowercase a through z, blank, or the special characters *, +, –, /, ,, ., ;, (,), =, ', or any figurative constant. The following example prints the currency sign as an "F" and displays numbers in the European manner.

```
SPECIAL-NAMES.
    CURRENCY SIGN IS "F"
    DECIMAL-POINT IS COMMA.
```

You could then describe an identifier as follows, using F as the currency sign and reversing the roles of the period and comma:

```
01  Francs                                    PIC FFF.FFF.FF9,99.
```

You must then reverse the comma and period when you write a constant:

```
MOVE 1311,24 TO Francs          [Francs contains "bbbbbF1.311,24".]
```

12.4.3   Underlining Numbers

Rarely Used

There are two additional techniques used in printing numbers, although they are not a part of the editing. Sometimes you need to underline a column of numbers to denote a total, and place a double underline under the total to highlight it.

```
1432
3216
----
5648
=====
```

You can create a single underline by printing a row of dashes. (You can also suppress line spacing, to overprint the underscore character (_), if you want the underscore on the same line.) You create the double underline by printing a line of equal signs (=) on the next line.

12.5   ANATOMY OF A REPORT

Essential

Reports often start out simple, often nothing more than a column listing. The following might represent a report generated for personal finances.

```
JOB         AJAX APPAREL        INCOME              86.23
TAX         FEDERAL             TAX            -17,462.37
RENT        BOB'S BATH HOUSE    UTILITIES           -0.50
```

Each line represents the lowest level of detail and corresponds to a record in a file. These lines are termed *detail lines* to distinguish them from summary lines, described later in this section.

The only constant in reports is that they change. The first thing you would likely add would be a page heading. Usually a page heading contains a title, a date, and a page number. You need an identifier to contain the page number. You may also need an identifier to contain the line number so that you can determine when a new page is needed, although the LINAGE clause can be used for this. Adding the page heading, the report might look like this:

```
                    MONTHLY FINANCE REPORT                    PAGE 1
                      DATE:  5/1/2004
     JOB            AJAX APPAREL        INCOME              86.23
     TAX            FEDERAL             TAX            -17,462.37
     RENT           BOB'S BATH HOUSE    UTILITIES           -0.50
```

The date in the heading can be different each time the report is generated, so it must come from an identifier.

In the preceding report, revenue and expenses are printed in the same column, with the sign used to distinguish them. You can make the report clearer by printing descriptions on each line and column heading:

```
CATEGORY  VENDOR           ITEM        TYPE         AMOUNT
JOB       AJAX APPAREL     INCOME      REVENUE       86.23
TAX       FEDERAL          TAX         EXPENSE    17,462.37
RENT      BOB'S BATH HOUSE UTILITIES   EXPENSE        0.50
```

Perhaps it would be even better to print the revenue and expense in separate columns:

```
CATEGORY  VENDOR           ITEM          REVENUE      EXPENSE
JOB       AJAX APPAREL     INCO            86.23
TAX       FEDERAL          TAX                       17,462.37
RENT      BOB'S BATH HOUSE UTILITIES                     0.50
```

Next, you would undoubtedly want some summarization, perhaps by category and vendor within category. You would also want a final line of grand totals. For this, you must sort the input file on category and vendor. The body of the report might look as follows:

```
CATEGORY  VENDOR           ITEM          REVENUE      EXPENSE
JOB       AJAX APPAREL     INCOME          86.23
JOB       AJAX APPAREL     INCOME          86.23
          TOTAL                           172.46
JOB       STAN'S PARKING   INCOME       1,900.22
          TOTAL                         1,900.22
TOTAL                                   2,072.68
TAX       FEDERAL          TAX                       17,462.37
TAX       STATE            TAX              3.23      4,336.34
          TOTAL                            3.23     17,462.37
TOTAL                                              17,462.37
GRAND TOTAL                             2,075.91    35,337,64
```

You would need to define identifiers to contain the column totals for the vendor, category, and grand totals. You might also want an identifier for each total to count the number of items totaled. This enables you to not print a total line when the total is for only one line.

When a new job or vendor is encountered, you have what is termed a *control break,* and you must print a line of subtotals. The summary lines are termed *con-*

trol footings, because they occur after a control break; that is, after the value of a key in the sort hierarchy changes. The control footing break occurs after a detail line is printed.

When a control footing break occurs, control breaks must be forced on all lower control items in the hierarchy in minor to major order. That is, if JOB is the category in the previous record and TAX is the category in the current record, you have a control break for the category, but first you must force a control break for the vendor. An end of report is treated like a control footing break for the highest-level sort key and forces control breaks in lower to higher order for all other sort keys. Then the grand totals are printed.

Because you have two columns in the report, you might want to add them together and print the total in a separate column. This is termed *cross-footing.* The body of the report might look like this:

CATEGORY	VENDOR	ITEM	REVENUE	EXPENSE	NET
JOB	AJAX APPAREL	INCOME	86.23		86.23
JOB	AJAX APPAREL	INCOME	86.23		86.23
		TOTAL	172.46		172.46
JOB	STAN'S PARKING	INCOME	1,900.22		1,900.22
		TOTAL	1,900.22		1,900.22
TOTAL			2,072.68		2,072.68
TAX	FEDERAL	TAX	17,462.37	17,462.37	
TAX	STATE	TAX	3.23	4,336.34	4,333.11
	TOTAL		3.23	21,798.71	21,795.48
TOTAL			3.23	21,798.71	21,795.48
GRAND TOTAL			2,072.68	35,337,64	33,264.96

Now you might want to clean up the report by eliminating redundant data. The category and vendor names need only be printed the first time they appear. You might also leave a line after the category totals. Printing the category and vendor names requires a control break, and because the information is printed before the detail lines, it is termed a *control heading.* The report body now looks as follows:

CATEGORY	VENDOR	ITEM	REVENUE	EXPENSE	NET
JOB	AJAX APPARE	INCOME	86.2		86.23
		INCOME	86.23		86.23
		TOTAL	172.46		172.46
JOB	STAN'S PARKING	INCOME	1,900.22		1,900.22
TOTAL			2,072.68		2,072.68
TAX	FEDERAL	TAX		17,462.37	17,462.37
	STATE	TAX	3.23	4,336.34	4,333.11
TOTA			3.23	21,798.71	21,795.48
GRAND TOTAL			2,072.68	35,337,64	33,264.96

The report is now less cluttered and looks clearer. To fit more columns across the page, you can print the category and vendor indented on separate lines like this:

CATEGORY	ITEM	REVENUE	EXPENSE	NET
VENDOR				
JOB				
AJAX APPAREL	INCOME	86.23		86.23
	INCOME	86.23		86.23
TOTAL		172.46		172.46
STAN'S PARKING	INCOME	1,900.22		1,900.22
TOTAL		2,072.68		2,072.68
TAX				
FEDERAL	TAX		17,462.37	17,462.37
STATE	TAX	3.23	4,336.34	4,333.11
TOTAL		3.23	21,798.71	21,795.48
GRAND TOTAL		2,072.68	35,337.64	33,264.96

The control heading is printed when a control item in the next record to be printed changes value from the previous record. It is printed before the detail line, but it takes its values from the detail record. This is termed a *control heading break*. A control heading break for an item in a hierarchy requires that control breaks also be forced for all lower-level control items in the hierarchy, in major to minor order. Thus, in the previous example, a change in the category causes JOB to be printed, and then a control heading break is forced for the vendor, causing AJAX APPAREL to be printed. The first detail line printed at the start of a report must cause a control heading break for all levels of the hierarchy. Control breaks occur in the following order:

1. Control footings first in minor to major order. Control footings relate to the previous detail line.
2. Control headings next in major to minor order. Control headings relate to the next detail line.
3. The next detail lines are printed.

Now you can step back and generalize the items that went into the report. There are many different types of reports, but most business applications programmed in COBOL have the form shown in Figure 12.2. You would program the report so that when it reads a new record and encounters a new category, it does the following:

- Prints the control footing for the old vendor and the vendor totals, adds the vendor column totals to the category totals, and resets the vendor totals to zero
- Prints the control footing for the old category and the category totals, adds the category totals to the grand totals, and resets the category totals to zero
- Prints the control heading for the category with the new category
- Prints the control heading for the vendor with the new vendor
- Prints the detail line for the item and adds its columns to the vendor totals

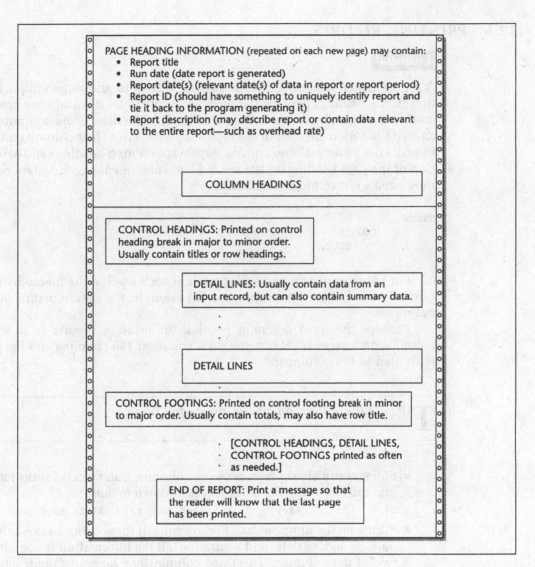

PAGE HEADING INFORMATION (repeated on each new page) may contain:
- Report title
- Run date (date report is generated)
- Report date(s) (relevant date(s) of data in report or report period)
- Report ID (should have something to uniquely identify report and tie it back to the program generating it)
- Report description (may describe report or contain data relevant to the entire report—such as overhead rate)

COLUMN HEADINGS

CONTROL HEADINGS: Printed on control heading break in major to minor order. Usually contain titles or row headings.

DETAIL LINES: Usually contain data from an input record, but can also contain summary data.

DETAIL LINES

CONTROL FOOTINGS: Printed on control footing break in minor to major order. Usually contain totals, may also have row title.

[CONTROL HEADINGS, DETAIL LINES, CONTROL FOOTINGS printed as often as needed.]

END OF REPORT: Print a message so that the reader will know that the last page has been printed.

FIGURE 12.2 Components of a generalized report.

In addition to control breaks, reports also have page breaks. A page break occurs when a page overflows. You may also cause a page break if you want a particular control break to start on a new page. When a page break occurs, you may print a *page footing* at the end of the current page. Then you skip to a new page and print the new *page heading* at the top of the next head. The page heading usually contains titles, a page number, a date, and column headings.

12.6   PRINTING REPORTS

Essential

A report should contain a title, describing what it is, and some unique identification in the heading, perhaps the program name, to tie it back to the program generating it. Paginate reports and date them with the date of the computer run, the date of the period covered in the report, or both. Print clear column and row titles to make the report self-descriptive. Repeat the column headings and at least a portion of the page heading on the second and subsequent pages. Indent row titles if they have a hierarchical relationship:

```
STATE
          COUNTY
               CITY
```

For columns of numbers, print totals at each level in the hierarchy unless the numbers would have no meaning, as, for example, the ages of people in a personnel report.

Perhaps the most common problem in printing reports is to exceed the columns on a page. What can you do if you need 150 columns and the print page is limited to 132 columns?

TIP   *To fit columns on a page, do the following.*

- Squeeze any blanks from between columns. Don't run columns together, but you can often squeeze several blanks down to one.
  ```
  23      15      64.7        Squeezed down to    23 15 69.7
  ```
- Eliminate the nonessential. For example, if three columns contain a starting date, an ending date, and a duration, all the information is contained in any two of the columns. The third column may be convenient, but it is also redundant.
- Print two or more lines, staggering the columns.
  ```
                  START DATE          FIRST 6-MO
                  END DATE            SECOND 6-MO
  DEPARTMENT 115
     JOE DOE      01/01/2001          100,000.00
                  12/31/2002          250,000,00
  ```
- Print two reports, in which the second report is a logical continuation of the columns of the first, so that the two reports form a complete report when placed side by side. Print all the page and column headings of the second

report, too, so that it can stand by itself. In practice, people will not lay the reports side by side, because it is awkward. You can print the second report on the next page by storing it in a table and printing it from the table after printing the first page. Or you can print it as a separate file so that it forms a completely separate report.

- Eliminate unnecessary lines from reports. You might not print a line containing all zeros. Don't print a total line if only one item went into the totals.

```
     HOURS                    Better as                 HOURS
ENG DEPT                                     ENG DEPT
    JOHN DOE           0                          MARY ROE        10
    MARY ROE         10
    DEPT TOTAL       10
```

Give careful thought to the credibility of reports. Column totals can be correct but appear wrong through rounding, and they also can be wrong but appear right through truncation. The former diminishes a report's credibility, but the latter shatters it if it is discovered. The first thing many people do when they receive a new report is to add up the columns by hand to check the totals. If people cannot understand how the numbers in a report are derived, they are quite justified in placing little faith in it.

You make reports more credible by printing numbers and totals in a logical sequence, so that a person can see how the totals are derived. This is not difficult with most reports, but it can be a problem in management reports. There, the reader often does not want to see the full detail but only a condensation of it. For example, it is logical to print totals at the bottom of a column of numbers, and this is also easier to program. However, the total may be the most important item to a manager, and you may need to print it at the top of the page.

If a report must print totals at the top of the page before the detail lines, there are three normal solutions. First, you can store the lines of data in a table, total the table, and then print the lines from the table. This may not work when the report becomes large, however, because of the size of the table that would be required. If this happens, you can pass through the file twice—the first time to compute the totals and the second time to print the report. However, this has limitations if there are many subtotals to compute.

The third alternative is to write the lines into a file with a sort key appended containing the report, page, and line number. When the last line is written and the total line is formed, you give it a page and line number so that it sorts in front of the detail lines. After the report is completed, you sort the lines, read the file, drop the sort key, and print the actual report.

In generating a report from a file, you usually must sort the file so that the lines will come out in the proper order. If only certain records are selected to go into the report, the sequence for this should be select, sort, and then report. Sorts are expensive, and selecting before sorting reduces the number of records sorted.

EXERCISES

1. Show what the following numbers will look like in the following statements.

```
01  W                              PIC $$,$$$,$$9.99CR.
    □  □  □
    MOVE 23655.97 TO W
    MOVE -2 TO W
    MOVE .01 TO W

01  X                              PIC Z,ZZZ,ZZ9.
    □  □  □
    MOVE 26531 TO X
    MOVE -4 TO X

01  Y                              PIC -****9.
    □  □  □
    MOVE -16 TO Y
    MOVE 327 TO Y
    MOVE -923945 TO Y

01  Z                              PIC $--,---,--9.99
                                   BLANK WHEN ZERO.
    □  □  □
    MOVE 35275.6 TO Z
    MOVE -247.96 TO Z
    MOVE ZERO TO Z
```

2. Print a table containing the square roots of the integers from 1 to 1000. Print 50 values per page in the following format:

```
SQUARE OF NUMBERS          PAGE xxx
NUMBER      SQUARE
  1           1
  2           4
  .
1000      1,000,000
```

3. Print a table containing the square roots of the integers from 1 to 1000. Print the square roots with five significant digits of accuracy to the right of the decimal point. Print 50 lines per page with each line containing two columns of values as shown. Print the page heading at the top of each new page.

```
          TABLE OF SQUARE ROOT      PAGE xxx
NUMBER      SQUARE ROOT           NUMBER      SQUARE ROOT
  1           1.00000               51          7.14143
  2           1.41421               52          7.21110
 ...            ...                 ...           ...
 50           7.07107              100         10.00000
```

Print a table showing the future value of an amount invested at 8 percent per annum in 1-year increments for 30 years. The equation for the future value is

Future value = amount $(1.08)^n$

where *n* is the year. Print the table in the format shown for amounts ranging from $100 to $1000 in $200-increments.

```
    FUTURE VALUE TABLE  PAGE xxx
AMOUNT: $100.00    INTEREST RATE: 8.00%
```

```
YEAR        FUTURE VALUE
 1             $103.00
 2             $116.64

 ...             ...
30            $1,006.27
```

4. Write a program to read in a line containing an initial investment, an interest rate, a number of years, and a starting date. The line has the following format:

```
        1|    |   |  |2 |  |  |
1234567890|1234|56|78|9|01|2|34|
aaaaaaa.aa|bb.b|cc|mm|/|dd|/|yy|
```

aaaaaaa.aa	The initial investment.
bb.b:	The interest rate.
cc	The period in years.
mm/dd/yyyy	The date.

Given this information, you are to produce the following report:

```
                    INVESTMENT ANALYSIS                    PAGE xxx
PREPARED ESPECIALLY FOR: your name
INITIAL  INVESTMENT: $xxx,xxx.xx     INTEREST = xx. x%        YEARS: xx
DATE        CURRENT BALANCE      INTEREST EARNED    NEW BALANCE
YEAR
xx/xx/xxxx     $xxx,xxx.xx             $xx,xxx.xx      $xx,xxx.xx
```

Allow 30 lines per page. The interest earned is computed as the current balance times the interest divided by 100. The new balance is the current balance plus the interest earned.

PART II

ADVANCED COBOL

CHAPTER 13

TABLES

13.1 OVERVIEW OF TABLES

Essential

For quick reference, the phrases that define tables must be coded in the following order:

```
OCCURS
DEPENDING ON
ASCENDING/DESCENDING KEY
INDEXED BY
```

A *table*, termed an *array* in other languages, is an arrangement of elements in one or more dimensions. Tables, powerful data processing tools, are much more common than one might expect. You can express the United States as a table containing 50 states as elements. The calendar can be represented as a table containing 12 months as table elements. Such a table has one *dimension,* that is, a single sequence of elements. The range of elements constitutes the *bounds* of the table; the bounds of the calendar table are 1 to 12.

Tables may have more than one dimension. A table with two dimensions is termed a *matrix* in other languages, with the first dimension referred to as the *row,* and the second dimension as the *column.* The seats of an auditorium are elements of a matrix, with rows and columns. COBOL tables may have a maximum of seven dimensions. You might make the auditorium table a three-dimensional table, with the third dimension representing the auditorium within the city. If you allow for 100 rows, 75 columns, and 10 auditoriums in the city, the table would have $100 \times 75 \times 10$ or 75,000 table elements representing auditorium seats.

To refer to a specific element, the table is *subscripted.* If the three-dimensional auditorium table is named *Seat,* you can refer to the twelfth seat in the fifth row of the third auditorium as *Seat*(5, 12, 3). The subscript may be an integer literal, an integer elementary data item, or a special data item called an *index,* described later in this chapter. In addition, the new ANSI standard permits it to be an arithmetic expression.

An important property of tables is their ability to hold several records in storage for computations. Suppose that a file contains numbers that are to be printed in a column of a report, with 50 lines per page. To print the sum of the numbers in the body of the report at the top of each page before the numbers themselves are printed, you can read 50 numbers into a table, sum the elements of the table, and print this total at the top of the page. Then you can print the 50 numbers from the table.

Next, suppose that 100 numbers are to be printed in 2 columns on a page, with the first 50 numbers in the left column and the next 50 numbers on the right. You could define a table of 100 elements to contain the page. However, it is easier to define a two-dimensional table with the first dimension representing the line on the page (1 to 50), and the second representing the column (1 or 2).

Furthermore, suppose that the first page of the report is to contain the total of all numbers in the report. You can define a three-dimensional table, with the first dimension representing the line on the page, the second dimension the column, and the third dimension the page of the report. By storing the entire report in a table, you can sum the numbers to print the total first, and then print the numbers from the table. A 100-page report would have $100 \times 2 \times 50$ or 10,000 table elements.

The use of tables may also reduce the number of statements required, which in turn may save coding time and central storage. But what is more important, it is easier to comprehend a few statements than many. As an example illustrating the benefits of a table, here is a record containing the population of the 50 states described without the use of a table.

```
01  Population-Count          PIC S9(11) PACKED-DECIMAL.
01  States.
    05  Alabama               PIC S9(11) PACKED-DECIMAL.
    05  Arkansas              PIC S9(11) PACKED-DECIMAL.
    .     .                     .    .    .    .
    05  Wyoming               PIC S9(11) PACKED-DECIMAL.
```

To compute the total population of all states, you would code the following:

```
MOVE ZERO TO Population-Count
ADD Alabama TO Population-Count
ADD Arkansas TO Population-Count
  .     .      .      .
ADD Wyoming TO Population-Count
```

Now suppose that you wish to determine the largest and smallest populations of the states. This would require the following:

```
01  Min-No                    PIC S9(11) PACKED-DECIMAL.
01  Max-No                    PIC S9(11) PACKED-DECIMAL.
```

□ □ □

```
      MOVE ZERO TO Max-No
      MOVE 99999999999 TO Min-No
      IF Alabama < Min-No
         THEN MOVE Alabama TO Min-No
      END-IF
      IF Alabama > Max-No
         THEN MOVE Alabama TO Max-No
      END-IF
```

This would be tedious to code, and should California be split into three states or the Virginias be reunited, the program would require several changes. You can reduce the amount of coding, make the operations more understandable, and allow for change by making the state populations a table. You specify a table with the OCCURS clause.

```
01  States.
    05  No-States        PIC S9(4) BINARY VALUE 50.
    05  Population        OCCURS 50 TIMES
                          INDEXED BY Ix
                          PIC S9(11) PACKED-DECIMAL.
```

Population is described as a table with 50 elements. *Ix* is an index data item used to index the table. The population is then summed and the minimum and maximum are computed as follows:

```
      MOVE ZERO TO Population-Count, Max-No
      MOVE 99999999999 TO Min-No
      PERFORM VARYING Ix FROM 1 BY 1 UNTIL Ix > No-States
        [Ix is used as a subscript to refer to individual elements of the table.]
        ADD Population(Ix) TO Population-Count
        IF Population(Ix) < Min-No
           THEN MOVE Population(Ix) TO Min-No
        END-IF
        IF Population(Ix) > Max-No
           THEN MOVE Population(Ix) TO Max-No
        END-IF
      END-PERFORM
```

Now if a new state is added, you can make the change in the Data Division rather than the Procedure Division.

13.2 FIXED-LENGTH TABLE DESCRIPTIONS

Fixed-length tables contain a fixed number of elements determined when the program is compiled and are the most common.

13.2.1 The OCCURS Clause

Essential

You describe fixed-length tables by appending the OCCURS to the data description.

```
nn  item                    PIC … OCCURS n TIMES.
```

For example:

```
05  A-Table                 PIC X(8) OCCURS 10 TIMES.
```

The *n*, an integer literal greater than zero, specifies the table size. You cannot code the OCCURS clause for level 01, 66, 77, or 88 data items. Neither can you code OCCURS for an item that is redefined. A redefined item can, however, be subordinate to an item with OCCURS. In the following example, *A-Table* is described as a single-dimensional table containing 30 elements.

```
01  Some-Thing.
    05  A-Table             OCCURS 30 TIMES
                            PIC S9(3) PACKED-DECIMAL.
```

Note that the following is invalid, because OCCURS cannot be coded for the 01 level.

```
01  Some-Thing             OCCURS 30 TIMES   [Invalid]
                            PIC S9(3) PACKED-DECIMAL.
```

Note also that OCCURS can be coded for a group item or an elementary data item.

```
01  Some-Thing.
    05  A-Table             OCCURS 30 TIMES
                            PIC S9(3) PACKED-DECIMAL.
    05  B-Table             OCCURS 30 TIMES.
        10  Thing-1         PIC X(4).
        10  Thing-2         PIC X(4).
```

Tables may have from one to seven dimensions. You describe multidimensional tables as records, with each dimension specified by a lower-level item. The following example describes *Y* as a 2 by 10 by 20 table.

```
01  A-Record.
    05  Level-1             OCCURS 2 TIMES.
        10  Level-2         OCCURS 10 TIMES.
            15  Y           OCCURS 20 TIMES
                            PIC S9(3) PACKED-DECIMAL.
```

You don't need to give names to levels where you have no use for the name. You could code the foregoing as:

```
01  A-Record.
    05                      OCCURS 2 TIMES.
        10                  OCCURS 10 TIMES.
            15  Y           OCCURS 20 TIMES
                            PIC S9(3) PACKED-DECIMAL.
```

13.2.2   Initializing Tables

Essential

You can assign all the individual elements of a table the same initial value with the VALUE clause. The following example initializes each element of the table to zero.

```
01  A-Record.
    05  A-Table             OCCURS 100 TIMES PIC S9(5)
                            PACKED-DECIMAL VALUE 0.
```

If the elements are each to contain different values, you can either move values to the elements or use the INITIALIZE statement described next. Alternatively, you can describe a record containing several data items with initial values and then redefine the record as a table. The following is an example of this.

```
01  A-Record.
    05  FILLER              PIC S9(5) PACKED-DECIMAL
                            VALUE 2.
    05  FILLER              PIC S9(5) PACKED-DECIMAL
                            VALUE 3.
    05  FILLER              PIC S9(5) PACKED-DECIMAL
                            VALUE 6.
01  Y REDEFINES A-Record.
    05  A-Table             OCCURS 3 TIMES
                            PIC S9(5) PACKED-DECIMAL.
```

You can use INITIALIZE to initialize a table, as shown in the following example. Note that indexes and FILLER data items are not initialized.

```
01  Record-Out.
    05  School              PIC X(25).
    05  FILLER              PIC X(10).
    05  Children            OCCURS 600 TIMES
                            INDEXED BY Ix.
        10  Ages            PIC S9(3) PACKED-DECIMAL.
        10  Names           PIC X(25).
□   □   □
    INITIALIZE Record-Out REPLACING ALPHANUMERIC BY SPACES
                            NUMERIC BY ZEROS
```

Same as

```
INITIALIZE Record-Out
```

Same as

```
MOVE SPACES TO School IN Record-Out
PERFORM VARYING Ix FROM 1 BY 1 UNTIL Ix > 600
   MOVE ZERO TO Ages IN Children IN Record-Out(Ix)
   MOVE SPACES TO Names IN Children IN Record-Out(Ix)
END-PERFORM
```

You can use INITIALIZE for a table that contains an OCCURS clause, but not an OCCURS DEPENDING ON, described later in this chapter. That is, you can't use INITIALIZE for a variable-length table.

You can initialize a complete table only by specifying a group item that contains the complete table. In the previous table, both of these would be invalid because they are not group items containing the entire table:

```
INITIALIZE Children        [Invalid]
INITIALIZE Ages            [Invalid]
```

13.2.3 Initializing Complex Structures

Sometimes Used

If the record is to be initialized from several places within the program, you can place the initialization in a paragraph and then perform it. Now consider the following record. The 600 elements of *Increment-Value* are to be set to values of 1 to 600, and the elements of *Decrement-Value* are to be set to values of 600 to 1. Executing the *B100-Initialize* paragraph does this.

```
01  Record-Out.
    05  Increments                OCCURS 600 TIMES
                                   INDEXED BY Ix.
        10  Increment-Value       PIC S9(3) PACKED-DECIMAL.
        10  Decrement-Value       PIC S9(3) PACKED-DECIMAL.
01  Dec-No                        PIC S9(3) PACKED-DECIMAL.
    □  □  □
B100-Initialize.
    MOVE 600 TO Dec-No
    PERFORM VARYING Ix FROM 1 BY 1 UNTIL Ix > 600
      SET Decrement-Value(Ix) TO Ix
      [The same SET statement that sets values for level 88 condition names also stores
      indexes, as described soon. You can't use indexes in MOVE, COMPUTE, ADD,
      and other arithmetic statements.]
      MOVE Dec-No TO Decrement-Value(Ix)
      SUBTRACT 1 FROM Dec-No
```

```
    END-PERFORM
    .
**** EXIT
```

The table is initiated in a loop, but if the record must be reinitialized many times, this would be wasteful. A more efficient way to accomplish this, at some cost in storage, is to define a new record that contains the same number of characters as the record to be written. You can initialize the original record only once and move it to the new record. Then, whenever you wish to initialize the original record, you can move the new record to it. This also works well when initial values are assigned to the first record or when you compute the initialization values within the program.

```
01  Zero-It                      PIC X(2400).
    [Same size as Record-Out.]
    ☐ ☐ ☐
    MOVE 600 TO Dec-No
    PERFORM B100-Initialize        [Initialize the original record.]
    MOVE Record-Out TO Zero-It
    [Save a copy of the original record after it is initialized.]
```

This initializes the record and saves a copy of it in *Zero-It*. Now you can initialize the record very efficiently by moving *Zero-It* back to it:

```
    MOVE Zero-It TO Record-Out
```

PROPOSED NEW ANSI STANDARD: Check Compiler to See if Implemented

The new ANSI standard lets you initialize tables directly. You can code the VALUE clause on an item that contains or is subordinate to an OCCURS clause. You can code more than one VALUE clause as follows:

```
    VALUE literal, literal, …, literal
```

Each literal is stored in successive elements of the table. You can also repeat an element some number of times.

```
    VALUE literal REPEATED n TIMES
    [The literal is stored in the next n elements of table.]
    VALUE literal REPEATED TO END
    [The literal is stored in the current element through the end of the table.]
```

You can specify the starting subscript at which to begin initializing elements of the table.

```
    VALUE FROM start IS literal, literal, …
    VALUE FROM start literal REPEATED …
```

[The *start* is any valid subscript value. Initializing starts at that element of the table.]

Finally, you can combine the forms by writing multiple VALUE clauses.

```
VALUE literal, literal, … literal
VALUE literal REPEATED TO END
```
[The *literals* are stored in successive elements of the table. The last *literal* is stored in the next table position through the end.]

```
01  A-Record.
    05  A-Table              OCCURS 100 TIMES
                             PIC S9(5) PACKED-DECIMAL
                             VALUE 1, 3, 3, 4, 5
                             VALUE 0 REPEATED TO END.
```

The table contains 1, 2, 3, 4, 5, and then 0 to the end.

13.2.4 Subscripting Tables

Essential

Earlier, the following $2 \times 10 \times 20$ table was defined.

```
01  A-Record.
    05                       OCCURS 2 TIMES.
        10                   OCCURS 10 TIMES.
            15  Y            OCCURS 20 TIMES
                             PIC S9(3) PACKED-DECIMAL.
```

Y must be subscripted to refer to a specific element. The subscripts correspond to the order of the OCCURS clauses. $Y(2, 10, 20)$ refers to the last element in the table. COBOL stores tables in row-major order, with the rightmost subscript increasing most rapidly. Thus, the elements of the Y table are stored in the order $Y(1, 1, 1)$, $Y(1, 1, 2)$, . . . , $Y(1, 1, 20)$, $Y(1, 2, 1)$, . . . , $Y(2, 10, 20)$. IBM COBOL limits the elements of a table to 16,777,215 bytes.

You can describe group items as tables. The following record describes 50 states, 5 rivers within each state, 20 counties within each state, and 10 cities within each county.

```
01  Nation.
    05  State                OCCURS 50 TIMES.
        10  State-Name       PIC X(25).
        10  River            OCCURS 5 TIMES PIC X(25).
        10  County           OCCURS 20 TIMES.
            15  City         OCCURS 10 TIMES.
                20  City-Name    PIC X(25).
                20  City-Size    PIC S9(7) PACKED-DECIMAL.
```

You write the subscripts after the last qualifier name of a record.

```
State(1) or State IN Nation(1)      [Refers to the first State group item.]
County(2, 3)
   [Refers to the third County of the second State group item.]
River IN State(2, 3)
   [Refers to the third River element of the second State group item.]
City-Name IN City IN County IN State IN Nation(4, 3, 2)
   [Refers to the City-Name element of the second City group item of the third
   County group item of the fourth State group item.]
```

Subscripts must be positive, nonzero integer literals or elementary data items that lie within the bounds of the table. That is, their value can range from 1 to the maximum table size. The subscript itself may be qualified but not subscripted. That is, $A(J$ IN $K)$ is valid, but $A(I(J))$ is not.

When a data item is subscripted, there must always be the same number of subscripts as there are dimensions in the table, that is, the same number of subscripts as there are OCCURS clauses.

```
A(I, J, K)        [Blanks required following the commas, as shown.]
```

13.2.5   Table Indexes

Essential

In addition to integers and elementary data items, a subscript can be an *index*, which is a special data type used only to refer to table elements, just as are subscripts. As such, they are generally more efficient as subscripts than are elementary data items. You describe indexes with the INDEXED BY phrase of the OCCURS clause. The following example describes *Bx* as an index for table *B*.

```
01  A.
    05  B                          PIC S9(3) PACKED-DECIMAL
                                   OCCURS 10 TIMES INDEXED BY Bx.
```

The index defined for a table can be used only to index that table. *Bx* preceding can be used only to index the *A* table. (IBM COBOL allows an index to be used for any table.) You can use indexes in combination with literals or elementary data items. For example, if B were a three-dimensional table, you could code:

```
MOVE B(index, identifier, integer) TO …
```

Arithmetic statements, such as ADD and COMPUTE, cannot operate on indexes. Instead, you use the SET statement. An index is a 4-byte binary item that contains values referring to the occurrence number of an element in the table. Internally, an index might, depending on the compiler implementation, contain a relative byte position of the element rather than the occurrence number 1 to *n*, but, aside from restrictions, you can treat the index as if it contained occurrence numbers. You can define several indexes for each dimension of a table, and only those defined can be used to index that dimension of the table. The general form of the INDEXED phrase is

```
INDEXED BY index-1, index-2, …, index-n
```

IBM COBOL permits 12 indexes to be defined for a single item. The indexes are any unique, valid COBOL name with at least one letter alphabetic, and they are defined as indexes for only that dimension of the table. The following example shows the specification of two indexes for each level of a three-dimensional table.

```
01  A.
    05  B                   OCCURS 4 TIMES
                            INDEXED BY Bx1, Bx2.
        10  C               OCCURS 6 TIMES
                            INDEXED BY Cx1, Cx2.
            15  D           OCCURS 10 TIMES
                            INDEXED BY Dx1, Dx2
                            PIC S9(3) PACKED-DECIMAL.
```

Note that INDEXED BY must follow the OCCURS clause. You can code them before or after any PIC clause.

```
Correct:                              Incorrect:
15  D PIC X(4) OCCURS 10 TIMES        15  D PIC X(4) INDEXED BY Dx
               INDEXED BY Dx.                        OCCURS 10 TIMES.
15  E OCCURS 10 TIMES                 15  E INDEXED BY Ex
        INDEXED BY Ex PIC X(4).                OCCURS 10 TIMES PIC X(4).
```

13.2.6   Relative Indexing

Essential

You can code both indexes and elementary data items plus or minus an integer literal. This is termed *relative indexing,* and it is the only arithmetic expression allowed as a subscript. Notice that you must leave a space before and after the plus or minus:

```
table(data-name ± integer, …)
```

(If either the *data-name* or *identifier* is signed, they must be positive.) The following indexes are then valid for array *D:*

```
D(Bx1 + 2, Cx1 - 3, Dx1)
```

If *Bx1* was set to 1, *Cx1* to 6, and *Dx1* to 7, the previous item would be the same as *D*(3, 3, 7). You can only code plus or minus an integer literal, not plus or minus an elementary data item or another index.

◄ 3.2.7 Index Data Items

Essential

An *index data item* is an index that is not associated with any table. You can use them only to save the values of other indexes. They are described by:

```
nn  index-name              INDEX.
```

For example

```
01  An-Index                INDEX.
```

The *index-name* is any unique, valid COBOL name. Index data items can contain only index values.

```
SET An-Index TO 1          [Invalid. Not set to an index value.]
SET An-Index TO Ix         [Valid if Ix is an index.]
```

Index data items cannot themselves be used to index a table. You can manipulate indexes and index data items only with the SET and SEARCH statements, in relational conditions such as in a PERFORM VARYING, and in the USING phrase. Index data items also participate in a group move with the MOVE statement, but you can move them only to other index data items. You cannot name an elementary index data item in a MOVE.

```
MOVE An-Index TO A-Num     [Invalid. Index item can't be named in a MOVE.]
```

13.2.8 The SET Statement

Essential

The SET statement manipulates indexes and has the following form.

```
SET index-1, index-2, …, index-n TO item
```

You can set one or more *indexes* to an *item*. The *item* may be an integer numeric literal or identifier, another index, or an index data item. Numeric literals must be positive nonzero integers.

```
SET Ix1 TO 10
SET Ix1, Ix2 TO Ix3
```

You cannot use the MOVE statement for indexes; you use the SET statement instead. You can also set one or more integer numeric identifiers to the current value of an index.

```
SET identifier-1, identifier-2, …, identifier-n TO index
SET A, B TO Ix1
SET C TO Ix2
```

You can increment or decrement one or more indexes with a value. The *value* can be an integer numeric literal or identifier with a positive or negative value.

```
SET index-1, index-2, …, index-n UP BY value
SET index-1, index-2, …, index-n DOWN BY value
SET Ix3 UP BY 3
SET Ix3, Ix4 DOWN BY 5
```

Indexes can appear in relational conditions, such as those in the IF statement, and they participate in the operation as if they were subscripts. If an index is compared to a nonindex item, COBOL automatically converts the index to a subscript value for the operation. Index data items, those not described for a table, cannot be converted to subscripts, because they are not described for a specific table. Therefore, you can compare them only to other indexes or index data items.

Functionally, indexes are a redundant language feature. They permit the compiler writer to make them more efficient than subscripts. The actual contents of the index are compiler dependent. In IBM COBOL, the index contains the relative byte location of the element within the table. COBOL must convert a subscript to the relative byte location each time the table element is referenced, and indexes eliminate this conversion. However, the gain in efficiency is often minimal. Such programming languages as FORTRAN, PL/I, C/C++, BASIC, Pascal, ALGOL, and APL, in which tables are used much more than in COBOL, do not have a special data type for indexes, and there is no complaint from them about efficiency.

The restrictions on indexes sometimes lead to convoluted programming that negates their efficiency. Index values are defined only for the bounds of the table (1 to the maximum entries in the table). If a table has 20 elements, the index for that table should contain only the values 1 through 20. Zero is not a valid value for an index, and the following statement is in error.

```
SET Ix TO ZERO          [Invalid]
```

In the following statements, IBM and PC COBOL give a result of 1, but other compilers may give a garbage result.

```
SET Ix TO 1
SET Ix DOWN BY 1        [A zero value is undefined.]
SET Ix UP BY 1          [An undefined value plus 1 is still undefined.]
```

Indexes can be zero or one more than the table size to terminate a PERFORM. The following is typical:

```
01  A-Record.
    05  A-Table              OCCURS 1000 TIMES
```

```
                   INDEXED BY An-Index
                   PIC S9(4) BINARY.

□  □  □
PERFORM VARYING An-Index FROM 1 BY 1
        UNTIL An-Index > 1000
```

Or

```
PERFORM VARYING An-Index FROM 1000 BY -1
        UNTIL An-Index < 1
```

The loop will terminate properly when *An-Index* is set to 1001 or 0. However, once outside the loop, these values are undefined. A value greater than the size of the table generally causes no problem, but zero values can.

TIP   *Don't use indexes if you need to retain the value of an index outside the loop. Use an identifier as a subscript instead.*

Indexes make debugging harder, because they cannot appear in DISPLAY statements. If *Ix* is an index, the following statement is illegal.

```
DISPLAY Ix
```

You must set a normal numeric data item to the index and then display the data item.

```
SET Some-Thing TO Ix
DISPLAY Some-Thing
```

These examples illustrate some of the problems in the use of indexes. The SEARCH statement requires that tables have indexes, but give careful consideration in using them for other purposes.

COBOL compilers generally don't generate code to check indexes or subscripts to see if they fall within the bounds of a table. (The Mainframe COBOL SSRANGE compile and run-time options cause subscripts to be checked.) The result is that indexing or subscripting beyond the bounds of a table will cause errors. If an item is moved from a table with an incorrect subscript, its contents are unpredictable, and this may not be discovered until later. If an item is moved to a table with an incorrect subscript, it may be moved into another data item or may even wipe out code within the program. The error may not manifest itself until later, when the other data item is used or the code is executed. If *Table-X* has 100 elements, the following statement might wipe out parts of the program itself:

```
MOVE 10000 TO A-Num
MOVE ZEROS TO Table-X(A-Num)
```

Zeros are moved to somewhere in the program, but not within *Table-X*.

13.3 VARIABLE-LENGTH TABLES

Sometimes Used

COBOL can describe tables in which the number of table elements is specified by a data item. For example, a census record for a person might contain a data item specifying the number of children, followed by a variable-length table containing their names. You use variable-length tables for variable-size I/O records, in which the record itself specifies the number of table elements to be transmitted. Such variable-size records reduce the record size and may increase the I/O and storage efficiency. You also use variable-length tables when the number of elements in a table may vary. Once you set the table length, a SEARCH statement referencing the table knows the table length and will search only the current size of the table. Chapter 22 describes how to use variable-length tables as variable-length character strings.

The OCCURS DEPENDING ON *size* clause describes variable-length tables. The *size* is a numeric integer data item that contains the current table length. COBOL allocates storage for variable-length tables based on the maximum occurrences that the table can have. Thereafter, the occurrences of the table vary depending on the contents of the *size* data item. When the table is written, only the number of table elements specified by the *size* data item are transmitted. The general form for the description of variable-length tables is as follows:

```
01  record-name.
    05  table                 OCCURS min TO max TIMES
                              DEPENDING ON size.
```

- The *min* is the minimum occurrences of the table. It must be a numeric integer literal of value zero or larger, but less than *max*. The zero value permits a table to have zero entries, allowing the SEARCH statement to work properly for an empty table. IBM and Micro Focus COBOL let you omit the *min* TO and a value of 1 is assumed for them.

- The *max* is the maximum occurrences of the table. It must be a numeric integer literal greater than *min.*

- The *size* is a numeric integer data item set to values from *min* through *max* to specify the current number of occurrences of the table. It cannot lie within the table being defined. That is, it cannot be within or subordinate to the item with the OCCURS DEPENDING ON. The *size* must also be in a fixed portion of the record. This means that it cannot follow an OCCURS DEPENDING ON within the same structure.

You can qualify *min, max,* and *size* but not subscript or index them. The following example describes *Table-X* as a table with a maximum of 100 elements, and it makes the current occurrences of *Table-X* depend on the contents of *Ix.*

```
01  A-Record.
    05  Ix                    PIC S9(4) BINARY.
```

[*Ix* must appear before *Table-X* in the record, because *Table-X* has an OCCURS DEPENDING ON.]

```
05  Table-X          OCCURS 1 TO 100 TIMES
                     DEPENDING ON Ix
                     PIC S9(5) PACKED-DECIMAL.
```

When *Ix* is assigned a value, the table acts as if it were described to be that size. If *Ix* is set to 75 and the record is written out, only 75 elements of table *Table-X* are written.

```
MOVE 75 TO Ix
WRITE Out-X FROM A-Record
```
[*A-Record* consists of *Ix* and 75 occurrences of *Table-X*.]

Items containing the DEPENDING ON clause and items subordinate to them can be assigned initial values. The initial values are assigned for the maximum number of occurrences.

In the ANSI standard, a group item containing a DEPENDING ON clause may be followed, within that record, only by items subordinate to it. Thus, a group item containing a DEPENDING ON clause must be the last group item of its level or higher in the record. For example, the following are not permitted in the ANSI standard:

```
01  A-Table.
    05  Size-1          PIC S9(4) BINARY.
    05  Size-2          PIC S9(4) BINARY.
    05  Part-1          OCCURS 1 TO 5 TIMES
                        DEPENDING ON Size-1.
        10  Part-2      OCCURS 1 TO 5 TIMES
                        DEPENDING ON Size-2
                        PIC X(4).
```
[Invalid. OCCURS DEPENDING ON can't be subordinate to the OCCURS in *Part-1*.]
```
    05  Part-3          PIC X(30).
```
[Invalid. OCCURS DEPENDING ON must be followed only by subordinate items.]

In IBM and PC COBOL, subordinate items can contain the OCCURS DEPENDING ON clause in their descriptions. You can also follow the OCCURS DEPENDING ON with nonsubordinate items. The preceding example would be valid in IBM and PC COBOL.

Nonrelational database management systems make extensive use of varying-size records. Each related portion of a record is termed a *segment*. In a variable-length table, the segment may be repeated—termed a *repeating segment*. There may be several repeating segments within a record, and the repeating segments may themselves contain repeating segments. For example, the record for a school might have a repeating segment for each administrator and a repeating segment for each teacher. Then, for each teacher segment, there may be a repeating segment for each student. IBM and PC COBOL permit several DEPENDING ON phrases to be described for items subordinate to group items with the DEPENDING ON phrase. This gives some of the facility required for databases, but database systems generally require a specialized language. However, COBOL serves as a host language to many generalized database management systems.

13.4   DYNAMIC TABLES

PROPOSED NEW ANSI STANDARD: Check Compiler to See if Implemented

The new ANSI standard lets you specify dynamic tables that can grow during execution. You code a dynamic table as follows:

```
01  record-name.
    05  table                        OCCURS min TO max TIMES
                                     DEPENDING ON size
                                     EXTEND  inc TO limit.
```

The *inc* is the number of occurrences to allocate when the table must be expanded. (If you omit BY *inc*, an amount defined by the compiler writer is used.) The *limit* is the maximum number subscript value for the table. If you omit TO *limit*, the table size is limited only by the amount of central storage. The table is initially allocated with enough storage for *max*. Thereafter, storage is allocated dynamically and may not be contiguous, but your program won't be aware of this.

You expand the table by first setting the *size* identifier to the new subscript value. Then when you reference a table element as a receiving item with a subscript or index that is outside the currently allocated table size, COBOL allocates the additional storage for the table. You deallocate table storage by executing the following SET statement:

```
SET OCCURS FOR table TO new-size
```

The *new-size* is the integer value of a literal, identifier, or arithmetic expression. It must be $\geq$ *min* and $\leq$ *limit*. You should then set the *size* identifier value to reflect the new table size.

13.5   THE SEARCH STATEMENT

Essential

The SEARCH statement searches a table for a specific entry. The simplest and most efficient way of retrieving elements from a table is to use a subscript or index to address the table directly. However, in many applications this is not possible. Suppose that a table representing a calendar contains 12 elements, for the number of days per month. Then suppose that you are to read in transactions containing a date and retrieve the number of days in the month. A date containing the month as a number from 1 to 12, such as 12/21/2001, would allow you to subscript the table directly. But what if the month is in text form, such as JANUARY or FEBRU-ARY? Then you must store the month name in the table, along with the days, and search the table for the matching month. The two usual means of doing this are a sequential search and a binary search. One further technique, the hash search, is described in the next section and is used less often.

COBOL provides the SEARCH statement to perform a sequential or binary search to locate elements in a table. It functions like the IF/THEN/ELSE statement: SEARCH searches a table for a specified element; if found, it takes one action; if not found, it takes another.

A *sequential search* examines each element of a table serially and may be used regardless of the order of the table elements. A *binary search* requires that the elements of the table be arranged in ascending or descending order. The binary search begins in the middle of the table. It continues to the middle of the lower or upper half of the table, depending on whether the current element was high or low. This continues until the element is found or the table is exhausted.

A binary search is more efficient for large tables than is a sequential search, although it requires that the table be in sort order. Suppose that you are trying to guess a number from 1 to 100, and that the number is 64. With a sequential search, you guess 1, 2, 3, . . . , 64, requiring a total of 64 tries. With a binary search, your first guess is 50 (too low). But you now know that the number must be in the range from 51 to 100. With the first guess you have cut the size of the table you need to search in half. Your next guess is halfway between 50 and 100, or 74 (too high). You continue with 62 (too low), 68 (too high), 65 (too high), 63 (too low), and 64 (found). The 64 is found with only 7 searches. Notice that with each guess, you cut the size of the table that must be searched in half. The larger the table, the more efficient the binary search becomes. To locate the number 643 in a table of 1000 elements would require 643 sequential searches, but only 9 binary searches.

To locate an element in a table with a sequential search, the number of searches is on the order of $n/2$, where n is the number of entries in the table. For a binary search, the number of searches is on the order of $n \log 2^n$. Note also that this assumes that the entry is in the table to find. If the entry is not in the table to find, the number of sequential searches is n, whereas the number of binary searches is still $n \log 2^n$.

A sequential search is slightly faster for small tables than is a binary search. A binary search becomes more efficient than a sequential search when there are roughly 60 elements in the table (Gear, 1974), excluding the time it may take to place the table in sort order for the binary search. Use a binary search if the table is in ascending or descending order. If a large, unordered table is searched often, sort it and use a binary search.

13.5.1   Sequential Search

Essential

You write the sequential SEARCH statement as follows:

```
SET index TO start
SEARCH table
  AT END imperative-statements
  WHEN condition imperative-statements
  .     .      .      .      .      .
  WHEN condition imperative-statements
END-SEARCH
```

Set the *index* of *table* to the subscript at which to begin the search, usually 1, before executing SEARCH. If *table* has several indexes, set the first index listed in the OCCURS clause, because it is used in the search. The search begins with this element, and COBOL applies the WHEN phrases in the order in which you code them. If any WHEN *condition* is true, the search terminates with the *index* pointing to the element satisfying the WHEN phrase, and the *imperative-statements* are executed. If no *condition* is true, the *index* is incremented by 1, and the search continues. If the entire table is searched without a *condition* being met, the AT END phrase executes, and the *index* has no predictable value.

The *table* must have the OCCURS clause and INDEXED BY phrase in its description. The table can also be subordinate to an item containing the OCCURS clause so that you can search different levels of a multidimensional table. The *table* cannot be subscripted or indexed in SEARCH. That is, SEARCH A(*Ix*) is invalid. If the initial *index* value exceeds the size of *table,* the AT END phrase is immediately executed.

The AT END *imperative-statements* is an optional phrase that causes the *imperative-statements* to execute if the entire table is searched without finding the element. Unless one of the *imperative-statements* is a GO TO, execution then continues with the statement following the END-SEARCH. Execution also continues there if the AT END phrase is omitted. In either case, the *index* has no predictable value.

The WHEN *condition imperative-statement* sets the conditions for selection. The *condition* may be a compound condition connected by the logical operations AND, OR, or NOT. The *imperative-statements* execute when a condition is true, and unless they contain a GO TO, execution then continues with the next executable statement following the END-SEARCH. The *index* points to the table element found. CONTINUE may be coded as the *imperative-statements,* and execution immediately continues following the END-SEARCH when an element is found.

The following table is set up to contain the names and ages of people.

```
01  Person-Record.
    05  Person                 OCCURS 1000 TIMES
                               INDEXED BY Ip.
```

```
10  Surname          PIC X(5).
10  Age              PIC S9(3) PACKED-DECIMAL.
```

The following statements search the table for a person named SMITH.

```
SET Ip TO 1
SEARCH Person
  AT END DISPLAY "SMITH NOT FOUND."
  WHEN Surname(Ip) = "SMITH"
      PERFORM A20-Found-Smith
END-SEARCH
```

The following statements find the first person less than 21 years old.

```
SET Ip TO 1
SEARCH Person
  AT END DISPLAY "NO ONE UNDER 21"
  WHEN Age(Ip) < 21 DISPLAY Surname(Ip)
END-SEARCH
```

Suppose you want to search the table to find all people less than 21 years old. For this, you begin the search with the first element of the table and perform the search within a loop.

```
SET Ip TO 1
MOVE "N" TO Quit-Flag
PERFORM UNTIL Quit-Flag = "Y"
  SEARCH Person
    AT END
        DISPLAY "NO MORE UNDER 21"
        MOVE "Y" TO Quit-Flag
    WHEN Age(Ip) < 21
        DISPLAY Surname(Ip)
        IF Ip = 1000            [Prevents setting Ip greater than table size.]
            THEN MOVE "Y" TO Quit-Flag
            ELSE SET Ip UP BY 1
        END-IF
  END-SEARCH
END-PERFORM
```

Suppose now that you wish to read in a list of names and add each unique name to the end of the *Person* table. There will be a varying number of elements in the *Person* table. One way to do this is to code the DEPENDING ON phrase in the *Person* table. Another method is to set the first element of the table to some unique characters, such as HIGH-VALUES. As each name is read, the table is searched for the name. If the name is found in the table, it is not stored, because it is already in the table. Another WHEN clause also looks for HIGH-VALUES and, if found, stores the name at that point in the table and sets the next element to HIGH-VALUES. The following example illustrates this technique.

```
MOVE HIGH-VALUES TO Surname(1)
```

Now assume that a record is read in, and the person's surname is contained in *The-Name*.

```
SET Ip TO 1
SEARCH Person
   AT END DISPLAY "Person TABLE FULL."
   WHEN Surname(Ip) = HIGH-VALUES
      MOVE The-Name TO Surname(Ip)
              [Now save the name in the next slot unless we are at the end of
              the table.]
      IF Ip < 1000
         THEN MOVE HIGH-VALUES TO Surname(Ip + 1)
      END-IF
   WHEN Surname(Ip) = The-Name CONTINUE
END-SEARCH
```

Now here is the same example, this time using the OCCURS DEPENDING ON.

```
01  Person-Record.
    05  No-People            PIC S9(4) BINARY.
    05  Person               OCCURS 0 TO 1000 TIMES
                             DEPENDING ON No-People
                             INDEXED BY Ip.
10  Surname                  PIC X(5).
10  Age                      PIC S9(3) PACKED-DECIMAL.
    □  □  □
MOVE ZERO TO No-People
```

No-People is the number of occurrences in the table. Now if you assume that *The-Name* contains a name, you can add it to the table by coding the following:

```
SET Ip TO 1
SEARCH Person
   AT END
      IF No-People = 1000
         THEN DISPLAY "Person TABLE FULL."
         ELSE ADD 1 TO No-People
              MOVE The-Name TO Surname(No-People)
      END-IF
   WHEN Surname(Ip) = The-Name CONTINUE
END-SEARCH
```

If you search a table containing a variable number of entries, you must always limit the search to the number of entries in the table. Otherwise, you would continue the search past the entries stored in the table, and because these entries contain unpredictable values, the results are unpredictable. The DEPENDING ON phrase limits the search. If you don't code it, limit the search with a WHEN clause by testing when the index exceeds the table size. Or, if you are using HIGH-VALUES to mark the end of the table, look for them.

```
SET Ip TO 1
SEARCH Person
```

```
        AT END DISPLAY "NOT FOUND IN TABLE."
        WHEN Surname(Ip) = HIGH-VALUES
             DISPLAY "NOT FOUND IN TABLE."
        WHEN ...
    END-SEARCH
```

A sequential search is more efficient if the most frequently retrieved elements are placed at the front of the table. If you were setting up a table to find the state name, you would place California first, New York second, and so on. The sequential search can also search a portion of a table. The following example searches elements 100 to 200 of the *Person* table to see if there is a person named "SMITH". The AT END phrase is omitted, because the search will stop before it reaches the end of the table.

```
    SET Ip TO 100
    SEARCH Person
        WHEN Ip > 200 DISPLAY "SMITH NOT FOUND."
        WHEN Surname(Ip) = "SMITH" DISPLAY "SMITH FOUND."
    END-SEARCH
```

You can append a VARYING *count* phrase to SEARCH to increment a *count* as each element is searched. You must then set *count* to an initial value, usually zero. The *count* retains its value after SEARCH executes.

```
    MOVE ZERO TO count
    SET index TO start
    SEARCH table VARYING count
      AT END imperative-statements
      WHEN condition imperative-statements
        .         .         .
      WHEN condition imperative-statements
    END-SEARCH
```

The *count* can be an index of this or another table, or a numeric integer identifier. If *count* is an index of this *table*, it and not the first index of the *table* is incremented. If *count* is an index from another table or an identifier, it along with the first index of the *table* is incremented. If SEARCH terminates without finding an element, *count* has no predictable value.

The VARYING phrase allows indexes or subscripts for other tables to be incremented in the SEARCH. This saves having to set them when the element is found.

13.5.2 Binary Search

Essential

The binary SEARCH statement requires that the table being searched be arranged in ascending or descending order based on selected data items (termed *keys*) of the table. Specify the keys in the data description as follows:

```
ASCENDING KEY IS key-1, key-2, …, key-n
```

Or

```
DESCENDING KEY IS key-1, key-2, …, key-n
```

Each *key* must name a table element. The *key* can name the table itself, and then there can only be one *key*. If the *key* does not name the table, there can be several keys. However, they must be subordinate to *table* and not be subordinate to, or follow, any other entries in the table that contain an OCCURS clause. Nor can the description of a key contain an OCCURS clause.

If you list more than one *key,* list them in decreasing order of significance. The *keys* can be DISPLAY, BINARY, PACKED-DECIMAL, COMP-1, or COMP-2 data items. The following table indicates that *Person* is in ascending order based on *Surname* and that the child of each *Person* is in descending order based on the contents of *Child*.

```
01  Person-Record.
    05  Person            OCCURS 1000 TIMES
                          ASCENDING KEY IS Surname
                          INDEXED BY Px.
        10  Surname       PIC X(5).
        10  Age           PIC S9(5) PACKED-DECIMAL.
        10  Children      OCCURS 5 TIMES
                          DESCENDING KEY IS Child
                          INDEXED BY Cx.
            15  Child     PIC X(5).
```

Code the binary SEARCH statement as follows:

```
SEARCH ALL table
  AT END imperative-statements
  WHEN key(index) = expression imperative-statement
    .     .     .     .        .          .
  WHEN key(index) = expression imperative-statement
END-SEARCH
```

Verbose form:

```
WHEN key(index) IS EQUAL TO expression
```

The *table* must have the OCCURS INDEXED BY clause and ASCENDING/DESCENDING KEY phrase in its description. The first index listed in the INDEXED BY phrase of *table* is used for the search if there are several, and if an element is found, the *index* points to that element. If an element is not found, the *index* has no predictable value.

The AT END *imperative-statements* is an optional phrase that executes the *imperative-statements* if the element is not found in *table*. Unless it is a GO TO, execution then continues with the next executable statement following the END-SEARCH. Execution also continues there if the AT END phrase is omitted. In either case, the *index* has no predictable value.

The WHEN *key*(*index*) = *expression imperative-statements* makes the selection. You must describe the *key* in the ASCENDING/DESCENDING KEY phrase for *table*. The *index* must be the first index listed in the INDEXED BY phrase, along with any other subscripts or literals you want. The *expression* may be a literal, identifier, or an arithmetic expression. The logical operation AND can join several comparisons. Any *keys* in the KEY clause may be tested, but if several *keys* are described, all preceding *keys* must be tested. The *imperative-statements* execute when the condition is true, and unless it is a GO TO, execution then continues following the END-SEARCH. The *index* points to the table element found. You can code CONTINUE as the *imperative-statements* and execution immediately continues with the next executable statement if an element is found.

The following example searches the *Person* table for the age of a person named "SMITH".

```
SEARCH ALL Person
   AT END MOVE ZERO TO Ans
   WHEN Surname(Px) = "SMITH" MOVE Age(Px) TO Ans
END-SEARCH
```

A table may contain duplicate entries, that is, elements with identical *keys*. This does not affect the search, but which entry of a duplicate entry it will find is unpredictable. It will not necessarily be the first of the duplicate entries in the table.

The binary search can also search a variable-length table. It is best to use the DEPENDING ON phrase to specify the current size of the table, and the SEARCH statement will not search beyond this. If you are not using the DEPENDING ON phrase, fill beyond the last entry in the table with HIGH-VALUES (table in ascending order) or LOW-VALUES (table in descending order). This enables the binary search to work properly.

Both the sequential and binary forms of the SEARCH statement can also search multidimensional tables so that a table may be subordinated to an item containing an OCCURS clause. You must set the *index* of the higher-level OCCURS clause before searching the lower levels. For example, if you code SEARCH ALL *Children* in the previously described *Person* table, *Px* must first be set and all table elements, *Children*(*Px*, 1 through 5), are searched. The following example searches all the *Children* of each *Person* and prints the *Surname* if a *Child* named "BOBBY" is found.

```
PERFORM VARYING Px FROM 1 BY 1 UNTIL Px > 1000
   SEARCH ALL Children
      WHEN Child(Px, Cx) = "BOBBY" DISPLAY Surname(Px)
   END-SEARCH
END-PERFORM
```

You can also use the sequential and binary SEARCH statements in combination to search a multidimensional table. The following example searches for each *Person* whose *Age* is greater than 50 and who also has a *Child* named "BETTY". Note that *All-Done* is used as a flag to terminate the search.

```
MOVE "N" TO All-Done
SET Px TO 1
PERFORM WITH TEST BEFORE UNTIL Px > 1000 OR All-Done = "Y"
   SEARCH Person
   [A sequential search finds the next person over 50.]
      AT END DISPLAY "ALL DONE."
            MOVE "Y" TO All-Done
      WHEN Age(Px) > 50
         SEARCH ALL Children
               [A binary search finds any child named "BETTY".]
            WHEN Child(Px, Cx) = "BETTY"
                DISPLAY Surname(Px)
         END-SEARCH
   END-SEARCH
   SET Px UP BY 1
END-PERFORM
```

13.6   HASH TABLES

Rarely Used

Sometimes it is impractical to use a sequential or binary search. Perhaps you must add to the table while it is being searched. You could still use a sequential search by adding new entries to the end of the table. For a binary search, you would locate where to add the new entry and move all the elements from there on down one slot to make room. However, the sequential search or updating the table for a binary search may be too slow.

An alternative is to use what is termed a *hash table*. Rather than searching the table for a match key, you compute a subscript to the table and use it instead. Suppose that you are using a table to retrieve a person's name, given a Social Security number. Suppose further that there are also transactions to add new employees. Assuming that there are 1000 employees to store, you need a technique that will convert the nine-digit Social Security numbers into numbers ranging from 1 to 1000.

The simplest method is to divide the Social Security number by 1000 and use the remainder, which will have a value from 0 to 999. Then add 1 to the remainder to bring it into the subscript range of 1 to 1000. The remainders are more evenly distributed if you divide by the largest *prime number* (a number divisible only by 1 and itself, such as 7 and 11) that is less than 1000. The largest prime number that is less than 1000 is 997.

Now to see how this works in practice. The number 555-44-1111 yields a remainder of 447 when divided by 997, and the number 555-44-2222 yields a remainder of 561. So far so good, but the number 666-44-2106 also yields a remainder of 447, the same as 555-44-1111. This raises the problem of *collisions*—when two numbers yield the same remainder. This means that you cannot use the subscript directly. Instead, you use it as the location at which to begin looking for a place to store the entry. This, in turn, requires that you initialize the table, probably with zeros, so that you can tell if an element contains an entry. You should also increase the size of the table to provide room for the collisions, perhaps to 1500 elements, and then divide by 1499 to compute the subscripts. The larger the table, the less the chance of collisions and the more efficient it becomes. The efficiency begins to drop off when the table becomes more than about 70 percent full.

There is still a problem at the end of the table. What if several Social Security numbers yield a subscript of 1500? You solve this by wrapping around to the beginning of the table. To retrieve an entry from the table, you compute the subscript from the Social Security number. Then you use this as the location at which to begin looking for the Social Security number in the table.

To illustrate a hash table, the following example uses the Social Security example to add and retrieve a person's name from a table given the person's Social Security number. First a table is defined, and then procedures are written to add new entries to the table and to search it. The table is defined as follows:

```
01   SS-Table.
     05   SS-Name               PIC X(25).
          [Name of person for storing and retrieval.]
     05   SS-No                 PIC 9(9).
          [Social Security number for storing and retrieval.]
     05   SS-Div                PIC S9(9) PACKED-DECIMAL
                                VALUE 1499.
          [Largest odd number not ending in 5 that is less than SS-Max-Size.]
     05   SS-Max-Size           PIC S9(4) BINARY SYNC
                                VALUE 1500.
          [Size of person array.]
     05   SS-Subscript          PIC S9(9) PACKED-DECIMAL.
          [Computed subscript.]
     05   SS-Person             OCCURS 1500 TIMES
                                INDEXED BY Ip.
          10   SS-Person-No     PIC 9(9).
          [Social Security number.]
          10   SS-Person-Name   PIC X(25).
          [Name of person.]
     □  □  □
*    First zero out the SS-Person-No elements.
     PERFORM VARYING Ip FROM 1 BY 1 UNTIL Ip > SS-Max-Size
       MOVE ZEROS TO SS-Person-No(Ip)
     END-PERFORM
```

Next, write a procedure to add entries to the table. The person's name must first be moved to *SS-Name,* and the Social Security number to *SS-No.* You perform the procedure as follows:

```
        MOVE Social-Security-number TO SS-No
        MOVE person's-name TO SS-Name
        PERFORM C10-Add-Name
```

The *C10-Add-Name* procedure is written as follows:

```
 C10-Add-Name.
 **************************************************************
 * PROCEDURE TO ADD ENTRIES TO Person TABLE.              *
 * IN:   SS-No contains Social Security number.           *
 *       SS-Name contains person's name.                  *
 * OUT:  Ip points to where SS-No stored.                 *
 *       SS-No stored in SS-Person-No(Ip).                *
 *       SS-Name stored in SS-Person-Name(Ip).            *
 **************************************************************
        COMPUTE SS-Subscript = FUNCTION REM(SS-No, SS-Div) + 1
        [Convert Social Security number to value from 1 to SS-Div by dividing it by
        prime number, keeping the remainder.]
        SET Ip TO SS-Subscript       [Search from SS-Subscript forward.]
        SEARCH SS-Person
          AT END
        [Not found from SS-Subscript to end of table. Wrap around to search from 1 up to
        SS-Subscript.]
            SET Ip TO 1
            SEARCH SS-Person
              WHEN Ip = SS-Subscript
                    [Wrapped around to SS-Subscript. Person not in table.]
                DISPLAY
                    "ERROR - SS-Person TABLE FULL, RUN TERMINATED."
                DISPLAY
            "INCREASE SS-Person- SS-Div, SS-Max-Size AND RECOMPILE."
                GO TO Z90-Stop-Run
              WHEN SS-Person-No(Ip) = ZEROS
                    [Found an empty slot. Store SS-No and SS-Name.]
                MOVE SS-No TO SS-Person-No(Ip)
                MOVE SS-Name TO SS-Person-Name(Ip)
            END-SEARCH
          WHEN SS-Person-No(Ip) = ZEROS
          [Found an empty slot. Store SS-No and SS-Name.]
            MOVE SS-No TO SS-Person-No(Ip)
            MOVE SS-Name TO SS-Person-Name(Ip)
        END-SEARCH
        SET SS-Subscript TO Ip

 **** Exit
```

You also need a procedure to retrieve a person's name given the Social Security number. The Social Security number is first moved to *SS-No*, and the name is returned in *SS-Name*. If the name is not found, *SS-Name* contains spaces. The procedure is invoked as follows:

```
    MOVE social-security-number TO SS-No
    PERFORM C20-Retrieve-Name
```

The *C20-Retrieve-Name* procedure is written as follows:

```
 C20-Retrieve-Name.
 ***************************************************************
 * PROCEDURE TO RETRIEVE A Person's NAME.                      *
 * IN:  SS-No contains Social Security number.                 *
 * OUT: If found:                                              *
 *          SS-Subscript points to entry in table.             *
 *          SS-Name contains person's name.                    *
 *      Not found:                                             *
 *          SS-Subscript contains ZERO.                        *
 *          SS-Name contains SPACES.                           *
 ***************************************************************
     COMPUTE SS-Subscript = FUNCTION REM(SS-No, SS-Div) + 1
```
[Convert Social Security number to value from 1 to *SS-Div* by dividing it by prime number, keeping the remainder.]
```
     SET Ip TO SS-Subscript        [Search from SS-Subscript forward.]
     SEARCH SS-Person
       AT END
```
[Not found from *SS-Subscript* to end of table. Wrap around to search from 1 up to *SS-Subscript*.]
```
         SET Ip TO 1
         SEARCH SS-Person
         WHEN Ip = SS-Subscript OR SS-Person-No(Ip) = ZERO
```
                    [Wrapped around to *SS-Subscript* or found an empty slot. Person not in table.]
```
             MOVE SPACES TO SS-Name
             MOVE ZERO TO SS-Subscript
         WHEN SS-No = SS-Person-No(Ip)        [Found person.]
             MOVE SS-Person-Name(Ip) TO SS-Name
             SET SS-Subscript TO Ip
         END-SEARCH
       WHEN SS-Person-No(Ip) = ZERO
```
[Reached an empty slot. Person not in table.]
```
         MOVE SPACES TO SS-Name
         MOVE ZERO TO SS-Subscript
       WHEN SS-No = SS-Person-No(Ip)        [Found person.]
         MOVE SS-Person-Name(Ip) TO SS-Name
         SET SS-Subscript TO Ip
     END-SEARCH
```

```
**** Exit
```

There still remains a problem if the key is alphanumeric rather than numeric. You solve this by moving the alphanumeric item to another alphanumeric item redefined as a BINARY data item. (It cannot exceed nine digits.) The following example illustrates this. The person's name, not the Social Security number, is used to compute the subscript.

```
       05  SS-Name             PIC X(25).
       05  SS-Short-Name       PIC X(8).
       05  SS-Convert          REDEFINES SS-Short-Name
                               PIC S9(9) BINARY.

   MOVE SS-Name TO SS-Short-Name
   COMPUTE SS-Subscript = FUNCTION REM(SS-Convert, SS-Div) + 1
```

Fortunately, hash tables are not often needed. For a table with few entries, a sequential search would be simpler and more efficient. If only a few entries are added to the table but you search it often, you might use a binary search. You would move all the entries in the table down to make room for a new entry. The hash table technique is also used for relative files, in which the entries are records stored in a file rather than elements of a table in memory.

13.7 READING IN TABLES

Essential

You often read a table in from a file. In the following example, a personnel file is read and the employee IDs are stored in a table, perhaps to validate transactions with a binary search. There are several things to note in this example. First, assume the payroll file has 1000-byte records, but that you need to save only the 10-byte employee ID. The table is a variable-size table, because the number of employees will change. If the table overflows, you display a message telling how to change the program. The payroll file must already be in sort on the employee ID in ascending order, and the program will check to ensure that this is true.

```
   WORKING-STORAGE SECTION.
   01  Old-Id                  PIC X(10).
   *                               Old-Id checks the sort
   *                               order of Input-File.
   **** Employee file.  Record length = 1000.
   01  Employee.
       05  Employee-Id         PIC X(10).
       05  FILLER              PIC X(990).
   **** Table of employee IDs.
   01  ID-Record.
       05  ID-Max              PIC S9(4) BINARY VALUE 1000.
   *                               Maximum IDs in table.
       05  ID-No               PIC S9(4) BINARY VALUE ZERO.
   *                               Current size of table.
       05  ID-Table            OCCURS 0 TO 1000 TIMES
                               DEPENDING ON ID-No
                               ASCENDING KEY IS ID-Id
                               INDEXED BY Idx.
           10  ID-Id           PIC X(10).
   □   □   □
   OPEN INPUT Pay-In
   MOVE LOW-VALUES TO Employee-Id, Old-Id
   PERFORM B20-Store-Ids WITH TEST AFTER
           UNTIL Employee-Id = HIGH-VALUES
```

```
        CLOSE Pay-In
          □   □   □
    B20-Store-Ids.
    *****************************************************************
    * PROCEDURE TO READ IDS AND STORE THEM IN THE TABLE.          *
    * IN:  Pay-In file open.                                      *
    *      ID-No points to last entry in table.                  *
    *      Old-Id contains previous ID.                          *
    * OUT: Pay-In file open.  One record read.                   *
    *      ID-No increased by 1.                                  *
    *      Employee-Id stored in Old-Id, ID-Id(ID-No).           *
    *      Employee-Id contains HIGH-VALUES if EOF.              *
    *****************************************************************
        READ Pay-In INTO Employee
          AT END MOVE HIGH-VALUES TO Employee-Id
          NOT AT END
            IF Employee-Id < Old-Id
              THEN DISPLAY
                "ERROR - PAYROLL FILE NOT IN SORT, RUN TERMINATED."
                  DISPLAY "OLD ID: ", Old-Id, "CURRENT ID: ",
                          Employee-Id
                  GO TO Z90-Stop-Run
            END-IF
            MOVE Employee-Id TO Old-Id
            ADD 1 TO ID-No
            IF ID-No > ID-Max
              THEN DISPLAY
                  "ERROR - ID-Table OVERFLOW, RUN TERMINATED."
                  DISPLAY "PAYROLL RECORD: ", Employee-Id
                  DISPLAY
                  "INCREASE ID-Max, ID-Table AND RECOMPILE PROGRAM."
                  GO TO Z90-Stop-Run
            END-IF
            MOVE Employee-Id TO ID-Id(ID-No)
        END-READ
          .
    **** Exit
```

Now, whenever an ID is to be validated, the following can be coded.

```
    SEARCH ALL ID-Table
      AT END statements-if-not-found
      WHEN ID-Id(Idx) = id statements-if-found
    END-SEARCH
```

13.8   TREE STRUCTURES

Rarely Used

Tree structures are occasionally needed in COBOL to represent hierarchical data. For example, a company may be divided into several divisions, with each division further subdivided. You can represent this organization with a tree structure.

Figure 13.1 shows a company's organization chart, in which each box represents an organizational unit, which is assigned a unique number.

One way to represent such a tree structure is to let the department numbers themselves specify the hierarchy. In Figure 13.1, the first digit represents level 1 of the organization, the second digit level 2, and the third digit level 3. The department table for such a numbering convention is shown in Table 13.1.

If the department table is sorted on the department number, it is also placed in hierarchical order. The COBOL statements necessary to contain this department table are as follows:

```
01  Department.
    05  Dept-Size          PIC S9(4) BINARY.
    05  Dept-Table         OCCURS 0 TO 100 TIMES
                           DEPENDING ON Dept-Size
                           INDEXED BY X-Dept.
        10  Dept-No        PIC X(3).
        10  Dept-Name      PIC X(25).
```

The table has a varying size, because departments are likely to be added or deleted. If the department table were contained in a file, each record would contain a department, and the records could be read into *Dept-Table*.

Tree structures must often be searched, but the search is usually to locate all the entries above or below a specific entry in the hierarchy. For example, if you were adding a new department, you would want to make sure that the departments above it in the hierarchy exist. In Figure 13.1, the number itself contains the hierarchy, so that if department 113 is added, you would search for departments 110 and 100. If you delete a department, you may want to delete all departments below it in the hierarchy. To search down in the hierarchy, you must find all records whose high-order digits match this one. For example, if you delete depart-

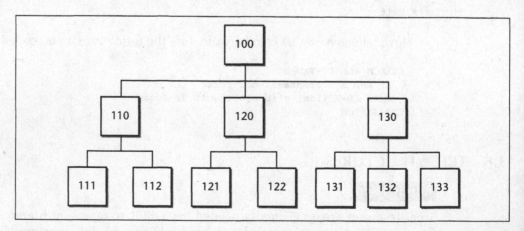

FIGURE 13.1 Organization chart represented by a tree structure.

TABLE 13.1 A Department Table

Department Number	Department Name
100	Computer Division
110	Operations Department
111	Computer Operators
112	Distribution
120	Programming Department

ment 110, you could search the table to find all departments that are numbered 11n and delete them, too.

The disadvantage of this technique, in which the numbers themselves specify the hierarchy, is that you may run out of numbers. Or you may want to transfer one number to be under another. For example, you may want to transfer department 111 to be under department 120. For this, you must store the full upward hierarchy for each record. Such a table would look as shown in Table 13.2.

The department numbers are arbitrary and signify nothing. To transfer department 111 under department 120, you change the record for department 111 as follows:

111   3   100 120 111   Computer Operations

Notice that the department number is stored twice in each record. This is redundant data, but it is necessary for sorting the department table on the department numbers into hierarchical order. The COBOL statements to contain the table would be as follows:

```
01  Department.
    05  Dept-Size          PIC S9(4) BINARY.
    05  Dept-Table         OCCURS 0 TO 100 TIMES
                           DEPENDING ON Dept-Size
                           INDEXED BY X-Dept.
        10  Dept-No        PIC X(3).
        10  Dept-Level     PIC 9.
```

TABLE 13.2 A Department Hierarchy Table

Department Number	Level	Hierarchy	Department Name
100	1	100	Computer Division
110	2	100 110	Operations Department
111	3	100 110 111	Computer Operations
112	3	100 110 112	Distribution
120	2	100 120	Programming Department

```
10   Dept-Hier.
     15   Dept-1        PIC X(3).
     15   Dept-2        PIC X(3).
     15   Dept-3        PIC X(3).
10   Dept-Name          PIC X(25).
```

It is easy to find all the departments above any department in the hierarchy, because the upward hierarchy is contained in each record. To find all the departments below a given department, search the table for those records whose hierarchy points to this department. For example, to find all departments belonging to department 110, which is a level 2 department, look for all records whose *Dept-2* is 110.

Tracing down in the tree structure is more complicated if the entire table cannot be contained in memory. You could read the entire department file sequentially to find the records below a given record in the hierarchy, but this is slow if the file is large. An alternative is to store for each department all those departments that belong to it in the hierarchy. The record for such a file would look as shown in Table 13.3.

The COBOL statements to describe the records in the file would be as follows:

```
01   Dept-Record.
     05   Dept-No                   PIC X(3).
     05   Dept-Level                PIC 9.
     05   Dept-Hier.
          10   Dept-1               PIC X(3).
          10   Dept-2               PIC X(3).
          10   Dept-3               PIC X(3).
     05   Dept-Subordinate-Count    PIC S9(3) PACKED-DECIMAL.
     05   Dept-Subordinate-Hier     OCCURS 0 TO 100 TIMES
                                    DEPENDING ON Dept-Subordinate-Count
                                    INDEXED BY X-Down.
          10   Dept-subordinate     PIC X(3).
```

This record would be especially useful for relative or indexed files, in which records can be accessed directly. To read all records above a given department, you would use the superior hierarchy as the key and read these records directly. To read all records below a given department, you would use the subordinate hierarchy and read these records directly. If necessary, you could use the subordinate

TABLE 13.3   A Department Tree Table

Department Number	Level	Superior Hierarchy	Subordinate Hierarchy
100	1	100	110 120 130
110	2	100 110	111 112
111	3	100 110 111	
112	3	100 110 112	
120	2	100 120	121 122

TABLE 13.4 A Department Binary Tree Table

Department Number	Level	Superior Hierarchy	Down Pointer	Side Pointer
100	1	100	110	—
110	2	100 110	111	120
111	3	100 110 111	—	112
112	3	100 110 112	—	—
120	2	100 120	121	130

hierarchy of the records that are read to go down to the next level in the hierarchy. This could continue until you have read all the records.

An alternative way of tracing down the tree structure is to keep only one down pointer and then keep a side pointer. (Such a structure is termed a *binary tree,* because each element has only two pointers.) Thus, you can go down one level in the hierarchy with the down pointer and then look at all items at this level with the side pointers. The table would look as shown in Table 13.4.

To find all the level 2 entries in the table given the department 100, you would use the down pointer to locate 110. Then you would use the side pointer to locate 120, then its side pointer to locate 130. The advantage of this type of organization over the previous one is that you need not guess the maximum number of entries at each level. Only one down pointer and one side pointer are needed. On the other hand, it is slower and more complicated to find all the entries at the next level down if the records reside in a file.

The COBOL statements to describe the records in the file would be as follows:

```
01  Dept-Record.
    05  Dept-No           PIC X(3).
    05  Dept-Level        PIC 9.
    05  Dept-Hier.
        10  Dept-1        PIC X(3).
        10  Dept-2        PIC X(3).
        10  Dept-3        PIC X(3).
    05  Dept-Down-Ptr     PIC X(3).
    05  Dept-Side-Ptr     PIC X(3).
```

This completes the discussion of records and tables. There are many other sophisticated record and data structures used in computing that generally require dynamic storage allocation and a facility for operating on storage addresses. Chapter 25 describes some of these.

EXERCISES

1. Define a table to contain numbers with a maximum magnitude of 999.99. The table is to contain 100 elements. Write the statements necessary to fill the table with the numbers from 1 to 100.

2. Define two numeric tables named *Hours* and *Salary* with dimensions 50 by 20. Multiply the corresponding elements of each table together and store the results in a table named *Wages* having the same dimensions. All elements are to have precision S9(7)V9(2).

3. Define a numeric table named *Tables* containing 200 elements. The largest number the table is to contain is 999.9999. Assume that the table is unordered and write the statements necessary to count the number of times the number 3.6257 appears in the table. Then write the statements to see if the number 0.7963 is in the table. Finally, assume that the table is in ascending numeric order and write the statements necessary to determine if the number 2.1537 is in the table.

4. Define a table named *City* to contain the population of each of 3 cities within each county, 30 counties within each state, and 50 states. What is the size of the table? Write the statements necessary to sum the total population for all states.

5. A single-dimensional table named *Population* contains 100 numeric elements. Define the table and sort the values of the table into ascending numerical order, writing your own sort.

6. Declare and initialize a table named *Calendar* containing 12 elements of 9 characters each to contain the names of the months. The first element would contain "JANUARY", and so on.

7. A table named *Lots* has 100 elements, and each element contains four characters. Count the occurrences of the characters "ABCD" and "CDBA" in the table.

8. Define a table named *Text-A* containing 50 elements of 9 characters each. Define two character data items named *Even* and *Odd* containing 225 characters each. Create two character strings from *Text-A* by concatenating all the even and all the odd elements and store them in *Even* and *Odd*.

9. A table named *Amount* has 100 elements. Sum the even elements from 2 up to and including element 50, and every third element from 15 to 100, but stop the summation if the total exceeds 1000.

CHAPTER 14

INPUT/OUTPUT CONCEPTS AND DEVICES

This chapter is critical to COBOL applications, especially those on the IBM mainframe. Skip this chapter only if you are familiar with the material.

14.1 INPUT/OUTPUT CONCEPTS

Essential

Input/output (I/O), the transmission of data between central storage and an input/output device, is often the most complex part of programming. It requires a knowledge of the data to be transmitted, the hardware devices, and the language features. The logic is deceptively complex, and the external hardware devices have physical limitations, such as storage capacity, that can cause problems.

COBOL applications are usually heavily I/O-oriented, and you should carefully select the proper I/O device for each file. Specify as little about the I/O device as possible within the program, leaving such details to system commands (JCL, AIX, OS/2, or Windows). By doing this, you can use a different I/O device or change a blocking factor without modifying the program. Then, if a disk file grows in size, requiring it to be moved to tape, or if a tape unit is changed to one of higher density, or if a program is tested with data on disk and then used to process records on tape during production, the program doesn't need to be recompiled.

COBOL input/output is record-oriented in that each READ or WRITE statement transmits a single logical record. A *logical record* is a logical unit of data that may contain several items of different data types. For example, a personnel record for a company might contain all the personnel data relating to an individual, such as name, age, and length of service. The words *record* and *logical record* are used interchangeably in the context of input/output.

The IBM mainframe blocks records. A *block* is a *physical record* that consists of one or more records stored as a unit on the I/O device for efficiency. Blocks are described in more detail later in this chapter.

253

14.2 RECORD FORMATS

The basic unit of an input/output operation in COBOL is the record. COBOL has three means of determining the length of a record. The record's length can be a constant, fixed length; it can be a variable length in which the record length is stored as part of the record; or it can be an undefined length in which a hardware marker denotes the end of the record.

14.2.1 Data Records

Individual fields with a record usually have a fixed length, but they can also be delimited by some character, such as a comma.

Tokenized or Delimited Data

A logical unit of related data is termed a *record*. A record in COBOL is unlike that found in other systems, such as C/C++ and UNIX. Typically, those systems use some character (*token*), such as a space or a comma, to separate the items of data (*tokenize* them). A record corresponds to a line and is typically delimited by a carriage return and new line characters. The data is transmitted as a continuous stream without regard to the record boundary. For example, typical data might be as follows, in which a comma delimits the items of data (this is termed *comma delimited data*):

```
Smith,John,102 Oak Street,Los Angeles,CA,90020,10000\r\n
Jones,Mary,77 6th Street,New York,NY,80010,15000\r\n
```

The \r\n represent the carriage return and new line characters. The problem with tokenized data is that it might contain the delimiter character. If the 10000 was written as 10,000, it would mess things up. Tokenized data is less efficient to process. The computer must scan down the line looking for the delimiter character to find where a data item begins and ends. The 10000 is a number recorded in character form, and the computer must convert this to its binary equivalent to do arithmetic on it. (You can't use a delimiter character for binary data because binary data might be any combination of bits, including that of any delimiter you might choose.)

COBOL Records

Although COBOL can process tokenized data as described in Chapter 22, its data is usually organized into record form. Rather than separating the items of data with a character, each data field is stored in fixed column positions, like this:

```
Smith    John   102 Oak Street   Los Angeles CA90020 1001110001000
Jones    Mary   77 6th Street    New York    NY90020 1110101001100
```

Notice that the 10000 and 15000 are stored as binary numbers, and would take either half or a full word of storage. The zip codes, because they don't participate in arithmetic operations, are stored as character data. The advantage of data in record form is that it is faster to process because the length of each data item is known and numeric data need not be converted from character to binary. No character need be reserved as the delimiter character. The disadvantage of record data is that you must decide how wide to make a field—not an easy matter for names and addresses—and it is relatively difficult to widen a field or insert a new field in the data. This is one reason why it is difficult to expand a two-digit year to four digits to solve the year-2000 problem.

14.2.2   OS/390 Record Formats and Blocking

Essential for Mainframe COBOL

OS/390 (and thus Mainframe COBOL) records have three forms: fixed-length, variable-length, and undefined-length. *Fixed-length* records all have the same length. For example, a file containing card images is fixed-length, because each card originally could contain 80 characters. Figure 14.1 illustrates fixed-length records.

Variable-length records, as their name implies, may have varying lengths. OS/390 appends 4 bytes to the front of the record to specify the record length and 4 additional bytes to specify the block size. For example, a personnel file containing employee names and the names of their dependents might be variable-length, because people have a varying number of dependents. Figure 14.2 illustrates variable-length records.

Undefined-length records also have varying lengths, but the record length is not contained in the record. The hardware separates records with a physical gap on the storage device, called an *interrecord gap* (IRG). Because a physical gap rather than special characters marks the end of a record, the record can contain any binary data. The computer is able to recognize this gap when transmitting a record, and thus it can distinguish between records. Undefined-length records cannot be blocked; each record constitutes a block. Undefined-length records are used when the record length is not known until after the entire record is written, as, for example, with data transmitted from an online terminal. They are also used to read files when you do not know the record format or even the record length of

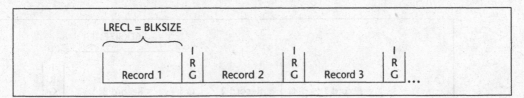

FIGURE 14.1   Fixed-length records.

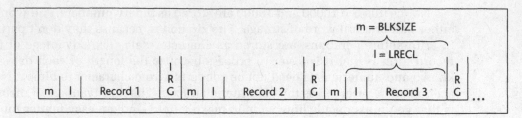

FIGURE 14.2   Variable-length records.

the records in a file. You can read the record as undefined and then display it to see what it contains. Figure 14.3 illustrates undefined-length records.

The system transfers data between memory and I/O devices in *blocks;* each block is separated by an interrecord gap. Several fixed- or variable-length records may be contained in a single block. Blocks of fixed-length records all have the same number of records in each block, except possibly for the last block. Blocks of variable-length records may have a varying number of records in each block. Only one undefined-length record can be contained in a block. A block, then, consists of one or more records to be transmitted at a time and stored on the I/O device as a physical record. Figure 14.4 illustrates blocked records.

You can also *span* records across several blocks. Spanned records allow the record length to exceed the block length so that the logical record is contained in two or more physical records. In OS/390, the maximum block length is 32,767 bytes. Spanned records let you exceed this. Spanned records are not a separate record format but a special form of either fixed- or variable-length records. (Undefined records cannot be spanned.) You specify spanned records in the JCL by appending S to the RECFM parameter. For example: RECFM=FS, FBS, VS, or VBS. Figure 14.5 illustrates spanned records.

The hardware can transmit data very quickly between memory and direct-access devices or magnetic tapes once the transmission of data begins. However, it may take quite long relative to the computer's speed to start the transmission, because of mechanical inertia. For direct-access devices, time is needed to position the access arm over the proper track and rotate it around to the start of the block. Blocking allows large, efficient groups of data to be transmitted at one time. Blocking also conserves storage space on the I/O device by limiting the number of interrecord gaps.

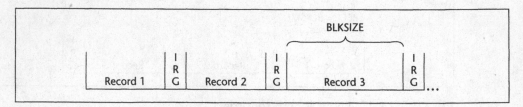

FIGURE 14.3   Undefined-length records.

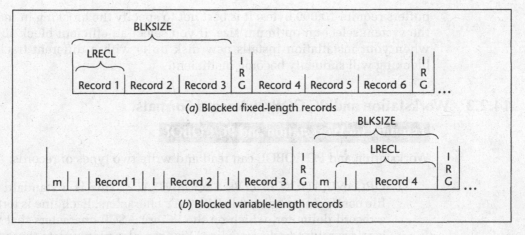

FIGURE 14.4 Blocked records.

The number of records per block is termed the *blocking factor*. The system reads a block of data into an area of memory called a *buffer*. When the last record of a block is processed, the system reads another block. The reverse occurs when data is written. The system provides several internal buffers so that while data is being processed in one buffer, the system can read the next block of data into another. This results in considerable efficiency because the I/O is *overlapped;* that is, data can be read or written simultaneously with computations being done in memory. Blocking is done only for hardware efficiency, and is unrelated to the way you want to process the data. The system does all blocking and unblocking, and there is no programming effort to block files. Consequently, programs can be compatible between Mainframe COBOL and other COBOL systems despite using entirely different blocking techniques.

The blocking factor for sequential files is likely to have more impact on the efficiency of the program than any other easily controlled factor. Block as high as possible within the constraints of the I/O devices. If a record containing 100 characters is blocked at 50 records per block, each block contains 5000 characters. Two

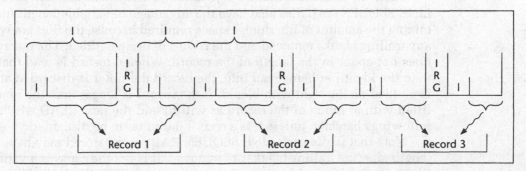

FIGURE 14.5 Spanned records.

buffers require 10,000 bytes. It is best not to specify the blocking in the JCL, to let the system select an optimum size. If you select an efficient block size yourself, when your installation installs new disk units with a different track size your blocking will suddenly become inefficient.

14.2.3   Workstation and PC COBOL Record Formats

Essential for Workstation and PC COBOL

Workstation and PC COBOL can read and write two types of records:

1. *ORGANIZATION IS LINE SEQUENTIAL.*   This is a standard ASCII text file containing displayable DISPLAY characters. Each line is terminated by a record delimiter, which on the PC are ASCII characters that represent a carriage return and a new line. You can also manipulate these files with a text editor.

2. *ORGANIZATION IS SEQUENTIAL.*   This is the typical file in OS/390. The data is stored as a single stream of data. It is left up to the program to know how long a record is. You can't manipulate these files with a text editor.

LINE SEQUENTIAL Files

The standard ASCII text files on the PC are essentially undefined, which means that they are fixed-length if the records all have the same length and variable-length if the lengths differ. These files are easily created, viewed, and modified by any text editor that can operate on ASCII files. You specify these files as LINE SEQUENTIAL in Workstation and PC COBOL. They do not default. You code the ORGANIZATION IS LINE SEQUENTIAL clause in the SELECT clause. In Workstation COBOL, don't code the BLOCK CONTAINS and LINAGE clauses or the WRITE AT END-OF-PAGE and WRITE BEFORE ADVANCING statements.

```
SELECT file-name ASSIGN TO ddname
   ORGANIZATION IS LINE SEQUENTIAL.
```

Make all Workstation and PC files that contain text be LINE SEQUENTIAL. LINE SEQUENTIAL files also have the advantage of variable-length files in minimizing the amount of file storage space required because the files are written with any trailing blanks removed and the record delimiter added. The record delimiter does not count in the length of the record. When a record is read that is shorter than the identifier being read into, the record delimiter is discarded and the data is padded on the right with blanks. If the record is longer than the identifier, it is filled with as much of the record as will fit and the next READ will begin at the following character, unless it is a record delimiter to be discarded.

Note that while each LINE SEQUENTIAL record stored may have a different length after the trailing blanks are removed, it is not the same as a variable-length file written with an identifier that contains the RECORD VARYING clause. For RECORD VARYING, you must use a SEQUENTIAL file.

SEQUENTIAL Files

SEQUENTIAL files are similar to OS/390 blocked files. The system collects records into a large block and writes them together. No text editor can know the block size, and so you cannot view or modify such files with a text editor. This is a real inconvenience in debugging. Not only can SEQUENTIAL files can be read and written faster than LINE SEQUENTIAL files, numeric data does not have to be converted from DISPLAY to numeric form to participate in arithmetic operations.

You must use SEQUENTIAL files in these instances:

- Where you want mainframe-type variable-length records.
- When your data might contain the record delimiter. This is always the case when you write binary or floating-point data.
- When you need the fastest I/O.

You get SEQUENTIAL as the default, or you can code the ORGANIZATION IS SEQUENTIAL clause in the SELECT clause.

```
SELECT file-name ASSIGN TO ddname
   ORGANIZATION IS SEQUENTIAL.       [This defaults if you omit it.]
```

14.3   FILES

Essential

You must open files before they can be used, and you should close them after processing is completed. (OS/390 calls a file a *data set.*) When a file is *opened,* the system creates all the internal tables needed to keep track of the I/O. It allocates storage for buffers, positions the file to the starting point, and generally readies the file for processing. *Closing* a file releases all buffers and tables associated with the file. It frees any tape drives no longer needed, deletes direct-access storage no longer needed, and generally cleans up after processing the file.

14.3.1   File Organization

Perhaps the most complicated part of COBOL input/output is the terminology. First, COBOL has three file organizations: sequential, relative, and indexed. The file organization determines how the records are stored. For a file with *sequential* organization, records are stored consecutively on the I/O device, and can only be retrieved serially, in the order that they are stored. In a file with *relative* organization, records are stored in what is essentially a table. You read or write records in any order based on their relative position in the file—first, second, third, and so on. For a file with *indexed* organization, each record has a *record key,* a portion of the record that uniquely identifies it. The system stores the records so that you can read or write them based on the record key. For example, in a personnel file, the employee ID might be the record key.

14.3.2   File Access Methods

COBOL also has three *access methods,* or means by which records in a file are read or written. *Sequential access* transmits the records one after the other in the order in which they are physically stored in the file. To transmit the last record, all the previous records must be transmitted. Sequential file organization can have only sequential access. Sequential access is optional for relative and indexed file organization.

Random access, often termed *direct access,* permits a single record to be transmitted in a file without disturbing the other records, and irrespective of its position in the file. (The term *random* means that any record can be read regardless of the previous record read, not that a record is selected at random when the file is read.) Thus, with random access you can read the last record in a file without having to read all the preceding records. Visualize a deck of playing cards. To locate the ace of hearts with sequential access, you deal one card at a time off the top of the deck until the card is found. For random access, you spread out the entire card deck, face up, so that you can see each card. Then you can select the ace of hearts directly. Only relative and indexed file organization can have random access.

A third access method, *dynamic,* is a combination of sequential and random access. It allows you to switch back and forth between the two. For example, you can use random access to retrieve a specific record, and then switch to sequential to read all the records that follow it. Only relative and indexed file organization can have dynamic access.

Sequential files are often sorted before processing to arrange the records in the necessary sequence. Relative and indexed files have a key with each record. For files with *relative* organization, the *key* is the record's relative position in the file and is not a part of the record. For files with *indexed* organization, the *key* is a part of the record. Records are stored in ascending order based on this key, and the system maintains a set of indexes to locate the record on the disk, called a *direct-access storage device* on the mainframe. *Disk* and *direct-access storage device* (DASD) are interchangeable terms.

The hardware devices for I/O include disks, printers, and tape drives. There are other devices, such as magnetic card readers and bar code readers, but they are specialized and less widely used.

In Mainframe COBOL, a tape reel or cartridge or a direct-access storage device unit is termed a *volume.* The volume has a volume label, and each file stored on the volume has a file label. For tape, the computer operators write the *volume label* containing the volume serial number as data on each volume. When your program requests a tape, the system matches it against the VOL=SER=*volume* parameter in the JCL to ensure that the operator has mounted the proper volume. The same is true for disk, but because disk units aren't mountable, you don't have to worry about an operator mounting the correct disk. For disk, you locate a file by giving the system its name and letting the system find the disk volume it is on.

14.4 INPUT STREAM DATA

Sometimes Used

The input stream is the source of the instructions directing the processing to be done on the computer. It may consist of keyboard input, but more often it is a file that is submitted to the computer by entering a command. In OS/390, you submit most files through ISPF commands.

On the IBM mainframe, 80-character lines in the input stream are a universal I/O medium because the primary computer input at one time was the 80-column punched card. Today, most terminals have 80-character lines, and so the standard remains.

In OS/390, lines are first queued on disk by the operating system. When the program reads a line, the system reads it from disk. This process, termed *spooling*, is necessary because several programs may be reading input lines concurrently. Input stream input is sequential, and you can update it with a text editor.

In Mainframe COBOL, input stream input is specified by the DD * statement. (Other COBOL systems require input to be stored in a separate file. They don't have the equivalent of DD * input.)

`//ddname DD *`
[Lines of data immediately follow.]

14.5 DIRECT-ACCESS STORAGE DEVICES

Essential for Mainframe COBOL

Direct-access storage devices are more versatile than tape. They have large capacity and fast access. They can contain sequential, relative, and indexed files. Direct-access storage derives its name from the way data is accessed. Unlike tape, you need not read the first nine records to get to the tenth. Direct-access storage devices today are all disk units. PCs have both hard disks and diskettes. They differ in speed and capacity, but not in how you program for them.

14.5.1 Disk Hardware

A disk device consists of a stack of rotating recording surfaces, similar to a stack of compact discs. Each disk surface contains many concentric tracks, each containing the same amount of data. A set of electronic read/write heads is connected to an access arm positioned on top of each disk surface. When a specific track is read or written, the hardware moves the access arm to position the read/write head over the track. This arm movement is called a *seek*. The read/write head looks for a special marker on the rotating track to tell it where the track begins. Thus, there are two physical delays in accessing a specific track: a *seek delay*, which depends on how far the access arm must be moved, and a *rotational delay,* which averages out to be one-half revolution.

These mechanical movements are the Achilles' heel of computing. Since the System/360 mainframe was introduced in 1964, the CPU speed, central storage, I/O data rates, and storage capacity have all increased by a factor of several hundred times whereas the seek and rotational delays have become only 3 to 7 times faster. This is one reason why, despite faster and faster PCs, it takes longer and longer to boot up Windows.

Because there is a read/write head for each disk surface, several tracks can be read without arm movement. The tracks that lie one above the other on different surfaces form an imaginary *cylinder,* in which all the tracks are accessible without arm movement once the cylinder is found.

At one time, mainframe disks were much larger than PC hard disks. Today, the mainframe has essentially the same hard disk as those on a PC. On the IBM mainframe, this is exemplified by the RAMAC disk storage based on redundant array of independent disks (RAID) technology. RAID groups several smaller hard disks into a single unit. Data can then be stored sequentially in strips across the several individual disks, rather than continuously on one disk, to reduce access time. The potential for hardware error is minimized by three levels of parity written onto a separate disk to allow all the data in an entire disk to be recovered, should it be lost.

14.5.2   Using Direct-Access Storage

Disks may be rewritten many times. Files can be deleted, allowing the space to be reallocated and reused. Alternatively, you may overwrite the data in an existing file. On the mainframe, disk storage is relatively expensive compared to tape. It gives immediate access, important in online applications. You often use it for temporary files and frequently used files. You must use it for relative and indexed files.

A major difference between OS/390 and other systems is that you must specify the amount of disk space to allocate to each file. The system terminates the program if the requested space is unavailable or if the program needs more space than requested. You allocate space with the SPACE parameter on the JCL DD statement. With tape, the entire tape volume is always available, and you don't reserve space. Estimating the disk space is a difficult task, particularly when a file tends to grow over time. In an OS/390 system, many users share the same disk volumes. There is no easy way to tell whether enough space will be available on a disk to run the program. Take special care in OS/390 production jobs to set up the JCL to reduce the risk of terminating because disk storage is not available. Delete all disk files in the last step in which they are used, to free up space for subsequent steps and for other jobs.

The mainframe problems of allocating space don't exist in VM, UNIX, or on the PC. They allocate space to files on demand. This is one reason why they are so much easier to use than the OS/390 mainframe.

4.6 MAGNETIC TAPES

Sometimes Used

Mainframe tapes consist of either tape reels or cartridges. A full two-tape cartridge contains roughly 10Gb (30Gb is compressed). Tape drives can also be attached to workstations and PCs, but they are rare. For them, you generally use diskettes, CD-ROM, or disk cartridges where tape would be used on the mainframe.

You can store a single file across several tape volumes, so that an unlimited amount of information can be stored. Tapes can contain only sequential files. You can also store several files on a single tape volume. The system separates them with file marks. In OS/390 JCL, you do this with the LABEL=*file-number* parameter on a DD statement. If any file is rewritten, all subsequent files on that tape reel are destroyed and must be rewritten. Thus, if a tape contains three files and the second file is rewritten, the first file is unchanged, but the third file is destroyed. You regenerate tapes by reading the old tape and applying any changes to produce a new tape. You create an automatic backup by keeping the old tape and the changes.

The system reads tapes by moving the tape past the read head to transmit the data. If an error is detected, the system attempts to reread the block several times before signaling an I/O error. The system notifies your program of the end of file if the file mark is read. The system writes a tape by transmitting data from memory onto the tape as it passes the write head. The data is immediately read back as it passes the read head to ensure that it is recorded correctly. The start of the tape contains a marker, which denotes the load point and allows a leader for threading. There is another marker at the end of the tape to mark the end of volume with enough space to allow unfinished blocks to be completely transmitted.

You may rewrite tapes many times, erasing the old data on tape as you write the new data. For safety, the operators can file-protect tape volumes, a hardware feature that physically prevents a tape from being written on.

Tape makes an excellent long-term storage medium, because it is inexpensive (as little as $10 a reel) and can contain vast amounts of information in a small storage space. Tapes may be faster or slower than direct-access storage, depending on the particular device. Automatic devices are available to load tape cartridges, but an operator must mount tape reels, and this may increase the turnaround time of the job.

14.7 FILE INTEGRITY

Essential

In crucial applications, such as an accounting or payroll system, many safeguards may need to be built in for file integrity. You need to ensure that the proper files are used and that the data they contain is correct. One way to ensure that the proper files are used and to protect their integrity is to write a header and trailer record in addition to the header and trailer labels written by the operating system. The header record might contain a date. This lets the program read the first record and check to see that the current file is supplied by comparing the data in the header record against a transaction date. The trailer record can contain any hash totals and record counts. (Hash totals are described later in this section.) It also gives positive proof that the file contains the last record it was intended to contain.

An additional safeguard of the file's integrity is to check the sequence of the records as they are read in. If a transaction is made up of multiple records, you can ensure that all the parts are present and that they, too, are in the proper order.

You should always validate source data entering a system to ensure that it is correct, or at least as correct as you can logically ensure it to be. The validation might include batch totals, hash totals, and field validation.

Do all validation in a single place. This makes the data consistent. You won't accept a transaction in one part of the program and reject it in another, as often happens when validation is done in several places. If the validation is changed, all the validation is in one place to change. Also, if you want to know what validation is done, it is all in one place to see.

Don't stop with the first error discovered in a transaction. Check for all possible errors before rejecting the transaction. This may result in some redundant error messages, but each pass through an editor should catch all possible errors.

14.7.1 Batch Totals

Sometimes Used

Batch totals ensure that the input is entered correctly. With each group of transactions, generally all those on a single input form, critical numeric fields are totaled by hand. This batch total and a transaction count are entered with the transactions so that if a transaction is lost or keyed improperly, the error can be detected. You can also add all the individual batch totals to obtain a grand total and a batch count. This gives an additional safeguard against losing an entire batch.

14.7.2 Hash Totals

Sometimes Used

The batch total is not so much a check against the computer doing something wrong as it is to ensure that transactions are not lost or entered improperly through human error. The usual internal safeguard against the computer making an error or dropping a record or transaction is the *hash total*. You create a hash total when the file is written by summing a numeric field within the record. You write this total as the last record in the file. Then, whenever the file is read, you sum the fields again and check this against the total in the last record. If the totals do not match, either a record was lost or a field was changed.

14.7.3 Field Validation

Sometimes Used

Batch and hash totals do not ensure that the data is correct—only that it is present. To ensure that the data is correct, you must validate individual fields. The secret of validating is to make few assumptions about the data. If a field is to contain numeric data, do not assume that it is numeric; it may contain invalid characters. The following validation checks may be made on individual fields and combinations of fields.

- *Character checking* ensures that fields that are to contain blanks do contain blanks and that nonblank fields are nonblank. Validate numeric fields to ensure that they contain only numeric data, and alphabetic fields only alphabetic data.

- *Field checking* performs a range check on numeric and alphanumeric fields to ensure that the data is within an acceptable range. Note that there may be two ranges—a range that is reasonable and a range that is valid. You can test a field to see that it contains only specific values by looking them up in a table or file. You can check fields for consistency. For example, if a person's age is less than 18 and he or she shows as a registered voter, there is likely to be an error. The Internal Revenue Service uses this technique extensively.

- *Cross validation* is done to ensure that dependencies in the data are observed. This often requires extensive logic. You might check for such things as a salary increase being within a prescribed range for an employee classification.

Alphanumeric fields are more difficult to validate. First, you may examine the field to see if it contains data. Blanks often represent the absence of data. Assuming there is data, you may be able to look values up in a table to validate them. When there can be many combinations of characters, as in names, addresses, and text, it is almost impossible to validate the data with the computer. You can sometimes use the ALPHABETIC test, but character data, such as a name, often contains nonalphabetic characters. You can also check the presence or absence of alphanumeric data, its length, and that it is left-justified. But humans are much better at validating text, and so to validate text, display it so that it can be proofread.

14.7.4 File Backup

Essential

In designing a system with files, give careful thought to recovering each file in the event that it is destroyed. Disk files can be deleted and tape files can be overwritten. The usual method of backing up files is to make a copy or to keep the old master file and the transactions. Copying a file takes extra effort and expense, whereas keeping the old master file and transactions requires no extra effort or expense. In the grandfather, father, son technique, you retain the master file and transactions for three or more cycles. This way you can go back one, two, or more previous cycles to recreate the new master file. Tape is generally the most convenient medium for this technique, but OS/390 provides generation data groups for disk storage to accomplish the same thing.

Commercial applications generally differ from scientific applications in file recovery. In scientific applications, there may be no means of regenerating a file. Telemetry data transmitted from a satellite cannot be recreated if it is lost. Consequently, in scientific applications, programmers often must recover as many records from a bad file as possible. In many instances, such as with telemetry data, it is not critical if some data is missing. In commercial applications, you would rarely try to recover records from a bad file. Rather, you would recreate it, because it is critical that none of the data be missing. The accounting books must balance, and all the employees must be paid.

14.8 THE VALIDATE STATEMENT

PROPOSED NEW ANSI STANDARD: Check Compiler to See if Implemented

Most of the items added to the new ANSI standard are items long a part of other languages. The VALIDATE statement is an innovative exception. With the VALIDATE statement, you specify the validation when you describe the data item. Then you execute the VALIDATE statement, naming the record, group item, or elementary data item. COBOL validates the data item and lets you display error messages about the results. It is a brilliant concept because the validation is placed with the data item where it is easy to find and easy to change. The VALIDATE statement itself is very simple:

```
VALIDATE identifier, identifier, …, identifier
```

You list the identifiers to validate. If you list a group item, all the items subordinate to it are also validated. Validation proceeds in the following steps. The new clauses are described following.

1. Format validation to check the value according to the PIC, SIGN, USAGE, and DEFAULT clauses.
2. Any DESTINATION clause is executed to store invalid values.
3. Content validation to check the value according to the CLASS and level 88 condition names.
4. Relational validation to check the value according to the ALLOW and INVALID clauses.

5. Error action as specified by the ERROR clauses to store values.

You specify the validation by coding the following clauses when you describe a group or data item. These items are ignored and have no effect except when the VALIDATE statement is executed.

14.8.1 The ALLOW Clause

You specify acceptable data values with the ALLOW clause that COBOL accepts, even if the value would cause other error checking to fail.

> **ALLOW** *literal* **OR** *literal* **OR** *literal* …
> [You can name a series of specific values. If the value of the data matches any literal, the data is valid. The absence of a match does not make the data invalid.]
> **ALLOW ONLY** *literal* **OR** *literal* **OR** *literal* …
> [Same as the previous, but if there is no match, the data is invalid.]
> **ALLOW WHEN** *condition*
> [You specify a condition that if evaluated to be true, makes the data valid.]
> **ALLOW ONLY** *literal* **OR** *literal* **OR** *literal* … **WHEN** *condition*
> [You can combine the literals with the WHEN. However, if you code ONLY with WHEN, you can code only one ALLOW clause for the item and any items subordinate to it.]

14.8.2 The CLASS Clause

The CLASS clause lets you specify the data class to use to validate the data. This is identical to the class condition described in Chapter 5. For example, if you specify NUMERIC for an alphanumeric item, COBOL checks the data value to see if it contains only valid numeric values.

> **CLASS IS** *class*

The *class* can be NUMERIC, ALPHABETIC, ALPHABETIC-LOWER, ALPHABETIC-UPPER, BOOLEAN, or a *class-name* in the SPECIAL-NAMES paragraph.

14.8.3 The DEFAULT Clause

If the data item is found to be invalid or if it is DISPLAY and contains all SPACES, the DEFAULT clause specifies a value to use for the remainder of the validation. Note that the value of the data item is not changed; only the value used for validation is changed.

> **DEFAULT IS** *item*

The *item* can be a literal, an identifier, or NONE. Coding NONE is the same as not coding the DEFAULT clause and doesn't change the value used for validation.

14.8.4 The DESTINATION Clause

The DESTINATION clause moves the value of a data item being validated to an identifier if the value is found to be invalid. (If you code the DEFAULT clause, the DEFAULT value rather than the data item's value is moved.) DESTINATION allows you to obtain and display invalid data values. You can also initialize the identifier before the VALIDATE and then test to see if the value has changed to determine if the data item was invalid.

```
DESTINATION IS identifier
```

14.8.5 The VARYING Clause

The same VARYING clause described in Chapter 18 for the report writer can be used for validation. It lets you specify a counter that you can use as a subscript to store different invalid data values in different elements of a table. The data item for which VARYING is coded must contain an OCCURS clause.

```
VARYING counter FROM expression BY expression
VARYING counter FROM expression          [BY 1 assumed.]
```

The temporary *counter* is automatically defined and exists only while the data item is being validated. The *expressions* must be arithmetic. They may reference the *counter,* and the values are converted to integer for execution. The *counter* is set to the FROM value and then is incremented by the BY value as each element of the table is validated.

14.8.6 The PRESENT WHEN Clause

The PRESENT WHEN clause is another clause borrowed from the report writer. It lets you give a condition under which the data item will be ignored for validation.

```
PRESENT WHEN condition
```

If the condition is evaluated as true, the value of the data item is validated. If false, it is not validated. You can't code PRESENT when on a level 01 or 77 data item.

14.8.7 The INVALID Clause

The INVALID clause lets you write a condition which, when the VALIDATE statement executes, determines whether the value of the data item is invalid.

```
INVALID WHEN condition
```

If the condition evaluates as true, the value is invalid.

14.8.8   Level 88 Condition-Name Checking

A new form of the level 88 condition name description can be used for validation. You can code a single value or a range of values.

```
VALID VALUE IS literal
VALID VALUES ARE literal THRU literal
```

Rather than specifying valid values, you can also specify invalid values.

```
INVALID VALUES …
```

You can add a conditional expression.

```
VALID/INVALID WHEN condition
```

Finally, you can code values and a condition.

```
VALID/INVALID VALUES … WHEN condition
```

For example:

```
05  No-Dependents      PIC S999.
    88  Check-Rec-2     VALID VALUE IS 2 THRU 30
                        WHEN Type-Rec = 2.
    88  Check-Rec-7     VALID VALUE IS 1 THRU 20
                        WHEN Type-Rec = 7.
```

14.8.9   The ERROR Clause

The ERROR clause lets you store valid values, generate error messages, or set error flags when an invalid data value is found. The first form lets you store values in the data item being checked.

```
ERROR STATUS IS value      [Item to move if invalid data.]
NO ERROR STATUS IS value   [Item to move if valid data.]
```

The second form lets you store a value, such as an error message or flag, in any identifier.

```
ERROR STATUS IS value FOR identifier
NO ERROR STATUS IS value FOR identifier
```

You can also specify the condition under which to store the value.

```
ERROR STATUS IS value ON condition FOR identifier
NO ERROR STATUS IS value ON condition FOR identifier
```

The *condition* can be FORMAT (format errors), CONTENT (invalid content), or RELATION (an ALLOW or INVALID WHEN condition). You can specify multiple ERROR clauses for the same data item.

```
01  Error-Msg.
    05  Error-Msg-1                  PIC X(30).
    05  Error-Msg-2                  PIC X(30).
    05  Error-Msg-3                  PIC X(30).
    □   □   □
    05  State-Code    PIC XX.
        ALLOW ONLY "CA" OR "WA" OR "OR"
        INVALID WHEN Rec-Type = "2"
        ERROR "XXX"
        ERROR "Invalid state code." ON CONTENT FOR Error-Msg-1
        ERROR "State code coded for rec type 2"
             ON RELATION FOR Error-Msg-2
        NO ERROR "Valid State Code" FOR Error-Msg-3
```

You can't code the ERROR clause if the data item has or is subordinate to an item that has an OCCURS DEPENDING ON clause.

CHAPTER 15

SEQUENTIAL INPUT/OUTPUT

Sequential input/output is at the heart of most legacy systems and is perhaps the most important part of COBOL. Don't skip this chapter.

15.1 ORDER OF INPUT/OUTPUT HEADERS AND CLAUSES

Essential

For reference, you must code the various headers and clauses for specifying I/O in the following order. Fortunately, you rarely need to code most of the FILE-CONTROL, I-O-CONTROL, and FD items.

```
IDENTIFICATION DIVISION.
PROGRAM-ID.  program-name.
ENVIRONMENT DIVISION.
CONFIGURATION SECTION.
INPUT-OUTPUT SECTION.
FILE-CONTROL.
    SELECT file-name
        [The order of the SELECT clauses doesn't matter.]
            ASSIGN TO …    RESERVE AREAS     ORGANIZATION IS …
            ACCESS MODE IS …    LOCK MODE IS …    PASSWORD IS …
            FILE STATUS IS ….        [Must terminate with a period.]
I-O-CONTROL.
        [The order of the I-O-CONTROL clauses doesn't matter.]
    SAME AREA, RECORD AREA, SORT AREA      RERUN ON …
    APPLY WRITE ONLY ….        [Must terminate with a period.]
DATA DIVISION.
FILE SECTION.
FD  file-name                [The order of the FD clauses doesn't matter.]
    EXTERNAL    GLOBAL    BLOCK CONTAINS …    RECORD CONTAINS …
    LINAGE IS …    RECORDING MODE IS …
    CODE-SET IS ….            [Must terminate with a period.]
WORKING-STORAGE SECTION.
LINKAGE SECTION.
```

```
PROCEDURE DIVISION.
DECLARATIVES.
section-name SECTION.
    USE AFTER … PROCEDURE.
paragraphs.
    statements
        .
END DECLARATIVES.
END PROGRAM program-name.
```

For sequential input/output, records are read and written in sequence. This is the simplest and most common form of I/O. You can perform it on all I/O devices, including disks, printers, and tapes.

15.2   FILE DEFINITION

Essential

You must specifically describe all files. OS/390 COBOL permits several I/O options to be coded in the program that can also be specified in the JCL. COBOL also has several anachronisms in the language described in Appendix C that remain from the past when there was no JCL to specify the I/O devices and their attributes.

Unless you specify otherwise, COBOL assumes files have sequential organization and access.

```
SELECT file-name ASSIGN TO ddname.
```

Same as:

```
SELECT file-name ASSIGN ddname
    ORGANIZATION IS SEQUENTIAL
    ACCESS MODE IS SEQUENTIAL.
```

15.2.1   The SELECT Clause

Essential

You must name each file, termed a *file-name,* in a separate SELECT clause in the Environment Division. The SELECT clause associates the external file with an internal name that you use in the COBOL program. By decoupling the external file name from the name you use to reference it in the program, the same program can operate on different files or the external file name can be changed without having to recompile the COBOL program.

For QSAM files (Queued Sequential Access Method, the regular sequential file) in Mainframe COBOL, the external name is a *ddname,* and you must code a JCL DD statement to give the operating system the external file name and other

necessary information about the file. You code the *ddname* as *ddname* or
S-ddname.

```
INPUT-OUTPUT SECTION.
FILE-CONTROL.
    SELECT file-name ASSIGN TO S-ddname
    □  □  □
//GO.ddname DD ...
```

For Mainframe COBOL VSAM (Virtual Sequential Access Method) sequential
files, prefix the ddname with AS-.

```
    SELECT file-name ASSIGN TO AS-ddname.
```

For VSAM-relative and -indexed files, omit the AS-.

```
    SELECT file-name ASSIGN TO ddname.
```

For Workstation and PC files, you associate the *ddname* in the ASSIGN clause
with a physical file name by using the facilities of the specific system. PC COBOL
provides two additional ways of specifying the physical file name that are not
compatible with IBM COBOL:

- By coding the external file name as a literal in the SELECT statement:
  ```
  SELECT file-name ASSIGN TO "file-name".
  ```
  For example:
  ```
  SELECT In-File ASSIGN TO "C:\COBOL\TEST\STUFF.TXT".
  ```

- By assigning the file to an alphanumeric identifier and moving a value to
  the item before opening the file. (This lets you obtain the file name during
  run time.)
  ```
  SELECT file-name ASSIGN TO identifier.
  □  □  □
  MOVE "file-name" TO identifier
  OPEN INPUT file-name ...
  ```
  For example:
  ```
  SELECT In-File ASSIGN TO What-File.
  □  □  □
  01 What-File              PIC X(30).
  □  □  □
  MOVE "C:\COBOL\TEST\STUFF.TXT" TO What-File
  OPEN INPUT In-File
  ```

The default file organization is SEQUENTIAL.

```
    SELECT file-name ASSIGN TO external-file
        ORGANIZATION IS SEQUENTIAL.
```

This is the same as:

```
SELECT file-name ASSIGN TO external-file.
```

To process text files in Workstation and PC COBOL, you add the ORGANI-ZATION IS LINE SEQUENTIAL clause to the SELECT clause as described in Chapter 14.

```
SELECT file-name ASSIGN TO external-file
    ORGANIZATION IS LINE SEQUENTIAL.
```

15.2.2   The SELECT OPTIONAL Clause

If the file may not exist when a file is opened for INPUT, I-O, or EXTEND, code the OPTIONAL clause so that COBOL doesn't fail the program if the file doesn't exist.

```
SELECT OPTIONAL In-File ASSIGN TO DDIN.
```

When you open such a file and it doesn't exist, you can test the file status by coding the FILE STATUS clause as described in Chapter 17.

15.2.3   Other SELECT Clauses

You must code the ORGANIZATION and ACCESS MODE clauses for relative and indexed files as described in Chapter 16. The remaining clauses are seldom used and are described in Chapter 17.

15.3   THE FILE DESCRIPTION (FD)

Essential

You further describe each file in the program with a File Description (FD) entry in the File Section of the Data Division. You must write the file's record description immediately following the FD entry.

```
DATA DIVISION.
FILE SECTION.
FD   file-name      [You must name the file-name in a SELECT statement.]
    BLOCK CONTAINS  0 RECORDS
        [Code this for Mainframe COBOL only. Other compilers ignore it. It specifies the
        blocking, and you should always code a length of zero. For writing data sets, the
        system selects an optimum block size when the file is written. For reading, the
        system obtains the block size from the data set label. Omit BLOCK CONTAINS for
        SYSIN/SYSOUT and VSAM files. If you omit BLOCK CONTAINS in Mainframe
        COBOL, records are not blocked, which is very wasteful. You can also code
        BLOCK CONTAINS integer CHARACTERS, rather than RECORDS, to specify the
        block size in bytes rather than records.]
    RECORD CONTAINS  integer CHARACTERS
```

[This specifies the record length in bytes. If you omit it, the system uses the length of the record that you describe following the SELECT. The literal *integer* should match the length of the *record* description that follows. COBOL ignores it if it does not. In Mainframe COBOL, you can code a value of zero and have the JCL specify the record length. You rarely need to code RECORD CONTAINS.]

[Terminate FD with a period.]

01 *record-description.*

[The *record-description* following the FD entry describes the record and defines its length. This record description area is termed the *record area.* Records become available here when they are read, and data is moved to this area before the records are written.]

There may be several *record-description* entries placed one after the other to describe the same input/output record. That is, each level 01 *record-description* implicitly redefines the previous. (For this reason, you can't code REDEFINES for a level 01 *record-description* here.) Variable-length records often require this, as do records that may have different formats. You reference a *record-description* when you write a record. If more than one file has the same *record-description* name, you must qualify these *record-description* names within the program: *record-description* IN *file-name.* Avoid this problem by making the *record-description* names unique.

```
FD   file-name BLOCK CONTAINS 0 RECORDS.
01   record-1-description.
01   record-2-description.
       .      .      .
01   record-n-description.
```

Choose file and record names that convey information to the reader. Pick names that make it apparent that the file name, record name, and *ddname* all relate to the same file. You might specify whether the file is input or output, perhaps by appending -I or -O to the file name. You might precede each record item with the *file-name.* If a file needs further documentation, place the comments immediately following the SELECT clause defining the file. The following example illustrates these suggestions.

```
     FILE-CONTROL.
         SELECT Pay-I ASSIGN TO PAY.
*                                        PAY is the current payroll
*                                        file for input.
         SELECT Rpt-O ASSIGN TO RPT.
*                                        RPT prints the payroll
*                                        listing for output.
     DATA DIVISION.
     FILE SECTION.
     FD  Pay-I BLOCK CONTAINS 0 RECORDS.
     01  Pay-I-Rec.
         05  Pay-Name                    PIC X(20).
*                                        Name of person.
```

```
        05  Pay-Address                    PIC X(60).
*                                          Person's mailing address.
        □ □ □
//GO.PAY DD …
//GO.RPT DD SYSOUT=A
```

15.3.1   The RECORDING MODE Clause

Rarely Used

Records are usually fixed-length, which is the default. You can specify different record formats, either explicitly or implicitly with the RECORDING MODE clause to specify the record format explicitly. The RECORDING MODE clause can specify fixed-length or variable-length records. For Mainframe COBOL, you can also specify undefined-length and spanned records. You code it as follows:

```
FD  file-name
                         F    [Fixed]
                         V    [Variable]
                         U    [Undefined. Mainframe COBOL only.]
                         S    [Spanned. Mainframe COBOL only.]
            RECORDING MODE IS _.
```

Here is an example:

```
FD  Pay-I BLOCK CONTAINS 0 RECORDS
    RECORDING MODE IS F.
```

You shouldn't need to code the RECORDING MODE clause, because the RECORD CONTAINS clause can tell COBOL whether the file is fixed-length or variable. In Mainframe COBOL, if the RECORD CONTAINS value is larger than the BLOCK CONTAINS value, the compiler knows you want spanned records. For U records, it is better to specify them with the RECFM=U parameter on the JCL DD statement. RECORDING MODE is ignored for VSAM files.

RECORDING MODE is ignored in Fujitsu COBOL. For Micro Focus COBOL, it is effective only if ORGANIZATION IS SEQUENTIAL is coded or implied. For ORGANIZATION IS LINE, RECORDING MODE is ignored, and trailing blanks are removed when characters are written.

15.3.2   Fixed-Length Records

Essential

You can specify fixed-length explicitly by coding RECORDING MODE IS F. If you omit RECORDING MODE, fixed-length records result if any of the following is true:

- RECORD CONTAINS *length* is coded in the FD. In Mainframe COBOL, if the RECORD CONTAINS *length* is greater than a nonzero BLOCK CONTAINS *length,* spanned records are assumed.

- All level 01 record descriptions for the file have the same length.
- None of the record descriptions contains an OCCURS DEPENDING ON.

That is, records are fixed-length unless you do something to make them variable-length.

```
FD  In-File BLOCK CONTAINS 0 RECORDS.
01  In-Rec                    PIC X(100).
        [This file is fixed-length.]
```

15.3.3   Variable-Length Records

Essential

You specify variable-length records as follows:

Explicitly, by coding RECORDING MODE IS V.

Explicitly, by coding RECORD CONTAINS *min* TO *max* CHARACTERS in the RD.

Explicitly, by coding a record description containing an OCCURS DEPENDING ON clause.

Implicitly, by coding several level 01 record descriptions for the same record, each having different lengths.

To determine the length of each record and block, OS/390 appends a four-byte field, containing the record length, to each record. It also appends a four-byte field, containing the block size, to each block. Exclude these fields in the count for the RECORD and BLOCK CONTAINS clauses, and do not provide space for them in the record descriptions; the operating system does this automatically. However, you must count these fields in coding any LRECL and BLKSIZE parameters in OS/390 JCL. A typical variable-length record might be described as follows:

```
FD  In-File BLOCK CONTAINS 0 RECORDS
        [Always code BLOCK CONTAINS 0 in Mainframe COBOL. Other systems ignore it.]
    RECORD CONTAINS min TO max CHARACTERS.
```

Verbose form:

```
RECORD IS VARYING IN SIZE FROM min TO max CHARACTERS.
```

You specify the smallest and largest record sizes in the form *min* TO *max*. The *min* cannot be less than one nor greater than *max*. It doesn't matter what values you code, because the compiler determines the record lengths from the length of the level 01 record descriptions.

```
01  In-Rec.
    05  In-Info              PIC X(98).
    05  In-Size              PIC S999 PACKED-DECIMAL.
```

```
05  In-Table                    OCCURS 0 TO 100 TIMES
                                DEPENDING ON In-Size PIC X(3).
```

The length of the variable-length record written by a WRITE, REWRITE, or RELEASE statement depends on the length of the record description referenced by the statement. If the record description is fixed-length, the variable-length record will have that length. If the record description contains an OCCURS DEPENDING ON clause, the length of the record will depend on the current size of the table.

Rather than have the record length depend on a record description, you can make it depend on a data item. For this, you code the RECORD phrase as

RECORD CONTAINS *min* **TO** *max* **CHARACTERS DEPENDING ON** *length*.

Verbose form:

RECORD IS VARYING IN SIZE FROM *min* **TO** *max* **CHARACTERS**
DEPENDING ON *length*.

The *length* must be an elementary unsigned data item in Working-Storage or the Linkage Section. You must store the number of characters in *length* before executing any WRITE, REWRITE, or RELEASE statement. Execution of any I/O statements leaves the contents of *length* unchanged. When a READ or RETURN statement is executed, the length of the record read is stored in *length*.

PC COBOL assumes ORGANIZATION IS SEQUENTIAL unless you specify something different. This writes the length of each record in front of each record, as is done in OS/390, allowing the record length to be determined when the records are read. For ORGANIZATION IS LINE SEQUENTIAL, PC COBOL removes trailing blanks from the record and writes the remaining characters. Any RECORD VARYING clause is ignored.

15.3.4   Undefined-Length Records (Mainframe COBOL Only)

Rarely Used

You must explicitly specify undefined-length records by coding RECORDING MODE IS U. The record description may contain the OCCURS DEPENDING ON clause, or there may be several level 01 record descriptions having different lengths. Omit the BLOCK CONTAINS clause, because undefined records cannot be blocked. COBOL ignores the RECORD CONTAINS clause and uses the record descriptions to determine the record length. A typical undefined-length record might be described as follows:

```
FD  In-File
    RECORD CONTAINS 200 CHARACTERS
    RECORDING MODE IS U.
```

```
01  In-Rec-1                              PIC X(100).
```
      [The record would probably need to contain a code to indicate which record
      description is applicable.]
```
01  In-Rec-2                              PIC X(200).
```

15.3.5 Spanned Records (Mainframe COBOL Only)

> **Rarely Used**

Spanned records are records in which the logical record length exceeds the block
size, requiring the record to be spanned across more than one block. You specify
spanned records by coding RECORDING MODE IS S. (They also result if
RECORDING MODE is not coded and the RECORD CONTAINS length is greater
than the BLOCK length, assuming the BLOCK length is nonzero.) The records may
be fixed- or variable-length. They are variable-length if

- You code RECORD CONTAINS *min* TO *max*.
- You code several level 01 record descriptions of different lengths for the file.
- You code a record description with the OCCURS DEPENDING ON clause.

In all other cases, the records are fixed-length. A typical spanned record might
be described as follows:

```
FD  In-File BLOCK CONTAINS 0 RECORDS
        [You must code BLOCK CONTAINS for spanned records.]
    RECORD CONTAINS 0 TO 200 CHARACTERS
        [This will be a variable-length record.]
    RECORDING MODE IS S.
01  In-Rec-1                              PIC X(100).
01  In-Rec-2                              PIC X(200).
```

Note that spanned records can also be specified in OS/390 JCL by coding
RECFM=VBS or FBS.

15.4 OPENING AND CLOSING FILES

> **Essential**

Opening a file allocates the buffers, loads the access routines into central storage,
creates or checks the file labels, and positions the I/O device to the start of the file.
Closing a file writes out any remaining records in the output buffers, writes an end
of file on output files, and for tape may rewind the tape.

    The OPEN statement must open files before being used, and the CLOSE state-
ment should close them after processing completes. (COBOL automatically closes
any open files at run termination.) You can open files more than once, as long as

you close them before opening them again. That is, open-close-open is valid, but open-open is not.

15.4.1   The OPEN Statement

Essential

You write the OPEN statement as follows:

```
          INPUT
          OUTPUT
          I-O
          EXTEND
    OPEN _____  file-name, file-name, …, file-name
```

These options affect the opening of the file as follows:

INPUT opens the file and positions it to its start point for reading.

OUTPUT creates the file if necessary and positions it to its start point for writing.

I-O opens the file for both input and output. This option is used for updating files.

EXTEND opens the file for output. If the file doesn't already exist, COBOL creates it. If it does exist, the system positions just past the last record in the file for writing. This allows you to add records to an existing file. EXTEND can also be accomplished by coding DISP=(MOD, . . .) in OS/390 JCL.

You can also open multiple files for INPUT, OUTPUT, EXTEND, and I-O with the same OPEN statement:

```
    OPEN INPUT   file-name, file-name, …, file-name
         OUTPUT  file-name, file-name, …, file-name
         EXTEND  file-name, file-name, …, file-name
         I-O     file-name, file-name, …, file-name
```

For example:

```
OPEN INPUT File-A, File-B OUTPUT File-C
```

If an OPEN statement is executed for a file that is already open, the USE AFTER EXCEPTION/ERROR procedure described in Chapter 17 is executed if provided.

The following are examples of OPEN statements:

```
    OPEN INPUT File-A
    OPEN OUTPUT File-B
    OPEN INPUT File-C, File-D OUTPUT File-E
```

15.4.2 The CLOSE Statement

Essential

You code the CLOSE statement as follows:

```
CLOSE file-name, file-name, ..., file-name
```

The system automatically writes labels and an end of file marker on an output file when it is closed. If you attempt to close a file that is not open, the USE AFTER EXCEPTION/ERROR procedure described in Chapter 17 is executed if provided.

The following are examples of CLOSE statements:

```
CLOSE File-A
CLOSE File-B, File-C
```

It is generally more efficient to open and close several files with a single statement. However, the system allocates buffers to each file, and the central storage requirement is greater if all files are open concurrently. You can read the same file several times by closing it and opening it again. You can also write a file, close it, open it again, and then read it.

```
OPEN INPUT or OUTPUT File-A
CLOSE File-A
OPEN INPUT File-A
```

In OS/390, you can delete a data set when you close it by coding DISP=(. . . ,DELETE) on the JCL DD statement. You can delete both normal and VSAM data sets this way.

If the file is contained on a tape volume, the tape is automatically rewound. To close a tape file without rewinding it in Mainframe COBOL, you can code CLOSE *file-name* WITH NO REWIND or code a JCL DD statement with either DISP=(. . . ,PASS) or VOL=(,RETAIN, . . .). This speeds processing when another file is to be read or written beyond the end of the first file.

```
CLOSE file-name WITH NO REWIND
```

Or

```
//ddname DD DSN=data-set-name,DISP=(OLD,PASS),...
```

Preventing a Second Open: The LOCK Clause

Rarely Used

To prevent a file from being opened a second time by the program during a run, close files with LOCK. (This is of marginal value, but it might protect against some programming errors, because if you didn't want a file opened a second time, you wouldn't code the program to open it.)

```
CLOSE file-name WITH LOCK
```

Forcing Tape Volume Switching: The REEL Clause

Rarely Used

To force volume switching to the next volume of a multivolume tape file, code the REEL clause. The file isn't closed when REEL is coded—only a volume switch occurs. For files not on tape or for single-volume tape files, CLOSE REEL is ignored. You code it as

```
CLOSE file-name REEL     or     CLOSE file-name UNIT
```

For an input file, REEL forces volume switch, and the next volume is mounted. If it doesn't contain any records, another volume switch occurs. For an output file, a volume switch occurs; the system mounts the next volume and positions it to its starting point for writing. OS/390 volume switching is automatic, so there is no need to code REEL for it.

15.5 READ AND WRITE STATEMENTS

Essential

Each READ statement reads a single logical record, and each WRITE statement writes a single logical record. There are two ways of reading or writing records. First, you can READ INTO or WRITE FROM an identifier. Or you can omit the INTO or FROM phrases and process the records directly in the record area; that is, in the buffer. The READ INTO and WRITE FROM are less efficient, because the record must be moved from the record area to the identifier, but they are perhaps easier to understand and are described first.

15.5.1 READ INTO Form

Essential

```
READ file-name INTO identifier
  AT END imperative-statements
  NOT AT END imperative-statements
END-READ
```

Verbose form:

```
READ file-name NEXT RECORD INTO identifier
```

The *file-name* is a file name described in an FD entry.

The *identifier* is a record whose length is long enough to contain the record. It can be in the Working-Storage or Linkage Section, or it can be the record description of another open file.

AT END *imperative-statement* provides statements to execute when an end of file is encountered—that is, when an attempt is made to read a record after the last record has been read. AT END is required unless the USE AFTER ERROR procedure described in Chapter 17 is specified for the file. (AT END can be omitted in Mainframe COBOL even without a USE AFTER.)

NOT AT END is optional and executes statements if no end of file is encountered, that is, if a record is read.

15.5.2 WRITE FROM Form

Essential

```
WRITE record-description FROM identifier
```

The *record-description* is described in the record area following the FD entry. The *identifier* is a record described in the Data Division that contains the record to write.

Remember that you must READ a *file-name* and WRITE a *record-description*. (The logic of this is that you read from the file and write from the record in central storage.) Also remember that the file must be open for INPUT for a READ and OUTPUT or EXTEND for a WRITE. The following example illustrates a single file that is first written and then read:

```
DATA DIVISION.
FILE SECTION.
FD  Pay-File BLOCK CONTAINS 0 RECORDS.
01  Pay-Rec                              PIC X(80).
WORKING-STORAGE SECTION.
01  Data-Rec                             PIC X(80).
PROCEDURE DIVISION.
A00-Begin.
    OPEN OUTPUT Pay-File              [Open the file for output.]
    MOVE SPACES TO Data-Rec          [Fill Data-Rec with some data.]
    WRITE Pay-Rec FROM Data-Rec      [Then write a record.]
    CLOSE Pay-File                   [Close the file.]
    OPEN INPUT Pay-File              [Now open the file for input.]
    READ Pay-File INTO Data-Rec
      AT END DISPLAY "END OF FILE"
    NOT AT END DISPLAY "RECORD: ", Data-Rec
      [The NOT AT END statements execute, because there is a record to read.]
    END-READ
    READ Pay-File INTO Data-Rec
      AT END DISPLAY "END OF FILE"
```

[The AT END statements execute, because there are no more records.]
```
    NOT AT END DISPLAY "RECORD: ", Data-Rec
END-READ
CLOSE Pay-File
```

When the end of file is detected in a READ and the AT END phrase executes, no record is read and the contents of *identifier* are unchanged. Once the end of file is detected, a subsequent READ to that file will abnormally terminate the program. (However, you may close the file, open it again, and then read it.)

The result of a READ INTO and WRITE FROM is as if the record were moved to or from the record area. In a READ, if the *identifier* is shorter than the length of the record being read, COBOL truncates the record on the right. If longer, it pads the *identifier* on the right with blanks. For a WRITE, if the *identifier* is shorter than the file's record length, COBOL pads it on the right with blanks; if it is longer, it truncates it on the right.

15.5.3 READ, WRITE in the Record Area

Essential

You can also process records directly in the record area (the I/O buffers) by omitting the INTO or FROM phrase. You access the records by the record names in the record area. (After a READ, the record is also available in the record area when the INTO phrase is coded.) The following example illustrates this with the previous *Pay-File:*

```
READ Pay-File                            [The record is available in Pay-Rec.]
   AT END DISPLAY "END-OF-FILE"
   NOT AT END DISPLAY "RECORD: ", Pay-Rec
END-READ
MOVE Pay-Rec TO Data-Rec                 [Move the record to Data-Rec.]
```

The WRITE works in the reverse. You must move the data to the record:

```
MOVE Data-Rec TO Pay-Rec                 [The data is moved to Pay-Rec.]
WRITE Pay-Rec                            [The data in Pay-Rec is written.]
```

The concept of processing data in the buffers is confusing. Figure 15.1 illustrates what occurs inside the computer when a READ statement is executed. The buffer is equal in length to the block size, and the figure illustrates a block containing three records. The OPEN, READ, and CLOSE do the following:

Prior to the OPEN. *Pay-Rec* has no predictable value.

After OPEN. Storage is allocated for the buffer and the first block is read in from the file. The contents of *Pay-Rec* are undefined.

After first READ. No data is transmitted, but *Pay-Rec* is made to point to record 1 in the buffer. An INTO phrase would move record 1 to *Data-Rec*.

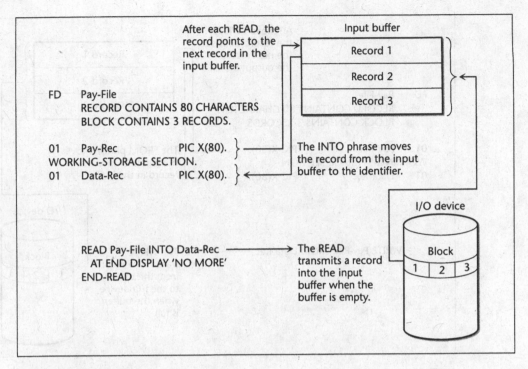

FIGURE 15.1 READ statements.

After second READ. No data is transmitted, but *Pay-Rec* is made to point to record 2 in the buffer. Record 2 is moved to *Data-Rec* if the INTO phrase is coded.

After third READ. Same as second READ, but *Pay-Rec* points to record 3 in the buffer.

After fourth READ. The next block is transmitted into the buffer, *Pay-Rec* is made to point to record 1 in the buffer, and an INTO phrase moves record 1 to *Data-Rec*.

After CLOSE. Storage for the buffer is released. *Pay-Rec* has no predictable value.

Figure 15.2 illustrates this process for the WRITE. The OPEN, WRITE, and CLOSE do the following:

Prior to the OPEN. *Pay-Rec* has no predictable value.

After OPEN. Storage is allocated for the buffer, and *Pay-Rec* points to record 1 in the output buffer.

After first WRITE. Any FROM phrase moves *Data-Rec* to record 1. No data is transmitted, but *Pay-Rec* is made to point to record 2 in the buffer.

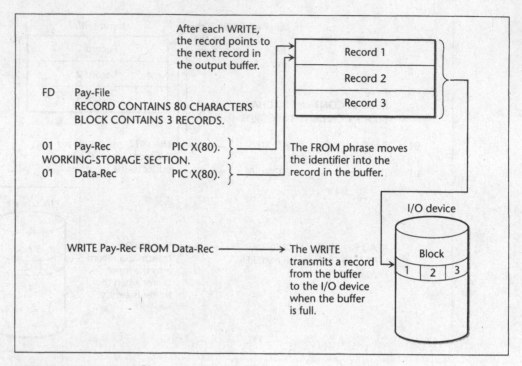

FIGURE 15.2 WRITE statements.

After second WRITE. Same as the first WRITE, but *Pay-Rec* points to record 3 in the buffer.

After third WRITE. Any FROM phrase moves *Data-Rec* to record 3. The buffer is transmitted to the I/O device as a block, and *Pay-Rec* is made to point to record 1 in the buffer.

After CLOSE. Any partially filled buffer is transmitted, and storage for the buffer is released. *Pay-Rec* has no predictable value.

Processing records in the record area is more efficient because COBOL does not move the data to another area. However, the READ or WRITE is harder to follow, because you must look back to the FD and locate the record to find out what is read or written. You must also remember the circumstances under which the record becomes unavailable. It is not difficult to write programs with this in mind, but someone can easily forget the restrictions when the program is modified. Records become unavailable under the following circumstances.

For a READ:

Opening the file does not make the record area available.

A READ makes a new record available and the old record unavailable.

An end of file makes the current record unavailable.

Closing the file makes the current record unavailable.

For a WRITE:

Opening the file makes the current value of the record unpredictable.

A WRITE makes the current record unavailable.

Closing the file makes the current record unavailable.

TIP *Don't process records in the buffer, because it introduces potential problems that are better avoided.*

The following examples illustrate some common errors:

```
WRITE Pay-Rec
MOVE Pay-Rec TO Some-Thing
   [Error. Pay-Rec contains unpredictable values.]


MOVE First-Record TO Pay-Rec
OPEN INPUT Pay-File
WRITE Pay-Rec
   [Error. Pay-Rec no longer contains First-Record. The OPEN destroyed its contents.]


READ Pay-File
  AT END MOVE Pay-Rec TO Last-Record
   [Error. Pay-Rec contains unpredictable values.]
END-READ


READ Pay-File
  AT END CONTINUE
  NOT AT END
     CLOSE Pay-File
     MOVE Pay-Rec TO Last-Record
   [Error. Pay-Rec contains unpredictable values.]
END-READ
```

To summarize, the READ INTO combines reading a *file-name* and moving the record into the *identifier,* and the WRITE FROM moves the *identifier* to the *record* and writes out the record. The following statements are logically equivalent:

```
READ Pay-File INTO A-Rec     Same as    READ Pay-File
   AT END CONTINUE                          AT END CONTINUE
END-READ                                 NOT AT END
                                            MOVE Pay-Rec to A-Rec
                                         END-READ
WRITE Pay-Rec FROM A-Rec     Same as    MOVE A-Rec TO Pay-Rec
                                         WRITE Pay-Rec
```

> **TIP** *Keep the number of READ and WRITE statements for each file to a minimum. If a file must be read or written from several places in the program, place the READ or WRITE in a paragraph and PERFORM it. This simplifies program maintenance, because there is only a single place where each file is read or written.*

15.6 MULTIPLE-FORMAT RECORDS

Sometimes Used

Sometimes a file may contain several record formats. For example, suppose that a variable-length record contains a 200-byte record when the first byte contains a 1 and a 100-byte record when the first byte contains a 2. The following example shows how such a file could be processed:

```
FD   Pay-File BLOCK CONTAINS 0 RECORDS
     RECORD CONTAINS 100 TO 200 CHARACTERS.
01   Pay-Rec-1.
     05  Pay-Type-1                     PIC X.
     05  Pay-1                          PIC X(199).
01   Pay-Rec-2.            [Pay-Rec-2 implicitly redefines Pay-Rec-1.]
     05  Pay-Type-2                     PIC X.
     05  Pay-2                          PIC X(99).
     □  □  □
     OPEN INPUT Pay-File
     READ Pay-File
       AT END CONTINUE
       NOT AT END
         EVALUATE Pay-Type-1
           WHEN "1"
             MOVE Pay-Rec-1 TO Big-Record
             PERFORM A10-Process-Big-Record
           WHEN "2"
             MOVE Pay-Rec-2 TO Small-Record
             PERFORM B10-Process-Small-Record
           WHEN OTHER DISPLAY "ERROR-RECORD TYPE NOT 1 OR 2."
         END-EVALUATE
     END-READ
```

15.7 SEQUENTIAL COPY

Essential

The following program illustrates sequential input and output by showing how to copy a file. The complete program is shown:

```
IDENTIFICATION DIVISION.
PROGRAM-ID.  COPY-PROGRAM.
```

```
ENVIRONMENT DIVISION.
INPUT-OUTPUT SECTION.
FILE-CONTROL.
    SELECT In-File ASSIGN TO DDIN.
    SELECT Out-File ASSIGN TO DDOUT.
DATA DIVISION.
FILE SECTION.
FD  In-File BLOCK CONTAINS 0 RECORDS.
01  In-Rec                          PIC X(100).
FD  Out-File BLOCK CONTAINS 0 RECORDS.
01  Out-Rec                         PIC X(100).
WORKING-STORAGE SECTION.
01  In-Record                       PIC X(100).
01  Record-Counts.
    05  In-File-No                  PIC S9(9) BINARY VALUE 0.
    05  Out-File-No                 PIC S9(9) BINARY VALUE 0.
01  EOF-In-Flag                     PIC X.
    88  EOF-In                      VALUE "Y".
PROCEDURE DIVISION.
A00-Begin.
    DISPLAY "BEGINNING COPY PROGRAM"
    OPEN INPUT In-File OUTPUT Out-File
    MOVE "N" TO EOF-In-Flag
    PERFORM WITH TEST AFTER UNTIL EOF-In
      READ In-File INTO In-Record
        AT END SET EOF-In TO TRUE
        NOT AT END
          ADD 1 TO In-File-No
          WRITE Out-Rec FROM In-Record
          ADD 1 TO Out-File-No
      END-READ
    END-PERFORM
    DISPLAY "In-File-No: ", In-File-No,
            " Out-File-No: ", Out-File-No
    CLOSE In-File, Out-File
    GOBACK.
END PROGRAM COPY-PROGRAM.
```

15.8   UPDATING SEQUENTIAL FILES

Sequential files are updated by copying the file and writing the updated records into the output file, or the file can be updated in place by rewriting specific records.

15.8.1   Sequential Updating

Essential

You update a sequential file by reading it sequentially and applying the transactions to it from another sequential file. The file being updated is termed the *old master file,* the file containing the transactions is termed the *transaction file,* and the updated file is termed the *updated master file*. You read the old master file, and if there is no transaction to update it, you simply write it out. Otherwise, you apply the transaction and then write it out. You must order the transactions and the records in the old master file on a record key. You use this record key to match a transaction in the old master file. A *record key* is a portion of the record that uniquely identifies it, such as the person's Social Security number in a personnel file. The keys may be composed of several noncontiguous fields within the record. The following example illustrates a sequential file update in which a *Master-In* file is updated by a *Trans* file to produce a *Master-Out* file. For simplicity, the entire record is considered to be the key.

```
INPUT-OUTPUT SECTION.
FILE-CONTROL.
    SELECT Master-In ASSIGN TO DDIN.
    SELECT Master-Out ASSIGN TO DDOUT.
    SELECT Trans-In ASSIGN TO DDTRANS.
DATA DIVISION.
FILE SECTION.
FD  Master-In BLOCK CONTAINS 0 RECORDS.
01  Master-In-Rec                    PIC X(10).
FD  Master-Out BLOCK CONTAINS 0 RECORDS.
01  Master-Out-Rec                   PIC X(10).
FD  Trans-In BLOCK CONTAINS 0 RECORDS.
01  Trans-In-Rec                     PIC X(10).
WORKING-STORAGE SECTION.
01  Master-Rec.
    05  Master-Key                   PIC X(10).
01  Trans-Rec.
    05  Trans-Key                    PIC X(10).
01  EOF-Master-Flag                  PIC X
    88  EOF-Master                   VALUE "Y".
01  EOF-Trans-Flag                   PIC X
    88  EOF-Trans                    VALUE "Y".
PROCEDURE DIVISION.
A00-Begin.
    OPEN INPUT Master-In, Trans-In, OUTPUT Master-Out
    MOVE "N" TO EOF-Master, EOF-Trans
    PERFORM WITH TEST AFTER UNTIL EOF-Master
    [All the master file records are read, along with any matching transactions.]
        READ Master-In INTO Master-Rec
          AT END SET EOF-Master TO TRUE
          NOT AT END
            PERFORM A20-Read-Trans WITH TEST BEFORE
                    UNTIL Trans-Key >= Master-Key OR
                          EOF-Trans
            IF (NOT EOF-Trans) AND Trans-Key = Master-Key
                THEN …
                    [The transaction matches the master file record. Update the master
                    file record with the transaction.]
            END-IF
            WRITE Master-Out-Rec FROM Master-Rec
        END-READ
```

```
      END-PERFORM
          .
  **** Exit
   A20-Read-Trans.
      READ Trans-In INTO Trans-Rec
        AT END SET EOF-Trans TO TRUE
        NOT AT END
          IF Trans-Key < Master-Key
            THEN DISPLAY "NO MASTER FOR TRANS RECORD."
                    DISPLAY "Trans-Key: ", Trans-Key
          END-IF
      END-READ
          .
  **** Exit
```

The preceding files can only be matched if they are in the same order based on their keys. You often need to check that the files are in the proper order and that there are no duplicate records. The following example shows how the previous *Master-In* file would be checked for this:

```
01  Old-Master-Key              PIC X(10).
 □  □  □
MOVE LOW-VALUES TO Old-Master-Key
 □  □  □
    READ Master-In INTO Master-Rec
      AT END SET EOF-Master TO TRUE
      NOT AT END
        IF Master-Key = Old-Master-Key
          THEN DISPLAY "DUPLICATE MASTER RECORDS."
                  DISPLAY "Master-Key: ", Master-Key
          ELSE IF Master-Key < Old-Master-Key
          THEN DISPLAY "MASTER OUT OF SORT."
                  DISPLAY "Master-Key: ", Master-Key
                  DISPLAY "Old-Master-Key: ", Old-Master-Key
                  END-IF
        END-IF
        MOVE Master-Key TO Old-Master-Key
         □  □  □
    END-READ
```

You usually apply transactions to an old master file by allowing records to be deleted, added, or changed. There may also be a *replace*, which is equivalent to a delete and an add. The operation, whether a delete, add, or change, should be specified within the transaction. The advantage of specifying the operation within the transaction is that you can detect errors. With the alternative—adding the transaction if it does not match a record in the old master file, and changing or replacing it if it does match—you couldn't detect the following errors:

Add. Error if the record already exists in the old master file.

Delete. Error if the record does not exist in the old master file.

Change. Error if the record does not exist in the old master file.

If there can be more than one operation on the same old master file record, the order should be add, change, and then delete. This may seem unnecessary. Why add a record and then change it in the same update run? However, transactions are often batched for a periodic update. It may be perfectly logical for one clerk to add a transaction on Monday, another clerk enter a change on Tuesday, and then process all the transactions on a Friday update run.

The delete and add are straightforward, because you either write or do not write a record, but the change operation is more difficult. With a change, you do not want to update all the fields (that would be a replace), but only certain fields. The usual way of changing a record is to establish a different transaction type for each field to be changed. In critical applications, you can require a change transaction to contain two values. One value can be the current contents of the field being changed to ensure that the proper field is changed, and the second value can be the change. Another way to update individual fields within the old master file records is to use the same transaction format as in the add transaction, but change only the fields that are nonblank in the transaction. The advantage of this is that the same input form used for the add can be used for the update. You simply fill in the record key and the fields to change and leave all the other fields blank. (You can redefine an alphanumeric data item over numeric fields to determine if they are blank.) The disadvantage of this technique is that if you wish to replace a field with blanks, you must indicate this by some means, such as asterisks in the field.

A common error in updating records is to update the record key and forget that this affects the sort order. In sequential updating, you write the master file out in the same order in which you read it. However, if the record key is updated, the record may no longer be in the proper sort order. Keep in mind that if you update the record key, you should re-sort the file.

15.8.2 Updating Files on Disk with REWRITE

Sometimes Used

Usually if a single record is changed in a sequential file, you must rewrite the entire file. However, it is possible to rewrite individual fixed-length records in files that reside on direct-access storage devices (disks). COBOL permits files to be opened for I-O (input-output), and they can then be both read and written. The REWRITE statement, coded like the WRITE, can rewrite a record that has just been read. The following shows how a sequential file might be updated using REWRITE.

```
FILE-CONTROL.
    SELECT Payroll-IO ASSIGN TO DDIO.
DATA DIVISION.
FILE SECTION.
FD  Payroll-IO BLOCK CONTAINS 0 RECORDS.
01  Payroll-Record                    PIC X(80).
WORKING-STORAGE SECTION.
01  Pay-Rec.
```

```
        05  Pay-Key              PIC X(20).
        05  Pay-Type             PIC X.
        05  Pay-Amt              PIC S9(5)V99.
        05  Pay-Rest             PIC X(52).
01  EOF-Pay-Flag                 PIC X.
    88  EOF-Pay                  VALUE "Y".
    □  □  □
        OPEN I-O Payroll-IO          [The file is opened for input/output.]
        MOVE "N" TO EOF-Pay-Flag
        PERFORM WITH TEST AFTER UNTIL  Pay-Key = HIGH-VALUES OR
                                       EOF-Pay
            READ Payroll-IO INTO Pay-Rec
              AT END SET EOF-Pay TO TRUE
              NOT AT END                 [A record has been read.]
                IF Pay-Type = "A"
                    [You may want to update only certain records.]
                    THEN MOVE ZERO TO Pay-Amt
                    [You can store any new values in the record.]
                        REWRITE Payroll-Record FROM Pay-Rec
                        [The last record read is rewritten.]
                END-IF
            END-READ
        END-PERFORM
```

The record rewritten must be the same length as the record read, because REWRITE overwrites the record in the file. Sequential files are often updated this way by reading a sequential file and executing REWRITE statements for the records to be rewritten.

REWRITE can also rewrite from the record area by omitting the FROM phrase:

```
REWRITE record-description
```

15.9 SEQUENTIAL UPDATE EXAMPLE

Essential

The next example shows how a master file is read and updated by a transaction file to create a new master file. This is a very common process for sequential files. For brevity, the transactions are not validated, but run statistics are printed. Assume you are given the following information:

1. Old master file:

```
File name: Old-Master
Record:    01  Master-Rec.
           05  Master-Key      [The record key.]
           05  Master-Fields   [The data fields.]
```

The file is in ascending sequence on *Master-Key*. There are no duplicate records.

2. Transaction file:

```
File name:  Trans-File
Record:     01  Trans-Rec.
                05  Trans-Key       [The record key.]
                05  Trans-Action    [Specifies the action.]
                                    D Delete the record.
                                    I Insert the record.
                                    U Update the record.
                05  Trans-Fields    [The data fields.]
```

A transaction can delete or update an inserted record. Insert must not have a matching record in master file. Delete and Change must have a matching record in master file. The file is in ascending order on *Trans-Key, Trans-Action.*

3. New master file:

```
File name:  New-Master
Record:     01  New-Master-Record
```

4. Hold-area record (to hold an inserted transaction so it can be changed or deleted by another transaction):

```
Record:  01  Hold-Area.
             05  Hold-Key      [The record key.]
             05  Hold-Fields   [The data fields.]
```

5. Program statistics:

Old-Master-Count counts master records read.

Trans-File-Count counts transactions read.

New-Master-Count counts master records written.

Trans-Change-Count counts records changed.

Trans-Add-Count counts transactions added.

Trans-Del-Count counts records deleted.

Trans-Error-Count counts transactions in error.

A complete program to perform this update is included here. It is a rather long example, but because it is such a common and important application, it is handy for reference. Rather than defining a separate end-of-file flag for each file, the record key itself is used by setting it to LOW-VALUES to indicate that a record has not been read and HIGH-VALUES to indicate an end-of-file. The advantage of this technique is that it simplifies the logic, letting you compare record keys without first determining whether an end-of-file has been encountered for the files. The disadvantage is that you must be sure that the record key cannot legitimately contain high or low values.

```
IDENTIFICATION DIVISION.
PROGRAM-ID.  UPDATE-IT.
ENVIRONMENT DIVISION.
INPUT-OUTPUT SECTION.
```

```
FILE-CONTROL.
     SELECT Old-Master ASSIGN TO "MASTER.TXT"
          ORGANIZATION IS LINE SEQUENTIAL.
     SELECT Trans-File ASSIGN TO "TRANS.TXT"
          ORGANIZATION IS LINE SEQUENTIAL.
     SELECT New-Master ASSIGN TO "MSTROUT.TXT"
          ORGANIZATION IS LINE SEQUENTIAL.
DATA DIVISION.
FILE SECTION.
FD  Old-Master BLOCK CONTAINS 0 RECORDS.
01  Old-Master-Record              PIC X(100).
FD  Trans-File BLOCK CONTAINS 0 RECORDS.
01  Trans-Record                   PIC X(101).
FD  New-Master BLOCK CONTAINS 0 RECORDS.
01  New-Master-Record.
    05  New-Master-Key             PIC X(5).
    05  New-Master-Fields          PIC X(95).
WORKING-STORAGE SECTION.
01  Master-Rec.
    05  Master-Key                 PIC X(5).
*       LOW-VALUES: No record. HIGH-VALUES: EOF.
        88  EOF-Master             VALUE HIGH-VALUES.
        88  No-Master-Rec          VALUE LOW-VALUES.
    05  Master-Fields              PIC X(95).
01  Prev-Master-Key                PIC X(5).
01  Trans-Rec.
    05  Trans-Key                  PIC X(5).
*       LOW-VALUES: No record. HIGH-VALUES: EOF.
        88  EOF-Trans              VALUE HIGH-VALUES.
        88  No-Trans-Rec           VALUE LOW-VALUES.
    05  Trans-Action               PIC X.
*       I - Insert, D - Delete, U - Update.
    05  Trans-Fields               PIC X(95).
01  Hold-Rec.
*       Hold-Rec contains inserted Trans-Rec until written.
    05  Hold-Key                   PIC X(5).
*       LOW-VALUES: Record deleted.  HIGH-VALUES: No record.
        88  EOF-Hold               VALUE HIGH-VALUES.
        88  No-Hold-Rec            VALUE LOW-VALUES.
    05  Hold-Fields                PIC X(95).
01  Prev-Trans.
    05  Prev-Trans-Key             PIC X(5).
    05  Prev-Trans-Action          PIC X.
01  Record-Counts.
    05  Old-Master-Count           PIC S9(9) BINARY VALUE 0.
    05  Trans-File-Count           PIC S9(9) BINARY VALUE 0.
    05  New-Master-Count           PIC S9(9) BINARY VALUE 0.
    05  Trans-Change-Count         PIC S9(9) BINARY VALUE 0.
    05  Trans-Add-Count            PIC S9(9) BINARY VALUE 0.
    05  Trans-Del-Count            PIC S9(9) BINARY VALUE 0.
    05  Trans-Error-Count          PIC S9(9) BINARY VALUE 0.
PROCEDURE DIVISION.
A00-Begin.
```

```
        DISPLAY "START OF UPDATE PROGRAM"
        OPEN INPUT Old-Master, Trans-File, OUTPUT New-Master
        SET No-Master-Rec, No-Trans-Rec TO TRUE
        MOVE LOW-VALUES TO Trans-Action
        SET EOF-HOLD TO TRUE
        PERFORM A00-Read-Master WITH TEST AFTER
            UNTIL EOF-Master AND EOF-Trans
        CLOSE Old-Master, Trans-File, New-Master
        DISPLAY "OLD MASTER RECORDS READ:     ", Old-Master-Count
        DISPLAY "TRANS RECORDS READ:          ", Trans-File-Count
        DISPLAY "NEW MASTER RECORDS WRITTEN: ", New-Master-Count
        DISPLAY "OLD MASTER RECORDS DELETED: ", Trans-Del-Count
        DISPLAY "OLD MASTER RECORDS CHANGED: ", Trans-Change-Count
        DISPLAY "NEW TRANSACTIONS ADDED:     ", Trans-Add-Count
        DISPLAY "TRANS ERROR COUNT:           ", Trans-Error-Count
        DISPLAY "END OF UPDATE PROGRAM EXECUTION"
        GOBACK.
    A00-Read-Master.
   ****************************************************************
   *   PROCEDURE TO READ ALL MASTER RECORDS.                     *
   *   IN:  MASTER, TRANS, New-Master files open.                *
   *   OUT: MASTER and TRANS file records read.                  *
   *       Master-Key, Trans-Key contain HIGH-VALUES when both   *
   *       reach EOF.                                            *
   ****************************************************************
   *             Get a master record.
        PERFORM A10-Get-Next-Master WITH TEST BEFORE
            UNTIL NOT No-Master-Rec
   *             Process transactions up to the master record.
        PERFORM A30-Get-Next-Trans WITH TEST BEFORE
            UNTIL NOT No-Trans-Rec
   *             If you are holding a record less than the
   *             transaction record, write it out.
        IF NOT No-Hold-Rec AND NOT EOF-Hold AND Hold-Key < Trans-Key
            THEN MOVE Hold-Rec TO New-Master-Record
                PERFORM A50-Write-Master
                SET EOF-Hold TO TRUE
        END-IF
        EVALUATE TRUE
          WHEN EOF-Trans AND EOF-Master
   *             EOF for both files.
                CONTINUE
          WHEN Trans-Key < Master-Key AND
              EOF-Hold OR No-Hold-Rec
   *             Apply transaction where it doesn't match a master
   *             record.
                PERFORM A60-Apply-Trans
                SET No-Trans-Rec TO TRUE
          WHEN Trans-Key < Master-Key AND
              NOT EOF-Hold AND NOT No-Hold-Rec
   *             Apply transaction where you have a record held.
                PERFORM A70-Apply-To-Hold
                SET No-Trans-Rec TO TRUE
```

```
          WHEN Trans-Key = Master-Key
*              Apply transaction to master record.
          PERFORM A80-Apply-To-Master
          SET No-Trans-Rec TO TRUE
      WHEN Trans-Key > Master-Key AND No-Master-Rec
*              Delete master file record.
          ADD 1 TO Trans-Del-Count
          SET No-Trans-Rec TO TRUE
      WHEN Trans-Key > Master-Key AND
          NOT No-Master-Rec
*              All transactions applied.  Write master record.
          MOVE Master-Rec TO New-Master-Record
          PERFORM A50-Write-Master
          MOVE Master-Key TO Prev-Master-Key
          SET No-Master-Rec TO TRUE
    END-EVALUATE
    .
**** Exit
 A10-Get-Next-Master.
 **************************************************************
 *   PROCEDURE TO READ NEXT MASTER RECORD.                    *
 *   IN:   MASTER file open.                                  *
 *   OUT: Master-Rec contains record.                         *
 *        Master-Key contains HIGH-VALUES if EOF.             *
 **************************************************************
     READ Old-Master INTO Master-Rec
       AT END SET EOF-Master TO TRUE
       NOT AT END
           ADD 1 TO Old-Master-Count
           PERFORM A20-Validate-Master
     END-READ
     .
**** Exit
 A20-Validate-Master.
 **************************************************************
 *   PROCEDURE TO VALIDATE MASTER RECORD.                     *
 *   IN:  Master-Rec contains record.                         *
 *   OUT: Master-Key set to LOW-VALUES if invalid.            *
 **************************************************************
     IF Master-Key < Prev-Master-Key
       THEN DISPLAY "ERROR--MASTER FILE NOT IN SEQUENCE:"
              DISPLAY "Prev-Master-Key: ", Prev-Master-Key,
                     " Master-Key: ", Master-Key
              GO TO Z90-Stop-Run
     END-IF
     IF Master-Key = Prev-Master-Key
       THEN DISPLAY "ERROR--DUPLICATE MASTER RECORDS:"
              DISPLAY "Master-Key: ", Master-Key
              ADD 1 TO Trans-Error-Count
              SET No-Master-Rec TO TRUE
     END-IF
     .
**** Exit
```

```
    A30-Get-Next-Trans.
    **************************************************************
    *   PROCEDURE TO READ NEXT TRANS RECORD.                     *
    *   IN:  TRANS file open.                                    *
    *   OUT: Trans-Rec contains record.                          *
    *        Trans-Key contains HIGH-VALUES if EOF.              *
    **************************************************************
        MOVE Trans-Key TO Prev-Trans-Key
        MOVE Trans-Action TO Prev-Trans-Action
        READ Trans-File INTO Trans-Rec
          AT END SET EOF-Trans TO TRUE
          NOT AT END
            ADD 1 TO Trans-File-Count
            PERFORM A40-Validate-Trans
        END-READ
        .
**** Exit
    A40-Validate-Trans.
    **************************************************************
    *   PROCEDURE TO VALIDATE TRANS RECORD.                      *
    *   IN:  Trans-Rec contains record.                         *
    *   OUT: Trans-Key set to LOW-VALUES if invalid.            *
    **************************************************************
        EVALUATE TRUE
          WHEN Trans-Key < Prev-Trans-Key
              DISPLAY "ERROR--TRANS FILE OUT OF SEQUENCE"
              DISPLAY "OLD-Key: ", Prev-Trans-Key,
                      " New-Key: ", Trans-Key
              GO TO Z90-Stop-Run
          WHEN Trans-Key = Prev-Trans-Key AND
              Trans-Action < Prev-Trans-Action
              DISPLAY "ERROR--TRANS ACTIONS OUT OF SEQUENCE"
              DISPLAY "OLD Key: ", Prev-Trans-Key,
                      " OLD ACTION: ", Prev-Trans-Action,
                      " New KEY: ", Trans-Key,
                      " New ACTION: ", Trans-Action
              GO TO Z90-Stop-Run
        END-EVALUATE
        IF Trans-Action = "I" OR "U" OR "D"
           THEN CONTINUE
           ELSE DISPLAY "ERROR--BAD TRANS ACTION.  KEY: ", Trans-Key,
                      " ACTION: ", Trans-Action
               SET No-Trans-Rec TO TRUE
               ADD 1 TO Trans-Error-Count
        END-IF
        .
**** Exit
    A50-Write-Master.
    **************************************************************
    *   PROCEDURE TO WRITE NEW MASTER RECORD.                    *
    *   IN:  Record stored in New-Master-Record.                *
    *   OUT: New-Master-Record written.                         *
    **************************************************************
```

```
          ADD 1 TO New-Master-Count
          WRITE New-Master-Record
          .
 **** Exit
  A60-Apply-Trans.
 ***********************************************************
 *   PROCEDURE TO APPLY TRANSACTION WHERE NO MASTER RECORD.   *
 *   IN:  Trans-Rec contains record.                          *
 *   OUT: Trans-Rec stored in Hold-Rec if insert.             *
 ***********************************************************
          EVALUATE Trans-Action
             WHEN "D"
                  DISPLAY "ERROR--DELETE WITH NO MASTER RECORD"
                  DISPLAY "IGNORING Trans-Key: ", Trans-Key
                  ADD 1 TO Trans-Error-Count
             WHEN "I" PERFORM A90-Trans-Add
             WHEN "U"
                  DISPLAY "ERROR--UPDATE WITH NO MASTER RECORD"
                  DISPLAY "IGNORING Trans-Key: ", Trans-Key
                  ADD 1 TO Trans-Error-Count
          END-EVALUATE
          .
 **** Exit
  A70-Apply-To-Hold.
 ***********************************************************
 *   PROCEDURE TO APPLY TRANS TO HOLD RECORD.                 *
 *   IN: Trans-Rec contains transaction.                      *
 *       Trans-Key = Hold-Key.                                *
 *       Hold-Rec contains previous TRANSACTION.              *
 *   OUT: Record applied to Hold-Rec.                         *
 *       Hold-Key set to HIGH-VALUES if Hold-Rec written.     *
 *                        LOW-VALUES if Hold-Rec deleted.     *
 ***********************************************************
          EVALUATE TRUE
             WHEN Trans-Key > Hold-Key
                  MOVE Hold-Rec TO New-Master-Record
                  PERFORM A50-Write-Master
                  SET EOF-Hold TO TRUE
                  PERFORM A60-Apply-Trans
             WHEN Trans-Action = "D"
                  SET No-Hold-Rec TO TRUE
                  ADD 1 TO Trans-Del-Count
             WHEN Trans-Action = "I"
                  DISPLAY "ERROR--INSERTING WITH MASTER RECORD"
                  DISPLAY "IGNORING Trans-Key: ", Trans-Key
                  ADD 1 TO Trans-Error-Count
             WHEN Trans-Action = "U"
                  MOVE Trans-Fields TO Hold-Fields
                  ADD 1 TO Trans-Change-Count
          END-EVALUATE
          .
 **** Exit
  A80-Apply-To-Master.
```

```
      **************************************************************
      *  PROCEDURE TO APPLY TRANS TO MASTER RECORD.                *
      *  IN:  Trans-Rec contains transaction.                      *
      *          Trans-Key = Master-Key                            *
      *       Master-Rec contains master record.                   *
      *  OUT: RECORD applied to Master-Rec.                        *
      *       Master-Key set to LOW-VALUES if deleted.             *
      **************************************************************
          EVALUATE TRUE
              WHEN Trans-Action = "I" AND No-Master-Rec
                  PERFORM A90-Trans-Add
              WHEN Trans-Action = "I" AND NOT No-Master-Rec
                  DISPLAY "ERROR--Add WHEN MASTER PRESENT: ",
                          Trans-Key
                  ADD 1 TO Trans-Error-Count
              WHEN Trans-Action = "D" AND NOT No-Master-Rec
                  MOVE Master-Key TO Prev-Master-Key
                  SET No-Master-Rec TO TRUE
                  ADD 1 TO Trans-Del-Count
              WHEN Trans-Action = "D" AND No-Master-Rec
                  DISPLAY "ERROR-DELETING DELETED RECORD: ", Trans-Key
                  ADD 1 TO Trans-Error-Count
              WHEN Trans-Action = "U" AND NOT No-Master-Rec
                  ADD 1 TO Trans-Change-Count
                  MOVE Trans-Fields TO Master-Fields
              WHEN Trans-Action = "U" AND No-Master-Rec
                  DISPLAY "ERROR--CHANGING DELETED RECORD: ", Trans-Key
                  ADD 1 TO Trans-Error-Count
          END-EVALUATE
          .
      **** Exit
       A90-Trans-Add.
      **************************************************************
      *  PROCEDURE TO INSERT A Trans-Rec RECORD.                   *
      *  IN:  Trans-Rec contains transaction.                      *
      *  OUT: Hold-Rec contains transaction.                       *
      **************************************************************
          ADD 1 TO Trans-Add-Count
          MOVE Trans-Key TO Hold-Key
          MOVE Trans-Fields TO Hold-Fields
          .
      **** Exit
       Z90-Stop-Run.
      **************************************************************
      *  PROCEDURE TO TERMINATE RUN IF ERROR.                      *
      *  IN:  All files open.                                      *
      *  OUT: RETURN-CODE set to 16.                               *
      *       All files closed.                                    *
      **************************************************************
          DISPLAY "RUN TERMINATED FOR ERRORS."
          MOVE 16 TO RETURN-CODE
          CLOSE Old-Master, Trans-File, New-Master
          GOBACK.
      END PROGRAM UPDATE-IT.
```

EXERCISES

1. An input file consists of 80-column lines divided into six fields, each alternating seven and nine characters in length. The last 32 columns of the lines are blank. The first two fields contain integer numbers, the next two fields contain numbers with two digits to the right of the assumed decimal point, and the final two fields contain character data. The numbers may be signed with a minus sign to the left of the leftmost digit, or they may be unsigned. The numbers also have leading blanks. Write a program to read this file in and store each column in a table. Store the numeric data as PACKED-DECIMAL. Assume that there can be a maximum of 100 records in the file, but print an error message and terminate the job if this number is exceeded. Print out the records as they are read in.

2. Copy a file containing 80 characters per record, and an unknown number of records. Exclude all records that contain the character "I" in the 63rd character position of the record. Print out the number of records read, number excluded, and the number of records written.

3. Define a record that contains a four-digit project number, a 25-character name, and an overhead percentage of precision PIC S9(5)V99 PACKED-DECIMAL. Read in a file of such records and print the number of duplicate project numbers. Check the sort sequence of the records to ensure that they are in order on the project number.

4. Read in a file containing eight integer numbers per line, 10 columns per number. The numbers are right-justified with leading blanks. Store the numbers in a two-dimensional table with the line number as one dimension and the numbers within the line as the other. Store the data as PIC S9(9) PACKED-DECIMAL. Allow for a maximum of 100 lines, print an error message, and terminate the run if this number is exceeded. Then do the following:

   - Print the number of records read.
   - Write out the entire table as a single record.
   - Read this single record back into an identical table.
   - Verify that the data was transmitted properly by comparing the first table with the second.

5. A file must be read that is set up as follows: Column 1 of the first line describes the format of the data contained in the lines that follow. If column 1 contains a 1, the lines following contain integer numbers in columns 1 through 5. If column 1 contains a 2, the lines following contain a decimal number in columns 1 through 10 with two digits to the right of the assumed decimal point. If column 1 contains a 3, the lines following contain integer numbers in columns 1 through 4. Read the file in, edit the data to ensure that it is numeric, and print an error message if any invalid data is found. The numbers may or may not be signed, and there may be leading blanks. Print out the number on each line as it is read.

6. Two files each have records containing 100 characters. Each file is in ascending sort order on the first 10 characters of the records. There may be duplicate records in each file. Read in the two files and merge them to write out a new file containing only records with unique keys.

7. A file contains 80-character lines. The first 10 characters of the record constitute the record key. Write a file containing only unique record keys. The input file is unsorted. Read the records in and store each unique key in a table. Allow for 1000 unique keys, and print an error message if there are more than this. Write the output file from the table.

8. The program listed for problem 9 was extracted from an actual program, and a very poor one at that. The program reads an old master file and a transaction file and writes out master file records for which there is a matching transaction. The program has been running for some time, but suddenly you are told that the last run did not write out enough records in the output file. The *Master-In* file is read, and only records that match records in the *Trans-In* file are written out in the *Master-Out* file. Any record in *Trans-In* is supposed to match a record in *Master-In,* but the transactions are prepared by hand. Both *Master-In* and *Trans-In* are in ascending sort order. They are sorted just before being read, so their sort order is likely to be correct. However, the program does not check for the sort order.

   Find the error in the program. Because the program has been running for some time, you might suspect that the error is caused by the data's not living up to the program's assumptions. Rewrite the program, following the rules of structured programming, and check for any data errors and print clear error messages.

```
01  Iskip                      PIC 9.
    □  □  □
    MOVE ZERO TO Iskip.
A10.  READ Master-In INTO In-Rec AT END GO TO A60.
    IF Iskip NOT = ZEROS GO TO A20.
    READ Trans-In INTO Trans-Rec AT END GO TO A50.
    GO TO A30.
A20.  IF Iskip = 2 GO TO A10.
    MOVE ZERO TO Iskip.
A30.  IF Trans-Rec NOT = In-Rec GO TO A40.
    WRITE Out-Rec FROM In-Rec.
    MOVE ZERO TO Iskip.
    GO TO A10.
A40.  MOVE 1 TO Iskip.
    GO TO A10.
A50.  MOVE 2 TO Iskip.
    GO TO A10.
A60.
```

9. The following program generates a master file for the sample program given at the end of this chapter. Run this program to generate the master file named *MASTER,* and then use a text editor to select a few transactions from it and store them in a file named *TRANS.* Insert an I, D, or U in column 6 to perform the actions you want, and modify the record keys in columns 1 through 5, as

needed. Then rewrite the sample program and simplify it to not check the files for sequence, don't allow a change transaction to modify an insert transaction, and test the program using the *MASTER* and *TRANS* files to create the *MSTROUT* file.

```
IDENTIFICATION DIVISION.
PROGRAM-ID.  UPDATE-IT.
ENVIRONMENT DIVISION.
INPUT-OUTPUT SECTION.
FILE-CONTROL.
    SELECT Master ASSIGN TO "MASTER.TXT"
        ORGANIZATION IS LINE SEQUENTIAL.
DATA DIVISION.
FILE SECTION.
FD  Master.
01  Master-Record.
    05  New-Master-Key            PIC X(5).
    05  New-Master-Fields         PIC X(95).
WORKING-STORAGE SECTION.
01  Master-Rec.
    05  Master-Key                PIC X(5).
    05  Master-Fields             PIC X(95).
01  The-Alphabet                  PIC X(26) VALUE
                                  "ABCDEFGHIJKLMNOPQRSTUVWXYZ".
01  I                             PIC S9(4) BINARY.
01  J                             PIC S9(4) BINARY VALUE 5.
01  K                             PIC S9(4) BINARY VALUE 1.
PROCEDURE DIVISION.
A00-Begin.
    DISPLAY "START OF GENERATE PROGRAM"
    OPEN OUTPUT Master
    MOVE ALL "-" TO Master-Fields
    PERFORM WITH TEST AFTER VARYING I FROM 1 BY 1 UNTIL I >= 100
        IF K > 26
            THEN MOVE 1 TO K
                SUBTRACT 1 FROM J
        END-IF
        MOVE The-Alphabet(6 - J:1) TO Master-Key(1:1),
            Master-Key(2:1), Master-Key(3:1),
            Master-Key(4:1), Master-Key(5:1)
        MOVE The-Alphabet(K:1) TO Master-Key(J:1)
        WRITE Master-Record FROM Master-Rec
        ADD 1 TO K
    END-PERFORM
    CLOSE Master
    DISPLAY "MASTER RECORDS WRITTEN: ", I
    GOBACK.
END PROGRAM UPDATE-IT.
```

CHAPTER 16

INDEXED AND RELATIVE FILES

Indexed and relative files are required for most online and many batch applications. Don't skip this chapter.

16.1 OVERVIEW OF INDEXED AND RELATIVE FILES

Essential

Indexed and relative files depend heavily on the facilities provided by the computer's operating system. Although they are included in the ANSI standard, their implementation varies among compilers and operating systems. In Mainframe COBOL, they are implemented as part of the VSAM file system. On AIX, OS/2, and Windows, they are implemented in Btrieve.

The advantage of indexed and relative files is their ability to access records randomly. To see how random access might be used, suppose that payroll transactions contain an employee's Social Security number and department. Suppose further that another file contains all the valid Social Security numbers, and yet another file contains all the valid department numbers. How could the Social Security and department numbers in each payroll transaction be validated against the Social Security file and the department file?

First, you might consider reading the Social Security file and the department file into a table to use the SEARCH statement. This is perhaps the best solution if the table will fit in memory, but the files may be too large for this. Next, you might sort both the payroll transactions and the Social Security file on the Social Security numbers. Then you could write a program to match the two sequential files to see if every Social Security number in the payroll transactions matches one in the Social Security file. You must also write a similar program to do the same for the department numbers. This is unduly complicated, and if there are only a few payroll transactions and the Social Security or department files are large, the method is inefficient. The problem is compounded if there are additional items to validate in the payroll transactions against other files.

Random access solves the problem. You can read each record irrespective of the previous record read. By making the Social Security and department files random-access, you can read payroll transactions and use the Social Security and department numbers as the keys to read records from the Social Security and department files. If a record is found, the payroll transaction is valid. If not found, the payroll transaction is invalid.

This example illustrates the advantage of random access in simplifying the logic where records in a file must be accessed in an unpredictable order. Another advantage of random access is that it is faster to update a few records in a large file than with sequential access. Online applications usually require random access, because they process relatively few transactions against large files that require fast retrieval or updating. An online reservation system could not exist with sequential access, because it would be too slow to update the files sequentially as each reservation is received. Nor can the reservations be batched to run a large group of them together, because any reservation must immediately update the file to avoid overbooking. Random access allows each reservation to update the file as it is received. Random access has the advantage when only a few transactions in a large file are updated. You might also use it when a single transaction must update multiple files or when a file must be immediately accessed or updated.

Random-access files can exist only on direct-access storage devices (termed *mass storage* in the ANSI standard and disk by the rest of the world). They can be accessed sequentially, randomly, or dynamically. For *sequential access,* you can read or write the records in random-access files serially, according to the order the records are physically placed in the file. Sequential access is often used to back up and restore the random-access files onto tape. You back up the file by reading it sequentially and writing it as a sequential file. You restore it by reading the sequential copy and writing it sequentially as a relative or indexed file.

With *random access,* you read or write individual records directly, regardless of where they are physically located in the file. *Dynamic access* is a combination of random and sequential access. You position to a particular record in the file with random access, and then you process the records sequentially from that point.

The two types of random-access files are indexed and relative. For *relative files*, the key is a sequential number (1 through *n*) that specifies the record's relative position within the file, analogous to the subscript of a table. For *indexed files*, the record key is a field within each record that uniquely identifies the record. The system sets aside a portion of the file to contain a directory that tells where the records are stored. To retrieve a record randomly, the system first searches the directory, termed the *index area,* to find the area where the record is stored. It then goes to that area to search for a record with a matching key. Indexed files are analogous to the way books are stored in a library. You search an index to find where the book is stored in the shelves.

Relative files, because you go to a record immediately without having to search an index, are faster for random access. Indexed files are easier to use, because the system maintains an index of where the records are stored rather than requiring you to tell where they are stored. Also, the separate index for indexed files makes it easier to expand the file when records are added.

You create relative files by writing them sequentially, and you cannot add records from then on, unless you reserved space with dummy records. To retrieve a record later, you supply the relative record key. For example, suppose that a personnel record for SMITH is written as the 100th record. For a relative file, you would specify the key of 100 to retrieve the record. Relative files are inconvenient and seldom used, because to access a given record you must somehow derive the key. (How would you know that the personnel record for SMITH was the 100th record?) Relative files are relatively inefficient for sequential processing, because the records cannot be blocked and the records might not be in a useful order.

Indexed files spare you the effort of determining the relative number of the record you want. The record key is a part of the record. You need not write indexed files in their entirety when you create them. You can add new records later.

You can update indexed and relative files in place, permitting records to be added, deleted, or changed without copying the entire file. Updating records in place simplifies the updating logic but leads to a serious backup problem. When you update a file in place, you change the original version of the file. If you must rerun the job, you must first restore the file from a backup copy, presuming you made a backup copy. Sequential files do not have this problem, because the original version of the file is not changed when it is updated, and you can use it to rerun the job if necessary. Therefore, while it is easy to update indexed and relative files, you must give more thought to backing up the files. The usual technique is to back up the entire file at some point and save all subsequent transactions.

Indexed and relative files are less efficient than sequential files for sequential access, and you shouldn't use them unless random retrieval of records is required. As an alternative to indexed files, you can read a small sequential file into an internal table and retrieve the records with the SEARCH statement.

16.2 STATEMENTS FOR INDEXED AND RELATIVE FILES

The same statements used for sequential files are also used for indexed and relative files, with the following additions.

16.2.1 The SELECT Clause

SELECT contains several additional clauses described later in this chapter. The RESERVE AREAS, PASSWORD, and FILE STATUS clauses described in Chapter 17 can also be coded for indexed and relative files.

SELECT for Indexed Files

```
FILE-CONTROL.
    SELECT file-name ASSIGN TO ddname
        ORGANIZATION IS INDEXED
        ACCESS MODE IS SEQUENTIAL or RANDOM or DYNAMIC
        RECORD KEY IS prime-record-key.
```

You describe the *prime-record-key* within the record description in the FD. It must be in the fixed portion of the record and can be qualified but not indexed. You can also describe alternate record keys for the file as described later in this chapter. The RELATIVE KEY clause is required when ACCESS IS RANDOM or DYNAMIC is coded. You can omit it for ACCESS IS SEQUENTIAL, unless you execute a START statement for the file.

There is also FILE STATUS clause in the SELECT clause that directs the system at the completion of each I/O statement to store both a two-character status code in a data item for normal I/O operations and a six-byte data item specific to VSAM. You should test the VSAM status codes after the completion of each VSAM I/O statement

```
SELECT file-name ASSIGN TO ddname
        FILE STATUS IS status, VSAM-status.
```

You describe the *status* and *VSAM-Status* in the Working-Storage or the Linkage Section as follows:

```
WORKING-STORAGE SECTION.
01  status.
    05  key-1    PIC X.
    05  key-2    PIC X.
```
[The system stores status code values in *status* before any USE AFTER ERROR procedures are executed. These status codes are described in Chapter 17.]
```
01  VSAM-status.
    05  key-1    PIC 9(2) BINARY.
```
[VSAM return code as a binary value. Values are 0, no error; 8, serious error and execution continues; 12, serious error and execution cannot continue.]
```
    05  key-2    PIC 9(1) BINARY.
```
[VSAM function code as a binary value. Values of 0 through 5 set only if *key*-1 not zero.]
```
    05  key-3    PIC 9(2) BINARY.
```
[VSAM feedback code as a binary value. Values of 0 through 255 set only if *key*-1 not zero.]

FILE STATUS is described in more detail in Chapter 17.

SELECT for Relative Files

```
FILE-CONTROL.
    SELECT file-name ASSIGN TO ddname
        ORGANIZATION IS RELATIVE
        ACCESS MODE IS SEQUENTIAL or RANDOM or DYNAMIC
        RELATIVE KEY IS relative-record-key.
```

Define the *relative-record-key* in Working-Storage as a PIC 9(9) BINARY item.

16.2.2 The ACCESS MODE Clause

The ACCESS MODE is one of the following:

SEQUENTIAL defaults if you omit ACCESS MODE. Records are read or written sequentially.

RANDOM requires that you supply a key to read or write a record.

DYNAMIC allows you to read the file with both SEQUENTIAL and RANDOM access. Writing is always RANDOM.

Because the ACCESS MODE is intimately associated with the READ and WRITE statements, the details are described later with them.

16.2.3 The FILE SECTION

You code the FILE SECTION as follows for indexed and relative files:

```
FILE SECTION.
FD  file-name                          [BLOCK CONTAINS is not needed.]
    RECORD CONTAINS length CHARACTERS.
```
[For fixed-length records. You can also omit RECORD CONTAINS if the record description supplies the needed information.]

Or

```
RECORD VARYING FROM min TO max CHARACTERS.
```
[For variable-length records.]

Or

```
RECORD VARYING FROM min TO max CHARACTERS
   DEPENDING ON data-name.
```
[For a variable-length record in which a field determines the record length. Remember that the *data-name* must not be contained within the *record-description*.]

For an indexed file, the record key is contained within the record.

```
01  record-description.
    05  perhaps-some-of-the-record PIC ….
    05  prime-record-key           PIC X(n).
```
[The *prime-record-key* must be an alphanumeric item within the record description for the file and lie within the fixed portion of the record. (That is, it cannot be in or follow a variable-occurrence data item.) Mainframe COBOL allows the key to be numeric (internal or external), alphabetic, numeric-edited, alphanumeric-edited, or floating-point (internal or external). Record key values must be unique and you cannot change them directly. (To change a record key, delete the record with the old key and then insert it with the new key.)]

```
    05  rest-of-record         PIC ….
```

If there is more than one record description for the file, you need to name the *prime-record-key* in only one of the record descriptions. However, each record description must have the *prime-record-key* in the same byte positions within the record.

For relative files, you must define the *relative-record-key* named in the RELATIVE KEY clause as an unsigned integer whose description does not contain a P. You can define it in Working-Storage, in the Linkage Section, or in the FD for a record description for another file.

```
WORKING-STORAGE SECTION.
nn  relative-record-key           PIC 9(9) BINARY.
```

16.2.4 The OPEN Statement

OPEN, in addition to EXTEND (only with ACCESS IS SEQUENTIAL), INPUT, and OUTPUT, lets you open files for I-O (input/output). This permits records to be updated in place.

```
OPEN I-O file-name
```

16.2.5 READ and WRITE Statements

The READ can be coded with the INTO phrase and WRITE can be coded with the FROM phrase to process data in Working-Storage, or you can omit the FROM and INTO to process the records in the record area.

```
READ file-name INTO identifier        or    READ file-name
WRITE record-desc FROM identifier     or    WRITE record-desc
```

When ACCESS IS DYNAMIC, COBOL needs to know whether you want to read sequentially or randomly. It assumes you are reading randomly unless you code NEXT to tell it you are reading sequentially.

```
READ file-name NEXT INTO identifier
```

The INVALID KEY Phrase (Not in ANSI Standard)

Files written on direct-access storage devices may exceed the amount of space for the device, or an invalid key may be used to write records in an indexed or relative file. You can detect these conditions by appending the INVALID/NOT INVALID KEY phrases to the READ, WRITE, REWRITE, DELETE, and START statements. (You can do the same thing with the USE AFTER ERROR PROCEDURE described in Chapter 17 and stay within the ANSI standard.) You code it as follows:

```
INVALID KEY imperative-statements
NOT INVALID KEY imperative-statements
```

Here is an example with the WRITE statement.

```
WRITE record-description FROM identifier
   INVALID KEY imperative-statements
   NOT INVALID KEY imperative-statements
END-WRITE
```

INVALID KEY is executed if an attempt is made to write a record outside the bounds of the file or if a record already exists with the same key. This can occur for a sequential file when there is insufficient storage space for the record. NOT INVALID KEY is optional and executes if the record is written. If neither INVALID KEY or USE AFTER ERROR is provided, the program abnormally terminates when an error occurs. INVALID KEY is not supported for VSAM sequential files or OS/2 Btrieve files.

ACCESS IS SEQUENTIAL
You write the READ and WRITE statements the same as for sequential files:

```
READ file-name NEXT RECORD INTO identifier
   AT END imperative-statements
   NOT AT END imperative-statements
END-READ
```

For INDEXED files, you must write the records in ascending order based on their record keys. For RELATIVE files, the system assigns a sequential number to each record when you write it and stores this number in the data item named in the RELATIVE KEY clause.

```
WRITE record-description FROM identifier
   INVALID KEY imperative-statements
   NOT INVALID KEY imperative-statements
END-WRITE
```

ACCESS IS RANDOM
You cannot write the AT END/NOT AT END phrases in the READ. Instead, you write the INVALID/NOT INVALID KEY phrases for both the READ and WRITE statements. For a READ, the INVALID KEY phrase executes if a record with the specified key cannot be found. For a WRITE, it executes if the key is invalid. You must code the INVALID KEY phrase unless you code the USE AFTER ERROR procedure described in Chapter 17.

Because an indexed file can have several keys, you can code a KEY phrase to name the key within the record that you want to read a record. Then you move a value to this data item. If you omit the KEY phrase, COBOL assumes you are using the *prime-record-key* named in the RECORD KEY clause. RELATIVE files have only one key, so you don't code the KEY phrase for them. Instead, you specify the record you want by moving a value to the data item named in the RELATIVE KEY clause.

```
MOVE value TO record-key
READ file-name RECORD INTO identifier
KEY IS record-key    [Omit for RELATIVE files.]
INVALID KEY imperative-statements
NOT INVALID KEY imperative-statements
END-READ
```

The WRITE statement is the same for both indexed and relative. Before executing the WRITE, you must store a value in the record key named in the RECORD/RELATIVE KEY clause for the file to identify the record to write.

```
MOVE value TO record-key
WRITE record-description FROM identifier
  INVALID KEY imperative-statements
  NOT INVALID KEY imperative-statements
END-WRITE
```

ACCESS IS DYNAMIC

You have the option of reading sequentially or randomly. First, you must open the file I-O. Then to read sequentially, you code the READ NEXT statement with the AT END/NOT AT END phrases.

```
READ file-name NEXT RECORD INTO identifier
  AT END imperative-statements
  NOT AT END imperative-statements
END-READ
```

To read randomly, you code the same READ as for ACCESS IS RANDOM:

```
MOVE value TO record-key
READ file-name INTO identifier
  KEY IS record-key [Only for INDEXED files.]
  INVALID KEY imperative-statements
  NOT INVALID KEY imperative-statements
END-READ
```

DYNAMIC can only write random access. Code the same WRITE as for ACCESS IS RANDOM:

```
MOVE value TO record-key
WRITE record-description FROM identifier
  INVALID KEY imperative-statements
  NOT INVALID KEY imperative-statements
END-WRITE
```

For ACCESS IS DYNAMIC, the various statements operate as follows:

OPEN positions the file to the first record.

START positions the file to the first record meeting the specified condition.

READ NEXT positions the file to the record following the record read.

WRITE, REWRITE, and **DELETE** statements have no effect on sequential reading.

16.2.6 The REWRITE Statement

The REWRITE statement locates a specified record in the file and replaces it with the contents of *identifier*. The *identifier* must have the same number of bytes as the record it is updating. You must open the file for I-O to use REWRITE.

For ACCESS IS SEQUENTIAL, you first read a record and then execute REWRITE to rewrite it.

```
REWRITE record-description FROM identifier
```

For ACCESS IS RANDOM or DYNAMIC, you first move a value to the record key and then execute the REWRITE.

```
MOVE value TO record-key
REWRITE record-description FROM identifier
   INVALID KEY imperative-statements
   NOT INVALID KEY imperative-statements
END-REWRITE
```

16.2.7 The START Statement

The START statement positions to a specific record in a relative or indexed file, letting you begin reading sequentially from that record. START can position to any record in the file, and you can execute START several times to reposition. You write START as follows:

```
START file-name KEY relational-operator record-key
   INVALID KEY imperative-statements
   NOT INVALID KEY imperative-statements
END-START
```

The *file-name* must be specified with ACCESS IS SEQUENTIAL or DYNAMIC, not ACCESS IS RANDOM. For indexed files, the *record-key* is either the RECORD KEY or ALTERNATE RECORD KEY. You can qualify the *record-key* but not subscript it. For relative files, the *record-key* must be the data name specified in the RELATIVE KEY clause for the file. For IBM and Micro Focus COBOL and the new ANSI standard, the relational-operator can be any comparison except the not equal (NOT =, UNEQUAL TO). Fujitsu COBOL and the current ANSI standard don't permit the less than.

You can omit the KEY clause, and COBOL finds the record with a key equal to the value you store in the data item named in the RECORD/RELATIVE KEY clauses:

```
MOVE value TO record-key    Same as    START In-File KEY = value
START In-File                                     INVALID KEY …
    INVALID KEY …                        END-START
END-START
```

You must also code the RECORD KEY clause (or ALTERNATE RECORD KEY clause described later in this chapter) for INDEXED files or the RELATIVE KEY clause for RELATIVE files, even if you code ACCESS IS SEQUENTIAL. That is, you must code the following:

```
FILE-CONTROL.
    SELECT file-name ASSIGN TO ddname
        ORGANIZATION IS INDEXED or RELATIVE
        ACCESS IS SEQUENTIAL or DYNAMIC
        RECORD KEY IS prime-record-key          [For INDEXED files]
        RELATIVE KEY IS relative-record-key.    [For RELATIVE files]
```

Then you must open the files for INPUT or I-O to use START.

```
OPEN INPUT file-name       or      OPEN I-O file-name
```

Next, move a value to the record key and execute the START statement.

```
MOVE value TO record-key
START file-name KEY = record-key
    INVALID KEY DISPLAY "CAN'T POSITION FILE"
END-START
```

PROPOSED NEW ANSI STANDARD: Check Compiler to See if Implemented

The new ANSI standard lets you start at the first or last record, in addition to specify any relational-operator except the not equal (NOT =, NOT EQUAL, or IS UNEQUAL TO). It also lets you specify the length of the key to examine for the start comparison.

```
START file-name FIRST
START file-name LAST
START file-name KEY relational-operator record-key
START file-name KEY relational-operator record-key
    WITH LENGTH arithmetic-expression
```

16.2.8 The DELETE Statement

The DELETE statement deletes records.

```
DELETE file-name RECORD
```

You must open the file I-O. For ACCESS IS SEQUENTIAL, you must first read the record and then execute the DELETE statement.

```
READ file-name INTO identifier
  NOT AT END DELETE file-name
[You can delete the record only if the READ is successful.]
END-READ
```

For ACCESS IS RANDOM or DYNAMIC, you first move a value to the record key to indicate the record to delete and then execute the DELETE statement:

```
MOVE value TO record-key
DELETE file-name
  INVALID KEY imperative-statements
  NOT INVALID KEY imperative-statements
END-DELETE
```

The DELETE statement does not disturb the contents of the record area for the file. Nor does it change the current position in the file. If you follow DELETE with a sequential READ, the deleted record is skipped, and the record following it is read. When a record is deleted, you can then add a new record with that key.

16.3 INDEXED FILES

The record keys in indexed files are a part of the record. Each record must have a unique record key, and the system stores the records in the file in ascending order based on this key. For example, a personnel file might have the person's name as the record key. You could read the file sequentially to process the records for each person in the file, one at a time in alphabetical order. You could also access records randomly by specifying the record key. You could read the record for Smith by presenting SMITH as the record key. You can position the file to a point in the file other than the first record to begin sequential processing. Thus, you could position the file to the record for SMITH and sequentially read all the following records.

A major advantage of indexed files is that records can be added or deleted. With sequential files, you add or delete records only by rewriting the entire file. You cannot add records to relative files, because the records have consecutive key numbers. Indexed files are slower to read sequentially than are sequential files, and slower to read randomly than are relative files.

The system maintains two files for each indexed file. One file holds the data records, and the other file holds record keys pointing to where the data records are stored. VSAM for Mainframe COBOL and Btrieve for AIX, OS/2, and Windows all use this technique, although the details of how the indexed and storage areas are organized are different. The PC COBOL compilers have their own access methods that are similar to VSAM.

You initially fill indexed files by writing them sequentially in the order of the record keys, and the system creates the separate index file containing record keys used to locate the records. It is much faster initially to write indexed files sequentially than it is randomly.

The system retrieves records randomly by searching the index to find the record's location and then using this to retrieve the record. You can update indexed files by replacing, adding, or deleting records. You replace records by overwriting the old record. The system dynamically reorganizes indexed files as they are updated. This is why it is faster initially to write them sequentially—the record keys are in order and no reorganization is necessary. When a record is deleted, the system physically removes it from the file. When a record is added, the system inserts the record in the data space and updates the index file.

When you update indexed files, the system writes the records into the file and updates the pointers. If the program abnormally terminates when the file is opened for OUTPUT, I-O, or EXTEND, the file may become unusable, because the pointers may not get updated. This is a serious problem if you do not have a backup. You should back up the file at some point and save all the transactions entered until a new backup is made.

16.3.1   Mainframe COBOL VSAM KSDS Files

In Mainframe COBOL, indexed files are VSAM KSDS (Keyed Sequential Data Sets). You usually create the files with the VSAM IDCAMS utility (Brown, 1998; IBM, 1996), but you can create them through JCL (IBM, 1996; IBM, 1997).

16.3.2   The ALTERNATE RECORD KEY Clause

You specify alternate record keys for a file by coding the ALTERNATE RECORD KEY clause, as follows:

```
FILE-CONTROL.
    SELECT file-name ASSIGN TO ddname
            ORGANIZATION IS INDEXED
            ACCESS IS SEQUENTIAL or RANDOM  or DYNAMIC
            RECORD KEY IS prime-record-key
            ALTERNATE RECORD KEY IS alternate-record-key
                    WITH DUPLICATES.   [WITH DUPLICATES is optional.]
```

The *alternate-record-key* is described as follows. It can be qualified but not indexed. If there is more than one record description for the file, you need name the *alternate-record-key* in only one of the record descriptions.

```
FILE SECTION.
FD  file-name
    RECORD CONTAINS …    or RECORD VARYING …
    □ □ □
01  record-description.
05  perhaps-some-of-the-record PIC ….
05  prime-record-key          PIC X(n).
```
[The relative position of the *prime-record-key* and the *alternate-record-key* doesn't matter.]

```
05  alternate-record-key PIC X(n).
```
[The *alternate-record-key* must be an alphanumeric item within the record description for the file. It must lie within the fixed portion of the record. (That is, it cannot be in or follow a variable-occurrence data item.) IBM COBOL allows the key to be numeric (internal or external), alphabetic, numeric-edited, or alphanumeric-edited. Unlike the *prime-record-key*, you can change the value of an *alternate-record-key*. The leftmost character position of any *alternate-record-key* must not be the same physical storage as the *prime-record-key* or another *alternate-record-key*.]
```
05  rest-of-record        PIC ….
```

Code the WITH DUPLICATES if there can be duplicate alternate record key values. You can also specify several alternate record keys.

```
SELECT file-name ASSIGN TO ddname
       ORGANIZATION IS INDEXED
       ACCESS IS SEQUENTIAL or RANDOM or DYNAMIC
       RECORD KEY IS prime-record-key
       ALTERNATE RECORD KEY IS alternate-record-key-1
              WITH DUPLICATES
       ALTERNATE RECORD KEY IS alternate-record-key-2
       ALTERNATE RECORD KEY IS alternate-record-key-3
              WITH DUPLICATES.
```

In IBM COBOL, you can specify a separate password for each ALTERNATE RECORD KEY. You must code any PASSWORD clause (described in Chapter 17) for it immediately following the ALTERNATE RECORD KEY/WITH DUPLICATES phrase.

The ALTERNATE RECORD KEY clause causes one or more additional indexes to be created to contain alternate record keys. Alternate record keys are a significant feature. They give COBOL the facility for inverting files, a facility generally found only in some generalized database management systems. If the term *inverted* is unfamiliar, the concept is not. Consider a telephone book. The primary index would be the names of people. You could invert the file using the telephone numbers as the alternate key so that you could look up a person's name given his or her telephone number. Because several people may have the same telephone number, the WITH DUPLICATES clause would be needed. A library is an even more familiar example of an inverted file. Libraries maintain catalogs with the book titles as the primary key. They then invert the file on the author so that a book can be retrieved by either its title or author.

You can use an *alternate-record-key* in the I/O statements as follows:

DELETE doesn't use the *alternate-record-key*.

START can name an *alternate-record-key*. This also makes the *alternate-record-key* the key of reference for any subsequent sequential READ statements. That is, once you use START to position to an *alternate-record-key*, READ statements will then read the file in the order of the *alternate-record-key*.

READ will read the file sequentially in the order of the *alternate-record-key* if you execute a START statement naming an *alternate-record-key*. For reading randomly based on the *alternate-record-key*, you can name an *alternate-record-key* in the KEY IS phrase. Note that only the first of a duplicate record written can be retrieved randomly when there are duplicate keys.

REWRITE doesn't use the *alternate-record-key*. You can change an *alternate-record-key* with a REWRITE, and the system will automatically update the alternate file index.

WRITE doesn't use the *alternate-record-key*. Just be sure to code WITH DUPLICATES if you will be writing records with duplicate alternate record keys.

When you code ALTERNATE RECORD KEY in Mainframe COBOL, you must use the IDCAMS utility to define the alternate record keys (Brown, 1998; IBM, 1996).

16.4   RELATIVE FILES

Rarely Used

You primarily use relative files when you must access records in random order and you can easily associate the records with a sequential number. You update a relative file by replacing or deleting records. You replace records by writing the new record over the old one. You assign the records numeric keys ranging in value from 1 through n indicating their relative position in the file. The first record has a key of 1. Thus, COBOL would assign a file containing 500 records keys from 1 through 500. The keys are not a part of the record. You supply them to read or write records.

You use relative files like tables. Their advantage over tables is that their size is limited by the amount of direct-access storage, rather than the more limited memory. However, it takes much more time to retrieve an element from a relative file than from a table. Relative files are best for records that are easily associated with ascending, consecutive numbers. For example, years (the years 1960 through 1980 could be stored with keys 1 through 21), months (keys 1 through 12), or the 50 states of the United States (keys 1 through 50).

If the records being stored cannot be easily associated with the keys, as in a personnel file, you can store some unique part of the record, such as the Social Security number, in a table along with the key. Then you can retrieve records by searching the table for the Social Security number to pick up the key. You could write the table as a sequential file and then read it back in when records are to be retrieved from the relative file. This increases the effort required to access the file, and you might instead consider using an indexed file.

In Mainframe COBOL, relative files are VSAM RRDS (relative record data sets). You usually create the files with the VSAM IDCAMS utility (Brown, 1998;

IBM, 1996), but you can also create them through JCL (IBM, 1996; IBM, 1997). VSAM RRDS files normally have only fixed-length records. VSAM can simulate variable-length records by using a KSDS (keyed sequential data set) rather than an RRDS. Mainframe COBOL also uses KSDS for indexed files. For variable-length Mainframe COBOL files, you must do the following:

- Code the SIMVRD run-time option:

```
// EXEC COBUCLG,PARM.GO=(your-parameters/SIMVRD)
```

- Specify RECORD VARYING in the FD statement for the file.

```
FD  file-name
    RECORD VARYING FROM min TO max CHARACTERS.
```

16.5   PROCESSING INDEXED AND RELATIVE FILES

Sequential files are updated by copying the file and writing the updated records into the output file, or the file can be updated in place by rewriting specific records.

16.5.1   Writing Indexed and Relative Files

In Mainframe COBOL, you can create VSAM files through JCL, but it is usually easier to create them using the VSAM IDCAMS utility program (Brown, 1998; IBM, 1996). In PC COBOL, the system creates indexed files when they are opened for OUTPUT (or EXTEND, if the file doesn't already exist).

Writing Sequentially

Indexed and relative files are usually first written sequentially, often by copying another sequential file. You sort the other file in the order the record keys are to have in the indexed or relative file, and then write the file sequentially. The following example illustrates this:

```
FILE-CONTROL.
    SELECT In-File ASSIGN TO INDD            [You copy this file.]
        ORGANIZATION IS SEQUENTIAL.
    SELECT Out-File ASSIGN TO OUTDD          [You create this file.]
        ORGANIZATION IS INDEXED or RELATIVE
        ACCESS IS SEQUENTIAL
        RECORD KEY IS Out-Record-Key.        [For INDEXED files.]
        RELATIVE KEY IS The-Record-Key.      [For RELATIVE files.]
        [The RECORD/RELATIVE KEY is only needed if you will be executing a START
        statement for the file. However, it is a good idea to code it.]
DATA DIVISION.
FILE SECTION.
FD  In-File.
01  In-Record                   PIC X(100).
```

```
FD   Out-File.
01   Out-Record.
     05  Out-Record-Key              PIC X(10).
     05  Out-Record-Data             PIC X(90).
WORKING-STORAGE SECTION.
01   In-Rec.
     05  In-Rec-Key                  PIC X(10).
     05  In-Rec-Data                 PIC X(90).
01   The-Record-Key                  PIC 9(9) BINARY.
```
[Needed only for a RELATIVE file.]
    ☐ ☐ ☐
```
     OPEN INPUT In-File, OUTPUT Out-File
     PERFORM WITH TEST AFTER UNTIL In-Rec-Key = HIGH-VALUES
        READ In-File INTO In-Rec
          AT END MOVE HIGH-VALUES TO In-Rec-Key
          NOT AT END
               WRITE Out-Record FROM In-Rec
```
            [Note that the WRITE FROM causes *In-Rec-Key* to be moved to *Out-Record-Key* when the WRITE is executed. For a relative file, this doesn't matter. COBOL will store the *relative-record-key* in *The-Record-Key*.]
```
                   INVALID KEY
                      DISPLAY "BAD KEY: ", In-Rec-Key
                      GO TO Z90-Stop-Run
               END-WRITE
        END-READ
     END-PERFORM
```

The INVALID KEY phrase executes if there is not enough space to store the record or if the indexed record keys are not in ascending sort order.

The following OS/390 JCL statement is required to write an indexed or relative file sequentially. There are other forms, but the following is typical:

```
//GO.ddname DD DSN=data-set-name,DISP=OLD
```

Writing Randomly
The following example shows how to write a file randomly. You must store a value in the RECORD/RELATIVE KEY IS clause data item.

```
     SELECT file-name ASSIGN TO ddname
            ORGANIZATION IS INDEXED or RELATIVE
            ACCESS IS RANDOM or DYNAMIC
            RECORD KEY IS prime-record-key.          [For INDEXED files.]
            RELATIVE KEY IS relative-record-key.     [For RELATIVE files.]
```
    ☐ ☐ ☐
```
     OPEN OUTPUT file-name     or     OPEN I-O file-name
     MOVE value TO record-key
     WRITE record-description FROM identifier
       INVALID KEY imperative-statements
       NOT INVALID KEY imperative-statements
     END-WRITE
```

16.5.2   Reading Indexed and Relative Files

Sequential files can be read sequentially, starting with the first record in the file, or you can position to a specific record and begin reading sequentially from there.

Sequential Reading

The records in indexed files are read sequentially in the order that they are stored, that is, in the order of their keys.

```
SELECT file-name ASSIGN TO ddname
      ORGANIZATION IS INDEXED or RELATIVE
      ACCESS IS SEQUENTIAL or DYNAMIC
      RECORD KEY IS prime-record-key            [For INDEXED files]
      RELATIVE KEY IS relative-record-key.      [For RELATIVE files]
```

The RECORD/RELATIVE KEY clause is only needed if you will be executing a START statement for the file. However, it is a good idea to code it. When you code the RELATIVE KEY clause for a relative file, COBOL stores the key of the record in the data item when you read it.

```
OPEN INPUT file-name      or      OPEN I-O file-name
READ file-name NEXT INTO identifier
[You can omit the NEXT for ACCESS IS SEQUENTIAL. You must code it for ACCESS
IS DYNAMIC.]
   AT END imperative-statements
   NOT AT END imperative-statements
END-READ
```

The following OS/390 JCL statement is required to read indexed or relative files sequentially. There are other forms, but the following is typical:

```
//GO.ddname DD DSN=data-set-name,DISP=SHR
```

Positioning for Sequential Reading

You can execute the START statement to position to a specific record within an indexed or relative file and then begin reading sequentially at that point. You must move a value to the RECORD/RELATIVE KEY data item (or ALTERNATE RECORD KEY data item) and then name this data item in the START statement. You must also open the file INPUT or I-O. The identifier specifying the key in the START statement can be qualified but not subscripted.

For an indexed file, it must have a length less than or equal to the *prime-record-key* for the file. For example, if you wanted to begin reading sequentially following the record whose key begins "SMI" in a file, such as SMITH or SMITHE, you could code the following:

```
FILE-CONTROL.
    SELECT In-File ASSIGN TO OUTDD
          ORGANIZATION IS INDEXED or DYNAMIC
```

```
        ACCESS IS SEQUENTIAL
        RECORD KEY IS In-Key.
□  □  □
OPEN INPUT In-File
MOVE "SMI" TO In-Key
START In-File KEY > In-Key
  INVALID KEY
     DISPLAY "NO RECORD IN FILE BEGINS WITH SMI"
     GO TO Z90-Stop-Run
END-START
READ In-File INTO In-Rec
  AT END …
END-READ
```

When fields of unequal length are compared, the longer field is truncated on the right to equal the length of the shorter for the comparison. The comparison ignores any PROGRAM COLLATING SEQUENCE clause.

For a relative file, if you wanted to begin reading sequentially following the fifth record in a file, you could code the following:

```
FILE-CONTROL.
    SELECT In-File ASSIGN TO INDD
           ORGANIZATION IS RELATIVE
           ACCESS IS SEQUENTIAL or DYNAMIC
           RELATIVE KEY IS In-Key.
□  □  □
01  In-Key                        PIC S9(9) BINARY.
□  □  □
OPEN INPUT In-File
MOVE 5 TO In-Key
START In-File KEY > In-Key
  INVALID KEY
     DISPLAY "5TH RECORD NOT IN FILE"
     GO TO Z90-Stop-Run
END-START
READ In-File INTO In-Rec
  AT END …
END-READ
```
[The fifth record is read.]

Random Reading
The following shows how you read records randomly:

```
    SELECT file-name ASSIGN TO ddname
           ORGANIZATION IS INDEXED or RELATIVE
           ACCESS IS RANDOM or DYNAMIC
           RECORD KEY IS prime-record-key.        [For INDEXED files]
           RELATIVE KEY IS retative-record-key.   [For RELATIVE files]
□  □  □
OPEN INPUT file-name    or    OPEN I-O file-name
MOVE value TO record-key
READ file-name INTO identifier
```

```
    INVALID KEY imperative-statements
    NOT INVALID KEY imperative-statements
END-READ
```

If you want other than the *prime-record-key* for an indexed file, you must add the KEY phrase to name the key. (You can also name the *prime-record-key*, but this is default if you omit the KEY phrase.)

```
READ file-name INTO identifier
    KEY IS alternate-key
```
[The *alternate-key* must specify a key defined for the record. It may be qualified but not subscripted.]
```
    INVALID KEY imperative-statements
    NOT INVALID KEY imperative-statements
END-READ
```

16.5.3   Updating Indexed and Relative Files

You can update indexed and relative files sequentially by rewriting the record just read or update them randomly by supplying the key of the record to update.

Updating Sequentially

You update indexed and relative files sequentially, just as you would a sequential file. You first read a record and then execute the REWRITE statement to rewrite it. The record rewritten must have the same length as the record read. For a relative file, omit the INVALID KEY clause. For an indexed file, the *prime-record-key* rewritten must be the same as that read. Here is an example:

```
SELECT In-File ASSIGN TO ddname
        ORGANIZATION IS INDEXED or RELATIVE
        ACCESS IS SEQUENTIAL or DYNAMIC
        RECORD KEY IS prime-record-key          [For INDEXED files]
        RELATIVE KEY IS relative-record-key.    [For RELATIVE files]
```

The RECORD/RELATIVE KEY is only needed if you will be executing a START statement for the file. However, it is a good idea to code it.

```
OPEN I-O file-name
READ In-File INTO In-Rec
    AT END MOVE HIGH-VALUES TO In-Rec-Key
    NOT AT END
        MOVE new-values TO In-Rec
        REWRITE In-Record FROM In-Rec
            INVALID KEY
                DISPLAY "CAN'T REWRITE RECORD: ", In-Rec-Key
                GO TO Z90-Stop-Run
        END-REWRITE
END-READ
```

Updating Randomly

You must open the file for I-O, and the record written must contain the same number of characters as the record in the file. (In IBM COBOL, the record can have a different length.) For an indexed file, you must not change the *prime-record-key* when you rewrite a record. If you need to change a *prime-record-key,* delete the record and write it with the new key.

```
SELECT file-name ASSIGN TO ddname
     ORGANIZATION IS INDEXED or RELATIVE
     ACCESS IS RANDOM or DYNAMIC
     RECORD KEY IS prime-record-key.            [For INDEXED files]
     RELATIVE KEY IS relative-record-key.       [For RELATIVE files]
□  □  □
OPEN I-O file-name
MOVE value TO record-key
REWRITE record-description FROM identifier
  INVALID KEY imperative-statements
  NOT INVALID KEY imperative-statements
END-REWRITE
```

Quite often, you update by first reading the record and then rewriting it:

```
MOVE value TO record-key
READ file-name INTO identifier              [First read the record to be updated.]
  INVALID KEY imperative-statements
END-READ
MOVE new-value TO identifier                [Change the values in the record.]
REWRITE record-description FROM identifier
  INVALID KEY imperative-statements
END-REWRITE
```

The DELETE statement deletes records in an indexed or relative file. You must open the file for I-O. The contents of the record description and the file position are not affected by execution of the DELETE statement. For ACCESS IS SEQUENTIAL, you must first successfully read a record with a READ statement. DELETE then deletes that record. Don't code the INVALID/NOT INVALID KEY phrases. For ACCESS IS RANDOM or DYNAMIC, the value in the *record-key* specifies the record to delete. Here is an example:

```
OPEN I-O file-name
MOVE value TO record-key
DELETE file-name
  INVALID KEY imperative-statements
  NOT INVALID KEY imperative-statements
END-DELETE
```

Once the record is deleted, the system logically removes it from the file so that you cannot read it. However, you may write it again.

EXERCISES

1. Describe several applications in which indexed and relative files might each be used.

2. Write a program to read a file, containing a charge number in columns 1 to 6, and create a relative file. Then write a program to read in each transaction in random order that contains a charge number in columns 1 to 6. Validate each charge number by looking it up in the relative file. Print an error message on the transaction if the charge number is not found in the file.

3. Repeat Exercise 2 for an indexed file. Assume that the charge number can be any alphanumeric characters.

4. Assume the same file described in Exercise 2. However, the transactions are to be used to update the file. Assume that column 7 of the transaction contains a D to delete the record in the file, an A to add the transaction to the file, and an R to replace the record in the file with the transaction. Any other character in column 7 is an error. Display an error message if the record to be deleted or replaced is not in the file, or if a transaction to be added already exists in the file. Do this exercise for either relative or indexed file organization.

5. Write a program to back up and restore the file described in Exercise 2 sequentially.

CHAPTER 17

SPECIAL PROCESSING FOR INPUT/OUTPUT

This chapter describes how to handle I/O errors, how to obtain file status information, and how to use the special I/O features in COBOL. The information applies to sequential, relative, and indexed files. Most COBOL programs won't use the features described in this chapter. You might skip this chapter and come back to it as needed.

17.1 I/O ERRORS AND FILE STATUS

You can detect and process I/O errors in COBOL in two ways. One way is to specify a procedure to invoke when the error occurs. The other method is to specify the names of data items into which COBOL will store codes indicating the result of an I/O operation. This method lets you detect the error in the mainline code.

17.1.1 The USE AFTER ERROR PROCEDURE

Sometimes Used

In the Declaratives, which immediately follow the Procedure Division name, you can add one or more sections to be automatically invoked when an I/O error occurs:

```
PROCEDURE DIVISION.
DECLARATIVES.
section-name SECTION.
    USE AFTER ....
paragraphs.
    statements
    .
section-name SECTION.
    USE AFTER ....
    □ □ □
END DECLARATIVES.
```

You code USE AFTER as follows:

```
                                    INPUT
                                    OUTPUT
                                    I-O
                                    EXTEND
                                    file-name, file-name, …, file-name
USE AFTER ERROR PROCEDURE ON _____.
```

Verbose form:

```
USE GLOBAL AFTER STANDARD EXCEPTION/ERROR PROCEDURE ON ….
```

The system executes the paragraphs in the section if an I/O error occurs on any of the named files. Coding INPUT, for example, would detect an I/O error on any input file. Coding *file-name* would detect only the errors on the specified file. You can code several USE statements, but if you code a *file-name,* it has priority over any generic specification, such as INPUT or OUTPUT, that would include that file name.

In the ANSI standard, the paragraphs within the sections cannot contain any statements that refer to nondeclarative procedures. Nor can nondeclarative procedures refer to any paragraph in the Declarative Section. IBM COBOL removes these restrictions.

Control is returned to the statement causing the error when the exit is made from the section—unless the error causes the program to terminate abnormally.

```
PROCEDURE DIVISION.
DECLARATIVES.
File-I-Error SECTION.
    USE AFTER ERROR PROCEDURE ON File-I.
File-I-Start.
    DISPLAY "ERROR ON File-I"
    ADD 1 TO Error-Count
    .
File-O-Error SECTION.
    USE AFTER ERROR PROCEDURE ON File-O.
File-O-Start.
    DISPLAY "ERROR ON File-O"
    ADD 1 TO Error-Count
    .
END DECLARATIVES.
    □  □  □
    READ File-I INTO X
      AT END MOVE "Y" TO EOF-File-I
      NOT AT END
          MOVE File-I-Rec TO File-O-Rec
          WRITE File-O-Rec
    END-READ
```

COBOL invokes a USE AFTER ERROR PROCEDURE for the following conditions:

- An I/O error occurs during a READ, WRITE, REWRITE, START, DELETE, OPEN or CLOSE.
- An end of file condition occurs, and the READ statement doesn't contain an AT END clause.
- An invalid key error occurs, and the READ or WRITE statement doesn't contain an INVALID KEY clause.
- An I/O error occurs that causes *key-1* of the FILE STATUS, described later in this section, to be set to 9.

Programs terminate if an open is unsuccessful, unless a USE AFTER ERROR PROCEDURE is coded, which can take action when an unsuccessful open occurs.

17.1.2 User Labels: The USE AFTER LABEL PROCEDURE (Not in ANSI Standard)

Rarely Used

IBM COBOL and PC COBOL allow you to create and process user labels for files (very rare). User labels are records written immediately after the standard header or trailer labels. The USE AFTER LABEL PROCEDURE declarative allows you to code paragraphs containing statements to read or write these labels and do whatever processing is needed.

Mainframe COBOL VSAM files cannot have user labels. To specify user labels, you must also code a LABEL RECORDS clause in the FD paragraph for the file. The LABEL RECORDS clause also lets you specify STANDARD labels (the default if you omit the clause), or OMITTED for no labels. The LABEL RECORDS clause is obsolete in the ANSI standard and is to be removed in the next revision. In Mainframe COBOL, it is better to code the LABEL parameter in the JCL DD statement to specify nonlabeled data sets, which can only be on tape. Consequently, you would need the LABEL RECORDS clause only if you have user labels. You code it as follows:

```
FD  In-File BLOCK CONTAINS …
                       OMITTED
                       STANDARD
                       record-name
    LABEL RECORDS IS/ARE. _____.
```

Code *record-name* if you have user labels. (If you have user labels, you must also have standard labels.) The *record-name* is then the name of the record description for the user label, and you describe it as a level 01 entry following the FD. The record length must be 80. Here is an example:

```
FD  In-File BLOCK CONTAINS …
    LABEL RECORDS My-Label.
01  My-Label.
    05  Some-Stuff                    PIC X(60).
    05  More-Stuff                    PIC X(20).
01  normal-record-name …
```

You describe both the regular records in the file and the label records with level 01 entries. Next, you code the USE AFTER LABEL PROCEDURE in the Declaratives Section in the same way as you code a USE AFTER ERROR PROCEDURE. You code the USE AFTER LABEL PROCEDURE as follows:

```
PROCEDURE DIVISION.
DECLARATIVES.
section-name SECTION.
    USE AFTER LABEL PROCEDURE …
paragraphs.
    statements-to-process-the-user-labels
    .
section-name SECTION.
    USE AFTER ….
    □  □  □
END DECLARATIVES.
```

INPUT or OUTPUT or I-O or EXTEND execute the procedures only if the file is opened as specified. You code the USE AFTER LABEL PROCEDURE as follows:

```
                                            INPUT
                                            OUTPUT
                          FILE              I-O
          ENDING          REEL              EXTEND
          BEGINNING       UNIT              file-name
USE AFTER _____  ____  LABEL PROCEDURE ON _____.
```

Verbose form:

```
USE GLOBAL AFTER STANDARD ___ ___ LABEL PROCEDURE ON ___.
```

- *BEGINNING/ENDING* specifies whether the procedure is executed for the BEGINNING label only, the ENDING label only, or both the beginning and ending labels (if neither BEGINNING nor ENDING is coded).

- *FILE/REEL/UNIT* specify when the procedures are to be executed for the beginning and/or ending labels. If none of these three are specified, the procedures are executed as if both REEL/UNIT and FILE were specified.

  FILE for BEGINNING executes only at the beginning of file for the first volume only. For ENDING executes at the end of file for the last volume only.

  REEL or *UNIT* for BEGINNING executes at the beginning of volume on each volume except the first. For ENDING executes at the end of volume on each volume except the last. Don't code REEL for disk files.

- *file-name* names a file for which user labels are to be processed. You can name several files in different USE AFTER LABEL PROCEDURE declaratives for different combinations of BEGINNING/ENDING and FILE/REEL/ UNIT. However, the file must not be simultaneously requested for execution by more than one USE procedure. The file can't be a sort file or have the LABEL RECORDS ARE OMITTED clause coded for it. You can code several *file-names*, separating them by spaces, so that their user labels are processed by the same statements. Here is an example:

```
Tape-Error SECTION.
    USE AFTER BEGINNING FILE LABEL PROCEDURE ON File-1, File-2.
```

Normally the system exits the Declarative following the last statement in the section. However, you can code a special GO TO MORE-LABELS statement to execute the procedure again, perhaps to read or write a second user label. The GO TO MORE-LABELS finishes reading or writing the current label and then reenters the procedure. Obviously, you would want to insert code to make the GO TO MORE-LABELS conditional so that the program does not go into a loop.

17.1.3 The FILE STATUS Clause

Rarely Used

The FILE STATUS clause in the SELECT clause directs the system to store a two-character status code in a data item at the completion of each I/O statement. You can test these status codes after completion of the I/O statement, either in a USE AFTER ERROR PROCEDURE or in normal program statements.

```
SELECT file-name ASSIGN TO ddname
       FILE STATUS IS status.
```

You must describe the *status* in the Working-Storage or the Linkage Section as a two-character alphanumeric field:

```
WORKING-STORAGE SECTION.
01  status.
05  key-1 PIC X.
05  key-2 PIC X.
```

The system stores status code values in *status* before any USE AFTER ERROR procedures are executed. The status codes are shown in Table 17.1.

IBM and PC COBOL also allow a second identifier to be specified in the FILE STATUS clause for VSAM or Btrieve I/O errors.

```
SELECT file-name ASSIGN TO AS-ddname
       FILE STATUS IS status, VSAM-status.
```

For Mainframe COBOL, the *VSAM-status* must be a group item of 6 bytes described as follows:

```
WORKING-STORAGE SECTION.
01  VSAM-status.
    05  key-1    PIC 9(2) BINARY.
    [VSAM return code as a binary value.]
    05  key-2    PIC 9(1) BINARY.
    [VSAM function code as a binary value.]
```

TABLE 17.1 System Status Codes

key-1	key-2	Cause
Successful Completion		
0	0	No further information.
	2	Duplicate key detected.
	4	Wrong fixed-length record.
	5	File created when opened. With sequential VSAM files, 0 is returned.
	7	CLOSE with NO REWIND or REEL, for nontape.
End of File		
1	0	No further information.
	4	Relative record READ outside file boundary.
Invalid Key		
2	1	Sequence error.
	2	Duplicate key.
	3	No record found.
	4	Key outside boundary of file.
Permanent I/O Error		
3	0	No further information.
	4	Record outside file boundary.
	5	OPEN and required file not found.
	7	OPEN with invalid mode.
	8	OPEN of file closed with LOCK.
	9	OPEN unsuccessful because of conflicting file attributes.
Logic Error		
4	1	OPEN of file already open.
	2	CLOSE for file not open.
	3	READ not executed before REWRITE.
	4	REWRITE of different size record.
	6	READ after EOF reached.
	7	READ attempted for file not opened I-O or INPUT.
	8	WRITE for file not opened OUTPUT, I-O, or EXTEND.
	9	DELETE or REWRITE for file not opened I-O.

TABLE 17.1   *(Continued)*

key-1	key-2	Cause
		Specific Compiler-Defined Conditions
9	0	No further information.
	1	Password or authorization failure.
	2	Logic error.
	3	Resource not available.
	4	VSAM sequential record not available or concurrent open error.
	5	Invalid or incomplete file information.
	6	No DD statement specified.
	7	VSAM OPEN successful and file integrity verified.
	8	Open failed due to locked file.
	9	Record access failed due to locked record.

```
05  key-3    PIC 9(3) BINARY.
    [VSAM feedback code as a binary value.]
```

17.2   SPECIAL I/O FEATURES

Rarely Used

The special I/O features in this section are all optional and seldom required. Some of them are compiler-dependent.

17.2.1   The I-O-CONTROL Paragraph

You can code the I-O-CONTROL paragraph to specify various I/O options. Terminate the last clause with a period. The options are described following.

```
INPUT-OUTPUT SECTION.
File-CONTROL.
    SELECT ...
I-O-CONTROL.
    SAME AREA or RECORD AREA or SORT AREA
    APPLY WRITE ONLY ....            [Terminate paragraph with period.]
```

The SAME AREA Clause (Not in Workstation COBOL)

The SAME AREA clause in the I-O-CONTROL paragraph illustrates how the desire to squeeze the last bit of efficiency from the system can result in making simple things complex. IBM COBOL treats SAME AREA as documentation for sequential files. (It is ignored for all files in Workstation COBOL.) You code SAME AREA as follows:

```
I-O-CONTROL.
    SAME AREA FOR file-name, file-name, …, file-name.
```

The SAME AREA clause causes the listed files to share the same storage for their access routines and buffers. You must not have the files open at the same time. In the following example, *File-A* and *File-B* could not be open at the same time, because they share the same storage. OS/390 allocates storage dynamically with the OPEN and releases it with the CLOSE, so any savings are minimal.

```
SAME AREA File-A, File-B
```

The SAME RECORD AREA clause allows several files to share the same record area. (You cannot code SAME RECORD AREA for a file that has RECORD CONTAINS 0 CHARACTERS specified.) The files may be open at the same time.

```
SAME RECORD AREA FOR file-name, file-name, …, file-name.
```

In essence, the records following the FD entry are implicitly redefined to each other for all the files listed. This allows a record to be read from one file and written by another without moving the data. The following example illustrates this.

```
I-O-CONTROL.
    SAME RECORD AREA FOR File-A, File-B.
DATA DIVISION.
FILE SECTION.
FD  File-A …
01  File-A-Rec                      PIC X(80).
FD  File-B …
01  File-B-Rec                      PIC X(80).
    □   □   □
    OPEN INPUT File-A, File-B
    READ File-A                     [Record is read into File-A-Rec.]
      AT END CONTINUE
    NOT AT END WRITE File-B-Rec
        [The record in File-A-Rec is also the File-B-Rec record, and it is written onto File-B.]
    END-READ
```

The APPLY WRITE-ONLY Clause (Not in ANSI Standard)

Mainframe COBOL allows the APPLY WRITE-ONLY clause to be written for QSAM output files with variable-length records. (APPLY WRITE-ONLY is treated as a comment in Workstation and PC COBOL.) It optimizes buffer and device space allocation. The savings are marginal. You code it as follows:

```
I-O-CONTROL.
    APPLY WRITE-ONLY ON file-name, file-name, …, file-name.
```

7.2.2   The SELECT Clause Options

For some systems, the SELECT clause lets you specify a password, change the number of buffers to use, and lock a file for exclusive use.

The PASSWORD Clause (Mainframe and Micro Focus COBOL Only)

Mainframe and Micro Focus COBOL permit a password to be specified in order to limit access to non-QSAM files. The password is a PIC X(8) item written into the file when it is created. You must supply the password thereafter to match the password of the file when the file is opened. The password can be specified only for VSAM files.

```
SELECT file-name ASSIGN TO AS-ddname
       PASSWORD IS password.
```

The *password* must be defined as a PIC X(8) data item in Working-Storage that will contain the password when the file is opened. For relative and indexed files, the password is associated with the record key and the PASSWORD clause must immediately follow the RECORD or ALTERNATE RECORD KEY data name with which it is associated.

```
01  password              PIC X(8).
```

The RESERVE AREAS Clause for Allocating Buffers

Buffers provide an area in which to block and unblock records. This allows the operating system to be reading or writing some buffer while the program is processing records in the other buffer, overlapping the I/O with the computations. If you omit RESERVE AREAS, the system assumes a default that is adequate in most instances. The RESERVE clause in the SELECT clause changes the number of buffers allocated to a file. You code it as follows, where the literal *integer* is the number of buffers to allocate.

```
SELECT file-name ASSIGN TO ddname
       RESERVE integer AREAS.
```

In OS/390, it is better to specify the number of buffers with the JCL BUFNO parameter.

```
//ddname DD DCB=(BUFNO=5,…
```

LOCK MODE Clause (OS/2 VSAM Only)

LOCK MODE tells whether an OS/2 file is in exclusive or shareable mode. Omit LOCK MODE to make it exclusive. For shareable mode, code the following:

```
SELECT file-name ASSIGN TO ddname
       LOCK MODE IS AUTOMATIC WITH LOCK ON RECORD .
```

17.3 THE FD CODE-SET CLAUSE (MAGNETIC TAPE ONLY)

The CODE-SET clause specifies the character codes of the characters on the tape if other than the computer's native mode. For example, you could use this to write an ASCII tape on the mainframe. You code CODE-SET as follows:

```
FD  file-name
    □   □   □
    CODE-SET IS alphabet-name.
```

You specify the *alphabet-name* in the ALPHABET clause of the SPECIAL-NAMES paragraph as described in Chapter 10.

CHAPTER 18

REPORT WRITER

Reports are surprisingly difficult to code, and the report writer both greatly simplifies the coding and makes reports easier to change. If your installation doesn't have the report writer or forbids its use, you can skip this chapter. Barring this, you should read this chapter.

Sometimes Used

Many examples have been presented throughout this book to illustrate the advantages of structured programming over conventional programming. The examples show the structured programming techniques to be better, but often the difference between structured programming and conventional programming is not dramatic. The COBOL report writer is not a part of structured programming, but its advantages over the conventional programming of reports are often dramatic.

TIP *The report writer greatly simplifies the writing of reports. Use it wherever possible.*

The report writer is a part of ANSI COBOL and the PC COBOL compilers also support it. IBM has made extensive enhancements beyond the ANSI standard to the report writer in Mainframe COBOL, and this chapter covers them.

The report writer generates reports with much less Procedure Division coding than printing each individual line, although the Data Division becomes more complex because it specifies the report format, the source of the data, and the totals to print. The entire report is parameterized, making it easier to change. Once the report format has been specified, the report writer automatically takes care of page breaks, page headings and footings, moving data to the print line, and column and row subtotaling and totaling.

Part of the reason why the report writer is easier to use for writing reports than the conventional manner with WRITE statements is that it knows that it is printing output on a printer, and it is adapted especially for this. For example, if WEEKLY STATUS is to print in column 60, you code it as:

```
05   COLUMN 60                      PIC X(13)
                                    VALUE "WEEKLY STATUS".
```

In Mainframe COBOL and the new ANSI standard, PIC is optional with the VALUE clause. They also allow you to abbreviate COLUMN as COL.

```
05   COL 60                         VALUE "WEEKLY STATUS".
```

When you omit PIC for a figurative constant such as SPACES, it is treated as a single character.

```
05  COL 10 SPACES.     Same as     05  COL 10 PIC X VALUE SPACES.
```

The main reason for using the report writer is to make reports easier to write and maintain. It will probably be less efficient than writing the report in the conventional manner because of the report writer overhead, but the loss in efficiency is negligible. Report writer programs are easy to maintain, but in practice, few programmers have become familiar with the report writer, which complicates maintenance. However, the report writer is not difficult to follow because it lays the entire report out in the Data Division, specifying the format, contents, and control breaks.

The report writer simplifies the deceptively complex logic required to compute totals and subtotals and roll them forward. The report writer performs these operations automatically, but if the report does not come out as expected, it may be difficult to discover the cause of the error. The logical flow and intermediate results cannot be printed with debugging statements, as would be possible if the report were programmed in the conventional way. The report is specified in the Data Division, and if there is an error, you have only your intellect to aid in debugging the problem. Mitigating this, though, the report writer produces an output that usually gives enough information for debugging.

Don't use the report writer for reports with complex formats, such as those in which different data requires different page headings. Nor should it be used where there are significant exceptions to be handled in the report, such as printing totals first, followed by the detail lines. The report writer is best for reports that have the same page heading format on each page and are composed of rows and columns. The columns can be cross-footed, and the detail lines can be summed to several levels with appropriate totals printed according to some specified hierarchy. Each level in the hierarchy can also have a heading line printed.

18.1   SAMPLE REPORT

Essential

The following simple example illustrates the report writer. A file containing the population of cities is read, and the report writer prints a report in the following format.

```
                        CITY LISTING
                                            PAGE nn

CITY:  name of city              population
CITY:  name of city              population
  □        □        □
```

The report writer writes a normal print file that must be opened before being used and be closed when the report is completed. The WRITE statement cannot write to the same file. The FD entry specifies a report name, and this report name is then defined in the REPORT SECTION.

```
INPUT-OUTPUT SECTION.
FILE-CONTROL.
    SELECT Rpt-File ASSIGN TO FILEO.
    [Rpt-File is the print file to which the report is written.]
    SELECT In-File ASSIGN TO MFILE.
    [In-File is the input file containing the cities and populations.]
DATA DIVISION.
FILE SECTION.
FD  Rpt-File BLOCK CONTAINS 0 RECORDS
    REPORT IS Cities.
    [The FD entry describes the print file. The REPORT clause names the report,
    Cities, to be written on the file.]
FD  In-File BLOCK CONTAINS 0 RECORDS.
01  File-Rec    PIC X(65).
    [A FD is required for the input file.]
WORKING-STORAGE SECTION.
01  Next-City.
    05   State         PIC X(20).
    05   County        PIC X(20).
    05   City          PIC X(20).
    05   Population     PIC S9(9) PACKED-DECIMAL.
    [The input file will be read into Next-City.]
REPORT SECTION.                    [REPORT SECTION describes the reports.]
RD  Cities      [A RD entry describes each individual report, Cities in our example.]
    PAGE 60 LINES               [The report size is 60 lines per page.]
    HEADING 1
    [HEADING specifies the line on which to print the first item. The page heading in
    this example begins on line 1.]
    FIRST DETAIL 5.
    [The body of the report begins on line 5. You can code this only if you code
    PAGE.]
01  TYPE PAGE HEADING.
    [The data items that follow describe the page heading report group. It is termed a
    report group because it may consist of several lines. The page heading is automat-
    ically printed at the top of each page. A report may consist of a report heading
    printed once at the start of the report, a page heading printed at the top of each
    page, control headings printed before a group of detail lines to title them, detail
    lines constituting the main body of the report, control footings for totaling detail
    lines, page footings to print something at the bottom of each page, and a report
```

footing to print something once at the end of the report, such as a grand total. Each item is optional, and this report has only a page heading and detail lines.]

```
05   LINE 1 COL 40                         PIC X(12) VALUE "CITY LISTING".
```
[CITY LISTING is printed in columns 40 to 51 of line 1. The LINE clause defines the start of a new line and tells where the line is printed on the page. COL specifies the starting column in which to print the data, and the PIC clause, if coded, specifies its format. Data to be printed can be literals specified in a VALUE clause, identifiers named in a SOURCE clause, or subtotals generated by the report writer specified in a SUM clause.]

```
05   LINE +2.
```
[The next line is spaced two lines beyond the last line. Note that relative line numbers in the form of +n are in Mainframe COBOL only.]

```
10   COL 95                                PIC ZZ9 SOURCE PAGE-COUNTER.
```
[The value of PAGE-COUNTER is printed in columns 85 to 87 of the same line. The SOURCE clause names the item to be printed and moves it to the print line according to the PIC clause. PAGE-COUNTER, automatically maintained by the report writer, is a special register described as PIC S9(9) BINARY SYNC containing the current page number.]

```
01   Dtl-Line TYPE DETAIL LINE +2.
```
[This line is a detail report group. It must be assigned a name, Dtl-Line here, and it is printed with the execution of each GENERATE statement that names it. Each line is printed two lines below the previous line.]

```
05   COL 1                                 PIC X(6) VALUE "CITY: ".
```
[CITY prints in columns 1 to 5.]

```
05   COL 8                                 PIC X(20) SOURCE City.
```
[The value of the identifier City from the input file prints in columns 8 to 27.]

```
05   COL 29                                PIC Z(8)9V
                                           SOURCE Population.
```
[The value of the identifier Population from the input file prints in columns 29 to 37.]

```
PROCEDURE DIVISION.
A00-BEGIN.
     OPEN INPUT In-File, OUTPUT Rpt-File
```
[The report file must be opened as with all files.]

```
     INITIATE Cities
```
[The INITIATE statement names the report and does all the housekeeping required to begin the report.]

```
     MOVE LOW-VALUES TO City
```
[The paragraph that reads the file is performed until an end of file terminates the loop.]

```
     PERFORM UNTIL City = HIGH-VALUES
        READ In-File INTO Next-City
             AT END MOVE HIGH-VALUES TO City
             NOT AT END GENERATE Dtl-Line
```
[The GENERATE statement prints the detail lines by naming the detail report group. The page heading automatically prints at the top of each page.]

```
        END-READ
     END-PERFORM
     TERMINATE Cities
```
[The TERMINATE statement names the report and does all the housekeeping required to terminate the report.]

```
        CLOSE In-File, Rpt-File          [Close the report file as with all files.]
        GOBACK.
**** End of program.
```

18.2   CONTROL BREAKS

Essential

Most reports need *control breaks* to print headings and totals. A control break occurs when a control item changes value. A *control item* is an identifier named in a CONTROL clause as described following. For the previous example, the file might be sorted on state, county, and city. A detail line is generated for each city. You might want to make the county a control break to print the total population for all cities in the county, and also make the state a control break to print the total population for each state by summing all the counties in the state. This is accomplished by *control footings.* In addition to the control footings, you might want to print a heading with each new state, and for each new county within a state. This is accomplished by *control headings.* When a control break occurs, the control footings print first to total the previous lines, then the control headings print to total the new detail lines, and then the detail lines print. The report is to appear as shown here.

```
                            CITY LISTING
                                                        PAGE nn
STATE                                                ⎫
   County                                            ⎬ Control headings
      CITY:   name of city           population      ⎭
      CITY:   name of city           population      ⎫ Detail lines
      □  □  □                                        ⎭
      COUNTY TOTAL                    population      ⎫
   □  □  □                                           ⎬ Control footing
STATE TOTAL                          population       ⎭
```

To accomplish this, code the report as follows:

```
REPORT SECTION.
RD  Cities
    PAGE 60 LINES
    HEADING 1
    FIRST DETAIL 5
    CONTROLS ARE State, County.
```

18.2.1   THE CONTROLS CLAUSE

Essential

The CONTROLS clause names the control items that are to cause the control breaks. The items are listed in order from major to minor, and the input file must be sorted in the same order. The control items can be fields in a record or in Working-Storage. The control break occurs only when the GENERATE statement is executed and the item has a different value than it had when the GENERATE statement was last executed.

```
01   TYPE PAGE HEADING.
     05   LINE 1 COL 40      PIC X(12) VALUE "CITY LISTING".
     05   LINE +2.
          10   COL 90        PIC X(4) VALUE "PAGE".
          10   COL 95        PIC ZZ9
                             SOURCE PAGE-COUNTER.
01   TYPE CONTROL HEADING FOR State LINE +2.
```
     [The control heading, spaced two lines beyond the previous line, is printed as each new *State* is encountered.]
```
     05   COL 1              PIC X(20) SOURCE State.
01   TYPE CONTROL HEADING FOR County LINE +1.
     05   COL 3              PIC X(20) SOURCE County.
```
     [This control heading prints when a new *County* is encountered.]
```
01   Dtl-Line TYPE DETAIL LINE +1.
     05   COL 5              PIC X(6) VALUE "CITY: ".
     05   COL 12             PIC X(20) SOURCE City.
     05   COL 33             PIC Z(8)9
                             SOURCE Population.
01   TYPE CONTROL FOOTING FOR County LINES +2.
```
     [This control footing prints the total of the previous county.]
```
     05   COL 3              PIC X(12) VALUE "COUNTY TOTAL".
     05   S1 COL 33          PIC Z(8)9 SUM Population.
```
     [The SUM clause sums the *Population* as each detail line is printed and resets it to zero after the footing is printed. The line is given a name, *S1* here, because it is referred to in a subsequent line.]
```
01   TYPE CONTROL FOOTING FOR State LINE +2.
```
     [This control footing prints the total for each state.]
```
     05   COL 1              PIC X(11) VALUE "STATE TOTAL".
     05   COL 33             PIC Z(8)9 SUM S1.
```
     [This SUM counter sums the previous *S1* SUM counter to give the county population.]

This completes the report changes. The Procedure Division need not be changed at all. The example illustrates a major advantage of the report writer—substantial changes can be made to reports solely within the Data Division where the changes are relatively easy. Had the report been written conventionally with WRITE statements, this change might have required scores of Procedure Division statements and taken days to debug.

18.2.2   Order of Control Breaks

When a control break occurs, it first causes a control break for all lower levels. The first GENERATE statement prints any REPORT HEADING report group, and then any PAGE HEADING report group, and then causes a control break for all control headings so that they print before the first detail line. The TERMINATE statement causes a control break for all control footings so that the final totals are printed at the end of the report. The control breaks occur in the following order:

1. Minor to major for the control footings.
2. Major to minor for the control headings.
3. The detail lines are printed.

Thus, when a GENERATE statement is executed and a new *State* is encountered to cause a control break, the following occurs:

1. Control footing for the old *County* prints the total for the previous *Cities* in the County, adds its sum to the *State* SUM counter, and resets the *County* SUM counter to zero.
2. Control footing for the old *State* prints the total for the previous *Counties* and in the *State* and resets the *State* SUM counter to zero.
3. Control heading for the *State* to print the new state.
4. Control heading for the *County* to print the new *County*.
5. Print the detail line for the *City* and sum its *Population* into the *County* SUM counter.

You can specify a FINAL control heading to print once when the first GENERATE statement is executed, perhaps to print something that is to go on the first page of the report. A FINAL control footing also prints once when the TERMINATE statement executes, perhaps to print the total for all the states. Code the CONTROLS clause in the RD entry as shown here. List the *data-names* in major to minor order. They can be subscripted, indexed, and have a subordinate item containing the OCCURS DEPENDING ON clause.

```
RD  report-name
    FINAL  or  REPORT      [FINAL and REPORT are the same.]
    data-name, data-name, …
    FINAL, data-name, data-name, …
    CONTROLS ARE _
```

There can be only a single item used for each control break. (The items can overlap.) To define a control break to occur when any one of several items change values, place them in a record and then name the group item in the CONTROLS clause. For example, if you want a control break to occur when either *Age* or *Weight* changes value, define them within the same group item.

```
05  Age-Weight.
    10  Age     PIC S9(3) PACKED-DECIMAL.
    10  Weight  PIC S9(3) PACKED-DECIMAL.
    □   □   □
RD  report-name.
    CONTROLS ARE Age-Weight.
```

The same control break will occur if either *Age* or *Weight* changes value. If the report is printed from a file, the record may not contain the proper record to produce the report. For this, define the record you want in Working-Storage and move the I/O record items to the record as each record is read.

18.3   REPORT GROUPS

Essential

The report groups have already been illustrated, but they provide several additional facilities. A *report group* is one or more lines printed together as a group, such as a page heading. A report group may also be a null group that is not printed, but is used for control breaks or for summing items to be printed. A report must contain at least one detail report group, and all other report groups are optional. The seven report groups are as follows:

1. *REPORT HEADING* is optional. It prints automatically once at the start of the report when the first GENERATE statement executes. You can specify a single REPORT HEADING group per report to print a cover sheet, distribution list, or any other information that pertains to the entire report. The REPORT HEADING starts on a new page.

2. *PAGE HEADING* is optional. It prints automatically at the top of each new page. You can specify a single PAGE HEADING group per report to print the page heading, page number, and column headings. A PAGE HEADING automatically prints when a page overflows, and you can also program it to occur either before an individual line is printed with the LINE NEXT PAGE clause or after a report group is printed with the NEXT GROUP NEXT PAGE clause. The first GENERATE statement prints the first PAGE HEADING following any REPORT HEADING. For this reason, page breaks should usually be caused by the NEXT GROUP NEXT PAGE clause in a control footing. If they are caused by a control heading, the report will begin with two page headings: one for the first GENERATE statement, and one from the first control heading break caused by the same GENERATE.

3. *CONTROL HEADING* is optional. A heading prints automatically above a detail line group when a control break occurs. You name control items in the CONTROLS clause, and a control break occurs when an item is presented with a changed value. A FINAL control heading break occurs only once when the first GENERATE statement is executed, to print a control heading at the start of the report. For each report, there may be a single CONTROL HEADING group for each control item and for FINAL.

4. *DETAIL* is required. The GENERATE statement prints each group of detail lines that constitute the main body of the report. There may also be several detail report groups in each report, useful if some detail lines are to be formatted differently than others.

5. *CONTROL FOOTING* is optional. It prints automatically following a detail report group to print totals when a control break occurs. The controls are identifiers named in the CONTROLS clause or FINAL. The FINAL control footing break occurs at the end of the report when the TERMINATE statement executes. For each report, there may be a single CONTROL FOOTING group for each control item and for FINAL.

6. *PAGE FOOTING* is optional. It prints automatically at the bottom of each page when a page break occurs. Only one PAGE FOOTING group may be specified per report, to print totals or remarks.

7. *REPORT FOOTING* is optional. It is prints automatically at the end of the report by the TERMINATE statement, perhaps to print a trailer sheet for the report. Only one REPORT FOOTING group may be specified per report. The REPORT FOOTING group does not automatically start on a new page.

The report groups are printed in the order shown in Figure 18.1. The PAGE HEADING automatically begins on a new page. The NEXT GROUP clause, described later, can specify the line spacing or a page break following each report group.

If report groups coded for different levels all have the same format, you can code just a single report group and name the levels for which it is to occur. For example, if you wanted the same report footings for a control break at the *State, County,* and *City* levels, you could code the following:

```
01  TYPE CONTROL FOOTING FOR State, County, City LINES +2.
```

18.4   RD ENTRY

Essential

You assign each report a name with the REPORT clause of the FD entry and then describe it with a RD entry in the REPORT SECTION. The RD entry specifies the lines on the page within which the report groups are printed and specifies the data items to be used for control breaks. The RD entry is followed by the description of each of the report groups in the report.

```
DATA DIVISION.
FILE SECTION.
FD  file-name BLOCK CONTAINS 0 CHARACTERS
    REPORT IS report-name.
```

Or

```
    REPORTS ARE report-name, report-name, ….
```
[You can write several reports consecutively on the same file.]
```
WORKING-STORAGE SECTION.
LINKAGE SECTION.
```

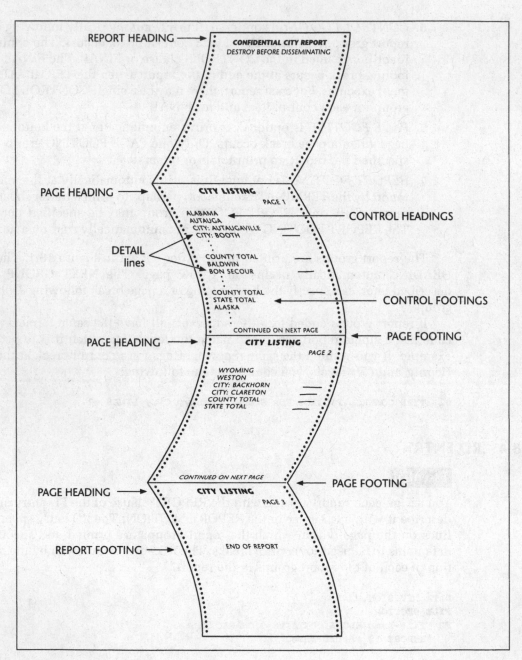

FIGURE 18.1 Report groups.

```
REPORT SECTION.
RD   report-name
     PAGE 60 LINES      or     PAGE LIMITS IS/ARE   n LINES
```
[PAGE specifies the number of lines per page, a maximum of 66 on most printers. If omitted, HEADING, FIRST DETAIL, LAST DETAIL, and FOOTING must also be omitted, and the report is printed single spaced with no page breaks.]
```
     HEADING IS 1
```
[Line number of the first item on each page. If omitted, 1 is assumed.]
```
     FIRST DETAIL 5     or     FIRST DE/BODY GROUP IS 5
```
[First line number of the report body on the page.]
```
     LAST DETAIL 40     or     LAST DE IS OR CH/OR CONTROL HEADING
```
[Last line number of the report body on the page. If omitted, FOOTING line is assumed.]
```
     FOOTING IS 50
```

Verbose forms:

```
     LAST CONTROL FOOTING IS 50     or     LAST CF IS 50
     LAST BODY GROUP IS 50
```
[Last line number of the control footing. The page footings begin on the next line. If omitted, LAST DETAIL line is assumed, unless it, too, is omitted, then the PAGE line number is assumed. Rather than a specific line number, you can code a relative line number (+n) to leave some number of lines for the control footing.]
```
     LINE LIMIT IS limit
```
[LINE LIMIT gives the maximum number of print columns in the report, not counting the carriage control character. The limit can be an integer literal or identifier. This lets the report writer warn you with a compilation message when you write a line longer than this. If you omit LINE LIMIT, Mainframe COBOL assumes a value of 256.]
```
     CONTROLS ARE clause     or     CONTROL IS clause
```
[Specifies the items used for control breaks and is described later.]
```
     OVERFLOW PROCEDURE IS clause.
```
[Tells what to do when an arithmetic error occurs while the report writer is preparing the report and is described later.]

The integer literal line numbers must be in ascending order and cannot exceed the PAGE size specified. Figure 18.2 illustrates the positioning of the report groups on the page as specified by the previous RD statement.

18.5   REPORT FORMAT

Essential

The report format is specified as a record following the RD entry. The report is composed of one or more report groups, each in turn composed of one or more lines. Lines within a report group cannot be selectively printed; either all the lines are printed or none. (The report writer cannot write lines longer than the line size of the printer.) The 01 level defines a report group with the TYPE clause. The

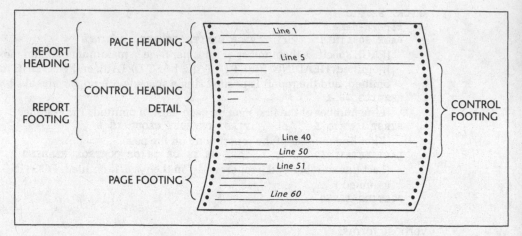

FIGURE 18.2   Line positioning of report groups.

LINE clause starts a new line, and it may be coded at the group level in which the several subordinate items are printed on the same line or at the detail level if the line consists of only a single detail item. The report may have levels from 01 to 48. Elementary items specifying data to be printed must have the COL clause indicating the starting column in which to print the data, a PIC clause specifying the format of the data, and a VALUE, SOURCE, or SUM clause to specify the source of the data. The following examples illustrate the composition of lines in a report.

```
01   TYPE clause LINE clause COL clause PIC clause VALUE clause.
       [This report group contains a single line with a single value.]
01   TYPE clause.   [This report group contains the following two lines.]
     05   LINE clause.
       [The first line of the report group contains the following two items.]
         10   COL clause              PIC clause SOURCE clause.
         10   COL clause              PIC clause VALUE clause.
     05   LINE clause COL clause   PIC clause VALUE clause.
       [The second line of the report group contains a single item.]
```

The following two detail lines are equivalent.

```
01   Dtl-Line TYPE DETAIL LINE +1.
     05   COL 10   PIC X(20) SOURCE State.
```

Or

```
01   Dtl-Line TYPE DETAIL LINE +1 COL 10 PIC X(20) SOURCE State.
```

You can assign each record a unique name. You must name the detail lines, and names are also required for subtotaling and in the USE BEFORE REPORTING directive, described later in this chapter.

```
01   group-name TYPE …
05   line-name LINE …
```

The report format is specified by the following clauses.

18.5.1   Specify the Type of Report Group: The TYPE Clause

Essential

You code the TYPE clause at the 01 level, where it is required. You can have any number of DETAIL report groups for a report, but only one of the other report groups. All of the report groups are optional. For a REPORT HEADING, and PAGE HEADING, you can code the following:

```
01   TYPE IS RH or REPORT HEADING
01   TYPE IS PH or PAGE HEADING
```

For a CONTROL HEADING, you specify an *identifier* or FINAL to trigger the control heading. Name the *identifier* or FINAL in the CONTROLS clause in the RD entry. To cause a control heading if either the *identifier* changes value or a page break occurs, code *identifier* OR PAGE. Only one control heading is produced if the *identifier* changes value when a page break occurs.

```
                         FINAL
                         identifier
                         identifier OR PAGE
   01   TYPE IS CH FOR _____
Or:
   01   TYPE IS CONTROL HEADING ON/FOR …
```

For a detail line, you must assign a name.

```
01   group-name TYPE IS DE    or    TYPE IS DETAIL.
```

For a CONTROL FOOTING, the CONTROLS clause in the RD entry must name the *identifier* or FINAL that is to trigger the control footing. You can list several identifiers to produce a control footing when any *identifier* changes value. The order in which you code them doesn't matter. To produce a control footing when any item in the CONTROLS clause changes value, code ALL instead of listing the identifiers.

```
                         ALL
                         FINAL
                         identifier, identifier, …, identifier
01   TYPE IS CF FOR _____
```

Verbose form:

```
TYPE IS CONTROL FOOTING FOR/ON …
```

For a PAGE FOOTING and REPORT FOOTING, you code the following:

```
01   TYPE IS PF or PAGE FOOTING
01   TYPE IS RF or REPORT FOOTING
```

18.5.2   Specify Starting Line on Page: The LINE Clause

Sometimes Used

The LINE clause specifies the start of the print line and where it is to print on the page.

```
                    line
                    +lines     or      PLUS lines
                    ON NEXT PAGE
LINE NUMBER IS _____
```

The *line* is a positive integer literal specifying the absolute line number. The *+lines* is a positive integer literal specifying the relative line number. NEXT PAGE creates a page break, printing any page heading. The item begins on the next page in the FIRST DETAIL line specified in the RD entry. You can code NEXT PAGE for a control heading, detail, control footing, and report footing types only, and only on the first line of the report group.

Within the report group, line numbers must be in ascending order. A relative line number cannot precede an absolute number.

```
Incorrect:        Correct:
 LINE +2           LINE 30
 LINE 30           LINE +2
 LINE NEXT PAGE    LINE NEXT PAGE
```

The line spacing is not difficult except when a new page occurs. LINE NEXT PAGE causes a page break, and the line is printed on the FIRST DETAIL *line.* An absolute line number less than the current line number also causes a page break, and the line is printed on the LINE *line* of the RD statement. A LINE *+line* will also cause a page break if the line will not fit on the page, and the line is then printed on the FIRST DETAIL *line.* If you code LINE +2 and the +2 would put the line off the page, the line prints on the FIRST DETAIL *line* of the next page, not the FIRST DETAIL *line* plus 2.

18.5.3   Specify Column in Which to Print: The COL Clause

Essential

COL specifies the starting column in which to print the elementary data item. The column number is a positive integer literal with values from 1 to the maximum print positions on the printer. Rather than specify a specific column, you can specify some number of columns to space over by coding *+columns.*

```
COL column      or      +columns
COL 64                  COL +6
```

Verbose form:

```
COLUMNS/COLS NUMBER/NUMBERS IS/ARE PLUS columns
```

You can code COL by itself on a line to shift over some number of columns without printing.

```
05  COL 10.
```
[This positions to column 10 in the line without printing anything.]

An entry with COL must have a LINE clause at the same or a higher level. If COL is omitted and either the OSVS precompiler option is on or the line has a data name, items are not printed. This enables you to total items for control footings without printing the values in detail lines. To suppress an entire detail line so that all items are totaled without a printing a line, see the GENERATE statement further on in this chapter. If the OSVS precompiler option is not on, COL +1 is assumed if you omit COL.

Rather than specifying a column position, you can code CENTER (or CENTRE), or RIGHT to justify the test. You can also code LEFT, but this is the default. For CENTER, if there is an even number of column positions, the extra character goes to the right.

```
05  COL RIGHT    VALUE "STUFF".
```
[STUFF will be right justified, based on the line length as specified by the LINE LIMIT clause.]

18.5.4   Specify the Size and Format of Printed Item: The PIC Clause

Essential

The PIC clause specifies the format of the data item. Only DISPLAY is permitted, and the PIC may contain any edit characters. Data items are moved to the print line and converted according to the PIC clause when they are printed. You can also code the JUST, SIGN, and BLANK WHEN ZERO clauses with the PIC clause.

```
PIC X(10).
PIC ZZZ9.99 BLANK WHEN ZERO.
PIC X(15) JUST.
PIC SZZZZZ9 SIGN IS LEADING "(" TRAILING ")".
```

A VALUE, SOURCE, FUNCTION, or SUM clause specifies the data to print. In Mainframe COBOL, you don't need to code PIC when you code a VALUE clause. A symbolic character is treated as a single character.

```
05   COL 10        VALUE "THE END".
```

Same as

```
05   COL 10        PIC X(7) VALUE "THE END".
```

If you are printing several values that can have different lengths, specify a variable format by enclosing the PIC values in < >. You can code just the <, and COBOL assumes the current item is variable up to the end of the PIC string or an edit character. PIC <999,999 is the same as PIC <999>,999. Code the > to end the variable part: PIC <99>9,999. Here, the *State* prints as 1 through 20 columns, depending on the length of the *State* data item. Then COBOL spaces over 2 columns and prints the *City* as 1 through 20 columns, depending on its length.

```
05   COL 10        PIC <X(20) SOURCE State.
05   COL +2        PIC <X(20) SOURCE City.
```

In addition, you can place characters to print in a PIC clause by entering them in quotes.

```
05   COL 10        PIC ZZZ9.99"% CHANGE"
                   SOURCE Temp-Amt.
```

If *Temp-Amt* contained a value of 25, this would print as 25.00% CHANGE.

18.5.5 Specify a Value to Print: The VALUE Clause

Essential

The VALUE clause assigns a literal value to the print line. You don't need to code a PIC clause for it. In the following, "ABC" prints in columns 30 through 32 and the value 10 in columns 41 through 42.

```
05   COL 30        VALUE "ABC".
05   COL 40        PIC ZZ9 VALUE 10.
```

18.5.6 Specify Data to Print: The SOURCE Clause

Essential

The SOURCE clause names an identifier to be moved to the print line and converted according to the PIC clause.

```
                  literal
                  identifier            [Can be indexed or subscripted.]
                  expression            [Like that in the COMPUTE statement.]
                  expression ROUNDED    [The expression is rounded.]
SOURCE IS _____      or    SOURCES ARE …
```

```
05   COL 20                    PIC ZZ9
                               SOURCE Population.
```

You can qualify, subscript, or index the identifier.

```
05   COL 30                    PIC X(10)
                               SOURCE State(Indx1).
05   COL 40                    PIC X(20)
                               SOURCE City IN State(10).
```

You can also code an arithmetic expression in the SOURCE. Write the expression the same as for a COMPUTE statement. ROUNDED is permitted.

```
05   COL 10                    PIC 999V99
                               SOURCE Jan-Cost / 31
                               ROUNDED.
```

The arithmetic expression can also contain the SUM clause described later. The SUM clause names a data item to sum whenever it is printed, and you can print this sum or perform arithmetic operations on it and display the result.

```
05   COL 60                    SOURCE SUM Population.
```
[This displays the sum of the *Population* field.]
```
05   COL 75                    SOURCE
                               SUM Population / No-Cities.
```
[This displays the average population of the cities, assuming *No-Cities* contains a count of the cities printed.]

If you display several items across the same line, you can specify multiple column positions and multiple SOURCE clauses.

```
05   COL 1 +2 +2              PIC X(20)
                               SOURCE State, County, City.
```
[Begins in column 1 and leaves 2 spaces after each X(20) field.]

Or

```
05   COL 1 OCCURS 3 STEP 22    SOURCE State, County, City.
```
[Begins in column 1 and spaces over 22 columns after displaying each of the three fields.]

The SOURCE clause provides the detail lines and control headings and footings with access to the data. When a control break occurs, data in the SOURCE items are as follows:

- **REPORT HEADING.** The data is the SOURCE value when the first GENERATE executes.
- **PAGE HEADING.** The data is the SOURCE value when the page break occurs.

- **CONTROL HEADING.** The data is the SOURCE value when the GENER-ATE executes. For a FINAL control heading, the data is the SOURCE value when the first GENERATE executes.
- **DETAIL.** The data is the SOURCE value when the GENERATE executes.
- **CONTROL FOOTING.** The data is the SOURCE value when the GENER-ATE executes unless the SOURCE item is named on the CONTROLS clause. Then the SOURCE value is the value from the previous detail line. This is handy because the control footing caused by a detail line prints totals related to the previous detail lines. For a FINAL control footing, the data is the SOURCE value when the TERMINATE executes.
- **PAGE FOOTING.** The data is the SOURCE value when the page break occurs.
- **REPORT FOOTING.** The data is the SOURCE value when TERMINATE executes.

The data presented to the report writer usually comes from a record read from a file, and the record often contains data that is to be printed in page headings, control headings, and control footings, in addition to the detail lines. Control foot-ings usually print the totals for the previous detail lines, and the source items should come from the previous record. For example, if the populations for states are printed and the previous detail line was for Alabama and the current detail line is for Arkansas, the control footing first prints the total for Alabama, and the source items must come from the previous record, which contained the name *Alabama*. The report writer does this automatically if the source item is listed in the CONTROLS clause.

Items listed in the CONTROLS clause retain their old values from the previ-ous detail line until after the control footings are printed. After the control foot-ings print, the new values from the current record are moved in and then the control headings and detail lines print. Data in the page heading that comes from the records should also appear in the CONTROLS clause because the page break may occur prior to printing the control footings.

18.5.7   Sum Columns and Rows: The SUM Clause

Essential

The SUM clause creates an internal counter to hold a sum and names the identi-fier or other SUM counter to be automatically summed. SUM may appear only in control footing report groups. The PIC clause specifies the size of the internal SUM counter and how it is to be edited to contain the totals. PIC may contain edit characters because the sum is kept internally as numeric data, and it is not con-verted according to the PIC clause until it prints. Code SUM as follows:

```
SUM OF item, item, …
```

The following sums the *Population*.

```
05   COL 10                      PIC ZZ,ZZ9.99 SUM Population.
```

The following sums the *Age,* but does not print it because the COL clause is omitted.

```
05                              PIC ZZ9 SUM Age.
```

SUM can name numeric data in your report by referencing the item's *data-name.*

```
05   Detail-Pop                 PIC Z(5)9 SOURCE Population.
05   Total-Pop                  PIC Z(5)9 SUM Detail-Pop.
```

Sum can also name another SUM counter by giving the *data-name* of the SUM counter. Qualify the data-name with the report name if there is more than one report.

```
05   Grand-Total-Pop            PIC Z(5)9 SUM Total-Pop.
```

SUM can also name an identifier from outside of the report. You can name an identifier or code an arithmetic expression. If SUM lists several items, each item is added to the SUM counter. SUM identifiers from outside the report can be qualified, subscripted, or indexed as necessary.

The SUM counter is added to any higher-level sums, printed unless COL is omitted, and reset to zero with each control footing break within which it appears, unless the RESET clause described later is coded. Items are added once from a detail line, even if they happen to appear more than once in the detail line. Items summed to a higher level must be assigned names.

```
05   item-name COL 120          PIC ZZ9 SOURCE Population.
```

Columns are totaled by naming the column item in the SUM clause. SUM can also total across the line to produce cross-footings by naming other SUM counters in the same line. This requires that the report items be assigned names, as illustrated in the following example.

```
01   TYPE DETAIL LINE +1.
     05   COL 10                 PIC 9(5).9 SOURCE Jan-June.
     05   COL 30                 PIC 9(5).9 SOURCE July-Dec.
01   TYPE CONTROL FOOTING FOR Yearly LINE +2.
     05   First-Half COL 10      PIC 9(5).9 SUM Jan-June.
     05   Second-Half COL 30     PIC 9(5).9 SUM July-Dec.
     05   Full-Year COL 50       PIC 9(5).9
                                 SUM First-Half, Second-Half.
```

The *First-Half* sum contains the total of the *Jan-June* column and the *Second-Half* sum contains the total of the *July-Dec* column. *Full-Year* contains the sum of *First-Half* and *Second-Half.*

SUM and SOURCE are easily confused. SOURCE prints the value of a data item. SUM sums the items it names and prints the total. It can name another a report item to sum, another SUM counter, an identifier from outside the report, or an arithmetic expression containing items from outside the report. Consider the following example.

```
01   Dtl-Line TYPE DETAIL LINE +1.
     05   S1 COL 1                    PIC S9(9) SOURCE Population.
01   TYPE CONTROL FOOTING FOR Country LINE +1.
     05   COL 1                       PIC S9(9) SOURCE Population.
```

The control footing doesn't sum the *Population*. It prints the *Population* from the next detail line. If coded as follows, it prints the sum of the *Population* for the *County.*

```
01   TYPE CONTROL FOOTING FOR Country LINE +1.
     05   COL 1                  PIC S9(9) SUM S1.
```

You could also print the sum in the control footing by coding the following:

```
01   TYPE CONTROL FOOTING FOR Country LINE +1.
     05   COL 1                      PIC S9(9) SUM Population.
```

To roll totals forward, such as for city, county, and state, the detail line would name the city value. The control footing for county would be the *data-name* for city, and the control footing for state would be the *data-name* for county. The following example illustrates this.

```
01   City-Line TYPE DETAIL LINE +1 COL 1 PIC S9(6)
                                SOURCE Population.
```
     [Prints each city's population.]
```
01   Cf1 TYPE CONTROL FOOTING FOR County
                                LINE +1 PIC S9(6)
                                SUM City-Line.
```
     [When a new county is encountered, this prints the total population for the cities within the previous county.]
```
01   Cf2 TYPE CONTROL FOOTING FOR State
                                LINE +1 PIC S(6) SUM Cf1.
```
     [When a new state is encountered, this prints the total population for the counties within the previous state.]

The control footings could also SUM *Population,* giving the same results.

```
01   Cf2  TYPE CONTROL FOOTING FOR State
                                LINE +1 PIC S9(6)
                                SUM Population.
```

The SUM *Population* is less efficient because COBOL must sum *Population* as each detail line is printed. SUM *City-Line* and *Cf1* need to sum only when the control footing is printed.

The internal precision of the SUM counter is defined by the maximum precision of the PIC clause of the item summed or the line containing the SUM clause, so that precision is not lost when items are summed. The following example illustrates this with a dollar amount whose sum is to be printed in whole dollars.

```
05  Cost                     PIC S9(5)V99.
    □  □  □
01  TYPE DETAIL-LINE +1.
    05 COL 10                 PIC -(6)9.99 SOURCE Cost.
01  TYPE CONTROL FOOTING FOR Month LINE +1.
    05 COL 10                 PIC -(6)9 SUM Cost ROUNDED.
```

Cost is printed in dollars and cents in the detail line. The sum is kept in dollars and cents and is rounded to whole dollars only when printed in the control footing.

If a SOURCE item appears in more than one detail report group, it is summed whenever any of the detail lines print. If the SOURCE item is to be summed only when one of the detail lines print, append the UPON phrase to the SUM clause to name the detail line from which to obtain the sum.

```
01  Line-A TYPE DETAIL … SOURCE Population.
01  Line-B TYPE DETAIL … SOURCE Population.
01  TYPE CONTROL FOOTING … SUM Population UPON Line-B.
```

The SUM counters are automatically reset to zero at the end of processing the group on which they are coded. To change this, perhaps for a running total, you can add the RESET phrase.

```
SUM items RESET ON identifier
```

The sum counters are not reset to zero until the *identifier,* which must be identified in a CONTROLS clause, changes value.

Another way of coding the SUM clause is as a term in an arithmetic expression in a SOURCE clause. The following prints the sum of the *Population* field divided by the *No-States* field:

```
SOURCE (SUM Population / No-States)
```

18.5.8   Line Spacing after Report Group: The NEXT GROUP Clause

Sometimes Used

NEXT GROUP specifies the starting line spacing following the last line of the report group. You can code NEXT GROUP only for report heading, detail, and control footing report groups with the TYPE clause at the 01 level.

```
                         line
                         +lines
                         NEXT PAGE      [Requires PAGE LIMIT clause be coded.]
          NEXT GROUP _____
```

Verbose form:

NEXT BODY DE OR CH GROUP IS PLUS *lines*/ON NEXT PAGE

The *line* is a positive integer literal specifying the absolute line number. The +*lines* is a positive integer literal specifying the relative line number. NEXT PAGE causes a page break.

NEXT GROUP is often used in a control footing to skip lines or to cause a page break when the next item is printed. It generally works better to do such spacing and page breaks in control footings with the NEXT GROUP rather than in control headings. The following example would cause any following items to begin on a new page.

01 TYPE CONTROL FOOTING FOR County NEXT GROUP NEXT PAGE.

The NEXT GROUP spacing is done only when the next line is printed. This prevents a needless page heading if nothing more is to be printed. NEXT GROUP NEXT PAGE causes a page break and the next line prints in the FIRST DETAIL *line*. NEXT GROUP +*line* also causes a page break if the next line would not fit on the page, and the *line* is printed in the FIRST DETAIL *line*. NEXT GROUP *line* causes a page break if *line* is less than the current line. If the next line to print contains a LINE + clause, it prints at the NEXT GROUP *line* plus 1. If the next line contains a LINE *line* clause, the line is printed on this line unless the LINE *line* is less than the NEXT GROUP *line*, in which case another page break occurs and the line is printed on the LINE *line* on the next page.

18.6 PROCEDURE DIVISION STATEMENTS

The INITIATE statement starts the report, the GENERATE statement prints the report, and the TERMINATE statement ends the report.

18.6.1 The INITIATE Statement

Essential

Execute the INITIATE statement before executing any GENERATE or TERMINATE statements. It sets the PAGE-COUNTER to 1, the LINE-COUNTER to 0, and all SUM counters to 0. Code INITIATE as follows:

```
INITIATE report-name, report-name, …
INITIATE Cities
```

18.6.2 The GENERATE Statement

Essential

The GENERATE statement prints the report. To print detail lines, name a detail line report group. The first GENERATE statement prints any report heading, followed by any page heading.

```
GENERATE detail-line
GENERATE Dtl-Line
```

To print summary reports, give a report name. You code it as follows:

```
GENERATE report-name
```

For *summary reporting,* the report writer performs the equivalent of a GENERATE detail line for each detail report group in the report, so that the summation includes all the detail lines. However, the detail lines themselves are not printed. The summation is done in the order in which the report groups are defined in the program. The control footings and control headings do print, so that the report contains summary lines with no detail lines. A GENERATE *Cities* could be executed for a city that is not to be printed, but is to be included in the totals. The following statement causes cities with a population less than 1000 not to be printed, but to be included in the totals.

```
IF Population < 1000
    THEN GENERATE Cities
    ELSE GENERATE Dtl-Line
END-IF
```

18.6.3 The TERMINATE Statement

Essential

You must execute the TERMINATE statement for the report after all GENERATE statements have been executed. It generates a FINAL control footing break, which causes a control break for all lower-level control footings, and produces any report footing. You code it as follows:

```
TERMINATE report-name
TERMINATE Cities
```

18.6.4 The USE BEFORE REPORTING Directive

Rarely Used

The need for USE BEFORE REPORTING to format lines has been greatly reduced by the new PRESENT/ABSENT WHEN and PRESENT/ABSENT AFTER clauses. You code the USE BEFORE REPORTING directive in the DECLARATIVES section to gain control just prior to printing a report group. Control is received after any summation and cross-footing is done. You code USE BEFORE REPORTING following a section name, and the section can execute any COBOL statements. When you exit from the section, the report writer continues as normal.

You can code USE BEFORE REPORTING for any report group, but there can be only one USE BEFORE REPORTING for each individual report group. The GENERATE statement prints detail report groups, which can be preceded by whatever statements are required. You code the USE BEFORE REPORTING as follows:

```
PROCEDURE DIVISION.
DECLARATIVES.
section-name SECTION.
    USE BEFORE REPORTING group-name.
    [Must immediately follow a SECTION.]
paragraph-name.
    statements.
END DECLARATIVES.
```

USE BEFORE REPORTING cannot contain INITIATE, GENERATE, or TERMINATE statements, and it cannot reference nondeclarative sections of the program. USE BEFORE REPORTING can perform computations on values before they print, perhaps to compute an average column for a row of sums.

You can execute the SUPPRESS statement to suppress the printing of a report group.

SUPPRESS PRINTING

This can suppress unnecessary totals, such as a line of zeros or a total formed from a single detail line. The report group is not printed, the LINE-COUNTER is not incremented, and the function of any NEXT GROUP is nullified. The suppression applies only to this instance of the report group; the report group will print the next time unless SUPPRESS is again executed.

Mainframe COBOL provides a PRINT-SWITCH special register for compatibility with older compilers. Moving a value of 1 to PRINT-SWITCH gives the same result as executing SUPPRESS.

```
MOVE 1 TO PRINT-SWITCH
```

Suppose that you wish to suppress the county total if there is only a single city in the county. Such a total is redundant to the detail line, and omitting such needless lines shortens the report.

```
01  No-Cities                    PIC S9(4) BINARY VALUE 0.
    □  □  □
01  County-Line TYPE CONTROL FOOTING FOR County LINE +2.
    □  □  □
```

```
PROCEDURE DIVISION.
DECLARATIVES.
A10-No-County SECTION.
    USE BEFORE REPORTING County-Line.
A20-Paragraph.
    IF No-Cities < 2
        THEN SUPPRESS
    END-IF
    MOVE 0 TO No-Cities
    .
END DECLARATIVES.
    □   □   □
    IF City NOT = HIGH-VALUES
        THEN GENERATE Dtl-Line
            ADD 1 TO No-Cities
    END-IF
```

If you have embedded programs, you can add the GLOBAL option to apply the USE BEFORE reporting to the main program and any embedded programs.

USE GLOBAL BEFORE REPORTING ...

18.6.5   LINE-COUNTER, PAGE-COUNTER, and COLUMN-COUNTER Special Registers

Sometimes Used

LINE-COUNTER, PAGE-COUNTER, and COLUMN-COUNTER are special registers automatically described in Mainframe COBOL as PIC S9(9) BINARY SYNC. LINE-COUNTER contains the line number of the last line printed or skipped. PAGE-COUNTER contains the current page number. COLUMN-COUNTER contains the current page number. The INITIATE statement sets LINE-COUNTER to 0 and PAGE-COUNTER and COLUMN-COUNTER to 1. They are automatically incremented by the report writer as lines are printed. You can move to the special registers, which you might use to change the page number. If there is more than one report, qualify the special register with the report name, such as LINE-COUNTER IN *Cities*.

18.7   PAGE HEADINGS

Essential

Page breaks cause several problems. The first GENERATE statement prints any report heading on a new page, immediately followed by the page heading on the same page. You must code the NEXT GROUP NEXT PAGE clause in the report heading to cause the first page heading to print on a new page. If the page break is caused by a LINE NEXT PAGE clause in a control heading, the report will begin with two page headings. The first GENERATE statement prints a page heading, and then prints the control heading, which will cause a second page break if it contains LINE NEXT PAGE. To solve this problem, cause the page breaks in the control footing with the NEXT GROUP NEXT PAGE clause so that the page break comes after a group of items.

The next item after a page break is printed on the NEXT DETAIL *line*. The only exception is when the preceding item contains a NEXT GROUP line clause and the current item contains a LINE + or a LINE *line* clause. A LINE + clause prints the item in the NEXT GROUP *line* plus 1. LINE *line* prints the item on this line— unless it is less than the NEXT GROUP *line,* in which case another page break occurs, and the line is printed on the LINE *line* on the next page.

Data in the page heading that comes from records should also appear in the CONTROLS clause because the page break may occur prior to printing the control footings. Neglecting this can cause the wrong information to print in a page heading. In the *Cities* report illustrated earlier in this chapter, suppose you wish to start each new state on a new page and to print the information from the *Next-City* record in the page heading. To cause such a page break, you simply code NEXT GROUP NEXT PAGE in the *County* control footing.

```
01   TYPE CONTROL FOOTING FOR County LINE +2
                             NEXT GROUP NEXT PAGE.
```

Suppose that the *Next-City* record contains the following data:

```
01   Next-City.
     05   State                 PIC X(20).
     05   County                PIC X(20).
     05   City                  PIC X(20).
     05   Population             PIC S9(9) PACKED-DECIMAL.
     05   Capital               PIC X(20).
```

You may wish to print both the *State* and the *Capital* in the page heading, as follows:

```
01   TYPE PAGE HEADING LINE 1.
     05   COL 1                 PIC X(20) SOURCE State.
     05   COL 30                PIC X(20) SOURCE Capital.
```

Now suppose that you have just printed the last city in Wisconsin and the next record is for the first city in Wyoming. This new detail line causes a control footing to print for Wisconsin, but if it will not fit on the page, a page break occurs and the page heading prints the proper value for *State* (Wisconsin) because it is in the CONTROLS clause and the new value for the record, Wyoming, has not been moved in yet. However, *Capital* is not in the CONTROLS clause, and the current value from the record, Cheyenne, prints rather than the previous value, Madison. There is no way to solve this incorrect page heading except to place all the page heading SOURCE items from the record in the CONTROLS clause. If the items do not appear within a group item in the record, describe a record in Working-Storage to contain them.

```
01  Page-Break.
    05  Page-State             PIC X(20).
    05  Page-Capital           PIC X(20).
```

The CONTROLS clause must then name *Page-Break* rather than *State*.

```
RD  Cities
    PAGE 60 LINES
    HEADING 1
    FIRST DETAIL 5
    CONTROLS ARE Page-Break, County.
```

You must change the page heading to print the new items.

```
01  TYPE PAGE HEADING LINE 1.
05  COL 1                      PIC X(20) SOURCE Page-State.
05  COL 30                     PIC X(20) SOURCE Page-Capital.
```

As each record is read, store the information in *Page-Break*.

```
READ In-File INTO Next-City
     AT END MOVE HIGH-VALUES TO City
END-READ
IF City NOT = HIGH-VALUES
   THEN MOVE State TO Page-State
        MOVE Capital TO Page-Capital
        GENERATE Dtl-Lines
END-IF
```

Because all the items in the page heading are named in the CONTROLS clause, the values from the previous record will be printed in any page break until all the control footings are printed. Then the values from the current record will be moved in so that the proper page heading will print for the control headings and detail line.

18.8 MULTIPLE REPORTS

Rarely Used

You can generate several reports concurrently on separate files. Simply define each file and report separately. The only difference is that you must qualify the special registers PAGE-COUNTER, COLUMN-COUNTER, LINE-COUNTER, and PRINT-SWITCH with the report name: PAGE-COUNTER IN *report-name*.

You can write several reports consecutively on the same file by specifying the report names in the FD entry. Then code the INITIATE, GENERATE, and TERMINATE statements for each successive report.

```
FD   file-name
     REPORTS ARE report, report, …, report.
```

You can also write a single report to two files at the same time, although you would rarely need this. To automatically write the same report to two files, code the same report name in each FD entry. Only two files can be written.

```
FD   file-name-1
     REPORT IS report-name.
FD   file-name-2
     REPORT IS report-name.
```

18.9   OTHER FEATURES

The report writer has a wide variety of other features for specialized use.

18.9.1   Print Values in Consecutive Fields

Sometimes Used

You can list consecutive literal fields with one COL clause. This is very handy for column headings.

```
05 COL 1 11 21 31 41                     VALUE "ONE" "TWO"
                                         "THREE" "FOUR" "FIVE".
```

This prints as:

```
ONE       TWO       THREE     FOUR      FIVE
```

Likewise, you can list several consecutive SOURCE items with one COL clause. The following prints the contents of *Val-One* in column 5, *Val-Two* in column 15, *Val-Three* in column 25, *Val-Four* in column 35, and *Val-Five* in column 45, all in PIC ZZ9 format. The COL clause line is given a name so that the SOURCE items it describes can be easily summed.

```
05   Total-Val COL 5 15 25 35 45 PIC ZZ9 SOURCE Val-One,
                                 Val-Two, Val-Three,
                                 Val-Four, Val-Five.
```

The following sums the five previous fields and prints the total in column 55, followed by the word TOTAL. Had the previous COL clause line not been given a name, the SUM clause would have had to list all five identifiers.

```
05   COL 55                              PIC ZZZZZ9 "TOTAL"
                                         SUM Total-Val.
```

Note that you can't mix VALUE and SOURCE items with the same COL clause.

18.9.2   Print Multiple Fixed-Length Columns: The OCCURS Clause

> **Sometimes Used**

If all the multiple fields are the same number of columns apart, you can list the starting column and add an OCCURS clause to indicate the number of columns and a STEP phrase to indicate the column width.

```
OCCURS n TIMES STEP columns
```

Verbose form:

```
OCCURS n TO m TIMES STEP/WIDTH/DEPTH columns LINES/COLUMNS/COLS
```

OCCURS cannot be coded at the 01 level.

```
05 COL 1 OCCURS 5 STEP 10      VALUE "ONE" "TWO"
                               "THREE" "FOUR" "FIVE".
```

This is the same as writing COL 1 11 21 31 41.

You can repeat a single literal value with the OCCURS clause. This is especially handy for drawing lines across the page.

```
05  COL 1 OCCURS 5 STEP 10      VALUE "  ------".
```

This prints the following line:

```
------    ------    ------    ------    ------
```

You can print multiple lines with one column stacked above another. As shown here, this is especially handy for column titles. You can code either VALUE or SOURCE clauses.

```
01  LINE 2 3.
    05  COL 1                  VALUE "  STATE   "
                               "POPULATION".
    05  COL 15                 VALUE "  COUNTY  "
                               "POPULATION".
    05  COL 25                 VALUE "|", "|".
```

This prints the following two lines:

```
  STATE      COUNTY   |
POPULATION  POPULATION |
```

You can also code OCCURS and STEP with the LINE clause.

```
01  LINE 1 OCCURS 2 STEP 1.
    05  COL 1 OCCURS 5 STEP 10    VALUE "    ------".
```

The OCCURS 2 in the LINE clause prints two lines. The STEP 1 prints them with single spacing. The line prints as follows:

```
------    ------    ------    ------    ------
------    ------    ------    ------    ------
```

18.9.3   Print a Variable Number of Columns: The VARYING Clause

Sometimes Used

If you want the lines or columns repeated a variable number of times, add the DEPENDING ON clause.

```
OCCURS min TO max DEPENDING ON identifier or expression
OCCURS max DEPENDING ON identifier or expression
```

The *min* and *max* are integer literals. If you omit *min* TO, the report writer assumes a value of 0 TO. The *min* TO *max* or 0 TO *max* establishes a range. When the item is printed, the report writer examines the value of the *identifier* or *expression* (both must be integer). A value of 0 prints no columns. If the value is not within the *min* to *max* range, it sets it to *max*, and then executes as if OCCURS *n* had been coded, where *n* is this value. An example makes this clear.

```
05  COL 1 OCCURS 1 TO 4 DEPENDING ON N-Cities STEP 10
                       VALUE "    ------".
```

If *N-Cities* contains 3 when the line is printed, this executes as if OCCURS 3 was coded. If *N-Cities* contains 0 or 5, it executes as if OCCURS 4 was coded. You can have any number of OCCURS clauses in a report, and they can be nested to any level to print values from multidimensional tables.

For tables, the VARYING clause can name an index and specify its starting value and the increment.

```
OCCURS n VARYING data-name FROM start BY increment
```

The *n* in an integer literal. The report writer automatically defines the *data-name*, so you must not define it yourself. The *start* and *increment* must be integer identifiers or expressions. The report writer sets the *data-name* to the *start* value and goes through its loop *n* times, adding the increment to the data-name each time. You can name the *data-name* in a SOURCE clause. If you omit the FROM or BY, values of 1 are assumed. In this example, the numbers 10, 20, . . . , 60 are listed as column headings.

```
05   COL 1                        PIC ZZ9 OCCURS 6
                                  VARYING Idx FROM 10 BY 10
                                  SOURCE Idx.
```

The columns print as follows:

```
10        20        30        40        50        60
```

You can code OCCURS and VARYING with either the COL or LINE clause.

18.9.4   Repeat Entire Horizontal Groups: The REPEATED Clause

Rarely Used

Suppose you wish to repeat entire groups side by side, such as the following addresses.

```
Mr. John Smith                    Mr. William Smythe
1715 Oak Street                   37 Descent Canyon Road
Via Vista, CA  90001              Mountain City, WA 82000
```

There is a REPEATED clause to do this. You define only the left-hand side and the report writer keeps the items in a buffer until the last item is received. Only then are they printed. Code the REPEATED clause as follows:

```
REPEATED n TIMES EVERY width COLS
```

Verbose form:

```
REPEATED n TIMES EVERY/WIDTH width COLUMNS
```

The *n* is the number of times to print the group across the page and the *width* is the number of columns from the start of one instance to the starting column of the next. You can omit the *n* TIMES, and the report writer calculates the number of times the group can be fit across the page. If you omit the EVERY *width* COLS, the report writer calculates how much space to leave for each group.

REPEATED is coded only at the 01 level of a body group, and the group must have a LINE clause. Here is an example to print an address group three times across the page.

```
01   Addr-Lines                   TYPE DETAIL
                                  REPEATED 3 TIMES EVERY 25 COLS.
05   Person-Name                  PIC X(20)
                                  SOURCE In-Person-Name(Idx).
05   Person-Addr1                 PIC X(20)
                                  SOURCE In-Person-Addr1(Idx).
05   Person-Addr2                 PIC X(20)
                                  SOURCE In-Person-Addr2(Idx).
```

Each time the detail group here needs to print, the report writer places the group in a buffer. When three groups have been generated, they are printed. When you have finished printing the groups (when another body group is printed or the TERMINATE statement executes) the remaining groups in the buffer are printed with blanks for the missing groups. The report writer keeps a special REPEATED-COUNTER register that is set to zero when the INITIATE statement is executed and incremented by one each time a group is placed in the buffer. When the buffer contains *n* groups, the groups are printed and REPEATED-COUNTER is reset to zero.

If you code the COL clause in the report group, the columns are assumed to be those for the left group. The report writer adds *width* to this for each successive group printed across the page.

18.9.5 Built-in Functions: The FUNCTION Clause

Sometimes Used

Rather than naming a variable with a SOURCE clause, you can code the FUNCTION clause to use one of the built-in report writer functions.

```
FUNCTION IS function-name
```

You can also write your own functions. The functions built into the report writer are as follows:

- **DATE.** This gives the current date in European format. The form of the date depends on the length of the PIC clause. PIC S9(5) yields *yyddd*. PIC S9(6) yields *ddmmyy*. PIC S9(7) yields *dd*MMM*yy*, where MMM is the first three characters of the month name. PIC S9(7) yields *ddmmccyy*, where *cc* is the century (19 or 20). PIC S9(8) yields *dd*MMM*ccyy*. PIC S9(13) yields *dd*M(9)*yy*, where the M(9) is the nine-character month name. PIC S9(15) yields *dd*M(9)*ccyy* in *ddmmyyyy* format.

- **MDATE.** This is the same as DATE, except it gives the date in U.S. format, with the month in front of the day.

- **YDATE.** This is the same as DATE, except it places the year in year/month/day order.

- **DAY.** This gives the current day of the week. PIC 9 yields an integer from 1 (Monday) to 7 (Sunday). PIC X(3) yields the first three characters of the day, such as MON. PIC X(9) yields the full name of the day.

- **MONTH.** This gives the current month. PIC X(3) yields the first three characters of the month, such as JAN. PIC X(9) yields the full month name.

- **TIME.** This gives the current time in the form *hhmmsstt*, where *tt* is hundredths of a second. If you code a PIC less than the full length, the value is truncated on the right.

- **CTIME.** This is the same as TIME except it gives a 12-hour clock followed by either AM or PM. For example, PIC 99":"99BXX might result in 04:30 PM.
- **STIME.** This is the same as TIME except the report writer uses the time when the job began execution rather than the current time.
- **STATE(*state*).** This gives the current U.S. state name as a PIC X(14) item. The *state* is either a PIC 99 item with values from 01 (Alabama) to 51 (Wyoming) or a PIC XX item with the two-character state abbreviation, such as AL or WY. (The values include one for the District of Columbia.)
- **STATEF.** This is the same as STATE except that it includes the overseas territories.
- **ZIP(*zip-code*).** This formats the zip code as a S9(9) PACKED-DECIMAL item for the United States and Canada in the form *nnnnn-nnnn*.

The report writer formats the value returned by the function according to the PIC clause. The following prints the date in the form *mm/dd/yyyy*:

```
05  COL 60                        PIC Z9/99/9999 FUNC MDATE.
```

18.9.6 Suppressing Printing Based on Data Values: The PRESENT/ABSENT WHEN Clause

Sometimes Used

The PRESENT/ABSENT WHEN clause lets you control when items print based on data values. For example, you might want to display a line only when the value of an item is greater than 100 or not display another line when the value of an item is 0. You code PRESENT/ABSENT WHEN as follows:

```
PRESENT WHEN conditional-expression
ABSENT WHEN conditional-expression
```

Obsolescent form:

```
PRESENT UNLESS        [Same as ABSENT WHEN.]
```

The *conditional-expression* is the same as that in an IF statement. PRESENT means to display the item only if the *conditional-expression* is true. ABSENT is the opposite and suppresses display of the item only if the *conditional-expression* is true.

You can write PRESENT/ABSENT WHEN at any level in any report group except the RD. If a condition at a higher level suppresses display, display of all the lower levels is suppressed and the report writer does not look at their PRESENT/ABSENT WHEN clauses. When you suppress lines and columns within a line, you may need to use relative line and relative column numbers rather than absolute numbers. When you sum items, any items suppressed by PRESENT/ABSENT WHEN don't get summed.

If the group for which you code PRESENT/ABSENT WHEN is a multiple control footing (one in which the TYPE CONTROL FOOTING clause has more than one item named), you code it as PRESENT/ABSENT WHEN CONTROL IS *item*. The item triggers the test. For example, suppose you had the following control footing:

```
01  TYPE CONTROL FOOTING FOR State, County, City LINES +2.
    □  □  □
    05  PRESENT WHEN CONTROL IS State.
        10  COL 1        PIC X(6) "State:"
        10  COL +1       PIC X(20) Source State.
```

If you have a line in which you want to display only one of several items, you could write separate entries and then control which to print by the conditional-expression. Alternatively, you can code several SOURCE, VALUE, or FUNCTION clauses in the same item and then make each subject to a PRESENT WHEN clause (ABSENT not permitted), as shown in the following example.

```
05  COL 1               PIC ZZZZZ9
                        SOURCE Avg-Income WHEN Type-Income = "A"
                        SOURCE Mean-Income WHEN Type-Income = "M"
                        SOURCE Max-Income WHEN Type-Income = "X" OR "Y"
                        SOURCE Ext-Income WHEN OTHER.
```

The WHEN OTHER acts as a catch all and determines the SOURCE if none of the other WHEN clauses displays the item.

18.9.7 Suppressing Printing Based on Items Printed: The PRESENT/ABSENT AFTER Clause

Sometimes Used

The PRESENT/ABSENT WHEN clause described earlier lets you control when items print based on data values. The PRESENT/ABSENT AFTER clause lets you control when report groups print based on events that have occurred within the report writer, such as a page or control break. For example, you can use it to print a page heading on only the first page. You code it as follows:

PRESENT BEFORE NEW *action*   or   **ABSENT AFTER NEW** *action*

PRESENT BEFORE means to display whatever group it is coded on until the *action* occurs. ABSENT AFTER is the opposite and means display it only after the action has occurred. The *action* is one of the following:

- **PAGE.** This indicates that a page break is the triggering event. You must code the PAGE option in the RD for this.

- **identifier.** This is an identifier named in a CONTROL clause in the RD that indicates that the control break for it or for a level above it is the triggering event. A control break for REPORT or FINAL will also be the triggering event.
- **PAGE OR** *identifier* (or *identifier* **OR PAGE**). This indicates that either is a triggering event.

```
01  Dtl-Line TYPE DETAIL LINE +1.
    05  COL 1 ABSENT AFTER PAGE OR Cities
                                PIC X(7) VALUE "CITIES".
    [Prints only the first time after a control or page break.]
    05  COL 9                   PIC X(20) SOURCE City.
    [Prints each time.]
```

These statements would produce the following report lines:

```
CITIES:  ABBEVILLE
         ALABASTER
         ALBERTVILLE
```

You code PRESENT/ABSENT AFTER in either a group or elementary level in a Detail, Control Heading, or Control Footing group, and you may nest clauses. (There is no need for it in a Report Heading or Report Footing because these print only once anyway.) When you code PRESENT/ABSENT AFTER *identifier* and the *identifier* determines when a control break occurs for a control heading or footing, that control level must be higher than the level in which the PRESENT/ABSENT AFTER *identifier* appears.

You can also code PRESENT/ABSENT AFTER identifier in a Page Heading or Page Footing group. You cannot code AFTER PAGE because this would put the PRESENT/ABSENT AFTER at the same level as the group it is controlling, and the report writer would have to print the group to find out if it needed to print the group.

You can also code PRESENT/ABSENT AFTER NEW, in which NEW is an optional word. For compatibility, you can code GROUP INDICATE, which is translated to mean PRESENT AFTER PAGE OR *lowest-level-control*. This means don't print the item with GROUP INDICATE coded until after the first page break and not until after the lowest-level control break occurs.

A final form lets you base the action on a group printing just after a page break has occurred and the page heading has printed.

```
PRESENT JUST AFTER NEW PAGE
```

You might use this to print the group upon which it appears only if the group comes immediately after the page heading on a page.

18.9.8 Checking for Arithmetic Errors: The OVERFLOW Clause

Rarely Used

The OVERFLOW clause of the RD entry operates for the report writer like the ON SIZE ERROR clause of the procedure division to gain control when an arithmetic error such as a zero divide occurs. It specifies the action when a report writer action results in an arithmetic error. You can code the following:

```
                                    OMITTED
                                    STANDARD
                                    REPLACE BY literal
                                    STOP literal
            OVERFLOW PROCEDURE IS  _____
        SUM OVERFLOW PROCEDURE IS  _____
```

OVERFLOW applies to items named in a SOURCE clause. SUM OVERFLOW applies to items named in a SUM clause. You can code them alone or together. The options are as follows:

- **OMITTED.** This suppresses testing for arithmetic errors.
- **STANDARD.** This is the default and the report writer checks for overflow and zero divide.
- **REPLACE BY** *literal*. This stores the literal as the result of an arithmetic operation causing an error. For example, REPLACE BY ALL "-" would store all dashes if a divide by zero occurred.
- **STOP** *literal*. This terminates the run by executing the COBOL STOP *literal* statement.

```
OVERFLOW REPLACE BY ALL "-'
SUM OVERFLOW REPLACE BY 0
```

18.9.9 Special Formatting: The STYLE Clause

Rarely Used

You code the STYLE clause on any level of item, including the FD, to specify special effects, such as highlighting, for printers and devices that support them.

```
STYLE IS style-name
```

The *style-name* can be UNDERLINE to underline, HIGHLIGHT to highlight, ALT-FONT to display the item in a contrasting type font such as italics, and GRAPHIC to display the item in a third contrasting font. The default is STYLE IS NORMAL. If you want the style to be in effect only when some condition is met, you can add the WHEN clause.

```
         STYLE IS style-name WHEN condition
    05   COL 1 STYLE IS HIGHLIGHT WHEN State = "WY"
                               PIC ZZZZZZ9
                               SOURCE is Population.
```

18.9.10 Counting Items Displayed: The COUNT Clause

Rarely Used

You can count the number of appearances of any report field or group item by coding the COUNT clause.

```
    COUNT OF data-name
```

The *data-name* can be the name of any REPORT SECTION entry except an RD. Because you are counting appearances, the *data-name* need not be a numeric item.

```
    05   COL 20              PIC ZZZ9 COUNT State.
```

To reset the count when a control item changes value, you code the following:

```
    COUNT OF data-name RESET ON identifier
```

Finally, you can code the COUNT with a SUM in an arithmetic expression.

```
    05   COL 10              PIC Z(6)9
                             SOURCE (SUM Population) /
                             (COUNT States) ROUNDED.
```

18.9.11 Last Line to Display Group on Page: The GROUP LIMIT Clause

Rarely Used

To specify the lowest permissible line position of a body group, code the GROUP LIMIT clause at the 01 level of the body group. The first line of the group must be a relative line number.

```
    01   TYPE CONTROL HEADING GROUP LIMIT IS 64 ...
```

18.9.12 Page Overflow: The MULTIPLE PAGE Clause

Rarely Used

If you want lines in a group that overflows a page to continue onto the next page, you can code the MULTIPLE PAGE clause on the 01 level for the item. This is especially handy when you are displaying elements of a table.

```
01   Personnel-Details TYPE DETAIL MULTIPLE PAGE.
     05   LINE OCCURS 0 TO 500 TIMES DEPENDING ON No-Lines.
```

You can code MULTIPLE PAGE for any report group except a page heading or footing. You cannot code it for a group that has a REPEATED clause.

18.9.13 Line Wrap: The WRAP Clause

Rarely Used

If a line does not fit on the width of a page, the report writer issues an error message. If you instead want the line to wrap around to the next line, you can code the WRAP clause as follows:

```
WRAP AFTER COL n TO COL m STEP s LINES
```

The n, m, and s can be integer literals or identifiers. AFTER COL n gives the rightmost column that any field can occupy before line wrap occurs. If you omit AFTER COL, the value of LINE LIMIT is assumed. TO COL m gives the column on the next line to begin printing in after line wrap. If you omit TO COL, column 1 is assumed. STEP s specifies how many lines to space forward for the wrapped line. If you omit STEP, a value of 1 is assumed to print on the next line.

Code the WRAP clause on an entry containing the LINE clause or on an entry having an entry below it with a LINE clause. You can code WRAP only on entries having relative column numbers. You will always get an error message if an absolute column number exceeds the width of the page.

18.9.14 The CODE Clause

Rarely Used

The CODE clause appends a nonprintable character to each print line preceding the line control character, perhaps to distinguish the report. Such a report could not be printed directly, but must be processed to remove the first character before it can be printed. You code it as follows:

```
RD   report-name
     □  □  □
     CODE IS mnemonic-name.    or    WITH CODE mnemonic-name.
```

You assign the *mnemonic-name* a character value in the SPECIAL-NAMES section. In COBOL 85, the value is two characters. For legacy systems, it is one character.

```
SPECIAL-NAMES.
    "character" IS mnemonic-name.
```

You can also write CODE *literal* to specify a nonnumeric literal. CODE *identifier* specifies an alphanumeric identifier and requires that you code either or both the BLOCK CONTAINS or RECORD CONTAINS n CHARACTERS. Because of the IBM preprocessor, you can't use CODE for it if the RD is followed by a record description entry.

EXERCISES

1. For the *Cities* report described earlier in this chapter, make the following modifications:
   - Print the total population for all states.
   - Print the cumulative population for each city with a county, each county with a state, and the cumulative populations of the states.
   - Suppress the line if any population is zero. Do this for each city, county, and state.
   - Do not print any totals if only one item is summed in the totals.
   - Do not print any city whose population is less than 10,000, but include the population in the totals.
   - Print a control heading before each group of cities in a county. Start each state on a new page.

2. Sketch out three separate reports for which it would not be appropriate to use the report writer.

3. What changes would you make to the report writer to enhance it?

4. Use the report writer to print a table containing the square roots of the integers from 1 to 1000. Print the square roots with five significant digits of accuracy to the right of the decimal point. Print 50 lines per page, with each line containing 2 columns of values as shown. Print the page heading at the top of each new page.

```
TABLE OF SQUARE ROOTS                       PAGE nnn

NUMBER  SQUARE ROOT    NUMBER    SQUARE ROOT
   1       1.00000       51         7.14143
   3       1.41421       52         7.21110
   □      □  □           □         □    □
  50       7.07107      100        10.00000
```

5. Write a program to read in a line containing an initial investment [PIC 9(7)V99], an interest rate [PIC 99V9], a number of years [PIC 99], and a starting date [*mm/dd/yyyy*]. Given this information, produce the following report using the report writer. For the date, assume 30 days per month. Allow 30 lines per page.

The interest earned is computed as the current balance times the interest divided by 100. The new balance is the current balance plus the interest earned.

```
PREPARED ESPECIALLY FOR: your name     PAGE nnn
INITIAL INVESTMENT: $n,nnn,nnn.nn     INTEREST: nn.n%     YEARS: nn
   DATE        CURRENT BALANCE     INTEREST EARNED    NEW BALANCE    YEAR
dd/mm/yyyy      $n,nnn,nnn.nn       $n,nnn,nnn.nn     $n,nnn,nnn.nn    nn
```

CHAPTER 19

PROGRAM ORGANIZATION

This chapter shows how to piece the COBOL statements together to form a complete program. Please don't skip this chapter.

19.1 STATEMENT GROUPINGS

Essential

COBOL has five groupings of statements: imperative statement groups, sentences, paragraphs, sections, and programs. An *imperative statement* group is one or more statements executed in sequence as if they were a single statement. You place them in the clauses of conditional statements, such as the IF, SEARCH, and READ statement to form a unit of code, and terminate them with the appropriate END group terminator or other key word, such as ELSE or WHEN. A conditional statement with its matching END group terminator also constitutes an imperative statement. A *sentence* consists of one or more statements that are terminated by a period. Sentences are vestigial remains in COBOL and serve no purpose today. A *paragraph* consists of all statements following a paragraph name, up to the next paragraph name. It groups statements together, enabling them to be executed by the PERFORM statement. A *section* consists of one or more paragraphs that are to be performed together. Additionally, sections allow portions of the program to be overlaid, sharing the same storage area. This is also a vestigial remains because central storage is no longer a scarce resource. Paragraphs and sections are called *procedures* in COBOL. A *program* is a collection of executable COBOL descriptors and statements.

19.1.1 Imperative Statement Groups

Essential

Imperative statement groups consist of one or more statements that are executed as a group and may be placed wherever a single imperative statement may go. You terminate the group after the last statement with an explicit or implicit scope terminator. The following example shows the use of imperative statement groups in an IF and a SEARCH statement:

```
IF A = B
   THEN MOVE 1 TO I
   COMPUTE J = K * 2
                    [Imperative statement group implicitly terminated by the following
                    ELSE.]
   ELSE MOVE 2 TO I
        MOVE ZERO TO J
                    [Imperative statement group terminated by END-IF.]
END-IF
SEARCH ALL Table-A
  AT END
     MOVE 1 TO I
     COMPUTE J = K * 2
                    [Imperative statement group implicitly terminated by WHEN.]
  WHEN Table-Element (Ix) = B
      MOVE 2 TO I
      MOVE ZERO TO J
                    [Imperative statement group terminated by END-SEARCH.]
END-SEARCH
```

19.1.2 Paragraphs

Essential

A paragraph consists of a paragraph name and all the statements that follow, up to the next procedure name. A paragraph collects statements into a unit to be executed by the PERFORM statement. A paragraph must end with a period.

```
PERFORM A10-Label-1
   □  □  □
A10-Label-1.
   MOVE A TO B
   MOVE D TO E                     [Paragraph]
   .
A20-Label-2.       [Next procedure delimits the previous paragraph.]
```

PROPOSED NEW ANSI STANDARD: Check Compiler to See if Implemented

The new ANSI standard provides the EXIT statement to exit a procedure, paragraph or section, from any point within the procedure.

```
EXIT
```

19.1.3 Sections

Sometimes Used

A section begins with a section name, followed by a paragraph name. It contains all paragraphs up to the next section name. You can use sections to define the range of the PERFORM statement, similar to paragraphs. Sections are redundant to paragraphs, except to segment programs. The following example illustrates a section:

```
A10-Part-2 SECTION.
A20-Part-2.
    MOVE A TO B
    .
A30-Part-2.
    MOVE C TO D
    .
A40-Part-2 SECTION.
```

[Section]

[The next section name delimits the previous section.]

COBOL requires paragraph names within a section to be unique, but you can use same paragraph name in different sections. You must then qualify the paragraph name: *paragraph-name* IN *section-name*. Within the section containing a duplicate paragraph name, you need not qualify the paragraph name.

TIP *To avoid confusion, never use duplicate paragraph names.*

Rarely Used

Sections can *segment* programs to divide a large program into smaller segments and reduce the central storage requirement. All computers today have very large central storage or virtual storage and there is no need for this. You can assign sections literal priority numbers from 0 to 99. Give the most frequently used sections the lower numbers. Sections having the same priority, termed a *program segment*, are grouped into a single overlay segment by the compiler. Thus, sections that frequently communicate with each other should have the same priority. Sections with priority number 0 to 50, and sections not assigned a priority, constitute a fixed portion and reside permanently in central storage during execution. Sections 51 to 99 constitute the *independent segments* and are loaded into central storage when required. You code sections as follows for segmentation:

```
segment-name SECTION priority.
A10-Task-A SECTION 55.
```

The system would not bring the code in the *A10-Task-A* section into central storage until required by it or one of the paragraphs it contains. When the section is brought into central storage, it may overlay some other idle section. This reduces the total central storage requirement of the program at some cost in extra I/O and slower execution.

TIP *Because of the extra cost and complexity, don't segment programs unless it is necessary to fit them into the computer, which is unlikely.*

19.2 MAIN PROGRAM

Essential

Most COBOL programs consist only of the main program, but you should divide larger programs into a main program and subprograms. (Subprograms are described in Chapter 20.)

19.2.1 Main Program Divisions and Their Order

The main program is divided into four divisions as follows:

1. Identification Division containing comments identifying the program, author, and date written
2. Environment Division naming the source and object computer and describes each file used by the program
3. Data Division describing all data items
4. Procedure Division containing the executable program statements

You code the four divisions as follows in the order shown here. Several descriptors serve only as comments. However, if you misspell such a COBOL word or omit the terminating period, it is an error. It is better to use a comment line denoted by an asterisk in column 7 for a comment, because the compiler does not check these statements for spelling and punctuation.

```
IDENTIFICATION DIVISION. [Required.]
PROGRAM-ID.  program-name.
        [Required to specify a one- to eight-character name for the program, first character
        alphabetic.]
AUTHOR.  comment-entry.
        [Optional and obsolete. It names the program's author. You code any comments in
        columns 12 to 72, and may continue onto several lines, still in columns 12 to 72,
        but you must terminate with a period. The comments may contain periods in addi-
        tion to the terminating period. (The comments in the following statements also
        have the same form.)]
INSTALLATION.  comment-entry.
        [Optional and obsolete. It names the installation.]
DATE-WRITTEN.  comment-entry.
        [Optional and obsolete. It gives the date the program was written.]
DATE-COMPILED.  comment-entry.
        [Optional and obsolete. It prints the compilation date.]
SECURITY. comment-entry.
        [Optional and obsolete. It describes the security level for the program.]
ENVIRONMENT DIVISION.                        [This entire division is optional.]
CONFIGURATION SECTION.                       [This entire section is optional.]
SOURCE-COMPUTER.  computer.
        [Optional. It names the computer on which the program is compiled and is treated
        as comments. Usual values are IBM-390 and IBM-PC.]
```

OBJECT-COMPUTER. *computer.*

    [Optional. It names the computer upon which the compiled program is to run and is treated as comments. You can also code a PROGRAM COLLATING SEQUENCE phrase, as described in Chapter 23.]

SPECIAL-NAMES.

    [Optional. Specifies a symbol other than the dollar sign ($) to be the currency symbol, and reverses the roles of the comma and period in numbers to enable them to be printed in the European manner. It also specifies mnemonic names used in the DISPLAY, ACCEPT, and WRITE statements. Described in Chapter 10.]

    ALPHABET *alphabet-name* **IS** …
    SYMBOLIC CHARACTERS …
    CLASS *class-name* **IS** …
    CURRENCY SIGN IS …
    DECIMAL-POINT IS …

.	[Terminate with period.]
INPUT-OUTPUT SECTION.	[This entire section is optional.]
FILE-CONTROL.	[Optional to specify the files.]
SELECT *file-name* **ASSIGN TO** *ddname*	
RESERVE *n* **AREAS**	[Optional to specify buffers.]
ORGANIZATION IS …	[Optional. SEQUENTIAL assumed.]
ACCESS IS …	[Optional. SEQUENTIAL assumed.]
LOCK MODE IS …	[Optional. OS/2 VSAM only.]
PASSWORD IS …	[Optional. OS/2 VSAM only.]
FILE STATUS IS …	[Optional to obtain file status.]
.	[Terminate each SELECT with a period.]
I-O-CONTROL.	[Optional to specify special I/O processing.]
SAME RECORD/SORT AREA FOR …	[Optional to share buffers.]
APPLY WRITE-ONLY ON …	[Optional to optimize buffers.]
.	[Terminate with period.]
DATA DIVISION.	

    [This entire division is optional, but it is difficult to conceive of a program without it.]

FILE SECTION.	[Optional to specify each file and its records.]
FD *file-name* …	[Code for each file.]
EXTERNAL	[Optional to make name available.]
GLOBAL	[Optional to make name available.]
BLOCK CONTAINS …	[Optional. Mainframe COBOL only.]
LABEL RECORDS ARE …	[Optional to specify labels.]
LINAGE IS …	[Optional to specify print page size.]
RECORDING MODE IS …	[Optional. Mainframe COBOL only.]
CODE-SET IS …	[Optional to specify ASCII or EBCDIC data.]
.	[Terminate with period.]
01 *record-name* …	[Must describe records for each file.]
WORKING-STORAGE SECTION.	

    [Optional to describe all data items and Working-Storage records.]

LOCAL-STORAGE SECTION.

    [Optional to describe local storage allocated when the subprogram is called and freed when control returns from the subprogram.]

LINKAGE SECTION.

    [Optional to describe subprogram parameters in a called subprogram.]

PROCEDURE DIVISION.

    [This entire division is optional, but it is difficult to conceive of a COBOL program without it.]

```
DECLARATIVES.
     [Optional. Provides a group of statements to receive control for error or I/O condi-
     tions.]
section-name SECTION.
    USE AFTER …
    .                                          [Period terminates section.]
paragraph-name.
    statements
    .                                          [Period terminates paragraph.]
END DECLARATIVES.
procedure-name.
    statements-in-program
    .                                          [Period terminates procedure.]
END PROGRAM program-name.
```

The END PROGRAM header is optional unless you nest programs or compile several at the same time for batch compilation, as described later in this section. However, something should mark the end of a program, so it is a good idea to code it.

> **PROPOSED NEW ANSI STANDARD: Check Compiler to See if Implemented**
>
> The new ANSI standard makes the IDENTIFICATION HEADER optional, so that a program can begin with the PROGRAM-ID paragraph.

19.2.2 Usual Statements Needed

Essential

The usual statements needed for a complete program are included here for reference. Many programmers keep a file of these lines on disk so that the fixed part of the COBOL program does not need to be rewritten each time.

```
IDENTIFICATION DIVISION.
PROGRAM-ID.  program-name.
ENVIRONMENT DIVISION.
INPUT-OUTPUT SECTION.
FILE-CONTROL.
    SELECT file-name ASSIGN TO ddname.
DATA DIVISION.
FILE SECTION.
FD file-name …
    BLOCK CONTAINS …                      [Mainframe COBOL only.]
01  record-name …
WORKING-STORAGE SECTION.
PROCEDURE DIVISION.
procedure-name.
    □   □   □
    .
END PROGRAM program-name.
```

The ANSI standard requires that the Procedure Division contain paragraphs. This means that there must be a paragraph name before the first statements in the program. IBM and PC COBOL don't have such a requirement.

19.2.3   Program Termination

Essential

The STOP RUN statement terminates execution, even if executed in a subprogram. It closes all open files.

```
PROCEDURE DIVISION.
paragraphs.
   STOP RUN.
perhaps more paragraphs.
```

19.2.4   The GOBACK Statement

Essential

IBM and PC COBOL provide a GOBACK statement (it is also in the new ANSI standard) that acts like a STOP RUN statement when executed in the main program and as an EXIT PROGRAM statement (described in Chapter 20) when executed in a subprogram. Because it can replace two statements, STOP RUN and EXIT PROGRAM, use it rather than them.

```
GOBACK
```

19.2.5   Debugging Aids

The debugging aids in COBOL are obsolete elements that are someday to be removed from the ANSI standard. However, they have survived three standard generations. This means that they can be used, but that you should not build your career on them. Their function will be provided by the new EVALUATE and IF compiler directives in the new ANSI standard, as described at the end of this chapter.

The WITH DEBUGGING MODE Clause

Essential

You can mark statements in the Procedure Division as debugging statements by coding a D in column 7. The DEBUGGING MODE clause in the SOURCE-COMPUTER paragraph determines whether to compile these statements. You code DEBUGGING MODE as follows:

```
ENVIRONMENT DIVISION.
CONFIGURATION SECTION.
SOURCE-COMPUTER.   computer WITH DEBUGGING MODE.
```

WITH DEBUGGING MODE causes all statements that have a D coded in column 7 to be compiled. You usually omit the WITH DEBUGGING MODE so that COBOL treats any statements with a D coded in column 7 as comments. If you copy in statements from a copy library with the COPY statement, place a D in column 7 of the first statement, and the system will treat all the copied statements as if they had a D in column 7.

This is a very useful feature of COBOL. Often, debugging statements are placed in a program during testing and then removed when the program goes into production. The implicit assumption in this is that once a program is debugged, bugs never reoccur. Unfortunately, the sad fate of all programs is that bugs occur during their entire life. Debugging statements should be an inherent part of any program and never removed. Coding a D in column 7 allows this.

```
D    DISPLAY "The-Value: ", The-Value
```

You can continue debugging statements such as this, but you must code the *D* in each continued line. You can place debugging lines anywhere within a program, following the OBJECT-COMPUTER paragraph.

The USE FOR DEBUGGING Declarative

Sometimes Used

You can code the USE FOR DEBUGGING in a Declaratives Section to receive control when specified actions occur in files, identifiers, and procedures. Paragraphs placed after the USE statement perform any debugging action or display debugging information. Upon exit from the section, program execution continues.

For USE FOR DEBUGGING to become active, you must do two things:

1. Cause them to be compiled by coding the DEBUGGING MODE clause on the SOURCE-COMPUTER paragraph. (This also causes any statements with a D coded in column 7 to be compiled. If the DEBUGGING MODE clause is omitted, any USE FOR DEBUGGING sections and any statements with a D coded in column 7 are treated as comments for the compilation.

2. Turn on the debugging section during execution. You do this in Mainframe COBOL by coding the DEBUG parameter for the GO step as a PARM. DEBUG is usually default, so you must code NODEBUG to turn the debugging off.

The ability to either compile or not compile the debugging sections and turn them on or off during execution is a very good feature. For efficiency during production of a mature system, you may elect not to compile the debugging statements. But early in the life of a system, you may choose to compile the statements but turn them off during production. In either case, the debugging statement can and should be a permanent part of the program.

The USE FOR DEBUGGING sections must immediately follow the DECLARATIVES paragraph header. You code them as follows:

```
PROCEDURE DIVISION.
DECLARATIVES.
section-name SECTION.
    USE FOR DEBUGGING ON event.
paragraph-name.                         [There can be several paragraphs.]
    statements
        .

section-name SECTION.
    USE FOR DEBUGGING ON event.
paragraph-name.                         [There can be several paragraphs.]
    statements                          [The statements can make no reference to
                                        nondeclarative procedures.]

END DECLARATIVES.
```

You code the USE FOR DEBUGGING statement as follows:

```
                    file-name              [Not in IBM COBOL]
                    procedure-name, procedure-name, …
                    ALL PROCEDURES
                    ALL identifier         [Not in IBM COBOL]
USE FOR DEBUGGING ON _____.
```

Code the *file-name* to invoke debugging for it after any OPEN, CLOSE, DELETE, START, or READ statements (unless the AT END or INVALID KEY phrases are invoked).

Code one or more *procedure-names* to invoke debugging just before the execution of the named *procedures*. You can't name a procedure that is in a USE FOR DEBUGGING section. That is, you can't debug your debugging.

ALL PROCEDURES invokes debugging before the execution of each procedure within the program. Don't code this if you code a *procedure-name*.

ALL *identifier* invokes debugging after the execution of any statement that references *identifier* during execution. (For WRITE, REWRITE, and GO TO DEPENDING ON, COBOL invokes it just before executing the statement. For a PERFORM VARYING or AFTER, COBOL invokes it immediately after the initialization or evaluation of the data item.)

COBOL executes the USE FOR DEBUGGING only once for a single statement (or a single verb for statement groups), regardless of the number of times a data item is referenced in a statement. This means that it would be executed once for a STRING or UNSTRING statement, regardless of the many steps within these statements. You can only code USE FOR DEBUGGING in the outer program, not in nested programs.

A special register named DEBUG-ITEM is automatically provided to define a record into which COBOL inserts information identifying the statement and procedure that caused the USE FOR DEBUGGING section to be invoked. COBOL first fills DEBUG-ITEM with SPACES and then moves the relevant information to it. You can only refer to it in a USE FOR DEBUGGING section. COBOL automatically defines it as follows:

```
01   DEBUG-ITEM.

     02   DEBUG-LINE                   PIC X(6).
```
[This will contain the statement sequence number of the statement that caused the execution of the debugging section.]
```
     02   FILLER                       PIC X VALUE SPACE.
     02   DEBUG-NAME                   PIC X(30).
```
[Contains the first 30 characters of the data item or procedure name that caused the execution of the debugging section.]
```
     02   FILLER                       PIC X VALUE SPACE.
     02   DEBUG-SUB-1                  PIC S9(4)
                                       SIGN LEADING SEPARATE.
     02   FILLER                       PIC X VALUE SPACE.
     02   DEBUG-SUB-2                  PIC S9(4)
                                       SIGN LEADING SEPARATE.
     02   FILLER                       PIC X VALUE SPACE.
     02   DEBUG-SUB-3                  PIC S9(4)
                                       SIGN LEADING SEPARATE.
```
[If the DEBUG-NAME item is subscripted, COBOL stores the subscript of each of the first three levels in DEBUG-SUB-1, DEBUG-SUB-2, and DEBUG-SUB-3. If there are more than three levels of subscripting, don't use DEBUG-ITEM.]
```
     02   FILLER                       PIC X VALUE SPACE.
     02   DEBUG-CONTENTS               PIC X (n).
```
[This contains descriptive information about the statement being executed. For example, it might contain "SORT INPUT" when a SORT/MERGE input section executes, and "FALL THROUGH" when execution falls through one procedure into another.]

You can write any statements you wish in paragraphs following the USE FOR DEBUGGING statement to display the contents of DEBUG-ITEM or other identifiers. You can PERFORM paragraphs contained in other USE FOR DEBUGGING procedures, but you cannot reference any paragraphs outside the USE FOR DEBUGGING procedures. Nor can statements outside USE FOR DEBUGGING refer to procedures within USE FOR DEBUGGING.

19.2.6 Main Program Communication with the Operating System

Each COBOL system has its own means of communicating with the operating system.

Command Line Input: PARM (Mainframe COBOL Only)

Mainframe COBOL passes parameters to the main program with the PARM parameter on the EXEC JCL statement. You code the EXEC statement as follows to pass a character string containing up to 100 characters to the main program. The qualifier GO indicates that the parameter is for the GO step.

```
//STEP1 EXEC COB2UCLG,PARM.GO='string'
```

You then code the main program as follows to receive the *string*. You can use any valid data names in place of *Parm*, *Parm-Length*, and *Parm-Value*.

```
LINKAGE SECTION.
01  Parm.
    05  Parm-Length                    PIC S9(4) BINARY SYNC.
    05  Parm-Value                     PIC X(100).
```

COBOL stores the length of *string* in *Parm-Length* and moves the *string* itself to *Parm-Value.* Code the USING parameter in the Procedure Division as follows:

```
PROCEDURE DIVISION USING Parm.
```

Mainframe COBOL also allows you to specify various run-time options to COBOL such as DEBUG through Parm. Code a slash (/) after the program parameters and then write the run-time options.

```
//STEP1 EXEC COB2UCLG,PARM.GO='string/DEBUG'
```

The PARM information is sometimes used in place of data read in from a file, but it is best to reserve it for programming aids, such as debugging flags. The following example illustrates such a use, in which the PARM can trigger a debugging trace or cause an end of file after some number of records are read in. If no PARM is coded, the program executes normally. You code the PARM as follows for load module execution:

```
//step-name EXEC PGM=program,PARM='tnnnnn'
```
    [The *t* is the debugging flag. Code Y to turn the built-in debugging on. *nnnnn* is the number of input records to read before causing an end of file on the input file. Code 99999 to read all records.]
```
//STEP1 EXEC PGM=RUN12,PARM='Y00020'
```
    [Debugging is turned on, and 20 records will be read.]
```
//STEP2 EXEC PGM=RUN12
```
    [Normal production run with no debugging.]

The program could then be coded as follows:

```
01  In-Count                          PIC S9(4) BINARY VALUE 0.
*                                      Counts the In-File records.
LINKAGE SECTION.
01  Parm.
    05  Parm-Length                    PIC S9(4) BINARY SYNC.
    05  Parm-Value.
        10  Parm-Debug                 PIC X.
*                                      "Y" turns debugging on.
        10  Parm-Cutoff                PIC 9(5).
*                                      Cutoff count
    05  FILLER                         PIC X(74).
PROCEDURE DIVISION USING Parm.
A00-Begin.
```
    [First, display any debugging information, or set the flags and cutoff count if there is no PARM.]
```
IF Parm-Length = ZERO
    THEN MOVE "N" TO Parm-Debug
```

```
            MOVE 99999 TO Parm-Cutoff
    ELSE DISPLAY "DEBUG FLAG: ", Parm-Debug
        DISPLAY "INPUT RECORD CUTOFF: ", Parm-Cutoff
                    [Then set debugging on if the flag is set.]
    END-IF
```

When the input file is read, the program checks the number of records read and forces an EOF if appropriate:

```
READ In-File INTO In-Rec
    AT END MOVE "Y" TO EOF-In
    NOT AT END
        ADD 1 TO In-Count
        IF (Parm-Cutoff < 99999) AND
           (In-Count = Parm-Cutoff)
            THEN MOVE "Y" TO EOF-In
        END-IF
END-Read
```

Within the program, you could execute various debugging statements when the debugging flag is set on:

```
IF Parm-Debug = "Y"
    THEN DISPLAY "The Value: ", The-Value
END-IF
```

This technique is an alternative to using the COBOL debugging aids, which may someday be removed from the standard.

Return Codes (Not in ANSI Standard)

Sometimes Used

Mainframe and PC COBOL allow a program within a job step to return a completion code to the operating system. You can then test this code in subsequent job steps to determine whether to execute those steps. Thus, if a file to be read by a program in a subsequent job step cannot be written, you can set the return code so that the subsequent job step is not executed.

You set the return code by moving a value to the special register RETURN-CODE, which is automatically defined as PIC S9(4) BINARY.

```
MOVE value TO RETURN-CODE
MOVE 16 TO RETURN-CODE
```

In Mainframe COBOL, the COND parameter coded on the EXEC statement tests the return code to determine whether the step should be executed:

```
//step-name EXEC program,COND.step-name=(n,comparison)
//STEP2 EXEC PAYROLL,COND.STEP1=(4,LT)
```

19.2.7   Nesting Programs

Rarely Used

COBOL allows you to nest one program within another. This feature complicates COBOL without providing any apparent advantage. It is difficult to envision why one would want to nest one program within another, because both programs must be recompiled if either requires recompilation.

TIP   *Don't nest programs.*

Nesting programs simply means that you place one program inside another, just before its END PROGRAM header. The names within the higher-level program and the nested program can be the same, and describe different things without conflict, because the names are known only within the programs. However, names described in the Configuration Section of the higher-level program, including alphabetic names, class names, condition names, mnemonic names, and symbolic characters can be referenced in the nested program.

You write nested programs as follows:

```
IDENTIFICATION DIVISION.              [This begins the higher-level program.]
PROGRAM-ID.  program-name.
ENVIRONMENT DIVISION.
DATA DIVISION.
PROCEDURE DIVISION.
[Main program statements here.]
IDENTIFICATION DIVISION.              [This begins the nested program.]
PROGRAM-ID.  nested-program-name.
ENVIRONMENT DIVISION.
DATA DIVISION.
PROCEDURE DIVISION.
[Nested program statements.]
END PROGRAM nested-program-name.      [This ends the nested program.]
END PROGRAM program-name.             [This ends the higher-level program.]
```

A higher-level program can contain several nested programs. Likewise, nested programs can have programs nested within them. You must place the nested program directly before the END PROGRAM header of the program in which it is to be nested.

Nested programs are invoked by the CALL statement described in Chapter 20. A program can only call a nested program if the called program is nested within it, or nested within another subprogram nested in it.

The position of the END PROGRAM header is important, because it can also be used to compile several programs together for batch compilation. Notice the difference here:

Nested program:
```
IDENTIFICATION DIVISION.                    [This begins the higher-level program.]
PROGRAM-ID.  program-name.
[Main program statements here.]
IDENTIFICATION DIVISION.                    [This begins the nested program.]
PROGRAM-ID. nested-program-name.
[Nested program statements here.]
END PROGRAM nested-program-name.            [This ends the nested program.]
END PROGRAM program-name.                    [This ends the higher-level program.]
```

Batch compilation of separate programs:
```
IDENTIFICATION DIVISION.                    [This begins the first program.]
PROGRAM-ID. program-name.
[Main program statements here.]
END PROGRAM program-name.                    [This ends the first program.]
IDENTIFICATION DIVISION.                    [This begins the second program.]
PROGRAM-ID. program-name.
[Nested program statements here.]
END PROGRAM program-name.                    [This ends the second program.]
```

You invoke a nested program with the CALL statement described in Chapter 20.

```
CALL "program-name"
```

To return control from a nested program, you execute the EXIT PROGRAM statement.

```
EXIT PROGRAM
```

The COMMON Clause

A nested program can be called only by a program in which it is either directly or indirectly nested. (An indirectly nested program is one nested several levels—like the branches of a tree structure.) If you want a nested program to be called by any program, even one on a different branch of the nested tree structure, code the COMMON clause in the PROGRAM-ID paragraph of the nested program. (Recursive calls are not allowed with COMMON.) You can code COMMON only for nested programs.

```
PROGRAM-ID.  program-name IS COMMON PROGRAM.
```

The INITIAL Clause

The INITIAL clause tells COBOL to initialize the program each time it is called. Data is set to its initial values, files are closed, and the program is placed in its initial state.

```
PROGRAM-ID.  program-name IS INITIAL PROGRAM.
```

You can code INITIAL with COMMON.

```
INITIAL COMMON    or      COMMON INITIAL
```

The RECURSIVE Clause

The RECURSIVE clause makes the program recursive so that a single copy of it can be invoked several times, even by itself. You can code RECURSIVE only for the outmost program, and it cannot contain nested programs. Data is allocated and initialized on the first entry to the program, and any recursive entries get the data in its last-used state.

```
PROGRAM-ID.  program-name IS RECURSIVE PROGRAM .
```

The GLOBAL Clause

You can also code the GLOBAL phrase for File Definitions (described in Chapter 20) and level 01 data items. (Any subordinate items automatically become global.) This allows them to be referenced in all subprograms directly or indirectly contained within them. (Note that you code COMMON on the PROGRAM-ID of the nested program. On File Descriptions and data items, you code GLOBAL on the higher-level program.)

If a nested program defines the same name as one declared GLOBAL in a higher-level program, COBOL uses the declaration within the nested program. All condition-names, indexes, and lower-level items within the level 01 item declared GLOBAL are also GLOBAL. IBM COBOL lets you code GLOBAL in the Linkage Section.

```
FD   file-name IS GLOBAL …
01   data-name IS GLOBAL …
```

If the data item contains a REDEFINES clause, GLOBAL must follow it and only the subject of the REDEFINES (*data-name*) is global.

```
01   new-data-name REDEFINES data-name GLOBAL …
```

19.2.8   Sharing Data and Files among Programs with the EXTERNAL Clause

Sometimes Used

There are three ways to share data and files in COBOL programs:

1. By nesting programs and using the GLOBAL phrase, as just described.
2. By coding subprograms and passing data as parameters in a CALL statement, as described in Chapter 20. (You can share data but not files this way.)
3. By coding the EXTERNAL clause for a File Description or Working-Storage data item, as described here.

Code EXTERNAL on a File Description (described in Chapter 20) or level 01 data item in Working-Storage, but not in the Linkage or File Sections. This makes the items external from the program and available to all programs and subprograms in the run. COBOL keeps storage for the EXTERNAL items separate from any program.

```
FD   file-name IS EXTERNAL …
WORKING-STORAGE SECTION.
01   data-name IS EXTERNAL …
```

Because EXTERNAL items are kept outside any program, any subprogram can use them as if they were part of that subprogram.

19.2.9   Writing the Program

There are several ways to make programs easier to update and change and to leave a record of what the program does. Chapter 4 suggested you organize programs into paragraphs and invoke them with PERFORM statements, so that the PERFORM statements serve as a table of contents to the program. The preceding section illustrated how PARM information could be used to turn debugging statements on and off. The next few paragraphs describe some other techniques, and the sample program that follows illustrates them all.

It is a good practice to build an audit trail into the program so that in a production run you can tell what processing was done in the program. This is especially important later in the program's life when someone less familiar with the program must track down an error. An audit trail is a way of identifying each transaction and tracing its flow through the system—where it came from and where it went. The audit trail should include the following:

Display any control statements or PARM information read.

Print a message when program execution begins and when it terminates. Describe the condition under which the program terminates, either normally or for some error condition. If it is a long-running program that operates in several phases, print a message at the end of each phase.

Count all records read and written for each file, and print these totals at the end of the program. You might also print all input and output transactions themselves, perhaps triggering such detail with a PARM value.

Build the debugging facilities into the program so that production programs can be tested without modification. The most serious bugs occur in production programs, and it is important to be able to quickly track down such errors. Programs are never completely debugged. After thorough testing, they reach a point at which bugs are no longer being discovered with the test data, but undiscovered bugs always remain in the program. Devise debugging aids that can be left in a production program at a minimal cost in efficiency. This also eliminates the annoying errors caused by removing debugging aids from a program in preparation for placing it in production.

The following example is a complete program that incorporates these ideas. They are not exhaustive, and you will undoubtedly devise better ones for your own programs.

```
//JR964113 JOB (24584),'JONES',CLASS=A
//STEP1 EXEC COB2UCLG,PARM.GO='00500PT'
//COB2.SYSIN DD *
 IDENTIFICATION DIVISION.
 PROGRAM-ID.  TESTPGM.
 ******************************************************************
 * This program reads in a file and selects records with an      *
 * "X" in column 80.  The selected records are written into an   *
 * output file.  The program serves no purpose but to illustrate *
 * how a simple COBOL program might be written.                  *
 * RETURN-CODE is ZERO for normal run; 4 for bad PARM field.     *
 ******************************************************************
 ENVIRONMENT DIVISION.
 CONFIGURATION SECTION.
 SOURCE-COMPUTER.  IBM-390 WITH DEBUGGING MODE.
 INPUT-OUTPUT SECTION.
 FILE-CONTROL.
      SELECT In-File ASSIGN TO DDIN.
      SELECT Out-File ASSIGN TO DDOUT.
 DATA DIVISION.
 FILE SECTION.
 FD  In-File BLOCK CONTAINS 0 RECORDS.
 01  In-File-Image                 PIC X(80).
 FD  Out-File BLOCK CONTAINS 0 RECORDS.
 01  Out-File-Image                PIC X(80).
 WORKING-STORAGE SECTION.
 77  In-File-Read                  PIC S9(4) BINARY VALUE ZERO.
 77  Out-File-Written              PIC S9(4) BINARY VALUE ZERO.
 77  In-File-EOF                   PIC X.
 01  File-Image.
 *                                 This is the line read in.
     05  FILLER                    PIC X(79).
 *                                 Columns 1 to 79 ignored.
     05  CC-80                     PIC X.
 *                                 Look for "X" in column 80.
 LINKAGE SECTION.
 ******************************************************************
 * The PARM field is set up to allow the program to be cut off   *
 * after some number of records has been read.  Code the         *
 * following on the EXEC statement to cut off early for debugging *
 * purposes, where nnnnn is the maximum number of records to     *
 * read.  Remember to code the leading zeros.  p is flag to      *
 * print input records read and output records written.  Code    *
 * "Y" to print, "N" to not print.                               *
 *                                                               *
 * // EXEC COB2UCLG,PARM.GO='nnnnnp'                              *
 *                                                               *
 * // EXEC COB2UCLG,PARM.GO='00100Y'   CUTOFF AFTER 100 RECORDS. *
```

```
*                                    PRINT RECORDS.              *
*********************************************************************
 01  Parm.
     05  Parm-Length                 PIC S9(4) BINARY SYNC.
     05  Parm-Field.
         10  Parm-Cutoff             PIC 9(5).
         10  Parm-Print              PIC X.
         10  FILLER                  PIC X(94).
 PROCEDURE DIVISION USING Parm.
 DECLARATIVES.
 Debug-It SECTION.
*        This provides a trace of the procedures invoked.
     USE FOR DEBUGGING ON ALL PROCEDURES.
 Debug-Procedures.
     DISPLAY DEBUG-LINE, DEBUG-NAME, DEBUG-CONTENTS.
 END DECLARATIVES.
 A00-Begin.
     DISPLAY "PROGRAM TEST EXECUTION BEGINS."
     PERFORM A10-Initialize
     MOVE "N" TO In-File-EOF
     PERFORM A20-Read-All-Records WITH TEST AFTER
             UNTIL In-File-EOF = "Y"
     PERFORM A40-Terminate
     GOBACK.
 A10-Initialize.
*****************************************************************
* PROCEDURE TO ADD INITIALIZE FOR RUN.                        *
* IN: All files closed.                                       *
*     PARM fields stored in LINKAGE SECTION.                  *
* OUT: Parm-Cutoff contains valid cutoff value.              *
*      In-File opened for input.                              *
*      Out-File opened for output.                            *
*****************************************************************
     IF Parm-Length NOT = 6
        THEN MOVE 99999 TO Parm-Cutoff
             MOVE "N" TO Parm-Print
        ELSE IF Parm-Cutoff NOT NUMERIC
                THEN DISPLAY "WARNING--BAD PARM RECORD COUNT: ",
                             Parm-Cutoff
                     MOVE 4 TO RETURN-CODE
                     MOVE 99999 TO Parm-Print
                ELSE DISPLAY "WILL CUTOFF AFTER ", Parm-Cutoff,
                             "RECORDS READ FOR DEBUGGING"
             END-IF
             IF Parm-Print NOT = "Y" AND Parm-Print NOT = "N"
                THEN DISPLAY
                        "WARNING--INCORRECT PARM PRINT FLAG: ",
                                Parm-Print
                     MOVE 4 TO RETURN-CODE
                     MOVE "N" TO Parm-Print
                ELSE DISPLAY "PARM PRINT FLAG: ", Parm-Print
             END-IF
     END-IF
     OPEN INPUT In-File, OUTPUT Out-File
```

```
        .
**** Exit
A20-Read-All-Records.
****************************************************************
* PROCEDURE TO READ ALL THE RECORDS IN In-File.               *
* IN: In-File opened for input.                               *
*     Out-File opened for output.                             *
*     In-File-EOF contains "N".                               *
* OUT: Records with X in column 80 written into Out-File.     *
*      Out-File-Written bumped by 1 if record written.        *
****************************************************************
     MOVE SPACE TO CC-80
     PERFORM A30-Select-A-Record WITH TEST AFTER
           UNTIL (CC-80 = "X") OR (In-File-EOF = "Y")
     IF In-File-EOF NOT = "Y"
        THEN WRITE Out-File-Image FROM File-Image
             ADD 1 TO Out-File-Written
             IF Parm-Print = "Y"
                THEN DISPLAY "Out-File: ", File-Image
             END-IF
     END-IF
        .
**** Exit
A30-Select-A-Record.
****************************************************************
* PROCEDURE TO ADD ENTRIES TO PERSON TABLE.                   *
* IN: In-File opened for input.                               *
*     In-File-EOF contains "N".                               *
* OUT: In-File-EOF set to "Y" if EOF for In-File or           *
*      Parm-Cutoff records read.                              *
*      In-File bumped by 1 to count In-File record read.      *
*      File-Image contains input record if no EOF.            *
****************************************************************
     READ In-File INTO File-Image
        AT END MOVE "Y" TO In-File-EOF
        NOT AT END
           IF (Parm-Cutoff < 99999) AND
              (In-File-Read = Parm-Cutoff)
              THEN MOVE "Y" TO In-File-EOF
                   DISPLAY "CUTOFF FOR DEBUGGING."
              ELSE ADD 1 TO In-File-Read
                   IF Parm-Print = "Y"
                      THEN DISPLAY "File-Image: ", File-Image
                   END-IF
           END-IF
     END-Read
        .
**** Exit
A40-Terminate.
****************************************************************
* PROCEDURE TO TERMINATE PROGRAM.                             *
* IN:  In-File-Read contains count of In-File records read    *
*      Out-File-Written contains count of Out-File records    *
*      written.                                               *
```

```
*        In-File and Out-File files open.              *
* OUT: End message and record counts displayed.        *
*        In-File and Out-File files closed.            *
***************************************************************
     CLOSE In-File, Out-File
     DISPLAY "NORMAL COMPLETION OF PROGRAM TESTPGM."
     DISPLAY "RECORDS READ:     ", In-File-Read
     DISPLAY "RECORDS WRITTEN: ", Out-File-Written
     .
**** Exit
 END PROGRAM TESTPGM.
//GO.DDOUT DD SYSOUT=A
//******** PLACE INPUT DATA FOLLOWING DDIN DD STATEMENT.
//GO.DDIN DD *
```

19.3   COMPILER-DIRECTING STATEMENTS

The compiler-directing statements let you copy in statements and modify them. The new ANSI standard lets you selectively compile statements.

19.3.1   The COPY Statement to Include Statements from a Library

Essential

The COPY statement is an excellent feature that copies source statements into a program from a library. COPY permits a single file description, record description, or paragraph to be used by several programs. This reduces coding and simplifies maintenance by ensuring that all programs use the same data names for files.

COPY is most useful in copying file and record descriptions. Keep all file and record descriptions used by more than one program in a copy library. (Except for source input and printed output, most files are used by more than one program.) Paragraphs are harder to share among programs, because they may use data that has a different data type or different names. There is also an inherent difficulty in publicizing and describing paragraphs so that others will know about them and know how to use them. Subprograms also let code be shared, as described in Chapter 20. They have a formal interface that makes them both easier to use and to describe how to be used. The ultimate in sharing, of course, are the object-oriented features of COBOL described in Chapter 27.

In Mainframe COBOL, the copy library is a partitioned data set, and the COPY statement specifies a member name. You must specify the LIB parameter for the compile step. You must include a JCL statement in the compile step to name the partitioned data set containing the library members.

```
//STEP1 EXEC COB2UCLG,PARM.COB2='LIB'
//COB2.ddname DD DSN=library,DISP=SHR
```

There may be several COPY statements within a program, coded as follows. Note that the period is required.

```
COPY member IN ddname.                    [Period required for COPY.]
```

All text contained in the member is copied into the program at the point at which COPY appears, replacing the COPY statement and the period following it. You can omit the IN *ddname,* and SYSLIB is assumed.

```
//STEP1 EXEC COB2UCLG,PARM.COB2='LIB'
//COB2.SYSLIB DD DSN=library,DISP=SHR
    □  □  □
    COPY member.
```

In PC COBOL, you code the COPY statement as follows:

```
COPY "file-name".
```
[The *file-name* is the actual name of the file containing the statements to copy, such as C:\COBOL\MY.LIB.]
```
COPY text-name
```
[The *text-name* is then associated with the external file name as a compiler option.]
```
COPY text-name IN library-name.
```
[The *library-name* is the name of a library containing the text.]

The text and lines in the file or member are copied into the program at the point at which COPY appears. The COPY statement is replaced in its entirety, including the period, by the copied text. The copied statements can themselves contain a COPY statement, as long as they do not name the member they themselves are in. You can place COPY wherever a word or separator may occur, but you must precede COPY with a space. You should usually place COPY on a line by itself. COBOL treats a COPY statement on a comment line as comments.

```
* COPY STATUS.                            [Treated as a comment.]
```

A COPY statement may, however, copy comments in. If a copy library named ENDCOM contained

```
******************
* End of program *
******************
    GOBACK.
```

and you coded this in your program:

```
Z90-Stop-Run.
    COPY ENDCOM.
```

the result would be as if you had coded

```
 Z90-Stop-Run.
******************
* End of program *
******************
    GOBACK.
```

The following example illustrates COPY statements in which two members, *PAYFD* and *PAY*, are copied into a program.

Member *PAYFD:*
```
FD   Pay-In BLOCK CONTAINS 0 RECORDS.
01   Pay-Rec                           PIC X(80).
```

Member *PAY:*
```
01   Pay.
     05   Pay-Name                      PIC X(25).
     05   Pay-Address                   PIC X(55).
```

The members may then be copied into a program:

```
COPY PAYFD.
COPY PAY.
```

The statements are then compiled as:

```
FD   Pay-In BLOCK CONTAINS 0 RECORDS.
01   Pay-Rec                           PIC X(80).
01   Pay.
     05   Pay-Name                      PIC X(25).
     05   Pay-Address                   PIC X(55).
```

COPY can also edit the text as it is copied into the program. The following example illustrates the need for this. Assume that a member named MFILE is contained in a COPY library as follows:

```
01   Door.
     05   Y                             PIC X.
     05   Z REDEFINES Y                 PIC 9.
```

The library member is copied into the program as follows:

```
COPY MFILE.
```

It would be compiled as:

```
01   Door.
     05   Y                             PIC X.
     05   Z REDEFINES Y                 PIC 9.
```

Suppose that *Door* should be renamed *Real-Thing.* You can do this by coding the COPY statement with the REPLACING phrase to edit the copied text.

```
COPY member REPLACING text BY new-text
                      text BY new-text
                       .    .    .
                      text BY new-text.
```

The *text* may be any COBOL word (except COPY), a literal, identifier, or pseudotext (explained later in this section). You can now edit the preceding example as it is copied:

```
COPY MFILE REPLACING Door BY Real-Thing
                     Y BY First-Thing.
```

It is compiled as:

```
01  Real-Thing.
    05  First-Thing                     PIC X.
    05  Z REDEFINES First-Thing         PIC 9.
```

You can also change any sequence of words in COBOL statements using pseudotext. *Pseudotext* consists of text enclosed by ==, the pseudotext delimiters. Here is an example.

Member *MFILE:*
```
01  Door.
    05  Y                               PIC X.
    05  Z REDEFINES Y                   PIC 9.
```

Then if you coded

```
COPY MFILE REPLACING ==Door== BY ==Real-Thing==
                     ==Y== BY ==First-Thing==.
```

the result would be:

```
01  Real-Thing.
    05  First-Thing                     PIC X.
    05  Z REDEFINES First-Thing         PIC 9.
```

The rules for coding, continuation, searching, and replacement for the REPLACING phrase are the same as for the REPLACE statement, described next.

19.3.2 The REPLACE Statement to Make Global Changes in Text

Rarely Used

The REPLACE statement allows you to specify a search-and-replace operation for your program. REPLACE does much the same thing as a global change using a text editor. The main differences are that the REPLACE statement operates after any COPY statement has been processed so that items in a Copy library are also changed. REPLACE also compares word by word, not character by character.

You can place a REPLACE statement anywhere in a program where a character string can occur, including any word, literal, and PIC string, as long as they are delimited by separators. REPLACE must be preceded by a period unless it is the first statement in the program. It must also terminate with a period. The change you specify is made from that point to the end of the item being compiled or until another REPLACE or REPLACE OFF statement is encountered. You code the REPLACE statement as follows:

```
REPLACE ==pseudotext-to-replace== BY ==new-pseudotext==.
```

The *pseudotext-to-replace* specifies the text you want to replace. You can continue the pseudotext onto another line. IBM COBOL, but not the ANSI standard, permits the pseudotext to replace to consist entirely of a comma or semicolon. The *new-pseudotext* is the replacement text. Case is ignored in the strings. Lowercase characters are the same as uppercase. The change is made only for compilation; the original source code is, of course, not changed. The resulting line after the replacement must not contain a REPLACE statement. That is, REPLACE can't be recursive.

The new pseudotext can be null:

```
REPLACE ==SOURCE-COMPUTER.  IBM-390.== BY ====.
```
[Changes all instances of the specified characters to a null, which will result in a blank line.]

You can specify several replacements with a single REPLACE statement:

```
REPLACE ==DAYS-YR== BY ==DAYS-IN-YEAR==
        ==DAYS-MO== BY ==DAYS-IN-MONTH==
        ==PIC S9(4) BINARY== BY ==PIC S9(9) BINARY==.
```

REPLACE and the pseudotext can begin in either area A (column 8) or B (column 12). The pseudotext can continue onto another line if necessary. To continue, code the text through column 72, code a hyphen in column 7 of the next line, and continue the text beginning in the B area, column 12. The two pseudotext delimiter characters (==) must appear on the same line.

In matching, COBOL begins matching at the leftmost source program text word following the REPLACE statement, and compares the words in the pseudotext with the words in the COBOL program. For matching, COBOL considers each separator comma, semicolon, or series of spaces to be a single space. If the words match, COBOL replaces the found text with the replacement pseudotext, and continues the search with the next word following the found text. If there is no match, COBOL continues the search with the next word in the source. COBOL ignores comment and blank lines for the search. If a line becomes too long during replacement, COBOL automatically continues the line.

To terminate the replacement before the end of the program, you can code another REPLACE statement or code the REPLACE OFF statement.

```
REPLACE OFF.                              [The period is required.]
```

19.3.3 The BASIS, INSERT, and DELETE Statements (Not in ANSI Standard)

Rarely Used

The BASIS statement lets you copy a complete program from a library for compilation. INSERT lets you insert lines into the copied program, and DELETE lets you delete lines. Because you can do all this and more with a text editor or a source management system, you are unlikely to need to use BASIS. In Mainframe COBOL, you code the same JCL for BASIS as you do for COPY, along with the LIB compilation option. BASIC and INSERT are not in Fujitsu COBOL.

Code the statements anywhere in columns 1 to 72. Just leave at least one space after the statement name.

- BASIS names a program in the library you want copied in.

  BASIS *program-name*
  [In Micro Focus COBOL, write the DOS file name and enclose it in quotations.]

- DELETE names the six-digit sequence numbers (with leading zeros) in columns 1 to 6 of the lines in the BASIS program to delete. You can write a single number, a series of numbers separated by a comma and space, a range of numbers separated by a hyphen, or a combination of these. The sequence numbers must be in ascending order. If a DELETE line is followed by COBOL statements, the COBOL statements replace the deleted lines.

  DELETE *sequence-numbers*
  [You can place COBOL source statements here if you wish.]

- INSERT adds source statements to the BASIS program. You name the six-digit sequence number (with leading zeros) in columns 1 to 6 of a source line in the COBOL program. The COBOL statements that follow INSERT are then inserted in the BASIS program after this line.

  INSERT *sequence-number*
  [Place COBOL source statements here.]

You must place the DELETE and INSERT statements in ascending order of the sequence numbers.

19.3.4 New ANSI Compiler Directives

PROPOSED NEW ANSI STANDARD: Check Compiler to See if Implemented

The new ANSI standard provides three compiler directives to define constants that replace names when the program is compiled and allow selective compilation of statements. You precede the compiler directives with an >>, and you can place them anywhere within a program.

The DEFINE Directive
The new ANSI standard provides a means of defining constants. You define a constant by coding the following:

```
>>DEFINE constant-name IS value
```

The value can be a literal or arithmetic expression containing literals.

```
>>DEFINE TABLE-A-SIZE IS 100
```

Now, wherever you code *TABLE-A-SIZE* in the program, the COBOL compiler substitutes the value of 100.

```
05  Table-A                            PIC S9(10)
                                       OCCURS TABLE-A-SIZE TIMES.
```
    [Compiles as if you coded OCCURS 100 TIMES.]

You can place the DEFINE directive anywhere in a program. To define a new value within a program, you add OVERRIDE.

```
>>DEFINE IS TABLE-A-SIZE 200 OVERRIDE
```

To turn the constant substitution off, you code OFF rather than a value.

```
>>DEFINE IS TABLE-A-SIZE OFF
```

The EVALUATE and IF Compiler Directives

You can selectively include or exclude COBOL statements from compilation by coding the EVALUATE and IF compiler directives. They are similar in form to their equivalent COBOL statements, except you precede them with >>. Conditional compilation is extremely useful for leaving debugging code in a program and selectively compiling it for production or testing. It can also be used to include and exclude statements appropriate to a particular platform, such as the mainframe or PC.

```
>>IF condition
[COBOL statements to compile if condition is true.]
>>ELSE                               [The ELSE is optional.]
[COBOL statements to compile if condition is not true.]
>>END-IF
```

The *condition* can be a literal, a constant name defined in a DEFINE directive, or an arithmetic expression containing these that evaluates to true or false. You can code *constant-name* IS DEFINED or NOT DEFINED to make the compilation depend on whether the constant-name is defined.

```
>>DEFINE DEBUG-ON IS "ON"
>>IF DEBUG-ON IS DEFINED          or   >>IF DEBUG-ON = "ON"
    DISPLAY "Input record: ", In-Rec
>>END-IF
```

You code the EVALUATE directive as follows:

```
>>EVALUATE arithmetic-expression
```
   [This expression is evaluated and compared with the value of the expressions in
   the WHEN phrases.]
```
>>WHEN arithmetic-expression
```
   [If the result of this expression equals that of the EVALUATE, the statements up
   to the next >>WHEN or >>END-EVALUATE are compiled. Then compilation
   resumes following the >>END-EVALUATE. This means that only the statements
   following a single WHEN phrase are compiled.]
```
[COBOL statements to compile if arithmetic-expressions are equal.]
 >>WHEN arithmetic-expression
[COBOL statements to compile if arithmetic-expression are equal.]
 □  □  □
>>WHEN OTHER
```
   [Optional. OTHER is effective in no previous WHEN phrase was selected.]
```
[COBOL statements to compile if no WHEN was selected.]
 >>END-EVALUATE
```

Like the IF, the arithmetic-expression can contain only constants or constant
names. The WHEN phrase can specify a range of values, and the WHEN is true
if the EVALUATE value lies within the range.

```
>>WHEN arithmetic-expression THRU arithmetic-expression
```

You can also code EVALUATE as follows:

```
>>EVALUATE TRUE
 >>WHEN condition
[COBOL statements to compile if condition is true.]
 >>WHEN condition
[COBOL statements to compile if condition is true.]
 □  □  □
 >>WHEN OTHER
[COBOL statements to compile if no WHEN was true.]
 >>END-EVALUATE
```

The items controlled by the directives can be any combination of COBOL
words, statements, comments, or other directives.

EXERCISES

1. Discuss the advantages and disadvantages of the required statements in
   COBOL.
2. Discuss the means and limitations of modularizing programs in COBOL.

CHAPTER 20

SUBPROGRAMS

Subprograms, called *subroutines* in other languages, are self-contained collections of statements that may be compiled separately from the main program and other subprograms. They allow code to be shared among different programs. Don't skip this chapter.

Subprograms can save compilation time because each may be compiled separately and, if changes occur, only one subprogram will need to be recompiled and not the remainder of the program. Subprograms can also break up a large program into smaller, more manageable units that are easier to modify and test. Several people can work on a program composed of separate subprograms at the same time without stumbling over one another. COBOL also has the intrinsic functions described in Chapter 21.

Subprograms, added rather late in its life, are used less in COBOL than in other languages. The packed-decimal data of COBOL are harder to pass in subprogram calls because all programs calling the subprogram must pass the data in the same precision and length. Programmers sometimes find it easier to include the statements as a paragraph than as a subprogram.

20.1 CALLING SUBPROGRAMS

The CALL statement invokes subprograms.

```
CALL subprogram
```

The *subprogram* can be an alphanumeric data item containing the subprogram name, or it can be a literal.

```
MOVE "SUB2" TO Sub-Name      Same as      CALL "SUB2"
CALL Sub-Name
```

There is one subtle distinction between the CALL using a literal and a CALL using a data item. When you use a literal in the CALL, COBOL looks for the subprogram when you link edit. When you use a data item, COBOL doesn't look for the subprogram until the program is executed.

Usually you pass a subprogram some data. The USING phrase does this by giving a list of data names as *parameters,* termed *arguments* in other languages. For example, the calling program might list three parameters:

```
CALL "TABLEPGM" USING BY REFERENCE A, B, C
```

20.2 WRITING SUBPROGRAMS

Essential

The called subprogram must describe a corresponding list of *parameters* in its Procedure Division paragraph. The parameters correspond item for item to the list of parameters in the calling program, although they may have different names. COBOL makes the parameters available to the subprogram through the parameter names.

```
PROCEDURE DIVISION USING A, B, C.
```

You write subprograms like a main program, with the addition of the Linkage Section, which describes the parameters in the CALL. The USING phrase of the Procedure Division header must also list these parameters in the order that they appear in the CALL. You write a subprogram as follows:

```
IDENTIFICATION DIVISION.
PROGRAM-ID.  subprogram-name.
```
[The *subprogram-name* is the name by which the subprogram is called. It has one to eight characters, first character alphabetic.]
```
ENVIRONMENT DIVISION.
CONFIGURATION SECTION.
INPUT-OUTPUT SECTION.                  [Code these only as needed.]
FILE-CONTROL.
DATA DIVISION.
FILE SECTION.
WORKING-STORAGE SECTION.
```
[The subprogram can describe whatever internal data it needs. The items described here in a subprogram are known only within the subprogram, and it doesn't matter if you use the same names as in other programs. COBOL assigns items initial values only once at the start of the run, not each time the subprogram is called. You can reinitialize items by executing the CANCEL statement for the

subprogram or by coding the INITIAL attribute in the PROGRAM-ID paragraph. Both are described later in this chapter.]

LINKAGE SECTION.

[The parameters passed by the calling program must be described here. Each data description must have the same data length and precision as those in the calling program. They should also have the same PIC, USAGE, SIGN, SYNC, JUST, and BLANK WHEN ZERO, but COBOL doesn't enforce this. Items declared in this section cannot be assigned initial values because they receive their values from the calling program. However, you can code the VALUE clause for level 88 condition names. COBOL associates the parameters by position and not by name. This means that the names do not need to be the same. IBM and PC COBOL allow a parameter named in the PROCEDURE DIVISION USING to have a REDEFINES clause in its description in the Linkage Section. The ANSI standard does not.]

PROCEDURE DIVISION USING *a1, a2, …, an.*

[You must list a parameter here for each parameter in the CALL. Then describe the parameter in the Linkage Section as a level 01 or 77 item. COBOL begins execution at the first executable statement in the subprogram.]

[Place subprogram Procedure Division statements here.]

END PROGRAM *subprogram-name.*

[END PROGRAM is optional, but you should code it.]

Subprograms may contain the same statements as a main program. A GO-BACK statement in the subprogram returns control to the calling program at the next executable statement following the CALL statement. Names described within a subprogram are known only within that subprogram, and you can use these names in the main program or other subprograms for other purposes.

Here is how a calling program might be written:

```
IDENTIFICATION DIVISION.
PROGRAM-ID. TESTPGM.
DATA DIVISION.
WORKING-STORAGE SECTION.
01  A.
    05  Dd                      OCCURS 5 TIMES INDEXED BY Idd
                                PIC X(20).
01  B                           PIC S9(4) BINARY.
01  C                           PIC X(20).
PROCEDURE DIVISION.
A00-Begin.
    MOVE 3 TO B
    MOVE SPACES TO C
    CALL "TABLEPGM" USING A, B, C
    [The structure A and two elementary data items, B and C, are passed to subpro-
    gram TABLEPGM.]
    GOBACK.
END PROGRAM TESTPGM.
```

The called subprogram might be coded as follows:

```
IDENTIFICATION DIVISION.
PROGRAM-ID. TABLEPGM.
DATA DIVISION.
WORKING-STORAGE SECTION.
LINKAGE SECTION.
```
[Because the parameters are associated by position and not by name, the names do not need to be the same. Thus, *A* in the calling program becomes *X* in the called subprogram, *B* becomes *Y,* and *C* becomes *Z.*]

```
01   X.
     05   Xx                        PIC X(20) OCCURS 5 TIMES
                                    INDEXED BY Ixx.
```
[Upon entry, the contents of *Xx* are undefined, because the calling program didn't assign them values.]

```
01   Y                             PIC S9(4) BINARY.
```
[Upon entry, *Y* contains 3.]

```
01   Z                             PIC X(20).
```
[Upon entry, *Z* contains SPACES.]

```
PROCEDURE DIVISION USING X, Y, Z.
```
[The PROCEDURE DIVISION header must contain the USING phrase and list the parameters being passed by the calling program.]

```
A00-Begin.
     PERFORM VARYING IXX FROM 1 BY 1 UNTIL Ixx > Y
        MOVE Z TO Xx(Ixx)
     END-PERFORM
     MOVE ZERO TO Y
     GOBACK.
```
[You can execute GOBACK anywhere in the subprogram. GOBACK returns control to the statement following the CALL in the calling program. Upon return, *Xx*(1) through *Xx*(3) will contain SPACES, and *B* will contain 0.]

```
END PROGRAM TABLEPGM.
```

You can share data by passing it as a parameter in the subprogram call. File names cannot be shared by passing them as parameters to a subprogram. IBM COBOL allows QSAM files (a blocked sequential file) to be passed. However, a COBOL subprogram can't process them; only a program written in another language can. You can share files by coding EXTERNAL on the FD, as described in Chapter 19.

Because subprograms are separate from the main program, it takes more effort to combine them with other subprograms for execution and to document them. Sometimes it is not apparent that a functional unit of code is a candidate for being shared with other programs as a subprogram until after the program is written. Then lifting out the code and making it into a subprogram requires maintenance. Subprograms require careful planning to be successful, both in defining the data that is to be shared and in determining the functional units of code that are candidates for being shared. Any data passed as parameters in a calling program must match the parameter data descriptions in the called subprogram. For example, if a subprogram expects a parameter of precision PIC S9(9)V99, but the calling program carries the value with precision S9(5)V99, you must move the item to another item of precision S9(9)V99 in the calling program before it can be used as a parameter in the subprogram call.

20.3 THE CALL STATEMENT

Essential

The general form of the CALL statement is as follows:

```
                              VALUE
                              CONTENT
                              REFERENCE
        CALL subprogram USING BY _____ a1, a2, …, an
```

The *subprogram* is a literal or alphanumeric data item containing the subprogram. In Mainframe COBOL, it is one to eight alphanumeric characters, first character alphabetic. If longer than eight characters, only the leftmost eight are used.

The *a1, a2, . . . an* are subprogram parameters. They can be any level of data item in the File Section, Working-Storage Section, or Linkage Section. You can also code the ADDRESS OF special register described in Chapter 25 as a parameter.

20.3.1 CALL BY REFERENCE

BY REFERENCE, the default, passes the address of the data item. This allows the subprogram to change the data item's value in the main program. You cannot pass literals when BY REFERENCE is used.

```
        CALL subprogram USING a1, a2, …, an
```

Same as

```
        CALL subprogram USING BY REFERENCE a1, a2, …, an
        CALL "SUBMAX" USING BY REFERENCE X, Y, Z
```

20.3.2 CALL BY CONTENT

BY CONTENT passes only the contents of the parameter. This means that while you can change the value of the parameter within the subprogram, the changed value is not passed back to the calling program. BY CONTENT causes COBOL to move the parameters to temporary storage, so passing large tables with BY CONTENT is less efficient than with BY REFERENCE. In IBM and PC COBOL, you can use nonnumeric literals as parameters when BY CONTENT is coded. The

LENGTH OF special register implicitly defined as PIC 9(9) BINARY can also be used as a BY CONTENT parameter. You cannot pass a function reference in a CALL.

```
CALL subprogram USING BY CONTENT a1, a2, …, an
```

PROPOSED NEW ANSI STANDARD: Check Compiler to See if Implemented

The new ANSI standard permits the arguments of a call to be literals or arithmetic expressions.

20.3.3 CALL BY VALUE

BY VALUE is similar to BY CONTENT, except it uses linkage that allows calls to non-COBOL languages, such as C/C++. The arguments can be binary, floating-point, pointer, or a single-byte alphanumeric character.

```
CALL subprogram USING BY VALUE a1, a2, …, an
```

20.3.4 Passing Parameters

You can code BY CONTENT, BY REFERENCE, and BY VALUE in front of any specific parameters to which they apply:

```
CALL "SUBMAX" USING BY REFERENCE X, BY CONTENT Y, Z
```
[*X* is passed by reference and *Y* and *Z* by content.]

The subprogram called can itself call other subprograms. However, COBOL programs are normally not recursive. That is, a called subprogram cannot directly or indirectly call itself or the program that called it.

When you pass numeric parameters, COBOL does not convert them if their types don't match. This means that the item in the calling subprogram must match the length, precision, and data type of the item in the called subprogram.

When you pass data BY CONTENT or BY VALUE, the item in the calling subprogram must match the length of the item in the called subprogram. The data type should also match, but it doesn't need to as long as you know what you are doing. That is, you can call a subprogram with an alphabetic item and receive the item as alphanumeric. If you pass the argument BY REFERENCE, the length doesn't need to match as long as you have some means of determining the length. (You could terminate a string with a special character or pass the length as a parameter.) BY CONTENT and BY VALUE move the item to temporary storage, so COBOL must know the length. BY REFERENCE passes the address of the item, which doesn't require COBOL to know its length.

20.3.5 Optional Arguments

> **PROPOSED NEW ANSI STANDARD: Check Compiler to See if Implemented**
>
> The new ANSI standard allows BY REFERENCE arguments to be optional. For example, suppose that a call has an argument that may not be needed, depending on the context. You code OMITTED for the missing argument.
>
> ```
> CALL "A-PGM" USING BY REFERENCE A, B, C
> ```
>
> Or
>
> ```
> CALL "A-PGM" USING BY REFERENCE A, OMITTED, C
> ```
>
> The Procedure Division header must denote any optional arguments with the OPTIONAL clause.
>
> ```
> PROCEDURE DIVISION USING BY REFERENCE X, OPTIONAL Y, Z
> ```

20.3.6 The RETURNING Phrase

The RETURNING phrase is coded on both the USING of the Procedure Division header and the CALL statement to specify that a single data item is to be returned with a value. This gives COBOL the potential ability to code functions, such as the intrinsic functions described in Chapter 21. The current COBOL has no means of invoking user-written functions in expressions, as can be done for the intrinsic functions. (The new ANSI standard does, as described in Chapter 21.) The RETURNING phrase is thus of little value in COBOL programs because you can always return values from a subprogram by using BY REFERENCE arguments. It is mainly used for calls to C/C++, or any language using the C/C++ linkage conventions.

```
CALL "Sub-PBM" USING A, B, C BY REFERENCE RETURNING Size
```

Here, *Size* must be defined in the data division of the calling program. Then in the called subprogram, you must code the RETURNING clause again.

```
PROCEDURE DIVISION USING A, B, C RETURNING D.
```

The *D* here must be defined in the Linkage Section as a level 01 or 77 item and have the same PIC, USAGE, SIGN, SYNC, JUST, and BLANK WHEN ZERO as *Size* in the calling program. Within the subprogram, you can store a value in *D*, and when you execute the GOBACK statement, control returns to the statement following the call, and *Size* in the calling program will contain the value you stored in *D* within the subprogram.

Only a single identifier can be named in the RETURNING phrase. Although the RETURNING phrase gives COBOL the ability to write functions, you must invoke them with a subprogram CALL rather than a function reference, which is inconvenient and prevents the function from being coded in an expression, which is the purpose of a function.

20.4 DYNAMIC SUBPROGRAM LOADING

Rarely Used

Subprograms can also be loaded into storage dynamically when they are first called. (In Mainframe COBOL, the DYNAM compiler option, described in Chapter 33, specifies dynamic loading.) The ON EXCEPTION phrase specifies imperative statements to execute if the subprogram can't be found or if there is insufficient storage for it. You rarely need to do this in Mainframe COBOL, because it is better just to let the program terminate and increase the region size.

```
CALL subprogram USING parameters
    ON EXCEPTION imperative-statements    or    ON OVERFLOW ...
    NOT ON EXCEPTION imperative-statements
END-CALL
```

20.5 THE CANCEL STATEMENT TO REINITIALIZE SUBPROGRAMS

Rarely Used

When a subprogram is loaded into memory, COBOL sets it to its initial state. That is, all the VALUE clauses of the Data Division are set, all the files it describes are closed, and all the PERFORM statements are set to begin with their initial values. Normally, COBOL does not reset subprograms to their initial state each time they are called. You can reset them to their initial state by coding the INITIAL clause in the PROGRAM-ID for the subprogram, as described in Chapter 19. Alternatively, you can execute a CANCEL statement in the calling program to reset a called subprogram to its initial state the next time it is called and close any files left open in the subprogram. Storage occupied by dynamically loaded subprograms is also made available. CANCEL is ignored if the subprogram has not been called. If the subprogram has been called, GOBACK must have been the last statement executed in the subprogram.

A subprogram can also execute a CANCEL, but not for itself or a higher-level calling program. CANCEL is coded as follows:

```
CANCEL subprogram, subprogram, ..., subprogram
```

As with CALL, the *subprogram* can be an alphanumeric data item or a literal.

```
CANCEL "SUBMAX"
```

20.6 THE EXIT PROGRAM AND GOBACK STATEMENTS TO RETURN FROM SUBPROGRAMS

Essential

Both the EXIT PROGRAM and GOBACK statements return control from a subprogram. On return from the subprogram, COBOL leaves intact all data items within the subprogram, and they retain their values if the subprogram is called again (unless you execute a CANCEL statement or code the INITIAL attribute in the PROGRAM-ID paragraph).

```
EXIT PROGRAM          or     GOBACK
```

In a subprogram, GOBACK operates the same as EXIT PROGRAM, and in a main program, it operates the same as STOP RUN. Because GOBACK is more general than EXIT PROGRAM or STOP RUN, use it rather than them. In a subprogram, STOP RUN terminates execution rather than returning to the calling program.

20.7 MULTIPLE ENTRY POINTS (NOT IN ANSI STANDARD)

Rarely Used

IBM and PC COBOL subprograms can have multiple entry points specified by the ENTRY statement within the subprogram. The ENTRY statement can also list parameters different from those in the PROCEDURE DIVISION USING phrase in number, order, and data type. You code the ENTRY statement as follows:

```
ENTRY "entry-name"
ENTRY "entry-name" USING a1, a2, …, an
```

The *entry-name* is the name of the entry point; one to eight alphanumeric characters, first character alphabetic. A CALL statement can then name this entry point. The CALL has the same format as a call to a subprogram: CALL *"entry-name"* USING *parameters*. The *a1, a2, . . . an* are subprogram parameters. They must correspond in number and order to the parameters of the CALL and be defined in the Linkage Section. Execution begins with the first executable statement following ENTRY. You can code BY REFERENCE or BY VALUE to specify how the parameters are passed.

20.8 PROCEDURE-POINTER TO CALL SUBPROGRAMS BY ADDRESS

Rarely Used

IBM and Micro Focus COBOL let you store the address of a subprogram or entry point in an identifier and use this identifier in the call statement. You must describe the identifier as USAGE PROCEDURE-POINTER. (The new ANSI standard defines it as USAGE PROGRAM-POINTER.)

```
01   Sub-Name                          PROCEDURE-POINTER.
```

Then you store the address of a subprogram or entry point in the identifier using the SET statement.

```
SET Sub-Name TO ENTRY "TABLEPGM"
```

Now you can code the call and use *Sub-Name* in place of the subprogram name.

```
CALL Sub-Name USING A, B, C
```

Same as:

```
CALL "TABLEPGM" USING A, B, C
```

The SET statement can also store an alphanumeric item containing the subprogram name, NULLS, or another PROCEDURE-POINTER data item.

```
01   Store-Name                        PIC X(10) VALUE "TABLEPGM".
01   Another-Ptr                       PROCEDURE-POINTER.
     □ □ □
     SET Sub-Name TO Store-Name
     SET Another-Ptr TO Sub-Name
     SET Sub-Name TO NULLS
```

If you cancel the subprogram with a CANCEL statement, the address of that subprogram stored in a PROCEDURE-POINTER identifier becomes invalid. The following example shows how COBOL can call a function written in C. The function returns the address of another function, which the subprogram then calls.

```
IDENTIFICATION DIVISION.
PROGRAM-ID  CALL-C.
DATA DIVISION.
WORKING-STORAGE SECTION.
01   Function-Val                      POINTER.
01   Function-Name                     PROCEDURE-POINTER.
PROCEDURE DIVISION.
A00-Begin.
     CALL "c-function" RETURNING Function-Val
     SET Function-Name TO Function-Val
     CALL Function-Name
```

20.9 THE LOCAL-STORAGE SECTION

Rarely Used

In IBM, Micro Focus COBOL, and the new ANSI standard, you can define local automatic storage for a subprogram that is allocated when the subprogram is invoked and freed on return. Place the Local-Storage section between the Working-Storage and any Linkage section. You can give data items initial values.

```
WORKING-STORAGE SECTION.
LOCAL-STORAGE SECTION.
01  A                          PIC S9(9) BINARY VALUE 25.
LINKAGE SECTION.
```

COBOL would allocate storage for A and initialize its VALUE when the subprogram is called. The storage for A is released when control is returned from the subprogram, and any value in it is lost. You can't code EXTERNAL on local storage data items.

20.10 COMPILATION OF SUBPROGRAMS

Essential

You can compile subprograms separately from the main program and other subprograms so that a change in a single subprogram does not require recompilation of the entire program. An END PROGRAM statement must follow each program or subprogram. The following is for Mainframe COBOL.

```
// EXEC COB2UCLG
//COB2.SYSIN DD *
[Main program]
 END PROGRAM program-name.          [Begins in column 8.]
[Subprogram]
 END PROGRAM subprogram-name.
```

EXERCISES

1. Write a subprogram to compute the future value of an amount invested at a given interest rate for a given number of years. The formula for this is:

Future amount = Investment $(1 + i)^n$

The i is the interest rate [PIC SV9(5)] and n is the years [PIC S9(3)]. Define the amounts as PIC S9(11)V99. Verify that the subprogram works properly by checking some results against a table of compound interest.

2. Write a subprogram that is to be called with a parameter consisting of a one-dimensional PACKED-DECIMAL table with a varying size controlled by an OCCURS DEPENDING ON clause. The subprogram is to find the minimum, maximum, and average of the elements in the table. The table is to have a maximum size of 500, and the elements are to have precision PIC S9(5)V99.

3. Write a subprogram to change a date stored in the form *yyyy/mm/dd* to the form *dd/mm/yyyy* or *mm/dd/yyyy*, depending on a flag supplied as a parameter in the call.

4. Write a single subprogram to convert distances into meters. The subprogram is to convert units of inches, feet, yards, and miles. (1 inch = 0.0254 meters, 1 mile = 1609.35 meters.) Assume PACKED-DECIMAL numbers and choose a suitable precision. Use a parameter as a flag to specify the conversion. Test the subprogram and verify that it works properly.

5. List at least 10 candidates to be made into general-purpose built-in subprograms or functions for COBOL. Select functions for business data processing problems similar to the built-in functions provided in FORTRAN, C/C++, or PL/I.

CHAPTER 21

FUNCTIONS

Functions are the most underutilized feature of COBOL. They were not a part of COBOL until recently and haven't made their way into the mainstream COBOL culture. Don't skip this chapter.

Essential

Functions were added late in COBOL's life in 1989. Consequently, they are not found in most legacy systems. They are extremely handy and should be used wherever possible.

21.1 HOW FUNCTIONS ARE USED

Essential

Functions are written in the form:

```
FUNCTION function-name(arguments)
```

For example, the function named FACTORIAL computes the factorial of an integer.

```
COMPUTE T-Val = FUNCTION FACTORIAL(6)
```

The function computes the factorial of 6 and returns the value, 720, which is then stored in *T-Val.* The following rules apply to intrinsic functions:

- The type of result (alphanumeric, numeric, or integer) and often the length depend on the function's arguments.
- The arguments can be identifiers, literals, or, for numeric functions, arithmetic expressions.

```
COMPUTE Min-S = FUNCTION MIN(0, Low-S, High-S / 10)
```

This means that one function can be the argument of another.

```
COMPUTE The-Days = FUNCTION DATE-OF-INTEGER(FUNCTION
       INTEGER-OF-DAY(Julian-Date
```

- Numeric functions can be coded wherever you can code an arithmetic expression. This means that you can code:

```
COMPUTE A = FUNCTION NUMVAL-C("$1,234.56 CR")
```

However, because you cannot code an arithmetic expression in a MOVE statement, the following is in error.

```
MOVE FUNCTION NUMVAL-C("$1,234.56 CR") TO A        <=== Error
```

- You can code an alphanumeric function wherever an identifier of that data type is permitted, except that the function cannot be a receiving field. The same is true for numeric functions, except that they can also be used wherever an arithmetic expression can be used.

```
COMPUTE T-Val = FUNCTION RANDOM *
                  Stat-Pop(FUNCTION MIN(1, Some-Num))
```

The following is in error because the function is a receiving field.

```
COMPUTE FUNCTION FACTORIAL(6) = T-Val
```

- The arguments must be of the proper data type for the function. When a series of arguments are listed, they must all have the same data type: numeric or alphanumeric. ANSI COBOL doesn't allow you to mix alphanumeric and alphabetic. IBM and PC COBOL do.

- Several of the numeric functions allow you to list multiple items as arguments. For these, you can also process all the elements of a table by naming the table and coding ALL rather than a subscript. For example,

```
COMPUTE T-Val = FUNCTION MAX(Stat-Pop(ALL))
```

would examine all the elements of the *Stat-Pop* table and return the maximum value.

- The function has a data type that determines the value returned. For example, the data type of FACTORIAL is integer numeric.

- You can reference-modify character data when coded as an argument.

- A function can be an argument of a function, and the functions can be recursive. Functions are evaluated from left to right, taking into account any parentheses. For example,

```
COMPUTE T-Val = FUNCTION FACTORIAL (FUNCTION FACTORIAL(3))
```

first computes the factorial of 3, which is 6. Then it calculates the factorial of 6, which is 720, and this value is stored in *T-Val*.

21.2 INTRINSIC FUNCTIONS

Essential

The intrinsic functions are built-in. They provide date and time, character, numeric, scientific, financial, statistical, and programming operations.

21.2.1 Date and Time Functions

The date functions use the Gregorian calendar for conversion to other forms. Monday, January 1, 1601 is day 1 of this calendar. The integer Gregorian date is the number of days, beginning on January 1, 1601, or the number of days following December 31, 1660. Thus, the integer Gregorian date 144,270 is December 31, 1995.

CURRENT-DATE	Get current date.
Argument	None.
Returns	PIC X(21) as *yyyymmddhhmmsstt±hhmm*.
	yyyy = Year
	mm = month (01 to 12)
	dd = day of month (01 to 31)
	hh = hour (01 to 23)
	mm = minutes (00 to 59)
	ss = seconds (00 to 59)
	tt = hundredths of seconds (00 to 99)
	±*hhmm* = hours and minutes ahead (–) or behind (–) Greenwich Mean Time (00000 if system does not have the facility)
	FUNCTION CURRENT-DATE might return "20021022083217 1200000".
WHEN-COMPILED	Same as CURRENT-DATE, but returns the date the program was compiled.
	FUNCTION WHEN-COMPILED might return "20011022083217 1200000".
DATE-OF-INTEGER	Get calendar date from integer Gregorian date.
Argument	DATE-OF-INTEGER(*integer-Gregorian-date*).
Returns	Eight-digit integer containing digits: *yyyymmdd*.
	FUNCTION DATE-OF-INTEGER(144270) returns 19951231.
DAY-OF-INTEGER	Get year and day of year from integer Gregorian date.
Argument	DAY-OF-INTEGER(*integer-Gregorian-date*).
Returns	Seven-digit integer containing digits: *yyyyddd*, where *ddd* is the day of year (1 to 366).
	FUNCTION DAY-OF-INTEGER(144270) returns 1995365.

INTEGER-OF-DATE	Get integer Gregorian date from date.
Argument	INTEGER-OF-DATE(*date*) where *date* contains numeric digits in the form *yyyymmdd*.
Returns	Seven-digit integer Gregorian date.
	FUNCTION INTEGER-OF-DATE(19951231) returns 144,270.

INTEGER-OF-DAY	Get integer Gregorian date from Julian date.
Argument	INTEGER-OF-DAY(*date*) where *date* contains numeric digits in the form *yyyymmdd*.
Returns	Seven-Digit integer Gregorian Date.
	FUNCTION INTEGER-OF-DAY(1995365) returns 144,270.

Proposed New ANSI Standard: Check Compiler to See if Implemented

DATE-TO-YYYYMMDD	Convert the date from *yymmdd* to *yyyymmdd* form.
Argument	DATE-TO-YYYYMMDD(*date, n*) where *date* is a 6-digit integer of the form *yymmdd* and *n* is an integer that when added to the year of the current date at the time of execution defines the ending year of a 100-year interval or sliding window into which the year of *date* falls. If the current year is 2002, an *n* of 10 defines a window from 1911 through 2012. Two-digit years of 11 through 99 would be 1900 and 00 through 12 would be 2000. An *n* of −10 defines a window of 1891 through 1992. Two-digit years of 91 through 99 would be 1800 and 00 through 92 would be 1900.
Returns	Eight-digit integer of the form *yyyymmdd*.
	FUNCTION DATE-TO-YYYYMMDD(851003, 10) returns 19851003.
	FUNCTION DATE-TO-YYYYMMDD(981002, −10) returns 18981002.
DAY-TO-YYYYDDD	Same as DATE-TO-YYYMMDD, except it converts Julian dates of the form *yyddd* to *yyyyddd*.
LOCALE-DATE	Return a character string containing the date in a format appropriate for a locale.

Argument	LOCALE-DATE(*date,locale*) where *date* is an eight-character alphanumeric or national string of the form *yyyymmdd*. The *locale* is a mnemonic name associated with a locale in the SPECIAL-NAMES paragraph.
Returns	The date as a character string formatted appropriately for the locale.
LOCALE-TIME	Return a character string containing the time in a format appropriate for a locale.
Argument	LOCALE-TIME(*time,locale*) where *time* is an 11-character alphanumeric or national string of the form *hhmmsstt±hh*. (This is the time format returned by the CURRENT-DATE function.) The *locale* is a mnemonic name associated with a locale in the SPECIAL-NAMES paragraph.
Returns	The time as a character string formatted appropriately for the locale.
YEAR-TO-YYYY	Same as DATE-TO-YYYYMMDD function, except it converts only a two-digit year, *yy,* to *yyyy*.

21.2.2 Character Functions

CHAR	Convert character to ordinal position of character in collating sequence.
Argument	CHAR(*integer*).
	The *integer* is the ordinal position of the character in the collating sequence and must be 1 to 256. Note that this is one greater than the ASCII or EBCDIC code for the character.
Returns	Single character as PIC X.
	FUNCTION CHAR(110) returns "m" in ASCII and "%" in EBCDIC.
LENGTH	Get length of a nonnumeric data item in alphanumeric, national, or Boolean character positions, depending on the class of the argument.
Argument	LENGTH(*item*) where *item* is a nonnumeric data item.

Returns	Nine-digit integer length of *item*. FUNCTION LENGTH("ABCD") returns 4.
LOWER-CASE:	Convert character in a string to lowercase.
Argument	LOWER-CASE(*string*). The *string* can be alphanumeric or alphabetic.
Returns	A character string of the same length *string*. The new string contains the characters converted to lower- or uppercase. FUNCTION LOWER-CASE("123aBCD+−") returns "123abcd+−".
UPPER-CASE:	Same as LOWER-CASE, but converts the characters to uppercase. FUNCTION UPPER-CASE("123abcD+−") returns "123ABACD+−".
ORD	Get the ordinal position of a character in the collating sequence.
Argument	ORD(*character*).
Returns	Three-digit integer that is the ordinal position of the character in the collating sequence. Note that this is one greater than the ASCII or EBCDIC code for the character. FUNCTION ORD("A") returns 66 in ASCII and 194 in EBCDIC.
REVERSE	Reverse the characters in a string.
Argument	REVERSE(*string*).
Returns	A string (same length as *string*) containing all the characters in reverse order. FUNCTION REVERSE("ABCD") returns "DCBA".

PROPOSED NEW ANSI STANDARD: Check Compiler to See if Implemented	
CHAR-NATIONAL	Same as CHAR, except it uses the national program collation sequence.
DISPLAY-OF	Return string to display national characters.
Argument	DISPLAY-OF(*string*, "*c*") where *string* is a string of national characters and "*c*" is a single character to substitute for nondisplayable characters found in *string*.
Returns	Alphanumeric string of same length as *string*. FUNCTION DISPLAY-OF("abcd~", "X") returns "abcdX", where abcd represent displayable national characters and ~ represents a nondisplayable character.
BYTE-LENGTH	Same as LENGTH, except it returns a length equal to the number of alphanumeric character positions (bytes).
Argument	BYTE-LENGTH(*item*), where *item* is any data item.
Returns	Integer length if *item*.
	FUNCTION BYTE-LENGTH("ABCD") returns 4.
LOCALE-COMPARE	Return the result of comparing two strings using a comparison appropriate to a locale.
Argument	LOCALE-COMPARE(*string-1*, *string-2*, *locale*) where *string-1* and *string-2* are alphanumeric, alphabetic, or national. The two need not be of the same class. The *locale* is a mnemonic name associated with a locale in the SPECIAL-NAMES paragraph.
Returns	A single character indicating the result of the comparison: "=", ">", or "<".
NATIONAL-OF	Return a character string containing the national character internal representation of the characters in the argument.
Argument	NATIONAL-OF(*string*, "*c*") where *string* can be alphanumeric or alphabetic and "*c*" is a character to use if *string* contains a character with no national equivalent.
Returns	A national string of the same length as *string*.

21.2.3   Numeric Functions

INTEGER	Get the largest integer value that is ≤ *number*.
Argument	INTEGER(*number*).
Returns	Largest integer value ≤ *number*.
	FUNCTION INTEGER(23.5) returns 23.
	FUNCTION INTEGER(−23.5) returns −24.
INTEGER-PART	Get the integer part of a number.
Argument	INTEGER(*number*).
	INTEGER-PART(*number*).
Returns	Value of *number* truncated to integer.
	FUNCTION INTEGER-PART(23.5) returns 23.
	FUNCTION INTEGER-PART(−23.5) returns −23.
MOD	Get the modulo value.
Argument	MOD(*integer-1*, *integer-2*).
Returns	Value of *integer-1* modulo *integer-2*. *Integer-2* must not be 0. The calculation is *integer-1*, − (*integer-2* × FUNCTION INTEGER(*integer-1 / integer-2*)).
	FUNCTION MOD(36, 5) returns 36−(5×(36/5)) = 36−(5×5) = 7.
	FUNCTION MOD(−27, 5) returns −27−(5×(−27/5)) = −27−(5×−6) = 3.
NUMVAL	Convert an alphanumeric string to numeric.
Argument	NUMVAL(*string*).
	The *string* contains characters representing numbers in the form ±*nnnnnnnnn.nn*. There can be a leading sign (±) or trailing sign (±, CR, or DB). Blanks may optionally separate the sign and the groups of digits. The decimal point is optional.
Returns	Numeric value of the string.
	COMPUTE A = FUNCTION NUMVAL ("+100233.56") stores numeric 100,233.56 in A.
NUMVAL-C	Same as NUM-VAL, except the string can contain commas and a currency symbol.
Argument	NUMVAL-C(*string*). The standard currency symbol is assumed.
	NUMVAL-C(*string, currency-symbol*) The currency symbol in *currency-symbol* is assumed. The

currency-symbol can be a nonnumeric literal or alphanumeric data item of any length. The *string* can contain commas and the currency symbol can be placed to the left of the leftmost digit (and to the right of any leading sign). If you specify the currency sign as a literal or identifier containing a single character, it and not the normal currency sign is assumed for the string.

Returns	Numeric value of the string.

COMPUTE A = FUNCTION NUMVAL-C ("$100,233.56CR") stores numeric—100,233.56 in A.

FUNCTION NUMVAL-C("+£100,233.56", "£") returns numeric 100,233.56.

ORD-MAX	Get the ordinal number (1 through *n*) of the argument with the maximum value. If several items contain the same highest value, the number of the first is returned.
Argument	ORD-MAX(*item, item, . . . , item*).

The *items* can be numeric or alphanumeric. Alphanumeric, numeric DISPLAY, and alphabetic can be mixed.

Returns	Number (1 through *n*) of the *item* with the maximum value.

FUNCTION ORD-MAX("AMN", "B", "C", "D", "AAZ", "M") returns 6.

FUNCTION ORD-MAX(9, 3, 27, 16) returns 3.

ORD-MIN	Same as ORD-MAX, except it returns the ordinal number of the argument with the minimum value.

FUNCTION ORD-MIN("AMN", "B", "C", "D", "AAZ", "M") returns 5.

FUNCTION ORD-MIN(9, 3, 27, 16) returns 2.

REM	Calculate the remainder of *number-1* / *number-2*.
Argument	REM(*number-1, number-2*).

The *number-2* cannot be zero.

Returns	Remainder of *number-1* / *number-2*.

FUNCTION REM(36, 5) returns 1.

FUNCTION REM(–27, 5) returns –2.

PROPOSED NEW ANSI STANDARD: Check Compiler to See if Implemented

ABS	Get absolute value of a number.
Argument	ABS(*number*).
Returns	Absolute value of the number as the same numeric data type as the argument.
	FUNCTION ABS(–7) returns 7.
BOOLEAN-OF	Return boolean value of an item.
Argument	BOOLEAN-OF(*item, length*).
Returns	BIT item with length specifying the length. The result represents the binary value equivalent of the absolute value of the item.
	FUNCTION BOOLEAN-OF(3, 4) returns B"0011".
HIGHEST-ALGEBRAIC	Returns the highest algebraic value that can be contained in the data item given as the argument.
Argument	HIGHEST-ALGEBRAIC(*numeric-item*).
Returns	Returns the same data type as the argument.
	FUNCTION HIGHEST-ALGEBRAIC(*item*) returns +999 for a PIC S999 item, whether it is PACKED-DECIMAL, BINARY, or zoned-decimal.
INTEGER-OF-BOOLEAN	Return the decimal value of a Boolean item.
Argument	INTEGER-OF-BOOLEAN(*boolean*).
Returns	Integer value of the Boolean value.
LOWEST-ALGEBRAIC	Same as HIGHEST-ALGEBRAIC, except it returns the lowest algebraic value.
NUMVAL-F	Return the floating-point value represented by a character string.
Argument	NUMVAL-F(*string*) where *string* contains an external floating-point number.
Returns	Floating-point value represented by the string.
	NUMVAL-F(".2745E-16") returns .2745E-16 as a floating-point value.
SIGN	Return the sign of a number.
Argument	SIGN(*number*).
Returns	Integer value of +1, 0, or –1 to indicate the sign of the item.

TEST-NUMVAL	Test that an argument is valid for the NUMVAL function.
Argument	TEST-NUMVAL(*string*).
Returns	Integer value of 0 if the string is valid. If not valid, returns the number of the first character in error.
TEST-NUMVAL-C	Same as TEST-NUMVAL, but tests that an argument is valid for the NUMVAL-C function.
TEST-NUMVAL-F	Same as TEST-NUMVAL, but tests that an argument is valid for the NUMVAL-F function.
Returns	Integer value of 0 if the string is valid, −1 if the item would have exponent overflow, −2 if item would have exponent underflow, or the number of the first character in error.

21.2.4   Scientific Functions

ACOS	Compute arccosine in radians.
ASIN	Compute arcsine in radians.
ATAN	Compute arctangent in radians.
COS	Compute cosine in radians.
SIN	Compute sine in radians.
TAN	Compute tangent in radians.
Argument	ACOS(*radians*). Any numeric value from −1 through +1.
	ASIN(*radians*). Any numeric value from −1 through +1.
	ATAN(*radians*).
	COS(*radians*).
	SIN(*radians*).
	TAN(*radians*).
Returns	Value in radians.
	FUNCTION COS(0) returns 1.
LOG	Get natural logarithm (base e).
Argument	LOG(*number*). The *number* must be >=0.

Returns	Number representing the logarithm to the base e or base 10.
	FUNCTION LOG(10) returns 2.30258.
LOG10	Same as LOG, except it gets the logarithm to the base 10.
	LOG10(*number*). The *number* must be >=0.
	FUNCTION LOG10(256) returns 2.40824.
SQRT	Compute the square root of a number.
Argument	SQRT(*number*).
	The *number* must be ≥ 0.
Returns	Square root of *number*.
	FUNCTION SQRT(9) returns 3.

Proposed New ANSI Standard: Check Compiler to See if Implemented

E	Return the value of e, the base of natural logarithms.
Argument	None.
Returns	FUNCTION E returns 2.71828 . . . in the same numeric class as the expression in which it is used.
EXP	Return the value of e^n.
Argument	EXP(*n*) where *n* is a numeric item.
Returns	Returns e^n in the same numeric format as the argument *n*.
	FUNCTION EXP(4) returns 54.598.
PI	Return the value of pi.
Argument	None.
Returns	Numeric type depends on context in which function is used.
	FUNCTION PI returns 3.14159. . . .

21.2.5 Financial Functions

ANNUITY	Calculate the annuity for an investment value of 1 at a given interest rate and number of periods.
Argument	ANNUITY(*interest-rate, integer-periods*).
	The *interest rate* is the percentage/100 and must be ≥ 0.
	The *integer-periods* must be > 0.

Returns	Annuity for an initial investment of 1, assuming the interest is applied at the end of each period.
	FUNCTION ANNUITY(.1, 1) returns 1.1.
FACTORIAL	Compute factorial of an integer.
Argument	FACTORIAL(*integer*).
	The *integer* must be ≥ 0.
Returns	Integer factorial.
	FUNCTION FACTORIAL(6) returns 6×5×4×3×2×1 = 720.
PRESENT-VALUE	Calculate the present value given a discount rate and a series of future values.
Argument	PRESENT-VALUE(*discount, amount, . . . ,amount*).
	The *discount* is a rate, percentage/100, and must be > −1.
Returns	Present value of the series of future period-end amounts.
	FUNCTION PRESENT-VALUE(0.1, 100, 100) returns 173.554.

21.2.6 Statistical Functions

MAX	Get the maximum value of a series of values.
Argument	MAX(*item, item, . . . ,item*).
	The *items* must all have the same data class. They can be alphabetic/alphanumeric, integer, or numeric.
Returns	Value of the *item* having the maximum or minimum value.
	FUNCTION MAX(10, 33, 4, 6) returns 33.
MIN	Same as MAX except that it gets the minimum value.
	FUNCTION MIN(10, 33, 4, 6) returns 4.
MEAN	Calculate the mean (average) of a series of numbers.
Argument	MEAN(*number, number, . . . , number*).
Returns	Arithmetic mean of the *numbers.*
	FUNCTION MEAN(10, 33, 4, 6) returns (10+33+4+6)/4 = 13.25.

MEDIAN	Calculate the median of a series of numbers.
Argument	MEDIAN(*number, number, . . . , number*).
Returns	Median value of the *numbers*.
	FUNCTION MEDIAN(10, 33, 4, 6, 9) returns 9.
	FUNCTION MEDIAN(10, 33, 4, 6) returns (10+6)/2 = 8.
	(If the number of items is even, the median is the average of the middle two numbers.)
MIDRANGE	Calculate the middle range ([minimum + maximum]/2) value of a series of numbers.
Argument	MIDRANGE(*number, number, . . . , number*).
Returns	Average of the minimum and maximum values of the series of *numbers*.
	FUNCTION MIDRANGE(10, 33, 4, 6) returns (33+4)/2 = 18.5.
RANDOM	Get pseudo-random number.
Argument	RANDOM or RANDOM(*starting-integer*).
	The *starting-integer* seeds the next set of random numbers. (You can select different integers to start different series of random numbers.) Coding RANDOM without an argument returns the next random number. (If no *starting-integer* was given to seed the random numbers, a seed value of 0 is used.) Usually, you first code FUNCTION RANDOM(*starting-integer*) to start a series of random numbers and then code FUNCTION RANDOM thereafter.
Returns	A pseudo-random number having a value from 0 to 1.
	FUNCTION RANDOM returns .377, .799, and so on. (The actual values depend on the implementation.)
	FUNCTION RANDOM(9) always returns .891. (The actual value depends on the implementation.)
RANGE	Calculate the range of a series of numbers, the maximum value of a series minus the minimum value.
Argument	RANGE(*number, number, . . . , number*).

	If any of the *numbers* are integer, all must be integer.
Returns	Value of the maximum value of the series minus the minimum value.
	FUNCTION RANGE(10, 33, 4, 6) returns 33−4 = 29.
STANDARD-DEVIATION	Calculate the standard deviation of a series of numbers.
Argument	STANDARD-DEVIATION(*n, n, . . . , n*).
Returns	Standard deviation of the *n*s.
	FUNCTION STANDARD-DEVIATION(10, 33, 4, 6) returns 11.605.
SUM	Sum a series of numbers.
Argument	SUM(*number, number, . . . , number*).
Returns	Arithmetic sum of the *numbers.* The value is an integer only if all the arguments are integers.
	FUNCTION SUM(10, 33, 4, 6) returns 53.
VARIANCE	Compute the statistical variance of a series of numbers.
Argument	VARIANCE(*number, number, . . . , number*).
Returns	Statistical variance of the numbers.
	FUNCTION VARIANCE(10, 33, 4, 6) returns 134.688.

21.2.7 Programming Functions

PROPOSED NEW ANSI STANDARD: Check Compiler to See if Implemented	
ALLOCATED-OCCURRENCES	Get number of occurrences for which space is currently allocated for a table.
Argument	ALLOCATED-OCCURRENCES(*table*).
Returns	Integer number of occurrences of *table.*
EXCEPTION-FILE	Get the I-O status value and file-name of file that had the latest exception. Can be specified only in a declarative procedure.
Argument	None.
Returns	134 alphanumeric character string with the first 2 characters containing the I-O status

	and the remaining characters the file-name, left justified in uppercase, padded on the right with blanks. If there was no I-O exception, the first two characters are 0 and the remaining characters are blank.
EXCEPTION-LOCATION	Return an alphanumeric string that specifies the location of the statement that caused the last I-O error. Can be coded only in a declarative procedure.
Argument	None.
Returns	127 uppercase characters containing the name of the paragraph containing the statement causing the last I-O error, the paragraph-name of the statement causing the error, and identification of the source line as specified by the implement. The three items are each delimited by a semicolon and a space.
EXCEPTION-STATEMENT	Return an alphanumeric string naming the statement that caused the last I-O error. Can be coded only in a declarative procedure.
Argument	None.
Returns	31 uppercase characters containing the name of the statement that caused the last I-O error.
EXCEPTION-STATUS	Return an alphanumeric string that names the exception condition that caused the last I-O error. Can be coded only in a declarative procedure.
Argument	None.
Returns	31 uppercase characters naming the exception condition causing the last I-O error.
STANDARD-COMPARE	Return the results of a comparison using the ordering specified in ISO/IEC 14651.
Argument	STANDARD-COMPARE(*item-1*, *item-2*) where either item can be alphabetic, alphanumeric, or national. They don't need to be the same.
Returns	Single character result of the comparison: "<", "=", or ">".

21.3 WRITING YOUR OWN FUNCTIONS

PROPOSED NEW ANSI STANDARD: Check Compiler to See if Implemented

The new ANSI standard brings the full power of user-written functions to COBOL. You code a function the same as a subprogram, except that you code FUNCTION-ID rather than PROGRAM-ID. Then you code RETURNING in the Procedure Division header to return the function value. Finally, you code END FUNCTION rather than END PROGRAM.

```
IDENTIFICATION DIVISION.
FUNCTION-ID.   function-name.
     □  □  □                           [Everything else same as a subprogram.]
PROCEDURE DIVISION USING a1, a2, ..., an RETURNING result.
[Place function Procedure Division statements here.]
END FUNCTION function-name.
```

To use a function, you first must specify it in a new Repository paragraph in the Configuration Section of the Environment Division. COBOL looks at the Linkage Section and the PROCEDURE DIVISION USING phrase to see what arguments and data formats to expect and what it is to return. You specify the function as follows:

```
ENVIRONMENT DIVISION.
CONFIGURATION SECTION.
REPOSITORY.
   FUNCTION function-name.
```

Then in the Procedure Division, you invoke the function the same as you would an intrinsic function. However, you can omit the word FUNCTION.

```
    FUNCTION function-name(a1, a2, ..., an)
```

Or

```
    function-name(a1, a2, ..., an)
```

The arguments may be literals, identifiers, other functions, or expressions, as long as the data type matches what the function expects. Code OMITTED for an omitted argument. The function type, that is, the type of value returned by the function, is the data type of the RETURNING *result* data item. Here is an example of a simple function that converts minutes to seconds.

```
IDENTIFICATION DIVISION.
FUNCTION-ID.  Min-To-Sec.
```

```
DATA DIVISION
LINKAGE SECTION.
01  Min                          PIC S9(9) BINARY.
01  Sec                          PIC S9(9) BINARY.
PROCEDURE DIVISION USING Min RETURNING Sec.
A00-Begin
    COMPUTE Sec = Min * 60
    EXIT FUNCTION
    .
END FUNCTION Min-To-Sec.
```

To use this function, you code the following in the main program.

```
IDENTIFICATION DIVISION.
PROGRAM-ID.  Some-Program.
ENVIRONMENT DIVISION.
CONFIGURATION SECTION.
REPOSITORY.
    FUNCTION Min-To-Sec.
WORKING-STORAGE SECTION.
01  Minutes                      PIC S9(9).
01  Seconds                      PIC S9(9).
PROCEDURE DIVISION.
A00-Begin.
    MOVE 32 TO Minutes
    COMPUTE Seconds = Min-To-Sec(Minutes)
    DISPLAY Seconds
    GOBACK.
END PROGRAM Some-Program.
```

You can have a different internal name for the function than the external name. You might do this if the external name has limitations, such as the mainframe in which an external name must be all uppercase with no dashes and a maximum of eight characters. In the Repository paragraph, you add the AS "*external-name*" to specify the external name.

```
FUNCTION function-name AS "external-name"
FUNCTION Min-To-Sec AS "CVTMTS"
```

In addition to placing the names of your own functions in the Repository paragraph, you can also add the names of the intrinsic functions. Then you don't need to code FUNCTION when you invoke the function. Add the INTRINSIC clause for an intrinsic function.

```
REPOSITORY.
    FUNCTION RANDOM INTRINSIC
    FUNCTION MIN INTRINSIC
    FUNCTION Min-To-Sec.
```

Now you can invoke the functions without the word FUNCTION.

```
COMPUTE T-Val = MIN(Min-To-Sec, 12) * RANDOM
```

Once you do this, the function name becomes a reserved word, and you can't use it as a data name. If you want to include all the intrinsic functions, code ALL rather than an individual function name.

```
FUNCTION ALL INTRINSIC
```

CHAPTER 22

ADVANCED CHARACTER MANIPULATION

The INSPECT, STRING, and UNSTRING statements perform search, replacement, and concatenation operations on character strings. Character manipulation is important in COBOL but not critical. Read this chapter on an as-needed basis.

> **Sometimes Used**

COBOL can do character manipulation, but this is not its strength. It lacks the simplicity and elegance in handling character strings found in C/C++, Visual Basic, Java, and PL/I. In most COBOL applications, character string manipulation is done to validate data, and for this, COBOL is entirely adequate. If your application is heavily involved in other types of character string manipulation, such as parsing, concatenation, and searching, COBOL may not be the proper choice as a language.

22.1 THE INSPECT STATEMENT

> **Sometimes Used**

The INSPECT statement can both count the number of specific characters or substrings in an identifier and replace them with other characters of the same length.

22.1.1 Counting Characters

The first form of INSPECT counts the characters in an identifier. INSPECT examines the characters in *identifier* from left to right, counting specific characters as specified by the FOR phrase.

```
                              CHARACTERS
                              ALL match-string
                              LEADING match-string
INSPECT identifier TALLYING count FOR _____
```

433

- The *identifier* is a group item or an elementary DISPLAY item to examine. COBOL treats it as alphanumeric data and ignores any internal sign for external decimal numbers.
- The *count* is an elementary numeric data item to count the number of matches. You must initialize it, because INSPECT adds to it.
- ALL counts all nonoverlapping characters in *identifier* that match the characters in the *match-string*. (A *match-string* of "AA" counts 2 and not 3 in an *identifier* containing "AAAABAB".)
- LEADING counts the number of times the *match-string* appears as the leftmost characters in *identifier*. That is, it counts the number of times the *match-string* appears consecutively at the beginning of the string. (A *match-string* of "THE" counts two in an *identifier* containing "THETHE THE".)
- CHARACTERS counts the number of characters in *identifier*. (An *identifier* of PIC *X*(9) counts nine.) This acts the same as the LENGTH OF special register.
- The *match-string* is a DISPLAY elementary data identifier, alphanumeric literal, or figurative constant. INSPECT treats figurative constants as a single instance of the character. (ZEROS is the same as "0".)

```
01  String-A                        PIC X(11)
                                    VALUE "MISSISSIPPI".
```

□ □ □
```
MOVE ZEROS TO Count-1
INSPECT String-A TALLYING Count-1 FOR ALL "S"
```
   [Adds 4 to *Count-1*; *Count-1* contains 4.]
```
INSPECT String-A TALLYING Count-1 FOR CHARACTERS
```
   [Adds 11 to *Count-1*; *Count-1* contains 15.]
```
INSPECT String-A TALLYING Count-1 FOR LEADING "M"
```
   [Adds 1 to *Count-1*; *Count-1* contains 16.]
```
INSPECT String-A TALLYING Count-1 FOR ALL "ISS"
```
   [Adds 2 to *Count-1*; *Count-1* contains 18.]

A single AFTER and a single BEFORE phrase may follow the FOR phrase to start the scan after some other character string is encountered and end the scan before the occurrence of another character string.

BEFORE INITIAL *stop-string*   Or   **AFTER INITIAL** *begin-string*

BEFORE coded without AFTER starts the counting with the leftmost character in *identifier* and continues up to but not including the characters matching those in the *stop-string*. If the *stop-string* characters do not appear in *identifier,* the matching terminates with the rightmost characters in *identifier* as if BEFORE had not been coded. Assume for the next several examples that *String-A* contains "MISSISSIPPI".

```
INSPECT String-A TALLYING Count-1 FOR ALL "I" BEFORE "IS"
```
   [Adds 0 to *Count-1*.]
```
INSPECT String-A TALLYING Count-1 FOR CHARACTERS BEFORE "IP"
```
   [Adds 7 to *Count-1*.]
```
INSPECT String-A TALLYING Count-1 FOR LEADING "M" BEFORE "S"
```
   [Adds 1 to *Count-1*.]

AFTER coded without BEFORE starts the counting immediately after the *begin-string* characters in *identifier* and continues to the rightmost characters in *identifier*. The FOR phrase is ignored if the *begin-string* characters do not appear in *identifier*.

```
INSPECT String-A TALLYING Count-1 FOR ALL "S" AFTER "IS"
   [Adds 3 to Count-1.]
INSPECT String-A TALLYING Count-1 FOR CHARACTERS AFTER "IP"
   [Adds 2 to Count-1.]
INSPECT String-A TALLYING Count-1 FOR LEADING "I" AFTER "S"
   [Adds 0 to Count-1.]
```

Both *begin-string* and *stop-string* may be DISPLAY elementary identifiers, alphanumeric literals, or figurative constants. You can code AFTER and BEFORE together. The AFTER string is found first, and then the scan terminates with the BEFORE string. The CHARACTERS, ALL, and LEADING apply to the substring established by any AFTER and BEFORE. The following example adds 2 to *Count-1*.

```
INSPECT String-A TALLYING Count-1 FOR ALL "I"
        AFTER "S" BEFORE "P"
```

There may be several ALL phrases in the INSPECT statement. (There can also be several LEADING phrases, but this makes sense only if you also code AFTER or BEFORE phrases to establish different ranges of characters to scan.)

```
INSPECT String-A
   TALLYING Count-1 FOR ALL "M"          [Add 1 to Count-1.]
                        ALL "S"          [Add 4 to Count-1.]
```

LEADING, CHARACTERS, and ALL can all be coded together, but it becomes very difficult to do this correctly. Each successive FOR phrase picks up where the previous one stopped, which may not be the first character position. For example:

```
INSPECT String-A
   TALLYING Count-1 FOR LEADING "M",
                  [Add 1 to Count-1. Now positioned following the leading "M".]
                        ALL "M"
                  [Add 0 to Count-1. No "M" characters follow the leading "M".]
```

Note also that any BEFORE and AFTER clauses are performed before any of the other FOR clauses is executed. For example:

```
INSPECT String-A
   TALLYING Count-1 FOR LEADING "M",
                  [Add 0 to Count-1. The following BEFORE "PP" clause is per-
                  formed first to position before the "PP". The next character is no
                  longer an "M".]
                 CHARACTERS BEFORE "PP",
                  [Add 8 to Count-1. This positions at the "PP" before any FOR
                  phrase is        applied.]
                        ALL "S"
                  [Add 0 to Count-1. No "SS" characters follow the "PP".]
```

You can write several ALL phrases, but it is best to have only one LEADING or CHARACTERS phrase following a FOR. There may also be separate *counts* for the FOR phrase.

```
INSPECT String-A
   TALLYING Count-1 FOR ALL "S"         [Add 4 to Count-1.]
            Count-2 FOR ALL "I"         [Add 4 to Count-2.]
            Count-3 FOR ALL "P"         [Add 2 to Count-3.]
```

Be careful combining CHARACTERS and LEADING, because their final position affects phrases that follow, as shown in this example:

```
INSPECT String-A
   TALLYING Count-1 FOR CHARACTERS BEFORE "SS",
               [Add 2 to Count-1. This positions to the first "SS".]
            Count-2 FOR LEADING "M",
               [Add 0 to Count-2. The "M" is no longer leading.]
            Count-3 FOR ALL "I"
               [Add 3 to Count-3. There are three "I" characters starting with the
               "SS".]
```

These forms of INSPECT are complex and make it possible to write statements that are almost indecipherable. INSPECT applies each FOR phrase as follows:

- The first FOR phrase is applied starting from the first character position (or wherever any BEFORE or AFTER phrase would place it).
- If the FOR phrase is not applied because of the BEFORE or AFTER phrase, or if there is no match in the FOR phrase, the next FOR phrase is applied. It starts at the same character as the previous FOR phrase (or wherever any BEFORE or AFTER phrase would place it).
- If a FOR phrase is satisfied, the appropriate count is incremented and the FOR phrases that follow are not applied. The next comparison begins with the first FOR phrase. It begins at the next character in *identifier* that is to the right of the rightmost character that participated in the match.
- If no FOR phrases match, the first FOR phrase is applied starting with the character position in *identifier* to the right of where the last comparison began.

The next example illustrates this form of INSPECT.

```
MOVE "ABCDEFGH" TO String-A
MOVE ZERO TO Count-1, Count-2
INSPECT String-A
   TALLYING Count-1 FOR ALL "AB",
                    ALL "C",
            Count-2 FOR ALL "EFG"
```

The INSPECT statement then operates as follows:

|AB|DCEFGH   FOR ALL "AB" matches the first two characters, and 1 is added to
|AB| *Count-1. Count-1* now contains 1 and the matching continues to the
              right of "AB" in *String-A.*

```
A|B|CDEFGH
 |A|B
 |C|
```
FOR ALL "AB" does not match, but ALL "C" matches, and 1 is added to *Count-1*. *Count-1* now contains 2, and the matching continues to the right of "C" in *String-A*.

```
ABC|D|EFGH
   |A|B
   |C|
   |E|FG
```
Neither "AB", "C", nor "EFG" match. The matching continues to the right of "D" in *String-A*.

```
ABCD|EFG|H
    |AB |
    |C  |
    |EFG|
```
Neither "AB" nor "C" match, but FOR ALL "EFG" matches, and 1 is added to *Count-2*. *Count-1* contains 2, *Count-2* contains 1, and the matching continues to the right of "EF" in *String-A*.

```
ABCDEFG|H
       |AB
       |C
       |EFG
```
Neither "AB", "C", nor "EFG" match. *Count-1* contains 2, *Count-2* contains 1, and the INSPECT statement has completed execution.

22.1.2 Replacing Characters

The second form of INSPECT replaces characters:

```
                           CHARACTERS
                           ALL match-string
                           FIRST match-string
                           LEADING match-string
INSPECT identifier REPLACING _____
   BY replacement-string
```

INSPECT examines the characters in *identifier* as specified by the REPLACING phrase and replaces them with the characters in the *replacement-string*. The *identifier*, ALL, LEADING, and CHARACTERS are exactly as in the first form. FIRST searches *identifier* for the first characters that match the characters in *match-string*. The *replacement-string* may be a DISPLAY elementary identifier, an alphanumeric literal, or a figurative constant. It must contain the same number of characters as in *match-string*, or one character for CHARACTERS. If it is a figurative constant, it assumes the length of the *match-string*.

```
MOVE "MISSISSIPPI" TO String-A
INSPECT String-A REPLACING FIRST "SS" BY "XX"
   [String-A contains "MIXXISSIPPI".]
INSPECT String-A REPLACING ALL "I" BY "Z"
   [String-A contains "MZXXZSSZPPZ".]
INSPECT String-A REPLACING LEADING "M" BY "Y"
   [String-A contains "YZXXZSSZPPZ".]
INSPECT String-A REPLACING CHARACTERS BY "W"
   [String-A contains "WWWWWWWWWWW". Same as MOVE ALL "W" TO
   String-A.]
```

You can also list several *match-strings* for ALL and LEADING:

```
MOVE "MISSISSIPPI" TO String-A
INSPECT String-A REPLACING ALL "I" BY "Z"
                           ALL "PP" BY "XX"
```

String-A would be changed to "MZSSZSSZXXZ". You can also append the BEFORE and AFTER to the REPLACING clause.

```
MOVE "MISSISSIPPI" TO String-A
INSPECT String-A REPLACING FIRST "SS" BY "XX" AFTER "SS"
   [String-A contains "MISSIXXIPPI".]
INSPECT String-A REPLACING ALL "I" BY "Z" BEFORE "S"
   [String-A contains "MZSSIXXIPPI".]
```

There may be several REPLACING phrases in INSPECT, such as the following. Note that you write the REPLACING only once.

```
MOVE "MISSISSIPPI" TO String-A
INSPECT String-A
  REPLACING LEADING "S" BY "Z" AFTER "I",
```
        [*String-A* contains "MIZZISSIPPI". Starting after I, there are two leading *S*s.]
```
          CHARACTERS BY "Y" BEFORE "I",
```
        [*String-A* contains "YIZZISSIPPI". Each new clause starts over.]
```
          CHARACTERS BY "X" BEFORE "P",
```
        [*String-A* contains "YXZZXXXXPPI". Character already changes are not changed a second time.]
```
          ALL "P" BY "W",
```
        [*String-A* contains "YXZZXXXXWWI".]
```
            "I" BY "N",
```
        [*String-A* contains "YXZZXXXXWWN".]

INSPECT applies the REPLACING phrases from left to right in the order they are written. The matching occurs in the same way as for the first format. Each FOR phrase is applied only if its BEFORE or AFTER phrase is satisfied. If any match occurs, the processing begins again with the first phrase immediately after the rightmost character in *identifier* that was replaced. If no match occurs, the comparison begins with the first FOR phrase, one character to the right of where the previous cycle started.

The TALLYING and REPLACING phrases may appear in the same INSPECT statement. The TALLYING phrase is first applied in its entirety, and then the REPLACING phrase is applied. The effect is exactly the same as if two INSPECT statements had been written.

```
INSPECT String-A
  TALLYING Count-1 FOR ALL "X" AFTER "Y",
  REPLACING ALL "X" BY "Z" AFTER "Y"
```

Same as

```
INSPECT String-A TALLYING Count-1 FOR ALL "X" AFTER "Y"
INSPECT String-A REPLACING ALL "X" BY "Z" AFTER "V"
```

TIP *If you want to have any hope of understanding what INSPECT does, write separate TALLYING and REPLACING statements.*

22.1.3 Converting Characters

The final form of the INSPECT statement allows you to specify a string of characters, each of which is to be converted to the corresponding character in another string:

```
INSPECT identifier CONVERTING "these-characters" TO "others"
```

The "*others*" must have the same number of characters as "*these-characters*".

```
MOVE "MISSISSIPPI" TO String-A
INSPECT String-A CONVERTING "ISP" TO "XYZ"
```

Any "I" is converted to "X", any "S" to "Y", and any "P" to "Z". *String-A* would contain "MXYYXYYXZZX". Notice that this form of the INSPECT is exactly the same as coding:

```
INSPECT String-A REPLACING ALL "I" BY "X"
                             "S" BY "Y"
                             "P" BY "Z"
```

You can also code CONVERTING with a BEFORE and AFTER phrase.

```
MOVE "MISSISSIPPI" TO String-A
INSPECT String-A CONVERTING "ISP" TO "XYZ" BEFORE "IPPI"
```

Here, *String-A* will contain "MXYYXYYIPPI". The CONVERTING phrase is often found in legacy systems to convert to upper- or lowercase. The UPPER-CASE and LOWER-CASE intrinsic functions described in Chapter 21 do this today and are much simpler to code.

22.2 THE STRING AND UNSTRING STATEMENTS

Sometimes Used

The STRING and UNSTRING statements manipulate character strings. *Character string manipulation* is very different from the operations that have been presented so far, and it requires several new concepts. To illustrate character string operations, consider a string such as "MARY HAD A LITTLE LAMB." One operation you might want to perform is to see if the string contains a given substring, such as "LAMB", and where in the string it is located. The location is indicated by the starting character position, such as 19 for "LAMB." Another operation that might be performed is to concatenate two or more strings by appending one to the end of another. Suppose that another string contained "ITS FLEECE WAS WHITE AS SNOW." By concatenating this string to the first, you form a new string containing "MARY HAD A LITTLE LAMB. ITS FLEECE WAS WHITE AS SNOW."

You might also want to break up a string into substrings. This is usually done by specifying the starting character position and the number of characters. By forming a substring of 11 characters, starting at the twelfth character, you form a new string containing "LITTLE LAMB". Next, you might want to replace a substring with another substring. You can do this either by specifying a starting character and the number of characters to replace, or by specifying a substring to locate and a string with which to replace it. In our string, you might replace "LAMB" with "TOFU" so that the string contains "MARY HAD A LITTLE TOFU." If the replacement string is not equal to the length of the substring it is replacing, it is more complicated. If you wanted to replace "LITTLE" with "BIG" in "MARY HAD A LITTLE LAMB.", you would do the following:

- Search the string to find where "LITTLE" begins.
- Form a substring of all characters up to this point and a substring of all characters following the "LITTLE".
- Concatenate the first substring "MARY HAD A" with "BIG" and then with the last substring "LAMB." to form "MARY HAD A BIG LAMB."

You also need substrings when you want to locate all instances of a substring within a string. Suppose you want to replace all instances of "MARY" with "JANE" in the string "MARY HAD A LAMB. MARY ALSO HAD A HORSE." You would first replace the first "MARY" with "JANE" to form "JANE HAD A LAMB. MARY ALSO HAD A HORSE." Then you would examine the substring beginning just beyond where you replaced and replace "MARY" with "JANE" so that "HAD A LAMB. MARY ALSO HAD A HORSE." becomes "HAD A LAMB. JANE ALSO HAD A HORSE." This would continue until no more "MARY" is found to replace.

COBOL is fair as a language for text editing. Its statements are directed more toward examining data items to see if they contain valid numeric or alphabetic characters and toward replacing invalid characters with valid ones. The INSPECT statement already described can locate substrings within a string and can replace substrings with strings of equal length. The STRING and UNSTRING statements described next can concatenate strings, replace substrings with strings, and form strings.

The STRING statement transmits characters from a send string into a receiving string, starting at a specified character position in the receiving string. STRING can transmit multiple send strings into a single receiving string. The UNSTRING statement transmits characters starting at a specified character position in a send string into a receiving string. UNSTRING can separate a single send string into multiple receiving strings. STRING and UNSTRING are both complex and difficult statements—perhaps the most difficult statements to be found in any programming language.

One alternative to STRING and UNSTRING is to use reference modification. For example, if you want to store the characters "AB" into the first two positions of the identifier A, you can code the following:

```
01  A                        PIC X(4) VALUE "WXYZ".
    □  □  □
    MOVE "AB" TO A(1:2)      [A contains "ABYZ".]
```

Another alternative to STRING and UNSTRING is to use the REDEFINES clause, described in Chapter 11, which can define one substring to overlay another. The following example also stores the characters "AB" into the first two positions of the identifier A:

```
01  A                        PIC X(4) VALUE "WXYZ".
01  A-2                      REDEFINES A
                             PIC X(2).
    □  □  □
    MOVE "AB" TO A-2         [A contains "ABYZ".]
```

Both these methods work only if a fixed number of characters are to be moved to a fixed position in the identifier. Use them wherever possible rather than STRING and UNSTRING, because they will be both more efficient and more understandable.

22.2.1 The STRING Statement

Sometimes Used

The STRING statement concatenates strings or substrings from one data item into another. The simplest form of the STRING statement transmits the characters in the *send-string* into the *receiving-string*. This acts like a MOVE, except that any characters beyond the length of the *send-string* in the *receiving-string* are not disturbed.

```
STRING send-string DELIMITED BY SIZE INTO receiving-string
```

The *send-string* is an alphanumeric literal, figurative constant, or DISPLAY identifier containing the characters to be transmitted. STRING treats figurative constants as single characters. You can reference-modify: *send-string*(n:m).

The *receiving-string* is the DISPLAY identifier into which the characters in *send-string* are transmitted. It cannot represent an edited data item or be described with the JUSTIFIED clause. Nor can it be reference-modified. Use the POINTER phrase, described in a subsequent paragraph, instead. Characters in *send-string* are transmitted from left to right into *receiving-string* until the rightmost character in *send-string* is transmitted or *receiving-string* is filled.

```
01   A                              PIC X(4) VALUE "WXYZ".
     □  □  □
     STRING "AB" DELIMITED SIZE INTO A          [A contains "ABYZ".]
```

Note that this differs from a MOVE in that the STRING does not disturb the "YZ" characters:

```
MOVE "AB" TO A              [A contains "ABbb".]
```

Note also that you can use a MOVE with reference modification to accomplish the same thing:

```
MOVE "AB" TO A(1:2)         [A contains "ABYZ".]
```

The DELIMITED SIZE phrase specifies that all characters in *send-string* are to be transmitted. Alternatively, you can terminate the transmission with *delimiter* characters as follows:

```
STRING send-string DELIMITED BY delimiter INTO receiving-string
```

The *delimiter* is a figurative constant, alphanumeric literal, or a DISPLAY elementary identifier containing characters. Transmission terminates if the delimiter characters are encountered in *send-string*. All characters in *send-string* are transmitted if *delimiter* is not encountered. If the *delimiter* contains more than one character, they are treated as a unit. That is, a *delimiter* of "AB" terminates when "AB" is encountered, not when an "A" or "B" is encountered. The *delimiter* characters themselves are not transmitted.

```
01   A                              PIC X(4) VALUE "WXYZ".
01   B                              PIC X(4) VALUE "ABCD".
     □  □  □
     STRING B DELIMITED "C" INTO A          [A contains "ABYZ".]
```

The specific position in *receiving-string* at which transmission is to begin is specified by the POINTER phrase:

```
                              SIZE
                              delimiter
STRING send-string DELIMITED _____ INTO receiving-string
       WITH POINTER position
```

The *position* is a numeric integer data identifier (but not literal) specifying the first character position (the first character is number 1) in *receiving-string* into which the *send-string* characters are to be transmitted. It is incremented by one as each character is transmitted. On completion of the statement, it points one character beyond the last character transmitted. The POSITION phrase is optional, and *position* 1 is assumed if it is omitted.

```
01  A                                  PIC X(4) VALUE "WXYZ".
01  B                                  PIC S9(4) BINARY VALUE 3.
     □  □  □
    STRING "AB" DELIMITED SIZE INTO A POINTER B
```
   [*A* contains "WXAB", and *B* contains 5.]

The STRING statement can also concatenate character strings by listing several *send-strings*. The strings are concatenated by appending one string to the end of another to form a new string. Thus, "AB" concatenated with "CD" yields a new string containing "ABCD". The POINTER clause is optional.

```
                                    delimiter
STRING send-string-1 DELIMITED _____,
                                    SIZE
                                    delimiter
        send-string-2 DELIMITED _____,
          .          .          .          .
                                    SIZE
                                    delimiter
        send-string-n DELIMITED _____
    INTO receiving-string POINTER position
```

For example:

```
STRING "AB" DELIMITED SIZE,
 "CD" DELIMITED SIZE
INTO A                          [A contains "ABCD".]
```

You can detect error conditions by appending the ON OVERFLOW phrase to the end of the STRING statement.

```
STRING "AB" DELIMITED SIZE INTO A
    ON OVERFLOW imperative-statements
    NOT ON OVERFLOW imperative-statements
END-STRING
```

You can code END-STRING even if you don't code an OVERFLOW phrase. The error condition occurs when *position* is less than 1 or greater than the size of *receiving-string*. If the ON OVERFLOW phrase is not coded, execution continues with the next executable statement when an error condition occurs. You can also code the NOT ON OVERFLOW phrase with or without an ON OVERFLOW phrase:

```
STRING "AB" DELIMITED SIZE INTO A POINTER B
    ON OVERFLOW PERFORM B30-Error
    NOT ON OVERFLOW PERFORM C30-Process
END-STRING
STRING "AB" DELIMITED SIZE INTO A POINTER B
    ON OVERFLOW PERFORM B30-Error
```

```
      END-STRING
      STRING "AB" DELIMITED SIZE INTO A POINTER B
        NOT ON OVERFLOW PERFORM C30-Process
      END-STRING
```

22.2.2 The UNSTRING Statement

Sometimes Used

The UNSTRING statement selects strings or substrings from one string and stores them in one or more receiving fields. The simplest form of the UNSTRING statement transmits the characters in the *send-string* into the *receiving-string* and is identical to the MOVE statement:

```
UNSTRING send-string INTO receiving-string
```

Same as

```
MOVE send-string TO receiving-string
```

The *send-string* is an alphanumeric DISPLAY identifier containing the characters to be transmitted. It cannot be reference-modified. Use the POINTER phrase instead.

The *receiving-string* is the DISPLAY identifier into which the characters in *send-string* are transmitted. You can reference-modify it: *receiving-string*(*n*:*m*). It cannot be an alphanumeric edited or numeric edited data item. If numeric, it cannot be floating-point or have a P in its PIC phrase. Characters in *send-string* are transmitted from left to right into *receiving-string* until the rightmost character in *send-string* is transmitted or *receiving-string* is filled. The transmission is performed as if it were a MOVE, so *receiving-string* is padded on the right with blanks if it is not filled.

```
01  A                        PIC X(2) VALUE "AB".
01  B                        PIC X(4) VALUE "WXYZ".
      □  □  □
    UNSTRING A INTO B         [B contains "ABbb".]
```

Note that this form of UNSTRING is identical to a MOVE:

```
MOVE "AB" TO B               [B contains "ABbb".]
```

You can also terminate transmission by *delimiter* characters specified in the DELIMITED phrase.

```
UNSTRING send-string DELIMITED BY delimiter
  INTO receiving-string
```

The *delimiter* is a figurative constant, nonnumeric literal, or DISPLAY alphanumeric identifier. (Note that you can't code DELIMITED SIZE for UNSTRING.) Transmission terminates if the *delimiter* characters are encountered in *send-string*. A *delimiter* containing more than one character is treated as a unit. The *delimiter* characters themselves are not transmitted. All characters in *send-string* are transmitted if the *delimiter* is not encountered. The following example shows how the DELIMITED phrase limits the characters transmitted:

```
01  A                         PIC X(5) VALUE "ABCDE".
01  D                         PIC X(6) VALUE "111111".
    □  □  □
    UNSTRING A DELIMITED "C" INTO D
```

D contains "ABbbbb". Like the MOVE, UNSTRING truncates the sending item on the right if it is longer than the receiving item and pads on the right with blanks if it is shorter.

You can specify several strings as the delimiter. Just connect them with OR.

```
UNSTRING send-string DELIMITED delimiter OR delimiter OR …
UNSTRING A DELIMITED "B" OR "C" INTO D
    [D contains "Abbbbb". Transmission stops if UNSTRING encounters either a "B"
    or "C" in A.]
```

You specify the *position* in *send-string* at which to begin transmission by coding the POINTER phrase.

```
UNSTRING send-string DELIMITED delimiter INTO receiving-string
         WITH POINTER position
```

The *position* is a numeric integer identifier specifying the first character position (the first character is position 1) in *send-string* from which transmission is to begin. Note that POINTER applies to the *send-string* in UNSTRING, not to the *receiving-string* as in STRING. It is incremented by 1 as each character is examined. If DELIMITED is coded and the *delimiter* is encountered, this is one character beyond the *delimiter* in *send-string;* otherwise it is one beyond the last character transmitted. The POSITION phrase is optional, and *position* 1 is assumed if omitted.

```
01  A                         PIC X(4) VALUE "WXYZ".
01  B                         PIC X(4) VALUE "1234".
01  C                         PIC S9(4) BINARY VALUE 2.
    □  □  □
    UNSTRING A INTO B POINTER C    [B contains "XYZb", and C contains 5.]
```

You can also count the number of characters stored in the *receiving-string* by including a COUNT phrase. You must also code the DELIMITED phrase when you code the COUNT phrase. Both the COUNT and POINTER phrases are optional.

```
UNSTRING send-string DELIMITED delimiter INTO receiving-string
      COUNT IN count
      POINTER position
```

The *count* is a numeric integer identifier that is set to the number of characters moved into *receiving-string*. The *count* does not need to contain an initial value, because the count is moved to it as if by a MOVE. (The *delimiter* characters are not counted.)

```
01  A                        PIC X(4) VALUE "WX Z".
01  B                        PIC X(4) VALUE "1234".
01  C                        PIC S9(4) BINARY VALUE 2.
01  D                        PIC S9(4) BINARY VALUE 10.
    □  □  □
    UNSTRING A DELIMITED SPACE INTO B COUNT D POINTER C
```
[The POINTER *C* in which *C* contains 2 starts the scan at the "X" in *A*. UNSTRING moves the "X" to *B* and stores 1 in *D*. UNSTRING terminates the scan when it encounters the blank, the second character scanned, and adds 2 to *C*. *B* contains "Xbbb", *D* contains 1, and *C* contains 4.]

The next form of UNSTRING retrieves the delimiter characters with the DELIMITER phrase:

```
UNSTRING send-string DELIMITED delimiter INTO receiving-string
      DELIMITER IN save-delimiter
      COUNT count
      POINTER position
```

The DELIMITER phrase (not to be confused with the DELIMITED phrase) specifies a DISPLAY identifier into which a *delimiter* is stored when encountered in *send-string*. The COUNT and POINTER phrases are optional. You must also code the DELIMITED phrase when you code the DELIMITER phrase.

The *save-delimiter* is a DISPLAY alphanumeric identifier into which the *delimiters* are stored when encountered. When a delimiter is encountered, it is moved to *save-delimiter* as if by a MOVE. If no delimiter is encountered, *save-delimiter* is filled with spaces.

```
01  A                        PIC X(6) VALUE "UVWXYZ".
01  B                        PIC X(6) VALUE "111111".
01  D                        PIC X(6) VALUE SPACES.
01  Count-1                  PIC S9(4) BINARY VALUE 10.
01  Pointer-1                PIC S9(4) BINARY VALUE 2.
    □  □  □
    UNSTRING A DELIMITED "Y" INTO B
          DELIMITER D
          COUNT Count-1
          POINTER Pointer-1
```

UNSTRING operates as follows. The POINTER *Pointer-1* tells UNSTRING to begin with the second character in *A*. UNSTRING moves the three characters up to but not including the "Y" to B. It encounters the delimiter "Y" and moves it to D. Because UNSTRING moved three characters, it stores 3 in *Count-1*. Because UNSTRING examined four characters, it adds 4 to *Pointer-1*. At the end of the statement, *B* contains "VWXbbb", *D* contains "Ybbbbb", *Count-1* contains 3, and *Pointer-1* contains 6.

UNSTRING can separate the *send-string* into several *receiving-strings*. The DELIMITER and COUNT phrases are optional with each *receiving-string*. A TALLYING phrase can specify a numeric integer identifier that is incremented each time a new substring is transmitted.

```
UNSTRING send-string DELIMITED delimiter
   INTO receiving-string-1 DELIMITER save-1 COUNT count-1,
        receiving-string-2 DELIMITER save-2 COUNT count-2,
        .       .       .       .
        receiving-string-n DELIMITER save-n COUNT count-n
        POINTER position
        TALLYING IN tally
```

The *tally* is a numeric integer identifier that is incremented as each successive *receiving-string* is filled. You must set tally to an initial value, usually 0, before executing UNSTRING.

Characters are first transmitted from *send-string*, beginning at the *position* specified, into *receiving-string-1*. When a *delimiter* is encountered, it is moved to *save-1*, *count-1* is set to the count of characters stored in *receiving-string-1*, the number of characters examined is added to *position*, and *tally* is incremented by 1 (assuming that DELIMITER, COUNT, POINTER, and TALLYING phrases are coded). Characters following the *delimiter* are transmitted into *receiving-string-2* until another *delimiter* is encountered. That *delimiter* is moved to *save-2*, *count-2* is set to the count of characters moved, the number of characters examined is added to *position*, and *tally* is incremented by 1. Transmission continues until all *receiving-strings* are filled, or all characters in *send-string* are transmitted. If *receiving-string-n* is filled before a *delimiter* is encountered, blanks are moved to *save-n*, and transmission continues into the next *receiving-string* with the character following the last character transmitted.

You can specify more than one *delimiter* by connecting them with OR. Transmission stops if any *delimiter* is encountered in *send-string*.

```
DELIMITED "A" OR "B" OR "C"
```

If two *delimiters* are encountered in succession, the next *receiving-string* is filled with blanks, and any count for it is set to zero.

You can code ALL before the *delimiter* to treat successive occurrences of the *delimiter* as a single occurrence. For example, DELIMITED ALL "A" OR ALL "B" would treat the *send-string* "WAAXBBBY" as if it were "WAXBY".

You can append the OVERFLOW phrases to the end of UNSTRING to detect overflow when *position* has a value less than 1 or greater than the size of *send-*

string during execution. ON OVERFLOW also executes when all receiving fields have been filled but not all characters in *send-string* have been examined. If ON OVERFLOW is not coded, execution continues with the next executable statement.

```
UNSTRING send-string DELIMITED delimiter
   INTO receiving-string-1 DELIMITER save-1 COUNT count-1,
        receiving-string-2 DELIMITER save-2 COUNT count-2,
        .          .          .          .          .          .
        receiving-string-n DELIMITER save-n COUNT count-n
        POINTER position
        TALLYING tally
        ON OVERFLOW imperative-statements
        NOT ON OVERFLOW imperative-statements
END-UNSTRING
```

You can code NOT ON OVERFLOW with or without ON OVERFLOW. The following example illustrates the execution of UNSTRING:

```
MOVE 1 TO P1
MOVE "BALLYbJAZZbTOPAZbA" TO Save-It
UNSTRING Save-It DELIMITED "Z" OR ALL "L"
   INTO B1 DELIMITER S1 COUNT C1,
        B2 DELIMITER S2 COUNT C2,
        B3 DELIMITER S3 COUNT C3,
        B4 DELIMITER S4 COUNT C4
   POINTER P1
   TALLYING T
   ON OVERFLOW PERFORM C60-Error
END-UNSTRING
```

Execution proceeds as follows:

- UNSTRING stores "BA" in *B1*, "L" in *S1*, 2 in *C1*, and adds 5 to *P1* (it must scan up to the "Y" to determine that there are no more "L"s) and 1 to *T*.

- UNSTRING stores "YbJA" in *B2*, "Z" in *S2*, 4 in *C2*, and adds 5 to *P1* and 1 to *T*.

- UNSTRING stores blanks in *B3*, "Z" in *S3*, 0 in *C3*, and adds 1 to *P1* and 1 to *T*.

- UNSTRING stores "bTOPA" in *B4*, "Z" in *S3*, 5 in *C4*, and adds 6 to *P1* and 1 to *T*.

- UNSTRING performs the *C60-Error* procedure because the "bA" characters weren't scanned. At the end, *T* contains 4 and *P1* contains 17.

Such a statement constitutes almost an entire program by itself, and you might have to make a flow chart of it to understand what it does. STRING and UNSTRING are difficult statements to write, and they make programs difficult to read.

TIP *Use STRING and UNSTRING sparingly, and include comments to explain what they are intended to do.*

As another, more practical, example, here is how UNSTRING can parse a tokenized data stream. Assume a record has been read in and stored in *In-Rec*. (The VALUE clause shows its contents.) The name is to be stored in *In-Name*, the city in *In-City*, and the zip code in *In-Zip*. The data is defined as follows:

```
01  In-Rec              PIC X(55)
          VALUE "Lewis N. Clark,Seattle,90066-2543".
01  In-Person-Info.
    05  In-Name         PIC X(55).
    05  In-City         PIC X(15).
    05  In-Zip          PIC X(10).
```

The following UNSTRING parses *In-Rec* and stores the three data items.

```
UNSTRING In-Rec DELIMITED ","
  INTO In-Name, In-City, In-Zip
  ON OVERFLOW DISPLAY "Bad data in record: " In-Rec
END-UNSTRING
```

Now UNSTRING can be used to take apart the first name, middle initial, and last name. We need the following additional data items:

```
01  First-Name          PIC X(10) VALUE SPACES.
01  Middle-Init         PIC X(10) VALUE SPACES.
01  Last-Name           PIC X(10) VALUE SPACES.
```

The UNSTRING statement takes apart the string.

```
UNSTRING In-Name DELIMITED SPACE OR ","
  INTO First-Name, Middle-Init, Last-Name
```

After execution, *First-Name* contains "LEWIS", *Middle-Init* contains "N", and *Last-Name* contains "CLARK".

At the beginning of this section, several types of character manipulation were discussed:

- Determine if a string contains "LAMB".
- Concatenate two strings together to form a new string.
- Find the string "LITTLE LAMB" in the concatenated string and move it to another string.
- Replace "LAMB" with "TOFU" in the concatenated string.
- Replace "LITTLE" with "BIG" in the concatenated string.

Here is a program that does each of these:

```
01  Point-1                      PIC S9(4) BINARY.
01  No-Moved                     PIC S9(4) BINARY.
01  Point-3                      PIC S9(4) BINARY.
01  Point-4                      PIC S9(4) BINARY.
01  String-1                     PIC X(23) VALUE
                                 "MARY HAD A LITTLE LAMB.".
01  String-2                     PIC X(29) VALUE
                                 "ITS FLEECE WAS WHITE AS SNOW.".
01  String-3                     PIC X(55).
01  String-4                     PIC X(55).
01  String-5                     PIC X(55).
    □  □  □
PROCEDURE DIVISION.
A00-Begin.
***************************************************************************
* See if String-1 contains "LAMB"                                        *
***************************************************************************
    MOVE ZERO TO Point-1
    INSPECT String-1 TALLYING Point-1 FOR ALL "LAMB"
```
[INSPECT adds 1 to *Point-1* because *String-1* contains one instance of "LAMB".]
```
***************************************************************************
*  Concatenate String-1 and String-2 into String-3.                     *
***************************************************************************
    MOVE SPACES TO String-3
```
[Clean out *String-3* before concatenating the strings into it.]
```
    MOVE 1 TO Point-1
```
[*Point-1* will point to where to copy the concatenated strings into *String-3*.]
```
    STRING String-1 DELIMITED "." INTO String-3 POINTER Point-1
```
[Get everything up to the period in *String-1*. STRING moves "MARY HAD A LITTLE LAMB" to *String-3* and adds 22 to *Point-1* so that it contains 23.]
```
    STRING ".  " DELIMITED SIZE INTO String-3 POINTER Point-1
```
[Concatenate". " to retain the period and two spaces following it. *String-3* now contains "MARY HAD A LITTLE LAMB. ", and *Point-1* contains 26.]
```
    STRING String-2 DELIMITED "." INTO String-3 POINTER Point-1
```
[Concatenate everything up the period in *String-2* to the end of *String-3*. *String-3* now contains "MARY HAD A LITTLE LAMB. ITS FLEECE WAS WHITE AS SNOW", and *Point-1* contains 54.]
```
    STRING "." DELIMITED SIZE INTO String-3 POINTER Point-1
```
[Stick a period on the end of *String-3*. *String-3* now contains "MARY HAD A LITTLE LAMB. ITS FLEECE WAS WHITE AS SNOW." *Point-1* now contains 55.]
```
***************************************************************************
*  FIND string "LITTLE LAMB" and move it to String-4.                   *
***************************************************************************
    MOVE SPACES TO String-4
```
[Clear out *String-4* before moving "LITTLE LAMB" to it.]
```
    MOVE 1 TO Point-3
```
[*Point-3* points to where "LITTLE LAMB" is in *String-3*.]
```
    STRING String-3 DELIMITED "LITTLE LAMB" INTO String-5
       POINTER Point-3
```

[It doesn't matter what goes into *String-5*. It is only important to know where "LITTLE LAMB" is in *String-3*. *Point-3* contains 12 and points to it.]

```
IF Point-3 > 1
    THEN MOVE String-3(Point-3:FUNCTION LENGTH("LITTLE LAMB"))
            TO String-4
```
["LITTLE LAMB" is found and moved to *String-4*.]
```
    END-IF
*******************************************************************
* Replace "LAMB" with "TOFU".                                    *
*******************************************************************
    INSPECT String-3 REPLACING ALL "LAMB" BY "TOFU"
```
[The INSPECT statement does this very simply.]
```
*******************************************************************
* Replace "LITTLE" with "BIG" and store in String-4.            *
*******************************************************************
    MOVE SPACES TO String-4            [Clear out String-4 before copying into it.]
    MOVE 1 TO Point-3                  [Point-3 will point to where the search begins in
                                        String-3.]
    MOVE 1 TO Point-4                  [Point-4 will point where to move the concate-
                                        nated characters into String-4.]
PERFORM WITH TEST AFTER UNTIL Point-3 > LENGTH OF String-3
```
[Continue until beyond the end of string *String-3*.]
```
    UNSTRING String-3 DELIMITED "LITTLE" INTO String-5
      COUNT No-Moved
```
[*No-Moved* counts how many characters were stored into *String-5*.]
```
      POINTER Point-3
```
[*Point-3* points the starting character in *String-3* to examine.]
```
    ON OVERFLOW
```
[This is executed if "LITTLE" is found in *String-3*. *String-5* contains everything from where the search started, up to but not including "LITTLE". *No-Moved* contains the number of characters moved to *String-5*.]
```
      MOVE String-5(1:No-Moved) TO
          String-4(Point-4:No-Moved)
```
[Move these characters to the end of *String-4*.]
```
    ADD No-Moved TO Point-4
```
[Bump *Point-4* up by the number of characters concatenated.]
```
    STRING "BIG" DELIMITED SIZE INTO String-4
        POINTER Point-4
    END-STRING
```
[Concatenate "BIG" to the end of *String-4* and bump *Point-4* up by 3 for the three characters.]
```
    NOT ON OVERFLOW
```
[Here when no "LITTLE" found. All the characters from the starting point to the end of *String-3* are moved to *String-5*. *No-Moved* contains the number of characters moved.]
```
    IF No-Moved > ZERO THEN
        MOVE String-5(1:No-Moved) TO
            String-4(Point-4:No-Moved)
```
[If any characters were moved to *String-5*, concatenate them to the end of *String-4*.]

```
                              ADD No-Moved TO Point-4
                    [This is not really needed, but Point-4 is updated anyway.]
              END-IF
          END-UNSTRING
      END-PERFORM
      [String-4 now contains "MARY HAD A BIG TOFU. ITS FLEECE WAS WHITE AS
      SNOW.".]
      GOBACK.
```

22.3 CHARACTER MANIPULATION

Sometimes Used

COBOL variable-length character strings are defined as a table of characters with an OCCURS DEPENDING ON phrase. The OCCURS DEPENDING ON form allows the INSPECT, STRING, and UNSTRING statements to operate on the current length of the character string.

```
01  S-A-Def.
    05  S-A-L                   PIC 9(9) BINARY.
    05  S-A.
        10  S-A-Item            OCCURS 1 TO 30 TIMES
                                DEPENDING ON S-A-L
                                PIC X.
```

You can also treat any character string as a variable-length character string by defining a numeric data item for the string that contains the string length.

```
01  S-B                         PIC X(12).
01  S-B-L                       PIC 9(9) BINARY.
```

When strings in this form are used in the INSPECT, STRING, and UNSTRING statements, use reference modification in the statement to identify the substring.

```
    INSPECT S-B(1:S-B-L) …
```

The next several examples all operate on character strings and use the following data items:

```
01  S-A-Def.
    05  S-A-L                   PIC 9(9) BINARY.
    05  S-A.
        10  S-A-Item            OCCURS 1 TO 30 TIMES
                                DEPENDING ON S-A-L
                                PIC X.
01  S-B                         PIC X(12).
01  S-B-L                       PIC 9(9) BINARY.
```

```
01   T-Num                         PIC 9(9) BINARY.
01   T-Char                        PIC X(30).
```

Assume for the examples that the following statements have initialized the data items.

```
MOVE 12 TO S-A-L
COMPUTE S-B-L = FUNCTION LENGTH(S-B)
```
[To generalize, the LENGTH intrinsic function is used rather than coding 12 as the length. Where a function reference can't be used, such as the FROM clause of PER-FORM, *S-B-L* will be used.]
```
MOVE "   4567890  " TO S-A, S-B
```
[Both *S-A* and *S-B* contain "bbb4567890bb".]

22.3.1 Null-Terminated Character Strings

Although COBOL does not directly support the null-terminated character strings found in C/C++ and Java, you can operate on them with EXAMINE, STRING, and UNSTRING. Suppose that we wanted to store the characters "What time is it?" in the identifier *S-B* previously defined. We could use STRING to move the data into it and store a null (X"00") as the terminator.

```
STRING "What time is it?" DELIMITED SIZE
       X"00" DELIMITED SIZE INTO S-B
```

In C/C++ notation, *S-B* contains "What time is it?\n". We could then use INSPECT to find out how many characters *S-B* contains.

```
COMPUTE S-B-L = 0
INSPECT S-B TALLYING S-B-L FOR CHARACTERS BEFORE X"00"
```

S-B-L now contains the length of the string, 16. We could concatenate "It is 10:45." to *S-B* as follows:

```
MOVE "  It is 10:45." TO S-B(S-B-L + 1:)
MOVE X"00" TO
    S-B(S-B-L + 1 + FUNCTION LENGTH("  It is 10:45."):)
```

Note that you cannot code the following because the identifier named in the INTO phrase cannot be reference-modified.

```
STRING "  It is 10:45." DELIMITED SIZE
       X"00" DELIMITED SIZE
       INTO S-B(S-B-L + 1:)      <==Error. Can't reference-modify.
```

UNSTRING can retrieve the string from *S-B*.

```
UNSTRING S-B DELIMITED X"00" INTO Other-Data
```

IBM and Micro Focus COBOL let you define a nonnumeric literal as a null-terminated string: *Z"string"*

```
01  A-String      PIC X(10) VALUE Z"ABC".
```

A-String would contain "ABC\n", where \n represents the null character. LENGTH OF *A-String* would return 3 as the length of the string because it doesn't count the null in determining the length of such null-terminated strings.

22.3.2 Find First Nonblank Character in String

Here is how to find the first nonblank character position in a string and store the position in *T-Num*. ZEROS are stored in *T-Num* if there is no nonblank character. The variable-length character string and *T-Num* are defined as follows. (It works the same for a fixed-length character string.)

```
MOVE 1 TO T-Num
INSPECT S-A TALLYING T-Num FOR LEADING SPACES
IF T-Num > S-A-L                    [Set to zero if all blanks.]
    THEM MOVE ZERO TO T-Num
END-IF                              [T-Num contains 4.]
```

Rather than using the INSPECT statement, you could also use a PERFORM VARYING statement to look at the characters one at a time to find the first nonblank character. This illustrates how PERFORM VARYING can operate on character strings. The example uses a fixed-length character string, but it works the same for a variable-length string.

```
PERFORM WITH TEST BEFORE
        VARYING T-Num FROM 1 BY 1
        UNTIL S-B(T-Num:1) NOT = SPACE OR
            T-Num > FUNCTION LENGTH(S-B)
END-PERFORM
IF T-Num > FUNCTION LENGTH(S-B)          [Set to zero if all blanks.]
    THEN MOVE ZERO TO T-Num
END-IF                              [T-Num contains 4.]
```

22.3.3 Find Rightmost Nonblank Character in String

To find the rightmost nonblank character position in a string, use the PERFORM to search the string from right to left.

```
PERFORM WITH TEST BEFORE
        VARYING T-Num FROM S-B-L BY -1
        UNTIL S-B(T-Num:1) NOT = SPACE OR T-Num = ZERO
END-PERFORM                         [T-Num contains 10.]
```

22.3.4   Left-Justify String

To left-justify a string, find the first nonblank character and move the substring starting there to temporary storage. Then move this result back.

```
MOVE 1 TO T-Num
INSPECT S-B TALLYING T-Num FOR LEADING SPACES
    [INSPECT stores 4 in T-Num, the position of the first nonblank character in S-B.]
IF T-Num > 1 AND <= FUNCTION LENGTH(S-B)          [Account for a null string.]
    THEN MOVE S-B (T-Num:) TO T-Char
          MOVE T-Char TO S-B
END-IF                        [S-B contains "4567890bbbbb".]
```

22.3.5   Right-Justify String

To right-justify characters, search from right to left for the first nonblank character. Then move the string to temporary storage so that this rightmost character becomes the rightmost character in the target string.

```
PERFORM WITH TEST BEFORE
        VARYING T-Num FROM S-B-L BY -1
UNTIL S-B(T-Num:1) NOT = SPACE OR T-Num = ZERO
END-PERFORM
    [T-Num now contains 10, the rightmost nonblank character position in S-B.]
IF T-Num > ZERO AND < S-B-L
    [Leave it alone if it contains all spaces.]
    THEN MOVE SPACES TO T-Char
    [Otherwise, clear out T-Char to contain rightmost characters.]
        MOVE S-B TO T-Char(S-B-L - T-Num + 1:)
    [Move S-B to T-Char, starting in byte 12 − 10 + 1 = 3. T-Char contains
    "bbbbb4567890".]
        MOVE T-Char TO S-B
END-IF                        [S-B contains "bbbbb4567890".]
```

22.3.6   Create Substring of Leftmost Characters

The next example moves the five leftmost characters of S-B to T-Char. T-Char will contain "bbb45".

```
MOVE S-B(1:5) TO T-Char    [T-Char contains "bbb45".]
```

22.3.7   Create Substring of Rightmost Characters

This example moves the four rightmost characters of S-B to T-Char. T-Char will contain "90bb".

```
MOVE 4 TO T-Num                [Number of rightmost characters wanted.]
MOVE S-B(FUNCTION LENGTH(S-B) - T-Num + 1:T-Num) TO T-Char
    [Starting in byte 12 − 4 + 1 = 9, 4 bytes are moved to T-Char. T-Char contains
    "90bb".]
```

22.3.8   Concatenate Characters to End of a Substring

This example concatenates the characters "THE" to the end of the six rightmost bytes of the string *S-B* ("7890bb") and stores the results in *T-Char*, which will contain "7890bbTHE".

```
MOVE 6 TO T-Num     [Number of rightmost bytes wanted.]
MOVE S-B(FUNCTION LENGTH(S-B) - T-Num + 1:) TO T-Char
    [Starting in byte 12 – 6 + 1 = 7, 6 bytes are moved to T-Char. It contains "7890bb".]
MOVE "THE" TO T-Char(T-Num + 1:)
    ["THE" is moved to bytes 7 to 9 of S-B. It contains "7890bbTHE".]
```

22.3.9   Find First Instance of a Character in a String

Here the *S-B* string is searched to get the position of the first "8", which is stored in *T-Num*. Zero is stored if there is no "8".

```
MOVE 1 TO T-Num
INSPECT S-B TALLYING T-Num FOR CHARACTERS BEFORE "8"
IF T-Num > FUNCTION LENGTH(S-B)
    THEN MOVE ZEROS TO T-Num
END-IF     [T-Num contains 8.]
```

22.3.10   Find First String in Another String

This is the same as the previous example, but a search is made for the characters "789".

```
MOVE 1 TO T-Num
INSPECT S-B TALLYING T-Num FOR CHARACTERS BEFORE "THE"
IF T-Num > FUNCTION LENGTH(S-B)
    THEN MOVE ZEROS TO T-Num
END-IF     [T-Num contains 7.]
```

22.3.11   Convert Characters to Upper- and Lowercase

The UPPER-CASE and LOWER-CASE intrinsic functions described in Chapter 21 convert to upper- and lowercase. The following converts the characters in *S-B*.

```
MOVE "AZ3THe 89Zzz" TO S-B
MOVE FUNCTION LOWER-CASE(S-B) TO T-Char
    [T-Char contains "az3the 89zzz".]
MOVE FUNCTION UPPER-CASE(T-Char) TO S-B
    [S-B contains "AZ3THE 89ZZZ".]
```

EXERCISES

1. Define an identifier named *Titles* containing 200 characters. Write the statements necessary to count the occurrences of the character strings "ABCD" and "EFG" in *Titles*.

2. Assume that you have read a line into an identifier named *Input-Rec.* The line contains integers enclosed between slashes, and the last number in the input is terminated by two slashes. The maximum integer is five digits, and the numbers are unsigned. A typical line would be as follows:

   /335/21/4/12562/1956//

   Write the statements necessary to retrieve each number from the line and display its value.

3. Define three identifiers named *Monday, Tuesday,* and *Wednesday* containing 10 characters each. Initialize each identifier with the appropriate name of the day. Then define an identifier named *Week* containing 30 characters. Write the statements to concatenate the three identifiers and store them in *Week*.

4. Define an identifier named *Maximum* containing seven characters. Assume that the identifier contains characters representing numbers such as −2, +6.9, −43.651, 7, .256426, and 7852390. Write the statements necessary to edit the number into proper COBOL form, and store it in an identifier defined as PIC S9(7)V9(7) PACKED-DECIMAL.

5. Assume that an identifier containing 200 characters contains English text. Change all instances of the abbreviations "MISS" or "MRS." to "bMS.". (Make sure that words such as "MISSISSIPPI" do not get changed.)

6. Do the same as in the preceding exercise, but change "MISS" or "MRS." to "MS.". Pad the shortened string with blanks.

CHAPTER 23

SORTING

Sorting consists of arranging items in ascending or descending order. Most business transactions are in some sort sequence. You should not skip this chapter.

23.1 SORT CONCEPTS

Essential

Typically, a sequential file must be sorted into some order for updating or reporting. For example, a personnel file may be sorted in descending order on age, then in descending order on salary within age, and then in ascending order on name within salary. The sort is performed on three items, termed *sort keys,* within each record: age, salary, and name. Table 23.1 shows how records in such a file would be sorted.

Sorting can be deceptively complex. For example, it should not be hard to sort names in a personnel file into alphabetic order—as long as you remember to sort on the last name first and then on the first name or initials. Then, it is customary to sort names such as O'Brian as if they were spelled OBRIAN. Also, names that begin with Mc, such as McDonald, should sort after Ma. Thus, something as sim-

TABLE 23.1 Sort Order of Records

Before Sorting			After Sorting		
Name	Salary	Age	Name	Salary	Age
ABLE	19,000	65	JONES	20,000	65
BAKER	19,000	65	ABLE	19,000	65
JONES	20,000	65	BAKER	19,000	65
NOBEL	25,000	50	SMITH	30,000	50
SMITH	30,000	50	NOBEL	25,000	50
WATTS	21,000	50	WATTS	21,000	50

ple as sorting names into alphabetic order does present problems. The usual solution is to carry the name twice in the file, once as it is (O'BRIAN), and once as it is to act in a sort (OBRIAN).

Perhaps the most common error in sorting is to confuse the sort order. For example, if a file is sorted on state and city, one may try to use it to produce a report by cities. After all, the file was sorted on cities. But this is in error, because the file is in sort by cities within state, not by cities. Thus, all the cities for Alabama will come first, then all the cities for Alaska. So to produce a report by cities, the file must be sorted again on just cities.

23.1.1 Methods of Sorting

There are three methods of sorting for COBOL programs: the COBOL SORT verb, an external sort, and writing your own sort. You should never have to write your own sort. (Should you wish to, an example is provided on the Web site in the answer to problem 7 for this chapter.) The external sort, invoked as a separate job step in OS/390, is not a part of COBOL but a part of the operating system. It is simpler than the COBOL sort, because you don't need to write a COBOL program to invoke it, and it is more efficient. You can also change an external sort without recompiling the program. The external sort for OS/390 is described later in this chapter. The COBOL sort, invoked by the SORT statement, is most useful in sorting an internal table or in sorting a file generated within a program. It is also useful when the records to be sorted must be selected or manipulated before being sorted or if only a single program is to read the sorted file.

23.1.2 Year-2000 Help

The external sort—either DFSORT, an IBM product; SyncSort, a Syncsort, Inc., product; or CA-SORT, a Computer Association International product—may be used. These sorts can sort four-digit years packed into two-digit storage and convert two-digit years internally for the sort into four-digit years using a fixed or moving 100-year window to determine the century. The sort products also have control statements to let you use these features when the sort is invoked with the COBOL SORT statement.

You can also use a sort input and output procedure to pack, unpack, and expand two-digit years to four digits by using the sort input and output procedures. An example of this is given later in this chapter.

23.2 SIMPLE SORT

Essential

A simple sort consists of sorting an input file to produce a sorted output file. You specify the input and output files with SELECT and FD entries. In addition, you specify the name of a sort file with a SELECT clause. Then you must write a Sort Definition (SD) entry to describe the records to be sorted and establish their sort keys. The SELECT and SD entries describing the sort file do not define a physical file. They just provide a way of describing the fields within the record of the file to be sorted. You can have several sort files within a program, several input files for each sort, and several output files.

You must also write SELECT clauses and FD entries to describe the input file you want to sort and the output file to write:

```
FILE-CONTROL.
    SELECT sort-file ASSIGN TO SORTWK.
    SELECT sort-in ASSIGN TO ddin.
    SELECT sort-out ASSIGN TO ddout.
DATA DIVISION.
FILE SECTION.
SD  sort-file.
01  record-description.
    05  data-item …
```
[The *record-description* describes the records being sorted. The SORT statement names *data-items* in the *record-description* upon which to sort.]
```
FD  sort-in.
01  record-description.
    05  data-item …
```
[You must write an FD for the input and output files as you would any other file. The SD and the FD for the input and output files describe the same records, and the record descriptions must have compatible record lengths.]
```
FD  sort-out.
01  record-description.
    05  data-item …
```

You invoke the sort in the Procedure Division by the SORT statement.

```
SORT sort-file
    ASCENDING
    DESCENDING
ON _____ KEY key, key, …, key
    ASCENDING
    DESCENDING
ON _____ KEY, key, key, …, key
  .     .    .     .     .    .
    USING sort-in, sort-in, …, sort-in
    GIVING sort-out
```

- The *sort-file* is the name in an SD entry describing the records to be sorted.
- The ON ASCENDING or DESCENDING specifies an ascending or descending order of the sort *keys*. List the *keys* from left to right in decreasing order of significance. You can write several ON phrases, placing them in decreasing order of significance in the sort.

- The *key* is one or more data items in the *record-description* of the *sort-file* on which the file is to be sorted, listed from left to right in decreasing order of significance. For variable-length records, the keys must be in the fixed portion of the record.
- The USING specifies the input file to sort. You can specify several *sort-in* files in the USING phrase.
- The GIVING specifies the output file into which the sorted output is to be written. Neither *sort-in* nor *sort-out* may be open when the sort is invoked. SORT automatically opens and closes them.

In Mainframe OS/390 COBOL, you must include the following DD statements to the execution step of the job.

```
//GO.ddin      DD ...
//GO.ddout     DD ...
//GO.SYSOUT    DD SYSOUT=A
//GO.SORTLIB   DD DSN=SYS1.SORTLIB,DISP=SHR
```

The following example sorts the *File-I* input file on ascending order on *Part-X* and *Size-X*, on descending order on *Name-X*, and on ascending order on *Cost-X*. The sorted records are written into *File-O:*

```
SORT Sort-A
   ON ASCENDING KEY Part-X, Size-X
   ON DESCENDING KEY Name-X
   ON ASCENDING KEY Cost-X
   USING File-I
   GIVING File-O
```

Records in the input file with duplicate keys are sorted together, but not necessarily in the same order in which they are read. To preserve the order in which they are read, you can add the WITH DUPLICATES phrase.

```
WITH DUPLICATES IN ORDER
```

You code it as follows:

```
SORT sort-file
   ON ...
   WITH DUPLICATES
   USING sort-in
   GIVING sort-out
```

The next example sorts an input file on *Sort-Age* in descending order and on *Sort-Name* in ascending order.

```
FILE-CONTROL.
    SELECT Sort-It ASSIGN TO SORTWK.
    SELECT File-I ASSIGN TO SORTIN.
    SELECT File-O ASSIGN TO SORTOUT.
FILE SECTION.
SD  Sort-It.
01  Sort-Record.
    05  Sort-Name                 PIC X(25).
    05  Sort-Age                  PIC S9(3)V99 PACKED-DECIMAL.
    05  FILLER                    PIC X(30).
FD  File-I …
FD  File-O …
PROCEDURE DIVISION.
A00-Begin.
    SORT Sort-It
       ON DESCENDING KEY Sort-Age
       ON ASCENDING KEY Sort-Name
       USING File-I
       GIVING File-O
```

The record descriptions for the SD and the FDs describing the input and output files must be compatible; that is, they must have compatible record lengths.

23.3 SORT INPUT PROCEDURE

Essential

You can write an input procedure to supply records to the sort by coding an INPUT PROCEDURE phrase in place of the USING phrase of the SORT statement. This lets you read the records from a file, selecting specific records or modifying them before the sort. You can also obtain them from an internal table or from data generated within the program. The input procedure is a normal procedure, such as one written for a PERFORM statement. You can only invoke the input procedure with the SORT statement. A RELEASE statement within the procedure, usually executed within a loop, passes a record to the sort each time it executes.

```
    SORT sort-file
       ON …
       INPUT PROCEDURE IS paragraph-name
       [You can also specify paragraph-name-1 THRU paragraph-name-2. In addition,
        you can specify a section name. Legacy systems required this.]
       GIVING sort-out
    □  □  □
paragraph-name.
    statements to create each record
    RELEASE record-description FROM variable
       [The RELEASE statement passes each record to the sort.]
    perhaps more statements
    .
**** EXIT
```

The sort will invoke the paragraph once to receive all the records. You execute the RELEASE statement to pass each record to the sort. After the last record has been passed, exit the procedure to allow the sort to proceed. You code the RELEASE statement as follows:

> *RELEASE* record-description FROM *identifier*

The *record-description* is the record description in the record area specified for the *sort-file* in the SD entry. The *identifier* is the record or data item containing the data to be passed to the sort. (You can omit the FROM phrase if you move the data directly to the *record-description* in the record area of the *sort-file*.)

The following example sorts an internal table:

```
FILE SECTION.
SD   Sort-A.
01   Sort-Record.
     05   Sort-Age               PIC S9(3)V99 PACKED-DECIMAL.
     05   Sort-Name              PIC X(25).
WORKING-STORAGE SECTION.
01   Table-Def.
     05   Table-A                OCCURS 100 TIMES
                                 INDEXED BY Table-X.
          10   Table-Age         PIC S9(3)V99 PACKED-DECIMAL.
          10   Table-Name        PIC X(25).
 □ □ □
     SORT Sort-A
       ON ASCENDING KEY Sort-Name
       INPUT PROCEDURE IS P20-Sort-Input
       GIVING File-O
 □ □ □
P20-Sort-Input.
     PERFORM VARYING Table-X FROM 1 BY 1 UNTIL Table-X > 100
        RELEASE Sort-Record FROM Table-A(Table-X)
     END-PERFORM
     .
**** EXIT
```

23.4   SORT OUTPUT PROCEDURE

Sometimes Used

COBOL also lets you write a procedure to receive the sorted records from the sort, rather than having the sort write them out into a file. You can then modify the sorted records, select them before you write them, or store them in an internal table. Specify the output procedure in the SORT statement by coding an OUTPUT PROCEDURE phrase in place of the GIVING phrase. A RETURN statement, usually executed inside a loop, returns the next sorted record each time it executes.

```
           SORT sort-name
              ON ...
              USING sort-in
              OUTPUT PROCEDURE IS paragraph-name
              [You can also specify paragraph-name-1 THRU paragraph-name-2. In addition,
              you can specify a section name. Legacy systems required this.]
           □    □    □
       paragraph-name.
           statements to prepare to receive sorted records
           RETURN sort-file RECORD INTO identifier
              [The RETURN statement retrieves each sorted record.]
             AT END imperative-statements
             NOT AT END imperative-statements
           END-RETURN
           more statements
              .
       **** EXIT
```

COBOL invokes the output procedure only once when the sorting is completed. You execute the RETURN statement to receive each record. The NOT AT END is optional.

```
           RETURN sort-file RECORD INTO identifier
             AT END imperative-statements
             [Executed when there are no more statements to return.]
             NOT AT END imperative-statements
             [Executed when a record is returned.]
           END-RETURN
```

The *sort-file* is specified in the record area for an SD entry. The *identifier* is a record or data item into which the sorted record is to be moved. You can omit the INTO phrase so that the data is available only in the *record-description* in the record area of the *sort-file*.

Terminate the output procedure by exiting the section, and control returns to the next executable statement following the SORT. (To stop passing records, even if more remain to be passed, simply exit the procedure.) The following example stores sorted output into the *Table-A* used in the previous example:

```
           SORT Sort-A
              ON ASCENDING KEY Sort-Name
              USING File-I
              OUTPUT PROCEDURE IS P60-Get-Record
           □    □    □
       P60-Get-Record.
           PERFORM VARYING Table-X FROM 1 BY 1 UNTIL Table-X > 100
             RETURN Sort-A INTO Table-A(Table-X)
                AT END DISPLAY "ERROR—NO RECORDS SORTED."
                     SET Table-X TO 100
                     [Exit the procedure when the AT END is reached.]
```

```
        END-RETURN
        END-PERFORM
              .
**** EXIT
```

23.5   SORT INPUT AND OUTPUT PROCEDURES: SORTING DATES WITH TWO-DIGIT YEARS

Essential

You can supply both an input and output procedure for the sort by coding both the INPUT and OUTPUT PROCEDURE phrases:

```
SORT sort-file
    ON …
    INPUT PROCEDURE IS input-paragraph-name
    OUTPUT PROCEDURE IS output-paragraph-name
```

To illustrate the use of sort input and output procedures, assume that we have a file containing a two-digit year in the date field. The record has the following description:

```
WORKING-STORAGE SECTION.
01  In-Rec.
    05  In-Data                 PIC X(30).
    05  In-Date.
        10  In-Yr               PIC 99.
        10  In-Mo               PIC 99.
        10  In-Dy               PIC 99.
    05  In-More-Data            PIC X(30).
    01  EOF-In-Flag             PIC X.
        88  EOF-In              VALUE "Y".
    01  EOF-Sort-Flag           PIC X.
        88  EOF-Sort            VALUE "Y".
```

We want to sort the year field as if it were four digits. We can use a 100-year window as described in Chapter 26 to determine the century from the year. Then we'll use an input procedure to convert the year to four digits for sorting. The output procedure will truncate the year to two digits and write out the record, so that the format of the output file is the same as the input, and the four-digit year is used internally only for sorting.

For example, if the end of the 100-year window were 1989, you would know that years 00 through 89 were years in the 1900s, and 90 through 99 were years in the 1800s. Likewise, if it were 2003, 00 through 03 would be years in the 2000s, and 04 through 99 would be years in the 1900s. Because almost no computer business applications predate 1960, the 100-year window method should be safe for them. Unless you have employees more than 99 years old, the 100-year window should work for birth dates, too.

We'll use a 100-year sliding window that is based on the current year plus some number of years, *n*. We'll get the current year, *yy,* as two digits, set *yy* + *n* as the end of the 100-year window that determines the century. For example, if *n* is 2 and the current year is 2003, the years are assumed to fall in the range 1906 through 2005. A data item named *N* is defined in Working-Storage to contain the number of years to add to the current year. We also need a data item to contain the current year.

```
01  N                       PIC S99 VALUE 2.
01  Curr-Yr                 PIC 9(4).
```

To sort the file, we define the sort record with a four-digit year as follows:

```
SD  Sort-File.
01  Sort-Rec.
    05  Sort-Data           PIC X(30).
    05  Sort-Date.
        10  Sort-Yr         PIC 9(4).
        10  Sort-Mo         PIC 99.
        10  Sort-Dy         PIC 99.
    05  Sort-More-Data      PIC X(30).
```

Then we write the SORT statement with a sort input procedure to convert the year to four digits and move the record to the sort record. An output procedure chops off the first two digits of the year and writes the record. You write the SORT statement as follows:

```
SORT Sort-File
   ON ASCENDING KEY Sort-Date
   INPUT PROCEDURE IS B10-Get-Records
   OUTPUT PROCEDURE IS C10-Write-Records
```

The input and output procedures are written as follows:

```
B10-Get-Records.
   MOVE "N" TO EOF-In-Flag
   OPEN INPUT FILE-I
   PERFORM UNTIL EOF-In
     READ File-I INTO In-Rec
       AT END SET EOF-In TO TRUE
       NOT AT END
           MOVE In-Data TO Sort-Data
           MOVE In-More-Data TO Sort-More-Data
           MOVE FUNCTION CURRENT-DATE(1:4) TO Curr-Yr
               [Get the current year.]
           MOVE In-Mo TO Sort-Mo      [Store the month and day.]
           MOVE In-Dy TO Sort-Dy
```

```
            COMPUTE Curr-Yr, Sort-Yr = Curr-Yr + N
                [Get the last year in the century window.]
            MOVE "00" TO Sort-Yr(3:2)
                [Sort-Yr contains just the century part.]
            IF In-Yr > Curr-Yr(3:2)
                [If the year we are looking at is greater than the year of the cutoff
                date, then it is last century.]
                THEN COMPUTE Sort-Yr = In-Yr + Sort-Yr - 100
                ELSE COMPUTE Sort-Yr = In-Yr + Sort-Yr
            END-IF
            RELEASE Sort-Rec
        END-READ
    END-PERFORM
    CLOSE FILE-I
    .
**** EXIT
   C10-Write-Records.
    MOVE "N" TO EOF-Sort-Flag
    OPEN OUTPUT FILE-O
    PERFORM UNTIL EOF-Sort
        RETURN Sort-File
            AT END SET EOF-Sort TO TRUE
            NOT AT END
                MOVE Sort-Data TO In-Data
                MOVE Sort-More-Data TO In-More-Data
                MOVE Sort-Yr(3:2) TO In-Yr
                    [Save only the two rightmost digits of the year.]
                MOVE Sort-Mo TO In-Mo
                MOVE Sort-Dy TO In-DY
                WRITE File-O-Rec FROM In-Rec
        END-RETURN
    END-PERFORM
    CLOSE FILE-O
    .
**** EXIT
```

Input and output procedures have many other uses. Consider the following sort problems:

A file contains more than one record type, and each type must be sorted on a key that appears in a different place in each record type.

A file contains more than one record type, and each record type is to be sorted on different sort keys into the same output file for later processing.

A variable-length record is to be sorted on a key that is in the variable portion of the record.

You can do all these items by appending a sort key to the front or end of the record. The sort keys must have the same length, and you control the sort order by placing the appropriate items in the appropriate fields of the sort key. The solution to problem 8 on the Web site gives an example of this.

23.6 SORTING INTERNAL TABLES

PROPOSED NEW ANSI STANDARD: Check Compiler to See if Implemented

Although you can sort an internal table by coding sort input and output procedures, the new ANSI standard provides a more direct way. You merely code the SORT statement as normal and name the table you want sorted rather than a sort file. You don't code an SD. The general form is:

```
SORT table-name
  ON ASCENDING/DESCENDING KEY key, key, …, key
  .   .    .    .    .   .    .    .
  ON ASCENDING/DESCENDING KEY, key, key, …, key
```

You can omit the ON phrases entirely, and COBOL uses the items described in the ASCENDING/DESCENDING KEY clause of *table-name* to sort in ascending order. If the table has no KEY clause, COBOL uses the entire length of *table-name* as the sort key. The following sorts *Table-A*:

```
WORKING-STORAGE SECTION.
01  Table-Def.
    05  Table-A                   OCCURS 100 TIMES
                                  INDEXED BY Table-X.
        10   Table-Age            PIC S9(3)V99 PACKED-DECIMAL.
        10   Table-Name           PIC X(25).
    □  □  □
        SORT Table-A ON ASCENDING KEY Table-Name
```

23.7 SORT SEQUENCE

Rarely Used

The SORT statement specifies the sort keys left to right in decreasing order of significance, and each ON phrase in decreasing order of significance:

```
SORT Sort-File
  ON ASCENDING KEY State, County
  ON DESCENDING KEY City
  ON ASCENDING KEY Precinct
  USING File-I
  GIVING File-O
```

This statement sorts states into ascending order, the counties within a state into ascending order, each city in a county into descending order, and each precinct within a city into ascending order. Numeric fields are sorted in order of their algebraic values, taking into consideration the sign. Alphanumeric fields sort from left to right, with each character compared according to the collating sequence of the character set. Table 23.2 shows the collating sequences, from low to high.

If you want a collating sequence other than that native to the computer (EBCDIC in Mainframe COBOL and ASCII in non-Mainframe COBOL), you can code the COLLATING SEQUENCE clause:

```
SORT file-name
    ON ...
    WITH DUPLICATES
    COLLATING SEQUENCE IS alphabet-name
    USING or INPUT PROCEDURE ...
    GIVING or OUTPUT PROCEDURE ...
```

The *alphabet-name* can be one of the following:

STANDARD-1 specifies the ASCII collating sequence.

NATIVE specifies the collating sequence native to the computer: EBCDIC for Mainframe COBOL and ASCII for non-Mainframe COBOL. This is the default if you omit COLLATING SEQUENCE.

EBCDIC specifies the EBCDIC collating sequence.

STANDARD-2 specifies the International Reference Version of the ISO 7-bit code defined in International Standard 646, 7-bit Coded Character Set for Information Processing Interchange.

literal specifies a collating sequence defined by the compiler writer.

You can also specify the collating sequence for a program in the PROGRAM COLLATING SEQUENCE clause of the OBJECT-COMPUTER paragraph. Coding the collating sequence there affects the entire program, including comparison operations in IF statements, condition-name conditions, and the sequence of the keys of random-access files, in addition to SORT statements. (Coding COLLATING SEQUENCE in a SORT statement overrides any PROGRAM COLLATING

TABLE 23.2   EBCDIC and ASCII Collating Sequences

EBCDIC	ASCII
Blank	blank
¢ . < (+ | & ! $ *) ; ¬ / , % _ > ? : # @ ' = "	! " # $ % & ' ( ) * + , – . /
a through z	0 through 9
A through Z	: ; < = > ? @
0 through 9	A through Z
	[\ ] ^ _ `
	a through z
	{	} ~

SEQUENCE coded in the OBJECT-COMPUTER paragraph.) The *alphabet-name* is the same as that in the SORT statement.

```
OBJECT-COMPUTER. computer-name
    PROGRAM COLLATING SEQUENCE IS alphabet-name.
```

23.8 SORT EFFICIENCY

Essential

Sorts are relatively expensive and can account for a large portion of the running cost of a system. Sorting and merging may consume 25 percent of today's computing capacity (IBM, 1995).

23.8.1 Efficiency Considerations

TIP *You may be able to dramatically reduce the cost of sorting by considering the following ideas:*

Sort with an external sort rather than with application program sort statements. The SORTD cataloged procedure is generally more efficient than a Mainframe COBOL sort.

Sort fewer records. Sort cost varies exponentially with the number of records sorted. That is, it costs more than twice as much to sort 1000 records as it does 500. You can reduce the number of records by using a sort input procedure to select records before you sort. For example, if you were working with census data and wanted to list only the names of people who live in Wyoming, you could first select the records for Wyoming and then sort. That way, you would sort only about 350,000 records rather than 200 million records.

Sort shorter records. The cost of a sort is proportional to the record length. When you select records with a sort input procedure, you can drop all the fields that you don't need to shorten the record length.

Perform a tag sort. This shortens the record length for random-access files having record keys. You create a small record containing only the random-access key needed to retrieve the record, along with the other fields of the record needed as sort keys. Then you sort these short records on the sort keys and later use the random-access key to retrieve the full records in the sequence wanted.

Reduce the number of sort keys. The cost of a sort is proportional to the number of sort keys. Perhaps you can't control the sort keys, but sometimes in the design of a record you can. Suppose you are sorting a data set on date.

If the date is stored as *ddmmyyyy*, three sort keys are needed to sort the date: *yyyy*, *mm*, and *dd*. But if you store the date in the record as *yyyymmdd*, the entire date can be treated as a single sort key to sort on date. By placing sort keys together in major to minor order and having them be the same format, you can treat several alphanumeric sort keys in a sort as if they were a single sort key.

Block big. On the IBM mainframe, large blocks reduce the amount of I/O; they reduce the CPU time required to transmit the blocks, and, properly chosen, they conserve storage space on tape or disk; another reason to let the system select the appropriate block size.

Sort data as binary or character fields. If fixed-point data contains only positive values, you can sort it as a binary or character field. CH is slightly faster than BI. If you know that packed-decimal or zoned-decimal fields contain only positive values, you can also sort them as binary or character fields. Use packed-decimal rather than zoned-decimal wherever possible.

Use the sort special registers. SORT-CORE-SIZE sets the central storage size for the sort, and the more central storage, the more efficient it is. You can also move values to the SORT-FILE-SIZE and SORT-MODE-SIZE to estimate the number of records and their size.

23.8.2 SORT Special Registers (Not in ANSI Standard)

Rarely Used

The special registers for the sort are:

SORT-CORE-SIZE sets the number of bytes of memory for the sort. It is defined as:

```
01  SORT-CORE-SIZE          PIC S9(8) BINARY VALUE ZERO.
```
The sort operates more efficiently with large amounts of central storage because it reduces the I/O.

SORT-FILE-SIZE estimates the number of records to be sorted. It is defined as:

```
01  SORT-FILE-SIZE          PIC S9(8) BINARY VALUE ZERO.
```

SORT-MODE-SIZE contains an estimate of the most frequent record length of variable-length records. It is defined as:

```
01  SORT-MODE-SIZE          PIC S9(5) BINARY VALUE ZERO.
```

SORT-CONTROL contains the *ddname* of a sort control file containing control statements to optimize the sort. (The statements do the same as the aforementioned special registers. If you specify both, the sort control file takes precedence.) The sort attempts to open the file with the *ddname* and uses any control statements it contains. You can include a DD statement with the *ddname* to point to a file containing the statements. SORT-CONTROL is defined as:

```
01  SORT-CONTROL            PIC X(8) VALUE "IGZSRTCD".
```

SORT-RETURN contains the return code for a sort. It is defined as:

```
01  SORT-RETURN           PIC S9(4) BINARY VALUE ZERO.
```

A value of 0 is successful, and a value of 16 means an unsuccessful sort.

SORT-MESSAGE specifies the *ddname* of a data set the sort program is to use in place of the SYSOUT data set. If you change this, you must include a DD statement with the *ddname* for the output. It is defined as:

```
01  SORT-MESSAGE          PIC X(8) VALUE "SYSOUT".
```

23.9 THE MERGE STATEMENT

Sometimes Used

MERGE allows several input files having identical record formats and arranged in the same sort order to be merged into a single output file in this same sort order. Merging yields the same results as if the several files were concatenated as input to a normal sort, but merging is more efficient because the input files are already in the proper sort order.

The MERGE statement is similar to the SORT statement. You must describe all input and output files as you would normal files, with SELECT and FD entries. Like the sort file, you must describe the *merge-file* with an SD entry. You write the MERGE statement as follows. The phrases are the same as for the SORT, and COLLATING SEQUENCE is optional.

```
MERGE merge-file
    ASCENDING
    DESCENDING
ON _____ KEY key, key, …, key
    ASCENDING
    DESCENDING
ON _____ KEY key, key, …, key
COLLATING SEQUENCE IS alphabet-name
USING merge-in-1, merge-in-2, …, merge-in-n
GIVING merge-out     or     OUTPUT PROCEDURE IS procedure-name
```

The *merge-file* is described in an SD entry.

The *merge-in* are two or more file names to be merged based on the order specified in the ON phrases. The files must be sequential or dynamic access mode. Records with identical keys in several files are merged in the order the files are listed in the USING phrase. The files must contain records of the same record type.

The *merge-out* names the output file to contain the merged files. Neither the *merge-in* or *merge-out* files may be open when MERGE is executed. MERGE automatically opens and closes the files named by USING and GIVING.

The *merge-in* files and the single *merge-out* file are normal files, and you must specify them with SELECT and FD entries. You can replace the GIVING phrase with the OUTPUT PROCEDURE phrase and write a procedure to receive the merged records. The output procedure must contain RETURN statements to retrieve the merged records. (No input procedure is permitted.) The SORT-CONTROL, SORT-MESSAGE, and SORT-RETURN special registers also apply to a merge.

23.10   EXTERNAL SORT

Essential—For Mainframe COBOL

External sorts are not a part of COBOL, but they are used in combination with many COBOL programs. An external sort is simpler and more convenient than a COBOL sort. You can change the sort order with a control statement, whereas a COBOL sort requires the COBOL program to be recompiled. However, if you change the sort order of a file, you must recompile the program reading it anyway. The following describes the IBM DFSORT Sort/Merge Program for the OS/390 MVS mainframe system.

You invoke OS/390 mainframe external sorts as a separate job step. The JCL is a cataloged procedure like the one following, but check with your installation, as there may be differences:

```
//stepname EXEC SORTD
//SORT.SORTIN DD DSN=input-data-set,DISP=OLD,…
    [SORTIN specifies the input data set to sort. It must be a sequential or VSAM data set.]
//SORT.SORTOUT DD DSN=output-data-set,DISP=(NEW,…
    [SORTOUT specifies the output data set to contain the sorted records. It must be a
    sequential or VSAM data set.]
//SORT.SYSIN   DD *
 SORT FIELDS=(1,4,CH,A,20,10,CH,D)
    [Code the sort statements in columns 2 through 71.]
/*
```

23.10.1   The SORT Statement

The SORT statement specifies the sort order as follows:

```
1,4,CH,A
        [Starting in character position 1, sort 4 CHaracters in Ascending sequence.]
20,10,CH,D
        [Starting in character position 20, sort 10 CHaracters in Descending sequence.]
```

The general form of the SORT statement is:

```
SORT FIELDS=(sort-key,sort-key,...sort-key)
```

The *sort-key* specifies the fields within the record to sort, their data types, and whether they are to be sorted in ascending or descending sequence. List the keys from left to right in the major to minor order in which they are to sort. The sort keys must all be within the first 4092 bytes of the record. Each sort-key has four parts: *start*, *length*, *format*, and *order*.

```
SORT FIELDS=(start,length,format,order,…)
```

The *start* specifies the starting byte position in the record. The first byte is 1. (For VB records, the first byte of data is 5.) For binary fields, specify *start* in the form *byte.bit*, where *byte* is the byte number and *bit* is the bit number within the byte. (The first bit is 0.) Hence, 4.2 indicates that the key begins in the third bit of the fourth byte. The first bit in a field is 1.0. The *length* specifies the length of the field in bytes. For binary fields, specify the *length* in the form *bytes.bits,* where *bytes* is the number of bytes and *bits* is the number of bits. Hence, 0.3 indicates that the key is 3 bits long. The *format* specifies the format of the sort field. Table 23.3 shows the formats permitted.

TABLE 23.3 Formats for Fields in Sorting

Format	Description	Signed	Length in Bytes
CH	EBCDIC character		1–4092
AQ	EBCDIC character, alternative collating sequence set by the ALTSEQ command		1–256
ZD	Zoned-decimal	Yes	1–32
PD	Packed-decimal	Yes	1–32
FI	Fixed-point	Yes	1–256
BI	Binary		1 bit to 4092 bytes
FL	Floating-point	Yes	1–256
CSF or FS	Signed numeric-character with optional leading floating sign	Yes	
CSL or LS	Numeric-character, leading separate sign	Yes	2–256
CST or TS	Numeric-character, trailing separate sign	Yes	2–256
CLO or OL	Numeric-character, leading overpunch sign	Yes	1–256
CTO or OT	Numeric-character, trailing overpunch sign	Yes	1–256
AC	ASCII character (Sequences EBCDIC using ASCII collating sequence)		1–256
ASL	ASCII numeric character, leading separate sign	Yes	2–256
AST	ASCII numeric character, trailing separate sign	Yes	2–256
D1	User-defined data type		1–4092

The *order* specifies the sequence:

A Ascending

D Descending

The following example sorts records into ascending sequence with two sort keys:

```
SORT FIELDS=(4,6,ZD,A,12,3,PD,D)
```

The sort order is:

1. 4,6,ZD,A—Bytes 4 to 9 as zoned-decimal in ascending sequence.
2. 12,3,PD,D—Bytes 12 to 14 as packed-decimal in descending sequence.

Code sort statements in columns 2 through 71. To continue a sort statement, break it after a comma but before column 71, and continue somewhere in columns 2 to 16 of the following line:

```
SORT FIELDS=(4,6,CH,A,12,3,CH,D)
             12,3,CH,D)
```

23.10.2 The MERGE Statement

Sometimes Used

The JCL for a merge is identical to that for a sort, except that instead of one //SORTIN DD statement describing the input, there are up to 16 //SORTINnn DD statements describing the data sets to merge. The data sets must have identical formats and be in the same sort sequence. You write a merge as:

```
// EXEC SORTD
//SORTIN01 DD …
//SORTIN02 DD …
   .      .     .
//SORTIN16 DD …
//SORTOUT  DD …                    [The system writes the output to this data set.]
//SYSIN    DD *
 MERGE FIELDS=(sort-key,sort-key,...sort-key)
/*
```

The //SORTINnn DD statements (maximum of 16) name the input data sets to merge and tell how many data sets are to be merged. The nn in the //SORTINnn DD statements must begin with 01 and continue in increasing, consecutive order: (01, 02, 03, but not 01, 03, 04). Other than coding MERGE in place of SORT, the MERGE statement is identical to the SORT statement.

23.10.3 Year-2000 Sort Fields

DFSORT also has an added feature to sort the year, the month, or the day when the date is stored as a single packed-decimal number or as a 2-byte character or zoned-decimal field. In addition, you can specify a fixed or sliding 100-year window to expand the two-digit year to four digits for the sort. The windowing technique is described fully in Chapter 26. Table 23.4 shows the new format fields for sorting dates.

Packed-decimal numbers are stored two digits per byte, with the sign in the rightmost half-byte as described in Chapter 28. When the date is stored as a single packed-decimal number, such as *yymmdd, yyddd, mmddyyyy,* and so on, the new formats give you the ability to sort portions of a packed-decimal number. They also allow two-digit years to be converted internally to four digits for the sort, using the windowing technique described fully in Chapter 26. The data in the file is not changed. You specify the windowing with a Y2PAST option. If you don't specify the Y2PAST option, an installation-defined value is used. The details of the new formats are as follows.

TABLE 23.4 Formats for Fields in Sorting Dates

Format	Description	Signed	Length in Bytes
Y2C, Y2Z	Two-digit, two-byte character or zoned-decimal year in form *yy.* Expanded to four digits for sort. Y2C and Y2Z are interchangeable.	No	2
Y2S	Same as Y2C and Y2Z, except blanks, binary zeros, and binary ones are considered to be special indicators rather than years. Expanded to four digits for the sort.	No	2
Y2B	Two-digit, one-byte binary year in the form *yy* as a binary number. Expanded to four digits for the sort.	No	1
Y2D	Two-digit, one-byte packed-decimal year in the form *yy.* Expanded to four digits for the sort.	No	1
Y2P	Two-digit, two-byte packed-decimal year in form *yy.* Expanded to four digits for the sort.	No	2
PD0	Signed packed-decimal number with first and last digit ignored. Used for sorting *mm, dd, ddd,* etc.	Yes	2–8

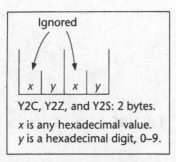

FIGURE 23.1 Data for Y2C, Y2Z, and Y2S formats.

Character and Zoned-Decimal Years—Expanded to Four Digits for the Sort

Y2C, Y2Z, and Y2S sort dates that contain two digits (*yy*) and occupy two bytes in either character or zoned-decimal form as shown in Figure 23.1. Y2C and Y2Z treat blanks (X'4040') and binary zeros (X'0000') as year values of 00 for the sort. Y2S treats blanks, X'0000', and X'FFFF' as special indicators and sorts them according to their hexadecimal values: X'0000' sorts first, then blanks, then the years, and X'FFFF' sorts last.

Binary Years—Expanded to Four Digits for the Sort

Y2B is a two-digit year (*yy*) stored as a binary number in a single byte, as shown in Figure 23.2. (A byte can contain binary value of 0–255.) Note that a code for a 2-byte binary year is not needed, because it can contain a four-digit year. If it contained only a two-digit year, the year would be in the rightmost byte, and you could sort it with Y2B.

Packed-Decimal Years—Expanded to Four Digits for the Sort

Y2D is a two-digit, 1-byte packed-decimal number representing a year in the form *yy*, as shown in Figure 23.3. It is used to specify the *yy* portion of a date within a packed-decimal number contained in a single byte.

Y2P, similar to Y2D, is also a two-digit, packed-decimal number representing a year in the form *yy*. However, it occupies two bytes as shown in Figure 23.4. It is used to specify the *yy* portion of a date within a packed-decimal number in which the *yy* crosses a byte boundary.

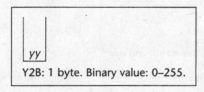

FIGURE 23.2 Data for Y2B format.

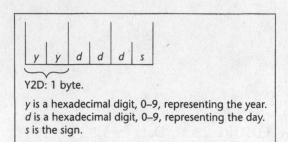

FIGURE 23.3 Data for Y2D format.

Packed-Decimal Months and Days—Not Expanded to Four Digits for the Sort

PD0 represents a 2- to 8-byte packed-decimal number representing a month or day in the form *mm*, *dd*, *ddd*, or whatever, in which the first digit and sign are ignored, as shown in Figure 23.5.

The Y2PAST Option

The Y2PAST option is applied to the Y2B, Y2C, Y2D, Y2P, Y2S, and Y2Z formats. If you don't specify the Y2PAST option for these fields, DFSORT uses an installation-supplied value. Y2PAST specifies either a fixed or sliding window, depending on the value you set. Values of 1000 through 3000 specify a fixed window. Note that with DFSORT, you specify the starting year of the 100-year window.

```
Y2PAST=1000 through 3000        [Denotes fixed window.]
Y2PAST=1960                     [The 100-year window is 1960 through 2059.]
```

Values of 0 through 100 specify a sliding window. The value is the number of years to subtract from the current year to form the starting year of the sliding window.

```
Y2PAST=0 through 100            [Denotes sliding window.]
Y2PAST=80
```
[If the current year were 1999, the 100-year window would be 1919 through 2018.]

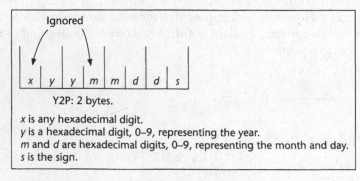

FIGURE 23.4 Data for Y2P format.

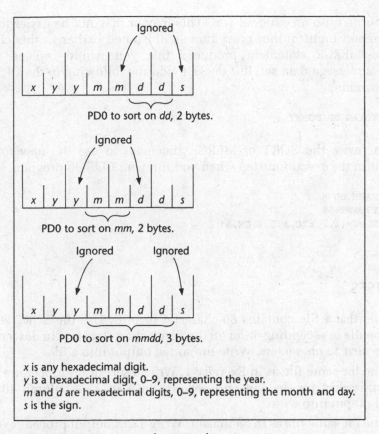

x is any hexadecimal digit.
y is a hexadecimal digit, 0–9, representing the year.
m and d are hexadecimal digits, 0–9, representing the month and day.
s is the sign.

FIGURE 23.5 Data for PD0 format.

You code Y2PAST on the OPTION statement as follows:

```
OPTION Y2PAST=98
SORT FIELDS=(1,2,Y2C,A,3,4,CH,A)
```

With the previous two statements, if you had the following date field in *yym-mdd* format in columns 1 through 6, it would sort as shown, assuming 1999 as the current year. The 100-year window is 1901 through 2000.

```
Appears in the file as:      Sorts as if it were coded as:
011221                       19011221
990604                       19990604
000426                       20000426
```

Using the New Sort Fields in a COBOL Sort

When you code a SORT or MERGE statement for Mainframe COBOL, the compiler generates a DFSORT SORT or MERGE statement. You can override this generated statement and supply your own to use the new sort fields. You would only do this if you couldn't use an external sort. This may or may not be easier than writing your own sort input/output procedure as illustrated earlier in this chapter. The SORT or MERGE statement produced that you would replace appears in DFSORT's message data set. If it doesn't, add the following to the DFSORT cataloged procedure:

```
//GO.SORTDIAG DD DUMMY
```

Then revise the SORT or MERGE statement to use the new formats, and include it in the execution step when you run your COBOL program.

```
//GO.DFSPARM DD *
 OPTION Y2PAST=98
 SORT FIELDS=(1,2,Y2C,A,3,4,CH,A)
/*
```

EXERCISES

1. Assume that a file contains 80-character records. Use the SORT statement to sort the file in ascending order on the first 8 characters and in descending order on the next 12 characters. Write the sorted output into a file.

2. Assume the same file as in Exercise 1. Write a sort input procedure to read the file, and select for the sort only records with an X in column 40. Write the sorted output into a file.

3. Assume the same file as in Exercise 1. Write a sort output procedure to print the keys of the sorted records, but do not write the sorted output into a file; store it in an internal table.

4. Assume the same file as in Exercise 1. Write a sort input procedure to read the file, and select for the sort only records with an X in column 40. Write a sort output procedure to print the keys of the sorted records. Also, because only the sort keys are used for output, shorten the record for the sort to a 20-character record containing just the sort keys.

5. Assume that a file contains 80-character records. Sort the file on the first 3 characters so that the records come out in the order shown.

   991
   992
   999
   981
   982
   989
   891
   899

6. Assume that you are called upon to develop a set of standards for the use of the sort. Give guidelines for the use of an external sort, an internal sort, and hand-coded sorts.

7. Write your own sort. There are many techniques for internal sorts, but the *bubble sort* is the simplest and is reasonably efficient for small numbers of records. In the bubble sort, you compare the first table element to each successive element. For an ascending sort, you switch the two elements if the first element is greater than the second. This bubbles the largest value to the top of the table. You repeat this for the second through the next-to-last element until the entire table is in the desired order. Write a bubble sort in which the 1000 elements of a table named *Amount* are sorted into ascending order. The bubble sort is not recommended for large files, because the number of operations it must perform increases as the square of the number of records.

8. Two record types must sorted into ascending order on state and town, which appear in different places in each record type. Write a program to append a sort key to the record in an input procedure for the sort and strip off the sort key in an output procedure as the file is written. The record format for the input file is as follows:

```
01  Rec-A.
    05 Rec-A-Type           PIC X.
*                           "A" for Rec-A.
    05 Rec-A-State          PIC X(20).
    05 Rec-A-Town           PIC X(10).
    05 Rec-A-Remainder      PIC X(100).
01  Rec-B                   REDEFINES Rec-A.
    05 Rec-B-Type           PIC X.
*                           "B" for Rec-B.
    05 Rec-B-Town           PIC X(10).
    05 Rec-B-State          PIC X(20).
    05 Rec-B-Remainder      PIC X(100).
```

CHAPTER 24

FULL-SCREEN I/O IN PC APPLICATIONS

Micro Focus full-screen I/O has become the de facto standard for COBOL on the PC. If you are writing applications in COBOL to run only on the PC, you should read this chapter.

Essential for the PC

Micro Focus full-screen I/O is also supported in Fujitsu and other COBOL compilers and in the new ANSI standard. Full-screen I/O is text based, which means you use the DISPLAY statement to display text at row, column positions. The person at the terminal can type in predefined input fields, and the ACCEPT statement retrieves what they typed. Full-screen I/O does not include graphics, windowing, icons, mouse input, or pull-down lists, although you can program the latter.

24.1   FULL-SCREEN I/O OVERVIEW

For full-screen I/O, you describe a screen in a new Data Division section, the *Screen Section*. In describing the data item, you give the row and column at which it is to display. Most PC terminals have 25 lines and 80 columns. You describe the screen as a collection of lines and columns in a data structure and then execute the DISPLAY statement to display the screen. You can then execute the ACCEPT statement to await input from the person at the terminal. In describing the screen, you indicate which items are input fields, and what the person at the terminal must do before the ACCEPT retrieves the input from the screen and stores it where you have specified. Here is a simple example.

```
DATA DIVISION.
WORKING-STORAGE SECTION.
01   The-Name                      PIC X(40).
01   The-Id                        PIC X(6).
```
   [Storage is defined for the items entered on the screen.]

```
SCREEN SECTION.
```
[This is a new section in which you describe the data to display on the screen.]
```
01  Screen-1                         BLANK SCREEN REQUIRED.
```
[Each 01 level in the Screen Section describes a screen. You name this screen in DIS-
PLAY and ACCEPT statements. BLANK SCREEN clears the screen before displaying
the items it affects. REQUIRED tells COBOL to not return until the person at the termi-
nal has filled something in all input fields.]
```
    05  First-Line LINE 5.
        10  COL 10                    VALUE "Enter your name: "
                                      HIGHLIGHT.
```
          [You specify lines and columns similarly to the report writer. You
          don't code a PIC with a VALUE clause. In addition, you can specify
          various video attributes, such as HIGHLIGHT and REVERSE-VIDEO.]
```
        10  COL 30                    PIC X(40) REVERSE-VIDEO.
    05  Second-Line LINE 7.
        10  COL 10                    VALUE "Enter your id: "
                                      HIGHLIGHT.
        10  COL 40                    PIC X(6) REVERSE-VIDEO.
    □   □   □
    DISPLAY Screen-1                  [Displays the screen.]
    ACCEPT Screen-1                   [Waits for input to be entered.]
```

You define each screen image as a level 01 item in the Screen Section. Each
screen image can have 1 to 25 lines of 1 to 80 columns each. You can also define
multiple input fields. You display the screen image with the DISPLAY statement.
The ACCEPT statement allows the person at the terminal to enter data, and stays
active until the person presses the ENTER key. That's really all there is to it. The
rest is detail.

24.2   SPECIAL-NAMES PARAGRAPH

For screen display and input, you can code the SPECIAL-NAMES paragraph as
follows:

```
ENVIRONMENT DIVISION.
CONFIGURATION SECTION.
SPECIAL-NAMES.
    CONSOLE IS CRT
```
        [This tells COBOL that all DISPLAY statements without an UPON phrase are full-
        screen. The result is that DISPLAY statements in which a row, column position is
        not specified all display in row 1, column 1.]
```
    CURSOR IS data-name
```
        [This is optional and names either a DISPLAY PIC 9(4) or 9(6) data item in
        Working-Storage that contains the cursor position after input. If PIC 9(4), COBOL
        stores *llcc* in the data item, where *ll* is the line the cursor is on and *cc* the col-
        umn. If PIC 9(6), *lllccc* is stored.]
```
    CRT STATUS IS data-name.
```
        [This is optional and names a DISPLAY PIC 99X item in Working-Storage that con-
        tains the terminal status after input. Table 24.1 shows the value stored in the first
        digit and Table 24.2 shows the values returned for the second and third digits.]

TABLE 24.1 First Digit Stored by CRT STATUS

1st Digit	Meaning
0	Terminator key or auto return from input field.
1	User-defined function key was pressed.
2	COBOL defined function key was pressed.
9	Error.

24.3 DEFINING THE SCREEN

You define each screen as a level 01 data item in the Screen Section header of the Data Division. You define the lines that make up the screen display as lower-level items belonging to the level 01 *screen-name*.

```
01   screen-name                       clauses.
     nn                                clauses.
```

You select level numbers to be subordinate to *screen-name* and describe what you want displayed in the traditional COBOL manner with a structure. You don't need to provide data names. For example:

```
01   Screen-Two.
     05   LINE 5 COL 2               VALUE "Ready to go.".
```

The elementary items specify the actual data to display. Higher levels in the structure can be used to specify the attributes of the elementary items, or you can specify the attributes for just the elementary item, which overrides any attributes from higher levels in the structure. You tell where to display data by specifying the line and column. Line 1, column 1 is the upper left corner of the screen. Most PC screens have 80 columns and 25 lines. Some clauses, such as BLANK LINE, can be coded only for an elementary item. Others, such as BACKGROUND COLOR, can be coded either for a group or for an elementary item. If coded for a group item, they apply to all items belonging to it. You can code the following *clauses* in any order.

TABLE 24.2 Second and Third Digits Stored by CRT STATUS

2nd Digit	3rd Digit	Meaning
0	0	Terminator key pressed.
0	1	Auto return from last item.
1	X"00"-X"FF"	Function key was pressed.
2	X"00"-X"FF"	Function key was pressed.
9	0	No items fall within the screen.

24.3.1 Clauses to Specify the Data

VALUE IS *literal*   [Code on an elementary item only.]

The standard COBOL clause. You can code this only for an output field. You can't code a PIC clause with it.

SIZE IS *size*   [Code on an elementary item only.]

Specifies the length of the item displayed on the screen. The *size* can be an integer identifier or literal. SIZE overrides the length implied by any PIC or VALUE clause.

PICTURE IS *string* **USING/FROM/TO** ...   [Code on an elementary item only.]

The *string* is the same as for any PIC. You must additionally code a USING, FROM, or TO clause to specify the data to display. You can't code a VALUE clause with PIC for a screen.

FROM *literal* or *identifier*
[Displays the item as an output field. You can code this with TO.]
TO *identifier*
[Defines the item as an input field. The item isn't displayed unless you also code FROM. FROM and TO can't name the same identifier. If you want to use the same identifier to display the data and receive it, code USING.]
USING *identifier*
[Acts as if FROM and TO were coded for the same identifier to update a field. You can't code FROM or TO with USING.]

The order in which you write PIC, USING, FROM, and TO doesn't matter.

24.3.2 Standard COBOL Clauses

BLANK WHEN ZERO   [Code on an elementary item only.]
JUSTIFIED RIGHT
OCCURS *n* **TIMES**
SIGN IS LEADING/TRAILING SEPARATE CHARACTER
USAGE IS DISPLAY

24.3.3 Clauses Specifying Where to Display

COLUMN NUMBER IS *column* or **PLUS** *columns* or **±***columns*
LINE NUMBER IS *line* or **PLUS** *lines* or **±***lines*

Code these only on an elementary item. They specify the column or line at which to display or accept input. The *columns* or *lines* can be an integer literal or identifier that specifies either an absolute or relative position on the screen. You can't use a relative position until you first display something to establish a position on the screen. The default is column 1 when a line is first displayed, and then the default column moves right and the default line moves down as items are displayed. The default line is also 1, the top line, and then the default line moves down as items are displayed.

Once data is displayed, if you omit LINE, the data displays on the current line, and if you omit COL, the data displays at the next column following the last data displayed.

Fujitsu doesn't allow you to abbreviate COLUMN as COL, but this will change because the new ANSI standard does allow it.

24.3.4 Clauses to Control Input

AUTO

Automatically moves to the next input field when the person at the terminal enters the last character in an input field. The person can't move from the field until they completely fill it.

FULL

Ignores the ENTER key and makes the person at the terminal enter something in all fields before returning control from an ACCEPT statement. Normally, control returns when the person presses ENTER.

PROMPT

Fills the input or update field with spaces when the item is displayed.

PROMPT CHARACTER IS *character*

Fills the input or update field with the single *character* when the item is displayed.

ZERO-FILL

Same as PROMPT, but for a numeric input or update field to fill it with zeros when the item is displayed.

REQUIRED

Makes the person at the terminal enter something for the field before control is returned from the ACCEPT statement.

SECURE

Makes the input item invisible on the screen for such things as entering passwords.

24.3.5   Clauses to Control the Display

```
BACKGROUND-COLOR IS color
FOREGROUND-COLOR IS color
```

These set the background or foreground color for the elementary or group item. The default background color is black and the foreground is white. The *color* is an integer literal having the following values:

Integer	Color	Integer	Color
0	Black	4	Red
1	Blue	5	Magenta
2	Green	6	Brown
3	Cyan	7	White

BELL   [Code on an elementary item only.]

Makes a sound like a bell when the item is displayed.

BLANK LINE   [Code on an elementary item only.]

Clears the entire line before displaying the item.

BLANK SCREEN

Clears the entire screen before displaying the item. You can code BACK-GROUND-COLOR and FOREGROUND-COBOL with it to set the background and foreground colors.

BLINK   [Code on an elementary item only.]

Blinks the item.

ERASE EOL or **EOS**   [Code on an elementary item only.]

ERASE EOL erases from the current column position to the end of line. ERASE EOS erases from the first column of the current line to the end of the screen.

HIGHLIGHT	[Code on an elementary item only.]
LOWLIGHT	[Code on an elementary item only.]
REVERSE-VIDEO	[Code on an elementary item only.]

HIGHLIGHT highlights and LOWLIGHT dims the item for which they are coded. REVERSE-VIDEO displays the item with the background and foreground colors reversed.

UNDERLINE [Code on an elementary item only.]

Underlines the item.

OVERLINE

Draws a horizontal line above the item.

24.4 THE DISPLAY STATEMENT

Once the screens are described, you display them with the DISPLAY statement.

DISPLAY *screen-name* [Displays the screen named.]
  AT LINE … [Optional to specify the line.]
  AT COL … [Optional to specify the column.]
  AT *data-name*
    [This replaces both AT LINE and AT COL. It names an identifier that contains the row and column position at which to display. The *data-name* has the same format as that in the CURSOR IS *data-name* clause.]
  ON EXCEPTION *imperative-statements*
  NOT ON EXCEPTION *imperative-statements*
    [Each EXCEPTION phrase is optional. Code END-DISPLAY if you code either of them.]
  END-DISPLAY [Needed only if you code an EXCEPTION phrase.]

The *screen-name* is the name of an 01 level entry described in the Screen Section. The AT LINE, AT COL, and AT *cursor* clauses are each optional and you can code them in any order. AT *cursor* names a six- or eight-digit DISPLAY item to contain the status information as described for the CRT STATUS clause.

Rather than using a screen-name, you can display any Working-Storage item by coding DISPLAY as follows:

DISPLAY *item* [Identifier or literal.]
  AT *clauses* [Same as previous DISPLAY.]
  UPON CRT or **UPON CRT-UNDER**
    [Tells COBOL that this is not an ordinary DISPLAY statement. You don't need to code this if the CONSOLE IS CRT clause is coded in the SPECIAL-NAMES paragraph. CRT-UNDER displays everything underlined.]
  MODE IS BLOCK
    [Treats the identifier as an elementary item. If it is a group item, it displays as a single alphanumeric item. Omit MODE IS BLOCK to display the individual elementary items when you name a group item.]
  WITH *options* [This is optional. See list following.]
  ON EXCEPTION *imperative-statements*
  NOT ON EXCEPTION *imperative-statements*
    [The EXCEPTION phrases are optional.]
  END-DISPLAY

The options can be any combination of the following:

BACKGROUND-COLOR	FOREGROUND-COLOR
BELL	HIGHLIGHT
BLANK LINES	LOWLIGHT
BLANK SCREEN	OVERLINE
BLINK	REVERSE-VIDEO
ERASE EOL	SIZE
ERASE EOS	UNDERLINE

24.5 THE ACCEPT STATEMENT

After you display a screen, you execute the ACCEPT statement to allow the person at the terminal to enter input. ACCEPT then returns with the new input values when the person presses the ENTER key or when an AUTO return is made. ACCEPT is coded similarly to DISPLAY.

```
ACCEPT screen-name        [Name the screen to retrieve input for.]
    AT LINE ...           [Optional to specify the line.]
    AT COL ...            [Optional to specify the column.]
    AT data-name
```
[This replaces both AT LINE and AT COL. It names an identifier that contains the row and column position at which to display. The *data-name* has the same format as that in the CURSOR IS *data-name* clause. ACCEPT then returns the position the cursor was at when it exits.]
```
    ON EXCEPTION imperative-statements
    NOT ON EXCEPTION imperative-statements
```
[Each EXCEPTION phrase is optional. Code END-DISPLAY if you code either of them.]
```
    END-ACCEPT                [Needed only if you code an EXCEPTION
                               phrase.]
```

Rather than using a *screen-name,* you can request input into any item in Working-Storage by coding ACCEPT as follows.

```
ACCEPT item               [Identifier or literal.]
    AT clauses            [Same as previous ACCEPT.]
    FROM CRT
```
[Tells COBOL that this is not an ordinary ACCEPT statement. You don't need to code this if the CONSOLE IS CRT clause is coded in the SPECIAL-NAMES paragraph.]
```
    MODE IS BLOCK
```
[Treats the identifier as an elementary item. Even if it is a group item, input is stored in it as a group item. Omit MODE IS BLOCK to accept input into individual elementary items when you name a group item.]

```
        WITH options                          [This is optional. See list following.]
        ON EXCEPTION imperative-statements
        NOT ON EXCEPTION imperative-statements
            [The EXCEPTION phrases are optional.]
    END-ACCEPT
```

The *options* can be any combination of the following:

AUTO	PROMPT
BACKGROUND-COLOR	REQUIRED
BELL	REVERSE-VIDEO
BLINK	SECURE
FOREGROUND-COLOR	SIGN
FULL	SIZE
HIGHLIGHT	SPACE-FILL
JUSTIFY	UNDERLINE
LOWLIGHT	UPDATE
OVERLINE	ZERO-FILL

UPDATE indicates that an input field will be updated, and that upon return, the data item will contain the new value. It is the equivalent of coding USING on the PIC clause.

24.6 FULL-SCREEN EXAMPLE

Here is a simple example of a full-screen application that asks the person at the terminal to enter their name.

```
IDENTIFICATION DIVISION.
PROGRAM-ID. FULLSCR.
ENVIRONMENT DIVISION.
CONFIGURATION SECTION.
DATA DIVISION.
WORKING-STORAGE SECTION.
01  The-Name                            PIC X(40).
01  The-Id                              PIC X(6).
SCREEN SECTION.
01  Screen-1                            BLANK SCREEN
                                        AUTO PROMPT REQUIRED
                                        BACKGROUND-COLOR 1
                                        FOREGROUND-COLOR 7.

    05  First-Line.
        10  LINE 5 COL 10                VALUE "Enter your name: "
                                         HIGHLIGHT.
```

```
          10  COL 30                        PIC X(40) REVERSE-VIDEO
                                            TO The-Name.

      05  Second-Line.
          10  LINE 7 COL 10                 VALUE "Enter your id: "
                                            HIGHLIGHT.
          10  COL 40                        PIC X(6) REVERSE-VIDEO
                                            TO The-Id.
PROCEDURE DIVISION.
    DISPLAY Screen-1
    ACCEPT Screen-1
    GOBACK.
END PROGRAM FULLSCR.
```

EXERCISES

1. Modify the full-screen example at the end of this chapter to write the name and ID into an output file. Program a loop to enable the person at the terminal to enter a name and ID, and then write out the record. Terminate the loop of the person presses ENTER without entering a name.

2. Write a subprogram to display a Lotus 1-2-3 type menu in which the various choices are displayed across the screen in a line. Write the subprogram to be called as follows:

   CALL MenuH(n, table, result)

   The n is a PIC 999 packed-decimal item containing the number of items in the menu to display. Each element of table contains the text to display for the menu choice. It is to have a maximum of ten PIC X(8) elements. The result is a PIC 999 packed-decimal item. Return the number (1 through n) if the item the person's cursor was on when they press ENTER. Begin the display of the menu in row 1, column 1.

3. Same as the previous problem, but as the person moves their cursor atop each new menu item, change its display to reverse video. Change the CALL so that the row and column in which to display the menu line are provided in the subprogram call.

4. Same as problem 3, but display the menu as a pull-down list by stacking the menu choices vertically rather than horizontally.

5. Write a subprogram to display a pop-up list. The subprogram call is to be as follows:

   CALL POPUP(row,col,text,result)

   The row and col are PIC 999 packed-decimal items that specify the row and column in which to display the text. The text is a PIC X(20) item. Display the text and then below it, place YES and NO buttons. Return a 1 in result if the cursor is on YES and 0 if it is on NO when the person presses ENTER.

6. Write a simple screen saver that displays a line of underlines (_) across all columns of the screen. Display the line in row 1, erase it, display it in row 2, and so on down the screen. Return to the top of the screen after displaying on the last row of the terminal. Terminate the loop with any keyboard input. Watch how fast the screen is painted, and then use the CURRENT-DATE function to wait approximately one second after displaying each line.

CHAPTER 25

POINTER DATA AND CICS

This chapter is essential for CICS. POINTER data also has uses aside from CICS, but they are rare. If you don't code for CICS, you might skip this chapter.

Sometimes Used

Pointer data consists of data items that contain the central storage address locations of other data items. COBOL pointer data is rather limited and doesn't have the full ability of address manipulation found in such languages as C/C++ or PL/I. The primary purposes of POINTER data are for subprogram calls and interfacing to the Customer Information Control System (CICS).

Pointer data defined as POINTER-PROCEDURE is provided to point to procedure names, as described in Chapter 20. Pointer data defined as OBJECT REFERENCE points to an object in object-oriented COBOL, as described in Chapter 27. Although described in other chapters, both of these forms of pointer data follow the same rules as the POINTER data described here.

25.1 DEFINING POINTER DATA

A POINTER is a 4-byte data item that can contain either zero (NULLS) or the storage address of another data item. You describe it as POINTER with no PIC clause:

```
01  An-Item                        USAGE IS POINTER.
```

You can code a VALUE of NULLS for a POINTER item. This is the only initial value permitted:

```
01  Another-Item                   POINTER VALUE IS NULLS.
```

Other than not coding the PIC clause, you describe a POINTER item like any other data item, and you can code it for any level except level 88. It can be the subject or object of a REDEFINES, it can contain an OCCURS, and you can code SYNC to align it on a full-word boundary.

If POINTER items are part of a group, the group still acts like an alphanumeric item. You can read or write pointers within group items. However, because POINTER items contain memory addresses, which will likely change each time a program is run, it wouldn't make sense to write POINTER items into a data set for later use in another run.

Because POINTER is not alphanumeric or numeric, you can't code BLANK WHEN ZERO and JUST RIGHT with it.

25.2 PROGRAMMING WITH POINTER DATA

POINTER data items can appear only in the following statements in the Procedure Division:

- Relational condition in IF, PERFORM, EVALUATE, and sequential SEARCH (but not a binary SEARCH) statements. You can compare POINTER items to NULLS or other POINTER items for equality only. That is, you can compare POINTER items only with = or NOT =. A POINTER item either is described as POINTER or is an ADDRESS OF special register item.
- Procedure Division header: The USING phrase may list POINTER items as subprogram parameters.
- CALL or ENTRY statements: Either a POINTER item or ADDRESS OF may appear in the USING phrase. Both may be BY CONTENT or BY REFERENCE.
- The SET statement can store POINTER data items. This will be described subsequently.

POINTER items have the following limitations:

Class test.   There is no class test for POINTER.

CORR.   POINTER does not participate in CORR operations.

MOVE.   You cannot name a POINTER item. Use SET instead.

SORT ASCENDING/DESCENDING KEY.   Cannot be a POINTER item.

You can also set a value of NULLS into a POINTER item with the SET statement. NULLS (or NULL) is a figurative constant used only with POINTER data. NULLS has a zero value and represents a null address for data items defined with POINTER or ADDRESS OF:

```
SET receiving-field TO sending-field
SET An-Item TO NULLS
```

ADDRESS OF is a special register implicitly defined as POINTER that obtains the address of level 01 and 77 items in the Linkage Section. An ADDRESS OF *data-name* exists for every 01 or 77 level data item in the Linkage Section, except those that redefine others (then ADDRESS OF is similarly redefined). You code ADDRESS OF as follows:

```
ADDRESS OF data-name
```

The *data-name* is a level 01 or 77 data item in the Linkage Section. (For AIX and the PC, the item as a sending field can be any level except 66 and 88 and can also be defined in Working-Storage.)

The SET statement for POINTER is as follows:

```
                            NULLS
        pointer-identifier  pointer-identifier
        ADDRESS OF identifier  ADDRESS OF identifier
SET _____ TO _____
```

Notice that the ADDRESS OF can be a sending or receiving item. You can pass it in a CALL statement both BY CONTENT and BY REFERENCE. When passed BY REFERENCE, you can use it to set the address of a level 01 or 77 item in the Linkage Section. This lets subprograms manipulate an item, given a pointer containing the item's address. You assign the pointer to a description of the item in the Linkage Section, and then you can manipulate it. An example will make this clearer. Suppose you have a subprogram that is called as follows:

```
01  Num-Blanks  PIC 9(9) BINARY.
    □  □  □
    CALL "NOBLANKS" USING BY CONTENT A-Pointer,
        FUNCTION LENGTH(Len-Item), BY REFERENCE Num-Blanks
```

Assume that the NOBLANKS subprogram counts all the blanks in the item pointed to it by *A-Pointer*. The length of the item is stored in *Len-Item*. (Don't worry now how *A-Pointer* and *Len-Item* came to contain their contents.) The subprogram is to store the number of blanks in *Num-Blanks*. You write the subprogram as follows:

```
IDENTIFICATION DIVISION.
PROGRAM-ID. NOBLANKS.
*****************************************************************
* SUBPROGRAM TO COUNT NUMBER OF BLANKS IN AN ITEM.            *
* CALL "NOBLANKS" USING BY CONTENT A-Pointer, Len-Item,       *
*                      BY REFERENCE Num-Blanks                *
* IN:  A-Pointer points to data item.         POINTER         *
*      Len-Item contains length of data item.  PIC 9(9) BINARY *
* OUT: Num-Blanks contains count of blanks in data item.      *
*                                             PIC 9(9) BINARY  *
*****************************************************************
DATA DIVISION.
WORKING-STORAGE SECTION.
```

```
01   Num-Item    PIC S9(4) BINARY.
```
[This is used as a subscript.]
```
LINKAGE SECTION.
01   A-Pointer   POINTER.
01   Len-Item    PIC 9(9) BINARY.
01   Num-Blanks  PIC 9(9) BINARY.
01   The-Item    PIC X(1).
```
[*The-Item* isn't passed as a parameter. It is included in the Linkage Section so that you can refer to the item pointed to by *A-Pointer* as a character string. You give it a length of 1 in the description, but its real length is contained in *Len-Item*, which is passed as a parameter.]
```
PROCEDURE DIVISION USING A-Pointer, Len-Item, Num-Blanks.
A00-Begin.
    SET ADDRESS OF The-Item TO A-Pointer
```
[This makes any reference to *The-Item* reference the item pointed to by *A-Pointer*. Now you can treat *The-Item* as if it were a data item passed as a parameter.]
```
    MOVE ZEROS TO Num-Blanks     [Set up to count nonblanks in Num-Blanks.]
    PERFORM VARYING Num-Item FROM 1 BY 1
            UNTIL Num-Item > Len-Item
```
[Look at each character and count it if it is blank.]
```
    IF The-Item(Num-Item:1) = SPACE
        THEN ADD 1 TO Num-Blanks
    END-IF
    END-PERFORM
    EXIT PROGRAM.
END PROGRAM NOBLANKS.
```

You can use ADDRESS OF to obtain the address of an item only in the Linkage Section in Mainframe COBOL. What if you want to obtain the address of any data item? You can write a subprogram to do this. Assume the subprogram is named GETADD and pass it an identifier (BY REFERENCE, so you get its address) and a POINTER variable in which the subprogram is to store the address of the identifier. Because the identifier will be defined in the Linkage Section, you can store its address in the POINTER item.

```
IDENTIFICATION DIVISION.
PROGRAM-ID. GETADD.
******************************************************************
* SUBPROGRAM TO OBTAIN THE ADDRESS OF AN ITEM.                   *
* CALL "GETADD" USING BY REFERENCE A-Rec, A-Pointer              *
* IN:  A-Rec is any data item:  DISPLAY, BINARY, PACKED, etc.    *
* OUT: A-Pointer contains the address of A-Rec.  POINTER         *
******************************************************************
DATA DIVISION.
LINKAGE SECTION.
01   A-Rec                      PIC X(1).
01   A-Pointer                  POINTER.
PROCEDURE DIVISION USING A-Rec, A-Pointer.
A00-Begin.
    SET A-Pointer TO ADDRESS OF A-Rec
```
[Store the address of *A-Rec* in *A-Pointer*.]

```
        EXIT PROGRAM.
    END PROGRAM GETADD.
```

To illustrate the use of pointers further, here is a subprogram that stores an item in another item, given a pointer to the other item.

```
    IDENTIFICATION DIVISION.
    PROGRAM-ID. STOREADD.
    ***********************************************************************
    * SUBPROGRAM TO STORE ITEM IN IDENTIFIER, GIVEN ITEM'S ADDRESS. *
    * CALL "STOREADD" USING BY CONTENT A-Pointer, Len-Item,        *
    *                       BY REFERENCE A-Rec                     *
    *  IN: A-Pointer contains address of item to store. POINTER    *
    *      Len-Item contains the length of item. PIC 9(9) BINARY   *
    * OUT: A-Rec contains the contents of item pointed to.         *
    *           Should be same PIC as data item, but data is       *
    *           moved to it without conversion regardless of its   *
    *           format.                                            *
    ***********************************************************************
    DATA DIVISION.
    WORKING-STORAGE SECTION.
    01  Num-Item    PIC 9(9) BINARY.
    LINKAGE SECTION.
    01  A-RecPIC X(1).
    01  Len-Item    PIC 9(9) BINARY.
    01  A-Pointer   POINTER.
    01  The-Item    PIC X(1).
    PROCEDURE DIVISION USING A-Pointer, Len-Item, A-Rec.
```
        [Set address of *A-Pointer* so you can access it as *The-Item*.]
```
        SET ADDRESS OF The-Item TO A-Pointer
```
        [Move the item a character at a time. Doesn't matter what kind of data the item contains.]
```
        PERFORM WITH TEST AFTER
                VARYING Num-Item FROM 1 BY 1
                UNTIL Num-Item > Len-Item
          MOVE The-Item(Num-Item:1) TO A-Rec(Num-Item:1)
        END-PERFORM
        EXIT PROGRAM.
    END PROGRAM STOREADD.
```

To show how the GETADD and STOREADD subprograms use POINTER data, the following example defines two records. It uses GETADD to get the address of the *Part-1* record and then uses STOREADD to copy the *Part-1* record to *P-Part-1*. (This accomplishes exactly the same thing as MOVE *Part-1* TO *P-Part-1*, and so the example is not particularly useful. The intent is just to show how POINTER data is used. A CICS subprogram or a subprogram written in another language can perform far more exotic operations using POINTER data.)

```
    01  An-Address                  POINTER.
    01  Part-1.
        05  Part-A                  PIC X(4) VALUE "1234".
```

```
        05   Part-B                    PIC S9(4) BINARY VALUE 10.
        05   Part-C                    PIC S9(6) PACKED-DECIMAL
                                       VALUE 20.
        05   Part-D                    PIC X(2) VALUE "YZ".
01  P-Part-1.
        05   P-Part-A                  PIC X(4).
        05   P-Part-B                  PIC S9(4) BINARY.
        05   P-Part-C                  PIC S9(6) PACKED-DECIMAL.
        05   P-Part-D                  PIC X(2).
        □  □  □
        CALL "GETADD" USING BY REFERENCE Part-1, An-Address
```
[Get the address of *Part-1* and store it in *An-Address*.]
```
        CALL "STOREADD" USING BY CONTENT An-Address,
             FUNCTION LENGTH(Part-1), BY REFERENCE P-Part-1
```
[Copy *Part-1* to *P-Part-1*.]

To give a flavor of how POINTER data can be used, the next example uses GETADD to obtain the address of a table of alphanumeric items and then uses STOREADD to store the addresses in another table. Data for the program is defined as follows:

```
01  Rec-Table.
        05   Rec-1                     PIC X(10) VALUE "1111111111".
        05   Rec-2                     PIC X(10) VALUE "2222222222".
        05   Rec-3                     PIC X(10) VALUE "3333333333".
        05   Rec-4                     PIC X(10) VALUE "4444444444".
        05   Rec-5                     PIC X(10) VALUE "5555555555".
        05   Rec-No                    PIC S9(4) BINARY VALUE 5.
```
[This is the number of items in *Rec-Table*.]
```
01  REDEFINES Rec-Table.
        05   Rec-Item                  OCCURS 5 TIMES
                                       INDEXED BY Rec-X
                                       PIC X(10).
```
[This redefines the record as a table.]
```
01  Ptr-Table.
        05  Ptr-Entry                  OCCURS 10 TIMES
                                       INDEXED BY Ptr-X
                                       POINTER.
```
[This is a table of pointers.]
```
01  Next-Rec     PIC X(10).
```
[This is used to obtain the contents of the *Rec-Table* items.]

Now we store the addresses of the *Rec-Table* entries into *Ptr-Entry*.

```
        PERFORM WITH TEST BEFORE VARYING Rec-X FROM 1 BY 1
             UNTIL Rec-X > Rec-No
          SET Ptr-X TO Rec-X
          CALL "GETADD" USING BY REFERENCE Rec-Item(Rec-X),
                                            Ptr-Entry(Ptr-X)
        END-PERFORM
```

Next, store NULLS in the next entry to mark the last address.

```
SET Ptr-Entry(Rec-No + 1) TO NULLS
```

To show some use for this, the next example gets each record pointed to by the *Ptr-Entry* table and stores it in *Next-Rec,* where it can be displayed. Notice how the value of NULLS is used to end the loop.

```
MOVE SPACES TO Next-Rec
PERFORM WITH TEST BEFORE VARYING Ptr-X FROM 1 BY 1
       UNTIL Ptr-Entry(Ptr-X) = NULLS
    CALL "STOREADD" USING BY CONTENT    Ptr-Entry(Ptr-X),
         FUNCTION LENGTH(Rec-1), BY REFERENCE Next-Rec
    DISPLAY "NEXT REC: ", Next-Rec
END-PERFORM
```

25.3   THE ALLOCATE AND FREE STATEMENTS

PROPOSED NEW ANSI STANDARD: Check Compiler to See if Implemented

The new ANSI standard provides the ALLOCATE statement to allocate dynamic storage and the FREE statement to release it. You code ALLOCATE as follows:

```
ALLOCATE n CHARACTERS RETURNING pointer
```

COBOL allocates the *n* characters of storage and returns the pointer to it in *pointer.* The *n* is an arithmetic expression, rounded up to an integer if necessary. The *pointer* is a POINTER data item. It contains NULL if you request zero characters or if the storage can't be allocated. Alternatively, you can allocate the amount of storage required to contain a data item.

```
ALLOCATE data-name RETURNING pointer
```

Normally, the storage contains unpredictable results. To fill it with binary zeros, you add the INITIALIZED phrase.

```
ALLOCATE … INITIALIZED RETURNING pointer
```

You release the storage back to the system with the FREE statement. FREE releases the storage and stores a value of NULL in *pointer-name.* If the *pointer-name* contains a value of NULL, FREE ignores it.

```
FREE pointer-name, pointer-name, …, pointer-name
```

25.4 CICS CONSIDERATIONS

A full description of the use of COBOL for CICS is beyond the scope of this book. See the "Selected Reading" section on the Web site for further information. COBOL programs communicate with CICS through subprogram calls. CICS permits only CICS I/O, and CICS I/O is all done through subprogram calls. Because all the I/O under CICS is done through subprogram calls, a COBOL program running under CICS cannot contain any of the following:

Environment Division. No FILE-CONTROL allowed except for a sort.

Data Division. No FILE SECTION allowed except for a sort.

Linkage Section. No JCL PARM input allowed.

Procedure Division

- DECLARATIVES: Only USE allowed is USE FOR DEBUGGING.
- CALL statement: No ON OVERFLOW or ON EXCEPTION phrases.
- Following statements not allowed:

ACCEPT	MERGE	REWRITE
CLOSE	OPEN	START
DELETE	READ	STOP
DISPLAY	RERUN	WRITE

SORT statements. They cannot contain USING or GIVING phrases, the SORT-CONTROL special register, and you cannot use sort control data sets.

Reserved words. The following additional words are reserved for CICS: CICS DLI EXEC END-EXEC

Compiler options. The following compiler options are required when the program is to run under CICS:

```
NODYNAM    RENT
RESLIB     LIB     [If program has a COPY or BASIS statement in it.]
```

The CICS translator always inserts a CBL statement as follows:

```
CBL RES,RENT,NODYNAM,LIB
```

There is also a WORD compiler option to specify either CICS or an installation-defined list of statements to be flagged at compile time. Coding WORD(CICS) flags any COBOL statements not supported by CICS. The default is NOWORD for no statements to be flagged.

PART III

BEYOND COBOL

CHAPTER 26

ALL ABOUT DATES

Great effort has been put into solving the year-2000 problem. This chapter covers some of the solutions and what problems they might cause. It also covers how to handle dates in COBOL.

26.1 THE YEAR-2000 PROBLEM

Essential

Many legacy applications carried the year as two digits to save file storage space. Most dates were also entered as two digits, and it was easy and natural to store the data in the form in which it was entered. All this worked wonderfully until the approach of the year 2000. Then it became a potential disaster. The two-digit year causes the following problems:

Incorrect sort order.   The year 2000 as a two-digit year sorts in front of all the 19xx dates.

Year used as a subscript.   If the year is used as a subscript into a table, the two-digit year is almost certain to cause problems.

Special values in the year field.   Some applications gave special meaning to values of 00 or 99 of the year. A value of 99 often indicated a date in the infinite future (no expiration date). Values of 00 and 99 were used to denote header and trailer records that would sort first and last when sorted on the year.

Incorrect date calculations.   Calculations on dates involving the year, such as duration between two dates, no longer work. Calculating 99 − 95 gives 4 years, which is correct. Calculating 00 − 96 gives −96, which is incorrect.

Leap-year determination.   This is unlikely to be a problem. The simple method of determining a leap year by seeing if it is evenly divisible by 4 will work for both a two- and four-digit year 2000. This is due to good luck. A year is a leap year if either of the following is true:

- It is evenly divisible by 400 (2000 and 00 are). The year 2000 is a leap year. Errors will result if the program compensates for this, but does not apply the following exception.
- It is evenly divisible by 4 (2000 and 00 are) and not evenly divisible by 100 (2000 and 00 are). This calculation alone would make the year 2000 not a leap year, except that it is evenly divisible by 400. Note that the simple calculation of determining a leap year by seeing if it is evenly divisible by 4 will work until the year 2100, which is not a leap year.

If the determination for leap year checks to see if the year is evenly divisible by 4 adds the additional sophistication that it not be evenly divisible by 100 but doesn't add the evenly divisible by 400 test, the calculation will be incorrect for the year 2000.

Date validation. Many programs check to see that a year field is entered. If an input field for the year is left blank, it is converted to zero. It was a common practice to check the year for a nonzero value to determine if the year was entered.

Determining the date format. Some programs were written to allow the date to be entered in either *mm/dd/yy* or *yy/mm/dd* order, that assumed mm/dd/yy order if the first two digits were 01 through 31.

Preprinted forms. Many input forms contain something like the following: Date _____ 19__. These forms will have to be changed. If the 19 was entered as part of the date, this, too, must be changed.

Year display in reports. People who accept a date like 10/20/99 may be upset by a date like 10/20/00. However, this may not be a real problem. Humans can easily cope with ambiguity. Anyone who can look at '99 and know that 1999 is meant can look at '00 and know that 2000 is meant. The question of how one can know that '01 is 2001 and not 1901 is moot. People determine this by the context. If someone sees Windows 98 advertised, they know it means 1998 and not 1898. There can be confusion with a date such as 02/03/04. Which is the year? Actually, it's easy. The year is almost always placed last. A more serious problem is which is the month and which is the day, and we've learned to live with that. Dates in reports are not a year-2000 problem. Any ambiguity of dates in reports was there before the year 2000.

Hardware chips. Many may not handle four-digit years or handle the year rollover from 99 to 00. This may turn out to be the most serious problem because the chips may have to be replaced. COBOL can't solve this problem.

26.2 SOLUTIONS TO THE YEAR-2000 PROBLEM

The first place to look for year-2000 solutions is in the products provided by the operating system, compiler, and vendors. There are products for packing dates in fields, sorting two-digit date fields, evaluating, testing, and on and on. Most of the software solutions use one of the following techniques. The first two techniques require changing the date in the file. The third technique, preferable for many applications, does not change the date in the file, but infers the century after the file is read using a windowing technique.

26.2.1 Expand the Date Field in the File

The most straightforward solution is to expand the year field from two to four digits. This solution is clean and final. No retrofitting should be needed. It requires that you copy and expand the file and modify all programs that read or write the file to handle the new record size, date format, and four-digit date field, which can be a major problem. The following code represents how the date field might be expanded.

```
05   Some-Date.
     10   Yr                    PIC 99.
     10   Mo                    PIC 99.
     10   Dy                    PIC 99.
□  □  □
05   New-Date.
     10   New-Yr                PIC 9(4).
     10   New-Mo                PIC 99.
     10   New-Dy                PIC 99.
□  □  □
read in old record
MOVE Mo TO New-Mo
MOVE Dy TO New-Dy
MOVE Yr TO New-Yr(3:2)
MOVE "19" TO New-Yr(1:2)
write out new record
```

For Julian dates in the form *yyddd,* you do the same thing and change the format to *yyyyddd.* The code shown here assumes that you are doing the conversion before the year 2000. Logic to determine the century is more complicated and is described later.

There are many problems with expanding the file. First, it must be done in one fell swoop. All programs that use the file must be changed at the same time. Hundreds of programs could be involved, and there is danger in changing any program. Then, all the files with the expanded date must be copied and converted at the same time. Converting a database that has online access would be extremely difficult. This leads to the extremely tense period when the cutover is made from the old format to the new format. When you expand the file, you must keep both the old and new file versions for testing and for the cutover into production. For large databases, there may not be enough disk space for this. There is also a source input problem because you must capture the proper century. If the input form contains only a two-digit year, you must expand this to capture the full four digits or provide some other means of deriving the century. Finally, there is the problem with what to do with the old files. Should archival files be converted? If not, all the old programs must be retained to access them.

After the conversion is done, problems will arise if all the references to the new date were not caught. You can also have problems if a program that hasn't been updated for the new file tries to read the program. It may be able to read the file, but the year field and everything that follows it in the record will be offset in a manner that the program doesn't know about, with the result that the program will be reading garbage. The same thing will occur when the updated programs try to read a file that hasn't been updated.

26.2.2 Pack the Date in the File

The big advantage of packing a four-digit year in the field in the file is that you don't have to copy or expand the file. By choosing an appropriate manner of storing the information, you can add logic to the program so that after a record is read, the program can determine whether the date is two or four digits and convert two-digit years to four-digit years on the fly. This solution requires that you put this code in all programs that read the file and change all the references to the old year to the new four-digit year. The following examples show this solution for various types of date storage.

Date Kept in Character Form
You redefine a new item as a four-digit half-word binary integer field over the two-digit year.

```
      05  Some-Date.
*           ***************************************************
*           ** NOTE: The year is redefined to be BINARY.  **
*           ***************************************************
          10  Yr                      PIC 99.
          10  Full-Yr                 PIC 9(4) BINARY
                                      REDEFINES Yr.
          10  Mo                      PIC 99.
          10  Dy                      PIC 99.
      01  Temp-Yr                     PIC 9(4) BINARY.
```

When you read a record, you look at the year to see if it has been converted. If not, you convert it.

```
      read in a record
      IF Yr(1:1) >= "0" AND <= "9"
         THEN COMPUTE Temp-Yr = Yr
            IF Temp-Yr < 60
               THEN ADD 2000 TO Temp-Yr
               ELSE ADD 1900 TO Temp-Yr
            END-IF
```
[For this example, the assumption is made that any dates from 60 through 99 are the 1900s and any dates 00 through 59 are the 2000s.]

```
            COMPUTE Full-Yr = Temp-Yr
END-IF
```

Then you must change all references to *Yr* to be references to *Full-Yr.* When the record is written, the new format is written in the file. All programs must be modified to add the preceding code to check the date to see if it is converted, and all references to the year in character form must be changed if the statements are affected by the four-digit binary year. Most shouldn't be.

Alternatively, you can redefine the full six-character year field as a single packed-decimal field.

```
*               ******************************************************
*               ** NOTE: The date redefined to be PACKED-DECIMAL.  **
*               ******************************************************
    05  Some-Date.
        10  Yr                      PIC 99.
        10  Mo                      PIC 99.
        10  Dy                      PIC 99.
    05  Full-Date                   PIC 9(6) REDEFINES Some-Date.
    05  New-Date REDEFINES Some-Date PIC 9(11) PACKED-DECIMAL.
    01  Temp-Date.
        10  New-Yr                  PIC 9(4) PACKED-DECIMAL.
        10  New-Mo                  PIC 99 PACKED-DECIMAL.
        10  New-Dy                  PIC 99 PACKED-DECIMAL.
```

As before, when you read a record, you look at the year to see if it has been converted. If not, you convert it.

```
read in a record
IF Yr(1:1) >= "0" AND <= "9"
    THEN COMPUTE New-Date = Full-Date
        IF New-Date < 600101
            THEN ADD 20000000 TO New-Date
            ELSE ADD 19000000 TO New-Date
        END-IF
        [The assumption is again made that any dates from 60 through 99 are the
        1900s and any dates 00 through 59 are the 2000s.]
        COMPUTE New-Yr = New-Date / 10000
        COMPUTE New-Mo = New-Date / 100 - New-Yr * 100
        COMPUTE New-Dy = New-Date - New-Yr * 10000 - New-Mo * 100
END-IF
```

For a date in Julian form, it is even simpler because there is enough space to store the year and day in separate packed-decimal fields.

```
    05  Julian-Date.
        10  Yr                      PIC 99.
        10  Dy                      PIC 999.
    05  New-Julian-Date REDEFINES Julian-Date.
        10  New-Yr                  PIC 9(5) PACKED-DECIMAL.
```

```
        10  New-Dy                      PIC 9(3) PACKED-DECIMAL.
   01  Temp-Date                        PIC 9(5) PACKED-DECIMAL.
```

Inside the program, you can convert the character date to a packed-decimal date as follows:

```
IF Yr(1:1) >="0" AND <= "9"
   THEN COMPUTE Temp-Date = Yr
        COMPUTE New-Yr = Temp-Date
        COMPUTE Temp-Date = Dy
        COMPUTE New-Dy = Temp-Date
   END-IF
```

Sorts on the date field should not need to be changed. They will sort in the proper order as long as you sort on the full date field. If you overlay the year field with binary, a sort on the year alone will still work. However, if you overlay the date with packed-decimal, a sort on the year alone will no longer work—the position of the year in the date field shifts, and you must modify the sort.

The main post-2000 year problems will be in programs that don't know the date is in the revised format. They will be able to read the file with no problem, but they will think the date is in character form when it is packed-decimal. Maintenance programmers might also reintroduce errors when they look at the date field and think it is still in character form, not noticing the REDEFINES. It would be a good idea to highlight this with comments, as was done here.

Because all the files will be converted at some point, there might be a temptation to remove the REDEFINES and just make the year field be four-digit binary integer. This is fine as long as you don't introduce any slack bytes into the record.

Date Kept in Packed-Decimal Form

If the date is kept in packed-decimal form, the year is already packed, and there is no place to store the extra two digits for the year. You need some other way to tell whether it is a year in the 1900s or the 2000s. You can take advantage of the fact that the month field contains only values from 1 to 12. You can add 12 to the month for years in the 2000s. By examining the month to see if it is greater than 12, you can tell if it is a year in the 2000s. (You could designate month values from 25 through 36 to be years in the 2100s, and so on. However, it is unlikely that your program will record such future dates, and if it does, you should expand the year in the file to four digits and be done with it.)

```
   05  Some-Date.
       10  Yr                       PIC 99 PACKED-DECIMAL.
*          ************************************************
*          ** NOTE: The month is 1-12 for 19xx dates.  **
*          **       It is 13-15 for 20xx dates.         **
*          ************************************************
       10  Mo                       PIC 99 PACKED-DECIMAL.
       10  Dy                       PIC 99 PACKED-DECIMAL.
   01  Full-Yr                      PIC S9(4).
```

When you read a record, you look at the month to see if it is a 1900s or 2000s year.

```
read in record
IF Mo <= 12
    THEN COMPUTE Full-Yr = Yr + 1900
    ELSE COMPUTE Mo = Mo - 12
         COMPUTE Full-Yr = Yr + 2000
END-IF
```

When you store the date back in the record, you must convert the year back to a two-digit number and record the century in the month field.

```
IF Full-Yr < 2000
    THEN COMPUTE Yr = Full-Yr - 1900
    ELSE COMPUTE Yr = Full-Yr - 2000
         COMPUTE Mo = Mo + 12
END-IF
write out record
```

A major problem with recording the century in the month field is that you cannot then use the date field directly for sorting. You would have to write a sort input and output procedure to convert the date for sorting, as described in Chapter 23.

As an alternative, you can take advantage of the fact that PIC 99 PACKED-DECIMAL occupies 2 bytes (see Chapter 28) because half a byte is reserved for the sign. A PIC 999 PACKED-DECIMAL item occupies the same 2 bytes, allowing you to use the left digit to represent the century: 0 for 1900s, 1 for 2000s, and so on. The advantage of this is that the date field can now be sorted directly. Here is how to record the century as a single packed-decimal digit:

```
05  Some-Date.
    10 Yr                      PIC 99 PACKED-DECIMAL.
    10 CYr                     PIC 999 PACKED-DECIMAL
                               REDEFINES Yr.
01  Full-Yr                    PIC S9(4).
```

When you read a record, add 1900 to the year (00 through 99 become 1900 through 1999 and 100 through 199 become 2000 through 2199).

```
read in a record
COMPUTE Full-Yr = CYr + 1900
```

When you write the record, the century is recorded in the year field by subtracting 1900 from the four-digit year.

```
COMPUTE CYr = Full-Yr - 1900
IF Full-Yr < 2000
    THEN COMPUTE CYr = Full-Yr - 1900
    ELSE COMPUTE CYr = Full-Yr - 2000 + 100
```

```
END-IF
write out record
```

For Julian dates, the options and procedures are essentially the same. You can take advantage of the fact that the *ddd* can range from 1 to 366, which lets you denote the year 2000 by adding 366 to *ddd*. Alternatively, you can change the packed-decimal description of the year from PIC 99 to PIC 999 and record the century in the left digit.

This solution sets little time bombs around for maintenance programmers. Any program not changed to revise the month and year would have problems. It would be easy for a maintenance programmer to miss the change and introduce a new error.

Store a Century Indicator in an Unused Field in the File

This is a bad solution and is mentioned only so that you will not attempt it. Many fields have unused fields somewhere in them, perhaps even slack bytes, that you could preempt to store a century indicator. Then you could change all the sorts to include the century indicator in a sort on the date field. When you processed the file in a program, the program could convert the date internally to a four-digit year as it read the records. The problem with this solution is that not all files have unused space. For future maintenance, it would be easy to overlook the century indicator because it would likely not be near the year field in the file. And finally, the other solutions are better.

26.2.3   Convert the Date Internally: Century Windowing

In many ways, this is the best technique. It requires no change to the data in the file, and can handle most date problems. The windowing technique defines a 100-year window, and the two-digit years are converted to four digits based on this. For example, if you define the date window to be from 1903 through 2002, two-digit years of 03 through 99 would be the 1900s and years of 00 through 02 would be the 2000s. The new ANSI standard has the DATE-TO-YYYYMMDD and YEAR-TO-YYYY functions, described in Chapter 21, to do this. Unfortunately, they will come too late for the year-2000 problem.

The windowing technique requires that the dates fall within a 100-year window. If the year is 03, how do you know it is 2003 and not 1903? However, this should not be a problem. Any existing data that carries the year as two digits has already assumed a 100-year window. How does the current application know that 89 is 1989 and not 1889? If there is special code to handle this case depending on the context, as for a birth date, the same technique can be applied to years in the 2000s.

This technique still leaves the problem of sorting. Because the date isn't changed in the file, the sorted fields will not be in the proper order. However, the sort vendors provide a means of specifying the windowing technique for a two-digit field so that it is expanded to four digits only for the comparison in the sort, without actually changing the date in the file to solve the sort problem. This is described in Chapter 23, and there is also an example of how to program this yourself with a COBOL sort.

Each program and sort that operates upon a particular date must be modified to use the same windowing technique. However, all the two-digit year solutions require that all the programs that reference the date be modified. With the windowing technique, all the sorts must also be modified. Different date fields can use different windows as appropriate. The windowing technique won't work for historical dates, but any current application with a two-digit year field already has this limitation. It might later become a problem where historical dates beginning in, say, 1960 are kept. This will lead to a problem with historical dates in the year 2060. Still, the windowing technique can be made to work for most business applications. Because almost no computer business applications predate 1960, you can assume that transaction dates are in the range from the current date back to 1960, and most business data will not be kept for 100 years. You are unlikely to have employees younger than 15 or older than 100, so an employee birth date must be in the range of the current date minus 15 to 100 years. A hire date might be in the range from the current date back 75 years.

There are two variations for the windowing technique: fixed and sliding. For a *fixed window,* you might internally convert dates with years 60 to 99 to be 1960 to 1999, and dates with years 00 to 59 to be 2000 to 2059. As time goes by, you might have to change the ranges. This method has little to recommend it because the *sliding-window* technique works as well and automatically slides the date range forward so that you don't have to constantly change it. With the sliding technique, you specify a window as the number of years in the past and in the future that constitute a window around the current date, as shown in Figure 26.1.

Should you choose the sliding-window method, here is one way to program it. You get the current year yy as two digits, and $yy + n$ marks the end of a 100-year cycle that determines the century. For example, if n is 2 and the current year is 2003, the years are assumed to fall in the range 1906 through 2005. *Some-Date* contains the date to convert in *yymmdd* form. The four-digit year is stored in *Full-Yr.*

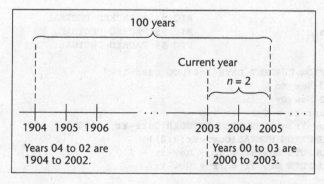

FIGURE 26.1   The sliding-window technique.

```
        05   Some-Date.
             10   Yr                    PIC 99.
             10   Mo                    PIC 99.
             10   Dy                    PIC 99.
   01   N                               PIC S99 VALUE 2.
   01   Curr-Yr                         PIC 9(4).
   01   New-Date
        05   New-Yr                     PIC 9(4).
        05   New-Mo                     PIC 99.
        05   New-Dy                     PIC 99.
        □   □   □
   MOVE FUNCTION CURRENT-DATE(1:4) TO Curr-Yr
```
[The current year is obtained from the intrinsic function here. In practice, you might enter the year as data so you could process old files. By entering the year as data, you automatically have the fixed-window technique.]
```
   MOVE Mo TO New-Mo              [Store the month and day in the new date.]
   MOVE Dy TO New-Dy
   COMPUTE Curr-Yr, New-Yr = Curr-Yr + N
```
[Compute the year that ends the 100-year window.]
```
   MOVE "00" TO New-Yr(3:2)        [New-Yr contains just the century part.]
   IF Yr > Curr-Yr(3:2)
```
[If the two-digit year is greater than the end year of the 100-year window, it belongs in the previous century.]
```
      THEN COMPUTE New-Yr = Yr + New-Yr - 100
      ELSE COMPUTE New-Yr = Yr + New-Yr
   END-IF
```

If the date is in packed-decimal, the same technique works, but you can't just zero out the two right digits of *New-Yr* to get the century part. Instead, you must divide it by 100 and then multiply it by 100.

```
        05   Some-Date.
             10   Yr             PIC 99 PACKED-DECIMAL.
             10   Mo             PIC 99 PACKED-DECIMAL.
             10   Dy             PIC 99 PACKED-DECIMAL.
   01   N                        PIC S99 VALUE 2.
   01   Curr-Yr                  PIC 9(4).
   01   New-Date
        05   New-Yr             PIC 9(4) PACKED-DECIMAL.
        05   New-Mo             PIC 99 PACKED-DECIMAL.
        05   New-Dy             PIC 99 PACKED-DECIMAL.
        □   □   □
   MOVE FUNCTION CURRENT-DATE(1:4) TO Curr-Yr
   MOVE Mo TO New-Mo
   MOVE Dy TO New-Dy
   COMPUTE Curr-Yr = Curr-Yr + N
   COMPUTE New-Yr = (FUNCTION INTEGER(Curr-Yr / 100)) * 100
   IF Yr > FUNCTION NUMVAL(Curr-Yr(3:2))
      THEN COMPUTE New-Yr = Yr + New-Yr - 100
      ELSE COMPUTE New-Yr = Yr + New-Yr
   END-IF
```

The windowing technique can be implemented a single program at a time, even before the year 2000. Because the format of the date in the file doesn't change, the new programs can process historic data. This method should present few maintenance problems during the life of the program. It will, however, be difficult to catch all instances where the year was referenced in a program and where it is used in a sort.

26.3 PROBLEMS CAUSED BY SOLUTIONS TO THE YEAR-2000 PROBLEM

Solving the year-2000 problem forces programmers to violate the old adage of "don't fix it if it isn't broken." Programs with two-digit years will work perfectly up to the year 2000, and then they will fall apart. Massive changes are required to solve the problem, and these changes will introduce new errors. There are two basic approaches to solving the problem. First, the file can be expanded for a four-digit year. This is a clean solution that solves the problem once and for all with no long-term maintenance problems. The other solution is to pack the year into the year field without expanding the file, or the program can determine the century internally from the two-digit year. This may initially be easier to implement, but it can leave long-term maintenance problems. Here are some of the typical problems that will be encountered:

Time spent analyzing solutions. Evaluating all the products and services available to solve the year-2000 problems will leave little time to implement any solutions. It may be easier to simply expand the date field for a clean solution than to evaluate all the ways you can avoid this.

Inadequate program testing. The code looks right, there are thousands of changes to make, we can't test everything, let's get on with it. Everyone knows this is wrong and almost everyone will do it in some form or other. It would be wise to distrust all year-2000-modified programs for the first few years of the twenty-first century.

Changes missed. You can use a cross-reference listing and a text editor to catch most references to dates, but you won't catch them all. For example, consider the following:

```
01  Rec-In.
    05   Some-Date.
         10   Yr                PIC 99.
         10   Mo                PIC 99.
         10   Dy                PIC 99.
    05   Test-Data REDEFINES Some-Date
                               PIC 9(6).
```

If you have modified a program containing this, you could look for references to the two-digit year in *Yr*. If it is moved to another identifier, you must also check all references to that, too. Then you must check all references to *Some-Date* so you catch such references to the year as *Some-*

Date(2:1). Don't overlook checking all references to *Test-Data,* which redefines *Some-Date.* Finally, you might easily overlook something like *Rec-In*(1:2), which also references the date.

Clever coding. Some of the solutions to the year-2000 problem suggested here encode the date field to determine the century. This would be easy to overlook by a maintenance programmer, and could be a problem over the life of the program.

Invalid assumptions in implementing solutions. This applies especially to making assumptions about the century by examining the two-digit year field. (An 03 must be 2003 and not 1903). If the assumptions made don't hold up over time, the problem is going to be extremely difficult to fix.

Validation. If the date validation rejects 00 as a valid year and this is changed, whatever the validation was to protect against can then happen. Solving the year-2000 problem may lead to future date validation problems.

Security. Many companies farmed out year-2000 changes, both domestically and to foreign countries. What were the motivations of the people making the changes? Were they people of good will? How did they feel about the company for which they were making changes? What were their political motivations? What were the opportunities for fraud? What might be implanted in the programs that came back? Some companies took more care to ensure that a virus didn't get on a PC used mainly for e-mail and games than they did with COBOL programs central to the operation of the company.

Maintaining the solutions. The year-2000 problems will seem less and less important after the year 2000, and they will quickly fade from memory. However, all the kludge solutions implemented to solve the problems must be maintained and must continue to run. As the year-2000 problems fade, maintaining these solutions will become more and more of a problem. After the year 2000, no programmer is going to see maintaining year-2000 solutions as a great career opportunity.

Integrating systems. Different applications may apply different solutions. Different divisions and companies will apply different solutions. With reorganizations, acquisitions, and expanding applications, these different solutions may come into conflict.

The unexpected. Unless you implement a clean solution by expanding the date field to four digits, the solution you implement may result in unanticipated problems. It is impossible to know beforehand what they might be because that would make them anticipated problems. The solution might run for months, and then an unusual transaction might bring a bug to light.

The year 10,000. Eight thousand years from now, will we be castigated for not foreseeing the need for a five-digit year? Who knows? Who cares?

26.4   OPERATIONS ON DATES

The ACCEPT statement described in Chapter 7 can retrieve the current time, date, and day of week. The intrinsic functions described in Chapter 21 can also operate on dates. Several additional operations frequently performed on dates are shown in this section. For example, the sequential day of the year is often used in data processing, because it makes it easier to calculate the number of days between two dates.

26.4.1   Determine Leap Years

The following code determines if it is a leap year:

```
01   The-Year                     PIC 9(4).
01   Leap-Year                    PIC X.
*                                      "N"-Not a leap year.
*                                      "Y"-Leap year.

  □   □   □
    MOVE "N" TO Leap-Year
    IF FUNCTION REM(The-Year, 400) = ZERO
        THEN MOVE "Y" TO Leap-Year
        ELSE IF FUNCTION REM(The-Year, 4) = ZERO
                AND NOT FUNCTION REM(The-Year, 100) = ZERO
                THEN MOVE "Y" TO Leap-Year
            END-IF
END-IF
```

26.4.2   Compute Age

The next few statements compute an age, given a birth date and a date:

```
01   Birth-Date.
     05   Bd-Yr                   PIC 9(4).
     05   Bd-Mo                   PIC 99.
     05   Bd-Dy                   PIC 99.
01   Current-Date.
     05   Cd-Yr                   PIC 9(4).
     05   Cd-Mo                   PIC 99.
     05   Cd-Dy                   PIC 99.
01   Age                          PIC S9(4) BINARY.
```

Check that to see if we are before or after the birthday by comparing the month/day fields.

```
    IF Birth-Date(5:4) > Current-Date(5:4)
        THEN COMPUTE Age = Cd-Yr - Bd-Yr - 1
        ELSE COMPUTE Age = Cd-Yr - Bd-Yr
    END-IF
```

26.4.3 Convert Calendar Dates to Julian Dates

These statements convert a calendar date to a year and day of year (1 to 366).

```
01  Julian-Date.
    05   Julian-Yr                PIC 9(4).
    05   Julian-Dy                PIC 9(3).
01  Julian-I-Date REDEFINES Julian-Date
                                  PIC 9(7).
01  Current-Date.
    05   Cd-Yr                    PIC 9(4).
    05   Cd-Mo                    PIC 99.
    05   Cd-Dy                    PIC 99.
01  Current-I-Date REDEFINES Current-Date
                                  PIC 9(8).
```

Subtract the integer Gregorian date for the date from the integer Gregorian date for January 1 of the year.

```
MOVE Cd-Yr TO Julian-Yr
COMPUTE Julian-Dy =
        FUNCTION INTEGER-OF-DATE(Current-I-date) -
        FUNCTION INTEGER-OF-DAY(Julian-I-Date) + 1
```

26.4.4 Convert Julian Dates to Calendar Dates

This set of code converts a Julian date to a calendar date:

```
01  Julian-Date.
    05   Julian-Yr                PIC 9(4).
    05   Julian-Dy                PIC 9(3).
01  Julian-I-Date REDEFINES Julian-Date
                                  PIC 9(7).
01  Current-Date.
    05   Cd-Yr                    PIC 9(4).
    05   Cd-Mo                    PIC 99.
    05   Cd-Dy                    PIC 99.
01  Current-I-Date REDEFINES Current-Date
                                  PIC 9(8).
```

Convert the Julian date to an integer Gregorian date and then convert this integer date to a normal date.

```
COMPUTE Current-I-Date =
  FUNCTION DATE-OF-INTEGER(
  FUNCTION INTEGER-OF-DAY(Julian-I-Date))
```

26.4.5 Compute Days between Two Dates

This subprogram computes the elapsed days between two dates:

```
01  First-Date.
    05  F-Yr                    PIC 9(4).
    05  F-Mo                    PIC 99.
    05  F-Dy                    PIC 99.
01  First-I-Date REDEFINES First-Date PIC 9(8).
01  Last-Date.
    05  L-Yr                    PIC 9(4).
    05  L-Mo                    PIC 99.
    05  L-Dy                    PIC 99.
01  Last-I-Date REDEFINES Last-Date PIC 9(8).
01  No-Days                     PIC S9(9) BINARY.
```

Convert the calendar date to integer days and subtract them.

```
COMPUTE No-Days = FUNCTION INTEGER-OF-DATE(Last-I-Date) -
                  FUNCTION INTEGER-OF-DATE(First-I-Date)
```

26.4.6   Determine the Day of the Week

The convention is to number the days of the week, beginning with Monday as 1. The following example determines the day of the week of an arbitrary date.

```
01  Current-Date.
    05  Cd-Yr                   PIC 9(4).
    05  Cd-Mo                   PIC 99.
    05  Cd-Dy                   PIC 99.
01  Current-I-Date REDEFINES Current-Date PIC 9(8).
01  Dy-Of-Week                  PIC S9(8) BINARY.
```

The simplest way to determine the day of the week is to convert the date to integer Gregorian. Because day 1 of integer Gregorian (1/1/1601) is a Monday, you can divide the days since then by 7 to determine the current day.

```
COMPUTE Dy-Of-Week =
    FUNCTION REM(FUNCTION INTEGER-OF-DATE(Current-I-Date), 7)
IF Dy-Of-Week = 0
    THEN COMPUTE Dy-Of-Week = 7
END-IF
```

If you wanted the text day (Monday, Tuesday, and so on), you could define the following table:

```
01  Dy-Table.
    05  Dy-Tbl-Values.
        10  Dy-Tbl-Mon          PIC X(9) VALUE "Monday".
        10  Dy-Tbl-Tue          PIC X(9) VALUE "Tuesday".
        10  Dy-Tbl-Wed          PIC X(9) VALUE "Wednesday".
        10  Dy-Tbl-Thu          PIC X(9) VALUE "Thursday".
        10  Dy-Tbl-Fri          PIC X(9) VALUE "Friday".
        10  Dy-Tbl-Sat          PIC X(9) VALUE "Saturday".
        10  Dy-Tbl-Sun          PIC X(9) VALUE "Sunday".
```

```
       05  Dy-Tbl REDEFINES Dy-Tbl-Values  OCCURS 7 TIMES
                                   PIC X(9).
```

You can then store the text day with the following:

```
MOVE Dy-Tbl(Dy-Of-Week) TO whatever
```

26.4.7 Convert Dates to Text Form

Sometimes you need to print a date like 20030426 as March 26, 2003. Here's how.

```
01  Current-Date.
    05  Cd-Yr                       PIC 9(4).
    05  Cd-Mo                       PIC 99.
    05  Cd-Dy                       PIC 99.
01  Formatted-Date                  PIC X(30).
01  Fmt-Dy                          PIC X(3).
01  Mo-Table.
    05  Mo-Tbl-V.
        10  Mo-Tbl-Jan              PIC X(9) VALUE "January".
        10  Mo-Tbl-Feb              PIC X(9) VALUE "February".
        10  Mo-Tbl-Mar              PIC X(9) VALUE "March".
        10  Mo-Tbl-Apr              PIC X(9) VALUE "April".
        10  Mo-Tbl-May              PIC X(9) VALUE "May".
        10  Mo-Tbl-Jun              PIC X(9) VALUE "June".
        10  Mo-Tbl-Jul              PIC X(9) VALUE "July".
        10  Mo-Tbl-Aug              PIC X(9) VALUE "August".
        10  Mo-Tbl-Sep              PIC X(9) VALUE "September".
        10  Mo-Tbl-Oct              PIC X(9) VALUE "October".
        10  Mo-Tbl-Nov              PIC X(9) VALUE "November".
        10  Mo-Tbl-Dec              PIC X(9) VALUE "December".
    05  Mo-Tbl REDEFINES Mo-Tbl-V OCCURS 12 TIMES PIC X(9).
```

The month can be indexed directly from the table.

```
IF Cd-Dy < 10                    [Eliminate any leading blank space from day.]
   THEN MOVE Cd-Dy(2:1) TO Fmt-Dy
   ELSE MOVE Cd-Dy to Fmt-Dy
END-IF
MOVE SPACES TO Formatted-Date
STRING Mo-Tbl(Cd-Mo) DELIMITED " ", " " DELIMITED SIZE
       Fmt-Dy DELIMITED " ", ", " DELIMITED SIZE
       Cd-Yr DELIMITED SIZE
       INTO Formatted-Date
END-STRING
```

26.5 STORING DATES AND TIMES

For the computer, it is best to carry the date in *yyyymmdd* order. This is the international standard (ISO, 1998), and it makes sorting much easier because the entire date field can be sorted as a unit. The standard date that we all use is based on the Gregorian calendar. It can be represented as year, month, and day, or in Julian form as year and day of year, where the days are numbered from 1 through 366.

In some applications, the date is kept as a number of days from some starting date. The INTEGER-OF-DATE function assumes a starting date of December 31, 1600, so a date of 1 is January 1, 1601. The international standards for storing dates encompass the following:

Gregorian dates	*yyyymmdd*	*yyyy-mm-dd*		
Julian dates	*yyyydddd*	*yyyy-ddd*		
Time of day	*hhmmss*	*hh:mm:ss*	*hhmmssZ*	*hh:mm:ssZ*

[The Z indicates that it is Coordinated Universal Time (UTC). Except for political differences and the date being maintained by a different organization, it is the same as Greenwich Mean Time.]

Date/time	*yyyymmddhhmmss*	
	yyyy-mm-ddThh:mm:ss	[The T separates the date and time.]
	yyyydddddhhmmss	*yyyy-ddddThh:mm:ss*

EXERCISES

1. The year-2000 problem resulted from abbreviating the year as two digits, and none of the current solutions proposed will work beyond the year 9999. While this is not a problem that will occur in our lifetimes, it represents the tendency of numbers to grow over time. What numbers that you carry about yourself might cause serious problems over your lifetime as they "grow." Consider such things as telephone area codes, telephone numbers, zip codes, social security numbers, credit card numbers, and so on. How might the growth of each of these affect computer systems?

2. Write a subprogram to accept start and end dates as PIC X(8) numbers in the form *yyyymmdd,* and calculate the number of week days between them. That is, exclude Saturdays and Sundays.

3. Same as problem 2, but in addition create a table containing the month and day of each legal holiday for an entire year, and exclude these days from the count.

CHAPTER 27

DEMYSTIFYING OBJECT-ORIENTED COBOL

This chapter explains the basics and benefits of object-oriented COBOL. If for no other reason than to know what people are talking about, you should read this chapter.

Object-oriented COBOL is often termed OOCOBOL or O-O COBOL, two of the least inspiring acronyms extant. Most of what is written about object-oriented programming is about design. Although it is important, the ultimate aim of design is to produce an object-oriented program, with its advantages over other forms of programming. This chapter covers the programming aspects. The main advantages of object-oriented programming are that it makes programs easier to change and code easier to share. Sharing code is the most cost-effective of all computing techniques. When you spend less than $100 for the Windows PC operating system, you get software that cost millions of dollars to develop. In languages like C/C++, programmers may spend more time selecting software to buy than they do in coding. This has never been the COBOL world: Object-oriented COBOL hopes to change this.

27.1 DESIGN PHILOSOPHIES

Programming has moved from top-down design to object-oriented design. They differ significantly.

27.1.1 Top-Down Design

Both structured and object-oriented programming are a combination of design and programming. When structured programming came into being, it was accompanied by a new design technique, top-down design. *Top-down* design, sometimes termed *stepwise refinement,* consisted of identifying the major functions of a program and decomposing these functions into smaller and smaller functional units until the lowest level was specified. Programs were written in the same order, with the highest level written first. The idea was to give discipline to the design and ensure that the most important part of the program, its overall design, was coded first. It also served to organize the program into digestible components consisting of functionally related parts that reflected the original design concept. Top-down design boiled down to worrying about designing the forest before you planted the trees.

There were several problems. First, the only time when you can know completely what needs to be programmed beforehand is when you have just finished programming it. Unfortunately, most systems are not immediately reprogrammed after they are completed, and for those that are, the person who wrote the first version is rarely invited back. Top-down design didn't take into consideration the catalytic effect that computer systems have on their users. Because the customer didn't get to use the system until it was complete, only then did they begin to find out what they really wanted. Their reaction to a new system they helped design often was as if space aliens suddenly imposed it upon them.

The customer cannot know beforehand in full detail what is needed. You can elicit all the known requirements, but not until the customer uses the system for some time will they really know in full detail what is wanted. This is not a communication problem. Programmers often write their own little systems for themselves, and these systems go through iterations just as they do when the end user and the programmer are different people. Change makes it impossible to know completely what the customer wants in advance. If the customer were able to tell you exactly what was needed, by the time the program was readied for production, the needs would have changed.

27.1.2 Object-Oriented Design

Object-oriented design is just the opposite. Object-oriented design argued that top-down design had two major limitations. First, it was difficult to adapt to changing needs. This was often reflected in statements like, "Well, if they would just tell us what they want and freeze the design, we could build the thing." The object-oriented philosophy argued that this will never happen because needs are dynamic. The second criticism of top-down was that it did not produce reusable code. All designs and programs become unique to an application, foregoing the most cost-effective technique, the reuse of code.

The object-oriented philosophy is that you should start by designing ways to plant trees, because you can then build any kind of forest. Besides, the customer probably didn't want a forest anyway—just a grove of trees. The difference is illustrated in Figure 27.1. Object-oriented programs concentrate on the data first, and then incorporate the functions that operate and manipulate the data as an inherent part of defining the data. In object-oriented terminology, a function is called a *method.* The design focuses on the lower level to develop general-purpose routines operating on common types of data. These can then be put together at a higher level for many different purposes. By including the concept of inheritance, whereby operations and data are inherited, the programs become more flexible.

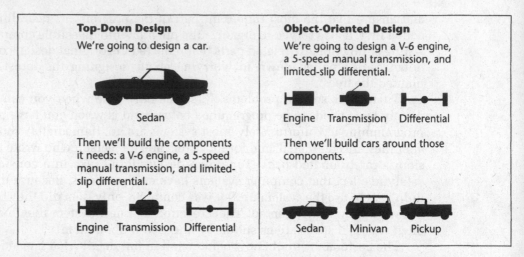

FIGURE 27.1 Top-down and object-oriented design philosophies.

Of course, neither top-down nor object-oriented design is likely the last word in programming. It is easy to see top-down used to specify the overall system, and then object-oriented used to design data and the common routines to operate on the data.

27.1.3   Object-Oriented and Structured Programming

Structured programming made programs easier to read and understand. Object-oriented programming doesn't. It may make them more difficult to understand, at least until programmers become accustomed to them. Object-oriented programming also adds effort to COBOL programming, but can be justified where code can be reused several times. This is a problem because many applications start out as one-time things, and then over time evolve into monster systems. The key to making potentially shared code useful is the documentation. Documentation needs differ for multiple-use object-oriented programs and single-use application programs. Single-use application programs are modified but not used, at least by the programmer. Shared programs are used but not modified. Consequently, for single-use application programs, the best documentation, aside from an end-user manual, is a system flowchart and comments in the source statements. By contrast for object-oriented programs, shared code isn't read, so the documentation must be external. A programming guide is essential to tell you what programs are available and how they can be used.

Structured and object-oriented programming are not alternatives. They are entirely separate and complimentary. Structured programming is a way of making programs more straightforward to write and more understandable to read. Object-oriented programming is a way of making the code for programs easier to change and easier to share. Structured programming doesn't make programs easier to change or share, aside from making them easier to understand. Object-oriented programming doesn't make programs more straightforward to write and more understandable to read, aside from hiding much of the code, until programmers become adept at it. The leap to object-oriented programming is major for COBOL because its programmers don't have the experience of coding functions to ease the way.

27.2 MINIMIZING THE IMPACT OF CHANGE

Because one of the main rationales for object-oriented programming is to make programs easier to change, the following briefly summarizes other ways of accomplishing this.

Write the program with change in mind.   Some try to achieve this by incorporating every conceivable requirement. But a program that has attempted to incorporate every conceivable situation would be terrible to change. Anyway, it is usually not the conceivable changes that give problems, but the inconceivable ones. The trade-off between being comprehensive and being flexible is difficult, but do not confuse the two by choosing one and assuming you have the other. They usually conflict.

Minimize the impact of outside forces.   Never read in a table without checking to see that it doesn't overflow. In reading any file, be prepared to handle an excessive number of records or no records at all. Protect programs against incorrect data. Validate the input data before accepting it, and validate it all in one place. The code required for validation is a potential source of error, and you minimize this code by validating only once in one place. This also makes it easier to change the validation.

Safety factors are used in engineering designs so that each component can withstand greater stress than the maximum expected. Stress in programs comes from growth. Computer programs should also have safety factors built into them to accommodate greater growth than expected. Each file and transaction in the system should have some unused space that is carried as filler. Then, if new data is required in the file or transaction, there is space for adding it without recompiling all the programs that read it.

Write clear, understandable programs.   Programs that can be understood are easier to change.

Drive the program with data.   Data is easier to change than programs.

Keep one copy of data.   The reason is expressed in the old saying, "A person with one watch always knows the time. A person with two watches never knows the time." Keeping one copy of data is an inherent design goal of all database systems.

Generalize programs.   For example, suppose you had the following table:

```
01  Dept-Tbl.
    05  Dept-Name                        PIC X(20)
                                         OCCURS 100 TIMES INDEXED BY Dx.
```

You might fill the table by reading in values from a file and check for table overflow.

```
read in a record
IF Dx = 100
    THEN DISPLAY "INCREASE Dept-Tbl and IF Dx = 100 STATEMENT"
        DISPLAY "AND RECOMPILE"
        GOBACK
    ELSE SET Dx UP BY 1
        MOVE name from record TO Dept-Name(Dx)
END-IF
```

The first step in generalizing is to make the maximum table size a data element so that you can more easily find and change it.

```
01  Max-Dept-Nos              PIC S9(9) VALUE 100.
    □  □  □
    read in a record
    IF Dx = Max-Dept-Nos
        THEN DISPLAY "INCREASE Dept-Tbl and Max-Dept-Nos AND"
            DISPLAY "RECOMPILE"
            GOBACK
        ELSE SET Dx UP BY 1
            MOVE name from record TO Dept-Name(Dx)
    END-IF
```

This is better, but the programmer must make changes in two places. It would be better to define a single item for both. The new ANSI standard lets you define constants to do this.

```
>>DEFINE MAX-DEPTS IS 100   [You could change the value once here.]
01  Max-Dept-Nos             PIC S9(9) VALUE MAX-DEPTS.
01  Dept-Tbl.
    05  Dept-Name            PIC X(20)
                             OCCURS MAX-DEPTS TIMES
                             INDEXED BY Dx.
```

If the maximum table size might change often, it would be even better to read in this maximum size from a file and dynamically allocate the table, as provided in the new ANSI standard. This way you could enlarge the table without having to recompile the program.

Write modular, reusable code. This is a main reason for object-oriented programming. It started with functions. These have been an essential part of most programming languages for over a quarter century, but came to COBOL only in 1985. Consequently, they have barely wound themselves into daily COBOL usage, although they are an excellent means of making programs more flexible. Thousands of programmers have written code to determine if a year is a leap year. Had this been made an intrinsic function (it hasn't), all that code with its potential for error would not need to have been written. With the new ANSI standard, you will be able to write your own functions. Until then, you must write subprograms that are more awkward to use because you must invoke them with a subprogram call. Functions are much more convenient to use because they can appear in expressions. For example, if a subprogram were written to convert Gregorian dates to integer date form and you wanted to determine the number of days between two dates, you would have to write something like the following:

```
CALL "INTEGER-TO-DATE" USING "19990406" GIVING Date-1
CALL "INTEGER-TO-DATE" USING "20030516" GIVING Date-2
COMPUTE Days-Diff = Date-2 - Date-1
```

With the intrinsic function INTEGER-TO-DATE, you can write all this in a single statement.

```
COMPUTE Days-Diff = FUNCTION INTEGER-TO-DATE("20030516") -
         FUNCTION INTEGER-TO-DATE("19990406")
```

You write less code, you don't have to define two temporary date items to contain the dates, and the single COMPUTE statement makes it clearer what you are doing because all the code is in one statement. Methods, the object-oriented equivalent of functions, have this same ability.

Encapsulate the data. This is the second reason for object-oriented programming. Suppose you have a program that reads in a file. In traditional COBOL, you read a record into a data structure and have the program operate directly on the data. If the data changes or the file changes format, the program must be changed. This is the Achilles' heel of traditional programming. When everything in a program has access to the data, it makes it easy to program but difficult to change.

With object-oriented programming, you can encapsulate the data to the point where all references to data items are through method (function) references. You might invoke a method to get the next record. The method would worry about opening the file before the first read, and reading the next record; whether it was a sequential or indexed file or even a database. The application program wouldn't care. It would just invoke a method that, in effect, says, "Get me the next record." Then you could encapsulate the fields within the record by accessing them through method references. If you wanted the date, you would invoke the date method. The method might return the date in text form (January 1, 2000), although the date was carried in *yyyymmdd* form in the file. The application program wouldn't know or care how the date was carried in the file. All it would know is that when it invokes the date method, it gets the date in the format it wants.

The advantage of this is that it makes programs easier to change. The application might start out with the method to read the next record from a sequential file on a PC. Over time, as the application grows, the file might be moved to the mainframe. The method to get the next record would have to be changed to retrieve the file from the mainframe, but the application would neither know nor care. Later, the application might go global, and the read method might be modified to dial up on the Internet and retrieve the record from a different continent. Again, the application program would be isolated from this. It just keeps requesting the next record and letting the get-next-record method worry about all the details.

Design to run on different platforms. Computing is not a static field. Programs always have longer lives than planned and migrate to different computers the way the upwardly mobile migrate to larger houses.

27.3 WHAT OBJECT-ORIENTED COBOL PROVIDES

Object-oriented COBOL gives you the ability to encapsulate data. You can define data, allocate it statically (at compile time) or dynamically (while the programming is running), and control access through methods. Static data, called *class data,* consists of data that are not replicated. File descriptions, record counts, constants, tables, and information about a file is an example. Dynamic data, called *object data,* is data that is replicated, similar to the way individual records in a file are replicated.

The second essential part of object-oriented programming is the ability to code methods, which are the object-oriented equivalent of subprograms or functions. Object-oriented programming encapsulates the code to make it available but invisible in the same way that the code in intrinsic functions is available but invisible. For example, when you invoke the CURRENT-DATE intrinsic function, you have no way of knowing where the function gets the current data. Nor can you change the current date. It is totally protected. In object-oriented programming, you can only access the encapsulated data with a method. Moreover, the method can have its own data that can either be reinitialized each time the method is invoked, or the data can retain its value through multiple invocations. This lets methods keep running counts and keep first-time flags.

For example, you might define a file in a method, along with the record description and a flag telling you whether the file is open. When the method is invoked, it would check the open flag, and if the file was not opened, it would open it. Then it would read a record. If there is no end of file, it would return the record. If an end of file were encountered, it could close the file, reset the open flag, and return a code to indicate the end of file. The method could also keep a running count of records read and validate the input records, check that they are in valid sort sequence, handle any I/O errors, and do all the necessary housekeeping for the file and its records. The program invoking the method need not know anything about the file. All it needs to do is request the method to return the next record or an indication that there was an end of file. Hundreds of programs could use this method and not have to duplicate all the tedious code contained in the method.

27.4   HOW SUBPROGRAMS EVOLVED INTO METHODS

To see how methods have evolved from functions, let's trace this evolution starting with a subprogram to convert a Gregorian date in the form *yyyymmdd* to text
form, such as *May 2, 2002*, from Chapter 26. Here is the subprogram.

27.4.1   Subprograms

```
IDENTIFICATION DIVISION.        [No longer needed in new ANSI standard.]
PROGRAM-ID. MoTextDate.
DATA DIVISION.
WORKING-STORAGE SECTION.
01  Fmt-Dy                          PIC X(3).
01  Mo-Table.
    05  Mo-Tbl-V.
        10  Mo-Tbl-Jan              PIC X(9) VALUE "January".
        10  Mo-Tbl-Feb              PIC X(9) VALUE "February".
            .       .                   .   .    .     .
        10  Mo-Tbl-Dec              PIC X(9) VALUE "December".
    05  Mo-Tbl REDEFINES Mo-Tbl-V OCCURS 12 TIMES PIC X(9).
LINKAGE SECTION.
01  Current-Date.
    05  Cd-Yr                       PIC 9(4).
    05  Cd-Mo                       PIC 99.
    05  Cd-Dy                       PIC 99.
01  Formatted-Date                  PIC X(30).
PROCEDURE DIVISION USING Current-Date, Formatted-Date.
A00-Begin.
    IF Cd-Dy < 10
        THEN MOVE Cd-Dy(2:1) TO Fmt-Dy
        ELSE MOVE Cd-Dy to Fmt-Dy
    END-IF
    MOVE SPACES TO Formatted-Date
    STRING Mo-Tbl(Cd-Mo) DELIMITED " ", " " DELIMITED SIZE
           Fmt-Dy DELIMITED " ", ", " DELIMITED SIZE
           Cd-Yr DELIMITED SIZE INTO Formatted-Date
    END-STRING
    GOBACK.
END PROGRAM MoTextDate.
```

For a program to invoke this subprogram, you would code the following:

```
CALL "MoTextDate" USING BY VALUE "20020502",
                       BY REFERENCE Report-Date
```

27.4.2   Functions

Using the features of the new ANSI standard, you could code this as a function.
Notice there are only three changes.

```
IDENTIFICATION DIVISION.              [You can omit this in the new standard.]
FUNCTION-ID . MoTextDate.             [Changed.]
DATA DIVISION.
WORKING-STORAGE SECTION.
01  Fmt-Dy                    PIC X(3).
01  Mo-Table.
    05  Mo-Tbl-V.
        10  Mo-Tbl-Jan        PIC X(9) VALUE "January".
        .  .                       .
        10  Mo-Tbl-Dec        PIC X(9) VALUE "December".
    05  Mo-Tbl REDEFINES Mo-Tbl-V OCCURS 12 TIMES PIC X(9).
LINKAGE SECTION.
01  Current-Date.
    05  Cd-Yr                 PIC 9(4).
    05  Cd-Mo                 PIC 99.
    05  Cd-Dy                 PIC 99.
01  Formatted-Date           PIC X(30).
PROCEDURE DIVISION USING Current-Date,
                             RETURNING Formatted-Date.  [Changed.]
A00-Begin.
    IF Cd-Dy < 10
       THEN MOVE Cd-Dy(2:1) TO Fmt-Dy
       ELSE MOVE Cd-Dy to Fmt-Dy
    END-IF
    MOVE SPACES TO Formatted-Date
    STRING Mo-Tbl(Cd-Mo) DELIMITED " ", " " DELIMITED SIZE
           Fmt-Dy DELIMITED " ", ", " DELIMITED SIZE
           Cd-Yr DELIMITED SIZE INTO Formatted-Date
    END-STRING
    GOBACK.
END FUNCTION MoTextDate.              [Changed.]
```

Now you can invoke the function in an expression, such as the following:

```
MOVE FUNCTION MoTextDate("20020502") TO Report-Date
```

27.4.3 Methods

We can easily turn the *MoTextDate* function into an object-oriented method by changing the FUNCTION-ID to METHOD-ID and the END FUNCTION to END METHOD. Because the Identification Division header is optional, it is omitted.

```
METHOD-ID . MoTextDate.               [Changed.]
    □   □   □                         [Everything else identical.]
END METHOD MoTextDate.                [Changed.]
```

Then instead of calling the method, you invoke it with the INVOKE statement, which is the equivalent of a CALL, except you also supply a pointer to the data on which the method is to operate. For now, assume we placed the *MoTextDate* method in a class named *The-Dates*. Class is described next.

```
CALL "MoTextDate" USING BY VALUE "20020502",
                        BY REFERENCE Report-Date
```

becomes

```
INVOKE The-Dates "MoTextDate" USING BY VALUE "20020502",
                        RETURNING Report-Date
```

Alternatively, you can invoke a method in-line, similar to the way you do a function.

```
MOVE FUNCTION MoTextDate("20020502") TO Report-Date
```

becomes

```
MOVE The-Dates :: "MoTextDate"("20020502") TO Report-Date
```

Except for coding METHOD-ID in place of FUNCTION-ID and END METHOD in place of END FUNCTION, a method is written identically to a subprogram function. And except for coding INVOKE rather than CALL or the slightly different form of in-line invocation in which you supply a pointer to the data, you already know what you need to know about coding a method. In object-oriented programming terminology, invoking a method is termed *sending a message.* If you think in terms of distributed processing in which the INVOKE references a method that may be on a different computer, calling this sending a message makes sense.

Methods by themselves add nothing new to COBOL. A method is nothing more than a function under a different name. The coding rules are identical, except for the small differences noted.

Now suppose that a department head hates commas and demands that reports for his department have the form 2 May 2002 rather than May 2, 2002. You would copy the *MoTextDate* method, changing only the name to *DyTextDate* (as good a name as any) and the STRING statement to the following:

```
METHOD-ID. DyTextDate.              [Changed.]
    □  □  □                         [Everything else identical.]
    STRING Fmt-Dy DELIMITED ".",    [STRING changed.]
        " " DELIMITED SIZE,
        Mo-Tbl(Cd-Mo) DELIMITED " ", " " DELIMITED SIZE
        Cd-Yr DELIMITED SIZE INTO Formatted-Date
    END-STRING
    GOBACK.
END METHOD DyTextDate.              [Changed.]
```

27.5   THE DETAILS OF OBJECT-ORIENTED PROGRAMMING

Now we have two similar methods that do slightly different things to the same data, a date. It would be nice to collect them, and all the other methods we might write to operate on dates, together. Object-oriented programming does this with what it calls the class.

27.5.1 The Class

A *class* describes a generic form of data, such as a date, along with the methods that operate on the data. To illustrate this, suppose we have various dates we want to display. Two of the dates might be today's date and the compilation date of the program. There is only one instance of each for a computer run. For such data, we describe it as part of the class and call it *class data*. We already have two methods to operate on it, *MoTextDate* and *DyTextDate*. Because these two methods belong to the class, we call them *class methods*. Figure 27.2 illustrates this. Now suppose that we read in a file containing records, and we want to store each of the records. Here we have multiple instances of a data field. We call such data an *object,* and each instance of the data is *object data*. We could also write methods to operate on the object data from a record. An obvious one would be to return the date field. A method that operates on the object data is called an *object method*. Figure 27.3 illustrates this.

Now let's see how all this is programmed. Unfortunately, because the ANSI standard for the object-oriented features has yet to be adopted, the different compiler vendors have had to implement their own versions. While they are similar, they are also all different and different from the proposed ANSI standard. For the examples here, the ANSI standard version is used.

You code a class as you would any COBOL program, with the four divisions. Because the Identification Division header is optional, it is omitted in the remainder of the examples. You start with the CLASS-ID paragraph, which is the equivalent of the PROGRAM-ID paragraph.

```
CLASS-ID. The-Dates INHERITS FROM Base.
```
          [This names the class as *The-Dates*. You create and delete objects using methods from a system-provided class named *Base*. The INHERITS *Base* lets the *The-Dates* class use the system-provided methods in *Base*. Besides naming *Base* here, you must also name it in the following REPOSITORY paragraph.]
```
ENVIRONMENT DIVISION.
CONFIGURATION SECTION.
REPOSITORY.
```

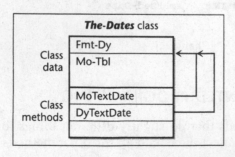

FIGURE 27.2 Class data and methods.

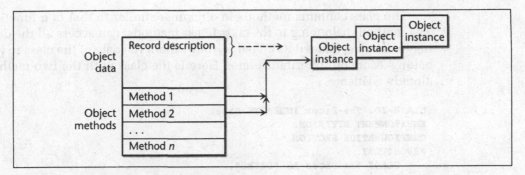

FIGURE 27.3 Object data and methods.

[This is the same REPOSITORY described in Chapter 21 for functions. You name each class used by the program and tell what file it is contained in.]

CLASS Base AS "*file-name*".

[This tells COBOL that the *Base* class is stored in the file named. (If you don't supply a suffix in PC COBOL, a suffix, ".CBL" in Micro Focus COBOL, is assumed.) This is similar to the SELECT clause in which you give the internal name of a file and connect it to its external name. This description connects the class to the external file in which it is stored.]

FACTORY.

[This is a new paragraph that denotes the start of the data descriptions and methods belonging to the class.]

DATA DIVISION.

WORKING-STORAGE SECTION.

[You describe the Working-Storage data for the class here—the class data. This is the static data for the class allocated during compilation. You can code it as you would any data, including assigning initial values to it with VALUE clauses.]

PROCEDURE DIVISION.

[You place the methods belonging to the class (class methods), such as *MoText-Date* and *DyTextDate* here. They have access to the data in the class Working-Storage.]

END FACTORY.

[You must code this to end the FACTORY paragraph.]

END CLASS The-Dates.

[You write END CLASS as you would write END PROGRAM.]

The class, as with all object-oriented components, is written much the same as a main program with the four basic COBOL divisions. When we include the *DyTextDate* and *MoTextDate* methods, we can move the month table (*Mo-Table*) out of the individual methods and up to the Working-Storage of the class so that we don't duplicate the same table in each of the methods. In this way, suppose the government decides to pay off the national debt by selling vanity month names to individuals so that January becomes Gates, the change can be made in one place. The tables could have been left in the individual methods, but any change would have to be made in two places.

The class contains methods in a manner similar to that of a function library. The methods belonging to the class (class methods) can access all the data belonging to the class (class data). That is, they *inherit* the data of the class to which they belong. More on inheritance later. Here is the class with the two methods we've already written:

```
CLASS-ID. The-Dates INHERITS Base.
ENVIRONMENT DIVISION.
CONFIGURATION SECTION.
REPOSITORY.
    CLASS The-Dates AS "DATES".
FACTORY.
DATA DIVISION.
WORKING-STORAGE SECTION.
        [The data that was in the DyTextDate and MoTextDate methods are placed
        following this.]
01  Fmt-Dy                      PIC X(3).
01  Mo-Table.
    05  Mo-Tbl-V.
        10 Mo-Tbl-Jan           PIC X(9) VALUE "January".
         . .                      .
        10 Mo-Tbl-Dec           PIC X(9) VALUE "December".
    05  Mo-Tbl REDEFINES Mo-Tbl-V OCCURS 12 TIMES PIC X(9).
PROCEDURE DIVISION.             [The methods are placed following this.]
METHOD-ID. DyTextDate.          [This is the first method.]
DATA DIVISION.
LINKAGE SECTION.          [Each method must still contain its own Linkage Section.]
01  Current-Date.
    05  Cd-Yr                   PIC 9(4).
    05  Cd-Mo                   PIC 99.
    05  Cd-Dy                   PIC 99.
01  Formatted-Date             PIC X(30).
PROCEDURE DIVISION USING Current-Date, RETURNING Formatted-Date.
      □  □  □
END METHOD  DyTextDate.
METHOD-ID. MoTextDate.          [Here is the second method.]
      □  □  □
END METHOD MoTextDate.
END FACTORY.
END CLASS The-Dates.
```

We've now defined a class named *The-Dates*. It is easy to think of additional methods we might place in it.

- Determine calendar days between two dates.
- Determine work days between two dates.
- Determine if a year is a leap year.

You can add methods as needed. The class, along with all its methods, is stored in a file. Assume the file name is DATES.CBL. Now let's see how the class and its methods can be used.

27.5.2　The Driver Program

All object-oriented programs must have a driver program. The driver program is an ordinary COBOL main program, with a couple of additions. It names the classes to use and starts things off.

```
PROGRAM-ID. TESTDATE.
ENVIRONMENT DIVISION.
CONFIGURATION SECTION.
REPOSITORY.
    CLASS Base AS "BASE"
    CLASS The-Dates AS "DATES".
        [Now COBOL knows that class Base in the file BASE.CBL and class The-Dates in
        the file DATES.CBL will be used.]
DATA DIVISION.
WORKING-STORAGE SECTION.
01  Date-Storage               PIC X(30).
PROCEDURE DIVISION.
A00-Begin.
    MOVE The-Dates :: "DyTextDate"("20030427") TO Date-Storage
        [The DyTextDate method is invoked to convert a date.]
    DISPLAY Date-Storage
    GOBACK.
END PROGRAM TESTDATE.
```

This is a lot of work to do what could have been done with functions, although encapsulating the data and the operations performed on it in the class do make the program easier to change. If the company were setting up standards, it might dictate that all dates in report headings be 30-character alphanumeric strings. All programs would define the date object and invoke a standard date function. The standard date function would know the preferred format of the date, such as 24 January 2003, January 24, 2003, 1/23/2003, 23/1/2003, or whatever. It would invoke the appropriate method to return the current standard date. Then when a new CEO dictates a different date form, only a single change need be made in a single method to effect the change in all reports throughout the company. Still, we could have done this with functions.

If this were all there were to object-oriented programming, letting several methods share the same class data, it would be no big deal. There is more to object-oriented programming—there are objects.

27.5.3　Objects

The *object* in object-oriented programming is one of those rare instances in which a computing term essentially retains its English language meaning. An object is a thing, or at least the generic description of a thing. We could organize employees, automobiles, or a pull-down list on a terminal screen in this same manner. As you might imagine, different people might define different objects. We humans have infinite capacity for classifying things that sometimes come from nature (the elements), but which more often come from our culture and history (cars, trucks, pickups, sport-utility vehicles).

An object consists of the data that describes a thing (its attributes and values) and the collection of methods that operate on the data. For example, we might call a date a thing or an entity, but in object-oriented programming, it is called an object. It belongs to a class, and a class describes only one object, but multiple instances can be made of that one object. The system creates an instance of an object (termed *object data*) using the data description to allocate dynamic storage and returning a pointer to the storage. You then write methods to store, retrieve, and manipulate the object data, supplying the pointer for the method as shown in Figure 27.4. Any number of instances of object data can be created. If an object were a record in a file, the class would contain an object with the record's description. You could store the file's records by creating an instance of object data for each record and using a method to store the data in the object. The form of an accounts receivable transaction might constitute a class, and the transaction description would be the object. This way, the class tells about the accounts receivable transactions in general, and the object provides the format of the transaction and contains the methods to operate on the transactions.

But why? You could also store the transactions in a table. The advantage of object-oriented programming is that the object contains both the data description and the code (methods) to operate on the data. When you write a program to store and retrieve data from a transaction, you as the programmer don't need to know the format of the data. You just invoke a method to store, retrieve, or manipulate the data.

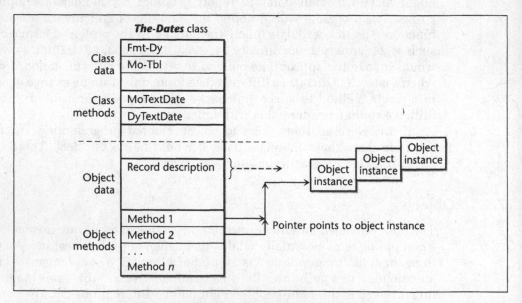

FIGURE 27.4 Class and object methods and data.

Object-oriented programming doesn't revolutionize sequential transaction processing. Transaction processing is more akin to the collision of different objects requiring a program to access data from two different objects at the same time, which is just what object-oriented programming tries to prevent. Object-oriented programming comes into its own when a variety of processing done on an object. This, of course, is just what happens in online systems where the user at the terminal decides what items to display on the screen, jumps back and forth among the items, and elects what processing to do.

Describing Objects

An object describes data and contains the methods that operate on the data. An instance of an object contains the actual data. When you describe an object, you give the template for an instance of the data in the form of data descriptions, in much the same way that a record description is a template for a file record. The record description doesn't contain the data for a particular record until you store the record in the data structure. Likewise, an object instance does not contain data until you create it (by allocating storage for it) and use a method to store data in it.

Here is the way you code an object. It begins with a new OBJECT paragraph.

```
OBJECT.                           [Starts the object description.]
DATA DIVISION.
WORKING-STORAGE SECTION.
[You place the data descriptions here that an instance of the
object is to contain.]
PROCEDURE DIVISION.
[You place the methods belonging to the object here.]
END OBJECT.                       [You end the object with this.]
```

Creating Objects

Objects are created by a system-supplied method called "NEW" that is part of the class *Base*. When you create an object, "NEW" allocates space to contain the data and returns a pointer to it. Because the data within an object is encapsulated, it can only be accessed by its methods. You must then write methods to store data values in the object and retrieve the data.

To illustrate how you create an object, let's take a simple example. First, you define the object by coding data descriptions inside the class. Here is the *The-Dates* class with an object defined to contain a single data item, a formatted date.

```
CLASS-ID. The-Dates INHERITS Base.
      □  □  □
END METHOD MoTextDate.
OBJECT.
DATA DIVISION.
WORKING-STORAGE SECTION.
01  Date-Storage                  PIC X(30).
PROCEDURE DIVISION.
[You place all the object methods here.]
END OBJECT.
END CLASS The-Dates.
```

Here is how you might create an object in the main program. Because COBOL returns a pointer (also termed a *handle*) that points to the object, you need a place to store it. You do this by defining a data item with a new data type, USAGE OBJECT REFERENCE. It has no PIC clause.

```
nn  name                          USAGE OBJECT REFERENCE.
01  Obj-Ptr                       OBJECT REFERENCE.
```

Here is a main program to create a single object.

```
PROGRAM-ID. TESTDATE.
ENVIRONMENT DIVISION.
CONFIGURATION SECTION.
REPOSITORY.
    CLASS Base AS "BASE"
    CLASS The-Dates AS "DATES".
DATA DIVISION.
WORKING-STORAGE SECTION.
01  Obj-Ptr                       OBJECT REFERENCE.
PROCEDURE DIVISION.
A00-Begin.
    INVOKE The-Dates "NEW" RETURNING Obj-Ptr
```
[This creates an object and stores the pointer to it in *Obj-Ptr*.]

The general form of this INVOKE statement is:

```
INVOKE pointer "method" RETURNING identifier
```

INVOKE *The-Dates* tells COBOL to look for the class *The-Dates*. From the REPOSITORY, it knows that *The-Dates* is stored in the file named DATES.CBL (in Micro Focus). COBOL then looks in *The-Dates* for the object. It sees the following data description.

```
01  Date-Storage               PIC X(30).
```

Normally, an object would have many more data descriptions than this, but this is enough to illustrate what happens. COBOL allocates the 30 bytes of storage needed and stores the pointer to the storage in *Obj-Ptr*. After execution, the program looks like Figure 27.5.

You can create many instances of an object. The following code creates 10 instances and stores the pointers in a table.

```
WORKING-STORAGE SECTION.
01  Obj-Table.
    05  Obj-Ptr                  OCCURS 10 TIMES INDEXED BY Ix
                                  OBJECT REFERENCE.
PROCEDURE DIVISION.
A00-Begin.
    PERFORM WITH TEST AFTER VARYING Ix FROM 1 BY 1 UNTIL Ix = 10
```

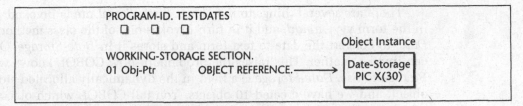

FIGURE 27.5 COBOL program after creating an object.

```
        INVOKE The-Dates "NEW" RETURNING Obj-Ptr(Ix)
    END-PERFORM
```

Destroying Objects

The storage for the objects is automatically released when the program terminates. You can also destroy an object during execution, releasing its storage, by invoking another system method named "FINALIZE".

```
        INVOKE pointer "FINALIZE" RETURNING pointer
```

COBOL releases the storage for the object pointed to by the first *pointer* and stores nulls in the second *pointer*. The following destroys the first of the 10 objects just created:

```
        INVOKE Obj-Ptr(1) "FINALIZE" RETURNING Obj-Ptr(1)
```

Using Objects

Now let's write two object methods, one to store a date in the object and a second to retrieve it. Here they are.

```
METHOD-ID. StoreDate.                [This stores the date in the object.]
DATA DIVISION.
LINKAGE SECTION.
01  Some-Date                        PIC 9(8).
PROCEDURE DIVISION USING Some-Date.
    MOVE The-Dates :: "MoTextDate"(Some-Date) TO Date-Storage
```
[This invokes the *MoTextDate* method of the *The-Dates* class to convert the eight-digit date into character form. It then moves the 30 characters to the *Date-Storage* pointed to by the pointer supplied when this method is invoked. *Date-Storage* is in the object's dynamically allocated storage.]
```
    GOBACK.
END METHOD StoreDate.
METHOD-ID. GetDate.                   [This retrieves the date in the object.]
LINKAGE SECTION.
01  Some-Date                        PIC X(30).
PROCEDURE DIVISION RETURNING Some-Date.
    MOVE Date-Storage TO Some-Date
    GOBACK.
END METHOD GetDate.
```

There are several things to note here. First, *StoreDate* is invoked with a date in the form *yyyymmdd,* and it in turn invokes one of the class methods, *MoText-Date,* to convert the date to text form and stores it in *Date-Storage.* One method can invoke another. This raises the problem of how COBOL knows which *Date-Storage* to use. *Date-Storage* is a field in the dynamically allocated storage for an object, and we have created 10 objects. You tell COBOL which object to use by supplying the pointer following the INVOKE. To invoke *StoreDate,* you would code the following:

```
INVOKE pointer "StoreDate" USING date
INVOKE Obj-Ptr(1) "StoreDate" USING "20030421"
```

StoreDate converts the "20030421" to "April 21, 2003" and stores this in the *Date-Storage* field of the first object, the one pointed to by *Obj-Ptr*(1). Here is the complete program with the two methods:

```
PROGRAM-ID. TESTDATE.
ENVIRONMENT DIVISION.
CONFIGURATION SECTION.
REPOSITORY.
    CLASS Base AS "BASE"
    The-Dates AS CLASS "DATES".
DATA DIVISION.
WORKING-STORAGE SECTION.
01  Obj-Table.
    05  Obj-Ptr                     OCCURS 10 TIMES INDEXED BY Ix
                                     OBJECT REFERENCE.
PROCEDURE DIVISION.
A00-Begin.
    PERFORM WITH TEST AFTER VARYING Ix FROM 1 BY 1 UNTIL Ix = 10
        INVOKE The-Dates "NEW" RETURNING Obj-Ptr(Ix)
    END-PERFORM
    PERFORM WITH TEST AFTER VARYING Ix FROM 1 BY 1 UNTIL Ix = 10
        INVOKE Obj-Ptr(Ix) "StoreDate" USING "20030421"
        [We store the same date in all 10 objects. This is just to illustrate how you store
        data.]
    END-PERFORM
    PERFORM WITH TEST AFTER VARYING Ix FROM 1 BY 1 UNTIL Ix = 10
        INVOKE Obj-Ptr(Ix) "FINALIZE" RETURNING Obj-Ptr(Ix)
        [Then we destroy all the objects. We've accomplished nothing useful except to
        illustrate objects.]
    END-PERFORM
    GOBACK.
END PROGRAM TESTDATE.
```

The entire *The-Dates* class stored in the DATES.CBL file now looks like this:

```
CLASS-ID. The-Dates INHERITS Base.
ENVIRONMENT DIVISION.
CONFIGURATION SECTION.
```

```
       REPOSITORY.
          CLASS The-Dates AS "DATES".
       FACTORY.
       DATA DIVISION.
       WORKING-STORAGE SECTION.
       01  Fmt-Dy                         PIC X(3).
       01  Mo-Table.
           05  Mo-Tbl-V.
               10  Mo-Tbl-Jan             PIC X(9) VALUE "January".
                   .    .    .    .
               10  Mo-Tbl-Dec             PIC X(9) VALUE "December".
           05  Mo-Tbl REDEFINES Mo-Tbl-V OCCURS 12 TIMES PIC X(9).
       PROCEDURE DIVISION.
       METHOD-ID. DyTextDate.
           □ □ □
       END METHOD DyTextDate.
       METHOD-ID. MoTextDate.
           □ □ □
       END METHOD MoTextDate.
       END FACTORY.
       OBJECT.
       DATA DIVISION.
       WORKING-STORAGE SECTION.
       01  Date-Storage                   PIC X(30).
       METHOD-ID. StoreDate.
       DATA DIVISION.
       LINKAGE SECTION.
       01  Some-Date                      PIC 9(8).
       PROCEDURE DIVISION USING Some-Date.
           MOVE The-Dates :: "MoTextDate"(Some-Date) TO Date-Storage
           GOBACK.
       END METHOD StoreDate.
       METHOD-ID. GetDate.
       LINKAGE SECTION.
       01  Some-Date                      PIC X(30).
       PROCEDURE DIVISION RETURNING Some-Date.
           MOVE Date-Storage TO Some-Date
           GOBACK.
       END METHOD GetDate.
       END OBJECT.
       END CLASS The-Dates.
```

Scope

Although the object belongs to a class and the class can have its own methods, the methods of the class cannot operate on the data belonging to the object (*MoText-Date* cannot access *Date-Storage*). Figure 27.6 illustrates this. However, the object's methods can operate on the data of the class. (*GetDate* can access *Mo-Tbl.*) Likewise, the class cannot use the methods of the object. (*MoTextDate* cannot invoke *StoreDate.*) The object can use the methods of the class. (*StoreDate* can invoke *MoTextDate.*)

The limiting of what data can be referenced and which methods can be invoked is termed *scope.* Object-oriented COBOL encapsulates data by limiting

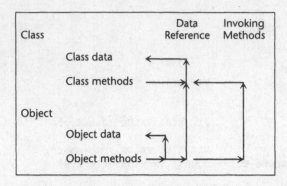

FIGURE 27.6 Scope of data and methods.

the scope so that data and methods can only be used by methods that inherit them.

Inheritance

The class and object represent a hierarchy, with the object lower in the hierarchy. One of the features of object-oriented programming is that items lower in the hierarchy *inherit* data and methods from things higher in the hierarchy. To inherit means that they get to use them. Inheritance is in only one direction, as shown in Figure 27.7.

Besides inheriting data, methods can inherit other methods. Thus, the method that determines calendar days between two dates might need to know if a year was a leap year. Because the method to determine leap year is a member of the same object, the method to determine days between dates inherits the leap year method and can use it.

Classes themselves can be organized into a hierarchy. Descendant classes are called subclasses and ascendant classes are called superclasses. Through inheritance, all subclasses inherit the objects, methods, and data from the classes above it. Consequently, any change to the data or method in a superclass makes the change automatically in all the subclasses.

In addition to objects inheriting from classes, the classes themselves can form a hierarchy. The CLASS-ID paragraph can specify that a particular class is to inherit the data, methods, and objects from another class.

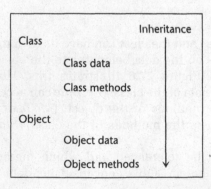

FIGURE 27.7 Inheritance of data and methods.

```
CLASS-ID. class-name INHERITS FROM other-class
                     INHERITS FROM other-class
              ...          ...          ...
                     INHERITS FROM other-class.
```

The class that inherits is termed the *subclass,* and the class it inherits from is the *superclass.* As with all inheritance, items higher in the hierarchy cannot access the data or methods lower in the hierarchy, but items lower in the hierarchy inherit the data, methods, and objects of those higher in the hierarchy. Thus the subclass inherits from the superclass as shown in Figure 27.8.

27.6   WHY OBJECTS

This raises the question of why we would want to go to all this trouble just to store a date. Why not store it in an identifier? We could, but what if there were several dates? Why then not store them in a table? We could, but what if we didn't know

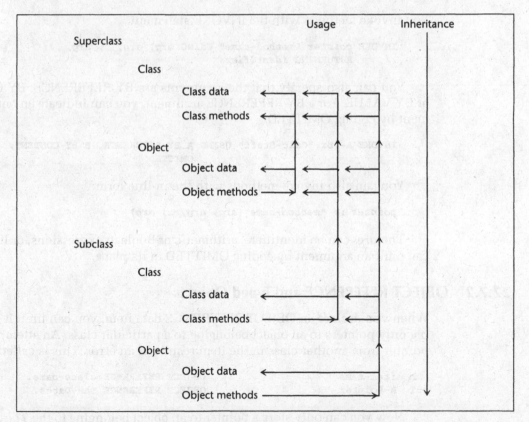

FIGURE 27.8   Inheritance of superclasses and subclasses.

how many there might be? Why not wait for the new ANSI standard to be implemented and use its dynamic table feature that lets you expand a table? We could.

In fact, there would be little reason to create an object for a single date or even a collection of dates. The same is true for transactions. In the batch transaction world of the traditional COBOL program, object-oriented programming benefits are muted, but do provide a convenient means of collecting similar functions together, such as the date functions. Objects don't have much of a payoff if they don't have an extended life inside the computer. The life of a transaction is brief. You read it in, apply it, and that's it. The data in most batch applications is similar. Where objects become worthwhile is when they hang around inside the computer, making it worth the effort to create them.

27.7   MORE DETAILS OF OBJECT-ORIENTED PROGRAMMING

We are now ready to move into the details of object-oriented programming.

27.7.1   Invoking Methods

You invoke methods with the INVOKE statement:

```
INVOKE pointer "method-name" USING arg, arg, …, arg,
       RETURNING identifier
```

You can also specify that the arguments are BY REFERENCE, BY CONTENT, or BY VALUE. For a BY REFERENCE argument, you can indicate an omitted argument by coding OMITTED:

```
INVOKE A-Ptr "Calc-Stuff" USING A BY REFERENCE, B BY CONTENT,
                              OMITTED
```

You can also invoke methods with the in-line form:

```
pointer :: "method-name"(arg, arg, …, arg)
```

The *args* can be identifiers, arithmetic or Boolean expressions, or literals. You can omit an argument by coding OMITTED in its place.

27.7.2   OBJECT REFERENCE and Typed Objects

When you declare an OBJECT REFERENCE data item, you can limit it to containing only pointers to an object belonging to a particular class. An attempt to store a pointer from another class in the item results in an error. This is called *typing*.

```
nn  item-name                    OBJECT REFERENCE class-name.
01  A-Pointer                    OBJECT REFERENCE The-Dates.
```

Now you can only store a pointer to an object belonging to the *The-Dates* class *in A-Pointer*. If you don't type the pointer item, you can store pointers in it from any class.

27.7.3   The SET Statement

You store one OBJECT REFERENCE item in another with the SET statement. (You can't use the MOVE statement, unless the OBJECT REFERENCE is a lower-level item in a group move.)

```
SET receiving-pointer TO sending-pointer
```

This stores the *sending-pointer* in the *receiving-pointer*.

```
SET Ptr-A TO Ptr-B            [The content of Ptr-B is stored in Ptr-A.]
```

27.7.4   Polymorphism

Because methods are meant to be shared, there is always the problem that methods written by different programmers might be given the same name. Even the same programmer may use the same name for similar functions. It is difficult to think of creative names to do common operations on values, such as get and store values. The problem of different methods having the same name is nicely solved by typing the pointers used in the INVOKE or in-line reference. Using the same name for different methods and selecting the proper method based on the context is termed *polymorphism.* For example, if another class named *Annual-Dates* also had a method named *DyTextDate* that did something entirely different from the *DyTextDate* method in the *The-Dates* class, there would be no problem if you typed the identifier containing the pointer. Here is an example.

```
01  A-Pointer                 OBJECT-REFERENCE The-Dates.
01  B-Pointer                 OBJECT-REFERENCE Annual-Dates.
    □  □  □
    MOVE A-Pointer :: "DyTextDate" TO Some-Storage
        [COBOL would use the DyTextDate method belonging to the The-Dates class.]
    MOVE B-Pointer :: "DyTextDate" TO Other-Storage
        [COBOL would use the DyTextDate method belonging to the Annual-Dates class,
        which would be an entirely different method.]
```

27.7.5   NULLS Figurative Constant

The NULLS figurative constant indicates the absence of a value for a pointer.

```
SET Ptr-A TO NULLS            [Ptr-A contains nulls pointing to nothing.]
```

27.7.6   The SELF and SUPER Pointers

Often in a method, you need to invoke another method to operate on the same object data. To invoke a method to operate on the object data, you must provide a pointer to the data. One way to do this is to pass the pointer as a parameter in the INVOKE statement. Suppose that you want to invoke *Method-A* using a pointer named *Some-Ptr*, and that inside *Method-A*, you want to invoke *Method-B* to operate on the same object data as *Method-A* is operating on. You could pass *Some-Ptr* as a parameter in the INVOKE.

```
INVOKE Some-Ptr "Method-A" USING A, Some-Ptr, RETURNING B
```

In the LINKAGE SECTION, *Method-A* would describe an item for the *Some-Ptr* parameter, say *A-Ptr*, and you could supply it as the pointer in invoking *Method-B*.

```
INVOKE A-Ptr "Method-B" USING A, RETURNING B
```

However, there is a simpler way. When you are inside a method, it is already pointing to the data you want. To supply this same pointer, you use the keyword SELF as the object reference. You could invoke *Method-A* without passing *Some-Ptr* as a parameter.

```
INVOKE Some-Ptr "Method-A" USING A, RETURNING B
```

Then inside *Method-A*, you could use SELF as the pointer to invoke *Method-B*.

```
INVOKE SELF "Method-B" USING A, RETURNING B
```

This is simpler and more direct.

Analogous to SELF is the SUPER pointer. It points to the class to which the object belongs. This provides access to class methods and data.

27.7.7   Comparing Pointers

You can compare pointers only for equality.

```
IF Ptr-A NOT = NULLS THEN …
IF Ptr-A = SELF …
IF Ptr-A = Ptr-B …
```

A pointer is either the relative or absolute storage address of the item to which it is pointing. Comparing two storage addresses to see if one is greater than or less than the other makes no sense. If the pointers are equal, they point to the same item; if not, they point to different items.

27.7.8   The PROPERTY Clause

Although the normal way of accessing object data is by invoking a method, there is a way to access the data directly as you would normal Working-Storage data. You can code the PROPERTY clause on the object's data description, and then qualify the reference to the data with an OF clause that supplies the pointer to the object instance. Here is how this works. Suppose that an object contains the following data item:

```
01  A-Date                      PIC X(10).
```

To make it directly accessible, you add the PROPERTY clause:

```
01  A-Date                      PIC X(10) PROPERTY.
```

Now suppose that we create an object instance and store the pointer to it in *A-Ptr*. A program can reference *A-Date* directly by coding:

```
    data-name OF pointer        A-Date OF A-Ptr
```

For example:

```
    MOVE "20031012" TO A-Date OF A-Ptr
```

The PROPERTY clause has three forms:

```
PROPERTY                    [You can change and retrieve the data.]
PROPERTY WITH NO SET        [You can retrieve the data but not change it.]
PROPERTY WITH NO GET        [You can change the data but not retrieve it.]
```

27.7.9 Statement Placement

Putting all the pieces together may appear complex, but it is actually quite simple. You place the statements as shown here.

Driver Program
```
PROGRAM-ID. program-name.
ENVIRONMENT DIVISION.
CONFIGURATION SECTION.
REPOSITORY.
    CLASS BASE AS "BASE"
    .       .       .
    CLASS class AS "file-name".
DATA DIVISION.
WORKING-STORAGE SECTION.
    .       .       .
PROCEDURE DIVISION.
[Procedure Division statements of driver program placed here.]
END PROGRAM name.
```

Class
```
CLASS-ID. class-name INHERITS BASE.
ENVIRONMENT DIVISION.
CONFIGURATION SECTION.
ENVIRONMENT DIVISION.
```

```
CONFIGURATION SECTION.
REPOSITORY.
    CLASS class-name AS "file-name".
FACTORY.
DATA DIVISION.
WORKING-STORAGE SECTION.
    □ □ □                              [Class data described here.]
PROCEDURE DIVISION.
METHOD-ID. method-name.               [Class methods placed here.]
[Method statements placed here.]
END METHOD method-name.
    □ □ □
END FACTORY.
OBJECT.
DATA DIVISION.
WORKING-STORAGE SECTION.
    □ □ □                              [Object data descriptions placed here.]
PROCEDURE DIVISION.
METHOD-ID. method-name.               [Object methods placed here.]
[Method statements placed here.]
END METHOD method-name.
    □ □ □
END OBJECT.
END CLASS class-name.
```

27.8   AN EXAMPLE OF OBJECTS

To illustrate an object-oriented program, the following simple application displays four dates on the screen and lets someone at the terminal select them by moving their cursor over them. When they do, the program displays the date at the bottom of the screen in text form. The screen might look like this, with four dates displayed and one selected to display in text form at the bottom of the screen. To end the program, the person moves the cursor over the "PRESS TO END" and presses ENTER.

```
20030407  20011028  20060914  19990228


      October 28, 2001          PRESS TO END
```

Here is the object for such an application.

```
OBJECT.
DATA DIVISION.
WORKING-STORAGE SECTION.
01  Date-Data.
    05  Date-Ptr              OBJECT REFERENCE.
    [This is a pointer that will point to the next object in the linked list. It is
    explained later.]
    05  The-Date              PIC 9(8).
    [The date is in yyyymmdd form.]
```

```
05  L-Row                        PIC 99.
05  L-Col                        PIC 99.
05  U-Row                        PIC 99.
05  R-Col                        PIC 99.
```

[These give the row and column positions of the box around the date where it displays on the screen. The program displays the date at the lower row, left column.]

```
PROCEDURE DIVISION.
[The methods that operate on this data will go here.]
END OBJECT.
```

Let's worry about the methods for the object later. For now, lets see how to create an object instance. We create objects by invoking the "NEW" method in class *Base*. It allocates storage for the instance and returns a pointer to it. We'll need an identifier to contain this pointer.

```
01  First-Ptr                    OBJECT REFERENCE.
```

The program displays four dates at a time on the screen. It could store the pointers directly in a table, but for illustration, we'll use a linked list in which *First-Ptr* points to the first object instance, and each instance contains a pointer to the next instance. The last instance contains a NULL pointer so we can know when we have reached the end of the list as shown in Figure 27.9. A linked list is not needed for this application, and is used only to illustrate some of the things that can be done with pointers.

In the program, the first object instance is allocated and its pointer is stored in *First-Ptr*. Then, as it creates each new instance, it stores a pointer to it in *Date-Ptr* in the previous instance. We're now ready to put all this together into a working program. An object-oriented program needs an ordinary COBOL main program (driver program) to start things off.

```
PROGRAM-ID. DATEPLAY.
ENVIRONMENT DIVISION.
CONFIGURATION SECTION.
REPOSITORY.
    CLASS BASE AS "BASE"
```

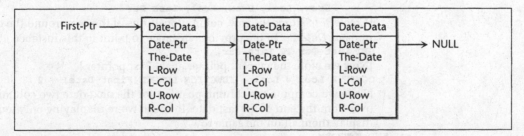

FIGURE 27.9 Linked list.

```
        CLASS BDates AS "BDATES".
```
[We'll code a class named *Bdates* to do all the work.]
```
DATA DIVISION.
WORKING-STORAGE SECTION.
01  Date-Tbl-Values.
    05  First-Date          PIC 9(8) VALUE 20030407.
    05  FILLER              PIC 9(8) VALUE 20011028.
    05  FILLER              PIC 9(8) VALUE 20060914.
    05  FILLER              PIC 9(8) VALUE 19990228.
01  Date-Tbl REDEFINES      Date-Tbl-Values.
    05  Date-Tbl-Entry      OCCURS 4 TIMES INDEXED BY Dx
                            PIC 9(8).
```
[We define a table containing four dates in *yyyymmdd* form.]
```
01  Lrow                    PIC 99 VALUE 2.
01  Lcol                    PIC 99 VALUE 4.
01  Urow                    PIC 99.
01  Rcol                    PIC 99.
```
[These contain the row, column positions of the box around the date. We start in row 2, column 4.]
```
01  First-Ptr               OBJECT REFERENCE VALUE NULLS.
```
[We need this to point to the first object. Thereafter, each object will point to the next.]
```
01  Last-Ptr                OBJECT REFERENCE VALUE NULLS.
```
[This contains the pointer to the previous object.]
```
01  Date-Ptr                OBJECT REFERENCE.
```
[This contains the pointer to the current object.]
```
PROCEDURE DIVISION.
    PERFORM WITH TEST AFTER VARYING Dx FROM 1 BY 1
            UNTIL Dx = 4
```
[We loop through four times to create an object for each date.]
```
    COMPUTE Rcol = Lcol + FUNCTION LENGTH(First-Date) - 1
    COMPUTE Urow = Lrow - 1
```
[This computes the row, column positions of the upper-right corner of the box around the date.]
```
    INVOKE BDates "NEW" RETURNING Date-Ptr
```
[This creates an object instance and stores the pointer to it in *Date-Ptr.*]
```
    IF First-Ptr = NULLS
        THEN SET First-Ptr TO Date-Ptr
```
[This saves the pointer to the first instance.]
```
    END-IF
    INVOKE Date-Ptr "CreateDate" USING Date-Tbl-Entry(Dx),
           Lrow, Lcol, Urow, Rcol, Last-Ptr
```
[*CreateDate* stores the row, column positions of the box around the date and updates *Date-Ptr* in the previous instance to point to this instance.]
```
    SET Last-Ptr TO Date-Ptr
```
[Now we store the current pointer as the last pointer.]
```
    COMPUTE Lcol = Lcol + FUNCTION LENGTH(First-Date) + 2
```
[Then we compute the column position for the next date two column positions over from the end of the last date. Because we're displaying only four dates, we'll display them all on the same row.]
```
    END-PERFORM
    INVOKE BDates "UserPlay" USING First-Ptr
```

[*UserPlay* lets the person at the terminal position their cursor under a date and press ENTER to display the date in text form.]

```
    GOBACK.
END PROGRAM DATEPLAY.
```

That is the entire driver program. The *Bdates* class is written and stored separately. To help you understand it, here are the methods it contains.

CreateDate stores the data in the object. It then links the current object to the last object in a linked list:

```
INVOKE pointer "CreateDate" USING date, lower-row, left-col,
                                     upper-row, right-col,
                                     last-pointer
```

- *pointer:* Pointers to the current object.
- *date:* 8-character date in form *yyyymmdd.*
- *lower-row, left-col:* Row (1 through 25) and column (1 through 80) on the terminal screen, 1 through 24 of the lower-left corner of the box.
- *upper-row, right-col:* Screen position of the upper-right corner of the box.
- *last-pointer:* Pointer to previous object—the object to link this object to.

DyTextDate converts a date in the form *yyyymmdd* to the text form of *dd month yyyy:*

```
INVOKE "DyTextDate" USING date, RETURNING formatted-date
```

- *date:* 8-character date in the form *yyyymmdd.*
- *formatted-date:* 30-character identifier. Date returned in the form *dd month yyyy.*

GetDates retrieves the date and row, column positions from an object, and stores them in a table:

```
INVOKE pointer "GetDates" USING i, RETURNING next-pointer
```

- *pointer:* Points to an object.
- *i:* Subscript to the table, 1 through *n*, where the data is stored.
- *next-pointer:* Points to the next object in the linked list. Contains NULLS if no more objects.

LinkDate links an object instance to the previous instance.

```
INVOKE last-pointer "LinkDate" USING pointer
```

- *last-pointer:* Points to the object to link to.
- *pointer:* Points to the object to link.

MoTextDate converts a date in the form *yyyymmdd* to the text form of *month, dd, yyyy.*

```
INVOKE "MoTextDate" USING date, RETURNING formatted-date
```

- *date:* 8-character date in the form *yyyymmdd.*

- *formatted-date:* 30-character identifier. Date returned in the form *month, dd, yyyy.*

UserPlay displays the date in each object of the linked list using the column, row positions stored in the object. It also displays "PRESS TO END" at the bottom of the screen. Then it positions the cursor on the first date on the screen and turns the screen over to the person at the terminal. The person can move the cursor from date to date. When they press the ENTER key, the text form of the date is displayed at the bottom of the screen. They terminate the program by moving the cursor to the PRESS TO END text and pressing ENTER.

```
INVOKE Bdates UserPlay USING pointer
```

- *pointer:* Points to the first object in the linked list.

With this out of the way, here is how the class is coded:

```
CLASS-ID. BDates INHERITS BASE.
ENVIRONMENT DIVISION.
CONFIGURATION SECTION.
SPECIAL-NAMES.
    CURSOR IS Csr-Loc
    CRT STATUS IS PF-Key.
    [Because we're using full-screen I/O, we need to name the data items that will
    hold the cursor location and the key pressed.]
ENVIRONMENT DIVISION.
CONFIGURATION SECTION.
REPOSITORY.
    CLASS BDates AS "BDATES".
FACTORY.
DATA DIVISION.
WORKING-STORAGE SECTION.
01  Csr-Loc                     PIC 9(6).
01  Csr-Loc-Parts               REDEFINES Csr-Loc.
    05  Csr-Row                 PIC 999.
    05  Csr-Col                 PIC 999.
    [This contains the data telling where the cursor is and what key was pressed as
    described in Chapter 24.]
01  PF-Key                      PIC 99X.
01  Fmt-Dy                      PIC X(3).
01  Mo-Table.
    05  Mo-Tbl-V.
        10  Mo-Tbl-Jan          PIC X(9) VALUE "January".
            .        .              .      .
        10  Mo-Tbl-Dec          PIC X(9) VALUE "December".
    05  Mo-Tbl REDEFINES Mo-Tbl-V  OCCURS 12 TIMES PIC X(9).
01  The-Objects-Table.
    05  Obj-Entries OCCURS 4 TIMES.
        10  S-Next-Ptr          OBJECT REFERENCE.
        10  S-The-Date          PIC 9(8).
        10  S-L-Row             PIC 99.
        10  S-L-Col             PIC 99.
```

```
          10   S-U-Row                    PIC 99.
          10   S-R-Col                    PIC 99.
```
[The data from the four objects is stored in this table.]
```
01   Formatted-Date                       PIC X(30) VALUE SPACES.
```
[This contains the formatted date at the bottom of the screen.]
```
01   End-Message                          PIC X(12) VALUE "PRESS TO END".
```
[This is displayed at the bottom of the screen.]
```
SCREEN SECTION.
01   Screen-1 BLANK SCREEN BACKGROUND-COLOR 1, FOREGROUND-COLOR 7.
```
[This describes the screen for the program. It displays four dates at a time plus the formatted date and a PRESS TO END message.]
```
     05   First-Line.
          10   LINE S-L-Row(1) COLUMN S-L-Col(1)
               REVERSE-VIDEO PIC 9(8) USING S-The-Date(1).
          10   LINE S-L-Row(2) COLUMN S-L-Col(2)
               REVERSE-VIDEO PIC 9(8) USING S-The-Date(2).
          10   LINE S-L-Row(3) COLUMN S-L-Col(3)
               REVERSE-VIDEO PIC 9(8) USING S-The-Date(3).
          10   LINE S-L-Row(4) COLUMN S-L-Col(4)
               REVERSE-VIDEO PIC 9(8) USING S-The-Date(4).
     05   Second-Line LINE 25 COLUMN 40 PIC X(12)
                                 USING End-Message.
     05   Last-Line.
          10   LINE 25 COLUMN 1 REVERSE-VIDEO
                                 PIC X(30) FROM Formatted-Date.
PROCEDURE DIVISION.
METHOD-ID. UserPlay.
DATA DIVISION.
01   I                                    PIC S9(5).
LINKAGE SECTION.
01   A-Ptr                                OBJECT REFERENCE.
PROCEDURE DIVISION USING A-Ptr.
A00-Begin.
     PERFORM WITH TEST AFTER VARYING I FROM 1 BY 1
               UNTIL A-Ptr = NULLS
          INVOKE A-Ptr "GetDates" USING I, RETURNING A-Ptr
```
[This retrieves the objects in the linked list and stores their data in a table.]
```
     END-PERFORM
     PERFORM WITH TEST AFTER
               UNTIL Csr-Row <= 25 AND Csr-Col >= 40 AND
                  Csr-Row >= 24 AND Csr-Col <= 51
```
[Now the program loops until it detects the cursor placed over the PRESS TO END box.]
```
     MOVE S-L-Row(1) TO Csr-Row  [This places the cursor on the first date.]
     MOVE S-L-Col(1) TO Csr-Col
     DISPLAY Screen-1            [This displays the screen and waits for the
     ACCEPT Screen-1            person to press ENTER.]
     MOVE 1 TO I
     PERFORM WITH TEST BEFORE
               UNTIL I = ZERO OR S-NEXT-PTR(I) = NULLS
```
[Then the program looks at each date to see if the cursor is positioned on it.]
```
          IF Csr-Row <= S-L-Row(I) AND Csr-Col >= S-L-Col(I)
               AND
```

```
                    Csr-Row >= S-U-Row(I) AND Csr-Col <= S-R-Col(I)
                    THEN INVOKE "MoTextDate" USING S-The-Date(I),
                              RETURNING Formatted-Date
                        MOVE ZERO TO I
```
[If the cursor is on a date, we convert the date and set I to zero to break the loop.]
```
                        ELSE ADD 1 TO I
```
[If the cursor is not on this date, we go look at the next one.]
```
              END-IF
           END-PERFORM
        END-PERFORM
        GOBACK.
  END METHOD UserPlay.
  METHOD-ID. MoTextDate.
  DATA DIVISION.
  WORKING-STORAGE SECTION.
  LINKAGE SECTION.
  01  Current-Date.
      05  Cd-Yr                        PIC 9(4).
      05  Cd-Mo                        PIC 99.
      05  Cd-Dy                        PIC 99.
  01  Fmt-Date                         PIC X(30).
  PROCEDURE DIVISION USING Current-Date, RETURNING Fmt-Date.
  A00-Begin.
      IF Cd-Dy < 10
          THEN MOVE Cd-Dy(2:1) TO Fmt-Dy
          ELSE MOVE Cd-Dy to Fmt-Dy
      END-IF
      MOVE SPACES TO Formatted-Date
      STRING Mo-Tbl(Cd-Mo) DELIMITED " ", " " DELIMITED SIZE
                     Fmt-Dy DELIMITED " ", ", " DELIMITED SIZE
                  Cd-Yr DELIMITED SIZE INTO Fmt-Date
      END-STRING
      GOBACK.
  END METHOD MoTextDate.
  METHOD-ID. DyTextDate.
  DATA DIVISION.
  WORKING-STORAGE SECTION.
  LINKAGE SECTION.
  01  Current-Date.
      05  Cd-Yr                        PIC 9(4).
      05  Cd-Mo                        PIC 99.
      05  Cd-Dy                        PIC 99.
  01  Fmt-Date                         PIC X(30).
  PROCEDURE DIVISION USING Current-Date, RETURNING Fmt-Date.
  A00-Begin.
      IF Cd-Dy < 10
          THEN MOVE Cd-Dy(2:1) TO Fmt-Dy
          ELSE MOVE Cd-Dy to Fmt-Dy
      END-IF
      MOVE SPACES TO Formatted-Date
      STRING Fmt-Dy DELIMITED " ",
             " " DELIMITED SIZE,
             Mo-Tbl(Cd-Mo) DELIMITED " ", " " DELIMITED SIZE
```

```
                    Cd-Yr DELIMITED SIZE INTO Fmt-Date
        END-STRING
        GOBACK.
    END METHOD DyTextDate.
    END FACTORY.
    OBJECT.
    DATA DIVISION.
    WORKING-STORAGE SECTION.
    01  Date-Data.                        [This is the data description for the object.]
        05  Date-Ptr          OBJECT REFERENCE.
        05  The-Date          PIC 9(8).
        05  L-Row             PIC 99.
        05  L-Col             PIC 99.
        05  U-Row             PIC 99.
        05  R-Col             PIC 99.
    PROCEDURE DIVISION.
    METHOD-ID. CreateDate.
    DATA DIVISION.
    WORKING-STORAGE SECTION.
    LINKAGE SECTION.
    01  T-Last-Ptr            OBJECT REFERENCE.
    01  T-The-Date            PIC 9(8).
    01  T-L-Row               PIC 99.
    01  T-L-Col               PIC 99.
    01  T-U-Row               PIC 99.
    01  T-R-Col               PIC 99.
    PROCEDURE DIVISION USING T-The-Date, T-L-Row, T-L-Col,
                             T-U-Row, T-R-Col, T-Last-Ptr.
    A00-Begin.
        MOVE T-L-Row TO L-Row
        MOVE T-L-Col TO L-Col
        MOVE T-U-Row TO U-Row
        MOVE T-R-Col TO R-Col
        MOVE T-The-Date TO The-Date
        SET Date-Ptr TO NULLS
        [The date and row, column positions are stored in the object.]
        IF T-Last-Ptr NOT = NULLS
           THEN INVOKE T-Last-Ptr "LinkDate" USING SELF
        END-IF
        [Then, unless the last pointer was NULLS, we store the pointer to the current
        object in the previous object.]
        GOBACK.
    END METHOD Createdate.
    METHOD-ID. LinkDate.
    DATA DIVISION.
    WORKING-STORAGE SECTION.
    LINKAGE SECTION.
    01  A-Ptr                 OBJECT REFERENCE.
    PROCEDURE DIVISION USING A-Ptr.
    A00-Begin.
        Set Date-Ptr TO A-Ptr
        GOBACK.
    END METHOD LinkDate.
    METHOD-ID. GetDates.
```

```
      DATA DIVISION.
      LINKAGE SECTION.
      01  I                             PIC S9(5).
      01  A-Ptr                         OBJECT REFERENCE.
      PROCEDURE DIVISION USING I, RETURNING A-Ptr.
      A00-Begin.
          SET S-Next-Ptr(I) TO Date-Ptr
          MOVE The-Date TO S-The-Date(I)
          MOVE L-Row TO S-L-Row(I)
          MOVE L-Col TO S-L-Col(I)
          MOVE U-Row TO S-U-Row(I)
          MOVE R-Col TO S-R-Col(I)
          SET A-Ptr TO Date-Ptr
          GOBACK.
      END METHOD GetDates.
      END OBJECT.
      END CLASS BDates.
```

27.9   WHEN TO USE OBJECT-ORIENTED PROGRAMMING

After you become comfortable with object-oriented programming, its use will become natural. Still, it does take more effort. You should create object-oriented programs when they will either be changed often (which is true for most programs), or when the objects may be used several times. More than this, object-oriented programming is best for interactive applications in which the objects have more than a transitory life. It does not lend itself well to batch jobs, the traditional field for COBOL.

27.9.1   Advantages of Object-Oriented Programming

The two main advantages of object-oriented programming are:

- It makes programs easier to change by modularizing parts of the program into methods and by encapsulating the data.
- It makes code easier to share by defining common data and the methods to operate on the data.

27.9.2   Drawbacks of Object-Oriented Programming

There are several drawbacks to object-oriented programming.

- It has enthusiastic converts. The attitude of some advocates is "Better to have never been born than to not do object-oriented programming." This does not always lead to rational decisions.
- Compilers are incompatible, and the new ANSI standard differs from them all. This will slowly change after the standard is finalized and the compiler manufacturers know what standard to conform to. However, to maintain

compatibility with existing applications, they may have to retain old features.

- It is difficult to retrofit legacy systems to make them object-oriented. Unlike structured programming, which can be implemented a few statements at a time, object-oriented programming is not incremental and is difficult to do piecemeal. There may also be little payoff, because a major advantage of object-oriented programs is that they can be shared, and the opportunity for sharing in old systems may be long past.

- Object-oriented programs may be more difficult to read. Rather than lines of code, they become a series of method invocations. If you know what the methods do, the program can be clear. If the methods haven't been well documented or the documentation is lost, the program can be extremely difficult to read.

- Object-oriented programming lends itself best to interactive applications, which has not been COBOL's strength. Although the new ANSI standard addresses this weakness, the changes are mostly features that were a part of the initial design of languages such as C/C++, Visual BASIC, and Java. These languages may be better suited to many interactive applications than COBOL.

There are strong reasons for not retrofitting many legacy systems. It may take effort away from solving the year-2000 problem and its aftermath, which is far more important. There may be little payoff, because a major advantage of sharing code is lost when the system is already developed. Converting legacy systems to be object-oriented is a major task that may introduce more problems than it solves. Finally, the ANSI standard is evolving, and until it is fixed, conversion to object-oriented COBOL will soon require further change to conform to the ANSI standard.

Object-oriented programs will be forced into playing catch up. All of this begs the question of whether object-oriented programming for COBOL is worth the effort. That has not been decided. The initial enthusiasm will wear off, and then the success of object-oriented programming will have to depend on what it delivers.

If the reason for converting a legacy system to be object-oriented is to add a graphical interface and make it interactive, there is an alternative. You can use the interface features provided by the compiler manufacturer to invoke functions written in other languages, such as C/C++ and Visual Basic. Not only does this let you use the features of these languages, it opens the door to the vast libraries of existing public domain and proprietary functions.

CHAPTER 28

INSIDE THE COMPUTER

You don't need to know the all the details of how a computer works, but knowing the basics of what is going on inside the computer will help you as a programmer and enhance your professional status.

28.1 NUMBERING SYSTEMS

The computer is a binary machine. Let's step back and see what this means. We humans are decimal machines. We do our numbers and calculations with decimal numbers—numbers with the base 10. This is a happenstance of biology. We have 10 fingers. Had we humans evolved with eight fingers, we would use the octal system, with the base 8.

Our ancestors first began to understand numbers by counting on their fingers. Over time, their descendants settled on a numbering system that began with no fingers (0—and it took a long time to catch on to the concept of zero); then they counted the first finger as 1, the second as 2, up to 9. For the last finger, rather than invent a new digit, they started over with 1 and placed a zero on the right for 10. If they had had eight fingers, they would have counted 0, 1, 2, and on up to 7. Then for the last (eighth) finger, they would have started over, appending a zero for 10. Some societies did develop octal numbering systems by counting the spaces between the fingers rather than the fingers, which seemed perfectly natural to them. Other societies counted with one hand and developed a pentagonal numbering system. The Maya, getting hands and feet into the act, used a base 20 numbering system. We perhaps owe the colder European climate that placed uncovered toes at risk for our base 10 system. Counting finger joints was common, leading to a wide variety of numbering systems. The record was perhaps held by the Torres Strait Islanders, who counted using parts of the body that it is best to not even think about to develop a numbering system based on 33.

We use different numbering systems all the time without giving it any thought. Time is base 60 (60 seconds per minute, 60 minutes per hour). The British until recently had a currency with a base 20 numbering system (20 shillings per pound). They also left us with a base 3 numbering system that the United States still uses: 1 foot; 2 feet; 1 yard; 1 yard, 1 foot; 1 yard, 2 feet; 2 yards, and so on. So numbers to the base 3, 5, 8, or whatever would have been as natural to us as the base 10, had we grown up using them.

28.2 BINARY NUMBERING SYSTEM

The computer uses the base 2, which needs only the digits 0 and 1, and which can be represented with an electrical charge. No charge is 0; a charge is 1. Think of it as a light bulb controlled by a switch. The switch or the light bulb is either on or off. Although the binary system is cumbersome for we humans to use, it is perfectly natural for a computer that does it at electronic speeds.

Let's see how numbers are represented in a numbering system with only the binary digits 0 and 1. (A binary digit is abbreviated to *bit.*) Table 28.1 shows the binary equivalents of decimal digits.

Now look at another property of numbers. In decimal, you multiply by the base (10) by appending a 0 to the right:

$$1 * 10 = 1 \text{ with a 0 appended, for 10}$$
$$20,395 * 10 = 20,395 \text{ with a 0 appended, for 203,950}$$

You can express the number 203,950 as

$$2 \times 10^5 + 0 \times 10^4 + 3 \times 10^3 + 9 \times 10^2 + 5 \times 10^1 + 0 \times 10^0$$

Remember that n^0 is 1 assuming that **n** is non-zero. Binary operates the same, except that you use 2 as the base rather than 10.

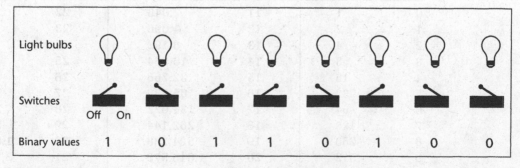

FIGURE 28.1 Binary data represented by light bulbs.

TABLE 28.1 Binary Equivalents of Decimal Numbers

Decimal	Binary	Decimal	Binary
0	0	7	111
1	1	8	1000
2	10	9	1001
3	11	10	1010
4	100	. . .	. . .
5	101	101,672	11000110100101000
6	110		

$$1 * 2 = 1 \text{ with a 0 appended, for } 10$$
$$110001011 * 2 = 110001011 \text{ with a 0 appended, for } 1100010110$$

You can express the binary number 1100010110 in decimal as

$$1 \times 2^9 + 1 \times 2^8 + 0 \times 2^7 + 0 \times 2^6 + 0 \times 2^5 + 1 \times 2^4 + 0 \times 2^3 + 1 \times 2^2 + 1 \times 2^1 + 0 + 2^0$$

In decimal, it is easier to refer to numbers in thousands (10^3), millions (10^6), and billions (10^9). When you refer to similar units on the computer, you use the closest number to a power of 2. As a result, 1000 becomes 1024 (2^{10}) or 1K, a million becomes 1,048,576 (2^{20}) or 1M or a Meg, and a billion becomes 1,073,741,824 (2^{30}) or 1G or a Gig. When someone says that a PC has a 64-megabyte memory, they are saying that it has $64 \times 1,048,576 = 67,108,864$ bytes.

Now let's see how to convert back and forth between binary and decimal. For this, you need Table 28.2, showing the powers of 2.

TABLE 28.2 Powers of 2

n	2^n	n	2^n	n	2^n
0	1	11	2,048	22	4,194,304
1	2	12	4,096	23	8,388,608
2	4	13	8,192	24	16,777,216
3	8	14	16,384	25	33,554,432
4	16	15	32,768	26	67,108,864
5	32	16	65,536	27	134,217,728
6	64	17	131,072	28	268,435,456
7	128	18	262,144	29	536,870,912
8	256	19	524,288	30	1,073,741,824
9	512	20	1,048,576	31	2,147,483,648
10	1,024	21	2,097,152		

28.2.1 Converting Decimal to Binary

To convert a decimal number to binary, you do the following:

1. Find the largest power of 2 (2^n) from Table 28.2 that is less than the number. Numbering the bits from left to right, set the nth bit to 1.
2. Subtract the 2^n value from the decimal number to get the difference.
3. If the difference is 0, quit. Otherwise, go back to step 1 and do it again using the difference.

Any bits not set to 1 are set to 0. Remember that for the conversion, you number bits right to left, starting with 0. Here's how to convert the number 203,950 to binary.

Decimal Number	Largest Value of 2^n Less Than Decimal Number	Difference
203,950	$2^{17} = 131,072$	72,878
72,878	$2^{16} = 65,536$	7,342
7,342	$2^{12} = 4,096$	3,246
3,246	$2^{11} = 2,048$	1,198
1,198	$2^{10} = 1,024$	174
174	$2^7 = 128$	46
46	$2^5 = 32$	14
14	$2^3 = 8$	6
6	$2^2 = 4$	2
2	$2^1 = 2$	0

You are done. The binary number is then $2^{17} + 2^{16} + 2^{12} + 2^{11} + 2^{10} + 2^7 + 2^5 + 2^3 + 2^2 + 2^1$. To write this in binary, you fill in the bits. Going from left to right, set the 17th, 16th, 12th, 11th, and so on bits to 1; all others down to the 0th (rightmost) bit are 0. The binary number is

110001110010101110

28.2.2 Converting Binary to Decimal

Let's convert the binary number back to decimal to verify that our algorithm works. Counting from right to left starting at 0 with the rightmost bit, you express the binary number as powers of 2.

$$2^1 + 2^2 + 2^3 + 2^5 + 2^7 + 2^{10} + 2^{11} + 2^{12} + 2^{16} + 2^{17}$$
$$= 2 + 4 + 8 + 32 + 128 + 1024 + 2048 + 4096 + 65,536 + 131,072$$
$$= 203,950$$

This is reassuring.

28.2.3 Hexadecimal Notation

Binary numbers are not only clumsy for we humans to express, but it is very easy to make an error in writing them. To get around this problem, we write binary numbers in hexadecimal, base 16 notation. The 16 hexadecimal digits are 0 through 9 and then A, B, C, D, E, and F. Table 28.3 shows the hexadecimal notation with its decimal and binary equivalents.

To express our binary number 110001110010101110, take the binary digits 4 bits at a time, right to left, |0011|0001|1100|1010|1110|, and replace each 4 bits with the hexadecimal equivalent:

```
|0011|0001|1100|1010|1110|
|  3 |  1 |  C |  A |  E |
```

You would write the binary number as 31CAE, which is much easier.

Note that data is always stored inside the computer as binary, not hexadecimal. Hexadecimal is only a notation that we humans find convenient for expressing binary.

28.3 CHARACTER DATA

Now let's see how the computer stores text. Computers today use 8 bits to store a single character. (However, for Japanese Kanji, which has many more characters

TABLE 28.3 Hexadecimal, Decimal, and Binary Equivalents

Hexadecimal Digit	Decimal Equivalent	Binary Equivalent
0	0	0
1	1	1
2	2	10
3	3	11
4	4	100
5	5	101
6	6	110
7	7	111
8	8	1000
9	9	1001
A	10	1010
B	11	1011
C	12	1100
D	13	1101
E	14	1110
F	15	1111

TABLE 28.4 Representation of EBCDIC Characters A, B, and Z

Character	Decimal Value	Value in Binary	Value in Hexadecimal
A	193	11000001	C1
B	194	11000010	C2
Z	233	11101001	E9

than our alphabet, 16 bits are required. The Latin alphabet is assumed here.) Table 28.4 shows how the characters A, B, and Z are represented in on the IBM mainframe with its EBCDIC (Extended-Binary-Coded-Decimal-Interchange Code) character set.

Unfortunately, it is not as simple as this. There are two character sets widely used: EBCDIC on IBM mainframe computers and ASCII (American Standard Character Code for Information Interchange) on most other computers, including PCs and UNIX systems. The representation for the characters A, B, and Z in ASCII is shown in Table 28.5. Notice that it takes two hexadecimal digits to represent the 8 bits of character storage.

The binary codes are different, as are many of the special characters, and even the sort order of the individual characters. This makes the IBM mainframe system inherently incompatible with most other computers. The computer can convert ASCII to EBCDIC and back, but most of the special characters get lost in the process. The common characters that don't convert to their equivalent are shown in Table 28.6.

The ASCII/EBCDIC sort sequences are also different so that the characters sort into a different order, making the incompatibility between ASCII and EBCDIC a serious matter. (A telephone book in ASCII might be in a different order than one in EBCDIC.) The order in which the characters sort is called the *collating sequence.* Table 23.2 gives the collating sequences.

Because both ASCII and EBCDIC use 8 bits to represent a character, they each have $2^8 = 256$ possible characters in their character set. The 8 bits of storage used to contain a character are termed a *byte,* and it is the basic unit of computer storage. It is also the minimum storage unit that the computer can directly address.

TABLE 28.5 Representation of ASCII Characters A and B

Character	Decimal Value	Binary Value	Hexadecimal Value
A	65	01000001	41
B	66	01000010	42
Z	90	01011010	5A

TABLE 28.6 ASCII/EBCDIC Problem Characters

ASCII	EBCDIC
!	|
[	¢
]	!
^	¬

28.4 BINARY NUMBERS

Binary numbers are stored in a word, a half word, or a double word. A *word* is 4 bytes (32 bits). (The new ANSI standard also allows them to be stored in a byte.) Table 9.1 shows the maximum value that can be stored for these. Binary data is mainly used to store integer values.

28.5 ZONED-DECIMAL NUMBERS

Because binary data is cumbersome for numbers other than integers, the IBM mainframe provides two other forms in numeric zoned-decimal and packed-decimal. Zoned-decimal numbers are a special case of character data. They consist of numeric digits with the rightmost digit carrying the sign. The hexadecimal code for the characters 0 through 9 are X"F0" through X"F9". The sign is carried on the left half of the rightmost digit. Hexadecimal "F" represents an unsigned number, "C" a plus sign, and "D" a minus. Using hexadecimal notation, the number 17,623.45 could be stored as follows in zoned-decimal. Note that the assumed decimal point is not stored as part of the data. Assume that the numbers are all stored in a PIC S9(5)V99 item.

```
"|F1|F7|F6|F2|F3|F4|F5|"     As unsigned 17623.45
"|F1|F7|F6|F2|F3|F4|D5|"     As -17623.45
"|F1|F7|F6|F2|F3|F4|C5|"     As +17623.45
```

You can do arithmetic on zoned-decimal numbers. COBOL converts them to packed-decimal for arithmetic operations.

28.6 PACKED-DECIMAL NUMBERS

Because only 4 bits are needed to represent the digits 0 through 9, two digits can be packed into a byte. Hence, the name *packed-decimal*. The digit 2 is 0010 in binary and the digit 9 is 1001 in binary, so the digits 29 can be represented within 1 byte. The sign is kept in the rightmost 4 bits of the number with "F" for unsigned, "C" for plus, and "D" for minus. The digits and sign are stored in bytes as follows, where *d* represents a digit and *s* the sign.

| *dd* | *dd* | *dd* | *ds* |

Using hexadecimal notation, the number 17,623.45 could be stored as follows in packed-decimal. The assumed decimal point is not stored as part of the data. Assume that the numbers are all stored in a PIC S9(5)V99 PACKED-DECIMAL item.

| 17 | 62 | 34 | 5F | As unsigned 17623.45
| 17 | 62 | 34 | 5D | As -17623.45
| 17 | 62 | 34 | 5C | As +17623.45

The IBM mainframe has hardware instructions to both perform arithmetic operations on packed-decimal data and convert them to zoned-decimal and character data for display. This makes them efficient in storage, display, and arithmetic operations.

Because it is easy to keep track of the decimal point when you represent numbers with digits, and because most business applications are in units that require a decimal point and finite precision (dollars are represented to hundredths—the penny) packed-decimal is ideal for most business applications. In addition, because the numbers in business applications are displayed on the terminal or printed in reports, the easy conversion to character data is a big bonus.

You can display numeric data only as characters. The computer can't display binary data in a meaningful form except by converting the binary number to characters. Let's follow this through with an example. Suppose you have the number 19,666 stored in binary as |0100|1100|1101|0010|. The hexadecimal representation of this is |4C|D2|.

The binary number occupies a half word or 2 bytes. If you told the computer to just display this number, it would think that each byte was a character and display that character. The left byte, with its hexadecimal value of 4C, displays as <. The right byte, with a hexadecimal value of D2, displays as *K*. If you tried to display the number 19,666 in binary directly, the computer would display <*K*, which makes no sense. Instead, COBOL converts the binary number to packed-decimal to zoned-decimal.

```
Binary              Packed-decimal           Zoned-decimal
|4C|D2| converted to |19|66|6C| converted to |F1|F9|F6|F6|C6|
```

From there, COBOL can edit the number to put on a leading sign, insert commas and decimal point, add a currency symbol, and so on to make it ready for display. Such conversion, especially from binary to character for numeric values, requires effort on the computer, and programmers avoid it as much as they can.

One way of avoiding it is to store numeric data as packed-decimal because the conversion from it to character is relatively easy; it can be done with a single machine language instruction.

28.7 FLOATING-POINT NUMBERS

You express a number such as −0.000333333 in floating point as an exponent part and a fractional part: -0.333333×10^{-3}. For single-precision, floating point occupies a full word of 4 bytes, as follows:

Bit 0	Sign of exponent with 1 for minus and 0 for plus
Bits 1-7	Exponent
Bit 8	Sign of number
Bits 9-31	Fractional part with 5 to 6 significant digits of precision

Double-precision floating-point numbers are identical, except that the number occupies two full words of 8 bytes. The fractional part consists of bits 9 through 63 with roughly 18 significant digits of precision.

28.8 MACHINE INSTRUCTIONS

Now let's take a typical COBOL COMPUTE statement and see how it is done on the computer.

```
COMPUTE A = B + C
```

The computer's memory is composed of a string of binary digits organized into bytes, nothing more. The binary digits can represent numbers, characters, and machine instructions. You've seen how numbers and characters are expressed. Now let's examine the computer instruction. The computer has a repertoire of machine instructions that tell the computer what to do. A language such as COBOL must be *compiled* to convert the COBOL statements into machine language instructions. The machine instructions for the COMPUTE statement must do the following:

1. Load a register with one of the numbers, *B.* The computer does integer arithmetic in a high-speed register. The IBM mainframe has 16 high-speed registers.

2. Add the other number, *C,* to the register.

3. Store the register into *A* as the result.

Bytes in the computer's memory are addressed consecutively: 0, 1, 2, 3, and so on. The number of bytes the computer can address, its *address space,* depends upon the number of bits that the computer instruction uses for storage addresses. For illustration, let's assume that *B, C,* and *A* are stored in the first 3 bytes of the computer as follows. *B* contains a decimal value of 100 and *C* a decimal value of 15.

Decimal Storage Address	Hex Storage Address	Identifier	Contents in Binary	Contents in Decimal
0-3	0000-0003	B	|0000|0000|0110|0100|	100
4-7	0004-0007	C	|0000|0000|0000|1111|	15
8-11	0008-000B	A	|0000|0000|0000|0000|	0

Then the three machine instructions that form the program are loaded somewhere else in the computer. Computer instructions may occupy several bytes. Let's assume the program was loaded starting at byte 1000 (in decimal).

Decimal Address	Hex Address	Instruction	Description
1000	3E8	L 5,0000	Load register 5 from address 0000 (identifier B).
1004	3Ec	A 5,0004	Add contents of address 0004 (identifier C) to register 5.
1008	3F0	ST 5,0008	Store register 5 into address 0008 (identifier A).

Now let's see these instructions as the computer sees them. The code for the L instruction (load register from address) is 58 in hex or |0101|1000| in binary, the code for A (add contents of address to register) is 5A in hex or |0101|1010| in binary, and the code for ST (store register into address) is 50 in hex or |0101|0000| in binary. The computer sees the following:

Decimal Address	Hex Address	Binary Value	Instruction
1000	3E8	|0101|1000|0101|0000|0000|0000|0000|0000|	L 5,0000
1004	3EC	|0101|1010|0101|0100|0000|0000|0000|0000|	A 5,0004
1008	3F0	|0101|0000|0101|1000|0000|0000|0000|0000|	ST 5,0008

This is the essence of how the computer actually works. Because the machine instructions themselves are expressed as bits, the computer doesn't know whether its storage contains bits representing numbers, characters, or machine instructions. If you branch to a storage area where a number is stored, the computer will try to execute it, often with strange results. This is why your PC may occasionally freeze, requiring you to reboot. The mainframe computer won't freeze; it will detect the problem and terminate the program.

When you compile a program, the compiler doesn't know in which part of central storage the program will execute. This depends on what else is currently running on the computer. To solve this problem, the computer assigns relative storage addresses. Then when the program is loaded to run, the system determines at what storage address to load the program, and provides the relative address so that the program can execute properly. For example, the system might decide to load the program at byte location 512,984, and it would tell the program that its relative addresses are relative to 512,984.

CHAPTER 29

READING PROGRAMS

Reading programs for debugging and maintenance is an important skill. This chapter tells how to do it.

29.1 READING FOR MAINTENANCE

For debugging, you will probably be familiar with the program because you wrote it, but for maintenance you may know nothing about the program. Begin by trying to understand generally what the program does. A user's manual, if one exists, is perhaps the best source. There may be an overview in the program documentation, and the introductory remarks in the program are another source. A system flow description or a JCL listing also tells a great deal about the program. Any detailed flow charts may also help, but be warned that flow charts are rarely kept up to date.

The next step is to identify the input and output: what is read and written. If you know what goes into a program and what comes out of it, you can make some fairly accurate assumptions about what must be going on inside the program. Get samples of the input and reports, if possible; study file layouts, input forms, and even data entry instructions. Locate the files used within a COBOL program by looking at the File Section, where they must all be listed.

At this level, the understanding depends on the documentation that is available. Don't depend only on formal documentation; use whatever is available. Talk to the people who receive the output of the program and who prepare the input. They often know more about the program than anyone if the original programmer is not available. Although they may not know programming, they know what the program does. They can often answer detailed questions from their long experience that might take days to discover by poring over the code.

29.2 READING A PROGRAM

Now, let's read a program. It is an actual program, not a good one, but typical, and it will serve as an example of how to read a program. It is not a structured program, but this will be typical of many programs you will read. First, look at the Identification Division:

```
000001 IDENTIFICATION DIVISION.
000002 PROGRAM-ID.  PAYYE.
000003* REMARKS.
000004* THIS PROGRAM COPIES THE PAY FILE AND EXCLUDES THOSE
000005* PERSONNEL RECORDS WHICH ARE NOT NEEDED IN NEW FISCAL YEAR
000006* RECORDS ARE NOT NEEDED FOR NEW FISCAL YEAR IF THE PERSON
000007* IS INACTIVE, DOES NOT HAVE A COST IN THE COST
000008* FILE, AND DOES NOT APPEAR AS A PERSON RESPONSIBLE FOR A
000009* PROJECT IN THE PROJ FILE.
000010 ENVIRONMENT DIVISION.
000011 CONFIGURATION SECTION.
000012 SOURCE-COMPUTER.   IBM-370.
000013 OBJECT-COMPUTER.   IBM-370.
```

The remarks are useful, and from them you can expect there to be four files: the *PAY* file in, the *PAY* file out, a *COST* file, and a *PROJ* file. The main loop within the program is probably controlled by reading the *PAY* file.

Next, look at the Input-Output Section, which lists the files:

```
000014 INPUT-OUTPUT SECTION.
000015 FILE-CONTROL.
000016     SELECT In-Pay-File ASSIGN TO PAY.
000017     SELECT In-Cost-File ASSIGN TO SCOST.
000018     SELECT In-Proj-File ASSIGN TO PROJ.
000019     SELECT Out-Pay-File ASSIGN TO PAYOUT.
```

The FILE-CONTROL paragraph lists each file, and as expected, there are four files. Evidently *In-Pay-File* is the *PAY* input file, *In-Cost-File* is the *COST* file, *In-Proj-File* is the *PROJ* file, and *Out-Pay-File* is the *PAY* file written out.

Next, look at the Data Division and the File Section, where the files are further described:

```
000020 DATA DIVISION.
000021 FILE SECTION.
000022 FD  In-Pay-File
000025     BLOCK CONTAINS 0 RECORDS
000024     RECORD CONTAINS 80 CHARACTERS
000025     LABEL RECORDS ARE STANDARD.
000026***** PAY FILE RECORD LAYOUT.  RECORD LENGTH = 80.
000027***** RELATIVE BYTE POSITION IN COLUMNS 75-77.
000028 01  Pay-Record.
00002      05  Pay-Key.
000030*                             RECORD KEY.
```

```
000031          10  Pay-Emp-Id      PIC X(9).
000032*                             PERSONS ID
000035      05  Pay-Name            PIC X(25).
000034*                             PERSONS NAME.
000035      05  Pay-Org-Person      PIC X(3).
000036*                             ORG OF PERSON.
000037      05  Pay-Salary          PIC S9(9)V9(2).
000038*                             ANNUAL SALARY IN DOLLARS.
000039      05  Pay-Status          PIC X(1).
000040*                             PERSONS STATUS.
000041*                             A-ACTIVE- I-INACTIVE.
000042      05  Pay-Date-Updated    PIC X(6).
000043*                             DATE RECORD LAST UPDATED.
000044*                             YYMMDD
000045      05  FILLER              PIC X(25).
000046*                             AVAILABLE SPACE.
```

We are in luck. The record descriptions have comments and it is relatively
easy to understand what the file contains.

```
000047 FD  In-Cost-File
000048     RECORD CONTAINS 80 CHARACTERS
000049     BLOCK CONTAINS 0 RECORDS
000050     LABEL RECORDS ARE STANDARD.
000051***** COST FILE RECORD LAYOUT.  RECORD LENGTH = 80.
000052***** RELATIVE BYTE POSITION IN COLUMNS 73-77.
000053 01  Cost-Record.
000054     05  Cost-Key.
000055          10  Cost-Emp-Id     PIC X(9).
000056*                             ID or PERSON.
000057     05  Cost-Chg             PIC X(4).
000058*                             CHARGE NUMBER.
000059     05  Cost-Obj             PIC X(3).
000060*                             OBJECT CODE OF PERSON.
000061     05  Cost-To-Date.
000062*                             CUMULATIVE AMOUNTS TO DATE
000065          10  Cost-Amt        PIC S9(9)V99.
000064*                             DOLLAR AMOUNT EXCLUDING FRINGE
000065*                             AND OVERHEAD
000066          10  Cost-Days       PIC S9(9)V99.
000067*                             DAYS WORKED
000065          10  Cost-Fringe     PIC S9(9)V99.
000069*                             DOLLAR AMOUNT OF FRINGE.
000070          10  Cost-Overhead   PIC S9(9)V99.
000071*                             DOLLAR AMOUNT OF OVERHEAD.
000072     05  Cost-Date-Updated    PIC X(6).
000075*                             DATE RECORD LAST UPDATED.
000074*                             YYMMDD
000075     05  FILLER               PIC X(14).
000076*                             AVAILABLE SPACE.
000077 FD  In-Proj-File
000078     BLOCK CONTAINS 0 RECORDS
000079     RECORD CONTAINS 80 CHARACTERS
```

```
000080      LABEL RECORDS ARE STANDARD.
000081***** PROJ FILE RECORD LAYOUT.  RECORD LENGTH = 80.
000082***** RELATIVE BYTE POSITION IN COLUMNS 73-77.
000085 01  Proj-Record.
000084     05  Proj-Key.
000085*                              RECORD KEY
000086         10  Proj-Chg          PIC X(4).
000087*                              CHARGE NUMBER.
000088     05  Proj-Chg-Title        PIC X(25).
000089*                              PROJECT TITLE.
000090     05  Proj-Act-Type         PIC X(1).
000091*                              ACTIVITY TYPE.
000092*                              D-DIRECT
000093*                              I-INDIRECT
000094     05  Proj-Person           PIC X(9).
000095*                              ID OF PERSON RESPONSIBLE.
000096     05  Proj-Amount           PIC S9(9)V9(2).
000097*                              TOTAL CONTRACT AMOUNT.
000098     05  Proj-Start-Date.
000099*                              CONTRACT START DATE.
000100         10  Proj-Start-Yr     PIC 9(2).
000101         10  Proj-Start-Mo     PIC 9(2).
000102         10  Proj-Start-Dy     PIC 9(2).
000103     05  Proj-End-Date.
000104*                              CONTRACT END DATE.
000105         10  Proj-End-Yr       PIC 9(2).
000106         10  Proj-End-Mo       PIC 9(2).
000107         10  Proj-End-Dy       PIC 9(2).
000108     05  Proj-Active-Flag      PIC X(1).
000109*                              ACTIVE FLAG.
000110*                              A - ACTIVE.
000111*                              I - INACTIVE.
000112     05  Proj-Date-Updated     PIC X(6).
000113*                              DATE RECORD LAST UPDATED.
000114*                              YYMMDD.
000115     05  FILLER                PIC X(11).
000116*                              AVAILABLE SPACE.
000117 FD  Out-Pay-File
000118     BLOCK CONTAINS 0 RECORDS
000119     RECORD CONTAINS 80 CHARACTERS
000120     LABEL RECORDS ARE STANDARD.
000121 01  Out-Pay-Rec.
000122     05  Out-Pay-Key           PIC X(9).
000123     05  FILLER                PIC X(71).
```

From this you can tell that all the files are sequential. The record descriptions are well documented, and you can easily tell what the files contain.

Now look at the Working-Storage Section, which will describe other data items used within the program:

```
000124 WORKING-STORAGE SECTION.
000125 01  FILLER COMP SYNC.
000126     05  In-Count              PIC S9(4) VALUE 0.
```

```
000127      05  Out-Count          PIC S9(4) VALUE 0.
000128      05  Drop-Count         PIC S9(4) VALUE 0.
000129 01  FILLER.
000130      05  Proj-Table-Size    PIC S9(4) COMP SYNC VALUE 1000.
000131      05  Proj-Table OCCURS 1000 DEPENDING ON Proj-Table-Size
000132          INDEXED BY Projx    PIC X(6).
```

In-Count, Out-Count, and *Drop-Count* are evidently counters, and you might guess that they count the *PAY* records read, dropped, and written. The *Proj-Table* is a variable-size table, and you will have to see how it is used. There are no input/output records described in Working-Storage, and so the READ INTO form cannot be used. The program processes the data in the buffers. As you read the program, you should keep this in mind for the potential problems it can cause.

Now look at the Procedure Division:

```
000133 PROCEDURE DIVISION.
000134 A10-Begin.
000135      OPEN INPUT In-Proj-File.
000136      SET Projx TO 1.
000137 A20-Read-Proj.
000138      READ In-Proj-File AT END GO TO A30.
000139      MOVE Proj-Person TO Proj-Table (Projx).
000140      SET Projx UP BY 1.
000141      GO TO A20-Read-Proj.
000142 A30.
```

The program begins with a paragraph name. You need to know if this is the start of a loop and how control gets back to *A10-Begin.* For this, you need the cross-reference list of paragraph names, such as the following:

```
THE LETTER PRECEDING A PROCEDURE-NAME REFERENCE INDICATES THE
CONTEXT IN WHICH THE PROCEDURE-NAME IS USED.  THESE LETTERS AND
THEIR MEANINGS ARE:
    A = ALTER (PROCEDURE-NAME)
    B = GO TO (PROCEDURE-NAME) DEPENDING ON
    E = END OF RANGE OF (PERFORM) THRU (PROCEDURE-NAME)
    O = GO TO (PROCEDURE-NAME)
    P = PERFORM (PROCEDURE-NAME)
    T = (ALTER) TO PROCEED TO (PROCEDURE-NAME)
    U = USE FOR DEBUGGING (PROCEDURE-NAME)
DEFINED     CROSS-REFERENCE OF PROCEDURES     REFERENCES
000134      A10-Begin
000137      A20-Read-Proj. . . . . . . . .    G000141
000142      A30. . . . . . . . . . . . .      G000138
000150      B10-Read-Pay . . . . . . . . .    G000163   G000167
000160      B20-Drop-Pay
000164      B30-Keep-Pay . . . . . . . . .    G000153   G000155
G000159
000168      C10-Level-Cost . . . . . . . .    P000154   G000173
000174      C20-Exit . . . . . . . . . .      E000154   G000169
G000172
000175      D10-End. . . . . . . . . . .      G000151
```

A10-Begin is not used, and so the beginning code does not start a loop but is executed only once. The first statement following *A10-Begin* opens the *In-Proj-File*. Then *Projx* is set to 1. *Projx* indexes the *Proj-Table,* and so you can expect to store values in it. Next, control passes through the *A20-Read-Proj* label, and you might expect this to be the start of a loop. Again, the cross-reference list tells you that only statement 141 refers to it, and it is apparent that it is a loop to read *In-Proj-File*. The file is read, and on encountering an end of file, control goes to *A30*. (Note that this is the only way to get to *A30.*) *Proj-Person* from *In-Proj-File* is stored in *Proj-Table,* with *Projx* used as the index. Then *Projx* is set up by 1 and control goes to *A20-Read-Proj* to read the next record. You don't know the sort order of *In-Proj-File,* and you must check to see whether there is an assumption of a sort order when *Proj-Table* is used.

Now you should examine the extreme cases within the loop. What happens if *In-Proj-File* is empty? Control goes immediately to *A30* with *Projx* set to 1. Notice that control always goes to *A30* with *Projx* set to one greater than the number of records read. You should keep this in mind, because it is a potential source of error. Now look at the other extreme, when more than 1000 records are read. There is no check to see if the table overflows, and this is a potential error that should be corrected. You might now expect the program to search for the person's employee ID in the *Proj-Table* rather than by reading the *Proj* file.

Let's see what happens next in the program:

```
000143      SET Projx DOWN BY 1.
000144      SET Proj-Table-Size TO Projx.
000145      CLOSE In-Proj-File.
000146      OPEN INPUT In-Pay-File.
000147      OPEN INPUT In-Cost-File.
000148      OPEN OUTPUT Out-Pay-File.
```

Projx is set down by 1 because it contains one more than the number of records read. Then *Proj-Table-Size,* the item that controls the size of *Proj-Table,* is set to *Projx.* This appears to be correct, but it contains a potential error. If *In-Proj-File* contains no records, *Projx* will contain 1, and setting it down by 1 yields a value of 0, but 0 is not a valid value for an index. You can correct the error by first setting *Proj-Table-Size* to *Projx* and then setting it down by 1.

The next statement closes the *In-Proj-File.* Lines 135 to 145 encompass the statements to read records from *In-Proj-File* into *Proj-Table,* and you might set them off with comments. Next, the program opens the *In-Pay-File* and *In-Cost-File* for input and the *Out-Pay-File* for output. Now to read some more of the program:

```
000149      MOVE LOW-VALUES TO Cost-Emp-Id.
000150 B10-Read-Pay.
000151      READ In-Pay-File AT END GO TO D10-End.
000152      ADD 1 TO In-Count.
000153      IF Pay-Status = "A" GO TO B30-Keep-Pay.
000154      PERFORM C10-Level-Cost THRU C20-Exit.
```

First, LOW-VALUES are moved to *Cost-Emp-Id*. It is not apparent what this is for, and you shall have to see. The programmer may not have realized it when he or she placed the MOVE here, but if it had preceded the OPEN for *In-Cost-File,* it would be in error. *Cost-Emp-Id* is in the record area, and there is no record area until the file is opened. Quirks such as this are the reason that it is bad to read and write from the record area.

Next, control passes through the *B10-Read-Pay* label to read *In-Pay-File.* Because *In-Pay-File* is the master file, you would expect *B10-Read-Pay* to be the start of the main loop of the program. Note from the cross-reference list that control can get back to here from statements 163 and 167. Remember this when you examine those statements. On encountering an end of file, control goes to *D10-End,* where you would expect the program to be terminated. If an end of file is not encountered, 1 is added to *In-Count.* You expected *In-Count* to count the *In-Pay-File* records, and apparently it did. Because an initial value was not moved to *In-Count,* you should check to see that it is assigned an initial value in the Working-Storage Section. On checking, you see that it is assigned a value of 0, as are *Out-Count* and *Drop-Count.*

The next IF statement goes to *B30-Keep-Pay* if the *Pay-Status* is "A". The program is to keep records whose pay status is "A", and so *B30-Keep-Pay* should write out the record. Let's look at the *B30-Keep-Pay* paragraph:

```
000164 B30-Keep-Pay.
000165     WRITE Out-Pay-Rec FROM Pay-Record.
000166     ADD 1 TO Out-Count.
000167     GO TO B10-Read-Pay.
```

Out-Pay-Rec is written from *Pay-Record.* The program writes the output record from the record area. Is this permitted? It turns out to be correct, but it is a bad practice. Then 1 is added to *Out-Count,* which you know has an initial value of 0, and this confirms the belief that *Out-Count* counts the *Out-Pay-File* records. Next, control goes to *B10-Read-Pay* to read the next record. This GO TO is one of the two references to *B10-Read-Pay.*

Now let's get back to the main line of the code with the PERFORM *C10-Level-Cost* THRU *C20-Exit.* Let's see what this paragraph does:

```
000168 C10-Level-Cost.
000169     IF Cost-Emp-Id NOT < Pay-Emp-Id GO TO C20-Exit.
000170     READ In-Cost-File AT END
000171        MOVE HIGH-VALUES TO Cost-Emp-Id
000172        GO TO C20-Exit.
000173     IF Cost-Emp-Id < Pay-Emp-Id GO TO C10-Level-Cost.
000174 C20-Exit.  EXIT.
```

First, *Cost-Emp-Id* in the *In-Cost-File* is compared with *Pay-Emp-Id* of the current *In-Pay-File* record. If it is not less than (greater than or equal to), control goes to *C20-Exit* to exit the paragraph. Otherwise, the next *In-Cost-File* record is read, and if an end of file is encountered, HIGH-VALUES are moved to *Cost-Emp-Id* and control goes to *C20-Exit* to exit the paragraph. The first time *C10-Level-Cost* is entered, *Cost-Emp-Id* contains LOW-VALUES, and this will cause the first *In-Cost-File* record to be read. Now it is clear why LOW-VALUES were moved to *Cost-Emp-Id:* to force the first record to be read. If an end of file is not encountered, the program checks to see if the *Cost-Emp-Id* is less than the *Pay-Emp-Id,* and if so, control goes to *C10-Level-Cost* to read another record. In essence, *In-Cost-File* is read until a record is found whose key is equal to or greater than the key of the current *In-Pay-File* record. Moving HIGH-VALUES to *Cost-Emp-Id* ensures that the first IF statement in the *C10-Level-Cost* paragraph will immediately go to *C20-Exit* without attempting to read more records.

Now let's get back to the main line of code following the PERFORM:

```
000155      IF Pay-Emp-Id = Cost-Emp-Id GO TO B30-Keep-Pay.
000156      SET Projx TO 1.
000157      SEARCH Proj-Table
000158        WHEN Pay-Emp-Id = Proj-Table (Projx)
000159            GO TO B30-Keep-Pay.
000160 B20-Drop-Pay.
000161      ADD 1 TO Drop-Count.
000162      DISPLAY "Pay-Key: ", Pay-Key.
000163      GO TO B10-Read-Pay.
```

The program returns from the *C10-Level-Cost* paragraph with the next *In-Cost-File* record equal to or greater than the current *In-Pay-File* record, or HIGH-VALUES if there are no more *In-Cost-File* records. Then, if the *Pay-Emp-Id* of the *In-Cost-File* record equals the *Cost-Emp-Id* of the current *In-Pay-File,* control goes to *B30-Keep-Pay* to keep the record. This is correct, but notice the assumptions that the program makes about the order of the *In-Pay-File* and the *In-Cost-File.* They must both be in ascending order on the *Pay-Emp-Id* and *Cost-Emp-Id,* respectively. The program does not check the sort orders, and this, too, is a potential source of error. What if there are duplicate records in *In-Pay-File* or *In-Cost-File?* You don't know if they are permitted, but the logic will work correctly if they exist. This is comforting.

If the *Pay-Emp-Id* doesn't equal the *Cost-Emp-Id,* the program sets *Projx* to 1 and searches the *Proj-Table* sequentially for an entry equal to *Pay-Emp-Id.* Because it is a sequential search, the program makes no assumption about the order of *Proj-Table,* and duplicate entries will not cause a problem. If *Pay-Emp-Id* is found in *Proj-Table,* control goes to *B30-Keep-Pay* to keep the record. If not found, control passes through the unused *B20-Drop-Pay* label, 1 is added to *Drop-Count,* the key of the record dropped is displayed, and control goes to *B10-Read-Pay* to read the next record. This is the second place from which control goes to *B10-Read-Pay,* and all the statements in the loop have been examined. The statements to read the *In-Pay-File* encompass statements 146 through 174, and it would be a good idea to enclose them in comments to show their beginning and end.

The last thing is to look at *D10-End,* where control goes when there are no more *In-Pay-File* records to read:

```
000175 D10-End.
000176     DISPLAY "PAY IN =" In-Count.
000177     DISPLAY "PAY OUT =" Out-Count.
000175     DISPLAY "PAY DROP =" Drop-Count.
000179     CLOSE In-Pay-File.
000180     CLOSE Out-Pay-File.
000181     CLOSE In-Cost-File.
000182     STOP RUN.
000183*** END OF PROGRAM ***
```

The program displays the count of records in, out, and dropped. Then it closes the three files and stops the run. This concludes the program. You have read the entire program, and it appears to be correct, although some potential errors were discovered. Notice how invaluable the cross-reference listing was to reading the program. This was a small program, but the same techniques apply to large ones.

29.3   CHECKING DATA ITEMS

As you read a program, you will encounter important data items, such as tables, flags, and counters. If the names do not adequately describe their contents, note where the items are declared and note your assumption of their use. Again, the cross-reference listing is essential to find all the places in the program where they are used. They let you see if your assumptions are correct and see whether the items reused for some other purpose. When you are sure what they contain, insert a comment where they are defined to explain their use.

Often at a particular place in the program, you will want to know what value a data name contains. By using the cross-reference listing to find all references to the data name, and by knowing the major flow of control, you can usually discover what value the data name contains. Here is how to use the cross-reference listing to verify that *In-Count* counts the *In-Pay-File* records. The cross-reference listing tells where it is defined and where it is used:

```
AN "M" PRECEDING A DATA-NAME REFERENCE INDICATES THAT THE DATA-
NAME IS MODIFIED BY THIS REFERENCE.
DEFINED    CROSS-REFERENCE OF DATA NAMES    REFERENCES
000126     In-Count. . . . . . . .    M000152  000176
```
          [It is defined in statement 000126.]
```
00125 01  FILLER COMP SYNC.
00126     05  In-Count            PIC S9(4) VALUE 0.
```
          [It is used in statement 152.]
```
00151     READ In-Pay-File AT END GO TO D10-End.
00152     ADD 1 TO In-Count.
```
          [It is also used in statement 176.]
```
00175 D10-End.
00176     DISPLAY "PAY IN =" In-Count.
```

In-Count is used only to count *In-Pay-File* records, and the count is displayed at the end of the program. As you read a program, annotate the source listing as you discover things. Later, you should insert some of these annotations as comments in the program, so that the reading the program the next time will be easier. These comments are often the best of all comments because they tell the reader what was not obvious when you read the program.

29.4 CHECKING FOR ERRORS

As you read the program, look closely for errors. Just because the program has run correctly does not mean that there are no errors. Several potential errors were found in the program just read. The following items suggest things that should be checked:

- In a division, look for a possible division by zero or a loss of precision.
- Look for expressions such as $A * (B / C)$ that should be changed to $(A * B) / C$ or the reverse. The intermediate results of (B / C) or $(A * B)$ could have a great affect on the result as described in Chapter 9.
- In a nested IF statement, look for a misplaced period or END-IF.
- In an arithmetic expression, check the accuracy, especially if it contains a division.
- Look at the compiler error listing, because there may be error or warning messages. This is especially important when you recompile an old production program, because a new compiler may discover previously undetected errors, or there may be changes in the language since the last compilation. If you are link editing to place a load module in a library, check the linkage editor listing to ensure that the module was added or replaced correctly.
- Be suspicious of conditional expressions. If NOT and OR appear in the same logical expression, they are usually coded incorrectly.
- Look for exceptional conditions for which there is no detection. If items are stored in a table, check to see that the table does not overflow. Check for indexes having the potential of being set to a zero value.
- Look for off-by-one errors. In the PERFORM VARYING, check that the loop executes the proper number of times. A PERFORM VARYING X FROM 1 BY 1 UNTIL $X = 10$ executes the loop 9 times, not 10 times as you might at first expect.
- Identify each file, where it is opened, read or written, and closed. Note any assumptions the program makes about the file's order.
- If you discover an error, do not be misled into believing that it is the last error. That makes it even more likely that there are more errors.

CHAPTER 30

COBOL IN DISTRIBUTED COMPUTING

This chapter gives an overview of COBOL in distributed computing. Even if you work only with legacy systems, you are likely to move portions of them to the PC or to another vendor's hardware. Don't skip this chapter.

Essential

Many companies have thousands or even millions of lines of COBOL code driving legacy applications such as payroll and accounts payable. These programs may have been running on the mainframe for decades, with only minimal changes. This chapter provides you with an insight into how this legacy COBOL code can be preserved, given a graphical facelift, and provided a new lease on life as a distributed application. There is also a sample program to show how an application can be segmented between a client computer and a server computer.

30.1 TRADITIONAL ENVIRONMENTS

Legacy applications are usually described as *mission critical* because of their importance to the company's line of business. They are often written in COBOL and run on a mainframe or midrange server computer in a traditional computing environment that consists of *centralized, homogeneous,* or *host-based* computing. The *host* consists of one computer, either a large mainframe or a midrange server. It is *homogeneous* in that the hardware and software are both supplied by one company, such as IBM or DEC. Unlike personal computers, any attached terminals are *dumb* and can't do any processing on their own. Components such as terminals and printers are directly connected or *hard wired* to the system.

Because it's usually controlled by the one central Information Systems (IS) department we all know and love, the traditional environment provides reliability, centralized management, and security for legacy applications. Also, because they're dealing with a proven performer, upper and middle managers are comfortable within a traditional environment.

30.2 DISTRIBUTED ENVIRONMENTS

A distributed computing environment is one in which at least some of the processing is performed by separate computers that may have *heterogeneous* hardware and software, that is, from more than one vendor. These computers are linked via a communications system consisting of hardware, software, and data transfer links. A communications system is more commonly known as a *network* and can be as small as a *local area network* (LAN), or as large as a *wide area network* (WAN) that spans a vast geographical area.

A distributed computing environment provides flexibility; more user options for legacy applications, including a friendly graphical interface; and easier integration of diverse business systems in this era of mergers, acquisitions, and downsizing. It also provides *scalability,* the ability to make an entire system or a single application larger or smaller, depending upon the business need.

30.2.1 Client/Server Computing Defined

In computing, a *client* is one who requests service and a server is one who *provides* the service. *Client/server* is a special application of distributed computing where cooperative interactions are initiated by the smaller client computer. Client/server systems are composed of three logical components: presentation, one or more databases (usually relational), and business logic. *Presentation* is always on the client, although it may originate on the server. The *database* is generally on the server. *Business logic* may be on the client, on the server, or on both.

The client may perform calculations and do other processing depending upon whether it has been configured to be a *fat* or *thin client*. In a typical client/server application, the larger server computer performs most of the programming logic and retrieves and stores the data.

Client/server has revolutionized computer processing in that at least some control has been transferred from the central IS department to the user. This is directly attributable to the development of the personal computer (PC). As users fell in love with their PCs, they became ready to embrace client/server processing. Because of a perceived or real loss of control, upper and middle management are not as comfortable in a client/server environment as they are in a traditional one.

A client/server application must be *interactive.* That is, the user must participate in the processing. The programming logic must be *segmentable,* in that the logic must be able to be split between the client computer and the server computer. For these reasons, batch applications are not normally suitable candidates for client/server processing. Therefore, not all legacy applications, which are heavily batch oriented, are suitable candidates for client/server processing. However, many of them lend themselves well to some form of distributed processing.

30.2.2 Typical Client/Server Applications

In a typical client/server application, the client presents the user with a menu of choices, the user selects one of the choices, and the client edits the choice to be sure it's valid. If it's not, the client displays a message to the user, and the user selects another choice or quits. If it's valid, the client sends the edited choice to the server over the network. The server performs most of the COBOL logic, which includes calling a relational database, accessing the data in both the relational database and flat files, and sending the results back to the client over the network. The client performs whatever additional calculations are needed on the results and presents the formatted data to the user.

30.2.3 Client/Server Models

The graphic in Figure 30.1 (originally from the Gartner Group and shown in modified form here) provides five models of client/server computing:

1. *Distributed presentation*, in which all of the application logic and data management occurs on the server. Presentation is done on both the client and the server.

2. *Remote presentation*, in which all of the application logic and data management occurs on the server. Only presentation is done on the client. This model is also called the *fat server*.

3. *Distributed function*, in which all the data management occurs on the server. The application logic is split between the client and the server.

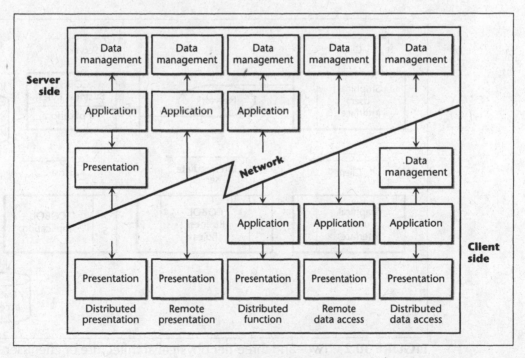

FIGURE 30.1 Five models of client/server computing.

4. *Remote data access*, in which only the data management occurs on the server. The client performs all of the application logic. This model is also called the *fat client*.

5. *Distributed data access*, in which data management occurs on both the client and the server. The client performs all of the application logic.

Most legacy COBOL applications fall between the distributed presentation and distributed function models of client/server.

A given client/server model may have two or three physical layers or tiers. The majority of legacy COBOL applications are physical *two-tier* architectures consisting of one or more clients providing user access and a single server providing business rules and data access. However, business rules may be written in COBOL and stored on an intermediate server, resulting in a three-tier physical architecture. Figure 30.2 depicts two- and three-tier physical architectures.

Client/Server under the Covers

Figure 30.3 shows what a typical client/server application that implements an interactive COBOL application looks like under the covers. The client's *graphical user interface* (GUI) is written in Easel or Mozart. These two products are also called *screen scrapers*, because they allow you to develop a GUI for a terminal-based legacy application with little or no change to the server code. They repre-

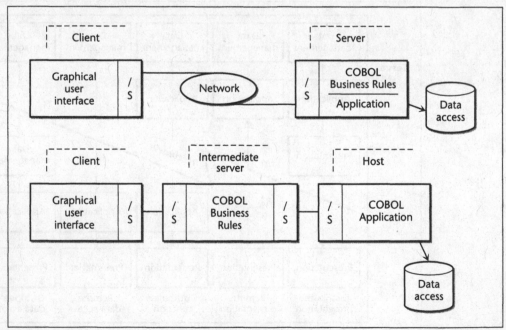

FIGURE 30.2 Two- and three-tier physical architecture of client/server systems.

sent an implementation of the distributed presentation model. If the client must perform more complex logic, the client application can be written in Visual Basic, Delphi, or PowerBuilder and be implemented as a distributed function or remote data access model.

In Figure 30.3, the client machine is a PC Pentium running Windows NT as the *client operating system*. Other client operating systems include the rest of the Windows family and IBM's OS/2. Generic Unix operating systems include DEC, Sun, and AIX (IBM's Unix). All except Windows 3.1 provide *preemptive multitasking,* which prevents any single program from monopolizing the system.

Notice the network protocol. A *network protocol* is a set of standards and rules that defines and enables communication and data transmission through a given network. The example in Figure 30.3 uses the IBM System Network Architecture (SNA) protocol. IBM shops have historically supported SNA. However, with the trend toward Internet processing, things are moving more in the direction of TCP/IP, which has become the de facto standard network protocol. Other popular network protocols include IPX/SPX, which supports Novell networks, and Net-BIOS, which supports LANs.

In Figure 30.3, the server is an IBM mainframe running MVS as the *server operating system.* For the mainframe, VMS is another choice, as is OS/400 for an IBM midrange server. For Intel processors, server operating system choices include Windows NT, NetWare 4.0, and OS/2. Generic Unix server operating systems include DEC, Sun, and AIX.

In Figure 30.3, CICS is the *transaction processing monitor* (TPM) that provides integrity and support for transactions. A *transaction* is a discrete activity within an online system. For example, an ATM transaction that debits your savings account and credits your checking account should be processed as one transaction. The entire transaction must complete successfully or none of it must

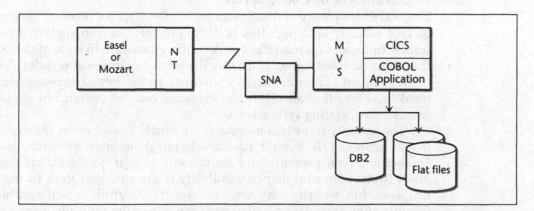

FIGURE 30.3 Client/server system implementing an interactive COBOL application.

complete. CICS now runs on all platforms and supports distributed transactions. A transaction processing monitor (TPM) increases performance by dramatically reducing the number of connections needed between the server operating system and the database.

Relational data access is provided by DB2, an IBM-developed relational database management system (RDBMS). Other RDBMSs include (but are by no means limited to) Oracle, Sybase, and Microsoft SQL Server. In Figure 30.3, the COBOL application also accesses data stored in sequential or flat files.

Client/Server Interoperability

While the industry has made great strides in creating *interoperable* systems via published and de facto standards, each of the aforementioned components is not necessarily compatible with every other component. Obviously, you can't run MVS on an Intel Pentium Processor, and NetBIOS, by itself, will not run across a WAN. For this reason, the design of your client/server system is a critical task that should be undertaken only by experienced designers. Above all, beware of vendor claims of interoperability and cost savings.

Advantages of Client/Server

There are numerous advantages to client/server processing. It provides increased user options and flexibility, including moving the processing closer to the user. It also removes the single point of failure, meaning that if the server goes down, the other servers can continue on without interruption. When the server comes back up, it rejoins the others on the network.

Client/server segmentation usually decreases the load on the overworked mainframe server and allows reuse of both COBOL legacy code and programming skills. It may also provide *portability*, the ability to move an application from one platform to another that is more suitable.

Disadvantages of Client/Server

There are also plenty of disadvantages to client/server processing. These include lack of security (although this is getting better), uneven support for distributed transactions, and increased network traffic. Above all, in spite of vendor claims to the contrary, client/server is usually the more expensive alternative. The management of client platforms usually proves to be the largest expense because of the need to ensure that all client platforms are current in terms of application programs and operating system software.

The security issue will become increasingly important as we move to an electronic economy. It doesn't take much imagination to envision the damage a Unabomber-type person could inflict with digital bombs rather than physical ones. It has been said that compatibility is the strongest force in the computing universe, but security may soon eclipse it. Mainframes will continue to exist because they have decades of experience in serving multiple users with security problems. Security is inherently easier in a centralized environment than in a distributed one.

Business Reasons for Client/Server

However, there are compelling business reasons to do client/server processing. You can provide a standardized interface across all applications, upsize or downsize a system depending upon business need, and use PCs that may otherwise sit idle much of the time. Above all, the competition is doing it.

30.3   INTERNET TECHNOLOGIES

The phenomenal growth of Internet technologies such as browsers and information servers has changed the focus of distributed computing from the PC to that portion of the Internet called the *World Wide Web.* The World Wide Web, which interlinks documents residing on information (HTTP) servers everywhere, provides an inexpensive and universal gateway to information. It has opened up the potential for global markets that were only dreamed of a few years ago. Instead of fat clients, there is the prospect of ultrathin clients containing only browser software such as Internet Explorer, Yahoo, and Netscape. Thin clients reduce high client management costs, one of the main drawbacks of client/server systems.

Internet technologies have also been incorporated into *intranets,* which are corporationwide networks, and *extranets,* which include not only corporations, but suppliers and customers as well. Some typical applications follow:

- An auto insurance company provides quotes to potential customers via the World Wide Web.

- Employees track savings and even change options in their 401(k) plans on the corporate internet.

- A company maintains an extranet with its suppliers for improved inventory control.

In Figure 30.4, note the *common gateway interface* (CGI). CGI enables communications between an HTTP server and resources located on that server's host computer. These resources usually consist of databases and various programs, including those written in COBOL. The HTTP server and the host computer may be the same physical machine, or they may be different machines.

CGI *script,* usually written in Perl, which is common to all Unix systems, adds interactivity to a Web page. The CGI script is normally confined to a specific function such as a response to a user's mouse click on a link or on an image on the client Web page. (Other technologies that add interactivity to Web pages include Java applets, plug-ins, helper programs, and Active X controls. They are beyond the scope of this book.)

It's hard to imagine how COBOL could fit into this scenario, but it can and does. In all three applications described previously, the underlying application could be written in COBOL. Micro Focus, a leading vendor in this area, offers *Net-Express,* a set of graphical tools that developers use to create Web-based applications. These include the following:

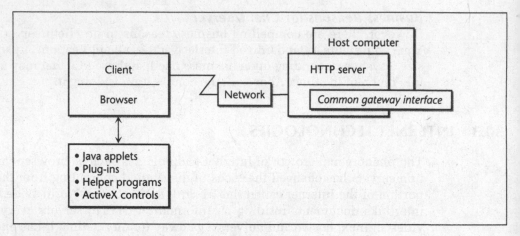

FIGURE 30.4 Common gateway interface.

- *Form Express,* a tool to render legacy COBOL applications Internet accessible
- *Form Designer,* a tool to generate a CGI program to convert COBOL code into the appropriate Internet format
- *Server-side scripting abilities* to create CGI applications with HTML in COBOL
- *Compile and link directives* that convert a single source program into CGI-compliant modules that can be used on any Web server, NSAPI.DLLs for Netscape web servers, and ISAPI.DLLs for Microsoft Internet Information Servers
- *Revolve 2000* to analyze legacy code to identify reusable components.

Other vendors now or soon will supply similar offerings. Your company may choose to use the World Wide Web only to furnish information to customers, or it may decide to develop a full-blown platform for selling its products. In any case, there are many compelling business reasons to combine Internet technology with your existing COBOL code. By doing do, you can reuse and leverage both COBOL code and existing programming skills. The quick development time allows you to reach more customers faster and improves your chances of getting there ahead of the competition. Above all, this strategy represents the wave of the future.

From the previous discussion, several conclusions fall out:

- Not all COBOL applications are candidates for distributed processing. Some batch applications, such as payroll, will remain batch applications.
- Although Internet and intranet applications will continue to grow rapidly, not all client/server applications are suitable for Internet technology.

- Some companies that have made big investments in client/server systems may decide not to migrate those systems to the Internet or an intranet.
- The market that supports Internet technology tools has not yet shaken out and will continue to change and grow.

EXERCISES

1. Explain three differences between a traditional computing environment and a distributed one.
2. Clarify the main distinction between generic distributed computing and client/server computing.
3. Enumerate the three logical components of a client/server system.
4. Name five physical components of a client/server system.
5. Point out three advantages and three disadvantages of client/server systems.
6. Cite two necessary characteristics that a legacy COBOL application needs in order to be considered a good candidate for client/server.
7. Explain why a thin client is normally an advantage in distributed processing.
8. Define the differences in scope among the World Wide Web, an intranet, and an extranet.
9. Name the specification that enables interactivity in a Web page.
10. Make the business case for combining Internet technology with existing COBOL code.

CHAPTER 31

APPLICATION PROGRAMMING INTERFACES

Sometime during your career, you are likely to use an *application programming interface* (API) to access systems such as CICS or SQL. Read this chapter when you use an API.

31.1 APPLICATION PROGRAMMING INTERFACES

COBOL is such a widely used programming language that vendors strive to make their products easily accessible to COBOL programs. Relational database management system (RDBMS) vendors like IBM and Oracle are no exception. A common approach is for the vendor to define an *application programming interface* (API) consisting of COBOL-like commands and statements that you place within a standard COBOL host program. The vendor also provides a special translator, commonly called a *precompiler,* to help prepare the resulting program for execution. The precompiler does the following:

1. Scans the COBOL program to find the API statements
2. Checks the syntax of the API statements
3. Converts the API statements into COBOL statements

The resulting COBOL statements call special run-time programs and also extract and save information from the API statements for the processing that happens outside of your program. An important (and sometimes the sole) output from the precompiler is a standard COBOL program with all of the embedded API statements replaced by true COBOL. This is the program that you go on to compile and prepare for execution, just as you would any standard COBOL program. The following portion of a program shows some API statements for an interface to Structured Query Language (SQL) and the expanded precompiled COBOL code they generate, in this case a record description.

API statements:

```
EXEC SQL
  INCLUDE PARTS
END-EXEC.
```

Expanded code:

```
EXEC SQL DECLARE TEST.PARTS TABLE
          (PartNo        CHAR (6) NOT NULL,
           Supplier      CHAR (20) NOT NULL,
           Phone         CHAR (10) NOT NULL)
******************************************************************
**  COBOL DECLARATION FOR TABLE TEST.PARTS **
******************************************************************
01   Parts-Row.
     10   PartNo                    PIC X(6).
     10   Supplier                  PIC X(20).
     10   Phone                     PIC X(10).
```

When you use vendor-produced APIs, you must learn the syntax of the product API, how it is combined with standard COBOL statements, and how to prepare for execution a COBOL program that contains the special-purpose statements. In the IBM world, two common examples of COBOL APIs are the CICS command language and the embedded SQL interface for DB2. This chapter uses the SQL interface for DB2 to illustrate the concept of embedded statements. These statements add power and flexibility to you COBOL program by allowing it to access relational table data. The objective here is not to teach you SQL, but to explain the elements needed by the DB2 precompiler. The steps to creating a COBOL program with embedded SQL statements are as follows:

1. Create any input and/or output tables using the SQL CREATE TABLE statement. The database administrator (DBA) usually performs this task. (Besides tables, other relational objects, such as views, can also be used in embedded SQL programs, but they are beyond the scope of our discussion.)

2. Use an optional DB2 facility, called DCLGEN facility, to produce one or more DECLARE statements, one of the elements used by the precompiler, and COBOL *host variables,* which accept or present values.

3. Precompile, compile, link and bind the program. *Binding* is the step that validates the relational database functions, checks database permissions, and creates an *application plan* or strategy for database access.

Figure 31.1 illustrates the precompile, compile, link, and bind steps.

31.1.1   Coding the Program

Let's look at a simple program with embedded SQL statements to retrieve and display the part number and supplier information from a DB2 table. Note that you

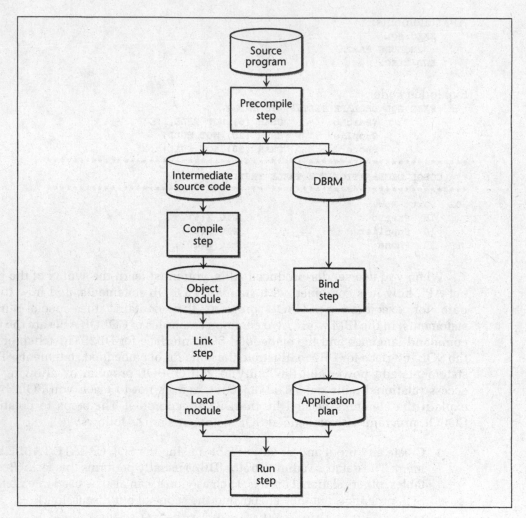

FIGURE 31.1 Precompile, compile, link, and bind steps.

don't need to code a COBOL SELECT statement in the Environment Division to assign an external name to the table. (Don't confuse the COBOL SELECT statement, which assigns an external name to a file, and the SQL SELECT statement, which retrieves columns from a table.) Neither do you need to provide file and record descriptions in the File Section of the Data Division as you would for an ordinary sequential file.

```
ENVIRONMENT DIVISION.
INPUT-OUTPUT SECTION.
FILE-CONTROL.            [No COBOL SELECT needed for a relational table.]
DATA DIVISION.
FILE SECTION.            [No FD and record description needed.]
```

Each SQL statement must begin with EXEC SQL and end with END-EXEC. You cannot use a COBOL COPY statement within EXEC SQL and END-EXEC. Use the INCLUDE statement instead.

```
EXEC SQL
INCLUDE PARTS
END-EXEC.
```

31.1.2   COBOL Host Variables

The INCLUDE statement calls a partitioned data set member named PARTS, which was previously generated with DCLGEN. DCLGEN is an optional facility that generates output for *host variables,* which are the COBOL structures used to contain DB2 data items. In DB2, running DCLGEN is the easiest and safest way to generate COBOL host variables, although you can code them manually. The following statements show the host variables generated by DCLGEN for the table TEST.PARTS.

```
**********************************************************************
** DCLGEN TABLE (TEST.PARTS)                                       **
**              LIBRARY (TESTDB2.DCLGENS COBOL (PARTS)             **
**              ACTION (REPLACE)                                   **
**              STRUCTURE (Parts-Row)                              **
**              APOST                                              **
**   This command created the following statements:               **
**********************************************************************
```

The initial comments in the statements describe a table named TEST.PARTS. The table declaration generated by this DCLGEN is stored as member (PARTS) in the partitioned data set TESTDB2.DCLGENS.COBOL. The main section of the DCLGEN follows in two parts. The first DECLAREs the table to the DB2 precompiler.

```
EXEC SQL DECLARE TEST.PARTS TABLE
       (PartNo       CHAR (6) NOT NULL,
        Supplier     CHAR (20) NOT NULL,
        Phone        CHAR (10) NOT NULL)
**********************************************************************
** COBOL DECLARATION FOR TABLE TEST.PARTS                          **
**   THE NUMBER OF COLUMNS DESCRIBED BY THIS DECLARATION IS 3      **
**********************************************************************
```

Then this part describes the corresponding *Parts-Row* record to COBOL. The data names (preceded by colons) become COBOL host variables into which the DB2 columns are received or presented.

```
01  Parts-Row.
    10  PartNo                    PIC X(6).
    10  Supplier                  PIC X(20).
    10  Phone                     PIC X(10).
```

31.1.3 The SQLCA and SQLCODE

Back in the example program, another INCLUDE statement defines a SQL communications area (SQLCA) that DB2 uses to pass return code information to the COBOL program.

```
EXEC SQL
    INCLUDE SQLCA
END-EXEC.
```

The following statements show the expanded SQLCA.

```
01 SQLCA.
   05 SQLCAID                    PIC X(8).
   05 SQLCABC                    PIC S9(9) BINARY.
   05 SQLCODE                    PIC S9(9) BINARY.
   05 SQLERRM.
```
   [Contains more descriptive information for the type of error that occurred.]
```
      49 SQLERRML                PIC S9(4) BINARY.
      49 SQLERRMC                PIC X(70).
   05 SQLERRP                    PIC X(8).
```
   [A set of six integer values. SQLERRD(3) indicates the number of rows inserted, updated, or deleted by the SQL statement.]
```
   05 SQLERRD                    OCCURS 6 TIMES
                                 PIC S9(9) BINARY.
   05 SQLWARN.
```
   [Contains eight variables indicating which SQL warning flags have been set.]
```
      10 SQLWARN0                PIC X.
      10 SQLWARN1                PIC X.
      10 SQLWARN2                PIC X.
      10 SQLWARN3                PIC X.
      10 SQLWARN4                PIC X.
      10 SQLWARN5                PIC X.
      10 SQLWARN6                PIC X.
      10 SQLWARN7                PIC X.
   05 SQLEXT                     PIC X(8).
```

The item you need to be most concerned about is SQLCODE, which DB2 uses hold the return code. It can have one of the following values:

SQLCODE	Interpretation
0	The operation was successful.
+100	Indicates either unfound data or the end of data.
Positive number > 0	The operation was successful, but some exceptional condition occurred.
Negative number	Indicates a serious error has occurred.

Check *SQLCODE* after each SQL statement, as in this example:

```
IF SQLCODE NOT = 0
   THEN MOVE "N" TO Part-Located-Sw
END-IF
```

For more extensive SQLCODE checking, you might program something like the following:

```
IF SQLCODE NOT = 0
   THEN MOVE "N" TO Part-Located-Sw
      IF SQLCODE = +100
         THEN ...              [Statements to determine if not found or end.]
      IF SQLCODE >= +0
         THEN ...              [Statements to determine the exception.]
      IF SQLCODE < +0
         THEN ...              [Statements to determine type of error.]
   END-IF
```

Each application is different, of course, but when the *SQLCODE* is a negative number, you'll probably want to end processing and even ROLLBACK processing (another SQL operation) that has already been done.

31.1.4   Programming Logic

Now let's return to the example program to look at the Procedure Division logic. The ACCEPT statement accepts a value entered by the user. This value describes a unique row to be read from the DB2 table.

```
DISPLAY "Type in the part number and press the Enter key"
DISPLAY "or type in xxxxxx and press the Enter key to quit."
ACCEPT PartNo
   [ACCEPT puts the desired value into the COBOL variable PartNo.]
IF PartNo = "xxxxxx"
   THEN MOVE "Y" TO End-Of-Query-Sw
END-IF
```

The SQL SELECT statement selects two columns from the TEST.PARTS table into the COBOL host variables defined previously with DCLGEN. Notice that the COBOL host variables are preceded by colons in the SQL statement. This is the API-defined way of making clear to the precompiler that these are the names of COBOL variables and not of DB2 objects.

```
EXEC SQL
   SELECT Supplier, Phone
          INTO :Supplier, :Phone
          FROM TEST.PARTS
          WHERE PartNo = :PartNo
```
[This statement will not appear in the compiled COBOL program. The precompiler will replace it with COBOL MOVE and CALL statements. The statement assumes that the table rows are unique and that the columns selected are NOT NULL.]

```
        END-EXEC.
        IF SQLCODE NOT = 0
            THEN MOVE "N" TO Part-Located-Sw
        END-IF
```

From a COBOL point of view, it is important to note that DB2 columns are selected into COBOL host variables by *position*, and not by name. In the example, the DB2 column and the COBOL host variable have the same name (*Supplier* to COBOL, *:Supplier* to SQL), but this is not required. The example also has only fixed-length character string columns, so the COBOL PIC clauses are straightforward. However, with numeric columns, each COBOL PIC clause must have a compatible numeric definition.

The WHERE clause tells DB2 to retrieve the only table row in which the value of the *PartNo* column matches the value placed in the COBOL host variable (*PartNo* to COBOL, *:PartNo* to SQL) by the ACCEPT statement.

Note again that the *SQLCODE* is checked for a return code and if it is not +0, an exception condition is performed. Here is the entire example program:

```
IDENTIFICATION DIVISION.
PROGRAM-ID.  PARTQUERY.
DATA DIVISION.
WORKING-STORAGE SECTION.
01  Switches.
    05  End-Of-Query-Sw             PIC X VALUE "N".
        88  End-Of-Query            VALUE "Y".
    05  Part-Located-Sw             PIC X VALUE "N".
        88  Part-LocatedVALUE "Y".
    EXEC SQL
        INCLUDE PARTS
    END-EXEC.
    EXEC SQL
        INCLUDE SQLCA
    END-EXEC.
```
        [The compiled program will display the expanded DCLGEN output.]
```
PROCEDURE DIVISION.
A00-Begin.
    PERFORM A10-Get-Parts UNTIL End-Of-Query
    GOBACK.
A10-Get-Parts.
    DISPLAY "Type in the part number and press the Enter key"
    DISPLAY "or type in  xxxxxx and press the Enter key to quit."
    ACCEPT PartNo.
    IF PartNo = "xxxxxx"
        THEN MOVE "Y" TO End-Of-Query-Sw
    END-IF
    IF NOT End-Of-Query
        THEN MOVE "Y" TO Part-Located-Sw
            PERFORM A30-Retrieve-Part-Row
            IF Part-Located
                THEN DISPLAY "  PART NUMBER       ", PartNo
                     DISPLAY "  SUPPLIER", Supplier
                     DISPLAY "  Phone     ", Phone
```

```
                        ELSE DISPLAY  "PART NUMBER NOT FOUND ", PartNo
                    END-IF
            END-IF
            .
    **** EXIT
    A30-Retrieve-Part-Row.
        EXEC SQL
            SELECT Supplier, Phone
                    INTO :Supplier, :Phone
                    FROM TEST.PARTS
                    WHERE PartNo = :PartNo
        END-EXEC.
        IF SQLCODE NOT = 0
            THEN MOVE "N" TO Part-Located-Sw
        END-IF
        .
    **** EXIT
    END PROGRAM PARTQUERY.
```

31.2 PREPARING AND RUNNING THE PROGRAM

Once the programming logic is the way you want it, the next step is to precompile
it. Refer again to Figure 31.1, which depicts the steps required to precompile,
compile, and run a COBOL program containing embedded SQL statements.

31.2.1 Precompile

The purpose of the precompile step is to produce two output files. One is a file of
intermediate source code that comments out each SQL statement and replaces it
with an equivalent COBOL statement. This file becomes the input to the COBOL
compile step. If the precompile process can't translate a given SQL statement into
an equivalent COBOL statement, it flags the statement and the step fails. The second file produced by the precompile is the *database request module* (DBRM). It
contains information about how the program will use the relational database (DB2
here). The DBRM is the input to the bind process.

31.2.2 Compile and Link

After the program precompiles, the next step uses the intermediate source file as
input to invoke the standard COBOL compiler. The intermediate *object module* is
produced as output. The object module becomes input to the *linkage-editor*,
which produces the load module as output.

31.2.3 Bind

The bind process uses the DBRM as input to validate the relational database functions and check permissions to make sure that you are authorized to access any

requested database objects, such as tables. It also decides on how DB2 will process each relational database request made by your program. The output of the bind process is an *application plan*. Both the load module and the application plan are used as input to the Run step.

31.2.4   DB2I versus JCL

DB2 provides a facility called DB2I that allows you to prepare and run the program interactively and to generate the DCLGEN. From the DB2I Primary Option Menu you set up the DB2I panels to point to your program libraries and name the options that you want to use. Then you need only supply the member name to prepare and run the program. Another option is to use garden-variety JCL statements to prepare and run the program in batch mode.

To recap, COBOL knows nothing about embedded SQL, but depends on the DB2 application programming interface (API) and the precompiler to convert the API statements into their equivalent COBOL counterparts. In the program preparation process, the output from the precompile step is used in both the COBOL compile and link steps and in the DB2 bind process. Both the COBOL load module and the DB2 application plan are needed to run the program.

EXERCISES

1. Name the steps needed (in the correct order) to prepare and run a COBOL program with embedded SQL statements.
2. Explain the difference between the compile step and the bind process.
3. Explain the purpose of the application plan.
4. Write a simple embedded SQL statement to INCLUDE a DCLGEN named PARTS.
5. Explain the purpose of the SQLCA.

CHAPTER 32

CROSS-SYSTEM DEVELOPMENT

The days of writing a COBOL program to run in only one environment are, for most applications, far in the past.

32.1 WHY CROSS-SYSTEM DEVELOPMENT

Even if a legacy system will continue to run on the mainframe, you will likely do development on the PC because of the following advantages:

The mainframe cost per MIPS (million instructions per second) may be hundreds of times more than on a PC, depending on whether you count the cost of the raised floor, water-cooling, operators, and systems programmers. The incremental cost of computing on a PC is essentially zero. You can run a PC all day for about the cost of burning a 60-Watt light bulb. The incremental cost of adding capacity with a PC is in the $1,000 range. On a mainframe, it might be 100 times this.

The PC response is faster and more consistent. Although a typical mainframe computer may be as fast or faster than a PC (and this is not at all certain), it supports many concurrent users, so that its effective response time is slower than a PC.

PC software is easier to use than that on a mainframe. Because a PC has a single user, the value of unused CPU cycles is zero. The PC can afford to spend most of its CPU cycles on the graphical interface of systems like Windows, which make the PC easier to use. The mainframe executes many concurrent programs, and if your program doesn't use the CPU cycles, another program can. The mainframe can't afford to devote most of its CPU cycles to making things easier for a single user.

The Workstation and Micro Focus compilers are essentially compatible with IBM Mainframe COBOL, and other compilers such as Fujitsu are ANSI-compatible. The compilers have compiler options to flag statements incompatible with the mainframe or the ANSI standard. Consequently, you can do your development and testing on a PC and then upload to the mainframe for final testing and production. The convenience of doing testing on the PC far outweighs the minor inconvenience of uploading and downloading the source code.

32.2 COBOL EDITORS

Many PC compilers come with additional tools that allow you to enter and manipulate both code and data. An online editor is one tool that will really increase your productivity by allowing you to edit, compile, run, and test COBOL code within the Windows environment. They let you plant breakpoints within a program, step through statements and execute them one at a time, and examine the contents of variables. These tools are especially wonderful for detailed debugging during development. They are less useful in the later stages of development or debugging production programs that may execute millions of statements before the bug is encountered. For this, it is better to include debugging statements directly in the program and use IF statements, or whatever, to activate them during execution when the conditions causing the bug are encountered. For example, if you get a zero divide in processing the 10,000th transaction in a file, debugging statements work much better than breakpoints and executing statements a step at a time.

Figure 32.1 shows the Edit mode for the Animator, which is part of the Micro Focus Personal COBOL toolset. (It's called the Animator because it allows you to view the code as it executes.) By default, the margins are set at 8 and 72, the space that COBOL legacy programs occupy. You can choose sequence numbers or not,

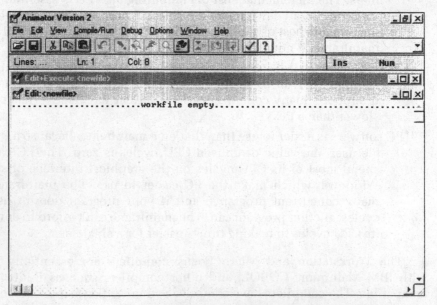

FIGURE 32.1   Edit mode of Micro Focus Animator screen.

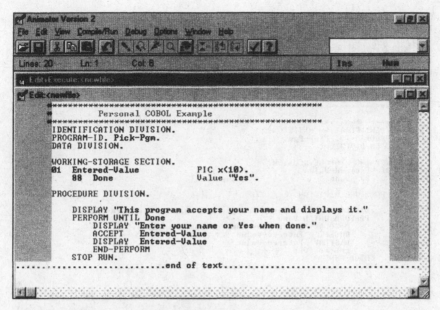

FIGURE 32.2   Animator screen with a simple COBOL program.

depending on what you select under Options. And you can access both Animator and COBOL syntax help by clicking the Help option on the toolbar menu.

Figure 32.2 shows a simple COBOL program. You can either type in the code line by line or copy in a file of previously written code. All COBOL statements and reserved words are color-coded for easy recognition.

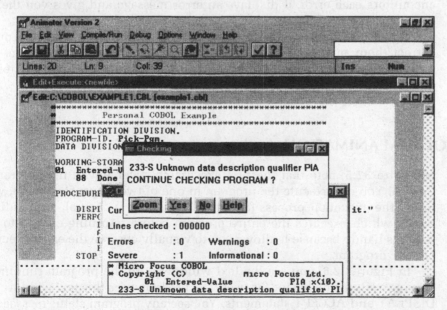

FIGURE 32.3   COBOL program with an error.

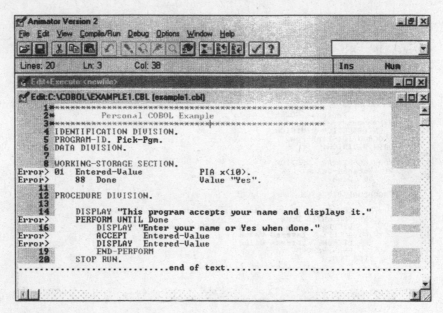

FIGURE 32.4   Errors highlighted in a COBOL program.

In Figure 32.3, an error has been keyed in and an attempt made to compile the program by choosing the Compile option from the toolbar menu. As the compiler encounters each error, it displays an error message and gives you the option of continuing on or quitting.

Figure 32.4 displays the program with all of the errors targeted. You can then correct them and repeat the process until you have a clean compile. Once you have a clean compile, you switch to Edit+Execute mode to run and test the program, while still being able to edit the source code.

32.3   PROGRAM ANIMATION

In Figure 32.5, note that the first executable statement in the program is highlighted. You can execute the program in one of two ways: *step* mode, which animates the execution process (and gives Animator its name), and traditional *run* mode, which executes the entire program before returning control to you. Step mode is handy because it allows you to visually observe the exact execution path of your program.

In Figure 32.6, you see the text window with the program running and displaying a simple dialog for the user. The program uses this text window to process DISPLAY and ACCEPT statements. You see any program status messages in separate pop-up windows.

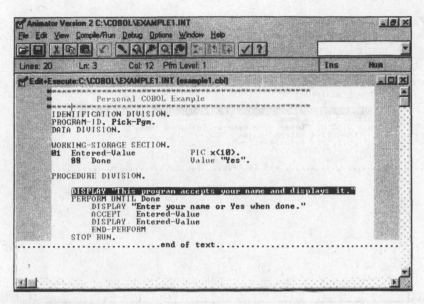

FIGURE 32.5 Stepping through program execution.

32.4 BREAKPOINTS

One of the most useful facilities of a PC COBOL editor is the ability to set *breakpoints*. A breakpoint is just what the name implies, a debugging facility that allows you to halt the program at a specified execution point. Figure 32.7 shows the COBOL program code with the breakpoint set, and Figure 32.8 shows the pro-

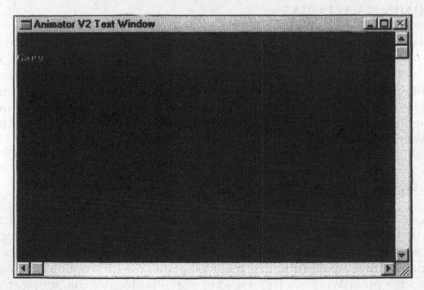

FIGURE 32.6 Dialogue screen.

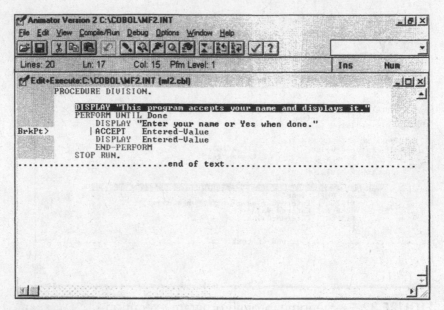

FIGURE 32.7 Breakpoint.

gram as it appears upon encountering the specified breakpoint. At this point, you can reaccess the code and examine, monitor, and perhaps even alter the value in any of the variables that are affected by the breakpoint, and then resume execution of the program or restart it as appropriate.

32.5 EXAMINING VARIABLES

In addition to watching which statements are executed, you can display the contents of variables as the program executes. You can request a pop-up window in which to name the variables you want to watch. Then as the program executes, you can request the pop-up window to display the name and value of the variables. With the combination of executing statements a step at a time and examining the value of variables as the statements execute, you can usually track down even the most complex bug.

32.6 GRAPHICAL USER INTERFACES

Your compiler tool may not work exactly like the Micro Focus product, but most will offer similar functionality. Your toolset may also include a *dialog system* or dialog manager. This tool allows you to create a *graphical user interface* (GUI) for your COBOL application that includes point-and-click options, pull-down lists, and the other Windows features so essential for today's computing environment,

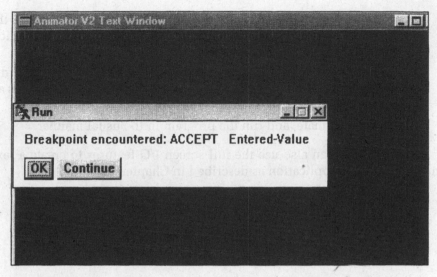

FIGURE 32.8 Dialogue screen with breakpoint encountered.

including the World Wide Web. A dialog system manages the details of the interface between the user and the COBOL program, allowing you to concentrate on the programming logic.

To create a graphical interface for your COBOL application using a dialog system, follow these general steps:

1. Begin by analyzing the data thoroughly and determining which items are essential for your application. Once you do this, all of the other steps fall naturally into place.

2. Specify the *data items* that the GUI will process. For each data item, you need to designate field name, type, size, and other properties using property lists that the dialog system provides.

3. Define the GUI *objects* that will process your data items. These objects include title bars, menus, buttons, and text entry fields. They provide the visual representation of the application to the user.

4. Join each data item to its GUI object by creating a *dialog.* Stated another way, a dialog specifies one or more *actions* to be taken in response to an *event* such as a key press or a mouse click. A dialog can pertain to a single object in a window, the entire window, or the entire application. The data item specification, GUI object definition, and any dialogs are saved together as a set and called by the application program.

5. Create one or more *copybooks* that provide data descriptions for the data items specified in step 2. Just as for a garden variety COBOL program, these copybooks are included in Working-Storage. The run-time facility of the

dialog system passes the data items as parameters. It also updates the value of data items if appropriate, performs all screen-handling functions, and returns control to the COBOL program.

6. Code the application program logic concentrating on the basic data processing tasks. Again, keep in mind that the dialog system handles all interface issues between the user and the program.

7. Compile, animate, and run the program in the usual manner.

Note that you can also use the full-screen I/O features to create a text-based interface for your application as described in Chapter 24.

CHAPTER 33

COMPILE, LINK, AND RUN PROCEDURES

In OS/390 COBOL, you invoke the COBOL compiler by naming an installation-supplied cataloged procedure that contains the necessary JCL statements. Read this chapter if you are programming for OS/390. Otherwise skip it.

Essential—for OS/390 Mainframe Only

To program in Mainframe COBOL, you must know Job Control Language (JCL). JCL is a rather complicated language used to execute batch COBOL jobs in OS/390 (Brown, 1998; IBM, 1997c). This chapter assumes that you know something about JCL. Even if you do most of your program development using the ISPF editor, you need to know about the COBOL cataloged procedures. The cataloged procedure name may vary with the installation and with the version of the COBOL compiler. The convention in naming is to append the cataloged procedure name with *C* to indicate compile, *CL* to indicate compile and link edit, and *CLG* to indicate compile, link edit, and go (run the program).

33.1   COMPILE

The compile procedure finds compilation errors and produces a program listing. It doesn't execute the program.

33.1.1   JCL for Compilation

You execute the IGYWC cataloged procedure to compile a COBOL program:

```
//JR964113 JOB (24584), 'JONES',CLASS=A
// EXEC IGYWC,PARM.COBOL='XREF,LIB'
```
            [IGYWC is the name of the cataloged procedure, but installations may have different names. The PARM.COBOL='XREF,LIB' specifies the XREF and LIB com-

piler options. The PARM.COBOL indicates that the PARM is to apply to the COBOL step. The convention is for COBOL to be the step name for the compile step, LKED for the link edit step, and GO for the execution step.]

```
//COBOL.SYSLIB DD DSN=copy-library,DISP=SHR
```
[You need SYSLIB only if you bring in members from a copy library.]
```
//COBOL.SYSIN DD *
[Place your COBOL program here.]
```

There are several compilation options beyond the scope of this book, but the options you are likely to need to use are these:

- *ADV* is default and tells COBOL to add one extra byte to each line in the FD file description of a file in which you code WRITE AFTER ADVANCING. NOADV requires you to account for the byte yourself.

- *ANALYZE* tells COBOL to check the syntax of embedded SQL and CICS statements. NOANALYZE is default.

- *APOST* indicates that you are using the apostrophe (') to enclose literals. QUOTE is the default for the quotation marks (").

- *CMPR2* generates code compatible with VS COBOL II Release 2. The ANSI 1985 COBOL standard introduced some incompatibilities with Release 2, and CMPR2 lets these programs compile properly. The default is NOCMPR2.

- *DATA(31)* is default; it allows storage to be acquired above or below the 16Mb line and requires either the RENT or RMODE(ANY) option in addition. DATA(24) requires the Working-Storage and FD area to be acquired below the 16Mb line.

- *DYNAM* causes a separately compiled program invoked with the CALL statement to be dynamically loaded at run time. NODYNAM is default. Don't use DYNAM with CICS.

- *FASTSRT* speeds up sorting by having the DFSORT program do all I/O rather than the COBOL program, saving overhead. NOFASTSRT is default.

- *LIB* lets your program use the COPY, BASIS, or REPLACE statements described in Chapter 19. NOLIB is default.

- *MAP* generates a listing of the items in the Data Division. NOMAP is default.

- *NAME* generates a link edit NAME statement for each object module, so that they can be link-edited as separate load modules for output to a partitioned data set. NONAME is default.

- *NUMPROC* specifies how the sign is carried in external decimal or packed-decimal numbers. NUMPROC(PFD) is considerably faster and assumes a single code on the high-order digit for − or +. NUMPROC(NOPFD) is default and allows four ways of coding a + and three ways of coding a −, which is the ANSI standard. NUMPROC(MIG) is used only to migrate from OS/VS COBOL to Mainframe COBOL.

- *OPT* generates optimized code. NOOPT is default.

- *RENT* generates reentrant code and is required for CICS. NORENT is default.
- *RMODE* indicates whether 24-bit addressing is used, which requires the program to run under the 16Mb line. RMODE(AUTO) results in 24-bit addressing if NORENT is specified and 32-bit addressing if RENT is specified. RMODE(24) specifies 24-bit addressing regardless of RENT or NORENT. RMODE(ANY) results in 32-bit addressing regardless of RENT or NORENT.
- *SSRANGE* generates code for run-time checking of index, subscript, reference modification, and variable-length group ranges for valid values. NOSSRANGE is default. The CHECK(OFF) run-time option can turn off checking during execution.
- *TRUNC* determines the way COBOL truncates numeric data when they are stored in a binary field. TRUNC(STD) is the default and the ANSI standard. It truncates the binary number to the number of digits specified in the PIC clause, not the number of digits the storage can contain. TRUNC(BIN) truncates the number to the size of the storage: byte, halfword, fullword, or doubleword. TRUNC(OPT) is a performance option that truncates the number of digits as STD or BIN, depending on which takes less effort.
- *VBREF* produces a cross-reference listing of the COBOL verbs with a summary of how many times each verb is used. NOVBREF is default.
- *XREF* produces a sorted cross-reference listing. NOXREF is default.

You can pass these options to the compiler with the JCL PARM parameter on the EXEC statement or with the CBL statement, described next.

33.1.2 Compiler-Directing Statements

- *CBL* lets you specify the COBOL compilation options on it rather than in the PARM of the JCL EXEC statement. You place the CBL statement before the Identification Division header. Code the statement in columns 1 to 72 and include several statements, if necessary, to contain all the options. Separate the options with a comma or space. Code the CBL statement as follows:

```
CBL option,option,...,option
CBL LIB,ADV,DYNAM,RENT
```

- **CBL* selectively generates or suppresses the source, object, and storage map listing for the compilation. The *CBL must begin in column 7 or beyond and be followed by a space. Code the *CBL statement as follows:

```
*CBL option
```

You can code only one option on a statement, but there can be several statements. The options are the following:

 SOURCE or *NOSOURCE:* Generate or suppress the source listing.

 LIST or *NOLIST:* Generate or suppress the object code listing.

 MAP or *NOMAP:* Generate or suppress storage map listing.

33.2 COMPILE, LINK-EDIT, AND GO

The compile, link edit, and go procedure is primarily for test runs. It compiles the program, link-edits it to produce an executable load module, and executes this load module. You usually don't save the load module for subsequent runs, although you can. The next section on the compile and link-edit procedure explains how to save the load module.

```
//JR964113 JOB (24584),'JONES',CLASS=A
// EXEC IGYWCLG,PARM.COBOL='XREF,LIB',PARM.LKED='XREF',
//      REGION.GO=nK
        [The PARM.COBOL='XREF,LIB' specifies parameters for the compile step.
        PARM.LKED specifies parameters for the linkage editor step. REGION.GO=nK
        specifies the amount of memory in units of 1024 bytes (1K) required by the GO
        step. REGION.GO=104K requests 104K.]
//COBOL.SYSLIB DD DSN=copy-library,DISP=SHR
//COBOL.SYSIN DD *
[Place the COBOL program here.]
//LKED . . .
[To save the load module, place the link-edit DD statements
described in the following procedure here.]
//GO.ddname DD ...
[Place all DD statements specified in SELECT clauses here.]
```

33.2.1 Linkage Editor Options

The linkage editor options that apply specifically to COBOL are the following:

- *AMODE 24* specifies 24-bit addressing and is the usual default. AMODE 31 specifies 31-bit addressing, allowing programs to run above the 16Mb line. AMODE ANY specifies both.

- *NOCALL* suppresses resolution of linkage editor references (subprogram calls and global data items) and is used when you are creating a subprogram library. CALL resolves the references and is default.

- *RMODE 24* requires the program to reside below the 16Mb line and is the usual default. RMODE ANY allows the program to reside above the 16Mb line, and requires AMODE 31 or ANY.

- *XREF* produces a sorted cross-reference listing of the linkage editor output. Omit XREF for no listing.

33.2.2 Run-Time Options

There are several run-time options. The following are the ones most used:

- *CHECK(OFF)* turns off run-time subscript checking generated with the SSRANGE compiler option. CHECK(ON) is default.

- *NODEBUG* doesn't compile lines with a *D* in column 7. DEBUG is default.
- *SIMVRD* allows a VSAM KSDS data set to be used to simulate variable-length records in a relative data set. NOSIMVRD is default.

You specify run-time options on the PARM parameter of the EXEC statement for the program. Code a slash before the first run-time parameter. If the PARM must specify both program and COBOL run-time parameters, code them as follows:

```
// EXEC PGM=program,PARM='program-parameters/run-options'
```

33.3   CREATING LIBRARIES

The compilation step creates what is termed an *object module,* which must then be link-edited to include all the necessary system routines and create what is termed a *load module.* The load module is executable and you can retain it to reexecute the program without the compilation and link edit steps. The following examples illustrate the JCL necessary to link edit a program, save the load module, and later execute it.

33.3.1   Creating Object Module Libraries

The following example shows how three COBOL programs, ONE, TWO, and THREE, are compiled and retained in object module form in a partitioned data set named A1000.LIB.OBJ. Partitioned data set member names must be one to eight alphanumeric (*A* through *Z, 0* through *9*) or national (@ *$* #) characters, beginning with an alphabetic (*A* through *Z*) or national character.

The IGYWC cataloged procedure is used to compile the programs and create the library. You must override the SYSLMOD DD statement to create the nontemporary data set.

```
//JR964113 JOB (24584),'JONES',CLASS=A
// EXEC IGYWC,PARM.COBOL='LIB'
//COBOL.SYSLIB DD DSN=copy-library,DISP=SHR
        [Include DD statements for copy libraries as needed.]
//COBOL.SYSIN DD *
[ONE source statements]
        END PROGRAM ONE.
[TWO source statements]
        END PROGRAM TWO.
[THREE source statements]
        END PROGRAM THREE.
//COBOL.SYSLIN DD DSN=A1000.LIB.OBJ,DISP=(NEW,CATLG),
//              UNIT=SYSDA,SPACE=(1024,(100,30,10))
        [The A1000.LIB.MOD data set is created, and the object modules are added as
        members named ONE, TWO, and THREE. The SPACE parameter is also overrid-
        den to allocate a more precise amount of space and to enlarge the directory space.]
```

Now you can include the A1000.LIB.OBJ library as input when you compile any COBOL. The following example shows how this is done.

```
//JR964113 JOB (24584),'JONES',CLASS=A
// EXEC IGYWCLG
//COBOL.SYSLIB DD DSN=copy-library,DISP=SHR
//COBOL.SYSIN  DD *
[Main COBOL source statements.]
//LKED.DD1     DD DSN=A1000.LIB.OBJ,DISP=SHR
//LKED.SYSIN  DD *
 ENTRY name
```
   [Even though the main routine is still loaded first, it is a good idea to tell the linkage editor the name of the entry point.]
```
 INCLUDE DD1
```
   [The A1000.LIB.OBJ library is included as additional input.]

33.3.2   Creating Load Module Libraries

The next example is the same, except this time ONE, TWO, and THREE are link-edited and stored in load module form in a partitioned data set named A1000.LIB .LOAD. Load module libraries are generally more efficient than object module libraries.

```
//JR964113 JOB (24584),'JONES',CLASS=A
// EXEC IGYWCL,PARM.COBOL='NAME,XREF'
```
   [The compile/link edit procedure is used. The NAME parameter causes the COBOL compiler to append linkage editor NAME statements to the object modules. This enables them to be link-edited as separate load modules for output in a partitioned data set. XREF produces a linkage editor cross-reference listing.]
```
//COBOL.SYSLIB  DD DSN=copy-library,DISP=SHR
//COBOL.SYSIN   DD *
[ONE source statements]
     END PROGRAM ONE.
[TWO source statements]
     END PROGRAM TWO.
[THREE source statements]
     END PROGRAM THREE.
//LKED.SYSLMOD DD DSN=A1000.LIB.LOAD,DISP=(NEW,CATLG),
//             UNIT=SYSDA,SPACE=(1024,(100,30,10))
```
   [The A1000.LIB.LOAD data set is created, and the load modules are added as members named ONE, TWO, and THREE.]

You can also include the A1000.LIB.LOAD library as input when any COBOL program is compiled, as shown in the following example:

```
//JR964113 JOB (24584),'JONES',CLASS=A
// EXEC IGYWCLG
//COBOL.SYSLIB DD DSN=copy-library,DISP=SHR
//COBOL.SYSIN DD *
[Main COBOL source statements.]
```

```
//LKED.DD1 DD DSN=A1000.LIB.LOAD,DISP=SHR
//LKED.SYSIN DD *
ENTRY name
```
[Although the main routine is still loaded first, it is a good idea to tell the linkage editor the name of the entry point.]
```
INCLUDE DD1
```
[The A1000.LIB.LOAD library is included as additional input.]

33.3.3 Creating Load Modules for Program Development

For program development, it is usual to compile a COBOL program and its subprograms and link-edit them into a single load module. In the example, the library is named A1000.PGM.LOAD, and the load module is named THING. The following JCL does this:

```
//JR964113 JOB (24584),'JONES',CLASS=A
// EXEC IGYWCLG
```
[The compile/link edit/go procedure is used.]
```
//COBOL.SYSLIB  DD DSN=copy-library,DISP=SHR
//COBOL.SYSIN   DD *
[Main COBOL source statements]
[ONE source statements]
[TWO source statements]
[THREE source statements]
```
[The absence of any END PROGRAM statements causes all the modules being compiled to be placed in a single load module.]
```
//LKED.SYSLMOD DD DSN=A1000.PGM.LOAD(THING),DISP=(NEW,CATLG),
//               UNIT=SYSDA,SPACE=(1024,(100,30,10))
```
[The A1000.PGM.LOAD data set is created to contain the load module named THING.]
```
//GO.IN    DD DSN=A1000.JUNK.DATA,DISP=SHR
[Place any DD statements for the GO step here.]
```

You can also place other programs in the A1000.PGM.LOAD library, as long as you give them different member names. You can now execute the program in a single step:

```
//JR964113 JOB (24584),'JONES',CLASS=A
//GO EXEC PGM=THING
//STEPLIB DD DSN=A1000.PGM.LOAD,DISP=SHR
```
[The STEPLIB DD statement describes the data set containing the program to execute. The JOBLIB DD statement could have been used as well.]
```
//IN DD DSN=A1000.JUNK.DATA,DISP=SHR
[Place any DD statements for the GO step here.]
```

33.3.4 Replacing a Single Subprogram in an Existing Load Module

One advantage of subprograms is that they can be compiled individually without having to compile the main program or other subprograms. Suppose that the ONE subprogram contains an error and must be replaced. You can compile just the ONE subprogram and replace it in the load module as follows:

```
// EXEC IGYWCLG
//COBOL.SYSLIB  DD DSN=copy-library,DISP=SHR
//COBOL.SYSIN   DD *
[ONE source statements]
//LKED.SYSLMOD DD DSN=A1000.PGM.LOAD(THING),DISP=OLD,SPACE=,UNIT=
```
[SYSLMOD is again overridden to describe the data set that is to contain the new load module. Because THING is already a member of A1000.PGM.LOAD, it is replaced by the new load module. By selecting a different name, you would add the new load module rather than replacing the old load module. The SPACE= parameter is coded to nullify the SPACE parameter on the overridden SYSLMOD statement, so that it does not change the secondary allocation specified when A1000.PGM.LOAD was created. The UNIT= is written because you want the system to locate the data set from the catalog.]
```
//LKED.DD1      DD DSN=A1000.PGM.LOAD,DISP=SHR
```
[The DD1 statement describes the library containing the old load module.]
```
//LKED.SYSIN   DD *
 ENTRY THING
```
[The main routine is no longer loaded first, and so you must tell the linkage editor that THING is the entry point.]
```
 INCLUDE DD1(THING)
```
[The old load module is included as additional input.]
```
//GO.IN         DD DSN=A1000.JUNK.DATA,DISP=SHR
```

APPENDIX A

CHANGES IN THE NEW ANSI STANDARD

The following proposed changes to the standard are incorporated in the book. The following includes only those changes not already in the IBM and PC compilers.

1. Extend the PIC string to 31 characters and make PIC optional for items with a VALUE clause that specifies an alphanumeric literal.
2. Extend numeric data to 31 digits.
3. Byte, half-word, full-word, and double-word binary data.
4. Single-, double-, and extended-precision floating-point data.
5. Standard arithmetic giving consistent results across different platforms is included.
6. Boolean data.
7. National characters.
8. User-written functions.
9. Compiler directives for conditional compilation and defining constants.
10. Exit and continuation from within an in-line PERFORM.
11. New intrinsic functions.
12. Initialized FILLER and initialization of data items to their VALUE clauses.
13. Elimination of B margin and free-form source statements.
14. Full-screen I/O.
15. Sort internal tables.
16. Automatically expand tables.
17. Validation criteria, specified in data descriptions, that is checked by executing the VALIDATE statement.
18. Object-oriented programming.

The following items not included in this book are also planned for the new standard.

1. Currency sign enhancements. You can specify a multiple-character currency symbol.

2. Dynamic-collating sequence. You can change the sort order of the collating sequence during execution.

3. Exception handling. This gives COBOL the ability to detect a wide variety of exception conditions.

4. New compiler directives for formatting listings. (The current compilers already have their own, and most programmers work from terminals rather than listings.)

5. File sharing and record locking. This lets you control access to a file that has multiple concurrent users. In practice, most such systems involve a database that you access with subroutine calls rather than COBOL statements.

6. User-defined data types. These let you specify new data types and apply this type to data descriptions.

7. A FORMAT clause in the FD to specify that records are formatted to an external representation, leaving the representation to the implementor. The implementors have already implemented this with ORGANIZATION LINE SEQUENTIAL in the SELECT clause.

8. Define symbolic constants.

APPENDIX B

COBOL RESERVED WORDS

The following reserved words are a compendium from IBM COBOL, Micro Focus COBOL, Fujitsu COBOL, ANSI COBOL 1985, and the new ANSI standard.

&	ALL	ASSIGN
(	ALLOCATE	AT
)	ALLOCATED-OCCURRENCES*	ATAN*
*	ALLOW	AUTHOR
**	ALLOWING	AUTO
+	ALPHABET	AUTO-HYPHEN-SKIP
–	ALPHABETIC	AUTO-SKIP
–>	ALPHABETIC-LOWER	AUTOMATIC
/	ALPHABETIC-UPPER	B-AND
;	ALPHANUMERIC	B-EXOR
<	ALPHANUMERIC-EDITED	B-LESS
<=	ALSO	B-NOT
=	ALTER	B-OR
>	ALTERNATE	B-XOR
>=	AND	BACKGROUND-COLOR
ABS*	ANNUITY*	BACKGROUND-COLOUR
ABSENT	ANY	BACKWARD
ACCEPT	APPLY	BASED-STORAGE
ACCESS	ARE	BASIS
ACOS*	AREA	BATCH
ACQUIRE	AREA-VALUE	BEEP
ACTUAL	AREAS	BEFORE
ADD	ARITHMETIC	BEGINNING
ADDRESS	AS	BELL
ADVANCING	ASCENDING	BINARY
AFTER	ASIN*	BINARY-CHAR

* These intrinsic function names become reserved only if they are declared as function names in the REPOSITORY paragraph.

BINARY-DOUBLE
BINARY-LONG
BINARY-SHORT
BIT
BITS
BLANK
BLINK
BLOCK
BODY
BOOLEAN
BOOLEAN-OF-INTEGER*
BOTTOM
BUFFER
BY
C01 through C12
CALL
CALL-CONVENTION
CANCEL
CBL
CD
CENTER
CENTRE
CF
CH
CHAIN
CHAINING
CHANGED
CHAR*
CHARACTER
CHARACTERS
CHAR-NATIONAL*
CICS
CLASS
CLASS-ID
CLOCK-UNITS
CLOSE
COBOL
CODE
CODE-SET
CODE-VALUE
COL
COLLATING
COLOR
COLS
COLUMN

COLUMNS
COM-REG
COMMA
COMMIT
COMMITMENT
COMMON
COMMUNICATION
COMP
COMP-0 through COMP-9
COMP-X
COMPLEX
COMPUTATIONAL
COMPUTATIONAL-0 through
    COMPUTATIONAL-9
COMPUTATIONAL-X
COMPUTE
CONFIGURATION
CONNECT
CONSOLE
CONTAINED
CONTAINS
CONTENT
CONTINUE
CONTROL
CONTROL AREA
CONTROLS
CONVERT
CONVERTING
COPY
CORE-INDEX
CORR
CORRESPONDING
COS*
COUNT
CRP
CRT
CRT-UNDER
CSP
CURRENCY
CURRENT
CURRENT-DATE*
CURSOR
CYCLE
CYL-INDEX
CYL-OVERFLOW

DATA
DATA-SUB-1 through DATA-
    SUB-4
DATE
DATE-COMPILED
DATE-OF-INTEGER*
DATE-TO-YYYYMMDD*
DATE-WRITTEN
DAY
DAY-OF-INTEGER*
DAY-OF-WEEK
DAY-TO-YYYYDDD*
DB
DB-ACCESS-CONTROL-KEY
DB-DATA-NAME
DB-EXCEPTION
DB-RECORD-NAME
DB-SET-NAME
DB-STATUS
DBCS
DE
DEAD-LOCK
DEBUG
DEBUG-CONTENTS
DEBUG-ITEM
DEBUG-LINE
DEBUG-NAME
DEBUG-SUB-1 through DEBUG-
    SUB-3
DEBUGGING
DECIMAL-POINT
DECLARATIVES
DEFAULT
DEFINE
DELETE
DELIMITED
DELIMITER
DEPENDING
DEPTH
DESCENDING
DESTINATION
DESTINATION-1 through
    DESTINATION-3
DETAIL
DEVICE

DIRECT
DISABLE
DISCONNECT
DISJOINING
DISK
DISP
DISPLAY
DISPLAY-1 through DISPLAY-9
DISPLAY-EXIT
DISPLAY OF*
DISPLAY-ST
DIVIDE
DIVISION
DLI
DOWN
DUPLICATE
DUPLICATED
DUPLICATES
DYNAMIC
E*
ECHO
EDIT-COLOR
EDIT-CURSOR
EDIT-MODE
EDIT-OPTION
EDIT-STATUS
EGCS
EGI
EJECT
ELSE
EMI
EMPTY
EMPTY-CHECK
ENABLE
END
END-ACCEPT
END-ADD
END-CALL
END-CHAIN
END-COMPUTE
END-DELETE
END-DISABLE
END-DISPLAY
END-DIVIDE
END-ENABLE

END-EVALUATE
END-EXEC
END-IF
END-INVOKE
END-MULTIPLY
END-OF-PAGE
END-PERFORM
END-READ
END-RECEIVE
END-RETURN
END-REWRITE
END-SEARCH
END-SEND
END-START
END-STRING
END-SUBTRACT
END-TRANSCEIVE
END-UNSTRING
END-WRITE
ENDCOBOL
ENDING
ENTER
ENTRY
ENVIRONMENT
EOL
EOP
EOS
EQUAL
EQUALS
ERASE
ERROR
ESCAPE
ESI
EVALUATE
EVERY
EXACT
EXAMINE
EXCEEDS
EXCEPTION
EXCEPTION-FILE*
EXCEPTION-LOCATION*
EXCEPTION-OBJECT
EXCEPTION-STATEMENT*
EXCEPTION-STATUS*
EXCESS-3

EXCLUSIVE
EXEC
EXECUTE
EXHIBIT
EXIT
EXOR
EXP*
EXP10*
EXTEND
EXTENDED-SEARCH
EXTERNAL
EXTERNALLY-DESCRIBED-
    KEY
FACTORIAL*
FACTORY
FALSE
FD
FETCH
FH-FCD
FH-KEYDEF
FILE
FILE-CONTROL
FILE-ID
FILE-LIMIT
FILE-LIMITS
FILES
FILLER
FINAL
FIND
FINISH
FIRST
FIXED
FLADD
FLOAT-EXTENDED
FLOAT-LONG
FLOAT-SHORT
FOOTING
FOR
FOREGROUND-COLOR
FOREGROUND-COLOUR
FORM
FORMAT
FORMATTED
FRACTION-PART*
FREE

FROM
FULL
FUNC
FUNCTION
FUNCTION-ID
GENERATE
GET
GIVING
GLOBAL
GO
GOBACK
GREATER
GRID
GROUP
HEADING
HIGH
HIGH-VALUE
HIGH-VALUES
HIGHEST-ALGEBRAIC*
HIGHLIGHT
HOLD
I-O
I-O-CONTROL
ID
IDENTIFICATION
IF
IGNORE
IN
INDEX
INDEX-1 through INDEX-9
INDEXED
INDICATE
INDICATOR
INDICATORS
INHERITING
INHERITS
INITIAL
INITIALIZE
INITIATE
INPUT
INPUT-OUTPUT
INSERT
INSPECT
INSTALLATION
INTEGER

INTEGER-OF-BOOLEAN*
INTEGER-OF-DATE*
INTEGER-OF-DAY*
INTEGER-PART*
INTERFACE
INTERFACE-ID
INTO
INVALID
INVOKE
INVOKED
IS
JAPANESE
JOB
JOINING
JUST
JUSTIFIED
KANJI
KEEP
KEPT
KEY
KEYBOARD
LABEL
LAST
LD
LEADING
LEAVE
LEFT
LEFT-JUSTIFY
LEFTLINE
LENGTH
LENGTH-AN*
LENGTH-CHECK
LESS
LIMIT
LIMITED
LIMITS
LIN
LINAGE
LINAGE-COUNTER
LINE
LINE-COUNTER
LINE-LIMIT
LINES
LINKAGE
LOCAL-STORAGE

LOCALE-COMPARE*
LOCALE-DATE*
LOCALE-TIME*
LOCALLY
LOCK
LOCKING
LOG*
LOG10*
LOW
LOW-VALUE
LOW-VALUES
LOWER
LOWER-CASE*
LOWEST-ALGEBRAIC*
LOWLIGHT
MANUAL
MASTER-INDEX
MAX*
MEAN*
MEDIAN*
MEMBER
MEMORY
MERGE
MESSAGE
METACLASS
METHOD
METHOD-ID
MIDRANGE*
MIN*
MOD*
MODE
MODE-1 through MODE-3
MODIFIED
MODIFY
MODULES
MORE-LABELS
MOVE
MULTICON
MULTICONVERSATION-
    MODE
MULTIPLE
MULTIPLY
NAME
NAMED
NATIONAL

NATIONAL-EDITED

NATIONAL-OF*

NATIVE

NCHAR

NEGATIVE

NESTED

NEW

NEXT

NO

NO-ECHO

NOMINAL

NONE

NORMAL

NOT

NOTE

NSTD-REELS

NULL

NULLS

NUMBER

NUMBERS

NUMERIC

NUMERIC-EDITED

NUMVAL*

NUMVAL-C*

NUMVAL-F*

O-FILL

OBJECT

OBJECT-COMPUTER

OBJECT-STORAGE

OCCURS

OF

OFF

OMITTED

ON

ONLY

OOSTACKPTR

OPEN

OPTIONAL

OPTIONS

OR

ORD*

ORD-MAX*

ORD-MIN*

ORDER

ORGANIZATION

OTHER

OTHERWISE

OUTPUT

OVERFLOW

OVERLINE

OVERRIDE

OWNER

PACKED-DECIMAL

PADDING

PAGE

PAGE-COUNTER

PALETTE

PARAGRAPH

PASSWORD

PERFORM

PF

PH

PI*

PIC

PICTURE

PLUS

POINTER

POS

POSITION

POSITIONING

POSITIVE

PREFIX

PRESENT

PRESENT-VALUE*

PREVIOUS

PRINT

PRINT-SWITCH

PRINTER

PRINTER-1

PRINTING

PRIOR

PROCEDURE

PROCEDURE-POINTER

PROCEDURES

PROCEED

PROCESS

PROCESSING

PROGRAM

PROGRAM-ID

PROGRAM-POINTER

PROGRAM-STATUS

PROMPT

PROPERTY

PROTECTED

PROTOTYPE

PUBLIC

PURGE

QUEUE

QUOTE

QUOTES

RAISE

RAISING

RANDOM*

RANGE*

RD

READ

READY

REALM

RECEIVE

RECONNECT

RECORD

RECORD-NAME

RECORD-OVERFLOW

RECORDING

RECORDS

RECURSIVE

REDEFINES

REEL

REFERENCE

REFERENCES

RELATION

RELATIVE

RELEASE

RELOAD

REM*

REMAINDER

REMARKS

REMOVAL

RENAMES

REORG-CRITERIA

REPEATED

REPEATED-COUNTER

REPLACE

REPLACING

REPORT

REPORT-NUMBER
REPORTING
REPORTS
REPOSITORY
REQUIRED
REREAD
RERUN
RESERVE
RESET
RETAINING
RETRIEVAL
RETURN
RETURN-CODE
RETURNING
REVERSE
REVERSE-VIDEO
REVERSED
REWIND
REWRITE
RF
RH
RIGHT
RIGHT-JUSTIFY
ROLL-OUT
ROLLBACK
ROLLING
ROUNDED
RUN
S01 through S05
SA
SAME
SAVED-AREA
SCREEN
SD
SEARCH
SECTION
SECURE
SECURITY
SEEK
SEGMENT
SEGMENT-LIMIT
SELECT
SELECTED
SELECTIVE
SELF

SELFCLASS
SEND
SENTENCE
SEPARATE
SEQUENCE
SEQUENTIAL
SERVICE
SESSION
SESSION-ID
SET
SHARED
SHARING
SHIFT-IN
SHIFT-OUT
SIGN
SIMPLE
SIN*
SINGLE
SIZE
SKIP1 through SKIP3
SORT
SORT-CONTROL
SORT-CORE-SIZE
SORT-FILE-SIZE
SORT-MERGE
SORT-MESSAGE
SORT-MODE-SIZE
SORT-OPTION
SORT-RETURN
SORT-STATUS
SOURCE
SOURCE-COMPUTER
SOURCES
SPACE
SPACE-FILL
SPACES
SPECIAL-NAMES
SQRT*
STANDARD
STANDARD-1 through
    STANDARD-4
STANDARD-COMPARE*
STANDARD-DEVIATION*
START
STARTING

STATION
STATIONS
STATUS
STEP
STOP
STORE
STRING
SUB-QUEUE-1 through SUB-
    QUEUE-3
SUB-SCHEMA
SUBFILE
SUBPROGRAM
SUBRANGE
SUBSCHEMA-NAME
SUBTRACT
SUCCESSIVE
SUFFIX
SUM
SUPER
SUPPRESS
SYMBOLIC
SYNC
SYNCHRONIZED
SYSIN
SYSIPT
SYSLST
SYSOUT
SYSPCH
SYSPUNCH
SYSTEM-DEFAULT
TABLE
TALLY
TALLYING
TAN*
TAPE
TENANT
TENNANT
TERMINAL
TERMINATE
TEST
TEST-DATE-YYYYMMDD*
TEST-DAY-YYYYDDD*
TEST-NUMVAL*
TEST-NUMVAL-C*
TEST-NUMVAL-F*

TEXT	TRANSFORM	VALID
THAN	TRUE	VALIDATE
THEN	TYPE	VALUE
THROUGH	TYPEDEF	VALUES
THRU	UNDERLINE	VARIABLE
TIME	UNEQUAL	VARIANCE*
TIME-OF-DAY	UNIT	VARYING
TIME-OUT	UNIVERSAL	WAIT
TIMEOUT	UNLESS	WHEN
TIMES	UNLOCK	WHEN-COMPILED
TITLE	UNSTRING	WIDTH
TO	UNTIL	WITH
TOP	UP	WITHIN
TOTALED	UPDATE	WORDS
TOTALING	UPON	WORKING-STORAGE
TRACE	UPPER-CASE*	WRAP
TRACK-AREA	UPSI-0 through UPSI-7	WRITE
TRACK-LIMIT	USAGE	WRITE-ONLY
TRACK-OVERFLOW	USAGE-MODE	WRITE-VERIFY
TRACKS	USE	YEAR-TO-YYYY*
TRAILING	USER	ZERO
TRAILING-SIGN	USER-DEFAULT	ZERO-FILL
TRANSACTION	USING	ZEROES
TRANSCEIVE	UUPPER	ZEROS

APPENDIX C

OBSOLETE COBOL ITEMS

C.1 OBSOLETE IDENTIFICATION DIVISION ITEMS

The following obsolete items are treated as comments.

```
AUTHOR.   comment-entry.
INSTALLATION.   comment-entry.
DATE-WRITTEN.   comment-entry.
DATE-COMPILED.   comment-entry.
SECURITY.   comment-entry.
```

C.2 OBSOLETE CONFIGURATION SECTION ITEMS

MEMORY SIZE was intended to specify the central storage size allocated to the program and is treated as a comment. Where this is appropriate, it is done through JCL today.

```
OBJECT-COMPUTER.   computer MEMORY SIZE n WORDS/CHARACTERS/MODULES
```

SEGMENT LIMIT was intended to specify which segments were permanently loaded (<*n*>) and which were loaded as needed in an overlay structure (>=*n*). It is treated as a comment.

```
SEGMENT LIMIT IS n
```

ON STATUS specified flags in the SPECIAL-NAMES paragraph of the Environment Division, which could then be tested in the Procedure Division:

```
SPECIAL-NAMES.
     environment-name ON STATUS IS on-name OFF STATUS IS off-name.
```

Environment-names, termed *UPSI switches,* are a holdover from the distant past when a computer operator could flip console switches that a program could test. The eight allowable *environment-names* were UPSI-0 through UPSI-7. For example:

```
SPECIAL NAMES.
     UPSI-0 ON STATUS IS Year-End.
```

```
     □   □   □
     IF Year-End THEN …
```

You set the switches at run time with the UPSI parameter. Each *n* represented one of the eight UPSI switches, UPSI-0 through UPSI-7. A value of 0 was off and 1 was on. The default was UPSI(0000000).

```
//STEP1 EXEC IGYWCLG,PARM.GO='UPSI(nnnnnnnn)'
```

C.3   OBSOLETE SELECT CLAUSE ITEMS

PADDING CHARACTER specified a character to pad unfilled blocks in sequential files, and is treated as a comment. Today's operating systems don't need this.

```
SELECT file-name ASSIGN TO ddname
       PADDING CHARACTER IS item.
```

The *item* is a one-character nonnumeric literal or identifier.

RECORD DELIMITER specified the method of determining the length of variable-length records, and is treated as a comment. Today's operating systems don't need this.

```
SELECT file-name ASSIGN TO ddname
     RECORD DELIMITER IS name.
```

The *name* can be STANDARD-1 for tape, and other values are intended to be installation-dependent.

C.4   OBSOLETE I-O-CONTROL CLAUSES

MULTIPLE FILE told the system that two or more files shared the same physical tape cartridge, and is treated as a comment. Operating systems today assume this.

```
MULTIPLE FILE TAPE CONTAINS file-name POSITION n file-name
POSITION n …
```

SAME SORT AREA was intended to optimize memory by sharing sort area space, and is treated as a comment. Operating systems dynamically allocate space, making this unnecessary.

```
I-O-CONTROL.
     SAME SORT AREA FOR file-name, file-name, …, file-name.
```

The *file-names* can be SORT or MERGE file names.

RERUN was intended to take checkpoints (a snapshot of the program's current state while the program is running) when writing sequential files. Mainframe COBOL supports this, but it is treated as a comment on other compilers. On OS/390, you specify checkpoints through OS/390 JCL.

```
RERUN ON ddname EVERY n RECORDS OF file-name.
```
[The system writes a checkpoint record for every *n* records of *file-name* processed.]
```
RERUN ON ddname EVERY END OF REEL or UNIT OF file-name.
```
[The system writes a checkpoint record whenever an end-of-volume occurs.]

Include a DD statement for each RERUN ON *ddname* listed.

C.5 OBSOLETE FD CLAUSE FEATURES

VALUE OF was intended to describe an item in the label record of the file, and is treated as a comment. Today's operating systems handle file labels.

```
FD  file-name
    VALUE OF system-name IS item.
```

LABEL RECORDS was intended to specify the presence or absence of labels of a file, and is treated as a comment. Today's operating systems handle file labels.

```
LABEL RECORDS IS/ARE STANDARD/OMITTED.
```

DATA RECORDS was intended to name the records belonging to a file described in the FD section, and is treated as a comment. Because the records that follow the FD are assumed to belong to the file, DATA RECORDS is not needed.

```
DATA RECORDS IS/ARE record-name.
```

C.6 OBSOLETE PROCEDURE DIVISION STATEMENTS

Stop *literal* supplied a literal to display on termination. This still works, but use a DISPLAY and GOBACK instead.

```
STOP literal
```

ALTER GO TO would win any award for the worst-conceived statement in any language. It changed the target of a GO TO statement. The GO TO must be the only statement in a paragraph. (This makes it the equivalent of what would be a labeled statement in other languages.) Suppose the following GO TO were coded in a paragraph named B100-Do-It.

```
B100-Do-It.
    GO TO B500-Do-More.
```

With the ALTER GO TO, you could change the target of the GO TO from B500-Do-More to some other paragraph name.

```
ALTER B100-Do-It TO PROCEED TO D300-Do-Something-Else
```

The GO TO *B500-Do-More* becomes a GO TO *D300-Do-Something-Else*. Programs that use the ALTER GO TO become almost impossible to read and maintain. Although the ALTER GO TO still works, replace any with EVALUATE or some other statement.

OPEN REVERSED told the system to position the tape at the end of the file, and then read the tape backwards, presenting the records in reverse order. This allowed you to read a tape file in reverse sort order. In practice, it was never used. It is still supported in Mainframe COBOL for a single-volume fixed-length record non-VSAM tape file. You can also request it in the JCL.

```
OPEN INPUT file-name REVERSED
```

OPEN WITH NO REWIND opened a tape file for INPUT or OUTPUT without rewinding it. It is still supported in Mainframe COBOL for single-volume non-VSAM tape files. You can also request it in the JCL.

```
OPEN OUTPUT file-name WITH NO REWIND
```

INDEX